Advance Praise

"*Assessing Trauma-Related Dissociation* takes an enormous step in providing clarity, instilling clinician confidence, and addressing the broad and specific features that require consideration during assessment of dissociative symptoms and disorders embedded in posttraumatic adaptation. In this book, Suzette Boon has distilled a lifetime of learning and packaged it into a very accessible, rich, and clinically grounded text that presents a thorough outline of the many considerations and multiple foci of trauma-related dissociation assessment. For anyone interested or engaged in the assessment of trauma-related dissociation, this book should be their first stop, regardless of how experienced they may be in the area."

> —**Martin J. Dorahy, PhD**, professor of clinical psychology, University of Canterbury, New Zealand, and coeditor, *Dissociation and the Dissociative Disorder: Past, Present, Future*

"An extremely practical and useful book to learn assessing and diagnosing dissociative disorders. The information is very well organized, easy to understand and integrate. Suzette Boon describes complex phenomena in a clear and precise way, addressing subtleties that can easily go unnoticed. *Assessing Trauma-Related Dissociation* is a gift for any clinician interested in improving their skills in assessment and diagnosis. A must-read."

> —**Dolores Mosquera**, psychologist at INTRA-TP, A Coruña, Spain

"This excellent book provides a highly accessible and comprehensive overview of the clusters of dissociative symptoms related to early childhood traumatic experiences. Each chapter highlights an aspect of the complexity of the TADS-I assessment, enriched with numerous examples and informed by a huge clinical experience. Clinical researchers and psychotherapists will find an extended analysis of differential diagnosis. An invaluable contribution to improving clinical diagnosis and therefore increasing the number of patients referred to an appropriate treatment plan."

> —**Manoëlle Hopchet**, clinical psychologist, psychotrauma therapist, and former president of the European Society for Trauma & Dissociation

Assessing Trauma-Related Dissociation

ASSESSING TRAUMA-RELATED DISSOCIATION

WITH THE

Trauma and Dissociation Symptoms Interview (TADS-I)

SUZETTE BOON

Norton Professional Books

An Imprint of W. W. Norton & Company
Celebrating a Century of Independent Publishing

This book is intended as a general information resource for professionals practicing in the field of psychotherapy and mental health. It is not a substitute for appropriate training or clinical supervision. Standards of clinical practice and protocol vary in different practice settings and change over time. No technique or recommendation is guaranteed to be safe or effective in all circumstances, and neither the publisher nor the author(s) can guarantee the complete accuracy, efficacy, or appropriateness of any particular recommendation in every respect or in all settings or circumstances. All case subjects and dialogues described in this book are composites.

Any URLs displayed in this book link or refer to websites that existed as of press time. The publisher is not responsible for, and should not be deemed to endorse or recommend, any website other than its own or any content that it did not create. The author, also, is not responsible for any third-party material.

Original title: Diagnostiek van traumagerelateerde dissociatie

Originally published as Diagnostiek van traumagerelateerde dissociatie
Copyright © 2022 by Suzette Boon
Published by Uitgeverij Mens!, Eeserveen, The Netherlands

For information about permission to reproduce selections from this book, write to Permissions, W. W. Norton & Company, Inc., 500 Fifth Avenue, New York, NY 10110

For information about special discounts for bulk purchases, please contact W. W. Norton Special Sales at specialsales@wwnorton.com or 800-233-4830

Manufacturing by Versa Press
Production manager: Gwen Cullen

ISBN: 978-1-324-05257-9 (pbk)

W. W. Norton & Company, Inc., 500 Fifth Avenue, New York, NY 10110
www.wwnorton.com

W. W. Norton & Company Ltd., 15 Carlisle Street, London W1D 3BS

1 2 3 4 5 6 7 8 9 0

To all the patients who were willing to share their dissociative experiences and participated in our assessment research

CONTENTS

Background

Trauma-related dissociative disorders have been steadily receiving more attention in therapeutic practice and in the clinical literature. Two conflicting problems are emerging with regard to the two most complex dissociative disorders—dissociative identity disorder (DID) and the first example in the DSM-5 listing of other specified dissociative disorders (OSDD-1; APA, 2013, 2022), which also describes a form of DID. On the one hand, diagnoses of such disorders are still too often overlooked. On the other hand, there is an increasing tendency to assign a diagnosis of this kind when the patient does not actually have the disorder. Both problems are largely due to insufficient knowledge among clinicians about diagnosing dissociative disorders. It is my hope that this book, based on 40 years of experience in both practice and research, will help clinicians better identify these disorders and distinguish them from other mental health disorders.

The book introduces a new diagnostic interview—the Trauma and Dissociation Symptoms Interview (TADS-I)—that will help clinicians to assess dissociative disorders. However, reading about the assessment is not enough; clinicians will also need practical training in conducting diagnostic interviews.

Since I first began treating patients with DID at a psychiatric outpatient department in the mid-1980s, together with my colleague Onno van der Hart, I became increasingly interested in the diagnosis and treatment of this then overlooked and highly underexposed group of patients. In the late 1980s, Nel Draijer and I began systematic research on the assessment of dissociative disorders. We conducted a study using the *Structured Clinical Interview for DSM-III-R Dissociative Disorders* (SCID-D; Steinberg, 1994a, 1994b; Steinberg et al., 1990). Our purpose was to gain a better understanding of the validity of dissociative disorders as defined in the DSM-III-R, specifically dissociative identity disorder (DID), formerly referred to as multiple personality disorder (MPD). We validated the SCID-D in the Netherlands and tested it for reliability (Boon & Draijer, 1991, 1993a, 1993b, 1993c; Draijer & Boon, 1999). The SCID-D was found to be valid and to have a high degree of inter-rater reliability. It was able to distinguish DSM-III-R (APA,

1987) dissociative disorders very well from other mental disorders, including related disorders such as borderline personality disorder (BPS; Boon & Draijer, 1993a, 1993c, 1995a). Our study found that patients with DID or dissociative disorder not otherwise specified (DDNOS), subtype I, which is listed as "OSDD Example 1" in the DSM-5 (APA, 2013, 2022), generally present with a coherent cluster of severe dissociative symptoms. This cluster of symptoms includes more than just amnesia and identity alterations, which are the criteria described in the DSM-IV and DSM-5.

In 1995, Nel Draijer and I published *Screening and Assessment of Dissociative Disorders* (Boon & Draijer, 1995a). Included was a description of the results of our research with the SCID-D, as well as methods for clinicians to use when screening for the presence of dissociative symptoms using the Dissociative Experiences Scale (DES; Bernstein & Putnam, 1986). Based on our research study, we gave clinical examples of patients' responses to the different questions in the SCID-D interview. The 1995 book also included chapters on differential diagnosis and on the assessment of the trauma history. We emphasized the importance of careful questioning during diagnostic assessment. At the time, we already noted substantial differences, not only in the quantity but also in the quality of examples of dissociative symptoms given by patients with and without dissociative disorder (Boon & Draijer, 1993a, 1995a, 1995b). For example, patients in the control group in our study mentioned other forms of depersonalization and derealization (especially temporary emotional detachment from themselves) and memory problems due to absorption (becoming completely absorbed in something); these symptoms did not indicate the presence of a dissociative disorder but were considered dissociative in nature by many clinicians. Later, these symptoms were described by Holmes and colleagues as forms of "detachment" (Brown, 2006; Holmes et al., 2005) (see Chapter 1).

In the early 1990s, the concept of dissociation was strongly influenced by the continuum idea; dissociative symptoms were thought to be on a continuum from normal symptoms that anyone may experience to pathological. At the time, however, we had already found evidence that dissociation did not seem to be on a continuum (Boon & Draijer, 1993a). Most clinicians do agree that dissociative disorders must always involve a cluster of pathological dissociative symptoms. van der Hart and colleagues formulated a narrower definition of the concept of dissociation: they speak of dissociation only in the presence of a "division of the personality" into different dissociative parts (van der Hart et al., 2006). Dissociative symptoms as such always stem from the presence of dissociative parts. van der Hart and colleagues do not consider the symptoms that would be classified as normal dissociation to be dissociative in nature. Chapter 1 discusses this topic in more detail. This book—following van der Hart and colleagues' terminology—refers to "division of the personality" and "dissociative parts of the personality."

In the early to mid-1990s, Nel Draijer and I were already describing patients who were confused about their symptoms and believed they had DID (Boon & Draijer, 1993a, 1993c, 1995a). Some had been imitating symptoms of DID intentionally; others had been wrongly diagnosed with DID by clinicians. These were mainly patients with severe personality problems. They had identity problems and also mentioned depersonalization and derealization symptoms. Finally, Nel Draijer and I described the differences between patients with genuine DID and those with imitated DID (Boon & Draijer, 1995a, 2003; Draijer & Boon, 1999).

Screening and Diagnosis of Dissociative Disorders was not translated at the time, nor was it reprinted. Also, unfortunately, the SCID-D is no longer published in the Netherlands and was only validated and available in a few European countries—albeit for a long time (Boon & Draijer, 1993a, 1994; Gast et al., 2001). A new version of the SCID-D will be published for DSM-5 and ICD-11 (Mychailyszyn et al., 2021). Although this version has recently been used in a small research study involving French-speaking patients in Switzerland and France (Piedfort-Marin et al., 2021), it has not been published yet.

Since 2006, I have focused on developing a new diagnostic interview. This was influenced by the fact that the SCID-D was not available in many European countries where I was teaching. In addition, the content of the SCID-D did not adequately match the categories of the ICD-10 dissociative disorders (WHO, 1992), because the interview lacked questions about somatoform dissociative symptoms and disorders. In addition, I found it useful to ask about various symptoms that could be trauma-related, including anxiety and PTSD symptoms, sleep problems, mood problems, suicidal ideation, and self-injurious behaviors. Not only do answers to questions about (possibly) trauma-related symptoms provide a broader clinical picture of a patient, but also they can help distinguish between dissociative disorders, other mental disorders, and false-positive DID diagnoses. This is explained in more detail in Chapter 5, which details the use of the TADS-I, and in Chapter 10, on false-positive DID.

I initially developed this new diagnostic interview with Helga Matthess, leading to a first unvalidated version, which was translated and distributed in Europe under the title *Interview for Dissociative Disorders and Trauma-related Symptoms* (IDDTS; Boon & Matthess, 2006; Nilson et al., 2019).

Since 2012, guided by different theoretical insights on the concept of dissociation, I have continued to work on this structured diagnostic interview, which is included in this book under the name Trauma and Dissociation

Symptoms Interview (TADS-I; Boon & Matthess, 2016). The section on possibly trauma-related symptoms has remained largely unchanged; however, changes were made in the structure and content of other sections of the interview. Currently, data are being analyzed from the first 53 interviews in the Netherlands, and research is being conducted with the TADS-I in several places in Europe, particularly in Italy and Poland (Cavalletti et al., 2021; Pietkiewicz et al., 2021).

Over the past 25 years, the differences of opinion have grown as to what exactly dissociation entails. As will become clear in Chapter 1, this discussion is important for identifying dissociative symptoms and disorders. However, regardless of the concept of dissociation they adhere to, clinicians should always probe carefully to clarify the meaning of examples given by their patients. For example, when a patient reports having memory problems, the clinician must be able to distinguish between memory problems that seem to arise as a result of absorption, daydreaming, or concentration problems on the one hand, and memory problems related to activities of a dissociative part of the personality on the other hand. Next, clinicians must learn to assess how the cluster of dissociative and other trauma-related symptoms aligns with dissociative disorders as described in DSM-5 or ICD-11.

The new edition of the *International Classification of Diseases* (ICD-11; WHO, 2019) has now also been presented online. The ICD is used in many European countries. Gysi (2020) published an excellent German-language book on diagnosing trauma-related disorders based on the ICD-11. Differences remain between the two psychiatric classification systems (DSM and ICD), as explained in Chapter 1.

The DSM-5 lists five dissociative disorders, while the ICD-11 lists nine. This book discusses all of these dissociative disorders, illustrating them with clinical examples. The focus is on DID and the first example of other specified dissociative disorder (OSDD-1, "partial DID" in IDC-11). Throughout this book, I will refer to OSDD-1, the form that has obvious similarities to DID. While there is overlap between OSDD-1 and partial DID, the criteria also show some differences that are discussed in Chapter 1. DID and OSDD-1 are the most common dissociative disorders in clinical practice. There are no research data yet on partial DID because this diagnosis was only recently included in the ICD-11.

For Whom Is This Book Intended?

This book, with the TADS-I interview, is intended primarily for clinicians who want to diagnose dissociative disorders or learn to do so. For colleagues who do not conduct their own diagnostic assessments in practice, the book provides a great deal of information to better recognize patients with dissociative symptoms and refer them to specialized colleagues. After all, not everyone is able or allowed to formally make a psychiatric diagnosis; scopes of practice vary from country to country, both within and outside Europe. Furthermore, in order to diagnose or exclude dissociative disorders, it is important for clinicians to have a broad knowledge of psychopathology to enable them to distinguish between dissociative disorders and any other mental disorders that may share similar features.

Finally, I wish to emphasize that reading a book on the diagnosis of dissociative disorders is not sufficient preparation for those wishing to learn how to diagnose such disorders in practice. Dissociative disorders are often difficult to diagnose, especially for clinicians who have seen only a few of these patients and who have no experience in treating dissociative disorders. Undergoing special training in conducting a diagnostic interview such as the TADS-I or the SCID-D is a prerequisite. During such training sessions, attendees will learn most from short video clips of patients with and without dissociative disorders. Interview practice and making and discussing a video recording of a diagnostic interview are also part of such training. Even after 35 years of experience in diagnosing dissociative disorders, I still find these disorders very difficult to assess in some cases. This finding is shared by colleagues with whom I discuss diagnostic dilemmas.

Structure of the Book

This book consists of 11 chapters, with the first chapter providing a general introduction to the concept of dissociation and the dissociative disorders of the DSM-5 and ICD-11. Next, the reader is given step-by-step information, using many case reports based on TADS-I interviews, on exactly how dissociative symptoms may present, how the clinician can screen for dissociative symptoms, and how to diagnose a dissociative disorder using the TADS-I. The last four chapters cover differential diagnosis and assessment of traumatic memories.

Apart from the TADS-I, several appendices are included for the purpose of scoring the TADS-I. The appendices also include a questionnaire on maladaptive daydreaming (Somer, Lehrfeld, et al., 2016). For ease of printing and to facilitate the accessibility of possible updates in the future, the TADS-I has also been made available to all users via a URL, tads-i .com/download, with the caveat that additional training in diagnostics is strongly recommended.

Chapter 1 discusses the challenges in diagnosing dissociative disorders. The different theoretical concepts about dissociation and the differences in the classification systems are causing significant confusion, as is the fact that patients with a dissociative disorder typically present to mental health services with symptoms other than the characteristic dissociative symptoms. The chapter also offers an overview of the DSM-5 and ICD-11 dissociative disorders.

Chapter 2 deals with the dissociative symptoms that indicate a division of the personality. Case reports are used to describe how patients may respond to the TADS-I questions for each dissociative symptom.

Chapter 3 describes depersonalization and derealization symptoms and other forms of alterations in consciousness, such as absorption and day-dreaming. Such symptoms occur in patients with dissociative disorders, but also in many patients with other mental disorders, as well as in the general population.

Chapter 4 provides an overview of the most commonly used self-report screening questionnaires on dissociative symptoms. The DES, a self-report questionnaire developed by Bernstein and Putnam (1986), is given exten-sive consideration. This scale is the most widely used screening tool glob-ally, and much research data are based on the DES.

Chapter 5 begins with a brief overview of the most commonly used diag-nostic interviews. This is followed by an explanation of the new diagnostic interview, the TADS-I, and its application.

Chapter 6 presents a number of completed interviews with patients with dissociative disorder, in order to show how patients with different dissocia-tive disorders may respond to TADS-I questions.

Chapters 7, 8, and 9 discuss key differential diagnostic dilemmas, illus-trated by case reports describing TADS-I symptom profiles of different patients. Not all other mental disorders are covered, but rather those that are often confused with dissociative disorders or those that may elicit dif-ferential diagnostic issues in clinical practice.

Chapter 8 focuses on the distinction between DID, DSM-5 OSDD-1, ICD-11 partial DID, and personality disorders, particularly borderline person-ality disorder (BPD). There is much overlap in symptoms between these disorders, and they may also co-occur. In clinical practice, distinguishing DID, OSDD-1, and partial DID from BPD—without comorbid DID, OSDD-I, or partial DID—often proves difficult.

Chapter 9 focuses on similarities and differences between the new DSM-5 subtype of posttraumatic stress disorder (PTSD) with dissociative symp-toms, the ICD-11 category of complex PTSD, and the dissociative disorders, specifically DID, OSDD-I, and partial DID.

Chapter 10 deals with false-positive DID diagnoses. Although the num-ber of false-negative DID diagnoses probably exceeds the false-positive ones, there is a great deal of confusion about what DID is exactly, not only among patients but often also among clinicians; incorrect DID diagnoses are becoming more common. A separate section is dedicated to false-positive and false-negative DID diagnoses within the forensic context.

Chapter 11 deals with the assessment of traumatic experiences and formulating a treatment plan. Officially, exposure to traumatizing events is not a diagnostic criterion for the various dissociative disorders, but it is for PTSD and CPTSD. Internationally, however, dissociative disorders are considered trauma-related disorders, particularly DID (APA, 2013, 2022; ISSTD, 2011). There is substantial empirical research confirming the relationship between trauma and dissociation, particularly in DID (e.g., Dalenberg et al., 2012; Dalenberg et al., 2014), which is discussed in Chapter 1. The careful exploration of a history of trauma and the tools that can be used to do so are discussed in this final chapter. A second section in this chapter emphasizes that a DSM-5 or ICD-11 diagnosis of dissociative disorder is only the first step toward an appropriate treatment plan. Individuals are more than their diagnoses. In order to make a proper treatment recommendation, the clinician will need to perform a broad diagnostic assessment. The nature and severity of the traumatic experiences, and in particular the degree of emotional neglect, are major factors in the treatment prognosis. In addition to these, however, there are many other factors to take into account. My colleagues and I have described these in detail in *Treating Trauma-Related Dissociation* (Steele et al., 2017), but it cannot be emphasized enough. All of them are important for a proper case conceptualization, prognosis, and treatment plan.

ACKNOWLEDGMENTS

My journey in the field of diagnosis and treatment of dissociative disorders began in the mid-1980s. Onno van der Hart, a dear colleague since 1978, introduced me to this field. This book would not have come about without the incredible support Onno gave me over the past few years. He read every chapter and tirelessly provided valuable comments, both in terms of content and wording. He also helped with corrections to the English version of this book. I am immensely grateful for his contribution and his ever-loyal support.

With Onno, I attended the first conferences of the International Society for Trauma and Dissociation (ISSTD) in Chicago in the mid-1980s, where we met the pioneers who inspired and supported us: Elizabeth Bowman, Bennett Braun, David Caul (1921–1988), James Chu, Philip Coons, Catherine Fine, Jean Goodwin, Richard Kluft, Richard Loewenstein, Frank Putnam, Colin Ross, and Roberta Sachs. Their work was of great significance and influence, and I will always be grateful to them.

With my friend and colleague Nel Draijer, I performed the first major diagnostic research study with the SCID-D, for which I received my PhD in 1993. She was a great support during this research and in the many years that followed. She also provided valuable comments on several chapters of this book, for which I am very grateful.

Desiree Tijdink, colleague and friend for 20 years, also read and commented on all the chapters. I am very grateful to her for all her work in improving the content of this book.

I have written two books with Kathy Steele, and this time around I really missed the enjoyable writing weeks in the United States and the Netherlands. The COVID-19 pandemic would have made that impossible this time, anyway! However, Kathy insisted from the beginning that this was my project and my expertise. Nevertheless, I was able to count on her support and I cherish our friendship and collaboration.

The development of the TADS-I has been a long process that began in 2006. Since then, colleagues all over Europe have translated previous versions of the TADS-I and invited me to give training sessions. Their enormous enthusiasm and dedication, their questions and comments have provided me with the stimulus and motivation to complete this book. I owe them all a debt of gratitude for the work and time they spent translating and organizing training sessions. Many of them have become dear friends with whom I regularly exchange ideas and knowledge, not only about diagnosis but also about the treatment of dissociative disorders.

In Germany, Helga Matthess developed the predecessor of the TADS-I with me—the IDDTS—and I am so grateful for that. Tina Overkamp and Susanne Nick contributed to later translations of the TADS-I. In Switzerland, Jan Gysi and colleagues produced the final German translation. In Norway, Ellen Jepsen and colleagues in Modum Bad and the colleagues at the outpatient clinic of Modum Bad in Oslo, including Ingun Holbaek, Katinka Salveson, and Harold Bækkelund, have been involved from the very beginning. Anne Suokas from Finland supported me in the development of the TADS-I from the outset. I really cherish our friendship and many years of working together. Maire Riis translated the TADS-I into Estonian and organized training sessions—I have had a close connection with her since 2006. In Sweden, Doris Nilsson performed scientific research with the IDDTS. Hakan Andersson, Christina Lander, Maud Nilsson, and Anna Gerge contributed to the Swedish translations, while Anna Gerge organized several training sessions in Stockholm. In Romania, Anca Sabau and her team contributed to both translations and training sessions—the same goes for Ildikó Szabó, Judith Molnár, and Zsófia Boytha in Hungary, and Lise Møller in Denmark. I want also to thank Dolores Mosquera in Spain, with whom I developed an important collaborative relationship and a friendship, while I am also indebted to Annabel Gonzalez and Doris Montalvo Moll for their work on the TADS-I. I would like to thank Hélène Delucci in France for translating the TADS-I into French and for initiating several training sessions, as well as Manoëlle Hopchet in Belgium. Hana Voytová translated the TADS-I into Czech-Slovakian and organized training sessions for Slovak and Czech colleagues. I thank my Russian colleagues Elena Kazenaya and Ekaterina Divid. They organized the first training sessions on the TADS-I in Moscow and translated the interview.

In Italy and Poland, there are two very active groups of colleagues who are also doing research with the TADS-I, which is a necessary contribution for its validation. I thank my Italian colleagues Giovanni Tagliavini and Maria Paola Boldrini for their support and commitment to the TADS-I and Matteo Cavalletti and his colleagues for their research and ideas regarding the graphical representation of scores. I thank Igor Pietkiewicz and Radek Tomalski for their commitment to translating the TADS-I into Polish and organizing training sessions and research in Poland. Our regular exchanges of thoughts and ideas are stimulating. Radek Tomalski has also helped me tremendously by finding all the research articles I requested.

My heart goes out to my Ukrainian colleague Karine Kocharyan and her colleagues to whom I taught diagnostics using the TADS-I just this past year and who are now going through terrible times.

There are many peers in and outside Europe who have made tremendous contributions in the field of diagnosis and treatment of dissociative disorders. While it is impossible to name them all, my gratitude goes to the contributions of Remy Aquarone, Bethany Brand, Richard Chefetz, Catherine Classen, Christine Courtois, Constance Dalenberg, Paul Dell, Martin Dorahy, Janina Fisher, Julian Ford, Steve Frankel, Jennifer Freyd, Steve Gold, Annabel Gonzalez, Jan Gysi, Judith Herman, Elizabeth Howell, Bessel van der Kolk, Ruth Lanius, Giovanni Liotti, Warwick Middleton, Andrew Moskowitz, Dolores Mosquera, Nelleke Nicolai, John O'Neil, Ellert Nijenhuis, Pat Ogden, Clare Pain, Olivier Piedfort-Marin, Simone Reinders, Vedat Şar, Roger Solomon, Eli Somer, David Spiegel, Marlene Steinberg, and Eric Vermetten.

There are too many colleagues in the Netherlands to mention personally. I am grateful to you all, not only for your support and interest but also for the pleasure of working together.

Marjolein Runhaar performed the pilot study of the TADS-I with me, while also conducting several interviews and helping me to collect the data. It was inspiring to collaborate with her and I owe her a huge debt of gratitude for all her voluntary work. Rik Knipschild was also involved in the study for a short time and helped develop the symptom profiles. Jolanda Treffers incorporated all changes of the different versions of the TADS-I in Dutch and English, for which I send her many thanks! The data from this pilot study will be analyzed with the help of Willie Langeland and Deborah Okundia Agho.

Many thanks are due to my publisher Carmijn zur Kleinsmiede and to Hilde Merkus and Hanneke Lustig for editing the original Dutch manuscript and translating it into English. The collaboration with all three was incredibly good. They have done a lot of work and made a huge contribution to improving the text. I thank Carmijn in particular for her generous effort to create a beautiful English text as well. The English translation was edited by Ineke Crezee in New Zealand, for which I am very grateful also.

Finally, I thank all the patients from whom I have learned so much since the late 1980s. Thank you for your trust, courage, and willingness to participate in research with the TADS-I. Without your cooperation, there would be no TADS-I. I sincerely hope that this book and the interview will contribute to a better recognition of dissociative symptoms. After all, this is crucial if we are to offer appropriate treatment.

Suzette Boon
August 2022

Assessing Trauma-Related Dissociation

CHAPTER 1

DSM-5 and ICD-11 Dissociative Disorders: Criteria and Dilemmas

Introduction

Patients with dissociative disorders often receive years of treatment at mental health facilities or in private psychotherapy practices, with dissociative symptoms frequently going unrecognized. This is particularly true for patients with dissociative identity disorder (DID) or other specified dissociative disorder (OSDD-1[1]). These patients generally do not present with dissociative symptoms but with symptoms such as anxiety, panic, depression, so-called psychotic symptoms, unexplained physical symptoms, and problems sleeping and eating. Some may have received a range of unsuccessful treatments for various disorders. In many countries, both within and outside Europe, dissociative disorders are not considered during diagnostic assessment. In addition, clinicians may have different understandings of what dissociative symptoms entail, because these often occur in the context of other mental disorders. In these cases, the underlying dissociative disorders remain untreated or are treated incorrectly, resulting in the persistence of the dissociative symptoms. The patient's presenting complaint, an eating problem for instance, may temporarily go into remission but will never completely disappear. This is because potentially trauma-related symptoms such as eating problems or self-mutilation are often related to dissociative parts of the personality. If a dissociative disorder were to be diagnosed in this instance, the dissociative organization of the personality becomes the focus of treatment. Then these parts would be involved in the treatment, which could lead to a lasting improvement of the symptoms.

According to the guidelines of the International Society for the Study of Trauma and Dissociation (ISSTD, 2011), the standard of care for the treatment of dissociative disorders involves a phase-oriented treatment comprising the following three phases: (1) stabilization, symptom reduction,

---

1   In this book, OSDD Example 1 will be referred to as OSDD-1.

and skills training. This first phase involves promoting a good therapeutic relationship, safety, stabilization, psychoeducation, symptom reduction, and skills building; (2) treatment of traumatic memories; and (3) reintegration of the personality and rehabilitation, grief, acceptance of any sequelae, and learning how to cope with them (Brown et al., 1998; ISSTD, 2011; Steele et al., 2017; van der Hart et al., 2006). During the course of therapy based on this model, the three phases are often likely to alternate as the trauma-related problems are the most complex.

Research has shown that phase-oriented treatment will improve everyday functioning of patients: they exhibit fewer self-harm behaviors and fewer signs and symptoms of PTSD and dissociation. In addition, the number of hospitalizations and costs of treatment will reduce (Brand et al., 2013; Brand & Loewenstein, 2014; Brand, Loewenstein, & Spiegel, 2014; Coons & Bowman, 2001; Myrick et al., 2017). Patients whose dissociative disorders are not treated will continue to experience dissociative symptoms and related problems, since their underlying dissociative organization does not change (Brand, Classen, Lanius, et al., 2009).

Dilemmas in Diagnosing Dissociative Disorders

Multiple factors contribute to the difficulty of diagnosing dissociative disorders. These are discussed below.

Different Definitions of the Concept of Dissociation

DSM-5 defines dissociation as a disruption of and/or discontinuity in the normal integration of consciousness, memory, identity, emotion, perception, body representation, motor control, and behavior. Dissociative symptoms can potentially disrupt every area of psychological functioning (American Psychological Association [APA], 2013, p. 291; 2022, p. 329).

The interpretation of the concept of dissociation still varies widely. It is a vague, unclear, and sometimes even controversial concept. When Nel Draijer and I started our research with the Structured Clinical Interview for Dissociative Disorders (SCID-D) in the 1980s and early 1990s (Boon & Draijer, 1993a, 1993b), the leading theoretical model of concept was that dissociation appears on a continuum, ranging from "normal" to "pathological" (Bernstein & Putnam, 1986; Cardeña, 1994; Carlson & Putnam, 1993). In those days, the majority of studies were performed with the Dissociative Experiences Scale (DES), a 28-item self-report questionnaire (Bernstein & Putnam, 1986). This questionnaire, based upon the continuum construct, includes the following subscales: absorption, depersonalization/derealization, and amnesia.

In 1996, a study was published that was based upon the DES-Taxon

(DES-T) tool, analyzing which symptoms from the DES best distinguish dissociative disorders from other disorders (Waller et al., 1996). The DES-T consists of eight items extracted from the DES and used to measure pathological dissociation. This study supported the idea of two continua: "normal and pathological dissociation." Today there is much debate as to whether these two continua actually exist and how they might be interrelated (Dalenberg & Paulson, 2009; Dalenberg et al., 2022; Leavitt, 1999). Based on her own research, Dalenberg suggests that absorption may be a substrate of pathological dissociation, given the fact that pathological dissociative symptoms show a high correlation with absorption in patients scoring within the DES-Taxon range (Dalenberg & Paulson, 2009; Dalenberg et al., 2022; Spiegel et al., 2011). However, such a correlation does not clarify whether there is a common basis starting point for both types of symptoms.

For many clinicians internationally, the continuum model is still an important theoretical principle, even though many scholars have raised concerns about this model (Boon & Draijer, 1993a, 1995a; van der Hart & Dorahy, 2009; Holmes et al., 2005; Steele et al., 2009; Steele et al., 2022; Nijenhuis, 2015; Rodewald, Dell, et al., 2011; van der Hart, 2021; van der Hart et al., 1991, 2006). In the continuum model, "normal dissociation" includes phenomena such as daydreaming, so-called highway trance, and being completely absorbed in a book, music, film, or in one's own thoughts or imagination, thus "absorption." "Pathological dissociation" includes phenomena such as severe amnesias, identity changes, and intrusions of dissociative parts, but also extremes of depersonalization and derealization. Some of these symptoms can also be observed objectively, but many are solely based on the patient's subjective experience. The intrusions of dissociative parts of the personality on executive functioning and self-image, for example, are also considered pathological core symptoms of DID (Dell, 2009a, 2009b). Pathological dissociative symptoms are characteristics of all dissociative disorders, in particular DID and OSDD-1 (formerly dissociative disorder not otherwise specified [DDNOS-1]) (Bernstein & Putnam, 1986; Butler, 2004, 2006; Dalenberg & Paulson, 2009; Waller, Putnam, & Carlson, 1996).

Instruments such as the DES present and measure qualitatively different phenomena—both absorption and symptoms associated with a division of the personality. Therefore, research that employs this widely used self-report questionnaire on dissociation creates a great deal of confusion when used to make general statements about the presence and severity of dissociative symptoms. Elevated DES scores can be based solely on absorption and some depersonalization symptoms without the presence of symptoms indicating a division of the personality.

As I described in the introduction, our own research with the SCID-D in the early 1990s (Boon & Draijer, 1993a, 1993b) found substantial differences between the descriptions of dissociative symptoms by patients with DID or DDNOS and those by a control group of patients with other mental disorders (Boon et al., 1993a; 1995a). The descriptions of dissociative symptoms by patients with other mental disorders were to a large extent vaguer and more varied. The memory problems reported by patients in the control group were mainly associated with absorption, but descriptions of depersonalization and derealization were also qualitatively different from the examples given by patients with DID or DDNOS. For example, when asked if she ever felt alienated from herself, a patient with a personality disorder explained: *When I'm stressed or very tired, I feel a little hazy, not very present and doing things sort of automatically.* Another patient, when asked if she ever lost time, described her experiences as follows: *Sometimes I'm lost in thought and I don't pay attention to the time, and then suddenly it's much later, time has gone by unnoticed.*

In contrast, all patients with DID or DDNOS described very clear examples of symptoms indicative of a division of the personality. When asked about alienation, one patient described her experiences as follows: *Sometimes it doesn't feel as if I'm in my body, I am outside, watching from a distance, for example when I am shopping.* From the examples of time loss, it was clear that another dissociative part had been present: *I often don't know exactly what I do during a day, then I want to go and do the shopping, but suddenly [I find that] my fridge is already filled!* Based on these distinctly different examples, we questioned the validity of the continuum idea (Boon & Draijer, 1993a; 1995a, 2013). This doubt is currently shared by many colleagues (Holmes et al., 2005; Nijenhuis, 2015; Rodewald, Dell, et al., 2011; Steele et al., 2009; van der Hart & Dorahy, 2009; van der Hart et al., 2006).

Holmes et al. (2005) suggested that we should speak of two qualitatively different forms of dissociation: detachment and compartmentalization. According to Holmes, symptoms such as depersonalization and derealization are related to the concept of detachment. These symptoms may occur on a continuum from relatively mild or short-term to chronic and severe forms, as is the case in depersonalization/derealization disorder. Also related to the concept of compartmentalization are symptoms such as dissociative amnesia, unexplained or pseudoneurological symptoms called somatoform dissociative symptoms, and pseudohallucinations, all of which are indicative of a division of the personality.

Other clinicians also view detachment as a dissociative phenomenon (Liotti, 1992, 2009; Farina et al., 2019), with Liotti describing the relationship between dissociation and disorganized attachment. According to these clinicians, a history of insecure or disorganized attachment can lead to feelings of not being there when in contact with others later in life, or a lowering of the level of consciousness in an attempt to maintain distance (see also Draijer & Langeland, 1999).

Based on the notion of two qualitatively different forms of dissociation, a new diagnostic screening tool was recently developed to further explore these different forms of dissociation: the Detachment and Compartmentalization Inventory (DCI; Butler et al., 2019). However, Butler and colleagues emphasize that in developing this self-report questionnaire they do not want to initiate a discussion about what should or should not be called dissociation. What they did want to explore was whether detachment and compartmentalization are actually different forms of dissociation.

Van der Hart and colleagues adopt the most radical position. Based on the theory of Pierre Janet (1889, 1907), they speak of structural dissociation of the personality, reserving the concept of dissociation for an actual division of the personality (van der Hart et al., 2006; van der Hart, 2021). In addition, they draw a fundamental distinction between dissociative parts of the personality that are stuck in traumatic experiences ("in trauma time"), so-called emotional parts of the personality (EPs), and parts that are focused on functioning in everyday life—apparently normal parts of the personality (ANPs). They distinguish three degrees of structural dissociation of the personality (Figure 1.1). They refer to the first degree as a primary structural dissociation, with one part of the personality, however rudimentary, stuck in trauma time while the other part continues to function in daily life, as in PTSD or in less complex somatoform dissociative disorders. The second degree, secondary structural dissociation, is characterized by the presence of multiple parts that are fixated in trauma time (EPs) and one part that keeps functioning in daily life (ANP), as in complex PTSD, OSDD-1, and partial DID. The third and most complex degree within this model, tertiary structural dissociation, involves DID that has multiple parts with tasks and functions in daily life (ANPs) and multiple parts stuck in trauma time (EPs).

In this theoretical model, trauma-related dissociative phenomena always result from a division of the personality. Thus, we must distinguish these dissociative symptoms from other more vague and, in the view of van der Hart and colleagues, nondissociative altered states of consciousness, such as absorption, imagination, and daydreaming, which may be associated with a narrowed or altered (lowered or raised) level of consciousness, but do not necessarily involve a division of the personality (Steele et al., 2009; Steele et al., 2017; Steele et al., 2022; van der Hart et al., 2006). In this theoretical perspective, the phenomena described as detachment by Holmes and colleagues would not necessarily be of a dissociative nature. These last forms of altered states of consciousness often occur in patients with other

Primary Structural Dissociation:
One part functioning in daily life (ANP);
one part stuck in the trauma time (EP)

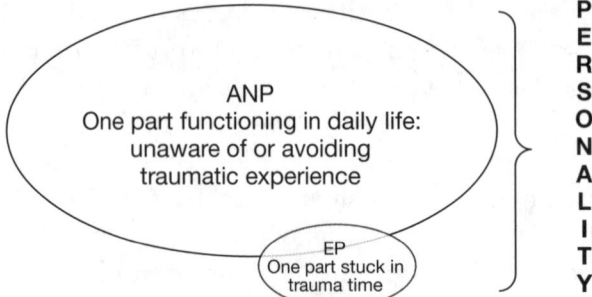

Secondary Structural Dissociation:
One part functioning in daily life (ANP);
several parts stuck in trauma time (EP)

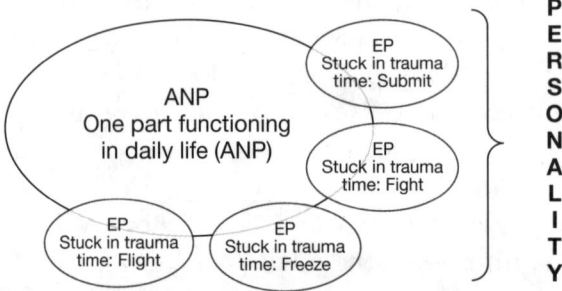

Tertiary Structural Dissociation:
More parts functioning in daily life (ANP);
more parts stuck in trauma time (EP)

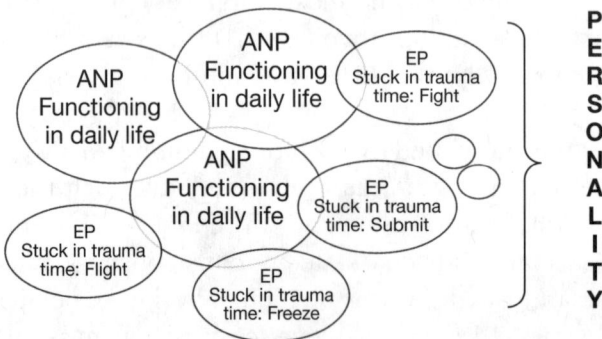

FIGURE 1.1   Three Levels of Structural Dissociation of the Personality: Primary, Secondary, and Tertiary Structural Dissociation

SOURCE: Adapted from van der Hart, O. (2000). *Psychic trauma: The disintegrating effects of overwhelming experience on mind and body.* 66th Beattie Smith Lecture, University of Melbourne, Department of Medicine.

mental problems, such as anxiety or depression. They may also occur in people who are either tired or sick, stressed or under pressure, or suffering from burnout symptoms. As mentioned above, absorption experiences may also occur—sometimes even in a positive sense—in people who have an excellent ability to focus and who can be extremely absorbed in an activity such as reading a book or listening to music, to the extent that they fail to notice much of what is going on outside themselves. Absorption experiences also include daydreaming and the trancelike phenomena sometimes experienced by runners or by children who become totally absorbed in their play. However, such relatively normal symptoms can become pathological in nature (Somer, 2002; Somer, Lehrfeld, et al., 2016; Somer, Somer, & Jopp, 2016a, 2016b; Somer et al., 2017), and Chapter 3 describes a number of examples. As a matter of fact, these other alterations in consciousness are common in patients with dissociative disorder but are also frequently found in patients with other mental disorders and in the general population.

Regardless of the theoretical beliefs of the clinician, it is important to distinguish between dissociative symptoms that refer to a division of personality (always pathological in nature), and other forms of alterations in consciousness (sometimes pathological in nature). For this reason, TADS-I includes a separate section containing questions about alterations in consciousness, narrowing of the field of consciousness and lowering of the level of consciousness, such as absorption, trancelike experiences, and daydreaming. This section of the interview also involves inquiring after symptoms of depersonalization and derealization that do not independently refer to a division of the personality but often occur in the context of other mental disorders and may be more indicative of processes of detachment. It should be noted that these symptoms may well be pathological in nature. In fact, chronic and severe depersonalization and derealization symptoms are the main features of depersonalization/derealization disorder in both DSM-5 and ICD-11.

Lastly, there is a relatively new theoretical model of dissociation, the 4-D Model by Frewen and Lanius (Frewen & Lanius, 2014, 2015; Lanius, 2015). Within this model, trauma-related symptoms are categorized into experiences that may occur in normal waking state (NWS) and experiences that occur in trauma-related altered states of consciousness (TRASC). This model compares the potential alterations in consciousness caused by traumatization on four phenomenological dimensions: time, thought, body, and emotion. It is designed to provide a transdiagnostic model to distinguish altered dissociative states of consciousness in different trauma-related disorders. The experiences in the normal waking state are ego syntonic, that is, they are "I-experiences." These are commonly seen. The experiences described in the TRASC are ego dystonic: nonself-referential. In the dimension of time, a further distinction is made between experiencing intrusive memories of a traumatic experience during NWS versus reexperiencing in which the person relives the trauma as if it were happening now—and is thus in a trauma-related altered state of consciousness.

The thought dimension involves the distinction between having negative thoughts about oneself (NWS) versus hearing voices with negative messages about oneself (where the voice is part of an altered state of consciousness or TRASC). The body dimension involves a distinction between hyperarousal and hypoarousal. Within this model, hyperarousal is considered nondissociative and appropriate to the normal waking state. Hypoarousal—focusing on experiences of depersonalization, freezing, paralysis—is considered dissociative and attributed to TRASC. Critics point out that the model is confusing and incongruent, particularly due to the view of hypoarousal as dissociative and hyperarousal as nondissociative, whereas hyperarousal can be equally dissociative (Dorahy & van der Hart, 2014).

After all, when there is a division of the personality, there will be parts that feel too little (e.g., overmodulation or overregulation of feelings with symptoms such as depersonalization or paralysis) and parts that feel too much and are often permanently in a state of hyperarousal (e.g., under-modulation, or underregulation of feelings). This can, for example, apply to the parts that hold anger but also to the parts that may be extremely anxious or sad (Dell, 2006a, 2006b; Dorahy & van der Hart, 2014; Steele et al., 2017; van der Hart et al., 2006).

Thus, positive dissociative symptoms, such as intrusions of dissociative parts that are highly emotional, are not considered dissociative within the model described above (see Chapter 2). In addition, no differentiation is made between depersonalization referring to a division of the personality (e.g., looking at oneself from a distance, an observing and an experiencing ego state) and depersonalization experiences that indicate a narrowing of consciousness or a state of absorption, but not a division of the personality. The following two chapters will discuss this in detail. However, a number of studies show that this model does differentiate between patients with and without PTSD and between patients with PTSD and PTSD plus a dissociative disorder (Frewen & Lanius, 2014, 2015; Frewen et al., 2015; Frewen et al., 2017; Bækkelund et al., 2018).

The debate on what should and should not be understood as dissociation and whether there are multiple distinguishable forms of dissociation has not been resolved to date. It is not my intention in this book to make a definite statement about this. However, TADS-I was developed to allow for careful research and more insight into different forms of alterations in consciousness in different patient groups, a prerequisite for reaching a correct diagnosis and thus indicating the right treatment.

By no means have all theoretical views of the construct of dissociation and its clinical implications been discussed here. I have limited myself to the various notions that are relevant to the diagnostic process. For a comprehensive discussion of the various theoretical views of the concept of dissociation and its clinical implications, I refer to a completely revised version of the standard work (Dell & O'Neil, 2009) on dissociation and dissociative disorders (Dorahy et al., 2022). With contributions from many renowned leaders in the field, this is the most complete new source of information in this area.

Two Distinct Psychiatric Classification Systems

A further factor that creates difficulties in the diagnosis of dissociative disorders concerns the differences in classification of dissociative disorders in the two most widely used psychiatric classification systems, which are the *Diagnostic and Statistical Manual of Mental Disorders* (DSM-5; APA, 2013; DSM-5-TR; APA, 2022) and the *International Classification of Diseases* (ICD-10; WHO, 1993; ICD-11; WHO, 2019).

Table 1.1 lists the dissociative disorders in both classification systems. For the sake of clarity, I have placed the diagnoses alongside each other. On the left, the correct order used in DSM-5 is maintained, while the ICD diagnoses are placed in the adjoining column. Please note that ICD-11 uses a slightly different order from DSM-5.

Patients with DID or OSDD-1 report many somatoform (sensorimotor) dissociative symptoms, such as paralysis of part of their body or entire lower body; sudden inability to speak, see, hear, or swallow. In addition, they often report non-epileptic seizures and unexplained pain symptoms (Boon & Draijer, 1993a, 1993b; Bowman, 1993a, 2006; Nijenhuis, 2004 (1999), 2009; Nijenhuis et al., 1997). DSM-5 categorizes these so-called conversion disorders as part of the somatic symptom disorders, failing to acknowledge the primarily dissociative nature of these disorders. The new Netherlands standard of care for conversion disorders, for instance, does not even mention dissociation or possible comorbidity with dissociative disorders at all. Anxiety and depression in particular are mentioned as common comorbid disorders in this standard of care (Akwa, 2017).

Clinicians using DSM-5 may therefore easily overlook dissociation in patients with a number of somatic or conversion symptoms. During the development of the DSM-5, there was discussion about categorizing the DSM-IV-TR conversion disorder as a dissociative disorder. Suggestions to this effect have not been followed up (Spiegel et al., 2013). However, the DSM-5 does mention comorbidity with dissociative disorders in conversion disorders.

TABLE 1.1

Dissociative Disorders in Accordance
with ICD-11 and DSM-5, Respectively

Dissociative disorders in ICD-11	Dissociative disorders in DSM-5*
Dissociative Identity Disorder (DID) (6B64)	Dissociative Identity Disorder (DID)
Dissociative Amnesia (6B61)	Dissociative Amnesia
Depersonalization/Derealization Disorder (6B66)	Depersonalization/Derealization Disorder
Partial Dissociative Identity Disorder (Partial DID) (6B65)	*In DSM-5 the first example of OSDD (see below) is comparable to this.*
Other Specified Dissociative Disorder (6B6Y)	Other Specified Dissociative Disorder (OSDD) 1. Chronic and recurrent syndromes of mixed dissociative symptoms 2. Identity disturbance due to prolonged and intense coercive persuasion 3. Acute dissociative reactions to stressful events 4. Dissociative Trance
Dissociative Disorder, Unspecified (6B6Z)	Unspecified Dissociative Disorder
Dissociative Neurological Symptom Disorder (6B60)	Conversion Disorder (Functional Neurological Symptom Disorder)
Trance Disorder (6B62)	*In DSM-5 an example of OSDD*
Possession Trance Disorder (6B63)	*In DSM-5 part of criterion A of DID*
Source: WHO. International Classification of Diseases 11th Revision (ICD-11). icd.who.int, Feb 2022.	*Source: Diagnostic and Statistical Manual of Mental Disorders (DSM-5 or DSM-5-TR). APA, 2013, 2022.* * Disorders in DSM-5-TR that have their origins in the DSM-5 are still called "DSM-5 disorders" in accordance with usage in the DSM-5-TR.

In ICD-11, conversion disorders are classified as dissociative disorders and are now referred to as dissociative neurological symptom disorders. In fact, the latter is an odd and confusing term as well; it includes the word neurological, whereas these disorders are in fact not neurologically identifiable, with functional, dissociative symptoms involved. In that respect, the ICD-11 term above is less appropriate compared to ICD-10, where these disorders were called dissociative disorders of movement and sensation (1992). In order to treat patients with such symptoms, it is of great importance to understand them as dissociative.

Both classification systems also fail to address the possibility that some pain symptoms may be dissociative in nature. Many patients with a dissociative disorder enter the mental health system with inadequately understood pain symptoms and other physical complaints, such as extreme fatigue; in DSM-5, this is also called a somatic symptom disorder. The physical symptoms are often related to early childhood abuse. For example, medically unexplained but intense abdominal pain may be associated with a form of (partial) reexperiencing by a dissociative part of an original sexual trauma during which this abdominal pain was experienced.

Unlike DSM-5, ICD-11 includes two separate dissociative disorders, trance disorder and possession trance disorder. These disorders should be distinguished from general, culturally accepted, normal trance and possession experiences. Both disorders are included in DSM-5, but dissociative trance is categorized as one of the other specified dissociative disorders, and experiences of possession are described as a cultural variety of DID. I will elaborate on this when discussing the separate DSM-5 and ICD-11 dissociative disorders in the next section of this chapter.

Finally, unlike DSM-5, ICD-11 includes a separate category called partial DID. I will address this diagnosis later in this chapter.

High Comorbidity

A third factor complicating the diagnosis of dissociative disorders is their high degree of comorbidity. Patients with dissociative disorders, particularly with DID or OSDD-1, typically report many symptoms of other mental disorders (Boon & Draijer, 1993a; Brand & Loewenstein, 2010; Carlson & Armstrong, 1994; Coons, 1984; Dell, 2009a, 2009b; Frankel, 2009; Kluft, 1985, 1991; Ross, 1995, 1997; Steinberg, 1994a, 1994b, 1995, 2004; Steinberg et al., 1993). Therefore, patients may be treated for the same symptoms, or indeed for a variety of symptoms, sometimes for many years, without a dissociative disorder being considered. A severe, not clearly dissociative symptom that is prevalent at the time of presentation will obviously affect the diagnostic process. In such cases, severe symptoms of this kind may require immediate intervention, for instance, when a patient presents to a clinic for eating disorders with severe underweight, or when a patient is admitted with severe suicidal or self-harming behavior. There is usually not enough time to explore whether there might be an underlying dissociative disorder that is affecting the presenting symptom. In fact, clinicians may not even consider the possibility of such an underlying disorder. When the presenting symptom is controlled or is fading, the patient is discharged from treatment without the dissociative disorder being recognized, let alone treated. The complaint may diminish temporarily but can resurface—sometimes out of the blue—when the dissociative part of the person associated with the symptom is activated or triggered.

Many comorbid symptoms in patients with dissociative disorders can be understood as trauma-related symptoms. After all, severe early childhood traumatization can lead to anxiety and mood problems, sleep problems, substance abuse, and so on. Even though it is this high comorbidity that calls for serious consideration of an underlying dissociative disorder, this very comorbidity will often also be the reason why the underlying disorder may be overlooked for many years.

If patients do not present with primary dissociative symptoms, how do they end up coming to the attention of the mental health professional and starting treatment? Patients may in fact present with the following symptoms or mental disorders:

- Sleep problems, difficulty falling and staying asleep, and in addition, all typical PTSD symptoms that may occur during sleep such as nightmares, reexperiencing, and flashbacks
- Symptoms associated with anxiety disorders: panic, obsessive-compulsive behaviors, specific phobias, and of course posttraumatic stress symptoms
- Symptoms associated with mood disorders: depression, suicidality, extreme mood swings
- Eating problems: anorexia, bulimia, obesity
- Substance abuse
- Psychotic symptoms: both short term and chronic. These may be dissociative symptoms that are mistaken for psychotic symptoms. Chapter 7, on differential diagnostics, will discuss these in more detail.
- Sexual problems
- Personality disorders: including associated problems with emotion regulation and attachment relationships
- Relational problems
- Unexplained physical symptoms and signs of conversion

Denial or Concealment

Patients with a dissociative disorder have a tendency to conceal or deny dissociative symptoms (Boon & Draijer, 1993a, 1995a, 2007; Loewenstein et al., 2017; Kluft, 1984, 1985, 1987a, 1987c; Kluft et al., 1988). Patients may not mention such dissociative symptoms out of fear or embarrassment unless explicitly asked about them. Even when asked, a patient may prefer not to talk about them or avoid reflecting on them and therefore provide limited or contradictory information during diagnostic assessment. van der Hart and colleagues refer to this as the phobia of mental actions or inner experiences and dissociative parts (van der Hart et al., 2006; Steele et al., 2017).

As a result, a dissociative disorder may not be diagnosed on initial examination due to a lack of clear information. This applies in particular to patients with DID because they are often initially unable to provide information about dissociative parts of their personality. Back then, we found that in more than half of the patients (20 out of 35) who had been diagnosed with dissociative disorder not otherwise specified (DDNOS in DSM-IV), the criteria of DID were met on follow-up examination after one year (Boon & Draijer, 1993a, 1995a). In this study, the nature and severity of the SCID-D scores in the DDNOS group showed no significant differences compared to the DID group. We suspected DID but were unable to assess it because the patients were not as yet able to provide information on dissociative parts.

Insufficient Diagnostic Training

During their residency in clinical psychology or psychiatry, most clinicians are inadequately trained in the recognition and treatment of dissociation and dissociative disorders (Boon & Draijer, 1995a, 2007; Draijer et al., 2012; Steele et al., 2017). This leads to underdiagnosis by those who never even consider dissociative disorder and overdiagnosis by clinicians who do not know how to distinguish dissociative symptoms that refer to a division of personality from other symptoms, such as extreme absorption and milder depersonalization symptoms. In addition, it can be difficult to distinguish between normal ego states or so-called borderline modes (Young et al., 2003) and dissociative parts of the personality. Inner conflicts or extraordinary fluctuations in emotions or thoughts occur in more than one mental disorder. Since the prevalence of trauma-related dissociative disorders is high (see Chapter 4), education and training in assessment and treatment of dissociative disorders should be a mandatory part of all clinical training programs.

Lack of Treatment Resources

Recently, many mental health institutions have been facing financial constraints and are increasingly heard to say that they cannot treat cases of DID, arguing that this would be too expensive and too much of a burden on the budget. Assessment of a dissociative disorder, especially DID, then creates a problem. Thus, the time-consuming process of assessing a dissociative disorder often is being avoided. As a result, these patients are again, as in the past, described as psychotic, or as having PTSD, or a somatization disorder, or borderline personality disorder, leaving the dissociative core of the pathology unidentified and untreated. It is hoped that this situation will improve in the Netherlands with the release of a standard of care for dissociative disorders (Akwa, 2020).

Dissociative Disorder Criteria in DSM-5 and ICD-11

As described earlier, there are differences between the dissociative disorders in DSM-5 and those in ICD-11. See Loewenstein and colleagues (2017) and Dell and O'Neil (2009) for comprehensive descriptions of the DSM-5 category of dissociative disorders. Spiegel and colleagues (2011) describe the considerations that led to proposals for modifications of the criteria for the dissociative disorders in DSM-5.

In 2019 the preliminary ICD-11 text was available online; it has been extended since then. When this chapter refers to ICD-11, it always refers to the February 2022 online version. Since the previous ICD version (ICD-10; WHO, 1992) was published 20 years earlier, it is understandable that ICD-11 has changed significantly from its previous iteration.

A number of disorders are now described more or less similarly in ICD-11 and DSM-5, although the criteria and the order and exact wording of the descriptions of the disorders are somewhat different at times. In this section I will describe these disorders and, where appropriate, I will explain discrepancies between the DSM and ICD descriptions.

DSM-5 comprises both a concise overview with the diagnostic criteria for the disorders and an expanded version (the manual) that provides much more information for each classification, some of which is incorporated into this chapter. In DSM-5, dissociative disorders are described in the DSM as a disruption or a discontinuity on the normal integration of certain functions (e.g., consciousness, memory, identity, emotion, perception, body representation, motor control, and behavior). Dissociative symptoms can potentially disrupt every area of psychological functioning (APA, 2013, p. 291, 2022, p. 329). ICD-11 adds that discontinuity may be complete, but is more commonly partial and can vary from day to day or even from one hour to the next.

Dissociative disorders are frequently found in the aftermath of trauma, and many of the symptoms, including embarrassment and confusion about the symptoms or a desire to hide them, are influenced by the proximity to trauma (APA, 2013, 2022). In ICD-11, the relationship between trauma and dissociative disorders is mentioned in DID, partial DID, and dissociative amnesia. ICD-11 states further: "Although a history of verbal or emotional abuse, neglect and other forms of childhood interpersonal trauma are associated with the development of depersonalization-derealization disorder, the association is not as strong as for other dissociative disorders" (WHO, 2019).

In describing the disorders, I have chosen to follow the order in DSM-5 and to begin with the DSM-5 criteria. Where descriptions of the disorders in the two classification systems differ significantly, I describe the differences separately. The ICD-11 dissociative disorders that are not included in DSM-5 are described immediately following my description of the DSM-5 disorders.

Dissociative Identity Disorder (DID)

Table 1.2 lists the ICD-11 criteria for dissociative identity disorder, with a comparison to the DSM-5 criteria. It should be noted that criterion sets in the DSM-5-TR that have their origins in the DSM-5 are still called "DSM-5 criteria" in the DSM-5-TR because the conceptual construction of the criteria has remained unchanged. The ICD-11 now includes DID as a separate classification for the first time. In the ICD-10, the diagnosis of multiple personality disorder (MPD) was marginalized as one of the other dissociative disorders. In addition, it was commented upon as being a very rare disorder, under debate as to whether it was an iatrogenic or culture-specific disorder.

TABLE 1.2 ICD-11 Criteria Dissociative Identity Disorder (DID) and Comparison With DSM-5	
ICD-11 Criteria Dissociative Identity Disorder (DID) (6B64)	**Comparison With DSM-5 Criteria* Dissociative Identity Disorder (DID)**
Disruption of identity characterized by the presence of two or more distinct personality states (dissociative identities), involving marked discontinuities in the sense of self and agency. Each personality state includes its own pattern of experiencing, perceiving, conceiving, and relating to self, the body, and the environment.	Criterion A similarly describes the fragmentation of identity and discontinuity in self-perception, but adds that in some cultures it is experienced as possession. In addition, it adds that symptoms may be self-reported by the patient or observed by others. Personality states may differ with regard to affect, behavior, consciousness, memory, perception, cognitive, and sensorimotor functions.
At least two distinct personality states recurrently take executive control of the individual's consciousness and functioning in interacting with others or with the environment, such as in the performance of specific aspects of daily life such as parenting, or work, or in response to specific situations (e.g., those that are perceived as threatening).	*This criterion is not included in DSM-5.*

continues

ICD-11 Criteria Dissociative Identity Disorder (DID) (6B64)	Comparison With DSM-5 Criteria* Dissociative Identity Disorder (DID)
Changes in personality state are accompanied by related alterations in sensation, perception, affect, cognition, memory, motor control, and behavior. There are typically episodes of amnesia inconsistent with ordinary forgetting, which may be severe.	Criterion A describes changes in sensorimotor function, perception, cognition, affect, memory, and behavior. Criterion B describes the presence of episodes of memory loss that do not correspond to ordinary forgetting.
The symptoms are not better accounted for by another mental disorder (e.g., schizophrenia or other primary psychotic disorder).	*This criterion is not included in DSM-5.*
The symptoms are not due to the effects of a substance or medication on the central nervous system, including withdrawal effects (e.g., blackouts or chaotic behavior during substance intoxication) and are not due to a disease of the nervous system (e.g., complex partial seizures) or to a sleep–wake disorder (e.g., symptoms occur during hypnagogic or hypnopompic states).	Criterion E also requires that the symptoms are not due to the effects of substances or to a medical condition, but does not mention mental disorders such as Sleep–Wake disorder.
The symptoms result in significant impairment in personal, family, social, educational, occupational, or other important areas of functioning. If functioning is maintained, it is only through significant additional effort.	Criterion C requires that there be distress and/or functional impairment, but does not mention the extra effort required to maintain functioning.
This criterion is not in ICD-11.	Criterion D requires that the phenomena not be part of cultural or religious practices or, in children, fantasy play or imaginary friends.
Source: WHO. International Classification of Diseases 11th Revision (ICD-11). icd.who.int, Feb 2022.	*Source: Diagnostic and Statistical Manual of Mental Disorders (DSM-5 or DSM-5-TR):* APA, 2013, 2022. ** Criteria sets in DSM-5-TR that have their origins in the DSM-5 are still called "DSM-5 criteria" in accordance with usage in the DSM-5-TR.*

The ICD-11 text differs from DSM-5 in the following ways:

- The second ICD-11 criterion is no longer included in the DSM-5 criteria (see Table 1.2). However, DSM-IV did include a similar criterion: "At least two of these identities or personality states recurrently take control of the person's behavior." This criterion was omitted from the DSM-5 criteria because it might suggest that DID would be characterized by invariably overt and visible switches from one dissociative part to another, which is often not the case, as will be explained in more detail in the next section.
- The addition in DSM-5 that it "may be described in some cultures as

an experience of possession," indicating a kind of transcultural form of DID, is not included in ICD-11. ICD-11 includes a separate diagnosis for possession trance disorder, discussed later in this section.

- There is an addition in DSM-5 (first criterion) that the signs and symptoms about the presence of multiple personality states may also have been "observed by others or reported by the individual." This addition is not included in the ICD-11 text, and is also discussed in the next section.

Dilemmas in Diagnosing DID

The diagnosis of DID is susceptible to both under- and overdiagnosis. In my view several factors are at play here: the high degree of comorbidity, flawed criteria that were changed slightly in each new revision of the DSM, and the fact that patients with DID often conceal their classic dissociative symptoms (the criteria for establishing the diagnosis) or show little awareness of them.

Diagnostic Criteria of DID

From the start, there has been discussion about the criteria for the diagnosis of DID, which was referred to as MPD at the time. The diagnosis of MPD was included in DSM-III in 1980. Since then, several revised editions of DSM have appeared, each time slightly modifying the criteria for DID. For example, the name of the diagnosis was changed from MPD to dissociative identity disorder (DID), and the criterion of amnesia did not appear in DSM-III-R, only to be added again in DSM-IV (APA, 1994). In DSM-5 it even was expanded upon. ICD-11 also includes the criterion amnesia.

Changes in DSM-5 From Previous Versions

A first modification in DSM-5 involves the omission of the DSM-IV-TR B criterion stating that at least two identities or personality states repeatedly take control of the individual's behavior. This addition was omitted in DSM-5 because it was considered to be too indicative of "overt switching" (see next section).

A subsequent modification consists of the DSM-5 amnesia criterion being more clearly defined and expanded upon to include the addition that there may be gaps in memory related to "everyday events."

A third important change in the DSM-5 criteria is the addition that in some cultures DID may involve an experience of possession.

A final and important change in criteria for DID concerns the addition that it may also involve a discontinuity in the normal integration of motor control. DID is now the only dissociative disorder in which a somatoform symptom may be present in addition to psychoform dissociative symptoms. However, DSM-5 does not do sufficient justice to somatoform dissociative symptoms overall. Many somatoform dissociative symptoms are still understood as conversion; this possibly results in a patient with DID being diagnosed with a comorbid conversion disorder or misdiagnosed with a conversion disorder.

Dilemmas Around the DSM-5 and ICD-11 Criterion of "Personality State"

As discussed, both DSM-5 and ICD-11 texts still reflect the dilemma as to how to interpret a personality state, a term that was used in both classifications, the difficulty being that—in sharp contrast to presentations portrayed in the media—different "personality states" are rarely directly observable during diagnostic assessment. Depictions in the media usually suggest that DID involves ongoing overt and dramatic changes between different "distinct personalities" with different clothing, habits, and the like. Such an image confirms the popular but mistaken idea that there may be totally separate people within one person. In fact, the clinical presentation of DID is completely different. Patients with DID are embarrassed by the fluctuations in behavior, thoughts, and emotions and the associated loss of control they experience, and they try to conceal these wherever possible.

Kluft (1985) was one of the first to note that diagnosing DID (then MPD) is difficult because there are generally no overt switches, much less during diagnostic assessment. In many cases, dissociative parts influence behavior as if from behind the scenes and is experienced by the person, but most of the time not noticeable to people around them. This phenomenon is also called passive influence. Kluft stated at the time that in many cases a diagnosis of DID (then MPD) could only be made when the patient answered questions about amnesia and Schneiderian symptoms in the affirmative (Kluft, 1987a; see Chapter 2 for descriptions of such symptoms). This involves the experience of behavior being influenced by a dissociative part within that is experienced as ego dystonic.[2] However, because of shame and anxiety about revealing this, patients usually will not mention it during diagnostic assessment unless explicitly asked.

A second unresolved dilemma relates to the fact that, even with all the changes in DSM-5 and the ICD-11, the criteria for DID are too limited, selectively emphasizing amnesia and the existence of two or more distinct personality states (Boon & Draijer, 1993a, 1995a, 2007; Coons & Bowman, 2001; Dell, 2006a, 2009a; Spiegel et al., 2013). Because clinicians usually cannot directly observe dissociative parts of the personality during diag-

---

2 Ego syntonic used in the sense of the "I experience," where the person experiences ownership over their thoughts, feelings, and actions, versus ego dystonic, where the person does not experience ownership over their thoughts, feelings, and actions.

nostic assessment, only the criterion of amnesia remains. Thus, the question remains: How can clinicians diagnose this disorder? In DSM-5, the criterion "perceiving personality states" now has been supplemented with the possibility that a patient independently reports experiencing "distinct personality states" or that others have observed this.

In my view, this has not made diagnosing DID any easier, for the very reason that many patients who have DID initially realize little or virtually nothing of the presence of dissociative parts, or they are extremely phobic about these and try to conceal anything that might point to the existence of such parts. They do experience the passive influence of parts but do not understand their origin. Therefore, they will not always observe or report these spontaneously and often will not answer relevant questions in the affirmative during the diagnostic interview. Patients who are confused about their symptoms and believe they have dissociative parts or DID, or who mimic DID, might be misdiagnosed based on these criteria (see Chapter 10, Incorrect (False-Positive) DID Diagnoses and Factitious or Imitated DID). Moreover, if the changes in personality are not dramatic, how can others (e.g., friends or family) distinguish the fluctuations in behavior of, say, a patient with borderline personality disorder from those of a patient with DID?

The Clinical Presentation of DID

If the current diagnostic criteria provide insufficient direction, then how does DID present itself during diagnostic assessment?

Critics of the current diagnostic criteria have called for the inclusion of polythetic[3] criteria for the diagnosis of DID, rather than the current monothetic[4] criteria (Dell, 2006a, 2009a; see also the detailed description of the proposed changes to the DSM-5 category of dissociative disorders by Spiegel et al., 2011; Spiegel et al., 2013).

DID is a polysymptomatic condition: empirical studies worldwide have described a much more extensive cluster of symptoms than are currently included in the DSM and ICD diagnostic criteria (Boon & Draijer, 1993a, 1993b; Dell, 2006a, 2009a; Dorahy et al., 2014).

As an example, based on our research with the SCID-D in 71 patients

---

3 A polythetic classification requires members of that class to have a large number of characteristics in common without necessarily having to share a specific characteristic. For example, when patients must meet 4 of 13 symptoms to classify for a disorder, they do not need to be the same 4.

4 A monothetic classification requires members of that class to share one or more specific characteristics. These characteristics are also a prerequisite for membership in that class. For example, in DID the specifically required characteristics are "the fragmentation of identity characterized by two or more distinct personality states" and "amnesia."

with DID, Nel Draijer and I described a coherent cluster of primary dissociative symptoms. This cluster included repeated episodes of various forms of amnesia in the present (i.e., not exclusively amnesia for autobiographical events in the past), depersonalization, derealization, and identity confusion, particularly related to the amnesia and to hearing voices (Boon & Draijer, 1993a, 1993b, 1995a, 2007). Some patients were able to describe dissociative parts, others just barely or not at all. However, almost all patients reported that they heard voices commenting, giving commands, or talking among themselves. Also, many patients reported somatoform dissociative symptoms, such as conversion symptoms and non-epileptic seizures. In all patients, clear, indirect indications of the existence of dissociative parts of the personality were found, such as coming across things they must have acquired or encountering evidence of actions they must have undertaken themselves, but without any recollection of any of these (see also Chapter 2). Finally, patients reported a range of secondary, possibly trauma-related symptoms, including anxiety and mood problems, intrusions of traumatic experiences, and other PTSD symptoms. Comorbidity was high; patients in the study by Nel Draijer and me had been under the care of mental health professionals with other diagnoses for an average of over 8 years before DID was diagnosed. On this basis, we formulated a cluster of symptoms that was more comprehensive than the ones included for DID in DSM-IV at the time.

Dell (2009a) argued that the fact that several clinicians had been developing their own lists of symptoms for DID based on empirical research was the clearest evidence that the monothetical DSM criteria do not provide sufficient direction to arrive at a correct diagnosis. Several studies using the Multidimensional Inventory of Dissociation (MID; Dell, 2006b, 2009a) consistently present evidence for polythetic criteria for DID (see Dell, 2009a, pp. 397–398). Based on empirical studies, Dell (2006a, 2009a) describes a list of 13 well-documented dissociative symptoms, broadly similar to what we described in 1993. This list is provided in Table 1.3. Based on these clusters of symptoms, the clinician is able to establish the diagnosis of DID reliably without having witnessed the patient switching between dissociative parts.

Ultimately, the recommendations for revisions of DSM-5 criteria for DID involved minor amendments and monothetic criteria (Spiegel et al., 2011; Spiegel et al., 2013). The rationale behind this choice, according to Spiegel and colleagues, is underpinned by the fact that, based on all empirical research to date, patients with DID constitute a fairly homogeneous group, with amnesia and the (subjective) experience of a division of the personality as central features. Spiegel and colleagues (Spiegel et al., 2011; Spiegel et al., 2013) argue that a long list of polythetic criteria would not simplify

TABLE 1.3
Thirteen Well-Documented Dissociative Symptoms in DID (Dell, 2009a)

Symptom	Empirical Studies
Primary Dissociative Symptoms	
1. Amnesia	32
2. Conversion	28
3. Voices	22
4. Depersonalization	20
5. Trance	17
6. Self-alteration	16
7. Derealization	14
8. Awareness of the presence of alters	10
9. Identity confusion	10
10. Flashbacks	8
Psychotic-like Dissociative Symptoms	
11. Auditory hallucinations	13
12. Visual hallucinations	11
13. Some Schneiderian first-rank symptoms	14
[-] "Made" actions	6
[-] Voices arguing	5
[-] Voices commenting	4
[-] "Made" feelings	3
[-] Thought withdrawal	2
[-] Thought insertion	2
[-] "Made" impulses	1

Note: Empirical Studies refers to the number of studies that have reported the occurrence of a particular dissociative symptom in individuals with DID. These passive-influence Schneiderian symptoms are correlated with DID. Three remaining Schneiderian symptoms (i.e., audible thoughts, thought broadcasting, and delusional perception) are not correlated with DID.

Made behavior, actions, and feelings are the experience that actions, impulses, or feelings do not come from the presenting part itself, but are, as it were, controlled by another part(s).

P. F. Dell, 2006, *Psychiatric Clinics of North America*, 29, pp. 1–26. Copyright 2006 by Elsevier B. V. Adapted with permission.

the diagnostic process. Nevertheless, the DSM-5 manual opted to include a comprehensive description of the complex presentation of DID in the text accompanying the criteria of DID. In practice, a clinician will need to find a cluster of psychoform and somatoform symptoms, as described in the next chapter and as highlighted in other empirical research (see Table 1.3 for an overview).

How Do Patients With DID Answer Questions About Possibly Trauma-Related Symptoms?

Patients with DID generally also report many other symptoms for which they have sometimes received years of unsuccessful therapy, usually because the underlying dissociative disorder was not identified. Many symptoms, such as anxiety, suicidal actions, self-harm, sleep problems, negative thoughts, obsessive–compulsive symptoms, eating problems, or medically unexplained symptoms are related to the original traumatization and are kept or experienced by parts that are stuck in trauma time (Steele et al., 2017; van der Hart et al., 2006). The dissociative part that is present during a diagnostic assessment is usually one that functions in daily life. That part suffers intensely from these symptoms, but also often feels as if the symptoms are beyond their control. Sometimes there is partial amnesia for behavior such as binge eating, suicide attempts, or self-mutilation because other dissociative parts are responsible for such behaviors. For this reason, TADS-I includes a separate section on possibly trauma-related symptoms, with questions about dissociative symptoms in conjunction with the trauma-related symptom (see Chapter 5 for a detailed explanation). In the course of this part of the interview, it often becomes clear in patients with DID that there is a dissociative organization of the personality with parts that have tasks and functions in daily life, and parts that are stuck in trauma time. Patients with DID often spontaneously respond that they are vaguely aware of a symptom but do not understand where it comes from and have no control over it, and they sometimes have no recollection at all of certain behaviors.

When asked about sleep problems, one patient replied: *Yes, I think I always sleep well but my partner says I wander at night.* When asked by the clinician what that wandering entailed, the patient replied:

> I seem to go to the kitchen at night and eat all sorts of things, but I really don't know. I have also found myself outside my house once, I had no idea where I was and how I got there.

Another patient answered when asked about self-mutilation:

> Sometimes I do it myself, but then there's a voice telling me to do it and sometimes it seems like I'm an observer, I see myself doing it. I don't want it, but it doesn't stop. There have also been times when I didn't remember [doing] it at all.

How Does DID Present in Someone Who Does Not as Yet Realize That They Have DID?

As described earlier, in assessing the diagnosis of DID, it is important to realize that not every patient can give information about the dissociative parts. In the past, we have referred to this as "the initial presentation of DID" (Boon & Draijer, 1993a; Dell, 2009b, p. 416). Others refer to it as "covert" DID (Dell, 2009b; Spiegel et al., 2011). Patients with this covert presentation report the same symptoms as those with DID, such as various forms of amnesia in the present, finding things in one's personal belongings that weren't there previously, hearing that they were present somewhere while having no recall of it, and a range of Schneiderian symptoms, such as hearing voices or the experience that their behavior is being influenced by something inside themselves. Such patients may also show other indications that the behavior is outside the person's control, comments from others that they find the person is behaving differently or strangely and the inability to reconcile certain behaviors. This often confuses patients. They feel embarrassed or tend to minimize or downplay their symptoms. They have no explanation for their symptoms or attribute them to psychosis or to neurological problems, such as dementia. In the Dutch study by Boon and Draijer (1993a), such patients often received the diagnosis of DDNOS, while the researchers suspected they had DID. In 20 of the 24 patients, it appeared that the diagnosis of DID could be confirmed after one year, because patients had gradually overcome the phobia for the dissociative disorder and the dissociative parts during therapy (Boon & Draijer, 1993a).

Prevalence of DID

Based on empirical research, the prevalence of DID in the general population is estimated to be 1.1% to 3.1%; in populations of psychiatric patients this estimation is 0.4% to 14% (Dorahy et al., 2014; Loewenstein et al., 2017; Şar, 2011). However, the study that found a prevalence of 14% was conducted in an acute admission ward in Turkey and stands out as the only one with a rate this high (Şar, 2011).

Explanations for the differences in the prevalence of DID in the above studies include the following:

1. The geographical location of the facility where the assessment took place. As an example, a relatively high prevalence of DID (6%) and of other dissociative disorders (30%) was found in a New York neighborhood with a high number of traumatized people (Foote et al., 2006);
2. The use of a range of diagnostic interviews (Friedl et al., 2000), generally leading to lower prevalence being found with the SCID-D than with

the dissociative disorder interview schedule (DDIS; Ross, Heber, Norton, et al., 1989);

3. Cultural differences in the interpretation of symptoms that may be a factor of influence (see also Dorahy et al., 2014). For example, prevalence in the United States and Turkey is multiple times higher than in many European countries. In Europe, Friedl and Draijer (2000) conducted a survey of newly admitted psychiatric patients in the Netherlands and found that 2% met criteria for DID; Gast and colleagues (2001) found 0.9% in a similar German study. Both studies were done using the SCID-D.

Early Childhood Traumatization in Patients With DID

DID is understood as a posttraumatic developmental disorder that arises in childhood, typically before the age of six (WHO, 2019; APA, 2013, 2022; Boon & Draijer, 1993a, 1993b; Coons et al., 1988; Dorahy et al., 2014; Kluft, 1984, 1985; Loewenstein et al., 2017; Middleton & Butler, 1998; Putnam, 1985, 1989, 1997; Ross et al., 1990a; Şar, 2011; Şar, Dorahy, & Krüger, 2017). All studies that examined the presence of early childhood traumatization in patients with DID found extremely high rates of abuse compared to other diagnostic groups (Loewenstein, 2018). In 10 studies of DID, childhood sexual abuse was found to occur in 70% to 100% (median 83%), childhood physical abuse in 60% to 95% (median 81%), and both sexual abuse and physical abuse in 77% to 100% (median 94%), often by multiple offenders over many years (see Loewenstein, 2018; Loewenstein et al., 2017). In the SCID-D study conducted by Nel Draijer and me involving 71 patients with DID, we found that 94% reported physical and/or sexual abuse (Boon & Draijer, 1993a, 1993b). Our study also revealed that a number of patients had no memories of their early childhood; for example, they reported amnesia for their life before the age of 12. Follow-up research showed that a number of these patients were still being abused by the original perpetrators at the time of the study and that a history of sexual abuse had begun at a very young age.

Of course, the etiology of DIS involves multiple factors in addition to early childhood traumatization. These include cognitive, neurobiological, systemic, and developmental factors (Freyd, 1994; Kluft, 1984, 1993; Putnam, 1989, 1997, 2006, 2016; Şar et al., 2017).

Controversy Over DID

Since the classification of DID first appeared in DSM (DSM-III; APA, 1980), there has been discussion as to whether this diagnosis actually exists. According to DSM-5, dissociative disorders and DID in particular occur often after a person has experienced traumatizing events. This is known as the trauma model.[5] This view is shared worldwide and is also the foundation of the International Society for the Study of Trauma and Dissociation (ISSTD) guidelines (APA, 2013, 2022; ISSTD, 2011; WHO, 2019).

The previous section referred to the empirical research supporting the trauma model. However, there are those who believe that DID is created through suggestion by practitioners and through the media. According to this socio–cognitive or iatrogenic model, highly imaginative patients may be influenced by suggestion and develop dissociative parts and also fabricate a history of trauma (Spanos, 1994; Lilienfeld et al., 1999). Finally, a so-called fantasy model is described. This model assumes that dissociation is a cognitive trait that leads to fantasy and confabulation of traumatic experiences (Giesbrecht et al., 2008; Lynn et al., 2012). Both the socio–cognitive and the fantasy model are very similar.

However, a large review of nearly 1,500 studies by Dalenberg and colleagues shows a robust relationship between trauma and dissociation, particularly in DID, and little empirical support for the fantasy model (Dalenberg et al., 2012; Dalenberg et al., 2014). Moreover, no study in clinical populations supports the fantasy model (Brand, Şar, et al., 2016; Brand, Vissia, et al., 2016; Brand & Frewen, 2017; Brand et al., 2018; Dalenberg et al., 2020; Loewenstein, 2018). Recent neurophysiological and neurobiological research also supports the trauma model and the existence of separate dissociative parts of the personality (Reinders et al., 2006; Reinders et al., 2012; Reinders et al., 2019; Reinders & Veltman, 2020; Schlumpf et al., 2013).

However, there are also patients who have come to believe—often jointly with their therapists—that they have DID, when in fact they do not. These patients may be differentiated from patients who genuinely have DID (Boon & Draijer, 1993a, 1995a; Brand et al., 2006; Brand, Tursich, et al., 2014; Brand & Chasson, 2015; Brand, Webermann, & Frankel, 2016; Draijer & Boon, 1999; Reinders et al., 2006; Reinders et al., 2012; Reinders et al., 2019; Visia et al., 2016). In the 1990s, Nel Draijer and I regularly saw patients with a false-positive diagnosis during our research with the SCID-D where there was uncertainty about the symptoms in both these patients and their clinicians. Recognizing these patients with factitious or imitated DID is very important, because in their case the iatrogenic/fantasy model applies. Hence, a robust differential diagnosis can overcome and resolve the dichotomy, and thus the controversy, about the diagnosis of DID.

---

5 The trauma model states that dissociation is a psychobiological state or trait that has a protective function in response to traumatic or overwhelming experiences (Loewenstein, 2018).

In Chapter 10, I explore the differences between patients with DID and patients who consciously or subconsciously mimic DID or think they have DID.

Possession Trance Disorder as a Cultural Variant of DID in DSM-5

Research into pathological possession in non-Western cultures has demonstrated phenomenological similarities to DID, including severe dissociative symptoms, such as amnesia for the state of possession, identity change, and a high prevalence of traumatic experiences in the past (Loewenstein et al., 2017; Spiegel et al., 2013; van Duijl et al., 2010).

Worldwide, two different manifestations of DID would thus exist: the classic Western-culture form of DID and a cultural variant of fragmentation of the identity (or a division of the personality), based on experiences of possession attributed to external entities, spirits, powers, or demons. This possession form of DID is thought to occur particularly in non-Western cultures, but also within specific religious communities in Western society. The non-possession form, the most commonly described form of DID, is based on the discontinuity in self-perception and sense of self-control resulting from the subjective inner experience of having more than one part of the personality. The two variants are not mutually exclusive though (for detailed descriptions see Loewenstein et al., 2017 and Spiegel et al., 2013), and the non-possession form of DID also occurs in non-Western cultures.

Over the past three decades, I have seen several patients from African countries, Suriname, and Afghanistan with a classic Western-culture presentation of DID. That is, these patients described a completely similar cluster of symptoms: amnesia, Schneiderian symptoms, and the presence of internally experienced dissociative parts that were able to take control of their behavior. All reported a history of sexual and physical abuse that had begun in childhood in their country of origin. Most of them had come to the Netherlands as migrants or refugees later in life. Apart from the cluster of dissociative symptoms, all reported severe PTSD and other trauma-related symptoms as well. There were no instances of possession attributed to external entities or ancestors in this group. Nel Draijer and Pauline van Zon have also reported on a Western form of DID in child soldiers (Draijer & van Zon, 2013).

It is debatable whether the classification of the possession form in the DSM-5 as a form of DID does justice to the much broader global phenomenon of pathological possession. Moreover, we are justified in asking whether they are the same phenomena. Based on a large literature review, During and colleagues (2011) have pointed out that it would be important to include thc two diagnoses as independent classifications in DSM as well. The reason the two diagnoses were not included as separate classifications may be due to the phenomenological similarities between the non-Western possession form of DID and the Western form of DID (see Spiegel et al., 2011). Van Duijl (2010, 2014), who has done extensive research in Uganda on the relationship between possession, dissociation, and trauma, points out that a major disadvantage of this classification, particularly with possession in non-Western cultures, is that local explanations and interventions—including, for example, collaboration with traditional healers—are overshadowed by a Western interpretation of the symptoms. She advocates a separate diagnostic category within the dissociative disorders for pathological trance and possession that is more globally identifiable and applicable to a broad patient group, similar to ICD-11 (van Duijl et al., 2010; van Duijl et al., 2014; van Duijl, 2014). Particularly in light of the worldwide increase in the movement of migrants and refugees to Western countries, it is important to better recognize the socio–cultural significance of trance and possession symptoms and not to treat them exclusively from a Western psychiatric perspective (van Duijl et al., 2013). In non-Western patients, the Cultural Formulation Interview, as included in DSM-5, can be a useful diagnostic adjunct to gain more insight into symptoms (DSM-5: APA, 2013, pp. 749–759).

Trance and possession experiences are also common in strict religious communities in Western countries where people speak in tongues or sometimes believe in possession by the devil or demons (Tobin, 2019). Research and case descriptions have shown though, that possession experiences are also regularly reported by patients with dissociative disorder (Goodwin et al., 1990; Ross, 2011, Şar et al., 2014).

Dissociative Amnesia

Table 1.4 lists the ICD-11 criteria for dissociative amnesia, with a comparison to the DSM-5 criteria. There is one difference in the wording of the DSM-5 text compared to the wording in ICD-10 and ICD-11. ICD-10 and ICD-11 wordings of dissociative amnesia emphasize that the amnesia is for recent traumatizing or stressful events. The DSM-5 description refers to amnesia for important autobiographical information, but not necessarily of a recent date or invariably of a traumatic or stressful nature. Thus, the definition in DSM-5 is broader. Both ICD-11 and DSM-5 add that the amnesia is primarily localized or selective for specific events. Rarely, there may be generalized amnesia for identity and life history (ICD-11). (See Table 1.5 for an overview.)

TABLE 1.4
ICD-11 Criteria Dissociative Amnesia and Comparison with DSM-5

ICD-11 Criteria Dissociative Amnesia (6B61)	Comparison with DSM-5 Criteria* Dissociative Amnesia
Inability to recall important autobiographical memories, typically of recent traumatic or stressful events, that is inconsistent with ordinary forgetting.	Criterion A also describes the inability to remember important autobiographical information, usually caused by stress or psychotrauma. It adds that this is usually localized or selective amnesia, or generalized amnesia for one's identity and life history. (See Table 1.5 for the different types of amnesia as defined by the DSM-5.)
The memory loss does not occur exclusively during episodes of trance disorder, possession trance disorder, dissociative identity disorder, or partial dissociative identity disorder and is not better accounted for by another mental disorder (e.g., posttraumatic stress disorder, complex posttraumatic stress disorder, a neurocognitive disorder such as dementia).	*This criterion is not included in DSM-5.*
The symptoms are not due to the effects of a substance or medication on the central nervous system (e.g., alcohol), including withdrawal effects, and are not due to a disease of the nervous system (e.g., temporal lobe epilepsy), another medical condition (e.g., a brain tumor), or to head trauma.	Criterion C specifies that the disorder cannot be attributed to the effects of substance use or to another neurological or medical condition. The examples differ slightly.
The memory loss results in significant impairment in personal, family, social, educational, occupational, or other important areas of functioning.	Criterion B also requires that the symptoms cause clinically significant distress and/or functional impairments.
Specifications in ICD-11	*Specifications in DSM-5*
With dissociative fugue (6B61.0)	*With dissociative fugue*
Dissociative amnesia with dissociative fugue is characterized by all of the features of dissociative amnesia, accompanied by dissociative fugue, i.e., a loss of a sense of personal identity and sudden travel away from home, work, or significant others for an extended period of time (days or weeks).	The specification *with dissociative fugue* is added when a person travels or wanders in association with the amnesia for identity and life history.
Without dissociative fugue (6B61.1)	
Dissociative amnesia without dissociative fugue is characterized by all of the features of dissociative amnesia occurring in the absence of symptoms of dissociative fugue.	
Dissociative amnesia unspecified (6B61.Z)	
Source: WHO. International Classification of Diseases 11th Revision (ICD-11). icd.who.int, Feb 2022.	*Source: Diagnostic and Statistical Manual of Mental Disorders (DSM-5 or DSM-5-TR)*: APA, 2013, 2022.
	* Criteria sets in DSM-5-TR that have their origins in the DSM-5 are still called "DSM-5 criteria" in accordance with usage in the DSM-5-TR.

TABLE 1.5	
Types of Dissociative Amnesia in DSM-5*	
Localized amnesia	Failure to recall all events during a circumscribed period of time. Usually the first few hours after a shocking event.
Selective amnesia	Failure to recall some, but not all, events during a circumscribed period of time.
Systematized amnesia	The memory impairment relates to a specific category of information, such as an abusive sibling or a particular room in the parents' house.
Generalized amnesia	The memory impairment affects the entire life history.
Continuous amnesia	Failure to recall the events up until the present experiences.

Source: Diagnostic and Statistical Manual of Mental Disorders (DSM-5 or DSM-5-TR): APA, 2013, 2022.

* Criteria sets in DSM-5-TR that have their origins in the DSM-5 are still called "DSM-5 criteria" in accordance with usage in the DSM-5-TR.

In the explanatory notes to the criteria, DSM-5 mentions that localized amnesia does extend beyond one specific event (e.g., months or years associated with child abuse or intense combat). Finally, it is mentioned that generalized amnesia is rare. Unlike in DSM-IV-TR, dissociative fugue is no longer an independent diagnosis but has become a subtype of dissociative amnesia, on the grounds of its extremely low prevalence. This was modified in ICD-11 as well.

Prevalence of Dissociative Amnesia

There are not many recent large-scale studies on the prevalence of dissociative amnesia (Loewenstein, 1991b; Loewenstein et al., 2017; Şar, 2014; Spiegel et al., 2011; Spiegel et al., 2013). Most of our understanding relies on extensive case reports or studies of small groups of patients with dissociative amnesia. The studies that are available give a prevalence of 1.8% to 7.3%. The higher prevalence was found in one study of Turkish women, in which 7.3% reported dissociative amnesia at least once in their lives (Şar et al., 2007).

Comorbidity and Differential Diagnosis

Dissociative amnesia is to be distinguished from amnesia in neurocognitive disorders, in brain injury, and in disorders related to substance dependence. Furthermore, dissociative amnesia is found as a symptom in posttraumatic stress disorder (PTSD), non-epileptic seizures (referred to as a conversion disorder in DSM-5), and especially in DID. This raises the question as to how prevalent dissociative amnesia is as a separate diagnosis, particularly without PTSD or acute stress disorder. After all, it is defined as a reaction to a traumatizing or stressful event. New research with large populations of patients will have to determine the answer to this question.

Coons and Milstein (1992) examined 25 patients with the DSM-III-R diagnosis of psychogenic amnesia (referred to as dissociative amnesia in DSM-5). This patient group reported many other symptoms in addition to amnesia including depersonalization, mood disturbances, substance abuse, somatoform dissociation, and personality disorders. A high rate of sexual and physical abuse in childhood was also reported. This patient group could be differentiated in several ways from patients with DID: they reported few auditory hallucinations, less self-mutilation, and less fugues. The patients in the study by Coons and Milstein (1992) also had lower mean DES scores and reported fewer severe-abuse histories. However, a limitation of this study (Coons & Milstein, 1992) was that it did not use structured interviews and that data on PTSD were missing. Looking at their study now, almost 30 years on, the clinical presentation of dissociative amnesia with high comorbidity is difficult to distinguish from the current DSM-5 classifications OSDD-1 or PTSD with the specification "dissociative subtype" and difficult to distinguish from what was then referred to as DDNOS Example 1. It is even possible to consider the previously described covert form of DID as a differential diagnosis for these patients. A similar study involving an adequate sample size and the use of semi-structured interviews might answer the question of whether, and if so, how often dissociative amnesia occurs as a separate diagnostic category.

Depersonalization/Derealization Disorder (DPDRD)

Table 1.6 lists the ICD-11 criteria for depersonalization/derealization disorder, with a comparison to the DSM-5 criteria. When compared to earlier versions of DSM and ICD, a number of substantive changes have been made to criteria in both DSM-5 and the proposed ICD-11.

In DSM-IV-TR, derealization was listed separately as one of the examples of DDNOS. Empirical studies have shown that depersonalization and derealization often co-occur. Based on these studies, there is little evidence for derealization as a separate phenomenon (Spiegel et al., 2011), hence the inclusion of depersonalization/derealization disorder in DSM-5.

In ICD-10, depersonalization/derealization disorder was not classified as a dissociative disorder but as one of the "other neurotic disorders." The ICD-11 does classify the disorder separately as a dissociative disorder. The criteria are similar to those in the DSM-5.

TABLE 1.6 ICD-11 Criteria Depersonalization/Derealization Disorder (DPDRD) and Comparison with DSM-5	
ICD-11 Criteria Depersonalization/Derealization Disorder (DPDRD) (6B66)	**Comparison With DSM-5 Criteria* Depersonalization/Derealization Disorder (DPDRD)**
Persistent or recurrent experiences of either or both depersonalization and derealization: • Depersonalization is characterized by experiencing the self as strange or unreal, or feeling detached from, or as though one were an outside observer of, one's thoughts, feelings, sensations, body, or actions. Depersonalization may take the form of emotional and/or physical numbing, a sense of watching oneself from a distance or "being in a play," or perceptual alterations (e.g., a distorted sense of time). • Derealization is characterized by experiencing other persons, objects, or the world as strange or unreal (e.g., dreamlike, distant, foggy, lifeless, colorless, or visually distorted) or feeling detached from one's surroundings.	Criterion A is entirely similarly described.
During experiences of depersonalization or derealization, reality testing remains intact. The experiences are not associated with delusions or beliefs that the individual is being controlled by external persons or forces.	Criterion B also describes that reality testing remains intact but does not mention delusions or feelings of being controlled.
The symptoms are not better accounted for by another mental disorder (e.g., posttraumatic stress disorder, an anxiety or fear related disorder, another dissociative disorder, personality disorder.	Criterion E also requires that symptoms are not better explained by another mental disorder, but also names schizophrenia as an example, and not personality disorder.
The symptoms are not due to the effects of a substance or medication on the central nervous system, including withdrawal effects, and are not due to a disease of the nervous system (e.g., temporal lobe epilepsy), head trauma, or another medical condition.	Criterion D also requires that the symptoms are not caused by the effects of substances or by a medical condition.
The symptoms result in significant distress or significant impairment in personal, family, social, educational, occupational, or other important areas of functioning. If functioning is maintained, it is only through significant additional effort.	Criterion C also requires suffering and/or functional impairments but does not mention the significant additional effort required if functioning remains intact.
Source: WHO. International Classification of Diseases 11th Revision (ICD-11). icd.who.int, Feb 2022.	*Source: Diagnostic and Statistical Manual of Mental Disorders (DSM-5 or DSM-5-TR):* APA, 2013, 2022. * Criteria sets in DSM-5-TR that have their origins in the DSM-5 are still called "DSM-5 criteria" in accordance with usage in the DSM-5-TR.

Comorbidity

During revisions of DSM, a recurring question over the years has been whether there is sufficient evidence for classification of a separate depersonalization disorder (DPD), now depersonalization/derealization disorder (DPDRD) in DSM-5. After all, depersonalization and, to a lesser extent, derealization are very common symptoms in other mental disorders, particularly anxiety, mood, eating, and personality disorders. Patients with psychotic disorders also report depersonalization and derealization. Finally, these symptoms also frequently occur with substance use, particularly cannabis.

The studies discussed below specifically concern depersonalization disorder. At the time Nel Draijer and I carried out our research with the SCID-D (Boon & Draijer, 1993a, 1993b), there was a lack of large-scale research on DPD. In the concluding remarks of her extensive literature review and her own research with the SCID-D, Steinberg (1991) argued that depersonalization disorder should remain in DSM-IV as a separate disorder. In the research Nel Draijer and I conducted (1993a, 1993b), we found chronic, severe depersonalization symptoms in a group of patients with Axis II personality disorder and a history of childhood sexual and/or physical abuse. The depersonalization symptoms reported by these patients appeared to be not so much a symptom of a personality disorder but rather a reaction to severe childhood traumatization and/or neglect. At that time, when assessed with the SCID-D, these patients reported no amnesia, no Schneiderian symptoms, and no identity confusion or identity alteration. Thus, there was no evidence of either DID or DDNOS. Moreover, the nature and severity of depersonalization in this patient group differed markedly from the depersonalization described by a control group with personality disorders but no history of trauma. However, only a small number of patients were involved in this study.

Our findings supported Steinberg's conclusions. Looking back now after almost 30 years, perhaps these patients would best fit the DSM-5 classification of CPTSD with depersonalization and derealization, possibly with secondary structural dissociation and thus an underlying division of the personality. CPTSD was not formally recognized in the 1990s and was even less frequently diagnosed in clinical practice than it is today. At the time, chronic depersonalization was a feature of the severe PTSD symptoms in the patients in the author's research (Boon et al., 1993a, 1993b). Since our research with the SCID-D, I have encountered the aforementioned presentation of chronic depersonalization many times. These are invariably patients with CPTSD symptoms due to physical or sexual abuse. Such patients also report chronic depersonalization involving loss of contact with their emotions as well as their bodies. During therapy it becomes apparent that there is a dissociation of the personality after all, with a part that functions in daily life and a number of parts that are stuck in trauma time and hold the emotions and physical sensations associated with the abuse. Sometimes patients' confusion about their identity increases once they become more aware of this in therapy. In such cases, some patients may hear voices in their heads from a number of child parts. One could say that depersonalization disorder was the initial presentation of OSDD-1 in these patients and in a few cases even of DID.

In the past two decades, several studies have been conducted with large groups of patients with depersonalization symptoms (Baker et al., 2003; Hunter et al., 2004; Simeon et al., 2003). From these studies, a clear clinical picture emerges that supports a separate diagnostic classification of depersonalization/derealization disorder (see also Simeon, 2009; Spiegel et al., 2011). The above studies also show that the onset and the course of the disorder were independent of any comorbid disorders. The onset of DPDRD is typically in late adolescence and becomes ongoing in nature (Hunter et al., 2017).

Prevalence of DPDRD

Prevalence studies mainly deal with the DSM-IV depersonalization disorder and show that DPD occurs in 2.5% (range 0.8 to 2.8%) of the general population and in 5% to 16% of the clinical population (Foote, Smolin, Kaplan et al., 2006; Hunter et al., 2004; Ross, Duffy, & Ellason, 2002). DPDRD is equally common in women and men.

Eliciting Factors

DPDRD is typically induced by severe stress, anxiety, or acute trauma. Chronic depersonalization that begins in adolescence seems more closely related to emotional neglect than to sexual abuse or physical maltreatment (Hunter et al., 2017; Loewenstein, 2018). In such cases, the symptoms are more consistent with detachment than with compartmentalization (see Holmes et al., 2005).

Other Specified Dissociative Disorder (OSDD), OSDD-1, and Partial DID

Table 1.7 describes the other specified dissociative disorder (OSDD) in accordance with DSM-5. Compared to earlier versions of the DSM, a number of substantive changes have been made to the DSM-5. First, the name of this diagnostic classification, formerly DDNOS, was revised and now corresponds to the name in ICD-11, namely other specified dissociative disorder. Furthermore, some of the examples now listed under the classification of OSDD were amended from those in DSM-IV-TR. An example was added regarding acute dissociative reactions of a transient nature; that was missing in earlier versions of DSM. One DSM-IV-TR example, Ganser syndrome (Example 6 in the DSM-IV-TR), was removed.

ICD-11 has changed significantly from ICD-10. The ICD-10 version had a category of "mixed dissociative disorders," involving combinations of dissociative disorders (or symptoms), without any examples. ICD-10 also had a category of "other dissociative disorders" that includes MPD (now DID) and Ganser syndrome. In contrast, ICD-11 includes DID as a separate classification, while Ganser syndrome has been left out. Instead of the "mixed dissociative disorders" category in ICD-10, ICD-11 includes an OSDD category, but without examples.

The first example in DSM-5 in the category OSDD appears to have become a separate and independent diagnosis in ICD-11 with the confusing name partial dissociative identity disorder—which I will discuss in more detail in the next section.

TABLE 1.7

DSM-5 Other Specified Dissociative Disorder (OSDD)*

- The symptoms are characteristic of a dissociative disorder and, while causing distress or impairments in functioning, do not fully meet the criteria of one of the other dissociative disorders.
- The clinician chooses to state the reason why those criteria are not fully met.

- The following examples of presentations can thus be specified as another specified dissociative disorder.

  1. Mixed dissociative symptoms which are chronic and recurrent:
- Identity disturbance
- Less-than-marked discontinuities in sense of self and agency

OR

- Alterations of identity or episodes of possession
- The patient reports no dissociative amnesia

  2. Identity disturbance due to prolonged and intense coercive persuasion (brainwashing, indoctrination).

  3. Acute, transient dissociative reactions to stressful events, lasting only a few hours to 1 month, with narrowing of consciousness; depersonalization; derealization; perceptual disturbances (e.g., time slowing, macropsia); micro-amnesias; transient stupor; and/or alterations in sensorimotor functioning (e.g., analgesia, paralysis).

  4. Dissociative trance: acute narrowing or loss of consciousness, manifesting as profound unresponsiveness to environmental stimuli, sometimes accompanied by minor stereotyped behaviors (e.g., finger movements) and transient paralysis or loss of consciousness. Exclude that this be part of a cultural or religious practice.

Source: Diagnostic and Statistical Manual of Mental Disorders (DSM-5 or DSM-5-TR): APA, 2013, 2022.

* Criteria sets in DSM-5-TR that have their origins in the DSM-5 are still called "DSM-5 criteria" in accordance with usage in the DSM-5-TR.

Residual Category OSDD and the Distinction Between DID and OSDD-1

One point of discussion regarding the residual category in DSM-5 concerns the fact that the examples described are not classifications with their own codes and criteria. With respect to DSM-IV, Dell (2009b) already noted that DDNOS-1 has no stature but is considered a separate diagnosis, both in empirical and epidemiological research and by many clinicians. As early as 1991, Spiegel, then chair of the Dissociative Disorders Work Group for DSM-IV, stated that something was very wrong with the nosology of dissociative disorders (Spiegel & Cardeña, 1991; see also Dell, 2009b). Spiegel made this statement because epidemiological studies had shown that DDNOS was by far the most prevalent dissociative disorder discussed in research, yet a residual category should never have the highest prevalence figures. The high prevalence involved almost exclusively DDNOS-1. Even today, there are virtually no prevalence data on the other five examples of this residual category DDNOS (Dell, 2009b).

This first example of the residual category DDNOS mostly involved a group of patients who presented with a cluster of symptoms that corresponded to the symptoms of DID in which, however, the dissociative parts of the personality either could not be observed during diagnostic assessment, or the patient was not yet able to talk about them. In such cases, a diagnosis of DDNOS was automatically assigned. Thus, these were mostly patients who actually had DID, but could not as yet be classified as such. As mentioned in this chapter, Nel Draijer and I named this phenomenon the initial or covert presentation of DID to differentiate the diagnosis from that of atypical dissociative disorders (Boon & Draijer, 1993a). Our 1993 finding still applies, since approximately 40% of all dissociative patients are diagnosed with DDNOS (Dell, 2009b; Spiegel et al., 2011).

This issue of covert DID patients needed to be addressed in DSM-5. The text has been modified so that researchers no longer need to observe switches in order to confirm a diagnosis of DID. Based on the criteria set out in DSM-5, one can now assign the diagnosis of DID when the patient reports the subjective experience of having parts or when the switching has been observed by others. This implies that the observed prevalence of DID might increase while that of OSDD might decrease. However, the wording in DSM-5 still does not cover the group of patients who cannot or will not talk about these dissociative experiences at all. In addition, the wording may unfortunately lead to more false-positive diagnoses due to the absence of the polythetic criteria, especially the criterion of intrusions.

DSM-5 OSDD-1 and ICD-11 Partial DID

In practice, the distinction between OSDD-1 and DID remains a challenge for clinicians. The only clear criterion that distinguishes OSDD-1 from DID is that the individual does not report amnesia (the B criterion of DID). The other criterion from OSDD-1, "less-than-marked discontinuities in sense of self and agency," is too vague for the clinician to make much use of it. Precisely because DID manifests so variably in clinical practice, it would be better if a subtype of DID were described as a diagnosis in its own right, with or without amnesia, similar to the diagnosis included in ICD-11—but under a different name. In ICD-11, partial DID is included as a separate diagnosis after the diagnosis DID; its criteria are shown in Table 1.8. These are more specific than those for OSDD-1 and contain the notable difference that amnesia is mentioned as a possible, briefly occurring symptom.

TABLE 1.8
ICD-11 Criteria Partial Dissociative Identity Disorder (Partial DID) (6B65)
Essential features
Disruption of identity characterized by the experience of two or more distinct personality states (dissociative identities), involving discontinuities in the sense of self and agency. Each personality state includes its own pattern of experiencing, perceiving, conceiving, and relating to self, the body, and the environment.
One personality state is dominant and functions in daily life (e.g., parenting, work), but is intruded upon by one or more non-dominant personality states (dissociative intrusions). These intrusions may be cognitive (intruding thoughts), affective (intruding affects such as fear, anger, or shame), perceptual (e.g., intruding voices fleeting visual perceptions, sensations such as being touched), motor (e.g., involuntary movements of an arm), or behavioral (e.g., an action that lacks a sense of agency or ownership). These experiences are experienced as interfering with the functioning of the dominant personality state and are typically aversive.
The non-dominant personality states do not recurrently take executive control of the individual's consciousness and functioning to the extent that they perform in specific aspects of daily life (e.g., parenting, work). However, there may be occasional, limited, and transient episodes in which a distinct personality state assumes executive control to engage in circumscribed behaviors (e.g., in response to extreme emotional states or during episodes of self-harm or the reenactment of traumatic memories).
Additional clinical features
The symptoms are not better accounted for by another mental disorder (e.g., schizophrenia or other primary psychotic disorder).
The symptoms are not due to the effects of a substance or medication on the central nervous system, including withdrawal effects (e.g., blackouts or chaotic behavior during substance intoxication), and are not due to a disease of the nervous system (e.g., complex partial seizures) or to a sleep–wake disorder (e.g., symptoms occur during hypnagogic or hypnopompic states).
The symptoms result in significant impairment in personal, family, social, educational, occupational, or other important areas of functioning. If functioning is maintained, it is only through significant additional effort.
Source: WHO. International Classification of Diseases 11th Revision (ICD-11). icd.who.int, Feb 2022.

The term "partial" is unfortunate because, in fact, this example involves a dissociative identity disorder with fewer dissociative parts, milder symptoms, and most importantly, a different organization of the dissociative personality. There seems to be one part that functions in daily life and parts that hold the traumatic memories. The description of partial DID is highly reminiscent of secondary structural dissociation as described by van der Hart et al. (2006) with one so-called ANP and multiple EPs: one dominant part that functions in daily life and other parts (nondominant) that take control only occasionally and only briefly, in response to extreme emotions or while reexperiencing a traumatic event. In ICD-11, amnesia may be present in this diagnosis and is not an exclusionary criterion.

Perhaps at some point a description will be provided in DSM and ICD that better represents the various ways in which DID can present in clinical practice than is the case now, possibly as subtypes of DID. Except for the name, the inclusion of partial DID as a separate diagnosis in ICD-11 is an improvement on what DSM-5 has.

Unspecified Dissociative Disorder

Table 1.9 describes the unspecified dissociative disorder in accordance with DSM-5. The ICD-11 does not provide a description of this.

TABLE 1.9
DSM-5 Unspecified Dissociative Disorder in DSM-5*
The symptoms are characteristic of a dissociative disorder and do cause suffering or impairments in functioning, but do not fully meet the criteria of one of the other dissociative disorders.   • The clinician chooses not to state the reason why those criteria are not fully met.   • The clinician describes symptoms, but these do not contain sufficient information to assign a more specific classification (e.g., emergency situations).
Source: Diagnostic and Statistical Manual of Mental Disorders (DSM-5 or DSM-5-TR): APA, 2013, 2022.   * Criteria sets in DSM-5-TR that have their origins in the DSM-5 are still called "DSM-5 criteria" in accordance with usage in the DSM-5-TR.

ICD-11 Dissociative Neurological Symptom Disorders

Table 1.1 of this chapter includes the proposed dissociative disorders from ICD-11. There are significant changes in ICD-11 when compared to ICD-10, and there is now more agreement with DSM-5. The main difference between the two classification systems lies in the dissociative neurological symptom disorders, which are categorized as conversion disorders in DSM-5.

According to ICD-11, dissociative neurological symptom disorder is characterized by persistent, involuntary motor, sensory, and cognitive symptoms that are dissociative in nature and are not consistent with a recognized neurological or medical condition and are not caused by the effects of a substance or medication. Table 1.10 summarizes the ICD-11 criteria of dissociative neurological symptom disorder and a comparison with DSM-5 conversion disorder.

TABLE 1.10	
ICD-11 Criteria Dissociative Neurological Symptom Disorder and Comparison With DSM-5 Conversion Disorder	
ICD-11 Criteria Dissociative Neurological Symptom Disorder (6B600)	**Comparison With DSM-5 Criteria* Conversion Disorder (Functional Neurological Symptom Disorder)**
Involuntary disruption or discontinuity in the normal integration of motor, sensory, or cognitive functions, lasting at least several hours.	Criterion A does not describe a required duration of several hours nor a change in cognitive functions—only disruption or discontinuity of motor or sensory functions.
Clinical findings are not consistent with a recognized disease of the nervous system (e.g., a stroke) or another medical condition (e.g., a head injury).	Criterion B requires that the clinical findings are not consistent with a known condition of the central nervous system or other medical condition.
The symptoms do not occur exclusively during episodes of trance disorder, possession trance disorder, dissociative identity disorder, or partial dissociative identity disorder. The symptoms are not due to the effects of a substance or medication on the central nervous system, including withdrawal effects, do not occur exclusively during hypnagogic or hypnopompic states, and are not due to a sleep–wake disorder (e.g., sleep-related rhythmic movement disorder, recurrent isolated sleep paralysis). The symptoms are not better accounted for by another mental disorder (e.g., schizophrenia or other primary psychotic disorder, posttraumatic stress disorder).	Criterion C requires that the symptom is not better explained by another mental disorder (which includes the disorders listed in these criteria of the ICD-11), nor by a medical condition.
The symptoms result in significant impairment in personal, family, social, educational, occupational, or other important areas of functioning.	Criterion D requires that there be significant distress or impairments in functioning due to the symptom or the need for medical examination.

Specifications in ICD-11	Specifications in DSM-5
With visual disturbance (6B60.0)	With special sensory symptom (visual, olfactory, or hearing disturbance)
With auditory disturbance (6B60.1)	
With vertigo or dizziness (6B60.2)	With anesthesia or sensory loss
With other sensory disturbance (6B60.3)	
With non-epileptic seizures (6B60.4)	With attacks or seizures
With speech disturbance (6B60.5)	With speech symptom (dysphonia, slurred speech)
With paresis or weakness (6B60.6)	With weakness or paralysis
With gait disturbance (6B60.7)	With abnormal movement (tremor, dystonia, myoclonus, gait disorder)
With movement disturbance (6B60.8)	
With cognitive symptoms (6B60.9)	
With other specified symptoms (6B60.Y)	
With unspecified symptoms (6B60.Z)	
	With mixed symptoms
	With swallowing symptoms
	Acute episode < ½ yr.
	Persistent > ½ yr.
	With psychological stressor (specify)
	Without psychological stressor
Source: WHO. International Classification of Diseases 11th Revision (ICD-11). icd.who.int, Feb 2022.	Source: Diagnostic and Statistical Manual of Mental Disorders (DSM-5 or DSM-5-TR): APA, 2013, 2022.
	* Criteria sets in DSM-5-TR that have their origins in the DSM-5 are still called "DSM-5 criteria" in accordance with usage in the DSM-5-TR.

Prevalence of Somatoform Dissociative Disorders

There are no prevalence studies of the dissociative disorders of movement and sensation in ICD-10 (1992) nor of the dissociative neurological symptom disorders in ICD-11. The vast majority of research and reports deal with conversion disorders and symptoms as defined in different DSM editions. Although differently named, they involve the same symptoms and disorders as described in ICD.

The exact prevalence of conversion/neurological-symptom disorders is unknown. DSM mentions that 5% of referrals to neurologists involve conversion symptoms. De Waal et al. (2004) found a 0.2% prevalence of conversion symptoms in Dutch primary care practices.

Major differences are described between the prevalence in Western and non-Western regions of the world, with conversion symptoms in particular being much more common, up to 31%, in third world countries (Ali et al., 2015). Conversion symptoms occur two to three times more often in women than in men.

Risk Factors

A history of childhood abuse is mentioned as a risk factor for the development of conversion disorder, but more recent stressful events or emotional conflicts are also cited (Roelofs et al., 2002). Sometimes existing neurological symptoms can also be a cause for the development of conversion symptoms.

Somatization, Conversion, and Dissociation

Why are conversion disorders not categorized as dissociative disorders in DSM? Since the classification of somatization disorder in DSM-III (APA, 1980), it has been argued that at least the so-called conversion disorder should be categorized among the dissociative disorders, as it was in DSM-II and also in both ICD-10 and the ICD-11 (Bowman, 2006; Brown et al., 2007; Kihlstrom, 1992; Kihlstrom et al., 1993; Nijenhuis, 2004, 2009; van der Hart et al., 2006). The earlier versions of DSM were more etiologically defined. From DSM-III onwards, the classification became purely descriptive. In that edition, the somatoform disorders were introduced, which included all mental disorders characterized by symptoms that resemble a somatic disorder but are psychological in nature. Apparently, this was done mainly for pragmatic reasons (DSM-IV; APA, 1994).

Three arguments for revising the classification in DSM are the following:

Numerous studies of conversion disorders show high comorbidity with dissociative disorders. Similarly, patients with dissociative disorder report many conversion symptoms and other medically unexplained physical complaints (Boon & Draijer, 1993a, 1993b; Brown et al., 2007; Şar et al., 2004; Spiegel et al., 2013; Spitzer et al., 1999). However, some of these studies show higher comorbidity with anxiety and mood disorders (e.g., Şar et al., 2004).

The same underlying mechanism is thought to play a role in the onset of symptoms. Conversion symptoms involve a disruption of the integration of bodily functions, in many cases related to traumatic experiences (Janet, 1907). In line with Janet (1907), Charles Myers also described very clear examples of this lack of integration of sensorimotor functions in soldiers he treated for shell shock during and after World War I (Myers, 1940; van der Hart et al., 2000). In other words, dissociative symptoms may disrupt every area of psychological and physical functioning (APA, 2013, 2022). Finally, conversion disorders are also found to show a high prevalence of past trauma.

However, several studies using self-report questionnaires, such as the

DES and the Dissociation Questionnaire (DIS-Q; Vanderlinden, van Dyck, Vandereycken et al., 1993), did not find a high correlation between so-called conversion symptoms, both non-epileptic seizures and other forms of conversion symptoms, and dissociation. Brown et al. (2007) explain this by pointing out that some of the items on these questionnaires concern absorption and depersonalization phenomena that refer to "detachment," while only a small number of items refer to dissociative pseudoneurological symptoms that would be more related to "compartmentalization," that is, a division of the personality (Brown et al., 2007; Holmes et al., 2005; Steele et al., 2009; van der Hart et al., 2004).

The question is whether this constitutes an adequate explanation because, in fact, patients in whom a division of the personality is diagnosed usually have high scores on these self-report questionnaires. In addition, the Somatoform Dissociation Questionnaire or SDQ-20, which asks about somatoform dissociative symptoms, has a high correlation with DIS-Q and DES. In a recent Dutch study, three groups were compared using a number of self-report questionnaires, including DIS-Q, SDQ-20, and SCL-90 (van der Hoeven et al., 2015). These included a group of patients with functional motor symptom disorders ("conversion disorders"), a group with neurologically explained motor disorders, and a healthy control group. The study indicated that the patients with functional motor symptom disorders appeared to be a very heterogeneous group. One third of these patients scored within the "normal" range on all questionnaires and no evidence of somatoform or psychoform dissociative symptoms was found. Furthermore, the Somatoform Dissociation Questionnaire-20 (SDQ-20) only found significant differences between patients with all forms of motor disorders and the normal control group. This study and others show that patients with so-called conversion disorders are a heterogeneous group; they do not always have the same underlying dissociative mechanism as Brown and colleagues hypothesize.

In a proposed amendment to DSM-5, Spiegel et al. (2013) suggested that conversion disorder might be separated into a somatic and a dissociative subtype. This was based on evidence that pure motor paralysis, as the only symptom, would have more in common with somatization and sensory symptoms, while non-epileptic seizures might be more related to dissociation. This idea has not been adopted in DSM-5, although the accompanying text does mention the relationship between conversion disorder and dissociation. Brown et al. (2007) advocate a distinction between somatic symptoms that are more related to anxiety and a preoccupation with physical health, versus conversion symptoms based upon a change in sensorimotor experiences that might indicate a dissociative organization of the personality. More research will need to show the extent to which conversion symptoms are always associated with an underlying dissociative structure of the personality. More research will also be needed to better understand the associations among other medically unexplained symptoms and dissociation.

What does this mean for clinicians using DSM-5? In my view, clinicians using DSM-5 will need to be aware of the possibility that so-called conversion symptoms and medically unexplained symptoms may be dissociative in origin, matching a dissociative disorder diagnosis such as DID, OSDD-1, or dissociative amnesia. A single somatic symptom disorder can also be dissociative in nature. Finally, there is a gap in both classification systems, in that there is an absence of positive dissociative symptoms such as pain symptoms that may be related to a traumatic experience (e.g., pain after rape or other experience of violence). Certainly not all medically unexplained symptoms (MUS) are likely to be dissociative in nature, but some of them are, and it is important that differential diagnostics take this possibility into account. After all, if the symptoms can be explained by the presence of a dissociative disorder, treatment can be focused on that. If this fails to be done, then there is a good chance that the patient will continue to have these symptoms.

ICD-11 Dissociative Trance Disorder

Table 1.11 contains a description of the ICD-11 dissociative trance disorder. The ICD-11 classifies dissociative trance disorder as a separate diagnosis, in contrast to the DSM-5, where dissociative trance is listed as Example 4 of OSDD.

TABLE 1.11
ICD-11 Criteria Dissociative Trance Disorder (6B62)
Occurrence of a trance state in which there is a marked alteration in the individual's state of consciousness or a loss of the individual's normal sense of personal identity, characterized by both of the following.   • Narrowing of awareness of immediate surroundings or unusually narrow and selective focusing on specific environmental stimuli; and   • Restriction of movements, postures, and speech to repetition of a small repertoire that is experienced as being outside of one's control.
The trance state is not characterized by the experience of being replaced by an alternate identity.
Trance episodes are recurrent or, if the diagnosis is based on a single episode, the episode has lasted for at least several days.
The trance state is involuntary and unwanted and is not accepted as a part of a collective cultural or religious practice.

The symptoms are not due to the effects of a substance or medication on the central nervous system (including withdrawal effects), exhaustion, or to hypnagogic or hypnopompic states, and are not due to a disease of the nervous system (e.g., complex partial seizures), head trauma, or a sleep–wake disorder.
The symptoms result in significant distress or significant impairment in personal, family, social, educational, occupational, or other important areas of functioning. If functioning is maintained, it is only through significant additional effort.
Source: WHO. International Classification of Diseases 11th Revision (ICD-11). icd.who.int, Feb 2022.

ICD Possession Trance Disorder

Table 1.12 contains a description of the ICD-11 possession trance disorder. This disorder is not included as a separate classification in DSM-5 but is included as criterion A in the diagnosis of DID.

TABLE 1.12 **ICD-11 Criteria Possession Trance Disorder (6B63)**
Occurrence of a trance state in which there is a marked alteration in the individual's state of consciousness and the individual's normal sense of personal identity is replaced by an external "possessing" identity. The trance state is characterized by behaviors or movements that are experienced as being controlled by the possessing agent.
Trance episodes are attributed to the influence of an external "possessing" spirit, power, deity, or other spiritual entity.
Trance episodes are recurrent or, if the diagnosis is based on a single episode, the episode has lasted for at least several days.
The possession trance state is involuntary and unwanted and is not accepted as a part of a collective cultural or religious practice.
The symptoms are not due to the effects of a substance or medication on the central nervous system (including withdrawal effects), exhaustion, or to hypnagogic or hypnopompic states, and are not due to a disease of the nervous system (e.g., complex partial seizures) or a sleep–wake disorder.
The symptoms result in significant distress or impairment in personal, family, social, educational, occupational, or other important areas of functioning. If functioning is maintained, it is only through significant additional effort.
Source: WHO. International Classification of Diseases 11th Revision (ICD-11). icd.who.int, Feb 2022.

Although pathological possession trance is probably the most common dissociative disorder in non-Western cultures, little systematic research using DSM or ICD criteria has been done among patients. Also, there is insufficient consideration of its diagnosis and treatment in Western training programs (Cardeña et al., 2009; Hecker et al., 2015; Spiegel et al., 2011; 2013). Also, little is known about the prevalence of these dissociative disorders.

Van Duijl (2010) conducted a systematic study of pathological possession in a rural community in Uganda. Individuals (n = 117) with pathological possession not only had significantly higher scores on the DES and SDQ-20 compared to a control group; they also reported significantly more traumatic experiences than the control group. Other research also shows a relationship between pathological possession and traumatic experiences (see Spiegel et al., 2011).

More research in the future will have to show whether the criteria in DSM-5 or ICD-11 can contribute to better understanding and treatment of trance and possession disorders.

CHAPTER 2

Dissociative Symptoms Indicating a Division of the Personality

Introduction

Chapter 1 described the different theoretical views on the concept of dissociation. In addition, it emphasized the importance of distinguishing between dissociative symptoms indicative of a division of the personality and other alterations in consciousness, such as absorption and depersonalization. It is the latter group of symptoms in particular that are the subject of debate as to whether they should be regarded as dissociative or not. When diagnosing a dissociative disorder, the clinician must at least be able to recognize the difference between the aforementioned symptoms. This chapter[6] discusses dissociative symptoms always indicating a division of the personality. Chapter 3 discusses the other alterations in consciousness.

Dissociative symptoms indicative of a division of the personality can be roughly divided into "positive and negative dissociative symptoms" (van der Hart et al., 2006). Negative dissociative symptoms reflect the absence or loss of functions that should theoretically be present. Positive dissociative symptoms come and go, and are temporary intrusions by dissociative parts, such as hearing voices or feeling nausea or pain coming from a dissociative part. Dissociative symptoms can also be divided into psychoform (cognitive–emotional) and somatoform (sensorimotor) symptoms. In complex dissociative disorders, clinicians should be aware that this division into positive and negative will depend on which dissociative part of the person they are speaking with; for example, one part may be experiencing terrible abdominal pain (positive symptom), related to an original sexual trauma, while another part may not feel anything at all (negative symptom).

---

6 The symptoms described in this chapter are most commonly reported by patients with DID, OSDD-1, and partial DID according to ICD-11. Research into partial DID is not available yet, but the wording of partial DID in ICD-11 is to some extent similar to that of OSDD-1 in DSM-5.

Usually, the part of the person that functions most in daily life—in older American clinical literature referred to as "host" and in the theory of structural dissociation as "ANP"—also reports the most diverse and alternating dissociative symptoms. It may be that one moment this host or ANP part has no feeling at all in the body, while experiencing severe pain due to an intrusion of sensation from a dissociative part the very next moment. Psychoform and somatoform symptoms can also be accompanied by severe depersonalization symptoms: not feeling anything at all, not limited to not feeling any emotions but also including not feeling one's own body.

Points to Consider During Assessment

When assessing dissociative symptoms that indicate a division of the personality, some general points of interest are important. Regardless of the type of diagnostic interview used by the person conducting the assessment, it is always important to understand what it is that the patient meant to say when they gave a certain answer and whether this is actually an example of a pathological dissociative symptom. Many patients will answer a certain question in the affirmative, for example, about memory loss, but on further questioning appear to mean something different from what was in fact being asked. Some patients may answer the questions briefly and very clearly, while others are verbose, providing many vague, unclear answers. A diagnostic interview with the latter patient can be extremely challenging and sometimes lengthy.

Further Questions in Case of Unclear or Ambiguous Responses

When supervising administration of the TADS-I or the SCID-D, I often noticed that the clinician was too easily satisfied with an affirmative or negative answer to a question. In such cases, the answers are not sufficiently explored by means of further questions, and the meaning of the answer given remains unclear. It is therefore important that patients always give several examples from past and present, in their own words, and that the clinician asks for further elucidation of the examples until the interpretation is sufficiently clear. Is it an example of a symptom indicative of a division of the personality, or is it more about absorption, or is it something else? This also means that the clinician often has to ask additional questions when the patient's example is unclear.

In the TADS-I, at the end of a section with questions on a particular symptom, the clinician checks whether this symptom occurs exclusively in the context of another mental disorder or fatigue, stress, and so on, in which case it is not part of a separate dissociative disorder.

Contradictory Responses During an Interview

Patients with dissociative disorders, especially those with DID, may give conflicting or vague answers during an interview. Frequently, the patient may give examples of a particular dissociative symptom that was previously denied. The opposite also may occur when a symptom that was initially confirmed is later denied or downplayed.

In fact, it is only at the end of the interview that the clinician can assess whether there is a cluster of dissociative symptoms. Chapter 6 explains this through a number of case reports.

Nonverbal Signs of Tension During an Interview

Questions relating to the dissociative organization of the personality can be particularly stressful for patients with dissociative disorders and may cause an internal struggle between different dissociative parts. This can be reflected in behavior, such as increased absent-mindedness, staring and not hearing the clinician, suddenly not being able to remember the question, restless motor activity in the body, or occasional muscle twitching in the face. Sometimes the patient also seems to be listening to voices. Many patients are unable to say much about their dissociative parts or find this too terrifying, because they hear voices telling them to shut up. They may dissociate, appearing not to hear the clinician or not to be fully present at this point.

If there is a lot of visible tension, the clinician can ask about it, for example: "Do you feel more tension due to this question?" When this is answered in the affirmative, the clinician can ask: "Can you describe what happens?" If there is a lot of tension, it helps to reassure the patient and explain that they are in control and that questions that elicit a lot of internal struggle or tension do not need to be answered. If the patient becomes anxious about losing control or going out of contact either before or during the interview, the clinician can discuss what they can do together to prevent or manage this.

During the hundreds of interviews I have done over the past 35 years, both using the SCID-D and the TADS-I, I have not often experienced a patient completely losing control. Only occasionally did patients go out of contact during the session for a somewhat long time (from minutes to, in one case, over an hour) and no longer heard me. On one occasion a familiar therapist was present, and the therapist and the patient had agreed that the former would touch the patient briefly if they were to go out of contact. On some occasions a patient suffered a non-epileptic seizure or was in danger of dropping out and going out of contact. In most cases, I was able to help the patient to reorient to the here and now by calling them by name and also clearly stating the place and date of the interview. When asked, the patient sometimes mentioned that *the voices* interfered more during the interview, that the voices forbade the patient from answering certain questions, or that *there was a lot going on inside their head.* A number of times there was clearly a switch to another part of the personality.

It is quite likely, however, that switches occuring during diagnostic assessment remain unnoticed by the clinician, as they are almost always very subtle.

Films, television series, the internet, and social media unfortunately paint a picture of DID with flamboyant or dramatic personality changes that are usually far removed from reality. Such dramatic personality changes apply to a small number (6–10%) of DID patients with a comorbid histrionic personality. (Boon & Draijer, 1993a, 1993b; Kluft, 1985). In the vast majority of patients, personality switches are usually hardly noticeable, especially when the person is first seen during a diagnostic interview.

I conducted most of my research interviews in one session, with one or sometimes several breaks. However, the patient may always ask for a break and the clinician should offer these. Chapter 10 discusses how some patients who think they have—or want to have—a dissociative disorder behave during the interview. They will sometimes dramatically show, without being asked, that they *don't remember* or *are not there anymore* because they have read about these symptoms or because they have observed in other patients that this can happen. Anxiety or tension while talking about difficult symptoms or dissociative parts is absent in these patients.

Avoiding Suggestive Questions

It is important to ensure questions are as open as possible. That way, patients present their own stories and are not led in a certain direction by the questions or the way they are asked. The clinician would also do best to adopt a neutral attitude; that is, not to reward some answers more than others, for example by nodding in agreement. In the design of the TADS-I, we tried to start, as much as possible, with an open-ended question, such as: "What has your mood been like in general over the past several years?" or "Do you generally have good recall?"

Questions Inquiring After Symptoms That May Indicate a Division of the Personality

The following is an overview of the most important dissociative symptoms that indicate a division of the personality, described by some as pathological dissociative symptoms (Dell, 2006a; see also Spiegel et al., 2013). I will explain the various groups of symptoms in more detail with the aid of short clinical vignettes. In order to assess the validity of the answers, it is very important that the patient provides the clinician with clear examples, preferably from the present or recent past, to assess whether a symptom is in fact dissociative in nature.

	TABLE 2.1 Psychoform and Somatoform Dissociative Symptoms	
Symptoms	Psychoform (Cognitive–Emotional)	Somatoform (Sensorimotor)
Negative	• Amnesia (loss of time, experiencing gaps in present and past); fugues; indications that one has done things one cannot remember; amnesia for personal information, such as name, age, address Amnesia must be distinguished from the inability to store information in the memory due to absorption or attention and/or concentration problems • Depersonalization (looking at the world and oneself from a distance); hearing oneself talk, but without control over the words • Derealization (not recognizing friends or familiar surroundings) • Loss of certain skills that the person normally possesses (e.g., driving, tying shoelaces, home-maintenance skills)	• Loss of sensation and motor control, such as anesthesia, analgesia, and sedation; conversion symptoms such as temporary inability to move, talk, swallow, see, hear, taste, or smell • Not being able to feel hot and cold properly; not being able to feel hunger and thirst properly • Loss of power in arms and legs • Paralysis of part of the body
Positive	• Cognitive and emotional intrusions by dissociative parts (thoughts or feelings that do not seem to belong to oneself or that come up seemingly out of nowhere) • Schneiderian first-rank symptoms (e.g., hearing voices) • Flashbacks of traumatic experiences • Having skills that the person normally does not have (e.g., speaking another language well, having certain knowledge, being able to play a musical instrument)	• Pain, involuntary movements, and tics • Non-epileptic seizures • Sensory perceptions such as hearing, smelling, or tasting things that are not there (based on intrusions by dissociative parts of the personality and often related to flashbacks of previous traumatic experiences)

Psychoform (Cognitive–Emotional) Dissociative Symptoms

Below is a discussion of the psychoform symptoms presented in Table 2.1.

Amnesia

Amnesia is an important characteristic of several dissociative disorders, particularly DID, and it is the only symptom in the diagnostic classification "dissociative amnesia" (with or without fugue). The memory gaps can apply to both current and past experiences. Amnesia is a difficult symptom to assess accurately, as it must be distinguished from the inability to store certain experiences in the memory due to absorption or attention and/or concentration problems and from memory problems due to substance abuse. Many patients with other mental disorders suffer from severe concentration problems, often temporarily, and will therefore answer questions about amnesia in the affirmative.

Another problem is that patients with DID, and also some with OSDD-1 or partial DID, may have very brief moments of amnesia. These are called micro-amnesia: a brief narrowing or lowering of consciousness for a few seconds during a diagnostic interview or during therapeutic sessions due to the influence/intrusions of other dissociative parts. Sometimes the clinician is able to observe this, especially when the patient seems to lose focus, lose the thread of the conversation, or is mentally absent for a while. At other times, such micro-amnesia is barely perceptible to the clinician or therapist. Moreover, patients are often barely aware of it themselves, especially when they have no awareness of having a dissociative disorder as yet. Again, a distinction must be made between these gaps on the one hand and absorption and being absentminded on the other. Studies of the clinical phenomenology of DID do show that in addition to these possible micro-moments, a cluster of severe other amnesia symptoms is reported, such as memory loss for things one appears to have done in daily life or fugues—having no memory of how one got to a certain place (Boon & Draijer, 1993a, 1993b; Dell, 2006a; Dorahy et al., 2014; Kluft, 1985; Loewenstein et al., 2017; Putnam et al., 1986; Ross, 1996; Ross, Norton & Wozney, 1989; Steinberg, 1995).

Dissociative amnesia is rarely an isolated symptom. It is usually a symptom of a more complex dissociative disorder, or it is part of a related disorder such as PTSD that is not classified as a dissociative disorder in DSM-5 and ICD-11. However, critics note that PTSD is characterized by many different dissociative symptoms, and some believe that the disorder should be classified among dissociative disorders (Dorahy & van der Hart, 2015; Nijenhuis, 2015; Rodewald, Wilhelm-Gößling, et al., 2011; Steele et al., 2017; van der Hart et al., 2006). The main reason why this was not done in DSM-5 is that traumatic experiences or a stressor are not criteria for a dissociative disorder, in contrast with PTSD and other stressor-related disorders where it is required (Spiegel et al., 2011).

Amnesia is also found in patients with non-epileptic seizures. This is usually amnesia for the seizure itself. As noted earlier, non-epileptic seizures are considered differently in DSM-5 versus ICD-11. In ICD, this is a dissociative disorder. When amnesia is reported in the context of PTSD (e.g., for reexperiencing a traumatizing event) or non-epileptic seizures, it is important to check whether other memory problems also occur (e.g., memory problems for everyday life experiences). PTSD and somatoform dissociative symptoms, such as non-epileptic seizures, occur frequently in complex dissociative disorders, such as in DID and OSDD-1 or partial DID (Bowman, 2006; Spiegel et al., 2013).

Finally, while asking about memory problems it is important to get an impression of the situations in which the amnesia occurs: Is amnesia reported only for events in the distant past, or in relation to reexperiencing traumatizing events, or for traumatic experiences? Or is the patient also giving examples of amnesia for tasks and functions that are part of daily life, for example, work, caring for children, social activities, or hobbies? When the latter is the case, one can speak of a more complex dissociative organization of the personality, with different parts having functions in daily life and parts stuck in trauma time (as in DID). In order to make a treatment plan, it is important, if possible, to gain insight into the dissociative organization of the personality during diagnostic assessment (Boon et al., 2011; van der Hart et al., 2006; Steele et al., 2017).

Like the SCID-D, the TADS-I includes direct questions about memory problems and questions that indirectly indicate the presence of gaps in memory. A direct question may be: "Are there ever periods where you have trouble remembering what you have done during the day or when you are missing a chunk of time?" The question about fugues would be: "Have you ever found yourself in a place while unable to recall how you had gotten there?" A fugue rarely occurs only once. For this reason, it is no longer a separate diagnosis in DSM-5 and ICD-11 but has been classified as a subtype of dissociative amnesia.

Fugues often occur in patients who meet criteria for DID and to a lesser extent OSDD-1. In these cases, a dissociative part takes over and goes somewhere. Another part is unaware of this and suddenly finds itself somewhere without knowing how it got there. For example, this may be a part that functions in everyday life that suddenly finds itself somewhere in town with a gap of several hours for which there is no recall. Meanwhile, another part, also functioning in daily life, has gone to the cinema with a friend. The first part was not present and has amnesia.

It can also be a part that is stuck in trauma time and suddenly flees from a situation that is threatening to that part. Other parts are unaware of this and may subsequently find themselves somewhere without knowing how they got there.

Indirect questions involve patients being confronted by others with a gap in their memory (e.g., *What an extraordinary movie we saw yesterday*) or finding indications themselves that they have apparently done things for which they have no recall (see examples in the next section).

Examples of Dissociative Amnesia in Patients With DID

When directly asked about memory gaps, one patient answered *I cannot recall what I have done on a certain day.* When asked if what he had done came back to him when he thought about it, he replied: *Only small bits.* He also said that sometimes he did not know his current age or where he lived. He was self-employed and always carried a checkbook that had his personal address to enable him to write invoices. Sometimes he had to look up his own address by consulting his checkbook.

He also gave an example of the opposite: *Sometimes I visit a new customer and know exactly what the problem is.* He found that very useful. He was afraid to reflect on the reason why he already knew what the problem was. He sometimes missed days in a row, especially when he was not doing well. *Then I go for a walk and eventually they* [the police] *find me somewhere, but I no longer recognize anyone. That is so awful for my son, that I don't recognize my own son in such situations.*

Another patient said she did not think her memory was that bad and that she often had discussions about it. There were gaps in her memory, but then she clung to her *knowledge*. The clinician asked her for an explanation. Such knowledge turned out to be a report by a voice in her head. She explained: *For example, Saturday did the groceries and Sunday visited such and such.* Her special *knowledge* turned out to be nothing more than a short message, without images and feelings, coming from another part. When asked how long the periods were lasting of which she had *knowledge* but no recall, she said that these reports could also pertain to entire days. She had no memory of those days, only a brief report by a voice in her head. But she concluded: *This way I won't lose time because I still have my knowledge.*

Yet another patient said,

> I didn't realize that my memory was bad at all; I only became aware of it when I had a burn-out and had to stay home. At work, my memory was always very good. But I am often so tired now that I also sleep a lot, especially when the children are at school. But then I sometimes find that I have done the laundry or some other chores. I don't remem-

ber doing that, but I guess I was very much absorbed in thoughts. I am really not that aware. I only get a little scared when I hear back from others, for example my husband, that we did things together that I can't remember. The children also confront me more and more with the fact that I have said or promised things that I do not remember.

When asked by the clinician if the children did not confront her before, the patient replied: *Yes, but they were much smaller then and I just said it wasn't true, but I can't get away with that now.*

One patient answered that she no longer had trouble with her memory and that it used to be worse. She said that she now only forgot *little things*, for example that she wanted to buy bread, but then it turned out that she had already done so. She still felt bad when she heard from her daughter that she had visited her, but that she herself had no recall for this. Asked by the clinician what she did in such situations, she replied that she pretended to remember and that that way her daughter did not notice this at all. *In fact, nobody really notices,* she said.

What these examples show is that many patients with DID tend to hide, minimize, or sometimes downplay their memory problems or find another reason for them. Sometimes the reason is sought in over-fatigue, a neurological disorder, or even early dementia. The loss of control is a source of fear and shame. It is mainly the indirect indications that are noticed first when dissociative patients appear to have done things they do not remember.

According to the theory of structural dissociation of personality, in all the examples given above there is tertiary structural dissociation of the personality, meaning the presence of several parts with functions in daily life and parts stuck in trauma time that is characteristic of DID (see Chapter 1 and Figure 1.1). The patients gave examples of gaps in their memory for everyday tasks and duties such as work, housework, and caring for the children. This means that there must be a complex division of the personality into parts that hold traumatic memories, feelings, and sensations and multiple parts with tasks and roles in daily life.

In contrast to the theory of structural dissociation of personality, as briefly described in Chapter 1 (Figure 1.1), DSM-5 and ICD-11 do not make a distinction between different levels of the dissociative organization of personality. DID is diagnosed when there is a division of the personality and when clearly different dissociative parts of the personality are present, regardless of the function of these parts.

The following are two examples of memory problems in patients with DID who might be said to have secondary structural dissociation. That is, one part fullfils tasks and functions in daily life—usually also the part that presents for help and is present during assessment—and several parts are stuck in traumatic experiences (van der Hart et al., 2006). When there is only one part with tasks and functions in daily life, amnesia is not reported for everyday functioning. The part of the person functioning in daily life may have amnesia only when a part is activated that is stuck in trauma time, resulting in a switch.

A young woman presented with non-epileptic seizures. She reported amnesia for all seizures. She described several seizures of different natures. In one type of seizure, she seemingly changed into a young girl. This had been observed repeatedly by her partner and a number of her friends; according to them, she could sometimes be stuck in this other dissociative part for several hours without being aware of it. She also described seizures in which she passed out and seizures in which she would scratch and bite. She had amnesia for these as well. Other than these seizures, she functioned in her work and daily life and was not aware of any memory problems. Throughout the TADS-I interview, she was able to answer clearly and consistently; there was not a single moment when she seemed to be out of contact or not hearing the questions. Also, no seizures occurred.

She did, however, say that she did not remember anything before the age of nine. She had fragmented memories of a very traumatic period of several months around the age of nine. Everything that happened in her life before that—school friends, holidays, home—was something she could not remember and had to reconstruct from photos or stories by others. Even when she saw photos, the memories did not come back. The patient had no idea what preceded her seizures and whether there were any triggers. Finally, she also said that she would scratch and bite in her sleep and then try to get her partner out of bed. This is what her partner told her although she was unaware of this behavior; it did not stop until someone woke her up.

Another patient was referred for a consultation using the TADS-I in relation to chronic PTSD. During a previous therapy session, she had repeatedly gone out of contact to such extent that the therapist could not reach her, and she did not seem to hear him. A number of times she had suddenly and briefly become very anxious, behaved childishly, and did not seem to recognize the therapist. She seemed to have amnesia for these moments and said she did not know what had happened, that she was often tense and felt ashamed of herself.

In the TADS-I questions on possibly trauma-related symptoms, she reported having very severe sleep problems. In addition to nightmares and flashbacks of early childhood traumatization, she had discovered that she must have gotten up regularly during the night. She had no recall of this. She found evidence that she had gone to the kitchen and eaten, she discovered that things have been moved around in her living room, and she found that things had been cleaned. Sometimes in the morning she had found drawings with unpleasant images that she did not recognize, which looked very childish. She confessed that she was so shocked by those that she threw them away. Sometimes, when she woke up, she did not know where she was and had difficulty getting oriented. But during the day she was doing well. She had a very good memory, except for what she called *that stuff* at night and what happened when she was with the therapist. She worked a lot and had her own ICT company that was doing well. As long as she was busy, there were no problems, she said. She therefore tried to plan everything as much as possible. No evidence of amnesia in her daily life was found during the interview.

In the first example above, a dissociative part of the person was seen repeatedly by the patient's partner. He described that part as *a little girl who was not afraid anymore and wanted to play children's games*. This dissociative part had never scratched or bitten, so the clinician suspected that, based on what had now been reported, there must be at least one other part that exhibited this behavior and was very afraid.

In the second example, the patient lived alone. Her dissociations had been observed by her therapist and looked as if she was reexperiencing a traumatizing event. On one occasion her therapist might have seen a dissociative part that was younger and afraid. The patient herself had found indirect evidence for the existence of dissociative parts: drawings and activities at night for which she had amnesia. Dissociative parts that have the function of holding traumatic memories are often active at night (Boon et al., 2011). On the one hand, this is because at night they *finally have time* especially if the part that functions in daily life has extreme control, as in the case of the patient in the second example. They do not have the opportunity to emerge until the evening and night, when the part that functions in daily life is exhausted or sleeping. On the other hand, parts are often active at night for fear of reexperiencing trauma or having nightmares. They remain busy in an attempt to avoid sleep. Being busy with something else is often a way for these parts to regulate emotions or keep them at bay. It is also known that food can have a function in regulating emotions, and the same is true of various forms of compulsive behavior, such as cleaning.

Absorption-Related Memory Problems

As described, many patients answer questions about memory problems in the affirmative. Amnesia related to the actions of another dissociative part of the personality must be distinguished from memory problems due to absorption or attention and concentration problems. Many patients without dissociative disorders report this type of memory problem. An additional complication is that patients with DID or OSDD-1 may also report absorption and concentration problems, in addition to having amnesia for the behavior of other parts.

The following are some examples of patients without a dissociative disorder who report memory problems due to absorption.

One patient described that she sometimes had a gap of hours: *Then suddenly it is hours later, the whole afternoon has passed.* On further questioning, it appeared that she had been lying on her sofa all afternoon in a gloomy mood. She had been channel surfing on the TV and had been thinking. She was aware of this, but she had lost an awareness of time. Such episodes appeared to occur frequently, always when she was feeling low. There were no further indications that she had done anything in those afternoons that she had no memory of. She did not give any other examples of amnesia.

Another patient replied to the question whether she had ever experienced being somewhere and not knowing how she got there: *Yes, I was suddenly outside somewhere and didn't know where I was.* The clinician then asked her if she remembered what had happened. It turned out that she had been on the phone with her mother, with whom she had a complex relationship. During that conversation, she had become very angry with her mother and had abruptly broken off the conversation. She was so angry that she had grabbed her coat and gone outside, angrily wrapped up in her thoughts. She had started walking and kept walking while lost in thought. This way she had ended up somewhere without realizing where she was, but she clearly remembered leaving her home. This patient said that she very often felt alone as a child and would then go into her own fantasy world. In those instances, too, there was no sense of time.

Yet another patient said that she had *a memory like a sieve.* She had become stressed out after a very painful divorce from her husband as well as the burden of the care for her young children. *I notice that my mind often wanders, and I have to pinch myself to stay in the present; this is particularly difficult when the children go to school, because I am alone then.* When asked if she had ever had such memory problems before, she replied in the negative. She also said that she had slept much better over the last few weeks, with the help of sleep medication, and therefore had fewer memory problems.

Forgetting Only Very Negative and Shameful Acts

It is not uncommon for patients with a personality disorder to have amnesia for an act they feel extremely ashamed of or for which they do not want to take responsibility. Sometimes there is also excessive alcohol consumption.

One patient described having an excellent memory, except when she became very aggressive and hit her partner and children. She concluded that this was *someone else inside her*, just like Dr. Jekyll and Mr. Hyde, the title characters in the classic novel by Robert Louis Stevenson. She reported no other memory problems; neither did she report any other symptoms indicative of DID or OSDD-1. It was evident that she had difficulty taking responsibility for her anger and impulsive actions. This type of amnesia, exclusively for intense negative affect and for incriminating and shameful behavior, may be a symptom of personality problems.

Patients with DID or OSDD-1 (or partial DID in accordance with the ICD-11) may have amnesia for embarrassing, aggressive, or self-injurious behavior, but also report memory problems for more neutral or sometimes even positive events. Of course, they usually report memory problems related to dissociative parts stuck in trauma time. This is discussed in more detail in Chapters 7, 8, and 9 on differential diagnosis.

Finally, when asking about memory problems, the clinician should always check whether these problems only occur in combination with or as part of other mental health problems. See Chapter 5 on the use of the TADS-I.

Depersonalization and Derealization

In addition to patients with dissociative disorders, patients with other mental disorders and even the general population commonly experience depersonalization and derealization symptoms (Foote, Smolin, Kaplan, et al., 2006; Hunter et al., 2004; Ross, Duffy, & Ellason, 2002; Simeon, 2009). Adolescents also report these symptoms frequently. In our research with the SCID-D, we found no significant differences in depersonalization and derealization phenomena between patients with dissociative disorders and patients with other mental disorders (Boon & Draijer, 1993a, 1993b, 1993c). In other words, we could not distinguish patients with dissociative disorders from patients with other disorders on the basis of reported depersonalization and derealization symptoms only. This is partly because many of these symptoms do not refer directly or clearly to a division of the personality, although the symptom may be related. I discuss this in more detail in Chapters 7, 8, and 9.

There are only a limited number of specific depersonalization and derealization symptoms that directly indicate a division of the personality, described below.

Finding Yourself Outside Your Body, as if Looking at Yourself or Someone Else From a Distance

This symptom involves the experience of being literally outside oneself (above or behind) and becoming an observer of oneself. This is described by Fromm (1965) as an "observing ego" and an "experiencing ego." Some patients say they see themselves; others are not sure at whom they are looking. The clinician should keep probing whether patients are indeed literally outside themselves. Many screening instruments, including the DES (Bernstein & Putnam, 1986) and the Dissociation Questionnaire (DIS-Q; Vanderlinden, van Dyck, Vandereycken et al., 1993), include this type of question. The question is often answered in the affirmative. When asked for an example, however, it turns out that patients mean to say that they are like a critical observer of themselves and judge their own behavior. This is a common experience, but not a dissociative symptom. It does not involve the experience of being literally outside the body and looking at oneself from the outside.

Examples of Depersonalization That Indicate a Division of the Personality

One patient reported that she actually very often found herself floating above herself. She used to think that everyone did that, until one day when she was in a restaurant with a friend. It was very crowded, and the tables were close together. She said to her friend: *Isn't it funny to see everything from above!* There was a silence and her friend looked at her blankly. The patient said that she then realized that her friend did not experience it that way. She saved herself from the situation by saying she was only joking. She was extremely shocked, and it was the first time she started to think she was crazy. She had likewise never told anyone that she talked with the voices in her head. She then started reading everything she could find and came to the conclusion that she was schizophrenic.

Another patient said:

> I see myself doing the shopping, I walk behind myself; that happens all the time at the checkout when there is a long queue. Then I am above myself in that line! Even now I am sometimes up there in that corner of the room, it happens suddenly and then I am back here on the chair opposite you.

A third patient reported:

> When I am at work, I sometimes see myself acting. I have to wash patients as a nurse, but I am really not able to wash men. Yet it automatically happens; I seem to be doing it anyway, but I am watching from the ceiling. Sometimes I find it so awful to look at, then it's as if I'm gone for a while. Back in the days when all that was going on, I also used to watch what was happening down there with that girl. Sometimes it was so horrible, I knew I could get away through a hole in the ceiling, so I no longer had to watch either.
>
> This still happens sometimes when I am with my husband. I know

very well that he does not do anything bad, but sometimes it happens very quickly. Sometimes I don't even recognize him; that's scary. Then I see my uncle. Fortunately, my husband doesn't notice, I think. We never talk about it, and he doesn't seem to realize.

The spontaneous examples of getting out of the body usually also provide insight into the dissociative organization of the personality. When it relates to everyday actions, such as work, shopping, or looking after children, this indicates the existence of another part with a function in daily life. In a therapeutic session, this is not always clear. It is quite possible that a dissociative part stuck in trauma time is activated and the part that functions in daily life leaves the body. In case there is a trauma history of sexual abuse, this also often occurs during sexual contact with the current partner. Then the part that functions in daily life describes being out of her body during sexual contact with her partner.

In the example of the patient who was a nurse, there were indications of the existence of a work part capable of washing men. In addition, there seemed to be another part that was present during sexual contact with her partner, in which the partner, in her experience, sometimes changed into the abuser of the past. This may mean that in the perception of that part of the patient she was back in the past and reexperiencing the original abuse—as if it happened now.

In patients with DID, the symptom of leaving their bodies can occur on quite an ongoing basis, both in seemingly normal situations, such as during work or social interactions, and also in situations that are obviously much more trauma-related. In patients with OSDD-1 (or partial DID in accordance with the ICD-11), out-of-body experiences are usually related to situations that are threatening or reminiscent of original traumatizing events. In such cases, the part that is stuck in trauma is often activated while the part that functions in daily life leaves the body.

Short-lived out-of-body experiences are also reported by patients in extremely stressful situations, such as near-death experiences and overwhelming experiences in war. Some patients also report such experiences when using cannabis. These experiences can therefore also occur—briefly and transiently—in patients who report no other dissociative symptoms on the TADS-I and do not meet the criteria of DID, OSDD-1, or partial DID (Pietkiewicz et al., 2019).

Hearing Oneself Talk, But Without Control Over the Content

Patients may have the experience of listening to themselves without having control over what they say. This occurs in patients with DID, OSDD-1, or partial DID when an intrusion of another dissociative part occurs. What is being said is experienced as ego dystonic—as not something the person would ever say. This may include all kinds of statements or remarks and certainly not just negative or angry ones.

One patient reported on this: *Sometimes I am in a meeting with colleagues and then I suddenly hear myself saying all kinds of things about subjects I know nothing about.*

Another patient remarked that he had heard himself saying that he liked certain television series, although he actually hated them.

Yet another patient said: *I sometimes hear myself using language that I am embarrassed about. I never get angry with people, but suddenly that can happen; it's terrible.*

It may be a sentence or a complete conversation about a topic that is alien to the patients or that they do not know anything about. In the first example, the alienation is clear. This also includes knowledge that the patient does not think they have.

This symptom, too, must be distinguished from more normal phenomena, in which a person realizes, for example, that they are speaking differently or are present in a different way than usual.

Oh dear, I'm rattling again, said a patient who often had this problem when she was under a lot of pressure or anxious. This patient was aware that she herself sometimes rattled; she knew she was doing that and did not experience it as ego dystonic. The experience described in this case does not represent a dissociative symptom.

Examples of Derealization That Indicate a Division of the Personality

Patients may feel unreal in their own familiar home. *Sometimes it's as if I am a visitor in my own home; nothing feels like mine.* This experience is usually the result of an intrusion of a dissociative part that is, for example, younger, did not grow up in the house, or does not feel at home there. But ideas on what home is like or feels like can also be very different when there are multiple parts active in daily life. In extreme cases, someone may no longer recognize their own home or partner and children; this is often associated with amnesia. Only when others tell the person about such episodes afterward does the person realize that they have no recall of those episodes.

One patient reported:

> I often wake up at night, not lying in bed. I find myself somewhere I do not recognize, and so I sit down on the floor and wait. Sometimes I smoke a cigarette. After a while it will get better, no idea how long it will take. At a certain point, I recognize my own bedroom again, I've already been living in my house for more than 20 years.

Different dissociative parts may have their own relationship or connection with the here and now, with current friends, partner, and children. This is illustrated by the following example:

> Sometimes I look at my children and think: Who are they? To my own horror I don't have any feelings for my children at such a point in time. They do not mean anything to me at that point. Sometimes I do remember who they are, but without feeling anything. And sometimes I really don't remember who they are. In my head I hear: But they are your son and daughter! And slowly it dawns upon me: Ah, yes, my son and daughter.

These experiences are frightening and embarrassing for the individual. It is worth noting that during assessment, patients do provide such examples when asked, albeit reluctantly.

Loss of Skills or Unfamiliar Skills

It is characteristic of a dissociative organization of the personality that dissociative parts have subjective experiences about who they are and what they can and cannot do. They also have different skills. Younger parts that are stuck in trauma time usually lack the skills and knowledge that fit the individual's current age and cognitive development. A child part that is stuck in trauma time at the age of four, for example, usually is not able to read, write, or tie their shoelaces. They will draw and write according to the developmental level of a 4-year-old. If an intrusion of such a part occurs, the patient may, as a grown-up part, suddenly experience loss of skills that they usually do possess. The grown-up parts, with their own tasks and roles in daily life, also possess different skills and capabilities. This is shown by the earlier example of the nurse who stepped outside herself and saw herself bathing male patients, and also by the patient who heard herself talk when she had the notion that she lacked the knowledge to do so. In patients who have little or no awareness of their dissociative disorder or are too ashamed to report it, the examples are usually not so obvious or dramatic; there are only subtle indications that another dissociative part may be active. Sometimes the clinician has to ask more questions, for example: "How do you think you have acquired such knowledge? Could it be that you have forgotten?" One patient hesitantly replied she had discovered that she had taken an entire palliative medicine course but was unable to recall a single detail.

Conversely, patients may say that they sometimes suddenly do not remember how the computer works, or how the washing machine works, or how the car starts. This may happen when a part that does not possess these skills influences the awareness and behavior of the part that functions in daily life.

Schneiderian Symptoms

At the beginning of the past century, German psychiatrist Kurt Schneider (1959) described the Schneiderian symptoms of schizophrenia—also known as positive symptoms or first-rank symptoms—as symptoms typical of patients with schizophrenia.

Some, but not all, Schneiderian symptoms are common in patients with dissociative disorder, even more so than in patients with schizophrenia (Kluft, 1987a; Ross et al., 1990b). They are also called "psychotic-like" or "pseudopsychotic" symptoms and often lead to misdiagnosis or nonrecognition of DID and OSDD-1 (Boon & Draijer, 1993a, 1993b; Dell, 2006a, 2006b; Kluft, 1987a). For example, patients with DID may be diagnosed with schizophrenia on the basis of hearing voices and feeling that their behavior is influenced from within.

These symptoms result from the activity and influence of dissociative parts (Brand & Loewenstein, 2010; Dell, 2009a, 2006a; Dorahy et al., 2009; Kluft, 1987a; Ross et al., 1990b; Steinberg & Spiegel, 2008). It is often the part that functions in daily life that is influenced by actions of other parts. These can be parts that are stuck in trauma time at moments when they are reliving a traumatic experience, but also parts with another function in daily life. Some Schneiderian symptoms may evoke feelings of extreme alienation or depersonalization in the part that functions in daily life.

During a diagnostic assessment, it is important to check whether these Schneiderian symptoms occur as part of a cluster of other dissociative symptoms. This is always the case in DID and OSDD-1. Patients with other dissociative disorders report few or no Schneiderian symptoms. Patients

---

TABLE 2.2

Common Schneiderian Symptoms in DID or in OSDD-1

Auditory hallucinations (including hearing voices commenting or talking to the person; hearing voices giving commands; hearing voices talking or arguing among one another)

Visual hallucinations (trauma-related)

Tactile hallucinations (trauma-related)

Olfactory and gustatory hallucinations (trauma-related)

Behavior, actions, or feelings that seem to be controlled by something or someone else

Thought insertion

Thought withdrawal

Delusions related to the trauma

---

with PTSD or CPTSD often do report some of these symptoms, in particular pseudo-hallucinations, in fact reexperiencing of the traumatizing event or events.

Table 2.2 lists the most common Schneiderian symptoms in patients with DID or OSDD.

Auditory Hallucinations

Hearing voices may be one of the most commonly reported Schneiderian symptoms in patients with DID or OSDD-1, but not all patients hear voices. Sometimes they report to have started hearing voices only after realizing that they have a dissociative disorder. *There has always been a lot going on in my head, hard to describe, like a murmur in the background. I tried to ignore it as much as possible. But it could be dead silent too*, one patient recounted.

Patients with DID, and to a lesser extent OSDD-1, may hear voices that talk to one another, sometimes about them: voices that give commands, often unpleasant ones such as to harm oneself; voices that make continuous comments about the patient's behavior or about another voice. Patients usually hear several voices and cannot identify them as familiar voices. Most patients report hearing the voices inside their heads, although research has shown that the voices may be external as well (Dorahy et al., 2009).

Many patients say that they were already hearing voices at a very young age and some thought that everyone experienced those. It was a shock for them to discover that this was not the case.

One patient explained it this way:

> I have been hearing voices since I was very young, at the age of eight I think. They gave me orders to do things. They could be nice too. I thought it was quite normal, really. I have never given it any thought. I received EMDR[7] treatment and seem to have said: "Stop it, stop it, I can't stand all these voices." There was an explosion of voices inside my head; it drove me crazy. I started to see weird things and was extremely frightened. It was only then that I realized it was not normal, really.

Patients with dissociative disorders who hear voices do have intact reality testing. They usually know that other people cannot hear the voices. Nor are the voices bizarre or strange—like being convinced that you are hearing the voice of Jesus through the TV, giving you commands. And it is usually possible for another person, like the therapist, to converse directly with such a voice. This rarely happens during diagnostic assessment—let alone

---

7 Eye Movement Desensitization and Reprocessing (EMDR)

at the request of the clinician—although it may happen that the patient, suddenly and often briefly, talks in a different voice (i.e., as a different part). Also, the influence of voices may sometimes be observable nonverbally during the assessment (e.g., because the patient seems to be listening to voices or has facial twitches), and patients may report that there are voices getting angry and telling them not to answer. In effect, these are dissociative parts that become angry, but not every patient realizes that this is the case.

Chapter 7, on differential diagnosis from psychotic disorders, discusses the differences between voices in psychotic patients or patients who suffer from schizophrenia.

Visual Hallucinations

Patients with DID or OSDD-1 frequently report seeing things that are not there. Usually these are flashbacks, so-called clips or fragments of traumatizing events in the past. Generally, they have intact reality testing and know that what they are seeing is related to previous traumatic experiences and is not real, but this is not always the case. Dissociative parts stuck in trauma time may be convinced that what they see is really happening at that moment; for example, that they really see the abuser in the room during a therapy session. In addition, the therapist or a known person may be perceived as someone else, often as an abuser from the past. Visual hallucinations may be distorted to the point of appearing delusional or psychotic. Finally, a patient may have amnesia for the original traumatizing events but still see flashbacks or visual fragments of that event stemming from a different part. This can be particularly frightening because the images do not make sense and are terrifying.

One patient reported on this:

> Often I can explain the images; that is frightening but at least I can tell myself that I am in the here and now and that it is not really happening. But sometimes I see really scary things and then I wonder if I am crazy and have a terribly bizarre imagination. It makes me start doubting everything: did I make it all up? But those images are really terrifying; I don't want to see them.

Tactile Hallucinations

A tactile or sensory hallucination involves feeling something on your body or skin that is not actually there. This is another experience regularly reported by patients who are reliving a traumatizing experience. One patient reported: *I can feel his hands around my throat again.* Another patient said:

At nights I keep having the feeling I am being touched; it's scary. I always sleep with the lights on so that when I wake up with that awful feeling, I can see where I am and that it is not real, that he is not there at all. He cannot even be, because he is long dead!

Both these patients could relate these experiences to past abuse. Sometimes someone cannot and that is even more frightening. Another patient reported that she always had the feeling that many bugs were crawling over her. She could not understand what it meant nor relate it to a traumatic experience; she thought she was *nuts*. Much later in the course of treatment, it became clear that as a child she had been locked up naked in a room with all sorts of crawling insects. She really had experienced such things repeatedly, but at the time of the interview she had amnesia for these experiences. Her sensations were based on the experiences of a dissociative part stuck in trauma time that sometimes reexperienced this situation.

Olfactory and Gustatory Hallucinations

This involves patients smelling or tasting things that are not there. This is another experience often reported as part of the reexperiencing of a traumatizing event. As with tactile hallucinations, it makes a lot of difference whether a patient knows that the smell or taste is an *old smell or old foul taste*. For example, one patient remarked:

I cannot stand the smell of cigars. Sometimes at night I smell them again so pungently; then I just have to go and check if anyone is smoking a cigar somewhere. I do know that it is not possible, but I can really smell it.

This patient knew that this smell had to do with an uncle who had abused him and who smoked cigars.

Not every patient knows what causes an experience in the present or whether there is a connection with a previous traumatic experience. Particularly patients who have a lot of amnesia often cannot explain the hallucinations. During a therapy session, one patient was convinced that there was a fire in the building. She could smell it quite clearly. The therapist did not smell it but was unable to convince her and had to explore the building with her. Even after it had been established that there was no fire, the patient still smelled it. She could not explain it, but she did say it happened to her often. A year later, treatment revealed that as a child she had once escaped from a burning house. For a long time, she had experienced amnesia for this event.

When a patient was asked whether he used alcohol, he replied: *Alcohol makes me sick straight away, not just from the smell but from the taste as well. I used to be forced to drink that and then everything went wrong.*

All the hallucinations mentioned above involve reexperiencing original traumatizing events. The more complex the dissociative disorder, the more amnesia there is, and the greater the chance that the patient is not or is no longer aware of the connection between the traumatizing event and the experiences in the present. The patient is affected by the reexperiencing of a dissociative part but is not in touch with or aware of that part. This makes patients vulnerable to being incorrectly labeled psychotic and to thinking that they are.

Made Behavior, Actions, and Feelings

Made behavior, actions, and feelings are the experience that actions, impulses, or feelings do not come from the presenting part itself, but are, as it were, controlled. Most patients say that they feel controlled from within, that a certain behavior or feeling *happens to them* and that they cannot influence it. Again, these are usually diverse behaviors or feelings, not just negative or shameful ones. The influence is exerted by other dissociative parts of the personality. A patient said, *I see my hands moving over the computer keyboard, but I can't type that fast at all.* Another patient said:

> Sometimes I suddenly feel panic. I have absolutely no idea what it is about: there is really no need! The same thing may happen with grief: my tears flow and seem to come from nowhere, I haven't the faintest, but I am completely overwhelmed without a clue why I am crying at all.

Something in me causes this, says another patient. And someone else said:

> I always have a shopping list at the supermarket, and I stick to it exactly, but sometimes I am driven to sections where I don't want to be. Sweets I don't like or unnecessary purchases. It feels like something in me is forcing me to go there anyway and put things in the basket. I often put them back quickly. And sometimes when I come home, they are in amongst my shopping after all.

Occasionally, patients feel that they are being influenced from the outside. This happens in particular to patients who have grown up in certain religious communities where influence by demons or other beings is preached. These communities speak of demonic possession or control of the body, sometimes even of so-called astral influence. These groups are also often the setting for exorcisms of such demons, which patients with

DID or OSDD-1 usually find extremely traumatizing (Bowman, 1993a; Fraser, 1993). In addition, the symptoms do not change after such treatments, and individuals will think they must be really bad for the treatment to have failed or that the demons have reasons to stay with them.

Thought Insertion

Many patients with DID, and sometimes those with OSDD-1, experience strange or unfamiliar thoughts suddenly coming up in their heads. These may be puzzling thoughts or thoughts that have absolutely nothing to do with the current situation. Moreover, such thoughts are experienced as being out of character. These are thoughts coming from other dissociative parts of the person. For patients not yet aware that they have a dissociative disorder, this can be strange and sometimes even frightening. A patient told me:

> I have had this thought for a few weeks now that I should buy a hamster, but I hate those creatures; they bite. I can't see why I have these thoughts. I think they are crazy.
>
> Sometimes when I am cuddling my children, I get the thought that I'd better hug them to death. That is a disgusting thought, and terrifying. It makes me stop cuddling [them] abruptly and they don't understand that at all.

Thought Withdrawal

Patients may report that sometimes, all of a sudden their head feels empty: *I was about to tell you something and now it is gone. My head is completely blank. It seems like something is taking away that thought and my words.* The clinician then asked if this happened often.

> It happens very often when I want to say something about the past. Sometimes I hear a very angry voice saying that it is not allowed, but sometimes it is as if everything I wanted to say is gone. Every thought.

In case of internal conflict about a certain subject, thoughts about that subject are often removed or blocked by a dissociative part. It usually has to do with the subject being considered *too difficult* by other parts or causing too much inner conflict, agitation, and emotion.

One patient called it *symptoms of drunkenness:*

> Sometimes I can't find the words, I know the first two words of a sentence but then I can't proceed to the rest, I can't get there. It's crazy. I want to say this thing, I know what it is, but it's gone.

Delusions Related to the Trauma

Sometimes patients report seeing images or experiencing sensations that could be understood as delusions if the clinician did not know they have a dissociative disorder. Fears related to real-life experiences can be distorted to the extent that they become psychotic-like experiences.

For example, one patient reported seeing bloody hands coming out of the walls of her room at night, trying to grab her. Afterward, she sometimes found herself hiding under a table so that the hands could not grab her. She might also sit on her balcony for hours, in the freezing cold, because the hands could not reach her there. During the time when she experienced this, she could not convince herself that it was not happening—it was real. It was not until the next day that she knew it was impossible and that triggered her fear of falling apart. It later became clear that she had been subjected to a very violent gang rape and had in fact seen bloody hands at the time. At night, these images sometimes became distorted.

Another patient was convinced that people would be able to trace him through Facebook and that they would try to influence him and find him. This patient had grown up in a strict religious community and had been abused by people from the church. He had been repeatedly told that God could see him wherever he was and whatever he was doing and that he would not be able to escape his fate.

Thought Broadcasting

This refers to the feeling that one's own thoughts can be heard by others. In fact, this is the only Schneiderian symptom that is not frequently seen in patients with DID or OSDD-1. Many traumatized patients fear that others can read their thoughts: this is more a function of the anxiety and shame about other people knowing what happened to them rather than a true psychotic symptom. These patients also often have the idea that they can read other people's thoughts. They may be more sensitive or alert than others and extremely vigilant about what they can expect from the other person. From a very young age, they have been focused on reading others, especially the behavior and facial expression of the abuser(s), in order to predict what might be about to happen to them. It has become a kind of habit to keep doing this, especially in one-on-one encounters. Although they often think that they have a very good sense of what someone else is thinking or feeling, they often turn out to be wrong because of old schemas and cognitions that often belong to parts stuck in trauma. They have to learn to correct their often distorted beliefs.

I can tell by looking at your face that you think I'm crazy, said a patient during a TADS-I assessment. *I do understand, I loathe myself too.* Such conclusions, based on one's own negative thoughts about oneself, are common among patients with a history of early childhood traumatization.

Somatoform (Sensorimotor) Dissociative Symptoms

Patients with complex dissociative disorders often exhibit a wide range of somatic symptoms for which no physiological cause can be found (Boon & Draijer, 1993a, 1993b; Bowman, 1993a, 2006; Bowman & Coons, 2000; Loewenstein & Goodwin, 1999; Nijenhuis, 2000, 2004, 2010, 2015; Ross, Heber, Anderson et al., 1989; van der Hart et al., 2006). As mentioned earlier, DSM and ICD have different diagnostic views on this. The ICD-11 also includes single somatoform dissociative disorders, which are categorized as conversion disorders in DSM-5.

Whenever a patient presents with a somatoform symptom, the clinician should always investigate whether this is part of a cluster of multiple somatoform and psychoform dissociative symptoms. Psychoform and somatoform symptoms often occur together. Earlier in this chapter, I presented the example of a patient with non-epileptic seizures for which she had amnesia. She also reported amnesia for her life before the age of nine.

A particular symptom can be experienced in several ways: as a physical experience, as something that is cognitively observed, or both at the same time. Here are two different answers to the question: "Have you ever had the feeling that your body or part of your body had changed? For example, that your body seemed larger/smaller or stronger/weaker?" (TADS-I, Question 192).

One patient answered: *I was in the car and wanted to drive home but my legs weren't able to reach the car's foot pedals.* When asked if he could elaborate, he replied:

> I look at my legs and they are simply shorter, very strange. But this happens to me regularly. I was frightened at first, but now I just ignore it. I wait for a while until it goes away, after some time. I can never actually feel my body. I can see it, but I have no feeling in my legs.

Another patient described the same symptom differently:

> I was in the car, and I had a strange experience. My legs couldn't reach the floor; I couldn't reach the car pedals. The same feeling I had as a little child, when you were sitting on a highchair and your legs were dangling, because you couldn't reach the ground.

And when the clinician asked, *Could you see your legs? Did they look shorter?* he replied: *No, I never look at my body; I loathe that. I just wait, I look at my phone sometimes. That helps and then after a while it goes away.*

In both cases, this is an intrusion of a younger dissociative part into the awareness of the part that functions in daily life and experiences the intrusion in different ways. In the first example, there is a loss of feeling in the body. The patient did not feel his legs. He thought that the length of his legs had changed. In the second example, the symptom was experienced as a physical sensation but without the perception of physical changes.

Loss of Physical Function

Perhaps one of the most frequent symptoms indicating a loss of physical function is the inability to feel the body or a part of the body and thus being unable to feel pain.

I am just a head, said a patient with a history of sexual abuse in her childhood. She was not able to feel her body at all.

Another patient said she could not feel the temperature of the water in the shower; she also had great difficulty drinking and eating enough in a day, as she had no sense of hunger or thirst.

Another patient said that he had apparently been walking with a broken foot for far too long.

> I seem to have a very high threshold for pain. I never noticed anything about my foot, until it suddenly became very swollen. I know I had had a bad fall, some days before, but my foot had not been bothering me.

In more extreme situations, a partial paralysis of the body may occur and patients may not be able to walk or move a body part even though no physiological cause is found. This can be short term but can also last for months and sometimes years.

Finally, some patients report shorter moments of loss of vision, hearing, smell, or taste. All these experiences are the result of intrusions from dissociative parts, usually parts that are stuck in trauma time.

Symptoms Caused by Intrusions of Dissociative Parts

Earlier in this chapter, in the section Schneiderian Symptoms of Schizophrenia, several examples were given of intrusions of dissociative parts; these caused a patient to have an experience of smelling or tasting something or experiencing something in the body for which no physiological cause could be found. This may sometimes be labeled as a psychotic symptom, especially when a patient is unaware of the original traumatizing event. In other cases, this sort of symptom is interpreted as part of PTSD, especially when the patient knows what the smell signifies and that the smell is part of a flashback of the original traumatizing event.

A patient may also describe their legs or arms moving without having control over them. One patient gave the following example:

The other day I was sitting on the bus. I usually sit in the back, close to a door where I can leave easily. A very loud man came in at a bus stop, who started yelling at the bus driver. I felt myself freeze. The bus moved on, but I was still hearing the yelling. Suddenly, my arm went up as if by itself and my hand pressed the stop button. I couldn't control it even though I didn't need to get out of the bus as yet. At the bus stop, my legs started walking. This was very strange because I couldn't stop that either. They were moving but didn't seem to be my own legs. It wasn't until I was outside the bus that I slowly started to feel better, but everything around me was still strange and unreal. I had to keep reminding myself where I was and that I could just wait for the next bus.

In this example, the patient could not control her arms and legs. This was most likely an escape reaction of one of her dissociative parts. She did realize what was happening, though. She described the experience of an intrusion of that part, but also the alienation from herself (*they didn't seem to be my own legs*) and later the alienation from her surroundings (*everything was strange and unreal*).

Another frequent symptom is the experience of medically unexplained symptoms (MUS), such as pain. This pain is usually related to a traumatic experience and is held by a dissociative part that is stuck in that pain. Many patients with a dissociative disorder regularly visit a medical specialist with unexplained pain symptoms. Others avoid doctors instead, because they have often been told that it is all *in their heads*. This can be hazardous, as they may walk around with a complaint that does have a physiological cause for which medical attention is needed.

Seizures or epilepsy without a medically identifiable cause, called non-epileptic seizures, also frequently occur in patients with dissociative disorders (Bowman, 1993a, 2006; Bowman & Coons, 2000). Often there is amnesia for the seizure, but not always. Some patients can still hear others during a seizure but are unable to talk; or they can see well but cannot stop the seizures.

The seizures may last for some minutes, but they may last longer. A neurological cause should always be investigated and excluded. Sometimes clear emotions are visible during a seizure (e.g., anger or sadness), sometimes a person completely disappears, and no contact can be made at all, as if he or she were in some kind of coma, a severe shutdown response.

Detecting the Presence of Dissociative Parts
of the Personality

As described in Chapter 1, the clinical picture of DID is very different from the way it is portrayed in various media. In the media, the image is often dramatic, with many separate personalities with completely different clothes, hairstyles, and behaviors. This image bears no resemblance to reality, which involves subtle, sometimes barely perceptible symptoms, without frequent overt switching from one dissociative part to another (Boon & Draijer, 1993a, 1993b; Kluft, 1985, 1987c; Loewenstein, 2018; Steele et al., 2017).

Rarely will a clinician notice different dissociative parts of the personality during a diagnostic interview. If patients are at all aware of the existence of dissociative parts, they will usually try to maintain control and avoid switching. Initially, many patients are unaware of the dissociative parts and have great difficulty thinking or talking about them. However, they can often report a cluster of dissociative symptoms that is indicative of the existence of dissociative parts.

The following is a summary of the major clues that indicate a dissociative division of the personality. Although patients with DID, OSDD-1, and partial DID do report a cluster of these symptoms, not all report exactly the same cluster:

- Examples of amnesia, both direct (missing time or being somewhere and not remembering how you got there) and indirect (finding clues that you must have done things, hearing from other people that you did things but having no recall for this)
- Various forms of influence by dissociative parts, such as:
  - Hearing voices; male, female, and/or children's voices
  - Having thoughts, feelings, wishes, or needs that seem strange or not your own
  - Doing things or following impulses that seem strange or not your own
  - Insecurity and confusion about yourself due to memory problems; hearing voices and having various wishes, desires, or behaviors that do not seem to be your own
  - Being outside your body and looking at yourself from a distance
  - Not recognizing acquaintances or relatives (or hearing that this has happened)
  - Having all sorts of strange physical sensations, such as the feeling that your body is being controlled, the feeling that your body is changing in shape (e.g., smaller, larger)

- Sudden changes in mood or behavior that are not comprehensible, or hearing about them from other people
- Sudden changes in your capabilities

Thus, it often happens that a patient reports a cluster of the symptoms summarized above without being able to say anything about the dissociative parts of the personality as yet. Conclusions about the possibility of a division of the personality are always based on the presence of several of the clues listed here, not just one.

Dissociative Parts of the Personality

Within the medical literature, dissociative parts of the personality are termed differently. Much of the older literature of the United States speaks of alter personalities or so-called alters. The DSM-5 and also the ICD-11 list "distinct personality states." Following Putnam (2016), some colleagues today also speak of discrete behavioral states (DBS), while others use the term "self states" (Bromberg, 2006; compare to Moskowitz & van der Hart, 2019). In this book I speak of dissociative parts of the personality. In my opinion, the different terms refer to the same phenomenon. In any case, clinicians agree that they are never separate "persons," even though many patients do experience them that way. Several dissociative parts may partially overlap, and they constantly influence each other. All dissociative parts have arisen in response to or adaptation to traumatization, whether they have a function in daily life or preserve traumatic memories. Moreover, there is overlap in functions: some parts hold traumatic memories but may also function in daily life. For a detailed discussion of dissociative parts and their functions, I refer to Steele and colleagues (2017).

A frequently asked question is what actually characterizes a dissociative part of the personality and how to distinguish this from an ego state, a borderline mode, or role playing. Some clinicians equate dissociative parts with ego states and speak of a continuum of ego states (Watkins & Watkins, 1993, 1997). Others believe that dissociative parts of the personality and borderline modes are the same thing (Huntjens et al., 2019a). Over the years, the first criterion in DSM required two or more "distinct personalities." The terminology was changed in the DSM-IV (1994) to "distinct identities or personality states" and has now been changed in DSM-5 to "distinct personality states."

The ICD-11 also speaks of distinct personality states. However, the fact that there is no definition of "distinct" anywhere is problematic. Even more problematic is that in the vast majority of patients observable switches between distinct personality states constitute one of the least common symptoms of DID (Dell, 2009a; Kluft, 1985; Loewenstein et al., 2017).

Dissociative parts can be distinguished from ego states and borderline modes because dissociative parts have their own sense of identity, self-image, autobiographical memory, and personal experiences, however limited these may be (Dorahy et al., 2014; Kluft, 1988, 2006; Moskowitz & van der Hart, 2020; Nijenhuis, 2015; Steele et al., 2017). Steele and colleagues describe this as follows:

> Dissociative parts have a strong first-person perspective—that is, a feeling of *I, me* and *my*—concerning at least one and sometimes all aspects of their experience, including thoughts, feelings, memories, fantasies, perceptions, predictions, moods, sensations, decision-making and behavior. (Nijenhuis & van der Hart, 2011; van der Hart et al., 2006)

Some parts, especially dissociative parts that hold traumatic memories or feelings, seem to be frozen in time, as it were. Such parts of the personality usually do not have access to cognitive and motor skills that the person does possess in an adult part that functions in daily life. In ego states or borderline modes, however, there is a shared sense of self; there is also continuity of memory and access to all the skills appropriate to the current adult age. Dissociative barriers between the different states of consciousness occur almost never, if ever.

It is mainly the presence of a cluster of dissociative symptoms, such as amnesia for the present, indications about influence by dissociative parts, and partial intrusions, that is highly but not exclusively decisive in distinguishing a dissociative part from an ego state or borderline mode. In DID, there must be a cluster of dissociative symptoms. Patients with borderline modes or ego states do not report this cluster of symptoms unless they are confused about the diagnosis or have a comorbid dissociative disorder.

All descriptions (in DSM-5 and ICD-11) of criterion 1 in DID involve the problem of the term "distinctness." The description of OSDD-1 in DSM-5, a kind of subtype of DID, creates even more confusion by speaking of an identity disorder associated with "less-than-marked discontinuities in sense of self and agency or alterations of identity" (APA, 2013, p. 306). This wording creates a gray area where it is not always clear whether there is a dissociative part or an ego state or borderline mode. This may lead to overdiagnosis and false-positive diagnoses by clinicians (see Chapter 10, Incorrect [False-Positive] DID Diagnoses and Factitious or Imitated DID). However, patients with dissociative disorders are usually unable to say much if anything at all about the dissociative parts, and they also present with other symptoms—and this is precisely why clinicians are even more likely to underdiagnose and to fail to recognize the very existence of dissociative parts.

As mentioned earlier, an individual matching the cluster of dissociative symptoms may not be able to say much, if anything, about dissociative parts.

Examples of Patients With Different Levels of Awareness of Dissociative Parts

Following are some examples of different patients with a symptom cluster consistent with DID. They differ greatly in the extent to which they have developed an awareness that they have dissociative parts. Some are not as yet able to talk about dissociative parts while others can.

One patient reported the full cluster of dissociative symptoms. He had severe amnesia and there were clear indications that he also did things at work or at home that he had no recall for afterward. He heard voices and reported a range of symptoms indicating the presence and influence of dissociative parts. However, he was unable to provide any information about these parts.

When asked what he thought had happened whenever he noticed that he had done something he could not remember doing, he replied that he was developing dementia, adding that he felt he was a little young for this. He had undergone extensive neurological assessments that had not revealed any dementia or neurological disorders. Nevertheless, he remained adamant that something must be wrong with his head. As did his wife, who thought that medication should be able to resolve anything.

Another patient described herself as absent-minded and believed that all her symptoms were aligned with a diagnosis of schizophrenia. She stopped responding when the clinician asked her some questions about possible dissociative parts.

There are also patients who have some knowledge and are able talk about parts, even if this is difficult for them. One patient described it as follows:

PATIENT: Perhaps it is another part of me, I don't know, but if my children keep being told things that I'd never tell them . . . that's weird, isn't it?

CLINICIAN: Can you tell me more about that?

PATIENT: Well, I know exactly what I like and don't like; for example, I don't want them to eat too many sweets; one ice cream a day is enough. But sometimes I find out that somehow, they'd had additional ice creams. I used to get very cross with them and accuse them of nicking. They would cry out angrily that I'd given it to them myself. Now I know that apparently there is another part that does that. That part also allows them to venture out further afield when they play outside. I'm very strict, maybe a little too strict sometimes, but I'm so afraid that something might happen to them.

This patient described other parts too, for example one that apparently sang in a choir:

> I don't really care for singing; I don't think I can sing very well either. But I seem to have joined a choir, nonetheless. At first, I wasn't aware of this at all. Now I am often aware of it and sometimes I see myself singing.

When asked by the clinician if she ever spoke to these parts of herself, she replied: *Well, no, I wouldn't know how; that's ridiculous.* So this patient had already been doing some thinking and was able to say more about some parts, although she had not as yet made contact with them.

Finally, there are patients who are already able to give a lot more details about their dissociative parts during the diagnostic examination and also have contact with some of them. One patient reported:

> Yes, I've known all that for a long time, but I thought it was crazy and I never said anything. I've been talking to some of them for a long time, I remember in high school. People would sometimes say that I was talking to myself, and I'd be shocked. But there are some that I really don't want; they truly don't belong to me at all, and they scare me.

These examples show that during diagnostic assessment, large individual differences exist in the extent to which a patient with a cluster of symptoms suggestive of DID realizes that they have dissociative parts. In general, discussing dissociative parts of the personality is more difficult and frightening for patients if these have never been discussed or asked about before.

Summary

This chapter has described psychoform and somatoform dissociative symptoms. When conducting a diagnostic interview, it is important for the clinician to realize that the most prevalent dissociative disorders, DID and OSDD-1, are diagnosed on the basis of a cluster of related symptoms. Only at the end of the interview can the clinician assess whether there is a dissociative disorder and, if so, which one. Even in less complex dissociative disorders (e.g., dissociative amnesia, depersonalization disorder, or a single somatoform disorder), this can only be determined at the end of the completed interview, because by then it will have become apparent if the patient has not reported any other dissociative symptoms.

CHAPTER 3

Other Alterations in Consciousness

Introduction

The TADS-I makes a deliberate distinction between dissociative symptoms indicating a division of the personality (particularly in DID, OSDD Example 1 [OSDD-1], and partial DID) and more common alterations in consciousness. The more common alterations may occur in patients with dissociative disorders and other mental health problems and in the normal population. These are sometimes milder or temporary depersonalization and derealization symptoms and alterations in consciousness as a result of absorption, daydreaming, or trance. Often these symptoms are associated with episodes of anxiety or stress, fatigue, and/or other mental disorders.

As described in Chapter 1, there is ongoing debate as to how these alterations in consciousness are related to dissociative symptoms that are indicative of a division of the personality, or whether in fact they are on the same dissociative continuum. Worldwide (and thus also in DSM-5 and the ICD-11), some of the alterations in consciousness described here—particularly depersonalization and derealization, but also trance—are considered dissociative symptoms. Moreover, these symptoms may be of such a severe and persistent nature that they result in the diagnosis of depersonalization/derealization disorder without reference to a division of the personality. In this case therefore, DSM-5 and ICD-11 do not distinguish between depersonalization symptoms that may indicate a division of the personality and other forms of depersonalization (see APA, 2013, p. 303). Some forms of absorption, particularly intense daydreaming, may also be pathological in nature and may severely impair the individual's functioning (Somer, 2002).

In order to make a correct diagnosis, however, it is important for the clinician to be able to distinguish between mild or temporary depersonalization and derealization symptoms and alterations in consciousness as a result of absorption, daydreaming, and trance on the one hand, and the symptoms indicative of a division of the personality (see Chapter 2) on the other hand. It is for this reason that a separate section of relevant questions was included in the TADS-I.

It is important to note that many of these other alterations in consciousness are also generally endorsed by patients who do report a cluster of dissociative symptoms indicative of a division of the personality. Moreover, it is not always clear in actual practice whether or not a particular symptom indicates a division of the personality. For example, patients with DID may stare for hours and not be very much aware of their surroundings because of an intense internal struggle. However, diagnostic assessment does not always reveal the internal struggle as the reason for the staring. Patients without DID may also answer in the affirmative when asked if they sometimes sit still staring for hours, but in their case it appears they were just very tired and lost in thought. In the first case, the absorption symptom needs to be part of a cluster of dissociative symptoms, including other symptoms indicating a division of the personality such as amnesia, hearing voices, and other indications of the existence of dissociative parts in order to confirm DID. In the second case, no symptoms referring to a division of the personality are reported, and a dissociative disorder can be excluded.

Depersonalization and Derealization

Depersonalization and derealization symptoms include the following:

Depersonalization:
- Feeling as if things happen in a dream
- Feeling like being in a movie
- Feeling as if not really present or participating
- Feeling of not being in contact with one's emotions or body
- Feeling as if acting like a robot or machine on autopilot
- Feeling as if one's head is empty or of being entirely empty

Derealization:
- Feeling that people are unreal or the world is unreal
- Feeling that you are looking at the world through a haze or through a crystal ball or as if inside an aquarium
- Feeling the world around is distorted or blurred, and far away
- Feeling no connection with people around you, even with loved ones

Examples of Depersonalization and Derealization
The following examples are from patients who, based on diagnostic assessment with the TADS-I, did not meet the criteria for DID, OSDD-1, or partial DID. Many had other mental health problems, in particular symptoms

of personality disorders, depression, and anxiety disorders. In one case, a depersonalization disorder was diagnosed in addition to a personality disorder as the symptoms were very persistent and severe.

Example 1

A patient with a history of emotional neglect and personality problems recounted the following:

> PATIENT: I often feel as though I'm sort of floating, as if I'm not really making contact with the ground.
>
> CLINICIAN: Are you outside your body at such times?
>
> PATIENT: No, it is not like that. It is more like a funny feeling. I do things because I must, but not quite consciously. I am not really experiencing it, not really in the moment and I cannot really enjoy the things around me. I have similar experiences in therapy, when I can't get in touch with my feelings. I do know I'm sad, you know, it's just that I cannot cry. This has emerged mainly since my breakdown after the breakup with my partner. I also tend to withdraw. And the world is frightening and strange. I think I may be disappointed in my ex-partner and don't really trust people anymore.

Example 2

Another patient described the following:

> Sometimes everything is a little unreal, as if it were all a dream. This happens especially when I am tense, or tired. It usually lasts only briefly. As soon as I am rested, it is over entirely, in fact. It feels just like I am not really in contact with myself and others then, but maybe I don't want to be either. I do perform certain activities on autopilot, but those are things like brushing my teeth. My thoughts are absent or elsewhere at those times.

Example 3

One patient reported having depersonalization symptoms after an accident. He had received EMDR treatment and said he no longer saw the accident happening again, but he still felt strange and unreal.

> It is like everything has happened in some sort of dream, and it still feels very unreal. It no longer wakes me up at night, and I don't see it happening any longer—that really is over since the EMDR. But I do need to pinch myself now and then and tell myself that I am still here. It all seems so strange, still. Sometimes I look at my wife and children

and they feel so far away. I have trouble getting in touch with my feelings not just about the accident, but about them as well. I have never experienced this in the past. Fortunately, it's been happening a little less over the past few weeks.

Example 4

A patient said that both her parents had psychiatric problems and that she had been the main caretaker for her mother and younger siblings.

> Ever since childhood, I have felt like a zombie at times. I always had to keep going, and at home you never knew what would be happening. This is still the case. I just keep going, as if on some autopilot. My mother was unpredictable; everything revolved around her. The best thing was to put up a kind of wall around me so that I wouldn't feel anything when she was being mean or belittling to me. Nor if she was being nice all of a sudden, because that could change at any time. I still have that wall around me, like a shell. The real Mary is behind it, but nobody sees her, [nobody] is allowed to see her. I always adapt to others and play a role in the outside world, but that is not the real me. I never feel like myself. Often, I don't even know who I am.

This patient described chronic depersonalization symptoms that appeared to be related to what Winnicot (1960) described as "false self" problems.[8] The symptoms were of such a lasting nature and so severe that she met the criteria for a depersonalization disorder.

Example 5

> I have been having panic attacks for many years. I get very scared and all of a sudden everything is completely unreal. I see things distorted and blurred, and it's very frightening. It makes me believe I am dying, that I am having a brain hemorrhage distorting my vision. I am never like this normally, but I really don't always understand what this panic is about. It can happen out of the blue.

---

8 Winnicott (1960) introduced the notions of "true self" and "false self." The true self would develop in the first months of life, when the child becomes aware of its vital functions: movement, touch, and the pleasure it derives from these. In a healthy situation, a child develops a realistic self-image and derives pleasure from what it does. Opposite to the true self is the false self, a kind of surface or role created by adapting to the wishes and expectations of parents or caretakers. The need to adapt can be so compelling that the true self needs to be hidden to avoid hurt and injury. This is described in the example of this patient.

This patient's derealization would exclusively appear during panic attacks.

Assessment of Depersonalization and Derealization Symptoms

When assessing symptoms of depersonalization and derealization, the following aspects are of concern for the clinician:

- Are the experiences temporary or ongoing?
- Do the experiences occur in the context of substance use, specifically recreational drugs or particular medications?
- Do the experiences occur as part of another mental disorder? For example: Does the patient report depersonalization or derealization during panic attacks, psychosis, a mood disorder, or as part of PTSD?
- Do the experiences exclusively occur when the person is ill or fatigued, tense, anxious, or distressed or after a disturbing or shocking experience (even without PTSD symptoms)?
- Are the experiences part of a cluster of dissociative symptoms indicating a division of the personality, such as amnesia, hearing voices, or other Schneiderian symptoms?

Absorption Experiences

The definition of absorption is being totally immersed in an activity or thoughts in such a way that one is not aware or is less than normally aware of one's surroundings. As described in Chapter 1, some self-report questionnaires on dissociation include symptoms of absorption. Extreme absorption may cause memory disturbances. One becomes so immersed in something that time passes by unnoticed. The clock suddenly shows a much later hour than expected. Absorption is sometimes comparable to extreme concentration or hyperfocus.

Examples of Absorption

I can be completely absorbed by a book or film, so that you can talk to me, but I will not hear you. Sometimes I am astonished afterwards about the amount of time that has passed. I love being able to shut myself off like this. I have been doing this ever since childhood. We had a hectic family and not much space at home. When [I'm] at work, it is a very convenient thing as well; I can concentrate very effectively, and I am not easily distracted.

During walks, I am always immersed in thoughts, and I can walk for hours. Fortunately, I know my way well and find it almost automatically. I do sometimes miss a turn because my mind is so immersed that I don't really pay attention. That does make me jump for a moment, because I don't know where I am. It also happens in the car, as if driving on autopilot; suddenly you are much further along the way than you realized.

The examples above relate to everyday and fairly common experiences, although not everyone can become so completely absorbed in thoughts or actions as described here. In some cases however, absorption can become more problematic and may overly interfere with daily functioning. In those cases, it may be associated with feelings of depression, emptiness, or loneliness.

A patient with borderline personality disorder and chronic depression responded as follows:

> I am easily bored and often feel gloomy. I have not been able to work, nor to continue the voluntary work I was doing. The days are quite long, but sometimes the hours just go by unnoticed while [I'm] sitting on the couch. My head is empty. Sometimes it starts with zapping [channels on] the TV, sometimes I sit and stare into nothing. I don't think I'm thinking about anything really, it just happens. I am okay with it, since it makes the time go by. After all, I can't do anything anyway. Everything I do fails.

In this case, absorption interferes with daily functioning, but this cannot be considered separately from the depression and borderline symptoms.

Daydreaming

Daydreaming is a special form of absorption. Daydreaming can take severe or pathological forms. Somer and colleagues (Somer, Lehrfeld, et al., 2016; Somer, Somer, et al., 2016a, 2016b; Somer et al., 2017) have investigated and continue to investigate maladaptive daydreaming, a form of daydreaming or escaping into a fantasy world for hours or even days from which the patient has great difficulty breaking free. The risk of addiction is not insignificant. Patients with this extreme form of daydreaming may have impaired memory as a consequence of the intense absorption, and they may feel strange and unreal despite the absence of a division of the personality. This form can lead to serious impairments in their daily functioning. Somer and colleagues (2017) regard this as a separate dissociative disorder and argue for further research and the inclusion of a diagnostic classification of Pathological Daydreaming in the section "Dissociative Disorders" in DSM.

Examples of Daydreaming

During the ongoing study with the TADS-I, a number of patients reported severe forms of daydreaming that interfered with their daily functioning.

One patient recounted the following:

> The last days before I went into therapy, I was in a daydream the entire day. I had trouble getting out of it. I have been doing that since childhood. I needed it because nobody was home for me. In my daydreams, there was always someone I could turn to. Sometimes I imagined a very sweet teacher at school who would comfort me when I was sad. When I got older, I used to play roles in films I had seen and could identify with. I still do that several times a week, especially when I feel anxious or very alone. Sometimes I am not quite so aware of my surroundings while daydreaming. During good times, I don't daydream at all. But when times are bad, I have no control over it. I feel very embarrassed about it and loathe doing it.

Another patient said:

> I am addicted to daydreaming, I think. I absolutely love it. I have been doing it for years and can sometimes hardly wait until I get the chance. I can get outraged by interruptions during a daydream, for example by the phone. But sometimes I don't even hear it, or I deliberately set it to silent mode. So far, I have been doing what I have to do in daily life, but not that much. I do go to therapy, and I exercise once a week. That's because my mentors tell me to. I experience great things in my daydreams. I am always a heroine type, like the tall slender girl who can beat anything and anyone. I like science fiction, so that is my type of heroine.

In this patient, too, daydreaming seemed to serve as protection from the emotional pain of loneliness. She had severe attachment problems, chronic anxiety, a very negative self-image, and was severely overweight. She was referred because her therapist suspected DID. She had reported memory problems, but these seemed to be limited exclusively to her daydreaming and other forms of absorption. No indications were found of the cluster of symptoms associated with the diagnosis of DID.

The TADS-I contains a number of questions about daydreaming. If clinicians develop the impression that there may be a pathological form of daydreaming, they are advised to use Somer's questionnaire as a supplement (Somer et al., 2016a). This questionnaire is included as an appendix with this book. It can also be downloaded free of charge in many different languages from the research group's website (see Appendix 5).

Trance Experiences

Trance experiences are described as a distinctive form of absorption and a narrowing of consciousness. In daily life, trance experiences may be indistinguishable from intense involvement in an activity such as music or dance, but also in running, for example. In addition, collective trance experiences are common in Western society, for example during large music festivals, whether or not enhanced by the use of drugs. Trance may also be a collective experience in some religious communities. The word "trance" is often associated with hypnosis. In non-Western societies, trance is a common and widely accepted cultural phenomenon. ICD-11 and DSM-5 speak of trance disorder or dissociative trance when the symptom does not occur within a generally accepted cultural context (Cardeña et al., 2009; Cardeña et al., 2022).

The TADS-I contains one question about trance. During diagnostic interviews, in which so far almost only Western patients participated, the question was frequently asked: What exactly is a trance? Is that different from what I have just described? These patients then referred to examples of intense absorption. Only patients who had been raised in a specific religious environment reported collective trance experiences during religious meetings or individual trance experiences during prayer sessions within the religious setting. To some of them, these experiences had been very frightening.

Examples of Trance Experiences

One patient recalled that during a certain period of his childhood, his mother would take him and his younger sisters to church services where people would speak in tongues: *Everyone became joyful, and we learned that this was a very special experience that we were going to be a part of.* He did acknowledge that people were no longer themselves and seemed in raptures during those meetings, but it also felt very uncomfortable. His father did not participate and was not very fond of this church. After his parents' divorce, he went to live with his father and stopped attending church. He has never visited a church community of this kind again. This patient reported occasional depersonalization experiences, especially during encounters with others.

Another patient described witnessing people becoming ecstatic and falling to the floor in her church community. In her case, this did not happen in the group, but rather in individual meetings with some people from the church, where they tried to exorcise the devil from her. *I was terrified and passed out, so everything went black,* she said. In her case, these experiences were found to be part of a cluster of dissociative symptoms consistent with a diagnosis of DID.

Trancelike experiences are common in patients with dissociative disorders, although they are not always described as such by the patients (Dell, 2002, 2006a; Ross, 1997). In dissociative disorder therefore, they constitute part of a cluster of symptoms.

Chapter 1 recommended using the Cultural Formulation Interview as included in DSM-5 as a diagnostic adjunct in non-Western patients (APA, 2013).

CHAPTER 4

Screening for Dissociative Symptoms Using Self-Report Questionnaires

Introduction

This chapter briefly describes several self-report questionnaires used in screening for dissociative symptoms. Not all self-report questionnaires have been included, only the widely used ones as well as an interesting recent one, the Detachment and Compartmentalization Inventory (Butler et al., 2019).

The Dissociative Experiences Scale (DES; Bernstein & Putnam, 1986) was validated in the Netherlands in several studies (Boon & Draijer, 1993a; Draijer & Boon, 1993b; Ensink & van Otterloo, 1989). This is the oldest, most widely used, and most researched questionnaire on dissociation worldwide. For this reason, the DES is discussed more extensively in this chapter than the other instruments. The DES and the Somatoform Dissociation Questionaire-20 (SDQ-20) were used in my research with the TADS-I (Boon & Draijer, 1993a; 1993b).

When Is Screening Advisable?

Screening for dissociative symptoms is not a standard procedure in mental health, the main reason being that patients rarely present with dissociative symptoms. Also, therapists often do not consider screening for dissociative symptoms due to unfamiliarity with dissociation. This really should be standard practice for patients with a history of chronic early childhood traumatization or patients with trauma- or stress-related problems. In addition, it is advisable to screen the patient groups below:

- Patients with medically unexplained physical symptoms (MUPS) or so-called conversion disorders.
- Patients hearing voices or experiencing psychotic symptoms and unresponsive to antipsychotic medications.

- Patients with varying medical or psychiatric diagnoses who are unresponsive or insufficiently responsive to first-line treatments.

The use of screening tools should never replace diagnostic assessments with structured clinical interviews, and no diagnosis should be made on the basis of screening alone. However, sometimes a careful interview does suffice, possibly using the answers from a self-report questionnaire (for an example, see the introduction to Chapter 5).

Screening Tools

When using a screening tool, it is important to ensure that the questionnaire is interpreted by a clinician who is able to distinguish between absorption and imagination experiences on the one hand and symptoms that may indicate dissociative symptoms indicating a division of the personality on the other hand. When there is any doubt about a score, it is possible to ask the patient to provide examples of a particular experience in their own words (see the section Practical Use of the DES as a Screening Tool, below).

The following is an overview of available screening tools.

Dissociative Experiences Scale (DES)

The DES is a short self-report questionnaire with 28 questions about possible dissociative experiences. It was developed in the United States in 1986 (Bernstein & Putnam, 1986). In the 1990s, the scoring system was modified for ease of use (DES-II; Carlson & Putnam, 1993). For each question, the patient indicates how often a specific experience occurs (a percentage between 0% and 100%). A special version, the Adolescent Dissociative Experiencing Scale or A-DES, was developed for adolescents (Armstrong et al., 1997).

As described in Chapter 1, the questionnaire is based on the continuum model of dissociation. The questionnaire has three subscales: (1) amnesia; (2) depersonalization/derealization; and (3) absorption/imagination (with absorption referring to becoming so absorbed in a particular experience that little or nothing else is consciously perceived, and imagination referring to intense mental images). If viewed from the continuum model of dissociation, the latter subscale covers the so-called normal forms of dissociation; these are often phenomena that go hand in hand with pathological dissociative symptoms, such as amnesia and hearing voices, but should be distinguished from them. It is precisely the absorption phenomena that do not refer to a division of the personality and that also occur frequently in patients who do not have a dissociative disorder.

Studies on the psychometric qualities of the DES show high reliability and validity (Carlson et al., 1993; Draijer & Boon, 1993b; Dubester & Braun, 1995; Ensink & van Otterloo, 1989; Frischholz et al., 1990; Frischholz et al., 1991; Holtgraves & Stockdale, 1997; Zingrone & Alvarado, 2001).

Meta-Analyses and Standard Scores in the DES

There have been two major meta-analytic studies of the DES. The first was published by van IJzendoorn and Schuengel (1996), while Lyssenko and colleagues (2018) recently published a second, larger meta-analysis of the DES. Their study included 216 studies, with data from more than 15,000 participants distributed across 19 diagnostic categories.

Of course, between 1996 and the recent (2018) study, more research with the DES has taken place that has been included. Also, more separate diagnostic categories have been studied and these also have been included in the 2018 study. For this reason, not all mean scores of the 2018 study can be compared with the earlier 1996 study by van IJzendoorn and Schuengel. However, the mean DES scores for DID—the diagnosis that consistently shows the highest DES scores, are comparable: 48.7 and 45.6, respectively. In the study Nel Draijer and I conducted with the SCID-D (n = 71) the mean DES score was 49.8 (Boon & Draijer, 1993a). Lyssenko included a category "DSM-5 dissociative disorders" (other than DID) with a mean score of 38.9, while in the earlier study by van IJzendoorn and Schuengel a category of DDNOS (mean 35.29) and unspecified dissociative disorder (mean 41.15) was included. Again, these data are quite comparable.

The PTSD scores of the 1996 and 2018 studies are also comparable. The original 1996 study by van IJzendoorn and Schuengel included a general category of personality disorders (with a mean DES of 16.80); the 2018 study by Lyssenko and colleagues lacks a general category of this kind, but patients with borderline personality disorder appear to have the highest mean DES after those with dissociative disorders and PTSD. Further examination of this borderline group shows that the elevated DES scores are mainly explained by high scores on the absorption scale and therefore do not indicate a division of the personality.

In both the 1996 and 2018 studies, the mean DES scores of patients with nearly all other mental disorders are below 20. Only eating disorders score slightly higher, which deviates from the 1996 study by van IJzendoorn and Schuengel—in which the mean scores of patients with (all) eating disorders were much lower.

How do scores of patients with mental disorders compare with those in the general population? Based on 11 studies with a total of 1,578 participants, the study by van IJzendoorn and Schuengel found a mean DES in the general population of 11.5. Students and adolescents (n = 5,676) had a mean score of 14. Recent Finnish and Portuguese studies for the general population found a mean DES score of 8 and 10, respectively (Espirito Santo & Pio-Abreu, 2009; Lipsanen et al., 2003).

Cutoff Scores for the DES

What does the above analysis imply for the DES cutoff score? In order to screen for dissociative disorders, the clinician must first determine the optimal cutoff score. This is determined by the ratio between sensitivity (the ability of a test to correctly identify the true positives or subjects with a dissociative disorder) and specificity (the ability to correctly identify the true negatives or subjects without a dissociative disorder).

In the early 1990s, various cutoff scores were used, based on limited data, the choice of which often depended on the objective. If researchers absolutely did not want to overlook any dissociative disorder in a study, they often chose a low cutoff score of 20. However, this does create the risk of including more false positives.

When we first compared the results of the DES with those of a validated clinical diagnostic interview, the SCID-D, we found an optimal cutoff score of 25 (Draijer & Boon, 1993b). Now, more than 25 years later, this cutoff score is still widely used. In the recent 2018 meta-analysis by Lyssenko and colleagues, the mean DES values of large groups of patients with various DSM-5 disorders show that, with the exception of borderline personality disorder (BPD), all groups with means above 25 have PTSD or a dissociative disorder. It is well known that borderline patients often have elevated DES scores. The meta-analysis by Lyssenko and colleagues (2018) involved 27 different studies involving 1,705 patients. Several studies have shown high comorbidity between BPD, PTSD, and dissociative disorders (Ford & Courtois, 2021; Korzekwa, Dell, & Pain, 2009; Korzekwa, Dell, Links, et al., 2009; Şar et al., 2003; Şar et al., 2006; van den Bosch et al., 2003). This is discussed in more detail in Chapter 8, on the TADS-I profiles in PBD, and Chapter 9, which deals with the differential diagnosis of dissociative disorders and personality disorders, PTSD, and complex posttraumatic stress disorder (CPTSD). Carlson et al. (1993) recommended 30 as the best cutoff score.

In our 1993 study with the SCID-D, using a cutoff score of 25, Nel Draijer and I found 7% false negatives and 14% false positives. During screening, a dissociative disorder would be missed in the first group, while the second group would have to be reassessed and then possibly excluded by means of a diagnostic interview. Many of the false-positive DES scores, of sometimes well over 25 or 30 were based on severe absorption and depersonalization symptoms. These patients did not have a dissociative disorder.

To be clear, having DES scores above 25 does not mean that the person has a dissociative disorder. Patients with mean scores above 25 only have an elevated risk for having a dissociative disorder.

A Critical Note

In the past 25 years I have seen a considerable number of patients with DES scores that sometimes far exceeded the 25 or 30 cutoff score who turned out not to have a dissociative disorder. At the time, Nel Draijer and I cautioned about possible false-positive DES scores (Boon & Draijer, 1995a) for the patient groups below:

Some manic or psychotic patients tend to score rather high on the DES. Upon further investigation it appears that this is clearly related to a state of disinhibition.

Patients who are in a state of crisis tend to score higher on self-report questionnaires—including the DES—than they normally would, because of their need for support and help.

Patients presenting their symptoms in an exaggerated manner also tend to make their symptoms seem more severe.

Mutual influencing may occur in certain patient groups, for example, in day treatment or clinical settings where there are many traumatized patients in a group, or where there is a lot of attention for dissociative symptomatology. Whenever patients have been in contact with DID patients, or whenever someone for some reason seems to have an interest in a DID diagnosis, a diagnostic interview is an absolute necessity. We often find very high DES scores—sometimes well over 60—in patients in this group, who turn out not to have a dissociative disorder after completing a diagnostic interview. However, this does not always involve a conscious amplification of dissociative symptoms. Some of these patients endorse some of the experiences mentioned in the DES, especially depersonalization and absorption. This may result in a high DES score.

Some adolescents also tend to score higher.

In the current study with the TADS-I—more than 25 years after our 1993 study with the SCID-D—the percentage of false-positive DES scores is much higher. Almost 60% of patients (16 out of 27) scored above and sometimes far above the cutoff score of 25 (ranging from 26.4 to 55.7); in the TADS-I they did not meet the criteria for a dissociative disorder or CPTSD. With a cutoff score of 30 in the DES, 51% of the patients in our TADS-I study scored significantly higher. This is a serious problem. Of patients who did have a dissociative disorder, 16% scored below the 25 cutoff score. In other words, 4 out of 25 patients had a false-negative DES score, while 2 had very obvious DID and another 2 had OSDD-1. Many of the patients with false-positive DES scores had particularly elevated scores on the subscales for absorption and depersonalization.

How can this be explained? The SCID-D study that we published in the 1990s was a validation study in which patients with dissociative disorders were compared to a randomly selected group of control patients with other mental disorders (Boon & Draijer, 1993a). The recent study with the TADS-I is a pilot study in which patients could either be referred to me or could self-refer for a second opinion in order to find out whether they had a dissociative disorder. Naturally, one can expect more false positives because it concerns a select group that is referred, unlike the random control group of patients in the earlier study. These were patients who, according to their therapists, might have a dissociative disorder or who suspected this themselves. Many of these patients had also read or heard about dissociation. Moreover, much has changed in the past 30 years with the arrival of the internet and social media. People have access to much more information about dissociative disorders than before, and the DID diagnosis has become more widely known. Lastly, as long as self-report questionnaires also contain many items on absorption or more general depersonalization experiences, patients—based on their absorption and depersonalization symptoms—may score above the cutoff scores. This is discussed in more detail in Chapter 10, on false-positive DID diagnoses.

Conclusion About the DES

The present study shows that the DES is not a reliable screening tool in the aforementioned select group of patients (Thomas, 2001). Whenever patients have high scores on the DES, a diagnostic interview is indicated. However, it may save time to first examine which items on the DES resulted in the elevated score before conducting a lengthy structured diagnostic interview. I will explain this further in the next section.

Practical Use of the DES as a Screening Tool

The DES can be used as a tool to get a first impression of the severity of dissociative symptoms. After the questionnaire has been completed, the clinician can discuss the answers with the patient. The aim is to get an impression of what the patient's responses actually mean. The clinician should also pay attention to the scores on the different subscales: For which items or subscales does the patient have an elevated score?

Items on the absorption subscale describe fairly common experiences, which may be found in the general population as well as in patients with other mental disorders. Below are some examples.

ITEM 1. Some people have the experience of driving or riding in a car or bus or subway and suddenly realizing that they don't remember what has happened during all or part of the trip.

ITEM 2. Some people find that sometimes they are listening to someone talk and they suddenly realize that they did not hear part or all of what was said.

Then there are several items that mainly describe depersonalization and derealization. Both patients with and without a dissociative disorder may have positive scores for these items. Also, people without a mental illness sometimes describe depersonalization and derealization in times of crisis, stress, or tension. The next item refers to a depersonalization experience.

> ITEM 7. Some people sometimes have the experience of feeling as though they are standing next to themselves or watching themselves do something and they actually see themselves as if they were looking at another person.

For this item it is important to differentiate between a more general feeling of being an observer of oneself or being critical of oneself, versus the experience of literally being outside one's body or looking at oneself from a distance (above oneself or outside oneself). In the latter case, one part (the observing part) is looking at another part (the experiencing or acting part)—an experience that is frequently described by DID patients (but also by some other traumatized patients).

The next item refers to derealization, which is another common phenomenon that is not limited to patients with dissociative disorders:

> ITEM 12. Some people have the experience of feeling that other people, objects, and the world around them are not real.

There are also items that describe experiences of amnesia directly or indirectly, such as the examples below:

> ITEM 3. Some people have the experience of finding themselves in a place and have no idea how they got there.
> ITEM 9. Some people find that they have no memory for some important events in their lives (e.g., a wedding or graduation).

For all amnesia items, the clinician has to ascertain whether they relate to absorption or involve actual amnesia.

Finally, some items that may also be related to amnesia describe experiences that are quite specific to patients with DID, such as the following examples:

ITEM 4. Some people have the experience of finding themselves dressed in clothes they don't remember putting on.

In this case, the person cannot remember getting dressed or having to get changed which indicates that another dissociative part of the personality may have done this.

ITEM 5. Some people have the experience of finding new things among their belongings that they do not remember buying.

This could mean that another dissociative part of the personality went to buy something; the part answering the question was not present and has amnesia.

ITEM 6. Some people sometimes find that they are approached by people they do not know who call them by another name or insist that they have met them before.

ITEM 8. Some people are told that they sometimes do not recognize friends of family members.

ITEM 10. Some people have the experience of being accused of lying when they do not think they have lied.

ITEM 25. Some people find evidence that they have done things they do not remember doing.

ITEM 26. Some people sometimes find writings, drawings, or notes among their belongings that they must have done but cannot remember doing.

All of these items refer to possible behaviors of dissociative parts for which the patient has amnesia. Nonetheless, patients without DID or OSDD-1 may also score positively on these items. Upon further questioning, the patients without DID or OSDD-1 sometimes appear to have interpreted the question differently from patients with the diagnosis. Therefore, the clinician should always ask patients to explain, in their own words, exactly what they meant. Do patients' answers indeed indicate a possible existence of dissociative parts of the personality? Or did they mean to say something completely different, or did they recognize the experience as dissociation, while their actual symptoms were different from what was meant by the question?

Case Report Illustrating the DES in a Clinical Interview

The following case report illustrates how clinicians can take a closer look at DES scores of patients who do not appear to have a dissociative disorder.

A 28-year-old patient presents for a diagnostic consultation. She has been receiving day treatment for a year. During this treatment, some problems have emerged. The patient has increasingly felt that she was getting stuck and was not making any progress. As the patient's behavior is constantly changing, the therapist decides to request a diagnostic consultation to determine whether she might have DID. It is known that the patient has a history of serious emotional neglect. Both her parents had psychological problems; they divorced when the patient was 6 years old. The patient and her older brother stayed with her mother. She was bullied at school and also by her older brother. She has been overweight since puberty.

The patient had an average score of 35 on the DES, which was well above the cutoff score. More clarity can be obtained by exploring the meaning of her responses to the individual questions on which she scored high. What did the patient have in mind when answering these questions?

For Item 3 (finding yourself in a place and having no idea how you got there; for which she scored 20) she said the following:

PATIENT: When I go somewhere by bike, I don't remember which route I cycled when I arrive.

CLINICIAN: Could you tell me a bit more about it?

PATIENT: Sometimes I am completely lost in my thoughts without paying much attention to what is going on.

CLINICIAN: Do you know where you are going when this happens?

PATIENT: Of course, I do. This may happen when I'm on my way to day treatment. Then I'm already thinking about what I want to say. And sometimes I'm late because I don't feel up to it. Then I've just left home too late.

CLINICIAN: You are aware that you departed from your home?

PATIENT: Yes, that is not what it is about. I'm just lost in thought when I'm en route.

For this item it is diagnostically important to differentiate between a real fugue and absorption phenomena. The item is actually intended to determine the presence of a fugue. In case of a fugue, patients suddenly find themselves somewhere but do not know how they got there—and usually do not know what they were doing there. There is amnesia for leaving their home. This is when one dissociative part of a person has left home; another part suddenly finds themself somewhere but has no memory of what happened before that. However, many patients who answer this question in the affirmative appear to mean something quite different. They remember very well that they left home but along the way they were lost in thought or describe a so-called highway trance.

Regarding Item 9 (having no memory of certain important events in life; score 15; these can be events in the past and present), the patient says: *I remember very little from before I was 12 years old.* When asked, she does remember her primary school period, who her teachers were, whom she liked and did not like. She then describes an incident with one of her teachers. And also how happy she was when, at the age of 10, she was given a bicycle to go to school. In fact, she is able to speak in fairly great detail about home, a friend, and her holidays. When asked again what exactly she meant by her answer to this item, she says: *Well, it's more like I feel that I have a bad memory. Some people remember so many details about the past, but not me.* There is no evidence of her actually missing things or not remembering certain events.

With regard to this item, it is important to differentiate between simply not having a particularly good memory and clear indications that there really is amnesia for an entire period or for important events in that period. In the latter case, one really does not remember anything or remembers only some fragments because another part of the personality was present at the time of the episode. Someone with DID, for example, answered this question:

> I love horse riding very much and I enjoy doing it. I just never understood how I learned to do it. I just do it. But it seems that I started when I was six, as there are photos of me on a pony, but I don't remember anything about it. Even when I look at those photos, I have no memory of it. But I have always pretended that I did remember.

This last answer clearly shows that this patient does not remember specific events such as horse riding at all. This is not the same as having a bad memory.

For Item 15 (not being sure whether things that they remember happening really did happen or whether they just dreamed them), the patient described: *I can get very absorbed in daydreams, which can be so real that it seems like I'm really living them. It sometimes happens that I can't remember whether I experienced something in my daydream or in reality.* This is also a case of extreme absorption, but not an indication of the existence of dissociative parts. However, the clinician should always be aware that such answers could also be given by patients with DID or OSDD-1; in such cases, in addition to these absorption symptoms, the patient also reports forms of amnesia that indicate a division of the personality.

For Item 17 (becoming so absorbed in a film or television program that one is unaware of events happening around oneself; score 25), the patient reports: *I get carried away in a movie very easily. I forget everything.* These items (on the absorption subscale) describe a phenomenon that also occurs in the normal population and that does not necessarily indicate a dissociative disorder. This patient also scored quite high on Item 18 (some people become so absorbed in a fantasy or daydream that it feels as though it were really happening).

For Item 20 (staring into space, thinking of nothing, and not being aware of the passage of time; Score 45), this patient describes:

> I catch myself staring and then I wonder what I've been thinking about, because I had just vanished for a moment. I don't take anything in and don't hear anything. It often happens when I am alone. Then I can just dream away.

This item is also part of the absorption subscale. Many patients describe moments like these, which can occur during daydreaming but also when they are tired or tense. The clinician may ask whether patients have ever found out afterward that apparently they have been doing things for which there is amnesia, instead of just sitting in a chair staring. This is often the case in patients with DID: sitting and staring is followed by a switch to another dissociative part that engages in certain activities. Much later, the patient comes to, sitting on the couch, unaware of what has happened.

For Item 23 (being able to do things with amazing ease and spontaneity that would usually be difficult; Score 55) the patient explains:

> Occasionally, when I go to parties or birthdays (I prefer to avoid them but sometimes I can't escape them) and I'm talking to someone, it suddenly goes well. I then find myself wondering: Why is it so easy now and why is it so often impossible?

This item calls for differentiating between ordinary differences in behavior and feelings—which are generally common phenomena—and differences due to the existence of different parts of the personality. In order to explore this, the clinician may inquire to what extent the other behaviors are associated with feelings of depersonalization or even partial amnesia. Although this may not always be clear, patients with DID might then describe this in the following way: *If I am honest, I am just looking at myself, as if I myself am not present, I am out of my body. Sometimes the evening is suddenly over, and I don't remember everything.* In the case of the patient described here, it turned out that she usually had a drink to feel more at ease.

For Item 27 (hearing voices inside one's head telling the person to do things, or commenting on things the person is doing) this patient also scored 25. She explains:

Yes, there is a kind of continuous commentary. For instance, when I have to do something difficult. I'm not even sure it's a real voice; it's a bit like my mother's voice, the way she can pick on me. It's a positive and a negative voice, or maybe a thought, a fight between the two. The negative one prevails. It usually wins; it keeps me doubting. This goes on for a very long time; even for little things; these thoughts can keep me occupied for a very long time.

For this item, it is important to distinguish between the voices during a psychosis, the voices of someone with DID, and the voices that are sometimes heard by patients with a personality disorder. Moreover, in DID there should be a cluster of dissociative symptoms, not just hearing voices. In this case, the patient is actually describing more of an internal struggle between something negative and something positive. At times, it is almost as if she is hearing her mother again.

For Item 24 (not being able to remember whether the person has done something or has just thought about doing that thing), the patient describes:

For example, when I am cleaning my house, I can sit and look at something, wondering whether I have cleaned it or not. I think cleaning is a very boring job and I always wander off. I guess I tend to get caught up in my own thoughts.

This item involves distinguishing between the presence of amnesia and possibly dissociative parts of the personality and memory problems that are caused by daydreaming, being absorbed in thoughts, or preoccupied with something else. Clearly, this patient describes being particularly absorbed in her thoughts or her own world of daydreams. This is how a patient with DID answered this question:

PATIENT: Sometimes I don't know whether I've done the laundry or not.
CLINICIAN: Could you clarify this?
PATIENT: Well, then I would have to go and check. I go to the attic, where the washing machine and dryer are. Then I see that the laundry is already clean, ironed, and folded, fortunately.
CLINICIAN: Can you then recall doing it?
PATIENT: Sometimes I do, in flashes, sometimes I don't. But then I am just happy it's done!

Case Evaluation

On further examination of the individual dissociative symptoms, this patient emerges as someone who daydreams a lot and is absorbed in her thoughts. Sometimes her daydreaming is so intense that she fails to notice her surroundings. The elevated DES scores are mainly on the absorption subscale; some of the other items she has clearly interpreted differently. Her fluctuating sense of self is consistent with borderline personality disorder.

In addition to exploring what the answers to the DES mean, it is also important to get as complete a picture as possible of what the patient thinks. Does the patient think he or she has a dissociative disorder? Has there been any influencing by a clinician or anyone else? After all, the likelihood of a false-positive DES outcome is greater when the patient, possibly in conjunction with the clinician or a close relative, has started to believe that he or she has a dissociative disorder. This may be entirely justified, in which case the disorder is diagnosed during further diagnostic assessment. However, it often turns out not to be the case. Usually, absorption and depersonalization symptoms are the reason for a patient or clinician to consider a dissociative disorder. The DES-II is available free of charge online at the website of the ISSTD free resources for nonmembers: http://www.isst-d.org/resources.

DES-Taxon (DES-T)

In 1995, Waller and colleagues introduced an abbreviated version of the DES consisting of eight items, with the aim of determining the severity of "pathological dissociation" (DES-Taxon). They assumed that there exist not one, but two continua of dissociative phenomena: a continuum of "normal dissociation" and a continuum of "pathological dissociation." The DES-T would be able to screen patients in the latter continuum. There is a calculator (Excel sheet) available online that, based on the items of the DES-II and the DES-T, calculates the probability of a person falling within the DES-Taxon parameters. In 1996, van IJzendoorn and Schuengel cautioned against the danger of response bias. The DES-T only contains items clearly indicating severe, pathological dissociative symptoms, which are so specific that van IJzendoorn and Schuengel argue they may lead to underreporting or overreporting. Several studies have demonstrated that the DES-T does not differentiate any better than the DES.

Dissociation Questionnaire (DIS-Q)

The DIS-Q (Vanderlinden, Vandereycken, et al., 1993) is a 63-item self-report questionnaire that was developed and validated in Belgium. Completing the DIS-Q takes about 15 to 20 minutes. The answers are scored on a Likert scale ranging from 1 ("not at all") to 5 ("very much"). The DIS-Q score is the quotient of the total score (ranging from 63 to 315) and the number of questions (63) and can therefore range from 1 to 5. DIS-Q scores higher than or equal to the 2.5 cutoff mark indicate an increased risk for dissociative symptomatology. In addition to the 63 items, the DIS-Q also enquires about age, gender, demographic status, and education. It also has questions about "severely stressful, life-threatening or traumatizing events in one's personal life," which can be specified in the various answer options: "serious physical injury, exposure to war, physical abuse, sexual abuse, emotional abuse, or other." The questionnaire consists of four subscales: (1) identity confusion and identity fragmentation; (2) loss of control over behaviors, thoughts, and feelings; (3) amnesia; and (4) increased concentration. The DIS-Q has a good reliability for internal consistency and test-retest. The list is much longer than the DES and is also less well-researched internationally.

Somatoform Dissociation Questionnaire (SDQ-20)

The SDQ-20 (Nijenhuis et al., 1996) is a 20-item questionnaire that measures somatoform manifestations of dissociation. The answers are scored on a Likert scale ranging from 1 ("this does not apply to me at all") to 5 ("this applies to me to an extreme extent"). The score is calculated by dividing the total by the number of items, and the cutoff mark is 32. The mean SDQ score for patients with somatoform disorders is 32; this is 43 for patients with DDNOS (now OSDD-1) and 55.1 for patients with DID. The Dutch version of the questionnaire has good psychometric qualities. There is also a shortened version, the SDQ-5, consisting of five questions with a cutoff score of 8 (Nijenhuis et al., 1997). The SDQ is the only self-report questionnaire with questions about somatoform dissociation and therefore complements the DES. The list is available free of charge in many different translations online at: dissociativedisorder.org/sdq-tec.

Cambridge Depersonalization Scale (CDS)

The CDS is a 29-item self-report questionnaire that focuses exclusively on symptoms of depersonalization and, to a lesser extent, derealization (Sierra & Berrios, 2000). The CDS enquires about the frequency and duration of each item over the last 6 months. The CDS correlates with the DES depersonalization subscale but is far more comprehensive than the DES subscale. The scale has good psychometric qualities, has been translated into several languages, and has been used in research.

The Multidimensional Inventory of Dissociation (MID)

The MID (Dell, 2006b) is a self-report questionnaire containing multiple scales that was developed specifically to assess the presence of pathological dissociative symptoms. It does not include any questions about normal dissociation. The MID focuses mainly on the diagnostic categories DID, OSDD-1, PTSD, and severe borderline personality disorder and not on dissociative amnesia and depersonalization disorder, although the MID does of course include questions on depersonalization and amnesia.

The MID consists of 218 questions with 168 dissociation items; the 50 remaining items were developed for validation purposes. The questionnaire is far more comprehensive than short self-report instruments such as the DES and the DIS-Q. Dell emphasizes that the MID should be followed by one, or sometimes more clinical interviews. The MID uses an 11-point Likert scale format and takes approximately 30 to 90 minutes to complete. The MID and its accompanying Excel-based scoring program generate both ratings on a subscale and categorical diagnoses (e.g., DID, DDNOS [OSDD-1], PTSD, and severe BPD). The MID measures 23 dissociative symptoms and 6 response sets that serve as validity scales: defensiveness, emotional suffering, rare symptoms, attention-seeking behavior, factitious behavior, and a severe borderline personality disorder index. It is the validity scales that distinguish the MID from all other self-report instruments.

The MID has two scoring systems: total score and severe dissociation score. The total score ranges between 0 and 100. A score of 30 or above is considered a cutoff indicative of probable dissociative psychopathology, whereas a score of 10 and below is considered an indication of a low level of dissociation. In one study (Dell, 2006b) involving 288 patients with DID, the mean total score was 50.6 and the mean severe dissociation score was 124. The average DID patient was experiencing 20.2 of the 23 symptoms.

The MID has been extensively researched and validated in the United States, Israel, and Germany (Gast et al., 2003; Somer & Dell, 2005). Dell developed an excellent website that offers a free download of the MID in several translations, as well as an extensive manual and the Excel scoring sheets in English (see www.mid-assessment.com). Recently, some webinar training courses about using and interpreting the MID have been organized, as can be seen on the Dell website.

Not long ago, a short, 60-item version of the MID was developed in Australia, which has been used for an initial survey carried out among students (Kate et al., 2021). The two reasons for developing this version were that (1) the MID is lengthy and (2) the shorter version might be better suited for research. However, the shorter version lacks much of the important information—such as the validity scales—that actually sets the MID apart from all other self-report instruments in a positive way. To date, the abbreviated version has only been studied in a student population.

Dissociative Symptoms Scale (DSS)

The Dissociative Symptoms Scale (DSS) is a relatively new self-report questionnaire consisting of 20 items. It was developed by Carlson (coauthor of the DES) and colleagues, who felt that a scale for moderately severe dissociation was still lacking (Carlson et al., 2018). Like the DES, it is based on the continuum idea of dissociation.

According to the authors, there was a need for such a new instrument, as the DES contains many items referring to mild dissociation, whereas the MID has items referring to the extreme end of the dissociation continuum. The DSS contains items falling within the following domains of dissociative experience:

1. Gaps in awareness or memory
2. Depersonalization and derealization
3. Trauma-related reexperiencing or intrusions in perceptions, cognitions, or behavior

The first study findings have indicated that the DSS is a reliable and valid scale for identifying moderate and severe dissociative symptoms.

Detachment and Compartmentalization Inventory (DCI)

Recently, a new self-report questionnaire, the Detachment and Compartmentalization Inventory (DCI), has been developed, aiming to distinguish between phenomena consistent with detachment and compartmentalization phenomena (Butler et al., 2019). As described in Chapter 1, there are various theoretical perspectives about what constitutes dissociation, with some authors referring to two qualitatively different forms of dissociation (Holmes et al., 2005; Brown, 2006) and others referring to dissociation only when there is a division of the personality (van der Hart et al., 2006; Nijenhuis, 2015; Steele et al., 2009; Steele et al., 2017).

The questionnaire consists of 22 items: 10 items measuring detachment, 10 items aiming to measure compartmentalization/a division of the personality and 2 validity items. The future will tell whether the questionnaire will do a better job of differentiating between patients with and without a dissociative disorder—particularly DID or OSDD-1—than the MID or the DES or other instruments, such as the SDQ-20.

Summary

Of all self-report questionnaires, the MID is currently the only instrument that focuses exclusively on dissociative symptoms indicating a division of the personality. However, it is a lengthy questionnaire; in my own experience, patients with DID do not always find it easy to complete. Clinicians may decide to use the MID during a diagnostic interview. Worldwide, the DES is the most commonly used short self-report questionnaire, but it measures pathological dissociation as well as absorption and other forms of detachment. If used in a general psychiatric population, the DES is a good screening tool for identifying dissociative symptoms and disorders. However, if the DES is used in a select population of patients who are either referred or who refer themselves for dissociative disorder diagnosis, the questionnaire appears to produce many false positives.

The DES can be used in patient interviews when asking them to provide examples for each item. In this way, the clinician can quickly get an impression whether the patient may be suffering from dissociative symptoms referring to a division of the personality, or other alterations in consciousness, such as depersonalization, absorption, or daydreaming. When the patient reports dissociative symptoms that may indicate a division of the personality, the next step is a diagnostic interview.

The SDQ-20 is an important addition for identifying somatoform dissociative symptoms mostly overlooked in other screening instruments.

CHAPTER 5

Assessment With the TADS-I

Introduction

Screening based on self-report questionnaires should always be followed by a diagnostic interview. However, careful assessment of the dissociative symptoms, possibly based on the responses to a self-report questionnaire, may suffice when the clinician is experienced and has a thorough knowledge of the clusters of symptoms associated with the various dissociative disorders. In that case, it will not always be necessary to perform a time-consuming structured interview. Assessment instead of a structured interview is particularly indicated for patients who are constantly dissociating and losing contact with the clinician, which would make it hard for the latter to administer a lengthy diagnostic interview.

An example: A 45-year-old woman was referred to me by an outpatient treatment center specializing in short-term intensive trauma therapy. She had been diagnosed with complex PTSD and had a history of childhood sexual abuse and a more recent exposure to violence. During the interviews leading up to exposure therapy, the patient had continuously gone out of contact, so it had been barely possible to talk with her. According to the referring clinician, she had either been unresponsive or had been crying constantly. Several times she had suddenly become extremely anxious and suspicious, seemingly unaware of where she was. She could hardly remember these episodes afterward. Thus, the clinician wondered if the patient had a dissociative disorder and arranged for a second opinion.

The patient's DES score was 40, with markedly increased scores for the absorption and depersonalization items, but also increased scores for several amnesia items. As the patient became unreachable very quickly and would barely be able to cope with a lengthy diagnostic interview, I decided to explore a limited number of symptom clusters in more detail, particularly amnesia and Schneiderian symptoms. Exploring these revealed that she had been suffering from what she called *blackouts* on a daily basis. These blackouts had not only occurred during therapy, but also while riding her bike to work. She had sometimes found herself in places without a clue as to how she had ended up there. She also indicated being very confused about who she was, as in her head she heard voices constantly telling her different things, sometimes in another language. Born in South America, she had been adopted in the Netherlands at the age of seven, and the conversations she heard in her head were in her native language of Spanish, as well as in Dutch. This had been scary for her, because she no longer spoke Spanish well, even though she could still understand it. Her partner, who was present at the interview, said that sometimes she did not seem to recognize him. In these situations, she would be very suspicious and angry with him. At times she could also be very scared and hide in a closet in their house.

The patient was anxious about the changes in her behavior, especially because she often heard voices in her head telling her that she should end her life or do something to her partner. She also affirmed that in those situations, it seemed as if she was no longer in control of her body—as if her body wanted to do something different than she herself wanted. Twice during our interview, the patient started to cry out loud like a small child and no longer seemed to be able to hear or see me. She was only able to return from this dissociative state with some difficulty. On one occasion she froze and was unable to move. She was still able to talk and told me that her head had suddenly gone completely blank. She said that she also froze like this at night and then found herself on a cold floor. She was then unable to get up, but it also felt as if something inside her did not want her to get up.

In one session of just over an hour, it was possible to obtain sufficient information about the important clusters of amnesia and Schneiderian symptoms without having to use an extensive diagnostic interview. She reported a lot of amnesia in her everyday life and several Schneiderian symptoms. The patient herself found it very scary to think about possible dissociative parts, but her partner confirmed that he regularly saw an angry part and a very scared part. On several occasions, he had also found her in the house doing childlike drawings. She would speak Spanish to him when this happened. But even when she appeared to be herself, he had experienced that her behavior tended to change: sometimes she was withdrawn and barely communicative, while at other times she would be unable to stop talking.

Based on the cluster of dissociative symptoms that she reported and the dissociative phenomena I had observed, as well as the additional information from her partner and the referring clinician, I was able to diagnose her with DID.

Loewenstein (1991a) gave an excellent overview of the different symptom clusters belonging to DID and his *Office Mental Status Examination* (OMSTE) offers relevant questions and examples of answers that are specific to DID patients. Questions are not limited to classic dissociative symptom clusters. Loewenstein also included questions about PTSD and somatoform dissociative disorder, as well as mood problems. Even though Loewenstein's article dates back to 1991, its questions and examples of answers are very instructive for clinicians who have not had any previous experience with DID.

Structured Interviews

Previously, two diagnostic interviews were developed for the assessment of dissociative symptoms and disorders: the *Dissociative Disorder Interview Schedule* (DDIS; Ross, Heber, Norton, et al., 1989) and the *Structured Clinical Interview for DSM-IV Dissociative Disorders* (SCID-D; Steinberg, 1994a, 1994b; Steinberg et al., 1990, 1991). The SCID-D is considered the gold standard worldwide. In 1987, Nel Draijer and I compared both interviews and decided to translate the SCID-D into Dutch and examine its reliability and validity (Boon & Draijer, 1991, 1993a, 1993b). What follows is a brief description of both interviews.

Dissociative Disorder Interview Schedule (DDIS)

Originally developed in 1989, the DDIS is a highly structured interview assessing for symptoms of any of the following DSM dissociative disorders: somatization disorder, borderline personality disorder (BPD), major depressive disorder, and dissociative disorders. The interview inquires after positive symptoms of schizophrenia, secondary features of DID, extrasensory experiences, substance abuse, and other aspects relevant to identifying dissociative disorders. Also included is a section with questions about experiences of abuse.

For several reasons, we decided not to translate and validate this interview in 1989, the main reason being the strict yes/no structure of the interview. The DDIS does not ask patients to give examples of the symptoms they confirm or deny; they respond with either "yes" or "no." Therefore, the clinician has no way of knowing exactly what a yes or a no means. This increases the risk for false-negative and especially false-positive dissociative disorder diagnoses. Data collected using the DDIS generally show a higher prevalence of dissociative disorders compared to the data collected with the SCID-D (Friedl et al., 2000). A second point of concern is a section in the middle of the DDIS interview that has detailed questions about childhood physical and sexual abuse. Here, without any introduction, the interview is posing extremely detailed questions (e.g., "Did the abuse involve oral sex?," "Was there any forced sex with animals?" etc.). This section in the interview is followed by the important sections about dissociative disorders. Apart from ethical considerations, one may wonder whether the authors had given any thought to the impact of such questions on patient responses during the rest of the interview and about the validity of obtaining trauma data in this way.

Internationally, a considerable amount of research has been conducted with this tool because it is short and structured and because, according to the authors, it enables us to diagnose dissociative disorders in no more than 30–45 minutes. I have my doubts. It is my experience that in most cases it is impossible to assess a dissociative disorder in a reliable manner in so little time without the patient giving examples. Recently, a self-report questionnaire of the DDIS was developed that possibly will be similarly susceptible to false-positive diagnoses.

Structured Clinical Interview for DSM-IV Dissociative Disorders, Revised (SCID-D-R)

The SCID-D-R (Steinberg, 1994a, 1994b, 1995, 2004; Steinberg et al., 1990, 1991) is a semi-structured interview specific to the assessment of dissociative disorders.

The SCID-D-R interview examines five dissociative clusters of symptoms: amnesia, depersonalization, derealization, identity confusion, and identity alteration. The nature and severity of each symptom cluster is determined using a severity rating based on the frequency of symptoms in the present or recent past. We translated the SCID-D into Dutch and validated it (Boon & Draijer, 1993a, 1993b). In our validation study, 45 patients with a dissociative disorder were compared to a control group of 45 patients with other mental disorders. All interviews were recorded on video. To establish its reliability, a random sample from a total of 90 interviews was scored by six raters (consisting of three psychiatrists and three psychologists). There was agreement among the six raters on the presence or absence of dissociative disorder in 98.8% of cases (kappa = .96) and on the type of dissociative disorder in 93% of cases (kappa = .70). The inter-rater agreement about the severity of individual dissociative symptoms was moderate to excellent. None of the patients with dissociative disorders had a dissociative amnesia or dissociative fugue diagnosis; leaving only patients with depersonalization disorder, dissociative identity disorder (DID), or dissociative disorder not otherwise specified (DDNOS).

Validation studies of SCID-D have also been conducted in Germany and Turkey (Gast et al., 2001; Kundakçi et al., 2014; Rodewald, 2005). A recent meta-analysis of 15 studies has confirmed both the reliability and validity of the SCID-D (Mychailyszyn et al., 2021).

So far, the SCID-D interview has not been revised for the DSM-5 dissociative disorders. Its current format offers no possibilities for clinicians to diagnose dissociative disorder as defined in ICD-11. However, a DSM-5 version that includes the ICD-11 diagnoses is expected to be released soon (Mychailyszyn et al., 2021).

The Trauma and Dissociation Symptoms Interview (TADS-I)

The *Trauma and Dissociation Symptoms Interview* (TADS-I; Boon & Matthess, 2016) evolved step by step. In 2006, together with my German colleague Helga Matthess, I started to develop the *Interview for Dissociative Disorders and Trauma-related Symptoms* (IDDTS), a precursor of the current TADS-I. There were several reasons for doing this. First, I had been teaching in several European countries where no diagnostic interviews were available for the assessment of dissociative disorders. In many of these countries the ICD-10 was used rather than DSM, which meant that the purely DSM-based SCID-D was not suitable, even if it was available in the language of that country. As mentioned above, somatoform dissociative disorders were not included in the DSM (not even in the latest edition, DSM-5) but they are in the ICD. Therefore, we decided to incorporate a section with questions about somatoform dissociative symptoms into the interview.

Moreover, our research with the SCID-D demonstrated that in addition to questions about dissociative symptoms it is useful to obtain a more complete clinical picture of the patient (Boon et al., 2007). It is evident from research into the clinical phenomenology of patients with dissociative disorders, in particular those with DID and OSDD-1, that besides a cluster of primary dissociative symptoms these patients also report numerous other trauma-related symptoms. As early as 1988, Nel Draijer and I decided to include some additional questions in our study, such as questions about self-harming, suicidality, and problems with sleeping and eating. We also added questions about memory problems and depersonalization associated with these symptoms. While answering these questions, the dissociative organization of the respondent's personality often became apparent, sometimes even before any direct questions were asked about primary dissociative symptoms. This will be explained in this chapter in the section on assessment of trauma-related symptoms.

Development of the TADS Interview

In 2006, while developing the new interview (IDDTS), I further expanded the section on trauma-related questions and included eight sections with questions on common comorbid problems in dissociative disorders: (1) eating problems; (2) sleep problems; (3) anxiety, panic, and PTSD symptoms; (4) mood- and emotion-regulation problems; (5) impulse control and self-injurious behavior problems; (6) self-image and identity problems; (7) problems in relationships with others; and (8) problems related to sexuality.

Questions about identity confusion were included in Section 7 of the IDDTS (and also in TADS-I). In the SCID-D, identity confusion was operationalized as a primary dissociative symptom, but this is not correct; it is a symptom that may occur as a result of the presence of different dissociative parts in DID or OSDD-1. However, different forms of identity confusion do occur in patients with personality problems and neurotic symptoms, as well as in patients with other diagnoses. This section contains several questions about the type of identity confusion, in part to better distinguish between confusion that may occur in patients with DID or partial DID (OSDD-1 in DSM-5) and patients with personality problems or other mental health problems. I will elaborate on this in the case reports in the following chapters.

The IDDTS has never been validated but was used in one Swedish study that was published recently (Nilsson et al., 2019). This study examined the severity of somatoform and psychoform dissociative symptoms in patients with various eating disorders compared to patients without eating disorders. Patients with eating disorders reported more somatoform and psychoform dissociative symptoms than the control group. Also, the severity of the eating disorder appeared to be associated with the severity of reported dissociative symptoms.

From IDDTS to TADS-I

In 2014, I carried out a major revision of the IDDTS. The main reason for this was to enable better differentiation between symptoms that indicate a division of the personality and symptoms associated with absorption and milder forms of depersonalization and derealization. Failure to make this distinction properly may lead to confusion. The structure of the IDDTS still relied too much on the continuum concept, as is the case with most other diagnostic interviews. As was described in Chapter 1, the continuum model of dissociation does not make a clear distinction between dissociative symptoms indicating a division of the personality and other alterations of consciousness.

Sometimes, elevated scores are reported on dissociation questionnaires and interviews based on absorption and milder forms of depersonalization even though no dissociative disorder is present. In order to better differentiate these other forms of alteration of consciousness, such as absorption, daydreaming, and most of the milder symptoms of depersonalization and derealization from symptoms that refer to a division of the personality, I have included a separate section with questions about these alterations in consciousness. I hope to demonstrate more clearly that patients who do not have a dissociative disorder (e.g., those with mood, anxiety, or personality disorders) often do report these other forms of altered consciousness, particularly absorption and depersonalization. This may contribute to better differential diagnostic assessment, particularly with respect to differences between symptom profiles of patients with dissociative disorders and those with disorders similar to these, such as bipolar disorder (BPD).

The Structure of the TADS-I

The interview consists of five parts plus an appendix with questions to ask in case a false-positive DID diagnosis is suspected (see Table 5.1). The first part covers demographic data, followed by questions about substance abuse. Part 2 contains questions about psychological symptoms that may be trauma-related: eating problems, sleep problems, mood and emotion

TABLE 5.1	
Overview of the Components of TADS-I	
Interview Parts	**Section**
Part 1: General	Biographical information
	Psychiatric treatment or psychotherapy/past history
	Substance use and medication
Part 2: Possibly trauma-related symptoms	Eating problems
	Sleep problems
	Mood and emotion regulation
	Anxiety and panic
	Self-injurious behavior
	Self-image and identity
	Relationships with others
	Sexuality
Part 3: Alterations in consciousness	Depersonalization
	Derealization
	Absorption, trance, and daydreaming
Part 4: Somatoform dissociative symptoms	Medical history, medically unexplained symptoms and dissociative neurological (conversion) symptoms
Part 5: Psychoform dissociative symptoms	Amnesia
	Schneiderian symptoms/intrusions
	Symptoms that possibly indicate a division of the personality
	Dissociative parts of the personality
Appendix	Suspected imitation of DID (or false-positive diagnosis by a third party)

regulation problems, anxiety and panic symptoms, self-injurious behavior, problems with self-image and identity, problems in relationships with others, and problems with sexuality. Part 3 proceeds with questions about other forms of alterations in consciousness that do not independently indicate a division of the personality: depersonalization and derealization, absorption, daydreaming, and trance symptoms. As described above, these symptoms do tend to be reported by patients with dissociative disorders but also often are endorsed by patients with other mental health problems. Some of these experiences also occur in the general population, particularly absorption phenomena. Part 4 has questions about somatoform (sensorimotor) dissociative symptoms, while Part 5 contains questions about psychoform (cognitive-emotional) dissociative symptoms.

Administering the TADS-I

The interview is generally administered in chronological order. Each section includes several questions with numbers presented inside a shaded or colored field. These are the mandatory questions within the section. Questions without a shaded field are follow-up questions and therefore optional where a previous question has been answered in the affirmative. The follow-up questions in Part 2 of the interview, concerning the relationship between the trauma-related symptom and any dissociative symptoms, are of course important to administer. It may be unclear whether a certain symptom is present. In that case, the clinician can ask additional questions in order to gain more clarity.

The administration of the entire TADS-I is time-consuming. This is because I decided to explore as completely as possible the problem areas where patients with a history of early childhood traumatization may suffer. In clinical practice, however, it is not always feasible to spend so much time on diagnostic assessment. For this reason, a minimal variant of TADS-I is also discussed below under number two in the following list, which in many cases will suffice. During my research to date with more than 60 patients, it was quite acceptable for the vast majority to do the entire interview in one session with one or more short breaks. The advantage of administering the entire TADS-I in one or several sessions is that it provides a broad clinical picture of the patient as a person, not just a diagnosis of a dissociative disorder.

Practical Guidelines for Administering the TADS-I

The following issues are of importance when administering the TADS-I:

1. It is not necessary to administer the complete interview in one session. It is fine to dedicate two or more sessions to this assessment

2. A minimum variant of the TADS-I is required to diagnose a dissociative disorder. When there is little time, the clinician may decide to administer only a part of the TADS-I. In such case, however, the questions about alcohol, drugs, and medication must always be asked. If a patient's biographical data are already known, these may be skipped. Strictly speaking, Parts 3–5 of the interview may be sufficient to establish a dissociative disorder diagnosis. However, it is strongly recommended that the clinician administer the following items from Part 2: sleep problems, mood and emotion regulation, anxiety and panic, and self-image and identity. These TADS-I sections contain many questions about PTSD symptoms and also probe for other dissociative symptoms. After all, dissociative disorders are chronic posttraumatic disorders. The section on self-image and identity contains many questions about confusion about the self, a symptom that may result from a dissociative organization of the personality but that can also be present in other mental health problems. The next section presents a closer look at the qualitative distinction between feelings of internal struggle and confusion in patients with DID or OSDD-1 and patients with other problems.

3. Subsequently, sections containing questions about somatoform and psychoform dissociative symptoms should always be administered (Parts 3–5).

4. For the sake of clarity, it is important that the clinician realizes that comorbid disorders cannot be formally established based on the questions about possibly trauma-related symptoms alone. There are not enough questions included to do so as it is not the aim of this part of the TADS-I. The main objective is to examine whether these symptoms are possibly trauma-related and occurring in the context of a dissociative disorder. Knowing which comorbid symptoms are present and how severe they are is also useful for making a treatment plan. The same is true for PTSD and complex posttraumatic stress disorder (CPTSD).

5. Questions on PTSD symptoms are included in various parts of the TADS-I. In order to diagnose PTSD or CPTSD, however, the patient's trauma history must be taken in addition to administering the TADS-I. This may be done using a structured trauma interview or a self-report questionnaire (see Chapter 11 on the assessment of traumatic experiences). Thus, it is not possible to formally diagnose PTSD and CPTSD on the basis of TADS-I. Questions about the patient's trauma history are deliberately not included in the TADS-I, even though a dissociative disorder is understood to be a trauma-related disorder. The main argument for this is that a dissociative disorder is diagnosed based on a cluster of dissociative symptoms. The presence of a trauma history is not a criterion in DSM or ICD.

6. In order to identify CPTSD symptoms, all questions in Part 2 should be administered, except for the last part about problems with sexuality. Although a separate CPTSD classification was not included in DSM-5, it has been in the ICD-11. The DSM-5 has included a separate subtype of PTSD with depersonalization and/or derealization symptoms. CPTSD in ICD-11 is characterized by PTSD symptoms plus severe and persistent (1) problems in affect regulation; (2) beliefs about oneself as diminished, defeated, or worthless, accompanied by feelings of shame, guilt, or failure related to the traumatic event; and (3) difficulties in sustaining relationships and in feeling close to others (Cloitre et al., 2013; ICD-11, WHO, 2019). If a CPTSD symptom cluster is reported, the clinician should then exclude a DSM-5 or ICD-11 dissociative disorder diagnosis, and thus should still administer Parts 3–5 of the interview. It is often difficult to distinguish CPTSD or PTSD dissociative subtype from OSDD-1. This will be addressed in Chapter 9.

7. If a patient presents with a problem that may be trauma-related, and the clinician wishes to further investigate the possibility of a dissociative disorder, it is recommended to at least include the questions from the relevant section with the presenting problem(s) in Part 2. For example if a patient has severe eating problems, be sure to ask the questions from the eating problems section as well.

8. There are two questions about daydreaming in Part 3 (Questions 127 and 128). When a patient experiences frequent daydreaming, the clinician might decide to follow up on this using the appendix on pathological daydreaming (Appendix 5).

9. If a patient with a non-Western background reports feeling possessed (Questions 179 and 180), it is advisable to also conduct the Cultural Formulation Interview as included in DSM-5 (DSM-5; APA, 2013, pp. 749–759). This interview and the additional modules are available as downloads on the website psychiatry.org.

10. If there are no indications to suggest the existence of dissociative parts of the personality in Parts 2–5, it will not be necessary to continue with Question 200 about dissociative parts. The existence of dissociative parts of the personality should not be suggested in any way.

11. When a false-positive dissociative disorder diagnosis (usually DID) is suspected, it is recommended to administer Part 2 in its entirety, followed by the appendix in Part 5 (Questions 207–214). A false-positive DID diagnosis may occur because the patient is convinced that they have a dissociative disorder, or because a clinician has wrongly established a dissociative disorder diagnosis (see Draijer & Boon, 1999). False-positive DID diagnoses will be discussed in detail in Chapter 10.

Lastly, several sections of the TADS-I focus on depersonalization, derealization, hearing voices, and amnesia. When the clinician administers the entire TADS-I, a lot of details and examples relating to one of these symptoms may have already been given in an earlier section of the interview. The clinician can then build on this information so it will not be necessary to ask the same question again. For example, sometimes depersonalization symptoms have been discussed already at length in the section on trauma-related symptoms. In that case the general questions about depersonalization that follow in the next section of the TADS-I can be skipped.

Assessing (Possibly) Trauma-Related Symptoms: TADS-I Part 2

The section containing questions about (possibly) trauma-related symptoms is usually the lengthiest part of the entire interview; however, in order to diagnose dissociative disorders, it is not formally necessary to complete this section fully. The questions are mainly intended to obtain additional information about a possibly dissociative organization of the personality. The answers also provide a clinical impression of any comorbidities and are helpful in making the treatment plan.

During our earlier research with the SCID-D, we noticed that patient's responses to some of the questions about eating problems, suicidality, and self-harm that we had asked before starting the SCID-D were indicative of a possible underlying dissociative disorder (Boon & Draijer, 1993a, 1993b). This is because dissociative parts stuck in trauma time suffer from different symptoms—such as depression, suicidality, and problems with eating and sleeping—that are related to traumatizing events. Sometimes, the part that is functioning in daily life itself has amnesia for the behaviors of dissociative parts, such as a suicide attempt, a binge eating episode, or self-mutilation, but also for other activities by these parts during the night (e.g., using the computer or cleaning). These behaviors may be experienced as ego dystonic (i.e., *that's not me*) and are beyond the control of the patient or, more precisely, of that part of the patient functioning in daily life.

Talking about difficult or shameful things, such as suicide attempts, self-mutilation, or other self-injurious behaviors sometimes results in an intensified internal struggle and physical agitation or observable dissociative responses. On one occasion, a patient suddenly began to stutter when asked questions about suicidality and then kept saying, *Wait a minute.* The clinician noticed that she tilted her head, looking upward and falling silent, only to come up with an answer quite suddenly. The more concrete these questions were about how she had planned a suicide attempt, the more this behavior and her anxiety increased. She seemed to be listening to something inside herself and her stuttering increased. The clinician then asked her if she heard something inside her head, after which she replied: *Yes, and I'm not allowed to tell.* The clinician then reassured her: "You don't have to tell anything you're not allowed to tell, and we can leave this question unanswered."

During the development of TADS-I, the possibly trauma-related symptoms section was expanded significantly. When asking about the various symptoms in this section of TADS-I, the clinician should always pay attention to whether there is any evidence of an underlying dissociative disorder. The question is whether certain symptoms originate from dissociative parts without the part or parts functioning in daily life being able to influence them or being aware of them. Usually, a part that functions in daily life is present during the interview, but other dissociative parts may influence the behavior from within, as was the case in the above example of the patient who started stuttering when asked suicide attempts. about suicidality. However, the extent to which the part that is being interviewed is aware of the existence of dissociative parts varies significantly. Initially, many patients are unaware of any dissociative parts, but they do notice that they have specific problems and are then able to indicate that they sometimes cannot control their behavior.

For instance, when asked about eating problems, one patient said the following:

PATIENT: I don't think I have any eating problems. But I do watch my weight very closely and try to eat very regularly.

CLINICIAN: So, what happens if you don't do this?

PATIENT: Well, I'm a very poor sleeper and then sometimes I start eating in the night.

CLINICIAN: Could you tell me a bit more about it?

PATIENT: Well, I don't really know. Apparently, I'm half asleep, but I notice it the next day.

CLINICIAN: What do you notice?

PATIENT: Well, then I have been eating and I find the leftovers.

CLINICIAN: What do you mean by that?

PATIENT: Occasionally I will find a frying pan and I notice that some eggs have disappeared from my fridge, and I must have been frying those at night. Sometimes it's more like empty bags of chips, and sometimes all my bread is finished. Whenever I've had a night like that, I just don't eat all day and that's how I keep an eye on my weight. It is very annoying!

Remarkably, this patient actually denied having any eating problems, but then provided examples of problematic eating behaviors for which she had amnesia. She attributed it to *being half asleep* as an explanation for her amnesia. A bit later, when asked whether she sometimes hears voices telling her to eat or not to eat, she replied: *They never interfere with my eating, but they do interfere with other things.*

This example illustrates that patients with dissociative disorders may sometimes describe dissociative symptoms as a response to questions about possibly trauma-related symptoms, in this case both amnesia for eating at night and hearing voices. However, this patient was unaware of the presence of dissociative parts that were eating at night. She attributed her problems to *doing things half asleep*. It was still too scary for her to realize that she had a dissociative disorder. During the interview it became clear that she had been experiencing more amnesia, also for behaviors in her daily life (e.g., at work), but she described herself as extremely forgetful and added that she might be suffering from early dementia. As described in Chapter 1, concealing, minimizing, or rationalizing symptoms is typical for patients with DID or OSDD-1, especially when they do not recognize or are unable to acknowledge such symptoms or when they do not want to be aware of the existence of dissociative parts. This avoidance may also be noticeable when patients are asked about possibly trauma-related symptoms.

When there is no underlying dissociative organization of the personality, Part 2 of the interview takes a very different course. Obviously, some patients, for example patients with a personality disorder and problems with impulse control, may feel ashamed about specific behaviors. However, they do not report dissociative symptoms, such as amnesia or hearing voices related to behaviors for which they feel ashamed. Their narrative is usually clear, consistent, and ego syntonic, a first-person narrative and there is no internal conflict noticeable or visible. The following is a summary of responses about eating problems reported by a 25-year-old patient with symptoms of a personality disorder.

> I don't have any eating problems now, but when I was fourteen, for a while, I dieted a lot, because I felt fat and ugly. Now I can see that I wasn't very happy at home and that I also wanted to upset my mom. She was controlling me in every way, but she had no control over my diet. This gave me a sense of power over her. I never really lost an extreme amount of weight; I think my lowest weight was 50 kilos. Once I had left home, it was no longer an issue. Nowadays, I can still go a bit overboard when I'm feeling down for a day or so, and I'll eat a bag of chips when I get home from work. But for years my weight has been stable at 58 kilos. It has helped me a lot to start exercising more and in therapy I have also learned what other things I can do when I feel down.

This patient was able to answer the various questions about eating problems calmly without any obvious internal conflict or hesitation. There was no evidence of underlying dissociative organization of the personality nor of dissociative problems such as amnesia or hearing voices.

Finally, it is important to realize that patients with an underlying dissociative organization of the personality may vary significantly. They do not all report the same trauma-related symptoms, and some are still so unaware of the underlying dissociative disorder that they report few dissociative symptoms or conceal or minimize them during Part 2 of the assessment. However, in the vast majority of patients with DID and OSDD-1, information about the underlying dissociative organization does emerge during the TADS-I interview.

Here is what the clinician should pay attention to for each section in Part 2. Once again, it is important to realize that these questions do not suffice to establish the existence of a separate, comorbid DSM-5 or ICD-11 disorder.

Eating Problems: Questions 10–22

Eating problems are common in patients with a dissociative disorder. In our study with the SCID-D, in a group of 71 patients with DID, we found that 76% (n = 54) reported a history of eating problems, while 34.9% (n = 22) had previously received a formal anorexia nervosa diagnosis and 53% (n = 35) reported binge eating with or without self-induced vomiting (Boon & Draijer, 1993a, 1993b). Many patients are hardly or not at all in touch with their bodies and are unable to feel whether they are hungry or very full. However, research has also shown that patients with eating disorders—particularly bulimia nervosa or mixed eating disorder—and a history of trauma report more dissociative symptoms than patients with other mental disorders (Vanderlinden, Vandereycken et al., 1993; Nilsson et al., 2019). In general, patients with eating disorders are not in touch with their bodies, and binge eating often occurs in a daze (Question 15c). This by itself does not indicate the existence of an underlying dissociative disorder. In their study involving 98 patients with eating disorders, Vanderlinden and colleagues found that a small subgroup (12%) reported pathological dissociative symptoms, particularly amnesia. Questions 16 (amnesia) and 22 (hearing voices) directly refer to a possible underlying dissociative disorder. If a dissociative disorder is suspected, the clinician may also ask further questions in order to establish whether there is amnesia for vomiting or the use of laxatives. This may be the case when a dissociative part of the person is responsible for the behavior.

One patient reported spontaneously:

> I try to do everything possible to keep the food down, but sometimes I can tell from the taste in my mouth that I must have vomited but

really don't remember having done so; I also know that I have laxatives in the house. I always throw them out when I find them, but then suddenly there is a new box, and I really didn't buy it.

Sleep Problems: Questions 23–39

Sleep problems are common in patients with dissociative disorders, especially with DID and OSDD-1. Sleep is most often disturbed by the presence of chronic PTSD symptoms and dissociative parts of the personality attempting to stay awake and delay sleep, for fear of reexperiencing traumatizing events and nightmares. Often patients with DID report that they think they have been sleeping but still wake up feeling very tired. Sometimes in the course of treatment it becomes clear that the parts functioning in daily life may think they have been asleep, but in fact other parts had been active during the night. There may also be a lot of conflict about who gets time when. Parts that don't get any time during the day, often the case in patients who have a full day job or take care of a family or small children, claim time at night (for a detailed description, see Boon et al., 2011, pp. 97–111). Patients with DID generally sleep too few hours per night. Sleep medication is often ineffective, sometimes because it is not taken correctly as a result of internal conflicts about taking medication. Some parts want to stay awake at all costs, not only due to a fear of nightmares or reexperiencing traumatizing events, but also because they fear to have no control over what might be done to them while they are asleep (since many patients were abused at night when they were children). Medication also seems to have varying effects on different dissociative parts. In some cases, the patient's day/night rhythm is reversed. Patients with chronic sleep deprivation sometimes describe *crashing* suddenly and then sleeping a lot for a few nights or even days.

The questions in this section are intended to ascertain whether the sleep problems do indeed have the quality of typical PTSD sleep problems (e.g., flashbacks, nightmares, hypervigilance, restlessness during sleep, chronic sleep deprivation). Additionally, some questions have been included that refer to the activities or presence of dissociative parts at night for which there is often amnesia in the part(s) that functions in daily life. Beyond the case of the patient who appeared to be eating at night (Question 33), these can be all kinds of activities, such as cleaning up, drawing, using the computer, sending emails, and so on. Ultimately, patients may sometimes wake up disoriented in time, place, or person. This is caused by intrusions of parts that are stuck in trauma time, sometimes also by reexperiencing a traumatizing event or a nightmare. Below are some examples.

One patient recounted that her therapist told her she had been sending emails in the night. She did not recognize these emails; they were full of grammatical errors and seemed to reflect a childish style of writing. She felt very embarrassed about this. One of the emails had been very angry. Most of these mails were sent during the night at times when she thought she had been asleep.

Another patient initially said that he was sleeping very well and added that he had not heard any differently from his wife. When asked if he had ever heard that he was restless in his sleep, he gave a different answer:

PATIENT: Yes, I seem to wander around the house at night.
CLINICIAN: How have you noticed this?
PATIENT: Well, the next morning my wife will tell me that she could hear me walking. We don't sleep together anymore, you see.
CLINICIAN: Can you remember that?
PATIENT: Well, not usually, but sometimes I wake up and I'm not in my bed. Sometimes I don't know where I am at all, and I don't recognize my house, even though I've lived there for 15 years. Also, I seem to have gone outside, but I can't remember anything at all.
CLINICIAN: What do you do when you wake up and you don't know where you are?
PATIENT: Sometimes I find myself sitting on the floor somewhere in my bedroom. Usually, I just wait and after a while I start recognizing the things around me. I used to be very scared when that happened, now I say to myself: "It's that thing happening again." It just happens very often; you get used to it.

Initially, this patient responded that he had no sleep problems, but after being asked more detailed questions on this subject, it appeared that he had nightmares almost every night and woke up disoriented in different places in his house, not recognizing where he was.

Not being able to recognize where you are occurs when consciousness is influenced or taken over by other, usually younger, parts that are stuck in trauma time. Apart from these psychoform symptoms, patients often describe somatoform symptoms. For example, one patient said that she was unable to move at all after waking up and would lie in bed completely frozen. Sometimes she was aware of where she was, at other times she was not. She sometimes believed she was in her parents' house and in a great panic that her father could enter any moment. Even though this patient had been taught in therapy to hold on to anchors—objects that represent the present, such as a photo of her children—that would help her orient herself in the present in such situations, she was not always able to do so immediately.

Summary of Questions 10–39

Patients with DID and some of the patients with OSDD-1 or partial DID will almost invariably report symptoms of PTSD when asked about sleep, and sometimes they also mention amnesia for nighttime activities. They often have nightmares or symptoms of reexperiencing and are therefore afraid to go to sleep. They also often report restlessness or being frozen or cramped at night.

Unless a comorbid PTSD has been established, patients with depersonalization disorder do not report sleep problems consistent with PTSD, nor do they report amnesia. This raises the question whether depersonalization disorder should be diagnosed in addition to PTSD, especially since a subtype of PTSD with depersonalization and derealization has been included in DSM-5. Patients who do not have CPTSD or a dissociative disorder do not report the aforementioned sleep problems. Of course, sleep problems also occur frequently in the context of other mental disorders. Patients may also frequently experience sleep problems in connection with stress and burnout. Then the symptoms will be different, involving worrying or ruminating and problems falling asleep and staying asleep, without the characteristic PTSD symptoms of nightmares, reexperiencing, and hypervigilance.

In order to differentiate sleep problems properly, it is important for the clinician to know how sleep problems manifest in the context of other mental problems, such as depression, psychosis, or stress and burnout.

Mood and Emotion Regulation: Questions 40–57

Patients with DID or OSDD-1 frequently report extreme mood swings, hyperactivity, depression, and suicidal ideation or actual suicide attempts. The different moods are commonly associated with various dissociative parts of the personality but may affect the moods of the parts that are functioning in daily life, and mood swings can be rather abrupt. Different dissociative parts of the personality often hold various emotions, such as intense fear, sadness, anger, or shame. There may be a sense of lacking control over these emotions, which is particularly experienced by the part that is functioning in daily life. However, the dissociative parts that hold specific emotions may also be activated and may suddenly feel very angry, fearful, sad, or ashamed. Patients with dissociative disorders often have poor self-soothing skills and emotion regulation; in this regard they resemble patients with disorders such as BPD. In contrast with these intense emotions that may occur rather suddenly, there may be feelings of numbness (Question 50) and emptiness (Question 57).

Some of the questions in this section are of a more general nature and may be answered in the affirmative by many patients, including those without dissociative disorders. Other questions are more specific and may indicate a dissociative organization of the personality. Question 44 (Have you ever experienced strong fluctuations in your capacities or your abilities as a result of your mood swings?) is an example of a more general question. An individual with a depression may answer that when depressed they are very unproductive and may not be capable of doing much. For Question 45 (Have you ever noticed that you could easily do things that you felt should be impossible, or that you are normally unable to do?) the same person might answer: *Yes, this sometimes happens when I'm feeling really good.*

One patient with a personality disorder replied to these questions as follows: *I have episodes of being very passive, nothing works out, and then I have moments when things are much easier for me.*

The purpose of Question 45 is to assess whether there may be dissociative parts with different capacities that make things seem to go very smoothly all of a sudden. It was a conscious decision to include this question as early as possible in this section so as not to provide patients with any suggestions. One patient with DID gave the following answer:

> Yes, I do experience this sometimes, but I'm not quite sure whether it has anything to do with my mood. I think it's unrelated. There are times when I speak French very well and fluently, but sometimes it seems as though I have forgotten all about it, and I cannot even remember the simplest words. It honestly makes me think I'm demented, but at 35?

In this patient, there was a part that was fluent in French, while other parts did not have the same command of the language.

The topic of suicidality involves some direct questions about dissociative symptoms that may be related to suicidal thoughts or suicide attempts. In DID, OSDD-1, or partial DID, a part that is functioning in daily life may be suicidal, but more often there are intrusions of feelings from parts that are stuck in trauma time. Some patients report amnesia for an attempted suicide or hearing voices while apparently watching themselves from a distance, outside their body, unable to influence their behaviors.

Finally, there is a question about hyperactive behavior. Working or otherwise being active all the time and hardly being able to stop is a recurrent symptom in patients with DID or OSDD-1. This behavior, which is often experienced by a part functioning in daily life, is usually a way of coping with a lurking fear of being overwhelmed by vehement emotions. As one patient with DID put it:

> I have always been working. If I don't work, I'm busy with other things, I'm incapable of sitting still and relaxing. It's like always run-

ning ahead of the tsunami. Stopping is terrifying, because then there are so many feelings. At one point I had broken my leg, which forced me to sit still. I thought I was going nuts. I immersed myself in a project then, so I would be working at the computer all day.

Anxiety and Panic: Questions 58–66

The questions about anxiety and panic largely cover PTSD symptoms and specific phobias or an avoidance of specific places or thoughts, and so on. As described earlier, almost all patients with DID or OSDD-1 also report PTSD symptoms; however, this is less often the case with patients with a depersonalization disorder. Research has shown that depersonalization disorder occurs mainly in patients with a history of emotional neglect or attachment problems (see Chapter 1).

Although trauma histories are not elicited in the TADS-I, this section does contain two questions about symptoms of reexperiencing traumatizing events and flashbacks. Patients are asked whether they know to what they call *bad images* relate. It is clearly not the intention that they then talk about the traumatizing event; rather, this question is meant to understand whether they are aware of a connection between the current symptoms of reexperiencing and earlier events. As patients may have amnesia for the traumatic events, they may consider their flashbacks to be *crazy fantasies* that they cannot place or understand.

As the section on sleep problems already inquired about symptoms of reexperiencing and flashbacks, patients may have provided sufficient details at this point. The clinician may then briefly touch on the subject again or skip the question. Finally, some questions in this section refer to a potential division of the personality (Questions 61d and 61e). Here is an example:

CLINICIAN: Earlier, when we were talking about sleep problems, you described unpleasant images or flashbacks at night but also during the day. Do you always know what events such images are related to?

PATIENT: I usually do. I know that I have been abused and it has something to do with that. But sometimes I don't know where it comes from and that frightens me a lot. I then say to myself: "You're crazy. You have a weird imagination," and I try not to think about it. It helps to keep myself really busy with something and to focus on other things.

The clinician should refrain from asking any further questions about the content of the bad images. Doing so may activate traumatic memories and upset the patient unnecessarily. It is sufficient to establish any PTSD symptoms and their severity. This patient reported symptoms consistent with all PTSD criteria. She explained that she was afraid to go to sleep because of the horrifying images; according to her partner, she was very restless and hypervigilant at night, and she avoided many *things, big and small* during the day.

Self-Destructive Behavior: Questions 67–72

This relatively brief section contains questions about various forms of self-destructive behavior. Self-destructive behaviors often occur in patients with dissociative disorders, but also with other mental disorders, such as borderline personality disorder. In the latter case, such behaviors often take place in a daze, a form of depersonalization, which does not necessarily indicate a division of the personality. In patients with DID or OSDD-1, it is mostly the parts that are stuck in trauma time that self-harm. Several parts may engage in different forms of self-harming behavior. In one patient, there was a part that would scratch and cut when it had not felt any sensations in her body for some time. Another part would burn her legs, in response to a voice urging her to do so. Yet another part disliked her body so much that it wanted to mutilate it. Finally, there was a part that started cutting when she felt extreme emotional pain.

These details only came to light during treatment. During the diagnostic interview this patient said:

> Sometimes it seems as if I observe the cutting and I can't stop it, I can see it happening, but I am outside my body. However, at other times I only discover it afterwards and I have no recollection [of it] at all. It's on my arms but that's always superficial. If it's on my legs it is very scary as these are deep cuts that need stitching. I don't remember doing that. I once found myself in a hospital in the emergency room, and I had lost hours of that day.

Another patient reported hearing voices urging him to drink bleach and drive at great speed on the motorway. He was quick to add that he did not listen to them, but he had once found himself with cuts and had absolutely no memory of inflicting those. When asked, he said that he recalled very little about that afternoon. Eventually, he indicated that these situations had occurred often.

One patient with BPD said:

> Sometimes I want to see blood. It calms me. It's not all that conscious, it can be a very impulsive thing. But of course, I know exactly where I keep the blades that I use to cut myself. As I am really trying to prevent it, I put them in a special place, so I cannot reach them easily.

I really only do this when I'm extremely upset, as for some strange reason, it calms me down.

This patient did not hear voices and did not have amnesia for the cutting. It was also an ego syntonic, first-person narrative (I-experience). She did however indicate that it sometimes happened in a kind of haze. During other parts of the interview this patient did not report any dissociative symptom that could be indicative of a division of the personality. She did report symptoms of absorption and depersonalization however.

Self-Image and Identity: Questions 73–85

This section of questions was designed to obtain an impression of the patient's self-image and potential identity problems. Many patients with early childhood traumatization have a negative self-image. It is one of the ICD-11 symptom clusters of CPTSD ("beliefs about oneself as diminished, defeated, or worthless, accompanied by feelings of shame, guilt, or failure related to the traumatic event"). The questions in this section may thus be answered in the affirmative by patients with and without dissociative disorders. In this section, only Question 79 (about internal struggles) has sub-questions that may indicate a dissociative organization of the personality. None of the other questions relate to specific indicators for a division of the personality.

Problems With Self-Image and Identity in Patients With DID and OSDD-1

Patients with DID and OSDD-1 in particular report a negative self-image (*I am a bad person*), although they cannot always explain to what it relates. The more amnesia for the original traumatizing events, the less connection the patient experiences with the cause of the negative sense of self. Patients with other dissociative disorders, like depersonalization/derealization disorder, are less likely to suffer from a negative sense of self.

As described earlier, identity confusion is not specifically a dissociative symptom. Identity problems and confusion about who one is or who one should be or would like to be occur in many mental disorders, particularly in personality disorders and gender dysphoria. They also occur frequently in adolescents. The quality of the examples does, however, vary quite significantly. Of all DSM-5 and ICD-11 dissociative disorders, patients with DID most frequently report confusion about who they are. Or they may be experiencing internal conflicts or an internal struggle, especially if there are several parts that are functioning in daily life and parts that are stuck in trauma time. Patients with DID often describe their confusion or internal struggle as an internal battle among several different thoughts, opinions, wishes, desires, and predictions. The conflict may take place between different voices inside their heads. The confusion about the self is also caused by amnesia for certain behaviors and by the different and often incomprehensible behaviors that patients do not recognize as their own.

The less the individual is aware of the dissociative disorder and of the existence of dissociative parts, the greater the confusion. One patient said that sometimes he did not understand at all how he had acquired certain knowledge in his work. He was an electrical fitter and visited customers whenever there were technical problems.

> I would get to a customer, step inside and already know exactly what the problem is, before having spoken to these people at all. I would also have the right equipment with me to fix the problem or do the repair. I find that very strange, but I don't think about it too long, because that would really drive me crazy. I must have talked with these people before, but I really have no recollection of it.

This example suggests that several parts may be involved in his work. Later on in his treatment, it became clear that there was a part that did the customer contacts and another, more technically inclined part that fixed the technical problems. The part of the patient present at the interview at first had no idea and also avoided thinking about it. Obviously, it confused him a lot.

Another patient stated that she did not understand herself at all because she had found library books at home on a wide range of topics, some of which did not interest her at all. She often could not recall being in the library either.

However, not all patients with DID report internal struggles or confusion about who they are. If there is only one part functioning in daily life, there are usually fewer intrusions from dissociative parts. Patients with this kind of dissociative organization of the personality experience more continuity in memory, sometimes do not hear voices, and suffer less from intrusions from dissociative parts. This is why these patients are sometimes less confused about who they are. Apart from the part functioning in daily life, the other parts serve to hold the traumatic memories. There may be intrusions of these parts during episodes of reexperiencing traumatizing events and flashbacks, but the patient—or actually the part that is functioning in daily life—is less confused about the things happening in the here and now. The person's self-image may vary, however. This is because dissociative parts stuck in trauma time tend to have a negative self-image or are insecure and also hold feelings of fear and distrust of others and the world.

A patient discussed earlier presented with non-epileptic seizures. During what she referred to as a *seizure*, she could switch to a 5-year-old child part.

She also described other seizures in which she would appear extremely anxious or would scratch and bite. She had complete amnesia for the seizures. She would find out what happened from her partner. During the TADS-I assessment, she reported no further amnesia in her daily life, she heard no voices, and reported no other Schneiderian symptoms. When asked about self-image and identity, she said the following:

CLINICIAN: Do you feel positive about yourself in general?

PATIENT: Fifty-fifty.

CLINICIAN: And when you don't feel positive about yourself, how do you feel?

PATIENT: On such occasions I feel very insecure, scared. All it takes is someone to look at me in the wrong way for it to happen. I will feel worried that I have done or said something wrong. Or that I don't look good.

CLINICIAN: Are you yourself able to feel that you have done something really well?

PATIENT: No, that's really hard. I would need to hear this from other people. I'm also afraid to express my opinion, I only do if I'm 100% sure.

CLINICIAN: Are you ever uncertain about your wishes and preferences?

PATIENT: No, not at all!

CLINICIAN: And are you ever insecure or uncertain about who you really are?

PATIENT: No, I think I know myself quite well.

This patient described herself as insecure but certainly not confused about who she was. At the time of the TADS-I interview, there was still an enormous dissociative barrier between her and the dissociative parts that held the traumatic memories and emotions for her. She later came to me for treatment; from the moment she started to make contact and connect with her dissociative parts, she became very uncertain about who she actually was. She suddenly became more aware of the different emotions, thoughts, and wishes of these parts, but that was confusing her also. Once she was able to regulate the emotions of these parts, things improved. The non-epileptic seizures also disappeared.

During the TADS-I study, as in my earlier research with the SCID-D, one group of patients with DID or OSDD-1 reported little or no confusion about their identities. Characteristic for this group was that they were extremely avoidant and phobic about their dissociative symptoms and were barely able to reflect on them. As in the example above, there was often a huge dissociative barrier between the part that functioned in daily life and participated in the interview and other dissociative parts.

Problems With Self-Image and Identity in Patients Without Dissociative Disorders

Patients with personality disorders, especially borderline, histrionic, or mixed personality disorders, also mention confusion about who they are. They may also continually experience internal conflicts. These are usually highly polarized conflicts between two sides within themselves: the good and the bad self, the active and the passive, the positive and the negative, the wish to live or to die. Also, these patients often describe a fluctuating sense of self. This sense of self and the confusion about the self are not related to having amnesia or based on intrusions of dissociative parts.

Patients with manic episodes or a psychotic disorder may also often describe confusion about the self that is specifically related to the manic or psychotic episode. Their behaviors and experiences during such episodes can cause a great deal of confusion. One patient who experienced her first psychotic episode said that she no longer knew who she was and then remarked that she was convinced that she was a famous singer. She said that nobody understood her anymore. Her confusion resolved as soon as the psychotic episode was over.

Lastly, patients with gender dysphoria also describe many identity problems. Several such patients participated in the TADS-I study. These patients did not describe confusion about various wishes or preferences and did not report any clusters of dissociative symptoms. Their confusion, sometimes associated with a lot of shame, concerned their gender identity.

Patients with DID can also be confused about their gender identity, as they often have dissociative parts that feel like women or girls and others that feel like men or boys. Their sense of self can therefore vary greatly depending on which part is influencing their consciousness or is in the foreground. However, these patients also report clusters of dissociative symptoms indicating a division of the personality. This distinguishes them from patients with gender dysphoria who do not report such clusters of dissociative symptoms.

Relationships With Others: Questions 86–94

This section of questions has been included to develop an understanding of the relationships with other people and attachment problems that may be involved. Many patients with early childhood traumatization have serious attachment problems and difficulty tolerating closeness to others or trusting them. It is one of the ICD-11 criteria for complex PTSD (difficulties in sustaining relationships and in feeling close to others). For this reason, this section contains a number of questions that are relevant to all patients with attachment problems.

For patients with DID, relationships can be particularly complicated because their dissociative parts may have different preferences and interests and consequently different acquaintances. Someone who is a friend of one part may be considered *stupid, annoying, uninteresting,* or even threatening by another part. Internal conflicts between dissociative parts can revolve around anything, but certainly involve partners, children, friends, and acquaintances.

For example, a patient with DID said during an assessment interview that she sometimes felt extremely uncomfortable when an old college friend suddenly showed up while she was having coffee with her neighbor. *Then I don't know what to do, it's as if one of them knows me in a different way than the other, but I don't understand. I feel panic.* When asked by the clinician how she solved this, she said: *Most of the time I disappear and I have no idea what happens next.* When the clinician then asked her whether she tried to find out later, she said: *No, I never dared to bring it up. I am sure it went well; it happens often and people never tell me I acted really crazy or something.*

Sexuality: Questions 95–105

The final section, comprising questions about sexuality, can be very challenging for patients who have been sexually traumatized. This is the case with many patients with DID, OSDD-1, and CPTSD. For this reason, the clinician may decide to skip this section. Another possibility is to go through the questions briefly and in a very structured way, without elaborating on examples.

The clinician should be aware that many patients with a dissociative disorder, especially those who have been sexually traumatized as children, may experience difficulties in their current sexual relationships. This may lead to complete avoidance of sexual contact and anything related to sexuality, including with one's own partner. When sexual contact does occur, it is often accompanied by dissociative responses, such as being out of the body, being completely numb, or having flashbacks of the original traumatizing events. There may even be complete amnesia for sexual contact, or patients may no longer recognize their partners but confuse them with the original abuser. Some parts of the person may be sexualized and may provoke, enjoy, or be compulsive about sex. Some patients have parts that prostitute themselves, whether or not commanded to do so by internal voices—that is, other parts. Finally, dissociative parts may perceive themselves in different ways, which may cause conflict or confusion about sexual identity. This section therefore involves a number of questions regarding dissociative responses during sexual contact in the present.

The above-mentioned problems are not exclusive to patients with dissociative disorders, such as DID and OSDD-1, but are generally associated with sexual traumatization.

Summary of Questions on Possibly Trauma-Related Symptoms

The questions about possibly trauma-related symptoms may provide significant understanding of the severity of comorbidities and of a possible underlying dissociative organization of the personality. The symptom profiles that have been included in the appendix contain some essential questions:

1. Is the symptom present, and how severe is it?
2. Is there any evidence of alterations in consciousness, such as depersonalization or absorption, associated with the symptom?
3. Is there any evidence of the presence of dissociative symptoms indicating a division of the personality associated with the symptom? These may consist of affirmative answers to the related questions, but often patients with DID or OSDD-1 spontaneously give examples that are indicative of a division of the personality. At this stage of the TADS-I, this may also become evident through nonverbal behavior.

In the following chapter, a number of TADS-I interview reports are included to show how the abundance of responses can be represented.

Assessing Alterations in Consciousness: TADS-I Part 3

For a comprehensive discussion of these symptoms, please refer to Chapter 3 of this book. Part 2 on possibly trauma-related symptoms has several questions on phenomena that may be associated with the symptom in question, such as depersonalization, amnesia, or hearing voices. If the clinician has already received information about a symptom, such as depersonalization, they can follow up on it in Part 3. For example:

CLINICIAN: When we talked about your mood earlier in the interview, you mentioned that you often feel completely cut off from your emotions. I am now going to ask you a number of questions about this kind of experience. Do you also sometimes feel very unreal? Can you give an example of this?

Boxes 5.1–5.3 list the main points that the clinician should pay attention to with regard to the various symptoms that are elicited in Part 3.

POINTS TO CONSIDER WHEN ASSESSING DEPERSONALIZATION

- Are symptoms of depersonalization chronic and persistent or intermittent?
- Do depersonalization symptoms always occur in conjunction with stress, fatigue, or other mental problems (e.g., psychotic episodes; mood, anxiety, or personality disorders) or do they also occur when these are not present?
- Do depersonalization symptoms occur only in association with negative, shameful, or impulsive behaviors (e.g., self-harm, binge eating, stealing, aggressive behavior)?
- Do depersonalization symptoms also occur during neutral or positive behaviors (e.g., singing in a choir, shopping, taking care of children)?
- Do patients give spontaneous examples that indicate a division of the personality (e.g., *I see myself doing the shopping, then I am out of my body and it is as if I am looking at myself from above*)?
- Do depersonalization symptoms occur exclusively as a result of substance use or medication?

POINTS TO CONSIDER WHEN ASSESSING DEREALIZATION

- Do derealization symptoms occur together with depersonalization?
- Are symptoms of derealization ongoing and persistent or intermittent?
- Do derealization symptoms always occur in conjunction with stress, fatigue, or other mental health problems (e.g., psychotic episodes; mood, anxiety, personality disorders) or do they also occur when these are not present?
- Do patients give spontaneous examples that indicate derealization as a result of intrusions of a dissociative part of the personality? For example: not recognizing one's own home or family or acquaintances, or experiencing them as odd; not being able to estimate distances properly; seeing the world from the perspective of a child: everything seems bigger, taller, higher.
- Do derealization symptoms occur exclusively as a result of substance use or medication?

POINTS TO CONSIDER WHEN ASSESSING ABSORPTION, DAYDREAMING, OR TRANCE

- Are symptoms of absorption, daydreaming, or trance ongoing and persistent or intermittent?
- Do the symptoms always occur in conjunction with stress, fatigue, or other mental health problems (e.g., psychotic episodes; mood, anxiety, personality disorders), or do they also occur when these are not present?
- Are there any episodes of daydreaming or trance phenomena the person has no control over?
- Absorption, daydreaming, and trance states may also cause memory problems. There is little or no awareness of time; hours may pass. These memory problems should be distinguished from memory gaps that are due to the presence of a dissociative part of the personality. Patients with DID or OSDD-1 may report both types of memory problems.
- For trance experiences, it is important to determine whether the experiences fit within the context of a culturally accepted practice (both Western and non-Western).
- Do the symptoms occur exclusively in conjunction with substance use?

Assessing Somatoform Dissociative Symptoms: TADS-I Part 4

A comprehensive discussion of these symptoms has been provided in Chapter 2 of this book. Box 5.4 lists the main points that the clinician should pay attention to with regard to assessing somatoform dissociation.

BOX 5.4

POINTS TO CONSIDER WHEN ASSESSING SOMATOFORM DISSOCIATIVE SYMPTOMS

- It is important to realize that the DSM-5 classification of somatoform dissociative symptoms is different from the ICD-11 classification.
- Has there been any physical/neurological assessment to rule out any organic cause for the symptoms?
- Have symptoms been ongoing or occurring intermittently? This may vary: negative somatoform symptoms are usually more ongoing in nature; positive somatoform symptoms may come and go.
- Do the somatoform symptoms occur in isolation or are they part of a cluster of psychoform and somatoform symptoms? The latter is often the case in DID, OSDD-1, and partial DID.
- Do the symptoms occur exclusively in conjunction with substance use?

Assessing Psychoform Dissociative Symptoms: TADS-I Part 5

A comprehensive discussion of these symptoms, particularly amnesia, Schneiderian symptoms, and dissociative parts of the personality, has been provided in Chapter 2 of this book. Boxes 5.5 and 5.6 list the main points that the clinician should pay attention to with regard to assessing psychoform dissociative symptoms.

BOX 5.5

POINTS TO CONSIDER WHEN ASSESSING DISSOCIATIVE AMNESIA

Differentiate between amnesia occurring as a result of the presence of dissociative parts of the personality ("personality states" in DSM-5 and ICD-11) versus memory and concentration problems stemming from absorption, strong emotions, stress, fatigue, depression, or other mental health problems. In the first instance, the memory is held by a dissociative part and should be accessible in therapy. In the second instance, there may be vague memories but often nothing is stored or accessible.

Forms of amnesia due to the presence of a dissociative part

- Regular amnesia in the present for tasks and functions that belong to daily life (e.g., work, taking care of the children, social activities, etc.). This is the form of amnesia that occurs in DID. One of the parts does things of which the presenting part and sometimes also other parts are unaware. Patients may find evidence that they must have done something but cannot recall doing it. The frequency may vary, and the gap can be hours or even days.
- Amnesia in the present related to reexperiencing trauma or flashbacks of traumatizing events. This form of amnesia may occur in DID, OSDD-1, ICD-11, partial DID, and CPTSD. The part that functions in daily life is absent, while parts ("personality states") that are stuck in trauma time are in the foreground and are usually reliving a traumatizing event.

- Amnesia in the present related to self-injurious behavior, suicidality, and aggressive behavior. When only this type of amnesia is reported for negative, undesired, or shameful behavior, it is important to check at the end of the TADS-I whether this amnesia is part of a cluster of dissociative symptoms consistent with a dissociative disorder or whether the symptom is more typical of a personality disorder (behavior consistent with a schema mode) and involves denial of undesired or antisocial behavior (see Chapter 8 on differential diagnosis).
- Amnesia for parts of past or childhood traumatizing events. This may occur in DID, OSDD-1, partial DID, and CPTSD as a result of the presence of dissociative parts ("personality states") that are stuck in trauma time.

Amnesia for a period or several periods in the past (e.g., no memory before 10 years of age; no memory of having completed certain training or educational programs). This occurs mainly in DID.

Rule out other causes of amnesia

- Rule out amnesia due to organic memory impairment (e.g., dementia).
- Rule out amnesia caused by substance abuse (e.g., alcohol, drugs).
- Rule out memory or concentration problems associated with another mental health issue (e.g., depression).
- Rule out memory or concentration problems as a result of stress, burnout, exhaustion, etc.

BOX 5.6

POINTS TO CONSIDER WHEN ASSESSING SCHNEIDERIAN SYMPTOMS

- Schneiderian symptoms are frequently reported by patients with DID and to a lesser extent by patients with OSDD-1 and partial DID. They are not or only very rarely reported by patients with other dissociative disorders.
- This concerns intrusions influencing the person's behavior, thoughts, wishes, emotions, etc., by other dissociative parts ("personality states"). The intrusions are usually experienced as coming from within (dissociative parts influencing behavior, thoughts, wishes, emotions, etc.).
- Some patients, especially those who were raised in strict Christian communities or sects, have additional fears of possibly being taken over by external demons.
- The vast majority of patients with DID report hearing voices, often from an early age. The voices are generally heard inside the person's head and can be male, female, or children's voices, or even babies crying. The voices often give commands, make comments, talk among themselves, or argue with one another. Some patients describe the voices as indistinct murmurs; others describe them as cacophonic.
- A key point to assess is whether reality testing is intact. In dissociative parts that are stuck in trauma time, sometimes this may not be the case, especially when they are not fully oriented in the present.
- During diagnostic assessment, there is usually a part that is functioning in daily life with intact reality testing.
- Patients with DID do not usually report strange or bizarre symptoms, such as the experience of being spoken to by someone on TV or the radio or by someone via a loudspeaker in a shop. The content of their delusions or pseudohallucinations is usually trauma-related.
- It is important to realize that the Schneiderian symptoms in DID, OSDD-1, and partial DID are part of a cluster of dissociative symptoms and do not exist in isolation.

The last two sections of the TADS-I deal with symptoms that indicate a division of the personality. Chapter 2 gives an overview of indications of the presence of dissociative parts. These last two sections are only relevant when the clinician has already found indications of the existence of dissociative parts of the personality earlier in the interview.

The clinician only asks the questions in the very last section if patients, people around them, or the referring clinician believe that DID is present and when the interview has thrown up doubts about the authenticity of the dissociative symptoms or presumed DID diagnosis. In all other cases it is not necessary to ask these questions.

Scoring the TADS-I

Scoring the TADS-I involves several steps:

1. Every symptom is first assessed for presence or absence. This is done on the basis of the patient's yes or no answer to the relevant question, where being able to give clear examples of the symptom in question is the deciding factor.
   a. *Absent.* A symptom is scored as absent when the patient reports not having that particular symptom, or in such a minor way that the presence of the symptom is considered not clinically significant, or when the patient is unable to provide clear, clinically significant examples related to the problem.
   b. *Present.* A symptom is scored as present when the patient describes a clinically significant problem and is able to provide clear examples of that problem in the present or recent past.
   c. *Unclear, or suspicion of false-positive response.* A symptom cannot be assessed because the patient is unable to provide clear information or examples related to the problem, while the clinician cannot say with absolute certainty that the symptom is absent. The patient also may report having a symptom—sometimes using exaggeration— although the clinician has doubts about the authenticity of the response or the examples. When the clinician suspects that there may be a false-positive response, they are advised to note this next to each answer.

2. If a symptom is scored as *present*, a number of additional questions about the symptom will usually follow, including a frequency question. To determine the frequency, the past year is considered, using the following guideline:

Seldom	Up to 3 times in the past year
Recurrent	Between 4 and 11 times in the past year
Monthly	At least once per month in the past year
Weekly	At least once per week in the past year
Daily	At least once per day in the past year
Unclear	

3. Then the severity of a symptom is assessed. In order to assess the severity of a symptom, the degree to which a symptom impairs social and professional functioning (the former DSM-IV Axis V GAF scale) is used as a criterion in combination with the frequency of a certain symptom. The severity score is assigned on the basis of the clinical judgment of the clinician with regard to the functioning and the frequency with which the symptom occurs. The interview itself only includes questions about the frequency.

    1 = *Minor.* Some minor phenomena or symptoms, or some minor problems with regard to social and/or professional functioning. The frequency of the symptom is described as a few times per year at most.

    2 = *Moderate.* Moderate phenomena or symptoms, or moderate problems with regard to social and/or professional functioning. The frequency of the symptoms is reportedly at least once a month.

    3 = *Severe.* Severe phenomena or symptoms, or severe problems with regard to social and/or professional functioning. The frequency of the symptom is daily or weekly (at least once a week) or the symptom is present most of the time (50% to 60%)

    4 = *Unclear, or suspicion of false-positive response.* It is unclear whether the symptom occurs in the manner described, for example in case of exaggeration or suspicion of a false-positive response.

4. Finally, based on the cluster of symptoms, it is determined whether the patient meets the criteria for a specific DSM-5 or ICD-11 dissociative disorder. The clinician may also determine whether the patient suffers from CPTSD symptoms. In the latter case, it is important to gain information about the trauma history. After all, CPTSD can only be diagnosed if the A criterion (exposure to trauma) is met.

Box 5.7 provides some examples of the assessment of amnesia. It should be noted that many patients with DID, OSDD-1, or partial DID tend to downplay or minimize their symptoms.

ASSESSING FOR AMNESIA: EXAMPLES

Severe amnesia for work-related tasks that occurs daily or weekly in patients who function well at work is scored as severe, even if there is no obvious serious impairment of professional functioning.

For example, when patients indicate that they *lost time for a number of days* on four occasions in the past year, and they have complete amnesia for these days, this must be scored as severe, even if the frequency of the phenomenon may not be monthly. Typically, patients who describe such a symptom also suffer from additional and other amnesia symptoms but may not always be able to talk about them or are sometimes unaware of shorter moments of amnesia.

Exaggeration or histrionic presentation is assessed according to the clinician's own impression of the severity. Or it should be scored as unclear if the clinician is unsure whether the symptom actually occurs or whether the response may be false-positive.

Moreover, with regard to amnesia, it is important to distinguish if possible between amnesia for current activities in daily life, for the past, or for reexperiencing.

In the latest revision of the interview (Version 1.12, also included in this book), a summary of the relevant symptom is included at the end of each section. An example of such a summary is given in Box 5.8.

TADS-I SUMMARY PER SYMPTOMS SECTION: EATING PROBLEMS EXAMPLE

Overall Severity Score: Eating Problems

0 = Absent

1 = Minor

2 = Moderate

3 = Severe

88 = Unclear

Subjective Distress Score: Eating Problems

0 = Absent

1 = Minor

2 = Moderate

3 = Severe

88 = Unclear

Are the eating problems accompanied by alterations in consciousness?

0 = No

1 = Yes

88 = Unclear

Are the eating problems accompanied by dissociative
symptoms indicating division of the personality?

0 = No

1 = Yes

88 = Unclear

Appendix 1 includes TADS-I symptom profiles that may help the clinician scoring and determining whether a symptom is present, including its frequency and severity. The clinician can also score whether the symptom co-occurs with alterations in consciousness (Part 3 of the TADS-I) or pathological dissociative symptoms that indicate a division of the personality (Parts 4 and 5). The symptom profiles in Appendix 1 serve as a tool to establish or exclude the existence of a dissociative disorder. Symptom profiles also have been created for PTSD and CPTSD diagnoses. An additional symptom profile has been created for the Schneiderian symptoms, especially for research purposes. Not all questionnaire items are included in the symptom profiles, but rather only those that refer to pathological manifestations of a symptom. Appendices 2 and 3 describe the DSM-5 and ICD-11 criteria for dissociative disorders. For each criterion, it is stated which questions should be answered in the affirmative in order to identify one of the DSM-5 or ICD-11 diagnoses mentioned above.

The TADS-I does not provide a total score that would automatically result in a DSM-5 or ICD-11 diagnosis. As with the SCID-D, the clinician conducting the interview and determining the nature and severity of the symptoms achieves a final assessment based on the cluster of reported dissociative symptoms. This may be supplemented with other available data, such as observations about the presentation of symptoms during the interview, available information about previous treatments, and collateral interviews.

CHAPTER 6

Case Reports of Dissociative Disorders Based on TADS-I Interviews

Introduction

This chapter contains five anonymized TADS-I reports compiled from interviews with patients with dissociative disorders. The purpose here is to provide concrete examples of the clusters of dissociative symptoms that are part of various dissociative disorders and the ways in which they are reported. The examples also serve to provide guidelines as to how to write a TADS-I interview report.

Case Report: A Patient With DID

Ms. B. is a 38-year-old woman who was referred to me for a second opinion. She was being treated in an outpatient program for patients with personality disorders. When her regular therapist was on holiday, she suffered a crisis and was seen several times by a clinician who was experienced in treating dissociative disorders, and who started to suspect that the patient might have a dissociative disorder.

The patient was not currently employed but had been working as a professional nurse for many years. She was living independently with her dog. Ten years ago, she had lived with a boyfriend for several years. She broke off the relationship herself but was unable to say exactly why. According to her, *it just didn't work out.*

General

First Impressions. The patient was cooperative and made a genuine effort to answer all the questions as well as she could. During the assessment there were nonverbal signs of an internal struggle, sometimes very obvious, sometimes more subtle: her face twitched continually, as may happen in patients with DID who are experiencing an internal struggle. Sometimes she did not hear the question or was absent for a while, and she regularly appeared to be listening to voices. This tended to get worse when topics were difficult for her to deal with, with the internal struggle seemingly getting worse as well.

Substance Use and Medication. The patient was not addicted to alcohol and had never used recreational drugs. Occasionally would she have a glass of wine at a party but stated that: *I actually try to avoid parties as much as I can. I prefer to be by myself.* Since she had stopped working, she had been having difficulties structuring her day. *Before, I used to be busy after work, with hobbies and sports; I now tend to reverse my days and nights.* The patient had never been addicted to medication. She had been using low doses of antipsychotic medication which, according to her, did not stop the voices, but calmed her down a bit.

Possibly Trauma-Related Symptoms

Eating Problems. The patient reported suffering from eating problems from a very young age. She had experienced episodes of anorexia, with her lowest weight being 42 kilos (92.5 lbs.). She also suffered from periodic overeating and vomiting. Her weight could fluctuate dramatically (by as much as 30 kilos). More recently, her weight had been fairly stable. The patient reported many dissociative symptoms relating to eating problems, such as amnesia for binge eating and vomiting. She said:

> I can never really tell whether I'm hungry or not, but sometimes it feels like I've got a hole in my stomach and I just have to keep eating. I sometimes discover that a lot of food was eaten during the night. I notice this the next day.

The patient also reported hearing voices interfering with her eating. As an adolescent she exercised excessively and used laxatives. Recently, the patient had been suffering from binge eating and often had memory loss for this. She mentioned that she had tried to keep control of her shopping and that she was often puzzled about the food and empty packaging she came across in her kitchen. It made her feel desperate and ashamed. *When I was still working, I was much more in control,* she added.

Evaluation of Eating Problems. The patient reported severe eating problems. Unprompted, she mentioned dissociative symptoms suggestive of a division of the personality: hearing voices interfering with her eating and amnesia for buying food and binge eating.

Sleep Problems. The patient reported many sleep problems consistent with complex PTSD or a dissociative disorder. She was sleeping very restlessly, very often waking up from nightmares. Sometimes she would see things that had happened in the past and she would no longer know where she was. When reexperiencing, she felt different, younger, and often did not recognize her bedroom; she relived the horrifying situations as if they were taking place in the here and now. Sometimes she would wake up not knowing what time she was living in, or she would have the feeling of not being in her own body. She would feel younger. *I may be 6 or 13 or 14,* she said. In addition to the binge eating that she mentioned earlier, she was doing other things at night of which she had no memory. Sometimes she would enter her living room in the morning and find the TV on a channel she would never normally watch herself. She did find it weird, as this sometimes included children's programs, too. She had found herself somewhere in the city at night, while she was sure that she had gone to bed. That scared her a lot. Recently, she had been trying to lock her front door with multiple locks and hide the keys.

Evaluation of Sleep Problems. There were severe sleep problems with many symptoms of PTSD. Again, the examples indicated the possible actions of dissociative parts of the personality: thinking you are asleep and apparently watching different types of TV programs at night, finding yourself in the city and not knowing how you got there (fugue).

Mood and Emotion Regulation. The patient described her mood as constantly fluctuating: she was unable to rely on herself as she never knew when her mood would change. She very much would have liked to do some volunteer work again, but was afraid to do so because she feared she would not be able to keep it up or might suddenly just not show up; she had experienced this several times.

> Then I'm not depressed at all and I get up fairly easily and I really feel like working, and then suddenly something happens—actually, I can't explain at all—sometimes hours have suddenly passed. I don't know what I've been doing, but I can see that work has phoned me to ask why I hadn't shown up. This is so embarrassing! If it only happens once, it is fairly easy to think of an excuse, but you can't keep doing this if it happens more often. I'm too embarrassed to go there again.

Her abilities also varied greatly: *Sometimes I hardly know how to work on a computer—which is ridiculous because I use it every day—but I don't think this has anything to do with my mood; it just happens suddenly.*

She would get upset easily, and it was hard for her to calm herself down. She had no control over her emotions. Sometimes she did not feel anything at all in situations where one usually would be feeling something, like at a funeral of a dear elderly friend. By contrast, in moments of stress or when there was occasion for panic, she was able to act very effectively, which was also the case when she was a professional nurse.

> This is really rather strange, because I wouldn't remember this afterwards; my colleagues would tell me that I had handled things so well and that I'd stayed very calm. I had no choice but to go along with it. Telling them that I didn't remember was not an option!

The patient often felt depressed and had attempted suicide several times. She usually did not remember anything about this. At one time, she found herself regaining consciousness in the emergency room. She explained: *Apparently, I had called the ER myself, telling them that I had taken too many pills.* She said this scared her very much, adding she did not want to die at all. She also said that these attempts had been coming *out of the blue.*

Evaluation of Mood and Emotion Regulation. The patient described highly fluctuating moods and suicidality. Also, her abilities to undertake certain tasks in daily life varied in a way that is often described by patients with DID. She felt this could not have been caused by her moods. She also experienced great difficulty regulating her emotions or calming herself.

Lastly, it became evident that she had been having a lot of amnesia, both for the suicide attempts and in daily life, not only in the past when she was still working as a nurse, but also more recently.

Anxiety and Panic. The patient often felt anxious when she was out, but also in her own house. *The worst part of it is that I've no idea what it's about. It happens all of a sudden. I feel like a small child and want to hide in a closet. I know I did this when I was little.* When asked by the clinician whether she still finds herself in a closet sometimes, she replied: *I no longer have a closet that is large enough for me to hide in, but I have found myself under my bed, petrified, without a clue as to how I got there.* She was able to connect some of the fears to a sexual trauma that happened when she was 15 years old, but more often she had no idea as to the source of her anxiety.

She also showed symptoms of avoidance. She would avoid all situations where many people are present. She would go shopping very early in the morning and would avoid going to the shops if she could. She bought her clothes online. She was afraid to go into fitting rooms. She had been isolating herself more and more. She reported episodes of reliving terrifying events with frightening images; some of these images were hard to trace back, which made them even scarier.

Finally, the patient reported hyperarousal: jumpiness, a strong startle reaction, and extreme vigilance.

Evaluation of Anxiety and Panic. The patient reported a range of anxiety symptoms consistent with severe PTSD. Again, she described symptoms indicating a division of the personality: she had amnesia and had found herself under her bed, petrified with terror. She also described possible intrusions by a child part (feeling like a small child who wants to hide in a closet).

Self-Injurious Behavior. The patient reported cutting herself frequently and often finding out that she had burnt herself. She sometimes had amnesia for this behavior. The patient often was aware that she was cutting herself and would look at herself feeling she was outside her body. She would be unable to stop the cutting on such occasions. She also heard voices telling her to cut herself. She always had amnesia for burning herself. She added: *Being a nurse I am glad I can try to take care of it as much as I can without others noticing it. But there have been times I had no choice but to visit the ER for stitches.*

Evaluation of Self-Injurious Behavior. A division of the personality was also evident from the patient's responses to questions about self-injurious behavior. The patient heard voices ordering her to cut herself, she was outside her body watching, and she had amnesia for burning herself. This probably indicated that multiple parts were self-damaging: possibly with one part doing the cutting and another part burning herself.

Self-Image and Identity. When talking about her self-image, she became increasingly uncomfortable. This was clear from the constant and visible twitching in her face. She would sometimes shake her head or easily go out of contact. The patient had a negative self-image and said she felt worthless every day.

The patient described feeling very insecure about her preferences because they could change so radically. She did not know who she was or how she should be. She was hearing voices all the time and it was as if they were arguing about every single subject. She added: *Have you ever been in a crowded media store where all the TVs are on? For me it's like they are all on different channels, all mixed up. It's driving me crazy.* The patient described a constant battle and chaos in her head, which was clearly noticeable during the interview. She was hearing many opinions in her head that did not feel like her own. Sometimes she heard herself expressing opinions that she did not agree with at all, as if she was hearing herself talk. She tended to conform to other people's wishes for fear of disappointing them.

She reported having feelings of shame and guilt. Sometimes, she was able to influence her own behavior, but often she was not able to do this at all. She would have no control over some of the things that happened, like not showing up at her volunteer job or hearing herself saying things with which she did not agree.

Evaluation of Self-Image and Identity. The responses to the questions in this section also indicate the existence of a division of the personality. In particular, she reports uncertainty about who she is because she hears voices and because things are happening beyond her ability to control, and for which she has amnesia.

Relationships With Others. The patient reported having a small network of friends and experienced having a stable friendship with them. However, she indicated having internal conflicts about her social contacts. Also, her opinions about the people she knew would vary greatly. She heard various voices telling her contradictory things about her friends.

She also found it very difficult to get together with acquaintances that she knew from various situations or worlds (e.g., former health care colleagues or contacts from dog-training classes). That was why she never invited people over for parties, as she would not know how to deal with it. *It's like I'm a different person with different people. It's so uncomfortable. Sometimes I'd forget what happened; it would be hours later and everyone would have left. I now try to avoid situations like that.*

She had difficulty trusting people and added that she was okay with having only a small network.

Evaluation of Relationships With Others. There was evidence for a division of the personality, possibly with multiple parts functioning in daily life, such as one part working in health care and another one attending dog-training classes. The patient reported experiencing a constant internal struggle about her social contacts and hearing voices interfering, consistent with DID.

Sexuality. The patient reported avoiding sexual interactions as much as possible. She had been in a relationship once, but she felt uneasy being touched, even when her boyfriend would just want to give her a hug. She would definitely feel bad when they had sexual contact. During sexual interactions with her partner she would either be outside her body or feel nothing at all. Often, she would also see horrible images that she was sometimes able to place, but sometimes not.

The patient also described quite compulsive thinking about sex, which she did not want to engage in at all. She would hear voices urging her to have sex or talking about sex. In the past she had ended up having sexual relationships without wanting to. Sometimes, she had found herself in bed with someone she did not know, without remembering how that had happened. In her adolescence, the patient had been confused about her sexual identity, but this was no longer the case.

Evaluation of Sexuality. Again, the patient reported many dissociative symptoms that indicated a division of the personality: hearing the voices of different parts of her personality, having the perception of being outside her body during sexual interactions, having amnesia before engaging in sexual contact.

Since the patient was participating in clinical research, I had to ask these questions—briefly. These questions may be skipped in clinical situations if it has been apparent during the interview that the patient often dissociates and if there is already a lot of evidence for a division of the personality consistent with DID or OSDD. Particularly in the case of childhood sexual traumatization, the questions about sexuality may trigger and distress patients.

Evaluation of Possibly Trauma-Related Symptoms At this point in the TADS-I interview I had been interviewing the patient for more than 90 minutes. We continued the interview after a short break. Her responses to the questions about symptoms that could be trauma-related had already provided much evidence for a dissociative organization of her personality, particularly for DID. The patient reported amnesia and hearing voices associated with virtually every trauma-related symptom and appeared to have amnesia also for everyday functioning.

The patient had already described many examples of depersonalization and derealization, so I was able to follow up on that.

Alterations in Consciousness

Depersonalization. The patient often felt disconnected from herself (a symptom of depersonalization). Sometimes, she heard herself talking and heard words coming out of her mouth that did not appear to be hers. *During the day, I sometimes feel like some kind of inflatable doll, that deflates in the night,* she explained. She also experienced depersonalization during her daily activities. She mentioned traveling by public transport as an example. She would go through the motions, while looking at herself from a distance. *I can see myself from above, sitting in the train,* she explained.

Derealization. Her surroundings often felt strange (a symptom of derealization). When this happened, she had difficulty recognizing her own house or street. She also reported that there was a wall between the world and herself, as if she were inside a bell jar.

Absorption. The patient did not endorse any symptoms of absorption and those questions were a bit confusing for her. She added that she was always trying hard to pay attention and stay alert. It felt like an inner compulsion to stay focused and in the here and now. However, she could become absorbed in a book or a movie, but only if she felt really safe.

The patient reported chronic depersonalization and derealization symptoms, occurring daily and often combined. These appeared to be severe, and a number of symptoms indicated a division of the personality.

When asked about absorption, she described an inner compulsion to stay alert, which could indicate an intrusion of a vigilant dissociative part of the personality.

Somatoform Dissociative Symptoms

The patient reported a high level of somatoform dissociation, specifically not feeling her body or involving her body appearing larger or smaller. On one occasion, she had been walking around for a week with a broken foot. She had felt no pain, but when the foot started to appear very swollen, a friend had urged her to go and see a doctor.

She also described symptoms of *freezing and feeling paralyzed*, for example when she found herself lying under her bed, but she could also experience such feelings of paralysis when lying in her bed or just during the day while talking to someone. She further described experiencing occasional muscle twitching or her whole body shaking.

She had previously had a neurological examination following a seizure that resembled epilepsy and for which she had amnesia. This examination had not uncovered epilepsy.

On a few occasions she had lost her voice, and this had lasted for several hours. She experienced brief moments of freezing or trembling of her body almost on a daily basis.

EVALUATION OF SOMATOFORM DISSOCIATIVE SYMPTOMS

The patient reported multiple somatoform symptoms occurring every day. These symptoms were indicative of intrusions by other dissociative parts, most likely parts that were stuck in trauma time.

Psychoform Dissociative Symptoms

Amnesia. The patient frequently had amnesia and would lose hours of time every day. She had found evidence of doing things she could not remember. She had found herself in places without knowing how she got there. The patient stated that she tried to think about it as little as possible.

She only remembered fragments of the past. There were many episodes, even in her normal daily life in the past, for which she had no memory. She appeared to have had memory problems from an early age. Even now, the patient would experience memory problems for everyday activities, such as housework or grocery shopping. She would plan to go to the supermarket, only to find out that she had already been there. Sometimes she was not able to recall whether or not she had walked the dog. Also, when she was still a practicing nurse, she would be unable to recall parts of her shifts, particularly when it was very busy. Sometimes she had to check whether or not she had written her handover notes. She added that she was quite surprised that no one had ever noticed. Eventually, she suffered burnout and stopped working.

In her interactions with friends, she experienced not being able to remember the content of their conversations; for example, when meeting again she could not remember what they had been talking about the previous time. She was very embarrassed about this. She also stated that she had learned how to deal with this and had many tricks to figure out what had happened.

Schneiderian Symptoms/Intrusions. The patient would hear many different voices, including children's voices and male voices. The voices told her to do things but were also talking about her among themselves, as if gossiping. The voices had no names, and she did not hear any voices outside herself; they were all in her head. Antipsychotic medication did not have any effect on the voices. The voices appeared to know each other; they would sometimes have terrible fights. The patient could have many different views on the same subject and had many sudden thoughts that were irrelevant to the situation. The patient also reported having sudden emotions that did not seem to be hers, and she was unable to understand or place these.

Symptoms That Possibly Indicate a Division of the Personality. Throughout the assessment, the patient continually gave examples of symptoms indicating a division of the personality: severe amnesia that was also present for functioning in daily life; varying perceptions of her body, either large or small; depersonalization symptoms, being outside of herself and watching herself doing things; having different opinions and views; and a highly fluctuating self-image that was not polarized, as between two black-and-white opinions, but was consistent with the different views of multiple dissociative parts.

The patient was unaware of the existence of any dissociative parts and indicated that it was too difficult for her to think about this. She avoided the subject during the interview, as the topic evoked a lot of fear and resistance in her.

EVALUATION OF PSYCHOFORM DISSOCIATIVE SYMPTOMS

The patient had a cluster of psychoform dissociative symptoms, including amnesia and Schneiderian symptoms, indicating a division of the personality consistent with DID.

Diagnostic Considerations

The symptoms reported by the patient were consistent with DID. She reported a cluster of somatoform and psychoform dissociative symptoms indicating a division of the personality involving multiple parts functioning in daily life.

The patient was afraid to reflect on her symptoms and was unable to answer the questions in the last part of the TADS-I about the existence of different dissociative parts. The tension increased enormously, which was also noticeable from nonverbal signals. She indicated not being able to think about it. I decided not to put any further pressure on her, nor ask for examples that might have indicated the existence of a dissociative part.

As described in Chapter 1, in our SCID-D research we would diagnose this group of patients as DDNOS Example 1 and we would refer to the "initial presentation of DID" (Boon & Draijer, 1993a). This case report is an example of this. During my TADS-I research, I saw a number of similar patients. Since patients with DID often present in the above manner during an initial diagnostic examination, Spiegel and colleagues proposed to broaden the DSM-5 criteria for DID to prevent the OSDD-1 category from being assigned to patients who actually have DID (Spiegel et al., 2011; Spiegel et al., 2013). DID may now be diagnosed when the patient self-reports having dissociative parts or when collateral reports reveal that others or partners have observed dissociative parts.

In the case of this particular patient, who tried to conceal her symptoms from the outside world at all costs and who was definitely unable to even consider the possibility of the existence of dissociative parts herself, there is still a problem. It is not possible to formally diagnose this patient with DID. However, in a case like this the diagnosis OSDD-1 is not really appropriate either, as the patient reported a lot of amnesia, which is not an OSDD-1 criterion. The criteria for ICD-11 partial DID do not match either. Although these criteria allow for incidental amnesia (e.g., for self-injurious behavior), this patient reported far more amnesia, including amnesia for daily events. In my TADS-I reports on similar cases, I chose to diagnose DID nonetheless, giving a detailed description of the dissociative symptoms and nonverbal presentation that were consistent with this classification.

When would a DID diagnosis be appropriate according to the DSM-5 in cases like the one above? Based on the present DSM-5 criteria, clinicians are able to diagnose DID when the patient is able to provide information about dissociative parts showing that these parts have their own autobiographical memories, their own first-person perspective, their own behavior, affects, cognitions, and sensorimotor functioning (see also as stated in the DSM-5; APA, 2013, p. 292, 2022, p. 330). DID may also be diagnosed when a partner, or someone else who knows the patient well, can provide additional information indicating the existence of dissociative parts. If the above patient had been able to answer the questions in the final paragraph about different parts of the personality, she might have done so as follows.

CLINICIAN: Have you ever had the feeling that different parts of you exist inside you?

PATIENT: Yes, this is a bit difficult, but I know that sometimes I am not there and someone else is.

CLINICIAN: Could you tell me a bit more about it?

PATIENT: Well, I may already have noticed this when I was in high school. Sometimes I would really panic, because I didn't remember whether I'd been to school or not, and was not able to remember what had happened. Then I heard a girl's voice in my head telling me that she had been to school.

CLINICIAN: Does this girl have a different name from yourself?

PATIENT: Um . . . yes, she calls herself Patricia. She was also there during my nursing studies, especially when I had to study a lot. I have difficulties concentrating and suddenly it's all gone. I've slowly come to understand that she is present when this happens.

CLINCIAN: Do you know of any other parts?

PATIENT: Well, I feel bad telling you this, but it wasn't me who bought my dog; it was just suddenly there. I really don't know how this happened. So this must have been done by another part who can access my money, because I did find a bank transfer to a breeder.

CLINCIAN: Do you know anything else about this part?

PATIENT: No, I was very shocked and very angry as it was quite a lot of money. But now I'm actually happy about it. I always wanted a dog, but I was afraid to buy one, because I thought I would never be able to take good care of it.

CLINCIAN: I presume this may have been an older part too?

PATIENT: Well, this part must have been able to access my money and be able to travel, as the breeder was in a completely different part of the country.

CLINICIAN: You also told me that you feel very small sometimes. Do you think there may be younger parts as well?

PATIENT: I know there are two girls; one is very scared and the other one seems to be more cheerful. Sometimes I can't pull myself away from a shop window displaying toys. That's really embarrassing. I feel smaller then too; I think this is when these girls are there.

CLINICIAN: I understand they are a different age than yourself. Do they have different names too?

PATIENT: Yes, but I'm not going to tell you because, really, I don't want to have anything to do with them. I think it's ridiculous and childish. I just ignore them.

CLINICIAN: Do you think these parts have different memories from your own?

PATIENT: I know very little about my high school days. Sometimes I hear things in my head. Sometimes I run into an old friend who will start talking about things that I can't remember at all. In some of these instances I'm suddenly not there anymore. I find myself at home later without remembering how I got home or what happened. I sometimes think this is when she's there.

CLINICIAN: You mean Patricia?

PATIENT: Yes, that one.

CLINICIAN: Do you dare to ask her if she was present when this happens?

PATIENT: No, I don't talk with them. I find this really strange. It's bad enough they're talking to me!

CLINICIAN: And what about the little girls. Are their memories different to yours?

PATIENT: I really don't dare think about that. There are gaps in the past, but doesn't everyone have those?

CLINICIAN: Earlier, you told me that you sometimes hear male voices too. Do you think there are any parts with a gender that is different from your own?

PATIENT: I try not to listen to those male voices. They scare me to death. They're all saying horrible things and tell me to do things that I don't want to do. They can't be parts of me. This is really very different from the girls and Patricia. Do you know enough now? I notice my head is getting more crowded by the minute. I really want to stop now.

The patient described several dissociative parts that had different memories from her own. There was a part that had been present since high school. Possibly this part took over at times when the patient had difficulty concentrating and also later, when she was training as a nurse, especially when she had to master theoretical knowledge. There was another part that had bought a dog, while the patient herself had wanted a dog, but had not dared to acquire one. She mentioned several younger child parts and also male parts that had scared her and that had commanded her to be self-injurious. In addition to all the information indicating a division of the personality, her explanation was enough to make a formal diagnosis of DID.

Case Report: A High-Functioning Patient With DID, Initially Presenting With Partial DID

Particularly patients who are functioning well and who are coping in busy jobs may present with rather covert dissociative symptoms. In these cases, there is initially insufficient information to diagnose DID. These patients are usually very much in control, certainly during the day, but less so at night. They tend to rationalize or downplay many of their symptoms. The following is an example.

Ms. A. was a 40-year-old woman who was referred when a dissociative disorder was suspected by her therapist, who had been treating her for a year. She was working full time and had her own business in natural cosmetics, employing several people. She had been living with her spouse for many years. The couple had no children.

Ms. A. had signed up for outpatient group therapy for recurrent feelings of depression and problems with eating. For instance, she found it very difficult to eat in public. She had had some EMDR sessions but had stopped those because she did not feel they were much help. They also confused her. The group sessions seemed to distress her too. Subsequently she had a few individual sessions with the group therapist, where, for the first time, she admitted cutting her leg but not remembering afterward. She also reported having been abused as a child, by an older boy living nearby, but she did not think her current problems had anything to do with this. *After all, I had a good childhood,* she added.

General

First Impressions. The patient was friendly and answered questions promptly. She made little eye contact and appeared to be businesslike.

Substance Use and Medication. She said she hardly drank any alcohol and had never used drugs. In the past, however, she used to drink a lot of wine and was once arrested for driving under the influence. This had really frightened her and since then she had rarely drunk again. She had been taking antidepressants for a while, but she had discontinued them because they had side effects and did not help her. She was not taking medication anymore.

Possibly Trauma-Related Symptoms

Eating Problems. The patient indicated sometimes having difficulty eating, especially in the company of others. This really bothered her, and she could not understand why this was the case. She could eat better when she ate alone. *But I've always been rather skinny, though not quite underweight, and there are all sorts of things I really can't swallow, like red meat: I feel disgusted* *by it, but I don't understand why.* She did not describe any binge eating. She did not hear voices and reported no amnesia related to eating.

Sleep Problems. The patient described being a very poor sleeper. She often did not dare go to sleep for fear of nightmares. She was awake a lot at night. *I sometimes really don't understand how I can work the next day. I get up feeling dead tired.* However, the patient reported no amnesia nor finding evidence for getting up and doing things at night. She also said that she was always able to recognize her surroundings.

Mood and Emotion Regulation. The patient explained that her mood could change and that she could suddenly feel completely hopeless, but once back at work everything would be fine again. She did not acknowledge any suicidal thoughts and had never attempted suicide. She said she was usually able to calm herself. *I talk to myself very sensibly. And when that doesn't work, my husband is very helpful in reassuring me.*

Anxiety and Panic. The patient's anxiety symptoms could be interpreted as PTSD symptoms. *As a child I was abused by a boy from my neighborhood. I think it has something to do with that,* she added. *I wouldn't really describe myself as an anxious person. In my job, I'm never afraid of anything!* The patient mentioned having had a few sessions of EMDR for her memories of being abused by the boy in her neighborhood, but this had not helped at all. *When the therapist told me to concentrate on a specific image, it simply vanished. I wasn't able focus on it at all. And I felt terrible after these sessions, so I stopped them.*

Self-Injurious Behavior. Sometimes the patient had problems with self-harming behavior.

> Yeah, that's really weird. Sometimes I feel so bad and empty that I start scratching my arm superficially. But I also cut my leg and those cuts are very deep. This scares me a lot because afterwards I don't remember doing this. When I come to I appear to have a really deep cut in my leg. I had to have it stitched up a few times. The first time I made a deep cut in my leg was after one of the EMDR sessions. I don't get it, because nothing really happened during the session!

Self-Image and Identity. The patient stated that she would think fairly positively about herself in general. *Actually, I'm not particularly concerned with myself,* she added. She said that she was not confused about who she was and that she was not experiencing any struggle within herself. She was generally very self-reliant and did not feel dependent on others.

Relationships With Others. The patient reported having no major problems in relationships with others. *I've been in a relationship with my partner for more than 15 years and I also have some good friends, one of them since primary school. But I'm basically always working, I don't have that much time for social contacts.*

Sexuality. The patient mentioned that she hardly has any sexual contact with her husband and added that, fortunately, they both had little desire for it. She did acknowledge having difficulties however, because she kept seeing images of the boy next door.

> I didn't experience that before, at least not that I can remember. It has suddenly started to occur, but I never let him know. I'm embarrassed about it. Actually, I don't feel anything at all, but I've always pretended to have sexual feelings. I can do without it.

EVALUATION OF POSSIBLY TRAUMA-RELATED SYMPTOMS

Although the patient mostly responded in an ego syntonic, first-person narrative way, giving the impression of always being present and in control, there were some indications for a division of the personality. She had amnesia for making deep cuts in her leg, which may indicate the presence of a dissociative part responsible for the cutting, while she herself was sometimes superficially scratching her arm. She never felt much while having sex with her husband but was too embarrassed to talk about it. This lack of feeling is a negative somatoform symptom. It is very common in patients who were sexually abused and have parts stuck in trauma time: they hold the feelings related to the abuse. During EMDR, the image she was asked to focus on had suddenly disappeared. This may indicate the influence of a dissociative part that made the image disappear. It is also striking that she avoided a lot of things or just did *not think about it much* or was *not very concerned about it,* as she put it.

Alterations in Consciousness

The patient acknowledged doing many things on autopilot (depersonalization).

> Doesn't everyone? When I go to work, I just turn a switch, it's as if I am different the moment I arrive at the office. Even if I got up feeling depressed or very tired; this suddenly seems to disappear, or maybe I'm just unaware of it. I don't feel much anyway, like feeling hungry or thirsty. I forget to drink. I often don't know whether I am actually happy, but I'm never angry.

The patient stated that, apart from this, she did not feel unreal. She also did not endorse any derealization symptoms. With regard to absorption, she reported being able to concentrate on her work really well but said that her energy would be totally gone afterward.

Somatoform Dissociative Symptoms

The patient described a number of negative somatoform dissociative symptoms. She had had pneumonia several times without feeling that she was actually quite ill. She was not able to feel pain well. *I seem to have a high pain threshold.* She also did not feel anything during sexual contact with her husband, and she experienced frequent headaches.

Psychoform Dissociative Symptoms

Amnesia. The patient described amnesia for some of the self-injurious behaviors, and on several occasions she had no memory of how she got home after a therapy session. *Then I really can't remember getting into my car. That's kind of weird, but I must have just been absorbed (or deep) in thought because of everything that came up in therapy. I'm on autopilot and suddenly I'm home.* She added that she had never had any memory problems in her daily life, not at work and not in her spare time, and she never forgot any appointments.

> I always prepare well and keep a meticulous diary. My diary tells me everything, I can't afford to lose it! By the time I get home in the evening it becomes a bit of a blur, but then I'm just tired. I sometimes work until after 8 p.m. Sometimes my husband says I act childish at home, and that he has to put me to bed like a small child. I don't really know what he means but I prefer not to ask. I'm kind of embarrassed about that. I can't remember it myself. I think I must be dead tired at those moments.

She also said that she could not remember all about the past and about what had happened exactly with the boy next door but added that many people have bad memories about the past.

Schneiderian Symptoms/Intrusions. The patient denied hearing voices. *These are my own thoughts. When I'm at work I can concentrate well and I'm also quite determined, but outside of work there can be chaos. I keep changing what I think or want, and this is rather tiring.* The patient did not describe any other Schneiderian symptoms.

Symptoms That Possibly Indicate a Division of the Personality. The patient denied having any dissociative parts.

I can be a bit crazy and very tired, which is when my memory doesn't function all that well. It's just the cutting in my leg that really worries me. It has to stop, but I haven't got a clue how to do this.

Diagnostic Considerations

During the interview it was striking how Ms. A. had explanations for everything that had occurred. She attributed many of her symptoms to fatigue. She was only really worried about cutting her leg. However, she did mention several symptoms that clearly indicated a division of the personality. She was still unable to reflect on that herself. She also reported feeling very embarrassed:

- The patient had amnesia for cutting her leg, while she was aware of the fact that she had been scratching her arm. There seemed to be a dissociative part making deep cuts in her leg, probably triggered by specific emotions. She also mentioned that the first time this happened was after an EMDR session where she claimed *nothing had happened*. It is likely the EMDR had triggered quite a few things that she was unaware of, resulting in the cutting by a part that was stuck in trauma time.
- Sometimes, the patient also had amnesia for driving home after therapy. Although her explanation was that she had been deep in thought, she also mentioned that she did not at all remember getting into her car and driving home. This would involve a lot more than just absorption. It is suggesting that—possibly because of things evoked in therapy—there was a dissociative part that was able to drive home.
- The patient mentioned that, at times, she could be so tired that her partner had to *put her to bed like a small child*. She attributed this to fatigue also and was too embarrassed to ask him about it. Judging by the way she was talking about this, she seemed to have more amnesia for this than she was willing to admit. She said everything was a bit hazier in the evening.
- The patient also described various forms of depersonalization, such as not being in touch with her emotions and often doing things on autopilot. At the office, she *turned a switch* and she appeared to be different.
- The patient mentioned a number of negative somatoform dissociative symptoms. She kept on going while having pneumonia and high fever without noticing or feeling anything. She was unable to feel hunger or thirst well. She did not feel anything during sex.
- Finally, the patient reported functioning well at work by being really well prepared, and with the help of her diary, but that outside work

there was often chaos; she would be unsure of what she wanted and had all kinds of contradictory thoughts. These may be various thoughts of dissociative parts. Despite her rationalizations, there were some indications of the existence of dissociative parts that were stuck in trauma time. It was unclear whether there were dissociative parts functioning in daily life. This may be inferred from the way she talked about her performance at work, being different upon entering her office, and also from the fact that there appeared to be another part that was driving home after therapy. However, the patient was unable to say much else about this.

Although I asked the patient's permission to speak with her partner, she adamantly refused. If her partner were able to describe what he had observed, this could have provided important additional information to support a DID diagnosis.

On the basis of the information so far, the patient at least met the ICD-11 criteria for Partial DID, while DID certainly could not be excluded. A diagnosis of OSDD-1 was not formally appropriate because the patient reported too much amnesia for cutting her leg and incidentally for driving home and for the evenings when she appeared to be younger according to her husband. In clinical practice, such patients often receive either a complex posttraumatic stress disorder (CPTSD) diagnosis based on their PTSD symptoms, or a diagnosis of OSDD-1 because of the presence of several dissociative symptoms. Previously (in DSM-IV), the first example of DDNOS was most appropriate as amnesia could be one of the symptoms. Officially, CPTSD is not a classification in DSM-5, but it is in the ICD-11. However, for a CPTSD diagnosis this patient was reporting too much amnesia, since it exceeded the amnesia for part of the abuse by the boy in the neighborhood. The differential diagnosis with CPTSD will be discussed in more detail in Chapter 9.

Follow-Up

I was able to follow this patient after the TADS-I examination as I became her therapist. In the course of her treatment, it became clear that she had DID and much more amnesia than she had realized or dared to tell me during the diagnostic assessment. In fact, there appeared to be several working parts at times taking control of her behavior: one part was theoretically strong and knew all about natural cosmetics, while another part mainly did the customer contacts. She gradually became aware of the fact that she had been experiencing more amnesia in her daily life than she had realized before.

The part that was driving her home after therapy turned out to be a helpful male part, who told her he was there to *take her away* whenever there was too much chaos: *She would otherwise be a danger on the road then.* The part that had been making deep cuts in her leg turned out to be an angry female part that blamed her for what had happened with the boy next door. There were also parts that were involved in her eating problems. One part was responsible for her inability to eat red meat. This turned out to be connected to early childhood traumatization that she initially could not recall at all. The abuse by the boy next door occurred much later. There were several child parts and eventually the patient had to realize that she had not only been abused by a neighbor boy but also by her father, her grandfather, and several other men. At the time of the diagnostic assessment, she had complete amnesia for this. As she dared to realize more and became less phobic of the dissociative parts, she could also understand that the voices in her head belonged to different dissociative parts and was able to very slowly begin to make contact with them.

Ms. A.'s case report is an example of how often highly functioning DID patients with this amount of control and rationalization can hide their dissociative symptoms, which complicates assessment. It is not always a matter of consciously hiding; Ms. A. was probably unaware of most of her dissociative symptoms and was too afraid to reflect on unexplained behaviors, such as the deep cuts. She was motivated, though, and genuinely wanted to gain control of her symptoms, in particular of her cutting. She also wanted to sleep better and was aware of the fact that she had PTSD symptoms. However, she was still unable to realize the severity and extent of her dissociative symptoms and abuse history and tended to downplay them (*doesn't everyone?*) or rationalize them (*it's only fatigue!*).

Case Report: A Patient With OSDD-1 (DSM-5) or Partial DID (ICD-11)

Ms. K. was a 28-year-old patient who worked full time in IT. She lived alone in a house she had recently purchased. When not working, she would enjoy numerous hobbies including gardening and horseback riding. The patient, who had received a CPTSD diagnosis, was referred for a second opinion. Her therapist had asked whether she might have a dissociative disorder with separate dissociative parts. This question had arisen because the patient would regularly have episodes of reexperiencing trauma during treatment sessions. She then would lose contact with the therapist, and it was hard to get her back in the here and now. Sometimes, she would be out of contact for almost an hour.

The patient had only received outpatient treatment for 2 years, after having started to suffer from nightmares and dissociative flashbacks after seeing a TV program at a friends house about abuse. This was just after her grandfather had died. The patient was sexually abused by her grandfather when she was a child. She had always known about it but had only started to suffer much more as a result of the abuse after he passed.

General

First Impressions. Ms. K. was able to establish a good rapport and able to clearly describe her symptoms. She was afraid she would start reexperiencing the trauma during the assessment and feared that she would go out of contact and not be able to orient to the here and now. We agreed that she would let me know when the interview was becoming too much for her or when tension was running too high. It was agreed that we would then stop the assessment and continue next time. This reassured her.

Substance Use and Medication. During high school, the patient drank heavily on the weekends for several years. While she had never experienced an alcoholic blackout, she reported having suffered from occasional dizziness and vomiting. She had stopped using alcohol when she felt that she was in danger of losing control. Her mother drank a lot, and the patient definitely did not want to be like her. She had never used any recreational drugs. At the time of the interview, she drank the occasional glass of wine on birthdays.

Possibly Trauma-Related Symptoms

Eating Problems. The patient reported being anorexic around the age of 16. She explained:

> I didn't want to gain too much weight and be like my mother. She is heavily overweight. I intentionally went on a diet, exercised a lot, and also used laxatives. My lowest weight at the time was 47.5 kilos [105 lbs.] and I stopped having periods.

Her weight had been rather stable for years by the time of the interview, but she would occasionally binge eat, eating all kinds of things in one go. She had no amnesia for the binge eating but she did tend to lose control; it all happened in a kind of haze and afterward she felt the compulsion to throw up everything. Sometimes she would still use a lot of laxatives, but only on the weekend so people would not notice when she had to go to the bathroom frequently. She was not hearing voices interfering with her eating.

Evaluation of Eating Problems. With regard to eating, the patient reported no dissociative symptoms indicating a division of the personality, such as amnesia or hearing voices related to her eating behavior. She described her symptoms in an ego syntonic, first-person narrative way. It was striking that she had been planning her laxative use so she would not be bothered by it at work. She did, however, report depersonalization related to the binge eating and felt some kind of urge to vomit.

Sleep Problems. The patient reported being able to fall asleep with the help of sleep medication most of the time but waking up every night and having frequent nightmares. She was usually aware of the nature of these nightmares, and they would not always be related to the abuse by her grandfather. For example, she would dream that a very close friend of hers had died. Apart from having nightmares, she would suffer from dissociative flashbacks. She knew this would often start when she experienced very anxious feelings and physical paralysis; after that she would no longer be aware of what was happening and have amnesia. Once she was oriented in the here and now again, her body would feel as if something bad had happened, and she would feel exhausted and confused, needing time before she was able to be fully present again. At such times, she would not immediately recognize her own house. These episodes of reexperiencing traumatic events could also occur during the day, always when she was home alone or during therapy.

She never found evidence of activities for which she had amnesia. After waking up, she would be frozen in her bed. She was only sleeping a few hours each night.

Evaluation of Sleep Problems. Dissociative flashbacks with full amnesia and disorientation while coming to in particular might indicate a division of the personality. The description suggested the presence of a dissociative part (personality state) that was stuck in trauma time. Similar episodes of reexperiencing trauma with amnesia had also been observed by her therapist.

Mood and Emotion Regulation. The patient said she was always wearing a *mask* at work.

> No one will notice anything, and I can keep it up until I'm home again; then it's coming off and I can't do another thing. Especially in the evening, I feel tired and listless. I'm fine as long as I can keep busy. I always make sure I have a very full schedule in the weekends, too.

The patient said that she was generally very much in control, as long as she was with other people. At home she would have no control over her anger, fears, and flashbacks.

The patient stated she was sometimes unable to be in touch with her feelings, but she had noticed that she had been feeling depressed and hopeless about her future. Several times, she had taken pills in combination with alcohol. According to her, this would happen when she was in another strange mood, upset, and also furious; *not at all like you see me now,* she added. She would be aware when she took the pills but would not feel like herself. She had no amnesia for any suicide attempts but also had no control over this mood; she described it like the haze she would experience while binge eating. *Something from inside is forcing me to do this.* She had never had her stomach pumped nor had she ever been hospitalized after an attempted suicide. *Apparently, I am not taking enough pills,* she commented. The patient had never heard voices instructing her to take pills.

She explained that it was better for her to be busy all week than to sit still. Sitting still would be scary and would always lead to unpredictable situations. On further questioning, it turned out she was referring to episodes of reexperiencing traumatic events or situations in which she would be suicidal or self-injurious.

The patient often felt empty but never bored.

Evaluation of Mood and Emotion Regulation. Again, the patient reported no obvious dissociative symptoms indicating a division of the personality, but the way she was talking about this other mood, in which she felt an *inner compulsion* to take pills, may be indicative of the so-called passive influence of a dissociative part that was suicidal. Such descriptions may also indicate a borderline mode, but so far there had not been any information suggesting the existence of a comorbid borderline personality disorder.

Anxiety and Panic. The patient explained that she never felt anxious during the day. *As long as I keep myself occupied, I don't feel anything, really.* But in the evenings, she was often very anxious and felt scared at home. She would suddenly feel very small: she knew she was an adult woman, but her body felt small, and she felt like a little child.

The patient further reported all of the PTSD symptoms, including dissociative flashbacks, jumpiness, a strong startle reflex, compulsive behaviors such as organizing her wardrobe by color, taking frequent showers, and feeling the urge to clean a lot. The patient had amnesia for part of the episodes when she was reexperiencing trauma. Finally, she tried to avoid everything that would remind her of her past abuse.

Evaluation of Anxiety and Panic. There were severe chronic PTSD and obsessive–compulsive symptoms. The fact that the patient felt very anxious at night, feeling as if she were a small child, including the experience of having a small child's body, may indicate a division of the personality and the influence of a dissociative child part. Moreover, the patient had amnesia for episodes of reexperiencing traumatic events.

Self-Injurious Behavior. The patient reported that she tended to cut herself frequently, especially when she was angry. She usually knew she was doing this, but sometimes she only remembered starting and nothing after that. Afterward, she noticed she had applied a bandage. She was not making deep cuts and had never had to go to an emergency room for stitches. As was the case with her suicidal behavior, the patient did not always feel in control of the cutting. It was hard for her to talk about the subject, and she would easily go out of contact. She could quickly be brought back in contact, but she was unable to explain what was happening internally. It was clearly observable that she was briefly out of contact and was unable to hear me. She said she never heard any voices instructing her to cut.

Evaluation of Self-Injurious Behavior. Although the patient reported cutting herself and being aware of it, there was also amnesia and she had briefly been out of contact with me during this part of the interview. Again, this may have been an indication of a division of the personality and possibly the existence of a dissociative part involved in the cutting.

Self-Image and Identity. The patient explained that she had negative feelings about herself half the time. She did not feel insecure at work; she knew she was doing a good job but was often unable to believe it. When she was with friends, she knew people thought more positively about her than she did, but it was hard to hold on to that thought when she was home alone. Then, all kinds of thoughts about herself would come up and she would start ruminating. She tended to adjust to what others wanted, particularly in social situations. She expressed shame about pretending to be someone she was not. *No one knows I sometimes feel so scared and dirty,* she said. *I just put on that mask again and nobody will notice who I really am.* There was an ongoing internal struggle about who she really was. She did not perceive this struggle like voices in her head; it was a struggle between different thoughts and feelings.

Evaluation of Self-Image and Identity. The patient described a lot of internal struggles about who she really was. She described an exterior (*a mask*) and an interior (*scared and dirty*) with an underlying negative self-image that did not match how others felt about her. Although the patient did not hear voices indicating that there might be a division of the personality, she described an ongoing struggle between different thoughts and feelings, which pointed in that direction. Moreover, it could not be ruled out that her feeling scared or dirty was consistent with dissociative parts that were stuck in trauma time and were influencing her self-image.

Relationships With Others. The patient described that she had stable relationships with others and that she had known some of her friends for many years. She felt her social network was large enough. Although she described some of her relations as superficial (*luckily they're not aware of what is behind my mask and I won't show them*), she was quite close with some friends.

Generally, she avoided conflicts and tended to adjust to others. The patient did not feel very dependent on others and said: *Actually, I try not to bother others too much and sort things out for myself. I usually manage.* The patient reported having few or very minimal problems in friendships.

Evaluation of Relationships With Others. It is not the primary purpose of this section to ascertain whether there is a division of the personality. The questions are intended to get an impression of whether there is a borderline organization including great instability in relationships with others. This was not the case with this patient. She had stable and long-lasting relations with friends. She did not describe having internal conflicts regarding various social contacts. Such conflicts may occur in patients with DID, because various parts functioning in daily life may not feel attracted to the same people and may have different opinions about particular people in their circle of friends.

Sexuality. The patient did not have difficulty with being touched by friends but did experience problems with sexual relationships. She avoided sexual contact and did not like to be touched in a sexual way. In the past she had had a number of sexual relationships and tended to adjust because sex was expected by the other person. She would shut herself off, or would feel numb, or would experience herself as if she was outside of her body during these contacts. She also described reexperiencing the abuse by her grandfather during sexual intercourse and not being able to clearly recognize her surroundings.

Evaluation of Sexuality. The description of her sexual relationships indicated a division of the personality. The patient described watching herself from a distance or no longer feeling things. Sometimes, she also did not recognize her surroundings. This pointed to the presence of at least one observing part and one or possibly several parts experiencing the sexual contacts, consistent with her self-reported intrusions of feeling *dirty*.

EVALUATION OF POSSIBLY TRAUMA-RELATED SYMPTOMS

Although the patient is clearly trying to maintain control and presents as one person, when the possibly trauma-related symptoms are assessed, several indications of a division of the personality are found. These are sometimes quite subtle clues, for example, of possible intrusions of dissociative parts with eating problems and suicidality. Sometimes the examples are clearer, with amnesia, derealization (not recognizing her own home when waking up or after reexperiencing a traumatic event), or depersonalization (experiencing herself and her body differently as small or being outside her body during sexual contact).

Alterations in Consciousness

Depersonalization. The patient particularly recognized the feeling of acting on autopilot; this was in essence the mask that she was putting on. It was hard for her to access her emotions. When riding a horse or working in her garden, she did feel more like herself and sometimes felt that she could take off her mask, only to put it back on again as soon as others were around. Her autopilot experiences occurred on a weekly basis and these feelings could be exacerbated by anxiety, pressure, and fatigue.

Derealization. The patient only experienced derealization immediately after having a dissociative flashback. On such occasions she would not know where she was nor recognize her surroundings. This also frequently occurred after waking up in the morning—she would not recognize her current home and sometimes thought she was back in her childhood home or at her grandparents' house.

Absorption. The patient described that she could be immersed in her thoughts without noticing the time passing (half an hour or a whole hour). This did not happen very often, *because I am always busy doing something*. The patient stated that she did not have a vivid imagination and did not tend to lose herself in daydreams.

EVALUATION OF ALTERATIONS IN CONSCIOUSNESS

In addition to chronic depersonalization, the patient notably describes derealization experiences that indicate the presence of a dissociative part that is stuck in trauma time (not recognizing her own home and thinking she is in her parents' house). She also describes severe absorption, but her examples do not clearly show whether there really is dissociative amnesia with another dissociative part present.

Somatoform Dissociative Symptoms

The patient reported losing her voice, no longer being able to move, not being able to see or hear, and having difficulty swallowing (all negative somatoform symptoms). These occurred particularly when she was having dissociative flashbacks. She would be present to some extent, but not really. At times, she could also be hypersensitive to sound and light (positive somatoform symptoms).

EVALUATION OF SOMATOFORM DISSOCIATIVE SYMPTOMS

The patient describes several somatoform dissociative symptoms that seem to be particularly related to the presence of a dissociative part stuck in trauma time.

Psychoform Dissociative Symptoms

Amnesia. The patient did not mention amnesia for the present, with the exception of partial amnesia for dissociative flashbacks. She stated that, in her view, she had forgotten things about the abuse and, really, about the whole period in which it had occurred.

> I never talked about it, for years. And nobody knew about it. On one occasion at a friend's house, I was watching a program on TV about abuse. I never watch programs like that myself, but it was hard for me to say that I didn't want to see it, and suddenly I heard myself telling her that my grandfather had done the same [to me]. I couldn't stop it. Since then, all kinds of memories have come back, not only about the abuse but also about my high school years—as if I had been hiding everything.

Schneiderian Symptoms/Intrusions. The patient was not hearing voices except her grandfather's, especially when she was reexperiencing being abused by him. She did feel that her behavior was sometimes influenced from within.

Symptoms That Possibly Indicate a Division of the Personality. The patient was able to mentally step out of herself or out her body, but did not do this deliberately, it just happened to her. She would be looking at herself. Sometimes she would see herself as she was now, but sometimes as she was when she was younger, like a small child. When she was feeling small, she did not actually see a smaller body—it was more a physical sensation. Friends who knew her well tended to have different experiences with her. According to the patient this was a result of her lowering her mask. As described earlier, the patient experienced a lot of internal struggles. She did not feel her skills varied: *I have always been very consistent in my work and in my hobbies,* she added.

Dissociative Parts of the Personality. The patient stated that she did not recognize having dissociative parts.

> I know that I was abused as a child. I try to avoid thinking about that as much as possible. I don't really understand why I told my friend. It would have been better if I hadn't told her. Since then, I've been having all these symptoms.

EVALUATION OF PSYCHOFORM DISSOCIATIVE SYMPTOMS

The patient reported amnesia for the past and amnesia for having dissociative flashbacks in the present. Sometimes, she left her body and watched;

she would then see herself as a child. She also described several examples of so-called passive influences of dissociative parts.

Diagnostic Considerations

There were several indications for the existence of trauma-related dissociative parts:

- Sometimes, the patient no longer recognized her surroundings, such as her bedroom. It would seem like she was looking through the eyes of a child part. This happened after waking up or after having a dissociative flashback. She also reported many somatoform symptoms, such as freezing and not being able to talk.
- The patient usually felt alienated from her body and did not feel much; she also said that she always wore a *mask* in daily life.
- The patient described that sometimes she was outside of her body and saw a small child being abused; at other times she would feel small.
- The patient heard herself telling her friend that she had been abused.
- The patient experienced inner urges to harm herself and sometimes had partial amnesia for it.
- The patient indicated that she had felt a kind of inner urge to take pills.
- The patient reported amnesia for the past that was more extensive than just for the abuse. She also had partial amnesia for dissociative flashbacks.

There was insufficient evidence for DID. The patient did not report amnesia for daily life. She also did not report hearing voices except her grandfather's and did not recognize having dissociative parts of her personality.

Based on the information she provided, the patient met the criteria for ICD-11 partial DID as there was clear evidence of dissociative parts stuck in trauma time. These parts sometimes were in the foreground and, at other times, were influencing her behavior from within. Finally, the patient also met the criteria for CPTSD. Again, it appeared that OSDD-1 in DSM-5 was problematic because the patient had amnesia in the present for most of her dissociative flashbacks. This had also been observed by her therapist who sometimes was unable to make any contact with her at all, for over an hour.

Case Report: A Patient With Depersonalization/ Derealization Disorder

Mr. L. was a 45-year-old man, married, with two children. Previously, he had been treated for anxiety disorder. He had been referred for a diagnostic consultation with suspected CPTSD or a dissociative disorder.

The patient grew up in a family with three children of which he was the oldest. From a young age he had taken care of his brother and little sister. His father was a truck driver and was away most of the time; his mother had psychiatric problems. *The atmosphere at home was always rather tense.* Often his mother would be lying in bed feeling depressed. *Sometimes she would be hysterical,* he added. This was frightening. She would threaten to kill herself or run away. On one occasion when he was an adolescent, he experienced her overdosing on pills and being taken away in an ambulance.

When his father was home, things were hardly better; his father was unable to cope with his wife's depression and would escape to the pub. He would not drink too much, but simply was not there. The patient did have a good relationship with his grandmother, his father's mother. The children would often be with her and he had fond memories of her.

The patient became independent at a young age and married young. He had two children. Around the age of 40, he was involved in a car accident in which he managed to escape a head-on collision just in time. He was not to blame for the accident and escaped with minor injuries. Afterward he developed symptoms of PTSD and other anxiety symptoms. He no longer suffered from episodes of reexperiencing the accident after EMDR treatment, but he said that after the accident he was never the same again. This was when many memories of his youth came back. *Before, I never used to dwell on things; I'd just carry on. It appears I can't do this anymore.*

He also found it difficult to make contact with his wife and children, as if there were a huge gulf between them. By then, the children were 18 and 20 years old and were leading their own lives.

General

First Impressions. The patient appeared to have a shallow affect. During the assessment it was possible to establish rapport to some extent. Sometimes it was difficult for him to put things into words or to give examples of the way he felt. He explained that he had never learned how to do this.

Substance Use and Medication. The patient never used recreational drugs and occasionally had a beer with friends on the weekends. He was not on any medication.

Possibly Trauma-Related Symptoms

Eating Problems. The patient did not report any eating problems.

Sleep Problems. The patient no longer had problems with sleeping. He explained that initially, after the accident, he had slept very poorly. He had suffered from nightmares and had kept seeing the accident. He had many flashbacks. After the EMDR treatment, these symptoms had disappeared. He could still wake up in the middle of the night and worry about the future. Thoughts would keep going through his head and he would worry about never being able to function as he had before the accident. However, in general he slept well again.

He remembered that he slept poorly as a child after his mother had attempted suicide. He added that this had passed and had never occurred again until after the accident.

Mood and Emotion Regulation. The patient explained that his mood was generally even. *I'm glad I'm not experiencing the extremes like my mother had.* He was never really depressed and said that—despite his difficult childhood—his life had been on track until the car accident. After the accident, he often wondered whether he would ever be okay again. It was all very different from before the accident. *I don't feel much at all, sometimes I'm like a robot.* He said that he never thought of suicide and would never end his life, because he did not want to hurt his wife and children.

Anxiety and Panic. The patient said that, since the accident, he occasionally suffered from anxiety. He did not report any current PTSD symptoms but said that sometimes he still had terrifying images of his wife or children having an accident. He would also be startled by the sound of police or ambulance sirens. He no longer saw images of his own accident but he would think there might be something wrong with the people he knew. He also said that, ever since the accident, he had often not been able to get in touch with his feelings at all; he felt very empty. He recognized this feeling from the time when he had still been living at home. According to him, it was then caused by him trying to shut himself off from *all the stuff going on* with his mother.

Self-Injurious Behavior. The patient reported no self-injurious behavior. He kept repeating that the bad example his mother had set had made him decide never to do such things.

Self-Image and Identity. The patient said that he really did not think much about himself or who he is. He was never confused about his identity.

> I never thought about these kinds of questions. Ever since I was young, I have gone my own way and wanted to have as little to do with my parents as possible. Until the accident, everything was going normally, as with everyone else.

Relationships With Others. The patient had been married for over 20 years. He said that he had a few friends from the time of his training as a gardener whom he had known for years. He also knew a lot of people from soccer.

> I am not very close to anyone. My wife sometimes complains that I am quiet and don't say much. But I'm not used to it, you see. I was better off not saying anything when I was still at home, because you never knew how she [his mother] would react.

The patient said he experienced few problems in relationships with others.

Sexuality. The patient did not report any problems with sexuality.

EVALUATION OF POSSIBLY TRAUMA-RELATED SYMPTOMS

When asking about possibly trauma-related symptoms, there were no indications of a division of the personality. However, the patient indicated several times that he was not very much in touch with his emotions and that it felt as if he was some sort of robot.

Alterations in Consciousness

Depersonalization. When asked, the patient recognized feeling disconnected from himself often.

> I seem to be the opposite of my mother. She was always screaming hysterically, or crying, or angry. I'm not very emotional; that has always been the case, but that has never bothered me. There's no need to be over the top. I hardly get angry either. But since the accident, all this has exacerbated. It's like nothing really affects me; I do everything on autopilot. Perhaps this has always been the case and I just never really thought about it. I remember having no emotions when my grandmother died. That's not normal, is it? She was the one person who was really there for us. My wife also tells me that I never show my emotions. She is finding it difficult.

After careful probing, it turned out that the patient's feelings of depersonalization had been present for a very long time. Also, his depersonalization symptoms appeared to be separate from anxiety and panic symptoms, but were of an ongoing nature, and appeared to have been aggravated by the accident.

Derealization. The patient did not report symptoms of derealization.

Absorption and Trance. The patient indicated that he had no experiences of absorption or trance. He stated that, as a child at home, he was always very much on the alert and was never able to become immersed in a book or movie.

EVALUATION OF ALTERATIONS IN CONSCIOUSNESS

The patient mainly describes chronic depersonalization experiences indicating detachment. He is not in touch with his emotions.

Somatoform Dissociative Symptoms

The patient did not report any somatoform dissociative symptoms.

Psychoform Dissociative Symptoms

The patient did not mention any psychoform dissociative symptoms. He did not report any amnesia and added: *I would rather say I remember things too well and since the accident I have been thinking about the past a lot more.*

He did not report any Schneiderian symptoms or any other symptoms that might indicate a division of the personality.

Diagnostic Considerations

Mr. L. reported chronic depersonalization symptoms consistent with a depersonalization/derealization disorder according to both DSM-5 and ICD-11. Although the symptoms had increased in both frequency and intensity following the car accident, they had been present prior to it. The PTSD had been treated and there were hardly any PTSD symptoms. The depersonalization symptoms did not appear to be exclusively related to symptoms of anxiety. A dysthymic disorder might have been considered as a differential diagnosis, but there was not enough evidence to support this.

Case Report: A Patient With Dissociative Neurological Symptom Disorder With Non-Epileptic Seizures (ICD-11) or Conversion Disorder With Attacks or Seizures (DSM-5)

Ms. J. was a 41-year-old woman who was referred to me by an outpatient trauma therapist for a second opinion. She had been in treatment for over a year, but both Ms. J. and her therapist felt that there had been little progress. Ms. J. was working in aged care; she was married, with two children, aged 6 and 8 years old.

Her symptoms had begun after she had been sexually approached by a confused patient with dementia. Although she had been able to handle the situation well at the time, symptoms of mostly physical tension had started immediately thereafter. She noticed that she would wake up completely rigid and sometimes was unable to move. Her therapist tried EMDR treatment for her memories of the event, but during treatment Ms. J. fell into a state that was much like an epileptic seizure. The EMDR treatment was discontinued, and her symptoms worsened. Although a non-epileptic seizure was suspected, Ms. J. was referred to a neurologist. No evidence of epilepsy was found. During treatment, Ms. J. had two more seizures whenever the therapist tried to further investigate whether there might have been earlier sexual abuse.

Ms. J. also began to experience increasing nightmares, jumpiness, and startlement as well as panic symptoms. Sometimes, images would come back to her of an uncle entering the bedroom when she was staying with her cousin. She thought she must have been young at the time, as she was 7 years old when her parents divorced, and after this she never saw her uncle and cousin again.

The referring therapist wanted to find out whether the non-epileptic seizures might have been part of a dissociative disorder.[9]

General

First Impressions. Ms. J. was in her early thirties. She established good contact and was able to express her symptoms accurately. She had read information about dissociative symptoms and she mentioned that she had recognized some of them.

Substance Use and Medication. The patient occasionally drank a glass of wine, but certainly not on a daily basis. She had never used recreational drugs and only used mild sleep medication if needed.

Possibly Trauma-Related Symptoms

Eating Problems. The patient never had eating problems.

Sleep Problems. The patient experienced a lot of problems with sleeping. She would often wake up with cramps and be unable to move well. She had a lot of nightmares, mostly about being chased or overpowered. She tended to go to bed too late because she dreaded going to sleep. According to her, the sleep problems had started after the incident at work. Her sleep pattern varied greatly. Sometimes she would fall asleep easily but wake up many times; at other times she would fall asleep very late and sleep through. In the morning she would still be very tired, as if she had hardly slept at all.

---

9 The classification system that is used in the Netherlands is the DSM-5. As we know, non-epileptic seizures are diagnosed in the DSM-5 as a somatic symptom disorder (conversion disorder)—ignoring their possibly dissociative nature.

There were no indications of her being active at night and having amnesia for it. She did not leave her bed. Her husband had not noticed much, but he was a deep sleeper. After waking up from a nightmare, she would need some time to orient herself in the present.

Mood and Emotion Regulation. The patient did not describe mood symptoms and would generally call herself a cheerful person. She indicated that she usually did not easily get upset and was able to soothe herself well when she was sad. She also experienced a lot of support from her husband. She never had any suicidal thoughts and never attempted suicide.

Anxiety and Panic. The patient said that she had never really been very anxious until the incident at work with the dementia patient. Even now she was managing quite well at work, although she had noticed that she was much more wary and more easily startled. She described PTSD symptoms with flashbacks of the man at work but also of her uncle. However, it was unclear to her what had actually happened with her uncle. She described sudden feelings of being in danger. She experienced cramping and a sense of threat, and in her nightmares she tried to run away but without being able to do so.

Self-Injurious Behavior. The patient had never intentionally hurt or injured herself and had never experienced other dangerous or destructive behaviors.

Self-Image and Identity. The patient generally had a positive self-image. She had no uncertainties about her likes or dislikes and was not uncertain about who she was as a person. She did not experience internal struggles. There was, however, some confusion about the seizures. She felt it was frightening and crazy that these had suddenly started. She wondered whether she was a simulator because she had the seizures mostly during therapy.

Relationships With Others. The patient had long-standing friendships with a number of girlfriends. She had lived with another partner for several years prior to her relationship with her current husband, to whom she had been married for 10 years. She generally had no difficulty trusting people and she was not afraid or conflict avoidant. She said she was quite good at standing up for herself and did not tend to always want to fit in with others.

Sexuality. The patient said that, at first, she did have trouble feeling safe in a sexual relationship, but she had thought that was just her inexperience. She had good sexual contact with her husband, but it had now become more difficult since the incident at work and the vague images of her uncle. Her husband was very understanding and patient, which helped her. *He doesn't mind just cuddling for now. The rest is not going very well at the moment.* The patient was not hearing voices, had no amnesia for sexual contact with her husband, nor had she had dissociative flashbacks in the past. However, she sometimes suddenly felt anxious, even though she knew she was with her husband.

The patient was never confused about her sexual identity.

EVALUATION OF POSSIBLY TRAUMA-RELATED SYMPTOMS

The patient described clear PTSD symptoms associated with physical tension symptoms and somatoform dissociation. No further indication of a division of the personality was found during this part of the TADS-I. Her narrative was ego syntonic, an I-experience, and there was no evidence of brief dissociative moments during this part of the interview.

Alterations in Consciousness

Depersonalization. The patient described mild depersonalization symptoms. She sometimes felt cut off from her feelings. Especially since the incident at work, she felt that she had been doing her work on autopilot quite often. She denied experiencing this at home with her husband and children.

Derealization. The patient did not endorse any derealization symptoms, except during seizures. Then, everything would be very far away. She would still hear her therapist but could no longer see her very well.

Absorption. The patient could be fully absorbed in a book or movie but not to the point of losing her sense of time. She was also able to stop reading or watching at any time.

EVALUATION OF ALTERATIONS IN CONSCIOUSNESS

The patient describes mild depersonalization and absorption symptoms. Her examples do not indicate a division of the personality.

Somatoform Dissociative Symptoms

Her main symptoms were the ones described earlier, involving tightening up and frequently cramping during sleep, as well as the non-epileptic seizures. The seizures had occurred several times, especially when there were triggers or continued questions about her uncle. During seizures she would go out of contact and usually fell to the floor. She would start kicking her legs. She explained that she could still hear everything but was unable to see well. She did not have amnesia for the seizures. She looked different when this happened: her face was distorted, and her voice sounded different. Sometimes she would make strange noises, but not always. The seizures lasted about 5 to 10 minutes. After the seizures she would have a lot of muscle pain and tension in her body and be very tired. It often took her days to fully recover.

The patient reported no other symptoms, such as complete loss of her voice or inability to hear or swallow.

EVALUATION OF SOMATOFORM DISSOCIATIVE SYMPTOMS

The patient reports chronic somatoform dissociative symptoms, particularly tightening up and cramping of her body at night. She has also had multiple non-epileptic seizures. It appears, moreover, that she had actually been waking up cramped for much longer, long before the incident at work.

Psychoform Dissociative Symptoms

Amnesia. The patient had a good memory and was able to give detailed information. She said she had never experienced doing things she did not remember. She also remembered her childhood well. The only thing she could not place were the images of her uncle. *They are all vague images with a lot of fear in my body,* she added. What she did recall was that she did not want to stay at her cousin's, even though she liked her. So there appeared to be amnesia present related to events with her uncle.

Schneiderian Symptoms/Intrusions. The patient was not hearing voices and did not describe any other Schneiderian symptoms. There were no other symptoms that might indicate a division of the personality except for the altered state of consciousness during seizures.

EVALUATION OF PSYCHOFORM DISSOCIATIVE SYMPTOMS

With the exception of amnesia for events with her uncle, the patient reports no other psychoform dissociative symptoms.

Diagnostic Considerations

Based on the assessment, there was no evidence of DID. The cluster of symptoms that is typical for DID was completely absent. There were also no indications for OSDD-1 or partial DID (e.g., she did not experience any passive influence phenomena from dissociative parts that were stuck in trauma time, nor stepping out of her body and seeing herself from a distance).

However, the patient did report significant PTSD symptoms and there was clear evidence of an altered state of consciousness (i.e., a dissociative part) during seizures. This case report illustrates that there was a dissociative division of the personality with one part functioning in daily life and most likely one part stuck in trauma time that surfaced during a seizure.

Formally, clinicians using the DSM-5 would diagnose PTSD and conversion disorder. In countries that use the ICD-11, the patient would be diagnosed with dissociative neurological symptom disorder with non-epileptic seizures, in addition to PTSD.

Summary

This chapter includes TADS-I reports from five patients with a dissociative disorder. The first two patients had DID, and they showed great differences in the extent to which they were able to talk about their symptoms. Chapter 7 will present more examples of different ways in which patients with DID present in mental health settings.

As described in Chapter 1, many patients with DID and OSDD-1 initially deny or downplay their symptoms. This is the result of nonrealization, the core of their serious traumatization (Janet, 1935): not being able and/or being unwilling to realize what has happened and what has been done to them. As a result, they often also avoid becoming aware of the division of their personality and the associated symptoms and are unable to say much about it during diagnostic assessment. Clinicians are faced with the task of assessing the patients' problems as best as they can while understanding the tendency these patients have toward nonrealization.

In a somatoform dissociative disorder, the symptoms are so obvious or annoying that the patient cannot avoid being aware of them, as was true of the last case discussed in this chapter. However, in this group of patients there is also the risk that they are unaware of their psychological problems, that is, the division of the personality and the underlying traumatization. For this reason, these patients often end up in somatic health care and remain there for a long time. When they are eventually referred for psychological treatment, the dissociative nature of their problems is not generally understood, partly because their dissociative symptoms are not understood as such in the DSM.

Finally, this chapter described the case of a patient with a depersonalization disorder. This disorder consists of symptoms of detachment that are not considered dissociative by some clinicians (e.g., Steele et al., 2022; van der Hart, 2021), as also described in Chapters 1 and 3. The depersonalization disorder is actually the odd one out, because there is no division of the personality, and, therefore, a different therapeutic approach is indicated.

CHAPTER 7

Challenges in Differential Diagnosis of DID, Partial DID, and OSDD-1

Introduction

Chapters 1 and 2 discussed the fact that dissociative identity disorder (DID) and Example 1 of the other specified dissociative disorders (OSDD-1, or partial DID in ICD-11) are polysymptomatic disorders, with patients presenting with diverse symptoms (Boon & Draijer, 1993a, 1993b, 1995a, 1995b; Dell, 2006; Draijer & Boon, 1995; van Dyck, 1992). The partial DID diagnosis, included in the ICD-11, is more or less similar to OSDD-1. As there have not been any trials with the ICD-11 dissociative disorder classifications, much of what is described in this chapter is based on earlier research and clinical experience with DSM-5 classifications and with earlier versions of the DSM. Chapter 6 explores how questions about possibly trauma-related symptoms were answered by patients with DID and to a lesser degree those with OSDD-1. It is precisely because of the multitude of trauma-related symptoms that dissociative disorders often go unidentified and patients are diagnosed incorrectly. Moreover, some patients with DID first present as with CPTSD, or OSDD-1, or even depersonalization/derealization disorder, because they are either concealing or insufficiently aware of dissociative symptoms indicating a division of the personality. However, often there is a clear comorbidity with DID, with DID going unrecognized. In a treatment study of patients with DID and DDNOS (n = 290) 89% of patients also met criteria for PTSD (n = 242), while 83% met criteria for a mood disorder (n = 226); 50% also had an anxiety disorder other than PTSD (n = 136), 30% had an eating disorder (n = 81), and 22% had a substance-related disorder (n = 61), while 22% had a somatoform disorder (n = 59) (Brand, Classen, Lanius, et al., 2009b).

The current chapter focuses on the challenges and dilemmas in differential diagnosis regarding the two most commonly described and complex dissociative disorders: (1) dissociative identity disorder (DID) and (2) other specified dissociative disorder (OSDD-1, DSM-5) or partial DID (ICD-

11). Previously, Nel Draijer and I published several articles and chapters on differential diagnosis based on our research with the SCID-D (Boon & Draijer, 1991, 1993c, 1995a, 1995b, 2011; Draijer & Boon, 1996, 1999). This chapter provides an overview based on our research with the SCID in the 1990s and, following this, many years of diagnostic assessments using the SCID-D and the IDDTS, as well as my own recent research with the TADS-I.

First, I again argue that the presentation of DID may differ during diagnostic interviews, which also has implications for differential diagnosis. Next, I identify the challenges regarding various diagnoses in the DSM-5 and ICD-11 that are often confused with DID and OSDD-1. For some diagnoses the criteria in the ICD-11 differ from those in the DSM-5, so that special attention is warranted where these differences may lead to further confusion. This chapter is primarily concerned with differentiation from other disorders previously included in the Axis I disorders.

Although it will always be possible to differentiate DID from other mental disorders by the presence of a specific cluster of dissociative symptoms, this cluster is not always easy to determine—after all, patients with DID present in many different ways and do not always spontaneously report the entire cluster of symptoms. OSDD-1 and partial DID (in the ICD-11) are harder to differentiate from other disorders precisely because the patient reports less amnesia, and also because amnesia is not even a criterion for OSDD-1 in DSM-5. In order to better identify the polysymptomatic nature of these disorders, a section with questions on possibly trauma-related symptoms was added to the TADS-I. The patient's responses to these questions will provide an additional source of information when performing differential diagnostic assessments (see also Chapter 5).

Table 7.1 lists the main differences in responses and presentations that clinicians should pay attention to when performing a differential diagnosis with a TADS-I.

Various Clinical Presentations of DID, OSDD-1, and Partial DID

Chapter 1 described the challenges caused by the different ways in which DID may present during the diagnostic interview. Nel Draijer and I saw a group of patients whom we diagnosed with DDNOS because they were unable to speak about their dissociative parts. We called this "the initial presentation of DID" (Boon & Draijer, 1993a, 1995a, 1995b; Spiegel et al., 2011). It may often be confusing for clinicians as to how these different presentations of DID can be distinguished from OSDD-1 and partial DID. I list the different presentations of DID below because a differential diagnosis requires clinicians to have a good understanding of these.

TABLE 7.1

Main Differences DID, OSDD-1,
and Partial DID Versus other Mental Disorders

Symptoms, Presentation	DID, OSDD-1, Partial DID	Other Mental Disorders
Possibly trauma-related symptoms (*Part 2 TADS-I*) Differentiate between: 1. Occurs in conjunction with dissociative symptoms indicating a division of the personality; 2. Occurs with symptoms of depersonalization/ derealization and/or absorption; 3. Occurs with both (1) and (2).	Some of the symptoms are always present, particularly PTSD symptoms. • Frequent indications of a division of the personality with symptoms such as amnesia or Schneiderian symptoms in conjunction with the trauma-related symptom • Depersonalization/derealization and/or absorption occur frequently and may or may not be in conjunction with the trauma-related symptom • Often partly ego dystonic narrative, particularly with DID	Some of these symptoms may be present. • No indication of a division of the personality: no amnesia, nor Schneiderian symptoms in conjunction with the trauma-related symptom • Depersonalization/derealization and/or absorption may occur, and may or may not be in conjunction with the trauma-related symptom • Ego syntonic, first-person narrative
Alterations in consciousness (*Part 3 TADS-I*) Depersonalization, derealization, and absorption do not differentiate dissociative disorders from other disorders	Almost always present, depersonalization in particular	Regularly present, may be disorder-related (i.e., depersonalization in anxiety disorders or mood disorders)
Somatoform dissociative symptoms (*Part 4 TADS-I*)	Often present	Absent, except for functional neurological symptom disorder, MUPS, DSM-5 conversion disorder
Psychoform dissociative symptoms (*Part 5 TADS-I*) Amnesia	Present in the form of dissociative amnesia	Absent: Memory problems as a result of absorption or difficulties with attention and/or concentration are not considered as dissociative symptoms
Schneiderian Symptoms/ Intrusions	Present	Absent, except for psychotic disorders—particularly hearing voices—and sometimes borderline personality disorder, but the symptoms differ in quality
Dissociative parts	Present	Absent
Presentation during assessment	• Frequent tension • Discomfort • Dissociation • Anxiety and feelings of shame • Minimizing, downplaying, or rationalizing of symptoms	• No tension • Able to speak about symptoms freely • Ego syntonic, first-person narrative, except for false-positive presentations

DID Presentation 1: Classic DID With Tertiary Structural Dissociation

The patient, a woman in her early 40s, reported the full cluster of symptoms indicating a division of the personality (including amnesia, forms of depersonalization, hearing voices, other Schneiderian symptoms, evidence of dissociative parts). The patient reported amnesia for actions and events in both present and past. The amnesia in the present (e.g., for work, household chores, social activities, and childcare) indicated the existence of several parts with tasks and functions in daily life and parts that were stuck in trauma time. The patient was at least partially aware of the existence of the dissociative parts and was able to say something about them. Based on what she was able to say, the parts appeared to have their own autobiographical memories and their own first-person perspectives (see Chapter 2). According to structural dissociation theory, there was tertiary structural dissociation.

Although this patient reported many comorbid symptoms, using a structured interview such as the SCID-D or TADS-I for patients like her should enable the clinician to differentiate between DID and any other mental disorders, based on a coherent cluster of dissociative symptoms indicating a division of the personality.

DID Presentation 2: Initial Presentation

During his diagnostic interview, the patient, a man in his 50s, reported the full cluster of symptoms indicating a division of the personality (including amnesia for daily life functioning, several forms of depersonalization, hearing voices and other Schneiderian symptoms, and indications for the existence of dissociative parts). In all respects, his presentation was similar to that described in Presentation 1. However, he was either unaware of the existence of any dissociative parts, or he was still very anxious, embarrassed, or phobic about them, and hence unable to report anything about them. The patient had other explanations for his dissociative symptoms such as: *there's something wrong with my head, maybe I have burnout or early dementia.*

Formally, this group of patients is difficult to diagnose when using DSM-5 and ICD-11 criteria. Even though there are numerous clear indications for the existence of dissociative parts, including parts functioning in daily life, patients are not able to report anything about these parts and thus do not meet Criterion A. Previously, this would have led to a DDNOS diagnosis. Nel Draijer and I referred to this as the initial presentation of DID. These patients report a lot of amnesia for tasks and functioning in the present and thus do not meet criteria for OSDD-1, nor for partial DID in the ICD-11. As in the first presentation, there is tertiary structural dissociation, meaning that there is evidence for the existence of multiple parts with tasks and functions in daily life as well as parts stuck in trauma time.

Based on the information on the cluster of dissociative symptoms and clear indications for the existence of dissociative parts, clinicians are able to differentiate DID from all other mental disorders and to tentatively diagnose DID in situations such as these. However, this is not formally possible, unless there is additional information that "the signs and symptoms may be observed by others or reported by the individual" (see Criterion A according to DSM-5). In this case, however, the patient did not allow collateral information to be collected from his family.

DID Presentation 3: DID With Secondary Structural Dissociation

During the diagnostic interview, the patient, a woman in her 30s, mentioned a cluster of symptoms indicating a division of the personality, but no amnesia for tasks and functions in the present. She did report gaps in her memory for the past, and sometimes she also had amnesia for having flashbacks during therapy sessions or for behaviors that were consistent with parts stuck in trauma time (e.g., no memory of binge eating at night or for self-mutilation). There was clear evidence for the existence of parts stuck in trauma time. The patient was more or less aware of this and was able to say something about these parts. The parts had their own autobiographical memories and their own ideas of themselves, others, and the world. According to the structural dissociation theory, there was secondary structural dissociation. Precisely because this form of DID includes no amnesia for tasks and functions in daily life (there is only one part functioning in daily life), it may initially be more difficult to differentiate this presentation from other mental disorders—especially when there is a lot of comorbidity. Sometimes the dissociative wall or barrier between the part functioning in daily life and parts stuck in trauma time is still so significant that the person—the part presenting during the diagnostic interview—does not hear voices from other dissociative parts.

This presentation of DID is therefore more difficult to differentiate from the partial DID classification included in the ICD-11, or from CPTSD. I will further discuss this in Chapter 9.

DID Presentation 4: DID With Full Co-Consciousness

The current first example of OSDD (OSDD-1) in the DSM-5 may, in principle, also relate to actual DID. This may be a presentation of a patient with DID (Presentation 4) who has progressed in treatment to the point where there is full co-consciousness. This implies that in fact there is a great deal of realization as to the existence of dissociative parts, because the part or parts of the person that function in daily life do not have or no longer have amnesia when other parts are present or influence behavior. Yet, these other parts sometimes do have control over the person's actions. In that case, DID applies, even though there is an awareness of the fact that the parts all belong to the same person. *I know very well that this part is me, that it belongs to me, but it really doesn't feel that way and I have no control over it; I hear this part crying, I see it acting, so I'm really aware of it, but it doesn't feel like me and I can't stop the crying.*

Partial amnesia for the trauma history may often still exist in these patients. There may be awareness of what happened, but the emotions and physical sensations are still held by dissociative parts that are stuck in trauma time and thus not integrated. This presentation usually involves secondary structural dissociation with one part functioning in everyday life and a number of parts holding the traumatic experiences. This picture should, however, be differentiated from imitated DID, which will be discussed in more detail in Chapter 10.

Dilemmas in OSDD-1

It is most difficult to understand what is actually meant by the DSM-5 description of OSDD-1. This example is meant for patients who experience identity disturbance but without very clear discontinuity in (less-than-marked) in their sense of self, agency or alterations of identity. (APA, 2013, 2022). What are these symptoms if none of the above forms of DID apply? How are these "less-than-marked discontinuities" identified? For example, how can they be distinguished from the discontinuities or identity diffusion associated with borderline personality disorder or associated with patients diagnosed with CPTSD? What cluster of dissociative symptoms is appropriate? DSM-5 does not provide an answer to this question, while the distinction is often difficult and confusing in clinical practice also (Steele, Boon, & van der Hart, 2017). This is a gray area, in which it may be difficult to determine the distinction between OSDD-1, CPTSD, PTSD with the specification "dissociative subtype," and borderline personality disorder with PTSD symptoms. In such cases the diagnosis that will be given depends mainly on the preference of the individual clinician. This will be discussed in more detail in Chapter 9.

In our earlier research with the SCID-D, as well as the current TADS-I research, and the experience I gained in clinical practice over the past 30 years, I primarily encountered the first four forms of DID and division of personality, with the DDNOS classification often assigned to Presentations 2 and 3. In Table 7.2, I have attempted to summarize the various ways in which DID, OSDD-1, and partial DID may present during diagnostic interviews.

Schizophrenia and Psychotic Disorders

Patients with DID or partial DID/OSDD-1 run the risk of receiving false-positive diagnoses of schizophrenia or psychosis based on having auditory hallucinations and other Schneiderian symptoms. Differential diagnosis

TABLE 7.2

Dissociative Symptom Clusters Associated With Various Presentations of DID, OSDD-1, and Partial DID

Symptoms	DID Tertiary Structural Dissociation	DID Secondary Structural Dissociation	DID Initial Presentation Tertiary or Secondary	DID Full Coconsciousness Secondary or Tertiary	ICD-11 Partial DID Secondary Structural Dissociation	OSDD-1 Secondary Structural Dissociation
Depersonalization, derealization, absorption	Usually present, at least depersonalization	Usually present, at least depersonalization	Usually present, at least depersonalization	Usually present, at least depersonalization	May be present	May be present
Somatoform dissociative symptoms	Often present	Often present	Often present	Often present	May be present	May be present
Amnesia for the present	Present	Only when reexperiencing or switching to a part that is stuck in trauma time	Present in tertiary structural dissociation or when reexperiencing or switching to a part that is stuck in trauma time	Absent	Only when reexperiencing or switching to a part that is stuck in trauma time	Absent / There is coconsciousness
Amnesia for the past	Present	May be present	Often present	May be present for part of trauma	May be present	May be present, also when patient is unaware of it
Schneiderian symptoms/ intrusions	Present	Present, but less frequently reported	Present in tertiary, to a lesser extent in secondary structural dissociation	Present	Present, but sometimes to a lesser extent than with tertiary structural dissociation	Not always evident during the interview, but may be present
Indications of division of the personality	Present	Present	Present	Present	Present	Not always evident during the interview
Realization of dissociative parts	Partly present	Partly present	Absent, unable to talk about parts, is unaware of them	Present	May be present, or patient may be unaware of them	May be present, or patient may be unaware of them

between dissociative disorders and psychotic disorders requires a good understanding of the overlap and differences between psychotic disorders and DID, the qualitative differences in hearing voices, and the differences in content of delusions and hallucinations.

Particularly clinicians in countries where ICD-11 is used should be aware that patients only require two out of seven criteria to receive a classification of schizophrenia. This means that patients with DID or partial DID could easily be missed or misdiagnosed and wrongly receive schizophrenia diagnoses. Thus, it is vital that clinicians explore symptoms as best they can, to determinee whether there is a cluster of dissociative symptoms, particularly amnesia.

Trauma, Dissociation, Psychosis, and Schizophrenia

In recent decades, there has been an increasing theoretical interest in the relationship between trauma, dissociation, and psychotic disorders (Moskowitz et al., 2019; Şar & Oztürk, 2019). Janet (1898), having already observed psychotic disorders involving a dissociation of the personality, spoke of a "hysterical" psychosis in this context. According to Janet, an episode of psychosis could be considered hysterical if its dissociative nature can be identified. His criteria were: (1) the psychosis includes dissociative phenomena (such as amnesia and anesthesia); (2) the psychosis belongs to—in the language of van der Hart and colleagues—a dissociative part of the personality that alternates with other dissociative parts; (3) thus, there is a division of personality; (4) there are unconsious phenomena (such as thoughts, feelings, expressions, and behavioral actions outside the personal awareness). Referring to Janet's pioneering studies, van der Hart and colleagues use the term "dissociative" psychosis to describe this type of psychosis (van der Hart et al., 1993; van der Hart & Witztum, 2019).

The importance of distinguishing this dissociative type of psychosis, according to both Janet and van der Hart and colleagues, is that it can in principle be treated with psychotherapy, sometimes including the use of hypnosis (van der Hart & Spiegel, 1993).

Ross has proposed a dissociative subtype of schizophrenia in which individuals must meet three of the following six criteria (Ross & Keyes, 2004; Şar et al., 2010; Ross, 2019):

1. Dissociative amnesia
2. Depersonalization
3. The presence of two or more distinct identities or personality states
4. Auditory hallucinations
5. Extensive comorbidity
6. Severe childhood trauma

Based on this proposal, the curious situation could arise that patients would meet the classification of dissociative schizophrenia based on the last three criteria, which do not measure dissociation. Laferrière-Simard and colleagues (2014) examined Ross and Keyes's (2004) criteria for dissociative schizophrenia. In a study of 50 patients with a psychotic disorder, they found only 4 patients who met one of Ross's proposed dissociative criteria. One patient met the criteria for DID while three reported depersonalization symptoms. Based on their findings, Laferrière-Simard and colleagues concluded that the first patient should have had DID as the main diagnosis and that there was little basis for a separate classification of dissociative schizophrenia.

In line with the findings of these colleagues and based on my own research and clinical experience, I have some questions about the concept of dissociative schizophrenia. After all, as soon as there is actually a division of the personality with amnesia as an important symptom and possibly other Schneiderian symptoms, it concerns DID, OSDD-1, or partial DID. The question then arises whether a potential classification as dissociative schizophrenia does not result in more confusion rather than creating more clarity.

The distinction between short-term trauma-related psychosis, perhaps to be regarded as a special form of PTSD, and other psychoses and schizophrenia seems more relevant because psychotherapy, possibly supplemented with hypnosis, seems to be a better fit in terms of treatment than medication exclusively. However, more research will be needed on the prevalence and nature and severity of the dissociative symptoms in short-term trauma-related psychosis. The literature on dissociative psychosis is mainly theoretical, with a number of case reviews (Janet, 1894/5; van der Hart et al., 1993; van der Hart & Witztum, 2019).

Several studies examined the prevalence of dissociative symptoms in patients with either a psychotic disorder or schizophrenia (Longden et al., 2020; Renard et al., 2016; Schäfer et al., 2019). Almost all of these studies are based on self-reporting using the DES. Although some of these studies show that schizophrenic patients have a higher mean DES score than patients without a mental disorder, it is striking that these scores are usually well below the DES cutoff score and in most studies even below the most conservative cutoff score of 20 (Schäfer et al., 2019). Patients with dissociative disorders (Lyssenko et al., 2018) have mean scores ranging from 38.9 (all dissociative disorders) to 48.7 (DID). Patients in the schizophrenia spectrum mainly report absorption, depersonalization, and derealization but no symptoms indicating a division of the personality. However, a significant number of patients with schizophrenia or a psychotic disorder report a history of early childhood traumatization (Braehler et al., 2013; Dorahy et al., 2009; Read et al., 2005; Şar et al., 2010; Schäfer et al., 2006, Scott et al., 2018).

A limitation of all these studies is that early childhood traumatization is not unambiguously defined. In addition, there are different views worldwide about the concept of psychosis and schizophrenia. As a result, in some countries a patient with DID is much more likely to be labeled psychotic or schizophrenic than in other countries.

Overlap and Differences Between Psychotic Disorders and DID

DID is often confused with a psychotic disorder or schizophrenia. On the surface, there are similarities between certain symptoms, especially since the vast majority of patients with DID are hearing voices and also report other Schneiderian symptoms (Brand, Spindler, & Cannon, 2019; Foote & Park, 2008; Kluft, 1987a; Laddis & Dell, 2012; Longden et al., 2020; Pilton et al., 2015; Ross et al., 1990b; Steinberg, 2019; Welburn et al., 2003). Several studies have shown that there is mainly an overlap of positive symptoms of schizophrenia, but not of negative symptoms (Ellason & Ross, 1995; Longden et al., 2020; Tschöke et al., 2011).

Absorption, depersonalization, and derealization symptoms are also common in DID, as well as in psychotic disorders and schizophrenia (Longden et al., 2020; Moskowitz et al., 2018; Renard et al., 2016). Although reality testing is usually intact in patients with DID, sometimes a patient can be briefly overwhelmed by traumatic memories, intrusions from dissociative parts, or flashbacks, any of which may distort reality. During such moments, the patient's consciousness is dominated by the experiences of dissociative parts stuck in trauma time. It is striking that even if the consciousness of one or sometimes more parts is distorted when, for example, reexperiencing a traumatizing event, other parts are well oriented in the here and now and often can also explain what is going on. However, these parts are not always immediately accessible. Often the part that is reliving a traumatizing experience must first calm down and only then can another part that is well-oriented in the here and now take over so that the patient's reality is not distorted any longer. In any case, it is important to distinguish these hallucinations from the psychotic experiences of patients in the schizophrenia spectrum. In this last group one cannot address another part with intact reality testing. Numerous examples of nonpsychotic hallucinations have been described in Chapter 2. However, on careful further questioning, the symptoms consistent with DID differ markedly in quality compared to the symptoms associated with psychotic disorders and schizophrenia. Moreover, DID can be differentiated from other disorders by the presence of a cluster of coherent disso-ciative symptoms indicating division of the personality, including amnesia and identity alteration or switching (Boon & Draijer, 1993a; Foote & Park, 2008; Steinberg et al., 1994; Welburn et al., 2003). This cluster of disso-ciative symptoms does not occur in patients with psychotic disorder and schizophrenia.

Qualitative Differences in Voice Hearing

The vast majority of patients with DID report hearing voices inside their head and occasionally outside their head. They are well aware that other people cannot hear these voices. Usually there are different voices and they often represent different genders. The voices may sound older or younger than the patient's voice. Female patients usually also hear male voices and vice versa. In addition, patients often hear children's voices or even the sounds of crying babies. In most cases, the voices are described as two or more voices having discussions about the patient, voices making negative comments about the patient's behavior, or voices commanding the patient to engage in self-injurious behavior or prohibiting the patient from continu-ing with their treatment and sometimes from continuing with the diagnos-tic interview. The voices may also ridicule the patient (i.e., the part that is functioning in daily life). However, kind or caring voices are also heard. Sometimes the voices speak in a different language or dialect.

Hearing voices is not linked to particular episodes, as is the case with psy-choses. Most patients report hearing the voices fairly constantly, although in general the activity of the voices tend to increase with higher stress lev-els or when difficult decisions have to be made. For example, during a diag-nostic interview patients may start hearing voices telling them not to talk or threatening to punish the patient after the interview.

Some patients describe a kind of murmur or background noise, while oth-ers say there is a cacophony or war going on in their head. Many patients reported that they had actually been hearing voices for a long time, often as children, but initially thought it was quite normal or that everyone else was hearing them too. At some point, there was a sudden realization that this is in fact *not normal*, causing fear and shame. The thought of *being crazy* may also arise because the voices have been interpreted by clinicians as psychotic during diagnostic assessment or treatment.

The voices are not an isolated symptom but occur as part of a cluster of dissociative symptoms, such as amnesia, other symptoms of passive influences (Schneiderian symptoms), depersonalization, derealization, and other evidence of division of the personality. Antipsychotics generally have no effect on hearing the voices.

Dorahy et al. (2009) compared voice hearing in 29 patients with DID with voice hearing in 34 patients with schizophrenia. In contrast to patients with schizophrenia, patients with DID more often reported that they heard voices before age 18, they heard more than two voices, and they heard both adults' and children's voices. Also, the patients with DID reported more visual, tactile, and olfactory hallucinations than the schizophrenia group. Sometimes the patients in this group also heard voices outside their head.

In DID, partial DID, and OSDD-1, there are no formal thought disorders. Unlike in schizophrenia or psychotic disorders, thinking in DID is not characterized by incoherence or marked disorganization nor disorganized speech. Some dissociative parts may appear flat or depersonalized. Reality testing is intact, except when dissociative parts that are stuck in trauma time temporarily dominate the patient's consciousness. The latter occurs mainly in a state of fear or panic, such as reliving traumatizing events. In such cases, the patient is temporarily overwhelmed by vehement emotions, may appear psychotic, may experience reality as distorted, and may sometimes exhibit disorganized behavior. However, this is generally of short duration.

Differences in the Content of Delusions and Hallucinations

In patients with DID, the hallucinations and delusional beliefs are usually linked to past traumatic experiences. The content of delusions and hallucinations is not bizarre, but when there is amnesia for the original traumatic experiences, the hallucinations may cause much confusion or the feeling of being crazy. In patients with schizophrenia and psychotic disorders, the delusions and hallucinations are often bizarre and usually unrelated to previous traumatic experiences. For example, one patient with a psychotic disorder thought that a famous soccer player was asking her out via the television. She believed that she heard him talking to her through the TV and she also saw a message in the subtitles that, according to her, was meant specifically for her. A patient with schizophrenia was convinced that, as a follower of Jesus, he was destined to save humanity from corrupt political ideas.

In Chapter 2, I presented several examples of delusions and hallucinations in patients with DID that could sometimes briefly impair reality testing. Recently, the first study appeared that compared delusional beliefs of patients with DID with those of patients with schizophrenia spectrum disorder (SPS), both in terms of content and the degree of conviction, preoccupation, and distress (Martinez et al., 2020). The delusional beliefs clearly differed in content. The SPS group reported more different types of delusions, especially self-referential delusional beliefs, whereas the DID group reported more mistrust delusional beliefs and characteristics. Additionally, depersonalization and derealization experiences in the DID group appeared to be a predictor for mistrust beliefs, whereas these experiences did not predict any delusions in the SPS group. Strong beliefs based on distrust can be understood as originating from the severe trauma histories reported by most patients with DID.

Table 7.3 summarizes the differences and similarities between patients with DID, partial DID, or OSDD-1, and patients with schizophrenia spectrum and other psychotic disorders.

TABLE 7.3 Differences and Similarities Between DID and Schizophrenia Spectrum Disorders		
Symptoms, Behaviors, Presentation	DID, OSDD-1, Partial DID	Schizophrenia Spectrum and Other Related Psychotic Disorders
Possibly trauma-related symptoms	Often in conjunction with indications of a division of the personality (e.g., amnesia, hearing voices)	Not in conjunction with indications of a division of the personality (e.g., amnesia, hearing voices)
Depersonalization, derealization, absorption	Usually present	Often present, particularly during psychotic episodes
Amnesia, fugues, indirect indications of amnesia`	Present, particularly with DID and to a lesser extent with partial DID and OSDD-1	Absent; sometimes absorption is mistaken for amnesia
Auditory hallucinations	Mostly present, particularly with DID Patients: 1. Usually hear voices of various sorts, both children's and adults' 2. Hear voices mostly inside the head 3. Hear voices continuously 4. Often hear voices starting before age 18 5. Hear voices belonging to dissociative parts	Can be present, in particular during psychotic episodes Patients: 1. Report fewer voices (no children's voices) 2. Hear voices inside and outside the head 3. Do not hear voices continuously, mostly during psychoses 4. Start hearing voices during their first psychosis

Other first order Schneiderian symptoms (positive symptoms)	Present, often having an "as if" quality[10] • Reality testing is intact, at least in one of the parts • Multiple coexisting realities belonging to several dissociative parts • Content, particularly mistrust relating to trauma and dissociative parts that hold these memories	Present, during psychotic episodes • Reality testing is not intact • There is a single reality • Content is often bizarre; self-referential delusions
Negative symptoms of schizophrenia, loss of initiative, chronic flattened affectivity, catatonic behavior	Absent; sometimes behaviors of depersonalized parts are mistaken for negative symptoms	Present, particularly in schizophrenia
Cognitive functions	Intact	Not intact; often formal thought disorders
Indications of dissociative parts	Present	Absent
Presentation during assessment	• Avoidance, anxiety, shame about talking about dissociative symptoms • Intrusions of dissociative parts • Dissociation frequently visible during assessment	• No avoidance or anxiety, speaking freely of dissociative symptoms • No intrusions of dissociative parts • No visible dissociation during the assessment

*For example, being confronted with behaviors or finding things that the patient bought or did for which there is amnesia.

Case Report: A Patient With Schizophrenia

Mr. A. was a 32-year-old man. He had been living in an assisted living facility for a few years now. Mr. A. had referred himself, as he was wondering whether he had a so-called split personality. He had read something about this on the internet. Mr. A., who was from a highly educated, religious family, had had his first psychotic episode at age 19 after he had just embarked on a computer programming course. During this first episode of psychosis,

---

10 As if quality of a (psychotic) symptom means that the person (or at least a part of the person knows (cognitively) that the experience (e.g., seeing little insects crawling over your arms) is not real or not really happening even though it feels very real. There is a cognitive correction that is not present in a true psychotic person.

he had received messages from the universe telling him to address the animal suffering in the world. He had been an inpatient in a psychiatric hospital for several months and never managed to finish his computer training. He would alternate between staying with his parents and being in various psychiatric institutions. It was only the last few years that he had been feeling better and was no longer hospitalized. He felt this may have been due to receiving antipsychotics by depot injection. Previously, he would stop taking his medication or start self doctoring.

General

First impressions. The patient appeared to have a friendly but shallow affect. The patient was severely overweight. Sometimes, he answered elaborately, and sometimes it was hard for him to give examples of the symptoms he experienced.

Possibly Trauma-Related Symptoms

The patient reported hardly any trauma-related symptoms, nor any dissociative symptoms in conjunction with the trauma-related symptoms he did describe. He denied using alcohol and recreational drugs at the time of the interview, but had been smoking weed for a while, just before he had his first psychosis. *I've since learned that that doesn't help much*, he added. The patient had difficulties with being severely overweight as a result of his medication. He used to be skinny and athletic. He had never had any eating problems. The patient explained the medication was helping him sleep well and that he had to be careful not to stay in bed too long. He spontaneously described having trouble with getting himself to do things and that he would sometimes sit in his room for days. The patient denied ever feeling anxious and did not describe any PTSD symptoms. He experienced a flat mood and felt this was caused by his medication. In the past, he had been suicidal a few times, unable to accept this life. He explained that this had happened mostly when he was still living at home.

The patient claimed that his parents had difficulty accepting his illness; no one in the family had ever experienced psychoses. His sisters and brother all had successful careers. He had been expected to do the same. He repeated that he had been doing much better since he had started living in an assisted living facility. The patient explained that it was especially during psychotic episodes that he no longer knew who he was. He had since realized that he would have what he called very *crazy thoughts* when this happened. He also said that he had been very disappointed with himself and what had become of him. Initially, he had tried to continue his studies, but this did not work out. When asked what he meant by *split personality*, he had no coherent answer. Eventually he did say: *Perhaps I was hoping you might have a different therapy. I'm really a totally different person when I'm psychotic. I read about dissociation on the internet and wondered whether this would be similar.*

The patient had a few friends he had met in the psychiatric setting. He was no longer in touch with his high school friends nor with the friends he had met at the start of his training. He had no sexual contacts and said he did not feel the need to have any at present.

Alterations in Consciousness

The patient did describe depersonalization and derealization symptoms during his psychotic episodes. He would feel different, and things would become unreal. He had never experienced being outside his body and looking at himself from a distance. His psychoses were often related to animal suffering and sometimes to people he felt had to be saved. When he was not psychotic, he did not experience any derealization but did report feeling like some kind of zombie. In his case, this seemed more consistent with negative symptoms of schizophrenia from which he was suffering substantially and possibly with his medication. The patient reported being able to spend hours gaming. He had always spent a lot of time on his computer, even in high school. In such situations he would hardly notice time passing by.

Somatoform and Psychoform Dissociative Symptoms

The patient did not report any somatoform dissociative symptoms and described few psychoform dissociative symptoms. For example, he did not describe having amnesia and appeared to have a good recall. During psychotic episodes he did hear a voice. He felt this was a kind of messenger from the universe who was passing messages to him. The messages always came from outside. Once or twice, he heard more than one voice. With a smile he added that this made sense since there was more than one prophet, too. During psychotic episodes, he would receive special orders and be convinced that he had a mission in this world.

The voices' influence diminished as soon as he took his medication or increased the dose of his medication. He added that he did not hear the voice when he was not psychotic, like during the current interview. Apart from hearing a voice during psychotic episodes, he acknowledged receiving messages, for example through music compositions on the radio that were specifically meant for him.

When asked about dissociative parts, he stated that he felt he had a different identity when psychotic. *I'm a totally different person then, which is why I thought of this split personality.* He then suddenly wondered whether he had been an animal in a past life. During psychotic episodes he often saw images of street dogs being horribly maltreated. He felt his psychotic episodes may have had something to do with this.

Summary and Conclusion

There was no indication of a dissociative disorder. Depersonalization, derealization, and hearing a voice or voices were consistent with the psychoses and differed in quality from symptoms that are described by patients with DID.

Depressive Disorders

Patients with DID, partial DID, or OSDD-1 report many symptoms that may be consistent with a depressive disorder. As described in Chapter 1, many of these symptoms, such as dysphoria, irritability, sleep disturbances, or feelings of guilt and despair, as well as suicidal thoughts and acts, may also be understood as trauma-related symptoms in patients with dissociative disorders. In those cases, symptoms are related to or held by specific parts of the personality. Moreover, the clinical pictures and patterns of symptoms may vary greatly, depending on the dissociative part of the personality dominating the patient's consciousness. Not all parts feel depressed or suicidal; these are specifically the parts that are holding the emotions related to the trauma. This implies there may be more and faster alternations or switches between depressive and nondepressive moods. Of course, there may be a comorbid depressive disorder. However, when there are depressive symptoms, suicidality, and, for example, symptoms of CPTSD, it is key to carefully examine whether there may also be a dissociative disorder such as DID, OSDD-1, or partial DID. If so, in addition to the symptoms consistent with a depressive disorder, there will be a cluster of dissociative symptoms, including amnesia and hearing voices, for example related to suicidal behaviors, but also to other nonsuicidal behaviors. Suicidal acts are often executed by parts that are stuck in trauma time. The part that is functioning in daily life may have amnesia for these behaviors. Patients may also report hearing a voice commanding them to commit suicide or being an observer of their own acts without being able to intervene. Patients may say: *That's not me. I can see it happening. I'm hanging right above it, without being able to prevent things from happening.*

Bipolar and Related Disorders

It was pointed out in DSM-5 that DID is often misdiagnosed as bipolar disorder, particularly bipolar II disorder. The reverse, where DID is suspected or considered when it is not present, may also occur but probably less often. It is especially the rapid mood swings in DID, caused by the various dissociative parts, that may be confusing. Patients with DID may also appear hypomanic, but their mood and behaviors are qualitatively different from bipolar disorder. Hyperactivity, constantly being busy, and not being able to stop one or sometimes several activities are frequent symptoms in patients with DID. Hyperactivity may be anxiety driven and may lead to avoidance behavior. Patients have a tendency to keep going, because stopping invokes a fear of being overwhelmed with painful emotions and memories. Several examples of this may be found in Chapters 5 and 6. Patients are essentially running ahead of a perceived tsunami. This behavior may be more pronounced around or during anniversary responses[11] of original traumatizing events. It is often the parts functioning in daily life that are continuously driven into urgent actions and become exhausted. These parts often are not conscious of any anxiety or other reasons to keep going; it has become a natural survival mode. The hyperactive mood in DID differs from that in patients who are truly hypomanic. They experience no anxiety but rather excessive high-spiritedness or euphoria, like walking on clouds, sometimes accompanied by thoughts of grandiosity.

In our study with the SCID-D (Boon & Draijer, 1993b, p. 129 ff.), Nel Draijer and I found that 12% (n = 5) of patients in a random control group (n = 45) without dissociative disorder had a cluster of moderate to severe dissociative symptoms on the SCID-D. All five patients met the criteria for schizoaffective disorder and four met the criteria for personality disorder on the SCID-D. However, the SCID-D severity scores do not distinguish between dissociative symptoms that indicate a division of the personality (i.e., "pathological dissociative" symptoms) and the other alterations in consciousness such as depersonalization, derealization, and absorption. As a result, patients may receive a relatively high total score on the SCID-D; that is, they may score "severe" on several of the five symptom clusters of the SCID-D without having a dissociative disorder. Patients mostly mentioned depersonalization and derealization—and to a lesser extent memory problems—during or shortly after psychotic or manic episodes. Some also mentioned identity confusion related to behavior in hypomanic or manic episodes. They did not endorse any symptoms indicating division of the personality. More recently, I used the TADS-I to examine bipolar patients who were suspected of DID but were not diagnosed as such based on their responses during the interview. In one case, the patient also had PTSD symptoms. An example of this is given below.

Case Report: A Patient With Bipolar II Disorder

The patient was a single woman in her mid-40s. She had a good relationship with her adult son. For years, she had been treated for bipolar II disorder

---

11 An anniversary response is an increase in symptoms (e.g., PTSD, dissociation, anxiety) on or around the day that the original traumatizing event took place.

and was alternating between depressive and hypomanic episodes. During a recent hypomanic episode, the patient was assaulted after a night out in a bar. Although she was able to flee and stated that, apart from being touched inappropriately, nothing had really happened, she developed several PTSD symptoms, in particular hypervigilance, flashbacks, and nightmares. After some hesitation, she told her psychiatrist about this, who referred her for EMDR therapy. During her first EMDR session she was unexpectedly overwhelmed by memories of earlier abuse. Her symptoms increased and she refused to receive further EMDR treatment. It turned out that for several months the patient had been sexually abused by her brother-in-law, when she was around 14 years old. She had not forgotten about this, but she had never mentioned it during treatment. During the interview she reported feeling shame as she had not resisted, but actually participated.

> I was in love with him, but also disgusted with myself. My older sister was pregnant and he told me that it was no big deal at all, that in many cultures men have multiple wives. But he also made me do things I didn't want to do at all. And he kept on saying that I enjoyed it and wanted it myself. So horrible. He threatened that it would destroy my sister if I ever told her. It was all my fault. He dropped me like a ton of bricks when he was able to have sex with her again.

Her early childhood was highly influenced by her mother's psychoses that resulted in frequent hospitalizations. Her dad used to work long days and was absent a lot of the time. She would be the one taking care of the household and her younger brother. Her older sister had left the house at an early age and it was her older sister's husband who had abused her. The patient had been emotionally deprived as a child.

Because the EMDR session did not go well and the patient scored high on the DES (with an average of 35), she was referred for a diagnostic interview.

General

First Impressions. The patient was open and somewhat disinhibited in her interaction. She was talking continuously but was aware of it and apologized for it. *I'm still very dysregulated*, she said. There was no discernable tension or dissociation during the interview.

Possibly Trauma-Related Symptoms

The patient reported drinking a lot occasionally, particularly when she was hypomanic. She had never experienced an alcohol blackout. There were also periods during which she did not drink at all. She had never used any recreational drugs.

The patient did not report any eating problems. She explained that she had various and alternating problems with sleeping. When depressed, she would wake up very early in the morning but would not have trouble falling asleep; when hypomanic, she would sleep less. At such times she would go to bed really late and hardly get any sleep, until she was completely exhausted. There were also periods in which she did not experience any sleep issues. She added that she had never had nightmares before and that she had not thought about her brother-in-law for years. Her sister had divorced shortly after the birth of their second child and the patient had never seen her brother-in-law again. Now she did have nightmares about her brother-in-law. She had mainly felt really bad and guilty about it but had never experienced this kind of sleep problem prior. She was very shocked that the memories had suddenly returned as a result of the EMDR session. She never found any evidence of getting up at night or doing things without remembering it afterward. She would also know exactly where she was when waking up from nightmares.

The patient denied having any anxiety or panic symptoms. Her mood would vary greatly, but her depressive or hypomanic episodes were of longer duration. She was never psychotic but she added she had sometimes been *on the verge.*

> When hypomanic, I can handle anything. It's a wonderful feeling. I'm not afraid of anything, but I also know that I have done some pretty foolish things. I used to quit taking my medication, but I no longer do this now. At some point I will have exhausted myself completely and the whole thing turns into a depression that may last for months.

The patient did feel suicidal but said that she would never end her life. She could not do that to her son. When asked whether her abilities might vary, she replied: *Well, of course, I'm a totally different person when I'm depressed. I can't get anything done and this is totally different from when I'm hypomanic.* The change in her abilities seemed to be related to her two extreme moods, which is different from what happens in patients with DID. The patient never self-harmed nor did she exhibit self-injurious behaviors. She said that her self-image would vary a lot, ranging from very positive to negative, something she felt was related to her mood changes. She also said that since having EMDR, she had been tormented by very negative feelings about herself and what she and her brother-in-law had done. The patient did not describe any internal conflicts. They used to be present but would always be related to her taking or not taking her medication.

The patient had stable and long-lasting friendships, more so with women than with men. She had had boyfriends several times but said she would never want to live with anyone again. The patient said she had used to end up in bed with men all the time when she was hypomanic. This had not happened for years by the time of the interview. *As my son grew older, I really didn't want this. I wanted to be there for him.* She said she never avoided having sexual relationships, but also never looked for them. The patient did not describe any dissociative symptoms related to sexual contacts, including with her brother-in-law at the time.

> In fact, I felt everything: arousal—it was exciting—even though I didn't want to do everything he wanted me to do. But then I felt disgusted with myself; I should never have done it. Now, this also happens in my nightmares; I become some kind of perverse whore.

EVALUATION OF TRAUMA-RELATED SYMPTOMS

The patient did not report any dissociative symptoms that may be associated with possibly trauma-related symptoms at any time. The patient did describe nightmares and some symptoms of PTSD, but no episodes of reexperiencing trauma. It was not as if she was reliving the abuse all over. It was more that she was overwhelmed by feelings of guilt and disgust with herself, which was also the theme of her nightmares.

Alterations in Consciousness

The patient mainly described feelings of depersonalization during hypomanic episodes.

> You're really not your normal self then. I feel strange, but in a pleasant way; it's like I'm in some kind of movie and my imagination is getting the better of me. I will have the most fantastic plans and ideas and my thoughts are going all over the place. Everything seems to be in overdrive.

The patient did not acknowledge derealization but did report signs of absorption. *When I'm hypomanic, I can walk for hours; I don't really feel tired and hardly notice where I am or where I've been walking. I get lost sometimes, when I'm completely absorbed in my thoughts and plans.* Sometimes, she would end up somewhere without remembering where she was or where she had been walking. These problems seemed to be related to absorption and depersonalization.

Somatoform Dissociative Symptoms

The patient explained she was not really in touch with her body during hypomanic episodes. She would go on and on without feeling hunger or thirst. She would also hardly feel how tired her body was. Apart from this, she did not report any somatoform dissociative symptoms.

Psychoform Dissociative Symptoms

The patient did not describe any examples of dissociative amnesia. She generally had a good memory. However, she did acknowledge having problems with concentration: when fully absorbed in her thoughts, she would not be aware of her surroundings and her perception of time would be distorted. This mainly happened during hypomanic episodes. She did not describe any Schneiderian symptoms. The patient never heard voices and never experienced psychotic episode. Only when asked whether something within herself might cause her to behave very differently did she say that she would feel very confused about her behavior during hypomanic episodes.

> When there's something inside me that I can't control anymore, it seems I can be two entirely different persons: one is very confident and can take on the world, and a depressed person who can't cope with things anymore. Of course, I know very well that this is all to do with my moods.

The description of her two moods and her perception of two seemingly different persons rather differ from the dissociative parts that are described by patients with DID.

Summary and Conclusion

There were no indications of DID, partial DID, or OSDD-1. During the interview, the patient described no dissociative symptoms indicating a division of the personality. All of her symptoms were consistent with bipolar II disorder. Apart from this disorder, the patient described some PTSD symptoms but did not meet the criteria for a diagnosis of PTSD. There were no indications she had been dissociating during the abuse and was now truly reexperiencing the abuse. The patient was mostly struggling with intense feelings of guilt and shame. Closer inspection of the relatively high DES score (35) mainly revealed elevated scores on absorption and depersonalization items.

Anxiety Disorders and Obsessive–Compulsive Disorder

Patients with DID, OSDD-1, or partial DID report numerous anxiety symptoms such as panic attacks, specific phobias or persistent thoughts, or obsessive–compulsive behaviors. The specific phobias are mostly related to the original traumas, but patients may not be aware of this at all. In the recent study with the TADS-I, all DID patients mentioned symptoms of anxiety; some experienced them daily, others indicated that this could vary a lot (Boon, 2021, unpublished data).

> I wouldn't call myself anxious. Well . . . this varies a lot, really. I often do things my friends say they would never dare to do, but I just do it. I don't really feel much, certainly no fear. But then again, on other moments, I find myself terrified, hiding in a closet. I often have no idea how I got there, but my heart is pounding in my throat, I feel very small and I really expect that at any moment someone will come and kill me. At such times I really don't dare come out of the closet. Sometimes, I stay in there for hours. Then, hours later, I find myself somewhere else in my house. And I really don't remember getting out of the closet.

This example shows that exploring anxiety symptoms may result in DID patients spontaneously reporting amnesia related to scary moments. It would appear that, when hiding in the closet, the patient may have been dissociated in a child part that was terrified and was influencing her thinking and acting at that moment. Examples like these are obviously not reported by patients with anxiety disorders unless there is a comorbid dissociative disorder.

Other compulsive symptoms, like compulsive washing or showering and also cleaning compulsions, are often reported by patients with DID, OSDD-1, or partial DID. Such compulsions usually belong to specific parts of the personality as well, and are often related to the traumatization, particularly sexual abuse. They are a strategy of one or several dissociative parts to cope with overwhelming fear. In addition to the compulsive behavior a cluster of severe dissociative symptoms is reported.

Both the SCID-D and TADS-I can successfully distinguish patients with anxiety and compulsive disorders from patients with dissociative disorders, as the first lack the typical cluster of dissociative symptoms.

Case Report: A Patient With Chronic Anxiety Symptoms

The patient was a 45-year-old single woman. She worked one afternoon per week as a volunteer. She had been severely emotionally neglected during childhood. Her mother had had serious mental health problems and her father had drunk a lot. As the oldest child, she carried a lot of responsibilities for her younger brother and sister. When she was an adolescent, one of her cousins had sexually assaulted her. The patient was treated for anxiety symptoms for several years. Her therapist wondered whether the patient had more dissociative symptoms, as she had reported having frequent depersonalization symptoms and was confused about her identity.

General

First Impressions. The patient made little eye contact and indicated that she was not feeling very comfortable. This changed somewhat during the interview: she seemed to relax a bit more and was able to articulate her symptoms well.

Substance Use and Medication. The patient never used alcohol or recreational drugs.

Possibly Trauma-Related Symptoms

The patient did not report any eating problems. She was a poor sleeper, particularly because she often worried about her life and her fears. With medication, she was able to sleep well. She suffered from nightmares or reexperiencing associated with the abuse by her cousin. She explained that she did not consider the abuse to be her biggest problem. It was more the thought that she was not allowed or able to exist in the way she wanted to.

Mood and Emotion Regulation. The patient became depressed when she finally moved out to live on her own at age 35. The family doctor prescribed antidepressants. She was no longer depressed at the time of the interview, but her world was still very small. She had often been depressed but had never attempted to end her life.

Anxiety and Panic. For as long as the patient could remember, she had been anxious, including a fear of dying or getting sick and then being at the mercy of other people. She had also suffered from panic attacks for a long time; they were occurring weekly at the time of the interview. These panic attacks would appear out of nowhere and were associated with nausea, palpitations, and dizziness. The patient also described having depersonalization and sometimes derealization during these attacks. The attacks would sometimes ebb away, but she would normally take medication (lorazepam) immediately. After an attack she was afraid to do anything and was unable, for example, to go to the supermarket for groceries. She would also find it hard to walk her dog. For years she had been avoiding many things and had lived at home to take care of her parents.

The patient described that, in addition to the anxiety symptoms, she also suffered from obsessive–compulsive behaviors. For example, she often felt compelled to count out a certain number of repetitions in her head or turn the lights on and off 20 times. She also feared actually having no right to exist.

Self-Image and Identity. The patient had a negative self-image and felt others did not really know her. *I don't dare to open up. I'm always afraid of what might happen if I did: that others will disapprove of me.* She felt that she did not know who she was and whether she was allowed to exist. She said she was always adapting to the other person and to what she thought others would expect of her.

The patient had had a number of friends since childhood, but felt her network was too small. She was still taking care of her parents a lot. She once had a boyfriend with whom she also had a sexual relationship. At the time, she was still strongly connected to her parents and family and not sufficiently independent. According to her, that was the reason she broke up with him. *I didn't really dare to connect with him. After this relationship, it just never happened again,* she explained, adding that she did not really miss it.

EVALUATION OF POSSIBLY TRAUMA-RELATED SYMPTOMS

The patient denied having symptoms consistent with PTSD or dissociative symptoms indicating division of the personality. Depersonalization symptoms frequently occurred in association with her panic attacks. Additionally, she described typical examples of being detached and having difficulty connecting with others. Her identity problems also differed in quality from those of a patient with DID, as they were not caused by inner conflicts between dissociative parts.

Somatoform and Psychoform Dissociative Symptoms

During the follow-up interview, the patient did not report any symptoms consistent with DID, OSDD-1, or partial DID. She did not report any somatoform dissociative symptoms. She had a good memory and did not report any dissociative amnesia. She never heard any voices and did not report any Schneiderian symptoms.

Conclusion

This patient appeared to have panic disorder and possibly avoidant personality disorder symptoms.

Substance-Related Disorders

Several studies have been conducted on dissociative symptoms with patients with alcohol and/or drug addiction. The following is an overview of the findings and an explanation of differential diagnosis.

Data on Dissociative Symptoms Among Patients With Alcohol and/or Drug Addiction

Research on the relationship between substance use and dissociative symptoms and disorders provides conflicting data. For example, several studies using the DES found no clear relationship between alcohol dependence and dissociative experiences (Langeland et al., 2002; Schäfer et al., 2007; Schäfer et al., 2010). Schäfer and colleagues conducted a large multicenter study in Germany of patients (n = 459) with different forms of substance dependence. When the DES was administered, all patients who participated in this study (the same as in the study by Langeland et al., 2002) were in withdrawal and were no longer using any substances. Slightly higher mean DES scores were found in patients with a drug addiction (mean DES 12.9 with a standard deviation [SD] of 11.7) than in those with an alcohol addiction (mean DES 9.9 with SD 8.8). The highest mean DES was found in the group that was both alcohol and drug dependent (mean DES of 15.1 with SD 11.3).

Although no diagnostic interview was used in these studies to identify or exclude dissociative disorders diagnoses, almost all DES scores were well below the various cutoff points (usually 20, 25, or sometimes 30). This would suggest a low prevalence of dissociative disorders in this population. However, there appeared to be a relationship between the level of mean DES scores and the severity of traumatic experiences in childhood, with higher scores in patients who reported childhood traumatization. One explanation for the low DES scores would be that some traumatized individuals might be less capable of mental dissociation and, therefore, more inclined to use substances, especially drugs, to feel less or to achieve some sort of "dissociative state" (Langeland et al., 2004).

Another study examined the relationship between PTSD, substance dependence, and dissociation with a range of instruments (Najavits & Walsh, 2012). This study included 77 female outpatients with PTSD and current substance abuse in the past month. The mean DES score was 19.44 with an SD of 19.26. The patients were then categorized into a high (DES > 30) and low (DES < 30) DES group. Twenty-one percent of the patients had a DES score higher than 30, and this group reported many more PTSD symptoms than the participants with DES scores lower than 30.

Other studies, particularly several Turkish studies, show a relationship between higher mean DES scores and substantial prevalence of dissociative disorders in addicted patients (Evren et al., 2007; Karadag et al., 2005; Tamar-Gurol et al., 2008). For example, a mean DES score of 24.5 (with an SD of 17.5) was found among inpatients (n = 215) successively admitted to an addiction treatment unit of a large psychiatric hospital in Istanbul, Turkey (Karadag et al., 2005). Over 36% had DES scores higher than 30. Based on examination with the DDIS or SCID-D, the prevalence of DSM-IV dissociative disorders in this group was 17.2% for all dissociative disorders. Among patients with substance dependence, several studies in North America found a prevalence of dissociative disorders of 15.0% (Dunn et al., 1995) up to as high as 39.0% (Ross et al., 1992). As noted for previous prevalence studies (see Chapter 1), the results are influenced by the diagnostic instrument used and possibly also by a different cultural interpretation of the symptoms (Şar, 2011). The DDIS typically gives higher prevalence scores (Friedl et al., 2000).

Data on Alcohol and Drug Addiction Among Patients With Dissociative Disorders

In our study of 71 patients with DID, over 32% reported ever having had alcohol problems, while 14% reported very severe addiction problems. Over 22% had used drugs, with 7% of them having had a severe drug addiction. Other studies found even higher numbers of patients with comorbid addiction problems (Ellason et al., 1996; Ross, Norton, & Wozney, 1989).

In a study examining the treatment of 280 patients with DID and DDNOS, 22% had comorbid addiction problems or substance dependence (Brand, Classen, Lanius, et al., 2009). Şar (2011) also points out the comorbidity involving addiction and dissociative disorders in an article on the epidemiology of dissociative disorders.

Implications for the Assessment

Thus, studies of the prevalence of dissociative symptoms and disorders among patients with addiction problems show inconsistent results. In studies involving patients with dissociative disorders, comorbid addiction problems are found in 20% to 40% of patients. This provides sufficient grounds for screening patients with addiction problems and PTSD for a possible dissociative disorder.

The clinician will need to carefully differentiate between symptoms indicating a division of the personality and symptoms that are due to substances, such as depersonalization and out-of-body experiences due to ketamine, or between blackout due to excessive alcohol abuse. In fact, in my studies with the SCID-D and TADS-I, I found that dissociative patients who also used substances were usually able to indicate the distinction very clearly. For example, a female patient with DID who occasionally used a lot of alcohol gave the following answers about amnesia:

PATIENT: Sometimes I wake up feeling very lousy. I feel nauseated and light-headed, and I have bad breath. Then I know it's been that way again.

CLINICIAN: What do you mean by that?

PATIENT: Well, it would seem that I have had way too much to drink again. I hate it and don't remember it. But there used to be times in the past when I was very aware of going to the bar, getting drunk, coming home, and the next day sort of blacking out.

CLINICIAN: Do you also have problems with your memory when you haven't been drinking?

PATIENT: Yeah, I used to think that everything was because of the alcohol, or that I simply had Korsakoff's or something. But I don't drink all the time, actually: it's episodes, and sometimes not at all for a few months, so I often don't know how it starts. I find out afterwards because I feel so awful. But there are lots of other things I don't remember, even when I haven't been drinking at all.

CLINICIAN: Can you give an example?

PATIENT: Well, I will not be able to remember what I did on a day, but then sometimes I seem to have done my administration or it may happen that I saw a friend and can't remember it. It can be anything really.

CLINICIAN: And how do you know that you haven't had any alcohol?

PATIENT: Oh, I really can't do any administration when I've been drinking, and this friend, she doesn't drink a drop at all and is just always nagging me to be careful with alcohol! Besides, I can clearly notice the difference in how I feel. It's a totally different thing when I've drunk so much: when I "come to," I feel really sick.

This patient reported different types of amnesia, sometimes related to alcohol abuse, but often without any relation to drinking alcohol. She sometimes remembered going out for a drink herself, but there seemed to be a part of her that was drinking a lot, of which she was unaware. Apart from amnesia, she had many other dissociative symptoms like hearing different voices. She said there was a lot of arguing in her head. Also, she often saw herself from a distance outside her body. She explained:

I'm not very fond of social situations and parties, but sometimes you have to go, I guess. Especially family parties, I hate those. Sometimes I would be hovering above myself the whole evening. Then I'm not in my body, and can I see myself. It's actually very strange. I don't feel anything either.

Another patient explained that he would be using ketamine at parties and would be going out of his body:

Sometimes I'm in a sort of dreamy daze and see all sorts of wonderful things, but there have also been times when things went completely wrong and I became very anxious, probably because I had mixed up all sorts of substances. I tend to use more when I'm really depressed.

This patient suffered from personality problems and otherwise reported very few dissociative symptoms. He had never experienced stepping out of his body without using any substance. He also reported no amnesia or Schneiderian symptoms.

It is possible to distinguish between patients with addiction problems and patients with dissociative disorders on the basis of the cluster of dissociative symptoms. When there is potential comorbidity, the clinician should carefully explore whether the symptoms only occur after using substances, or also in situations in which the patient has not used any. When there is severe daily substance abuse, this distinction will be hard to make. However, many patients with DID or OSDD-1 have one or more parts that use substances and other parts that never use or even hate it. Consequently, they would definitely not be using on a daily basis but only periodically and would therefore be much better able to distinguish between dissociative symptoms and the effects of substances.

Attention-Deficit/Hyperactivity Disorder (ADHD)

In the recent 10 to 15 years, the diagnosis of ADHD has received more attention and is made more frequently. As yet, there has not been any research into the relationship between or comorbidity of dissociative disorders and ADHD. However, it is striking that more and more patients with dissociative disorders previously had been diagnosed with ADHD. It is not always clear whether they actually had ADHD or whether symptoms of a dissociative disorder were assumed to be part of ADHD. The confusion is caused by the overlap between some of the symptoms, such as attention and concentration problems, forgetfulness, impulsiveness, and hyperactivity. Also, patients with ADHD sometimes suffer from excessive irritability and emotional outbursts. On the surface, many of these symptoms also occur in patients with complex dissociative disorders and CPTSD. When mainly attention and concentration problems are reported in the absence of symptoms of hyperactivity, it will be difficult to distinguish whether these symptoms belong to PTSD or ADHD in patients with a history of severe early childhood traumatization. Although overlapping psychological symptoms occur in patients with ADHD and DID/OSDD-1 from a young age, the symptoms differ in quality and background. Based on the absence of a cluster of dissociative symptoms, it is possible to distinguish ADHD from DID and OSDD-1. When a dissociative disorder is diagnosed, the ADHD diagnosis will often turn out to be incorrect. However, the two disorders may also co-occur.

Autism Spectrum Disorder (ASD)

As yet, there has not been any research on the comorbidity of dissociative disorders and autism spectrum disorder (ASD). A number of symptoms of ASD and DID or OSDD-1 overlap, and this may be confusing. Some of these symptoms are listed below:

- Taking things too literally is a symptom of ASD. However, in DID and OSDD-1, parts that are stuck in trauma time may also take certain things literally.
- Not being able to look people in the eye is a symptom of ASD. Looking people in the eye is also difficult for many patients with DID or OSDD-1, with embarrassment or shame playing a particularly large role. In ASD, this mainly concerns the inability to make contact. Generally, in patients with DID or OSDD-1, making eye contact is also difficult for dissociative parts that are stuck in trauma time but certainly not for all parts stuck in trauma time. Therefore, the way in which patients make contact can vary greatly.
- Getting upset when things are going differently than expected is consistent with ASD. Many patients with DID and OSDD-1 also need everything to be as predictable as possible: unexpected things can greatly unsettle patients. For this reason, these patients stick to routines, just like patients with ASD.
- Being readily overstimulated is a symptom of ASD as well as DID and OSDD-1. This involves external sensory stimuli, internal flooding, chaos, and too much information. Hypersensitivity to sensory stimuli may involve sound, light, smell, or taste, as well as tactile stimuli such as being touched or feeling something on the skin. Sensory hyposensitivity, also called under-responsivity, occurs when patients are unable to feel pain, cold, or heat well. In patients with dissociative disorders, this is caused by early childhood traumatization and PTSD symptoms. Some parts feel nothing or not enough while other parts feel too much. In patients with ASD, hyposensitivity is more likely to arise from information-processing problems. Sometimes it is difficult to distinguish whether hyposensitivity is a result of trauma or part of ASD (van der Kolk, 2014).

DID and OSDD-1 can be distinguished from ASD by the presence of a cluster of dissociative symptoms, which is lacking in ASD. For example, amnesia and Schneiderian symptoms (including hearing voices) are not part of autism spectrum disorders.

Gender Dysphoria

The DSM-5 includes the diagnosis of gender dysphoria. This refers to people who were assigned a sex at birth that does not fit the gender with which they identify. Patients with DID and sometimes OSDD-1 often have dissociative parts with different genders. Females with DID report male personality parts, both adult males and boys, and males with DID often have parts that are either girls or women.

In DID, the parts that identify with a different gender than the one the person was assigned at birth usually arise as a survival strategy during certain traumatizing experiences. For example, male parts in a female patient often believe they were not abused. They also believe they have no breasts, a form of pseudohallucination similar to anorexic patients who see a very big body in the mirror. In patients with DID, it is clear that the parts with another gender were functional at the time of the abuse. Many adult patients have difficulty with or are very much embarrassed about dissociative parts of another gender. Though uncommon, it is possible for a male part in a female patient to present itself at a gender change clinic. It is critical for gender clinics to have sufficient knowledge about dissociative disorders, as it is quite possible that only part of the person wants a gender change.

I once made a clear DID diagnosis in a young woman, Anita, who was in her early 20s. A few years later, I did a new diagnostic assessment at the request of a gender clinic where the patient had by then requested gender transition as a young man, Daniel. During the original SCID-D interview this patient had described multiple parts including a boy part called Daniel. The psychiatrist the patient had been seeing for a year had come across my earlier SCID-D report when going through the medical records, but he had never noticed any dissociation during his weekly meetings with the patient. The patient explained that he did not feel like he belonged in a female body and that this had always been the case. However, the psychiatrist had some experience with dissociative disorders and wanted to know if DID was still present. During this second SCID-D interview—more than three or four years after the earlier one—Daniel initially denied all dissociative symptoms or had other explanations for them. He described himself as forgetful and dreamy in nature, which had caused the memory problems; this was why he sometimes lost hours of time. For example, he had no memory at all of the earlier SCID-D interview. He admitted to having inner dialogues but felt that *everyone had those*. He denied having any depersonalization and derealization symptoms. He denied having different parts but said he recognized female and male sides in himself. Again, he was convinced that everyone had that. His feminine side liked ballet very much and so he had started doing ballet where he himself also liked to dance in a tutu. He also stated that he sometimes found out afterward that, apparently, he had been to ballet classes but did not remember going. In answer to my final question as to whether he thought I had previously incorrectly diagnosed DID, and what he thought was happening now, he replied: *I don't believe you made an incorrect diagnosis although I can't remember the conversation we had. But I think it's no longer an issue now.* In the follow-up interview, I informed Daniel that, in my opinion, there were still many symptoms that indicated a dissociative disorder—possibly DID. He did not seem to be very shocked about this. The treating psychiatrist offered to continue the sessions with him without moving on to more invasive medical treatment. The patient also agreed to this. In the end, the patient withdrew his request for transition and reentered treatment for the dissociative disorder elsewhere.

Gender dysphoria can be distinguished from DID because it lacks the cluster of dissociative symptoms found in DID. I examined a number of patients with gender dysphoria using the TADS-I. They did report symptoms of depersonalization and one patient also suffered from recurrent depression. None of them had ever had memory problems. They were not hearing voices, nor did they describe any other Schneiderian symptoms.

Summary

In this chapter, I discussed a number of former Axis I disorders that are frequently confused with DID and OSDD-1. However, this by no means implies that all such disorders have been addressed. For example, Chapter 5 details that eating problems or eating disorders often occur in patients with DID and OSDD-1. Chapter 5 describes differences between patients with eating problems with and without comorbid dissociative disorders. It also describes specific sleep problems that are common in patients with DID and OSDD-1. In general, it is important for clinicians to have a good understanding of the possible comorbidities in patients with dissociative disorders.

CHAPTER 8

Distinguishing DID and OSDD-1 From Borderline Personality Disorder

Introduction

Many patients with DID or OSDD-1 exhibit features of comorbid personality disorders, particularly of Clusters B and C (Boon & Draijer, 1993a, 1993c; Brand, Classen, Lanius, et al., 2009; Brand, Armstrong, et al., 2009; Dorahy et al., 2014; Ellason et al., 1996; Horevitz & Braun, 1984; Korzekwa, Dell, & Pain, 2009; Korzekwa, Dell, Links, et al., 2009; Loewenstein et al., 2017). This is not surprising, given the related etiologies with histories of insecure attachment, affective neglect, and sexual or physical abuse.

Research on comorbidity of personality disorders and dissociative disorders has mainly focused on the prevalence of borderline personality disorder (BPD) with DID and DDNOS (now OSDD-1) or, conversely, on the prevalence of dissociative symptoms and dissociative disorders in patients with BPD. This is not surprising, given the overlapping clinical phenomenology of these disorders and that BPD is thought to be a trauma-related disorder by many clinicians (Ball & Links, 2009; Herman et al., 1989; Mosquera et al., 2012; Mosquera & Steele, 2017; van der Hart et al., 2006; van der Kolk et al., 1994). As early as the 1980s, Herman and van der Kolk described BPD as a developmental disorder related to early childhood trauma (Herman et al., 1989; Herman & van der Kolk, 1987).

A recent meta-analysis by Lyssenko and colleagues (2018) revealed that the mean DES score among patients with BPD was the fourth highest. This was higher than the mean DES score of BPD patients in the study by Zanarini and colleagues (2000a). Data reported on by Lyssenko and colleagues originated from 27 different studies of 1,705 BPD patients; the mean DES score they found was just above the 25 cutoff point. There were no data for a general category of personality disorders in this recent meta-analysis; however, such data were described by van IJzendoorn and Schuengel (1998) in their earlier meta-analysis of the DES. The latter found a mean DES score of 19.61 in a group of patients with personality disorders, which is just below the most conservative cutoff point of 20 and also lower than was found in BPD patients in the study by Lyssenko and colleagues (2018).

As is highlighted in Chapter 4, it is important to identify which of the DES subscales are contributing to the elevated scores in BPD patients. Further analysis of the elevated DES scores in the meta-analysis by Lyssenko and colleagues (2018) revealed that these were mainly symptoms of absorption and depersonalization and to a lesser extent symptoms indicating a division of the personality. Nevertheless, the relationship between BPD and particularly DID has been a topic of debate for many years. Some clinicians consider BPD to be a dissociative disorder (e.g., van der Hart et al., 2006; Howell & Blizard, 2009; Mosquera et al., 2012), while others feel that DID is more a borderline disorder with dissociative parts of the personality being borderline modes (Huntjens et al., 2019a, 2019b; Huntjens et al., 2020).

In this chapter, I aim to describe that DID and BPD are different and distinguishable from each other. This is relevant because these differences have implications for treatment (Brand, Loewenstein, et al., 2019; Nijenhuis et al., 2019). Several studies show that one third of BPD patients barely even report dissociative symptoms (Zanarini et al., 2009). However, patients may also present with a BPD diagnosis but during the course of therapy may turn out to have DID.

Studies of BPD as a Comorbid Disorder With Dissociative Disorders

Most studies have focused on the prevalence of comorbid BPD in DID or DDNOS Example 1 (now OSDD-1). In the early 1990s, Nel Draijer and I discovered that out of 71 patients with DID, 40% met five BPD criteria while 25% met four of the criteria (Boon & Draijer, 1993a, 1993b). Since the criterion of dissociative symptoms was added to the BPD criteria in 1994 in DSM-IV, creating a phenomenological overlap in symptoms, an even higher prevalence of comorbid BPD has been found in patients with DID and DDNOS.. Several studies reported percentages of comorbid BPD that ranged from 30% to as high as almost 80% (Boon & Draijer, 1993a, 1993b, 1993c; Dell, 1998; Ellason et al., 1996; Foote et al., 2008; Korzekwa & Dell, 2022; Korzekwa, Dell, & Pain., 2009; Korzekwa, Dell, Links, et al., 2009; Ross et al., 1991; Ross et al., 2014; Şar et al., 2003). However, it should be noted that the very high outcomes for comorbidity of BPD were found primarily in specific populations, such as patients with a history of sexual abuse or other early childhood abuse. Also, the outcomes were partially influenced by the diagnostic tools that were used. Therefore, questions may arise about the validity of these data. Caution is needed in generalizing some of these findings, particularly data relating to very high comorbidity.

However, comorbidity may lead to underdiagnosis of dissociative disorders, especially when severe dissociative pathology is not routinely explored. It appeared that a number of patients with DID and OSDD-1 (DDNOS in the DSM-IV) were initially diagnosed with BPD based on a number of corresponding symptoms such as problems in emotion regulation, suicidality, and self-harming behaviors. In some cases, BPD symptoms—for example severe affect dysregulation and self-harm—turned out to be part of DID. On further examination, it turned out that there was no BPD but rather something else, such as an avoidant personality disorder. Given the overlap in symptoms, it is surprising that DSM-5 makes no mention of DID nor of any other dissociative disorders in the section on differential diagnosis for BPD; it also does not mention dissociative disorders as frequently co-occurring with BPD (APA, 2013, 2022).

Research on Dissociative Symptoms and Dissociative Disorders Among Patients With BPD

In their review, Zanarini and Jager-Hyman (2009) described two generations of studies of dissociative symptoms in BPD patients. The first generation of studies was done between 1968 and 1990 and found symptoms of depersonalization and derealization in about half of BPD patients. Based on those results, a ninth BPD criterion was added to DSM-IV in 1994, referring to short-term, transient, stress-related episodes of depersonalization and derealization. However, these first-generation studies did not use standardized instruments to diagnose dissociative symptoms.

The second generation of studies used the DES. These studies showed a wide variety of DES scores in which three subgroups of BPD patients could be distinguished fairly consistently. Zanarini et al. (2000a) examined 290 BPD patients with a mean DES score of 21.8 (SD 18.6). However, one in three patients reported hardly any dissociative symptoms (DES < 10), while one third showed mild dissociative symptoms (DES between 10 and 29) and one third reported severe dissociative symptoms (DES of 35 or higher). This demonstrates that the severity of dissociative symptoms in BPD patients is heterogeneous. These findings were confirmed in several studies (Korzekwa, Dell, Links, et al., 2009; Scalabrini et al., 2017).

Zanarini and colleagues (2000b) found a number of risk factors predictive of high scores on the DES: (1) inconsistent care by primary caregiver, (2) sexual abuse by primary caregiver, (3) witnessing sexual violence as a child, and (4) a history of rape as an adult. Furthermore, in this 10-year disease progression study, in which the DES was administered every 2 years, it was found that in part of the last group (DES scores with a mean score of 40), the high DES scores barely decreased over time, while scores of the patients with initially less extreme DES scores did decrease. This corroborates the hypothesis that dissociative symptoms will not decrease as long as severe comorbid dissociative disorders are left unrecognized and untreated (Korzekwa, Dell, & Pain, 2009).

Several studies have been done on the prevalence of dissociative symptoms and disorders in BPD patients using a structured interview (SCID-D) for dissociative disorders, in addition to a wide range of screening instruments. In two studies involving outpatients with BPD (Korzekwa, Dell, Links, et al., 2009; Şar et al., 2003), over two thirds of patients also met the DSM-IV criteria for dissociative disorder, while one quarter of the group met the DSM-IV criteria for DID. These studies were limited by the small number of patients and selection bias. For example, the study by Korzekwa et al. (2009) took place in an outpatient clinic where severely traumatized patients were treated. In their BPD group 86% of the patients with a comorbid dissociative disorder also met the criteria for PTSD; so caution is needed in generalizing these findings. This study probably involved a subgroup similar to the third group (the patients with the highest DES score) in the study by Zanarini et al. (2000a, 2000b).

Korzekwa, Dell, Links, et al. (2009), like Zanarini, described three subgroups of BPD patients in terms of dissociative features in which the severity of dissociation was mostly related to the severity of psychotrauma or history of abuse and the severity of attachment problems.

In 1993, Nel Draijer and I compared patients with DID or DDNOS with patients who had cluster B personality disorders, particularly BPD, and also found three groups of patients (Boon & Draijer, 1993a, 1993c):

1. A BPD group with hardly any dissociative symptoms, similar to Zanarini's first group. This group consisted of BPD patients from the SCID-D validation study control group.
2. A second group consisting of BPD patients who had been referred for suspected dissociative disorder, which was then excluded. This second group did report frequent and sometimes chronic depersonalization and absorption symptoms and often PTSD symptoms.
3. A third group consisted of BPD patients with DID or DDNOS. This last group reported the full cluster of severe dissociative symptoms, including amnesia and Schneiderian symptoms.

These three groups differed significantly with regard to the nature and severity of dissociative symptoms. In particular, amnesia, Schneiderian symptoms, and identity alterations appeared to be distinguishing symptoms; however, depersonalization and derealization were not (Boon & Draijer, 1993a, 1993c). The nature and severity of trauma histories also differed significantly between groups, with the most severe traumatization seen in the group of DID patients and mainly emotional neglect seen in the BPD group without DID. Nel Draijer and I also encountered some dilemmas in the severity rating of the SCID-D symptom clusters; for example, the questions on depersonalization and derealization symptoms did not distinguish between more general symptoms and those indicating division of the personality. Another SCID-D cluster, identity confusion, did not always quantitatively differentiate BPD from DID and was often severe in both disorders. However, descriptions of identity confusion by patients with DID were completely different in quality compared to those presented by BPD patients. In patients with DID, confusion was related to other dissociative symptoms, such as amnesia and Schneiderian symptoms, and to the influence of dissociative parts; patients spontaneously described a struggle between multiple voices, thoughts, or parts, and being confused about their own behavior for which they had amnesia. The BPD patients described an ongoing polarized internal struggle between two thoughts or sides (good/evil, life/death, etc.). Both groups could be scored "severe" on the SCID-D for identity confusion because they were confused about who they actually were; however, this confusion was based on different phenomena (Boon & Draijer, 1993a).

In a study comparing DID and BPD patients using the Multidimensional Inventory of Dissociation (MID), Laddis and colleagues (2017) described different processes underlying dissociative pathology in both disorders. This study confirmed the qualitative differences between DID and BPD symptoms also described earlier. There was overlap in symptoms, such as identity confusion and memory problems, but there were also clear qualitative differences. The dissociative symptoms in DID were caused by the presence of dissociative parts of the personality, whereas in BPD most dissociative experiences involved detachment or severe absorption or were influenced by stress or rapid changes in emotional states of consciousness.

In short, the existing studies clearly show that BPD involves a heterogeneous group of patients: a first group without dissociative symptoms; a second group with mainly absorption and/or depersonalization symptoms, and sometimes also PTSD symptoms; and a third group with severe dissociative symptoms indicating division of the personality. This last group consists of patients with DID, OSDD-1, or partial DID, and sometimes also

CPTSD (discussed in the next chapter). Various symptom profiles are shown in Table 8.1 at the end of this chapter. We found a fourth group of patients, in particular patients with borderline or theatrical personality disorders, with extremely high scores on self-report questionnaires, which seemed to indicate exaggeration or imitation. Extensive diagnostic testing with the SCID-D or the TADS-I show that these are patients with false-positive diagnoses of DID. In a number of cases, the incorrect DID diagnoses are made by clinicians; in other cases DID imitations by patients led to an incorrect DID diagnoses by clinicians. A large proportion of this group had read a lot of information on the internet and reported textbook examples of dissociative symptoms during the diagnostic assessment (Boon & Draijer, 1993a, 1993b, 1995a, 1999; Draijer & Boon, 1999; Pietkiewicz et al., 2021). False-positive cases are discussed in Chapter 10.

General Points to Consider in Differentiating Dissociative Disorders (With or Without BPD) From BPD

Since there are different groups of BPD patients, different profiles are found during diagnostic assessment. Borderline patients with a history of physical and sexual abuse and CPTSD have different symptom profiles on the TADS-I and also on the SCID-D than BPD patients with a history of only emotional neglect. Different TADS-I symptom profiles are also found in all other personality disorders, especially in clusters B and C. In our study with the SCID-D, we found that the retrospectively reported abuse histories in the DID group were significantly more severe and had an earlier onset than those in the BPD group (Boon & Draijer, 1993a, 1993c).

Box 8.1 lists a number of important issues for clinicians to bear in mind when administering the TADS-I or any other diagnostic interview. These concerns will help clinicians differentiate between the various BPD groups and also other personality disorders. The most difficult task is to differentiate between OSDD-1 and the second group of patients who have BPD and CPTSD and PTSD symptoms. Sometimes, even careful diagnostic examination will not provide enough information to make the distinction (see also Chapter 1). I will discuss this in more detail in Chapter 9, which is about similarities and differences between PTSD, CPTSD, and the dissociative disorders.

So far, there has not been any research on the new ICD-11 diagnostic classification of partial DID. The criteria for partial DID may also pose diagnostic dilemmas in the differential diagnosis of BPD. The distinction between what are labeled modes and dissociative personality states, as described in ICD-11 in particular, will not be easy to make (see Chapter 1).

BOX 8.1

POINTS TO CONSIDER IN DIFFERENTIAL DIAGNOSES

1. *Possibly trauma-related symptoms:* It is important not only to check for evidence of alterations in consciousness such as depersonalization or absorption, but also for evidence of division of the personality in relation to the symptom (see Chapters 2 and 3).

2. *Sleep problems and anxiety and panic:* Questions about these contain questions about PTSD. Is there any evidence of PTSD, and if so, do the PTSD symptoms appear to be related to early childhood trauma, more recent trauma, or both? By themselves, bad dreams and nightmares are insufficient indications of PTSD. PTSD really involves reexperiencing trauma and flashbacks of traumatic experiences.

3. *Self-image and identity:* It is important to consider whether there is a polarized internal struggle between two sides (e.g., between good and evil, black and white) that may indicate borderline splitting or a struggle between multiple voices, dissociative parts, or thoughts. Confusion about identity, as well as confusion about sexual identity and negative self-image or gender dysphoria, frequently occurs in patients with BPD, but also in patients with other personality disorders and in patients with dissociative disorders. It is also possible to differentiate between a highly variable, unstable self-image (BPD) and a predominantly negative self-image (CPTSD) and most patients with dissociative disorders (see also Chapter 9).

4. *Somatoform dissociative symptoms:* Severely detached BPD patients commonly have little contact with their bodies; feelings of numbness are common, but there is no evidence of a division of the personality.

5. *Psychoform dissociative symptoms:* When assessing memory problems, it is essential to distinguish well between concentration and memory problems due to absorption or depersonalization on the one hand and dissociative amnesia due to the presence of dissociative parts on the other. Some BPD patients report amnesia exclusively for unwanted or shameful behavior or in stressful situations when they are completely outside their window of tolerance. Likewise, some patients with antisocial characteristics report amnesia only for antisocial behaviors.

6. *Schneiderian symptoms:* Some BPD patients may also hear voices. Some experience this only during brief psychotic episodes; others may hear continuous or frequent negative comments about themselves. BPD patients with PTSD may sometimes hear the abuser's voice when reexperiencing traumatizing events. The quality of voice hearing varies. Patients with DID often hear a cacophony of different voices that they have been hearing since a young age, or a lot of murmuring between all sorts (see also differences with psychotic disorders in Chapter 7). Most BPD patients, if hearing voices at all, only report hearing one or two voices, often familiar to them (e.g., a critical or angry parent).

7. *Presentation:* In contrast to many patients with DID, and sometimes to a lesser extent patients with OSDD-1, patients with BPD have no difficulty discussing their symptoms. Some of the BPD group feel chronically unseen and are actually eager to talk about their symptoms.

8. *Trauma history:* Although questions about traumatic experiences are not included in the TADS-I (nor in the SCID-D), it is important to assess a history of trauma in a proper way—at another moment in time (see Chapter 11). In doing so, be sure to make a distinction between trauma caused by a lack of loving, care, and attention (i.e., emotional neglect, being unseen as a child) and trauma caused by sexual and physical violence or experiencing violence from a young age (usually in combination with neglect). One group of BPD patients (Group 1) had mainly experienced the first form of traumatization, sometimes accompanied by experiences of bullying or isolation. The other two groups of BPD patients (Groups 2 and 3) had usually experienced a combination of neglect and sexual and/or physical abuse or other experiences of violence. In DID and OSDD-1 with or without comorbid BPD, there is almost always a combination of neglect and forms of early, severe physical and/or sexual abuse and/or other violent experiences.

BPD Patients Without Comorbid PTSD

Clinicians should be aware that every BPD patient is different, not only with regard to the nature and severity of possibly dissociative symptoms but also regarding their overall symptom profile. Indeed, for a DSM-5 diagnosis of BPD, the patient needs to meet five out of nine criteria. This alone makes for a lot of possible combinations of symptoms that may lead to a BPD classification.

TADS-I Profile for BPD Patients Without PTSD or CPTSD

The TADS-I symptom profile of a patient with borderline personality disorder can be distinguished clearly from the profile of patients with DID and OSDD-1. Below is a discussion of this.

Possibly Trauma-Related Symptoms

In general, any combination of potentially trauma-related symptoms is possible. These symptoms may sometimes be accompanied by mild depersonalization, derealization, and absorption. However, when assessing possibly trauma-related symptoms, dissociative symptoms indicating a division of the personality are not reported by the patients.

There are no PTSD symptoms; the sleep problems, if any, are of different nature and quality than those described by patients with PTSD and DID. Patients may describe vivid dreams or nightmares related to neglect or frequent rumination about not being seen, but they do not report reliving the past. They also do not describe hypervigilance, extreme jumpiness, or constantly waking up at night. Instead, these patients often sleep a lot and for lengthy periods, sometimes on medication.

Depression, including suicidal thoughts or attempts, anxiety, self-injurious behaviors, and substance abuse are common symptoms.

Problems with self-image and relationships with other people are at the core of the diagnosis, often including severe fear of abandonment.

Identity problems are often severe but have a different quality than what is seen in patients with complex dissociative disorders (especially DID). There is often a polarized struggle between what patients describe as *the good me and the bad me*, between life and death and black and white. This may involve two sides of the self arguing; sometimes the person addresses the bad part of the self with another name. Some may have strong feelings of not being seen, especially as a child. There may be confusion about the way one should behave or be like and uncertainty about one's identity and who one wants to be. There may also be uncertainty or confusion about one's sexual orientation.

Alterations in Consciousness

There may be mild to severe depersonalization and derealization symptoms, but the examples provided during the assessment are primarily related to detachment and feelings of estrangement from oneself and others. Patients do not report examples of depersonalization or derealization that might indicate division of the personality, such as literally being outside the body and perceiving oneself from the outside. However, depersonalization and detachment may be severe enough to warrant a DSM-5 or ICD-11 diagnosis of depersonalization/derealization disorder.

There may be attention and/or memory problems associated with absorption/imagination and sometimes daydreaming. Daydreaming may be very severe and may take pathological forms, sometimes related to the desire to be different and ideal and thus to have an ideal life with ideal relationships. This often is in contrast to the patient's reality, which is characterized by inactivity.

Usually, with the exception of daydreaming that can occur on an ongoing basis, the alterations in consciousness are mainly related to periods of stress or fatigue.

Somatoform Dissociative Symptoms

Patients may occasionally report somatoform symptoms, such as numbness, pain symptoms, or other conversion symptoms.

Psychoform Dissociative Symptoms

Amnesia. Any memory problems reported are usually related to absorption and sometimes depersonalization. Some patients report amnesia for negative behaviors (e.g., outbursts of anger) or chaotic behavior. They do not report fugues or periods of true loss of time caused by dissociative parts; personal details such as name, age, and address are not forgotten.

Patients do not show any reluctance or reservation to talk about memory problems. This does not appear to be stressful for them and they can talk freely about all symptoms. Passive influence of dissociative parts is not present.

Schneiderian Symptoms/Intrusions. Voice hearing may be reported, but typically involves one or two voices and never many different voices as in DID. The voices are usually of people who are familiar to the person; there is often the voice of a punishing parent. Again, there is no reluctance or internal struggle when patients are asked questions about voice hearing; patients do not experience any difficulties talking about this. For many patients it is unclear whether they are actually hearing voices or just having thoughts or making negative inner comments about themselves, which in schema therapy is known as the punitive or demanding parent mode (Young et al., 2003).

The other Schneiderian symptoms are mostly absent.

Dissociative Parts of the Personality. There are no indications of dissociative parts of the personality. However, there may be a regressive desire to be small, to be taken care of, and to not have any responsibilities. In addition, patients may experience childlike emotional states, such as being small and vulnerable, alone, unloved, or very angry. Patients may interpret these childlike emotions and needs as dissociative parts (see Chapter 10). However, they are rather ego states or what Young and colleagues call "borderline modes" (2003). These ego states do not have their own separate memories and their own first-person perspective: they are experienced as self, as ego syntonic (see also the description in Chapter 1).

Negative or impulsive behaviors for which there may be memory problems are sometimes considered to be not self (anger, eating attacks, stealing, sexual acting-out).

These patients, especially BPD with theatrical features, may lose themselves in roles or constantly adapt like chameleons to other persons or situations. They have no amnesia for these roles and are well aware of them; the behavior is also experienced as ego syntonic, an I-experience, although the behaviors are not always controlled. Destructive behaviors may be experienced as ego dystonic (i.e., "not me").

Presentation

There is generally no stress, shame, or phobic fear associated with talking about difficult topics, such as self-injurious behaviors and suicidality, loss of time, or identity confusion.

There are no visible nonverbal signs of dissociation during the interview, no emotional responses to the interview, and no internal voices interfering with or disturbing the conversation.

Trauma History

There is usually a history of emotional neglect or emotional abuse: a parent or parents who were unavailable or had addiction problems or other mental disorders and sometimes aggression or frequent parental arguments. Sometimes patients report histories of bullying at school.

Case Report: A Patient With Borderline Personality Disorder (BPD)

Ms. J. was a 32-year-old woman who participated in an outpatient day treatment program for BPD. She was single: a relationship with a boyfriend had ended several months prior. She was emotional when talking about this. She had been diagnosed with BPD and agreed with the diagnosis. She started college after graduating high school, but failed and had had several jobs since then. She explained that she was never able to maintain jobs for very long. She had been referred because she had recently had black-outs and her therapist wondered whether she might also have dissociative problems.

The patient said that for a period of time she drank a lot of alcohol. This was together with her boyfriend. They also used party drugs; she stopped using them as a condition for participating in the treatment program. In the past she used to have alcohol-related blackouts.

Possibly Trauma-Related Symptoms

The patient did not report having problems with sleeping: *On the contrary, I sleep rather too much.* She reported having nightmares sometimes. *They are always about me being alone and abandoned by someone, or not being able to find anyone. They're terrible dreams; I'm always relieved when I wake up again.*

She explained that being alone was one of her biggest problems: she was unable to cope with it. After waking up from such dreams, she was immediately well-oriented in the here and now. She would sometimes be afraid to go back to sleep again for fear of having more bad dreams. The patient did not describe any PTSD symptoms; she had not been reexperiencing trauma or having flashbacks.

The patient reported having eating problems during her adolescence.

> My parents were in a messy divorce at the time and my mother left. She left us with my father, just like that. He totally ignored me and was very fond of my older brother. I felt like I didn't matter at all. That's when I started dieting. I remember thinking I was fat and ugly and that my father didn't like me for that reason. I also started having binges, especially when I felt very depressed and alone. Eating offered me some sort of comfort. I remember going to the supermarket to buy all sorts of unhealthy food like chips and all kinds of sweet stuff.

The patient was able to give a very clear and detailed first-person narrative and there was no evidence of a division of the personality. She had no amnesia and never heard voices related to her eating problems. She did report episodes of binge eating, which were sometimes taking place in a kind of haze.

> I could sit alone in my room for hours, thinking or switching channels on the TV. Then I would eat all that junk, almost without noticing, until I felt so nauseated and sick that I had to throw up. This actually

always happened when I was feeling very lonely. In fact, the eating problems disappeared when I went back to live with my mother at seventeen. The relationship with my mom was restored then; my brother had already left home by then.

When describing anxiety symptoms, it once again appeared that her biggest fear was being abandoned and that several relationships with boyfriends had failed because of this. She feared relationships would never work out and that she would always be alone. Her moods tended to undergo extreme changes, but things had improved since she had been on medication. When she was not on medication, her moods would fluctuate from extremely happy and joyful to extremely unhappy.

> Again, the best example is this friend I had. I would feel extremely happy, for example when we had a nice evening together and I had cooked a delicious dinner and set the table beautifully. But then he would call it off last minute, or forget about it, and it would be like the world had collapsed. I would fall into the deepest abyss and was either inconsolable or furious.

At times, she had been very depressed and had also had suicidal thoughts, but she never actually attempted to kill herself. However, at moments when her world collapsed, she would see no perspective at all. The patient had a very unstable self-image:

> I often just feel like a loser, nothing works out, but it does vary. I have noticed that I can also feel very good. I will suddenly be very active then and undertake all sorts of things. When things were going well with my boyfriend, I felt strong and capable of doing almost anything.
>
> When asked whether she ever experienced an internal struggle, she answered: This is going on all the time; there's always a Yes-No conflict within me. It started with having these binges (eating or not eating). I'm terribly black-and-white: I would either feel that something is absolutely great, or the total opposite. Sometimes I really don't get why I keep changing so much.

The patient had a number of women friends but, in the course of time, some friendships had suddenly ended after conflicts. She had the most violent conflicts with men with whom she had had intimate relationships. *I would sometimes really behave like an angry, hysterical little child, especially when my boyfriend went his own way. Or when he didn't want to join me in doing something. That would often be a trigger.* She explained that she had no problems with sexuality but often adjusted to the wishes of the other person. *I've often had sex because it was something that was expected from me, not because I wanted to. I think I very often did it to make the man stay with me, but of course it doesn't work that way.* Now that she had been undergoing intensive treatment for over a year, she was starting to think more and was better able to set limits for herself.

EVALUATION OF POSSIBLY TRAUMA-RELATED SYMPTOMS

The patient mentioned a range of symptoms appropriate to her borderline issues. She was able to tell a clear ego syntonic, first-person narrative. She had only suffered from eating problems during adolescence and had had mild symptoms of depersonalization, particularly during binge eating episodes. She also described having absorption symptoms of being wrapped up in thoughts for hours on end. There was no evidence of symptoms indicating division of the personality. She had had intense fights, especially with her last boyfriend. She believed this is when what she called *the dissociation* started, because she could not remember some of the fights.

Alterations in Consciousness

The patient described sometimes feeling she was floating when very emotional: *As if I am not really there.* When asked whether she was outside her body then, she replied: *No, that's not what I mean, I never have that, it's a kind of floating feeling.* She also reported that she sometimes acted like a robot, especially when she was experiencing a lot of tension. The patient did not report experiences of derealization. However, she could be introverted and absorbed in thoughts or sometimes daydreams. In her adolescence, this sometimes lasted for hours, but this was no longer the case.

EVALUATION OF ALTERATIONS IN CONSCIOUSNESS

The patient described mild depersonalization and absorption symptoms, especially when stressed.

Somatoform Dissociative Symptoms

The patient described tension headaches and a lot of stress-related pain in her neck and back. Apart from this, she did not endorse any truly somatoform dissociative symptoms.

Psychoform Dissociative Symptoms

Amnesia. The patient reported multiple blackouts during the recently ended relationship with her boyfriend. Although she drank a lot of alcohol with this boyfriend, she indicated that she had also had a blackout once when she had not been drinking too much. During a violent conflict with this boyfriend, she had attacked him and hit him hard. She remembered exactly how he was provoking and infuriating her, but she could not remember anything about her beating him. She was terribly embarrassed because her boyfriend had sustained bruised ribs. A similar situation had occurred after this incident. *This is totally unlike me really, because I hardly ever get this angry,* she explained. The patient had never had blackouts previously in her life except in this relationship or when she had had too much to drink. She did not report any other amnesia symptoms. In fact, her memory was very good. She had also never experienced a fugue or forgotten personal information. Apart from having a meltdown with her ex-boyfriend twice, she found no evidence of doing things she could not remember.

Schneiderian Symptoms/Intrusions. The patient had never heard voices and did not report any other Schneiderian symptoms. When asked about dissociative parts, the patient replied:

> Well, I'm not so sure about that. My boyfriend said I was very different when I was so raging mad. He said I was a different person and that he had started reading on the internet about it. He then came up with this story about dissociation. I can only think that he was baiting me like my father used to do; he knew exactly how to hurt and infuriate me. It's like I can still hear my father with all his critical comments. He used to run me into the ground, and my boyfriend did exactly the same. I actually believe that it has everything to do with this.

On further questioning, the patient described sometimes feeling very small and dependent and at other times being enraged. She was well aware of this, although she found it difficult to control her often angry impulses. The clinical picture she described corresponded with the fluctuation of moods seen in BPD but not with having dissociative parts of the personality.

Conclusion

There was no indication of DID nor of any other dissociative disorder. The patient described some depersonalization and absorption symptoms but did not mention any symptoms indicating division of the personality. The blackouts occurred in a state of extreme hyperarousal: *Everything went black.* Moreover, it cannot be completely ruled out that alcohol was involved after all. The patient recognized the explanation of the schema mode model (Young et al., 2003) and agreed with it. After the diagnostic interview, she realized that she mainly had problems in intimate relationships with men and that she still wanted to heal some old wounds from the relationship with her father.

TADS-I Profiles of Other Personality Disorders

Patients with other personality disorders exhibit dissociative profiles very similar to that of the patient with BPD described above. In patients with histrionic personalities, the presentation is usually more dramatic or exaggerated. These patients also describe playing roles, like a little dependent girl, a seductive woman, or an efficient organizer at work. One patient described this as follows:

> I feel like a chameleon, I always adapt to every situation. I can behave in very different ways; this is so natural to me. I love it! But don't we all play roles in our lives? Doesn't everyone behave differently in different conversations, like with the garbage man or at the opera? Yes, I sometimes tend to lose myself in a role and completely let myself go, especially in relationships with others. I guess my behavior can be quite annoying then. I know very well that I am doing this but I can't stop it; it has a lot to do with how I feel. I can get very attached to someone when I feel very small, but when angry I behave like a cold, corporate bitch! But don't ask me who I really am! I would have no idea because it always changes depending on the situation. Sometimes I feel very empty inside when I am alone.

This patient did not report any symptoms indicative of a division of the personality: she reported no amnesia or PTSD symptoms. She was not hearing voices and did not report other Schneiderian symptoms. There were no indications of dissociative parts. Her dramatic presentation of the symptoms and significant subjective distress were both considerable. She also had relatively high scores on self-report questionnaires (including a DES score of 35.70), with no evidence of a dissociative disorder. There was probably some exaggeration.

Case Report: A Patient With BPD With Antisocial and Narcissistic Traits

The patient was a 25-year-old male. He had been treated in an outpatient unit for several years for depressive symptoms and impulsive, aggressive actions. He had several times been briefly psychiatrically hospitalized, but this had not helped and had resulted in even more tension and aggression or in very regressive behavior. The patient had great problems in social interactions, experiencing many conflicts with other people. After finishing high school, he failed his further education at a technical college. He had argued with his teachers and was expelled. After that he had a number of jobs where he kept having conflicts with the managers and then left or was fired.

The patient used large amounts of medication (sedatives such as oxazepam; 50 mg) and drank frequently. He was aware that alcohol played a role in the aggressive outbursts. He was also aggressive when he had not been drinking. *I simply have a short fuse; people just have to be considerate of me. If you say something wrong, you'll know it. I won't let people hurt or insult me.*

The patient described regularly having suicidal thoughts and walking along the railroad. He added that he sometimes remembered very little about these episodes. On further inquiry it appeared that he had taken many benzodiazepines on those occasions. He had also been accused of stealing at work a number of times, which he claimed he could not remember very well. *Yes, that's what they say, well I really don't remember that exactly. I have worked for large cleaning companies and in an IKEA warehouse. They don't even notice when something is missing. They're all big capitalists.*

Memory problems occurred only after excessive use of alcohol or benzodiazepines; the patient was unable to name any other examples.

The patient stated that he had no negative self-image. He was convinced that he was capable of many things but just was not given the opportunities. Failures were always caused by others. *Apparently, they always have it in for me, but this has always been the case in my life.*

The patient reported feelings of depersonalization and derealization, also when not using benzodiazepines.

> I feel like an outsider and I don't belong anywhere. I'm like a machine, but if someone pushes the wrong button on the machine, I explode. Sometimes the world is very far away and a bit foggy, or it feels like I'm in a fishbowl.

Depersonalization and derealization symptoms occurred mainly when he was experiencing a lot of stress or after using substances; symptoms were severe. The feelings were not ongoing. The patient felt he was *a kind of Dr. Jekyll and Mr. Hyde*; he had read the classic Robert Louis Stevenson novel in high school. All aggressive and antisocial behaviors were attributable to Rob, a name he had given himself. He made Rob responsible for these behaviors and explained that they were completely out of his control. *I am not like that at all!* He also felt that the aggressive behaviors and thefts were always provoked by others. He said he was not confused about it, since he was not that person. He was very aware of who he was and what he was capable of, but did feel confused about his sexual identity. He described having homosexual feelings, but that also made him very anxious and aggressive.

The patient was not hearing voices and did not describe any Schneiderian symptoms. Apart from the part named Rob who represented his bad self, there was no evidence of any dissociative parts. *I have no control over when I turn into Rob, it just happens.* When asked whether he knew what Rob was doing, he replied: *Well, usually I do, but I can't stop it. Sometimes I notice it afterwards.* In the latter case, he appeared to have been drunk or taking a lot of benzodiazepines.

Conclusion

There was no DID, OSDD-1, or partial DID. This was a patient with BPD and antisocial traits. He reported memory problems for antisocial behaviors such as aggressive actions and stealing, which he attributed to another personality he had named Rob. Although he gave the impression that he had feigned his memory problems because he was unwilling to take responsibility for these behaviors that he claimed were *always provoked by others*, some of these also may have been related to alcohol and drug use. He reported no other symptoms indicating a division of the personality. He was genuinely confused about who he actually was, but had little ability to reflect on his feelings of confusion. His homosexual feelings evoked a lot of anxiety. He said he did not want to be a *sissy*.

During the interview, the patient behaved defensively, sometimes somewhat belittling or angry. He said that he had already expected the outcome that he did not have a dissociative disorder, and it was a waste of his time to go through such an examination again. There were no signs of dissociation, and he was able to answer all the questions despite his dismissive attitude.

The patient had a sad history. His mother had a psychiatric disorder and committed suicide when he was 16 years old. His father had drunk a lot of alcohol since then. He was an only child and only remembered being close to a grandmother, but she died when he was 10 years old. He hardly ever saw his father.

Summary

General symptoms of depersonalization and derealization frequently occur in patients with personality disorders. These symptoms, usually related to severe detachment, may be so chronic and severe that patients meet the criteria for a depersonalization/derealization disorder. In addition, many of these patients report symptoms of absorption, often with related memory problems. These absorption phenomena may also become pathological in nature, if patients lose themselves in daydreaming and no longer have control over this (Somer, 2002; Somer et al., 2016a, 2016b).

Many patients with personality problems are confused about their identities, sometimes including their sexual identities. Patients frequently mention feeling empty or bored. If there is identity confusion, patients often have polarized perceptions of themselves as either good or bad. Some patients have difficulties recognizing their bad selves as a part of them; they cannot take responsibility for their negative behaviors. These patients do not report symptoms indicating a division of the personality, although they do experience themselves shifting from the good self (*me*) to the bad self (*not me*).

When there is comorbid PTSD or CPTSD, the symptom profiles are different (see Chapter 9). The following chapter will describe symptom profiles of patients with the DSM-5 dissociative subtype of PTSD and the ICD-11 CPTSD. Of course, these may coexist with personality disorders. Table 8.1 contains an overview of symptom profiles in BPD with and without CPTSD and/or a dissociative disorder.

TABLE 8.1

Dissociative Symptoms in Various Groups of BPD Patients With and Without CPTSD Or Dissociative Disorder*

Symptoms, Behavior	BPD	BPD plus (C)PTSD	BPD plus OSDD-1	BPD plus DID
Possibly trauma-related symptoms (comorbidity) (TADS-I Part 2)	May be present; no indication for a division of the personality in conjunction with trauma-related symptoms	Present; at least PTSD, sometimes indication for a division of the personality in conjunction with some of the trauma-related symptoms	Present; at least PTSD, CPTSD often with indication for a division of the personality with some of the trauma-related symptoms	Present; at least PTSD, CPTSD mostly with indication for a division of the personality in conjunction with some of the trauma-related symptoms
Identity problems/ confusion	Often present; polarized as good/evil, internal conflict	Often present; polarized as good/evil, internal conflict	May be related to trauma-related parts; amnesia, voices, sometimes also polarized	Confusion about different voices, thoughts, acts, amnesia, often internal conflict between more than two voices
Alterations in consciousness (TADS-I Part 3)	May be present	Regularly present	Often present	Often present

continues

Symptoms, Behavior	BPD	BPD plus (C)PTSD	BPD plus OSDD-1	BPD plus DID
Depersonalization; experiencing self as strange or unreal (detachment)	May be present	May be present	Often present	Often present
Derealization; surroundings unreal	May be present	May be present	May be present	May be present
Absorption	May be present	May be present	May be present	May be present
Trance and Daydreaming	May be present	May be present	May be present	May be present
Somatoform dissociative symptoms (TADS-I Part 4)	May be present; no indication for a division of the personality, tension-related	May be present; sometimes indications for a division of the personality	Regularly present; with indications for a division of the personality	Regularly present; with indications for a division of the personality
Psychoform dissociative symptoms (TADS-I Part 5)	Absent	May be present	Present	Present
Amnesia				
Direct and indirect indications of having done certain things	Absent; concentration problems and problems due to absorption are sometimes wrongly interpreted as dissociative amnesia	May be present; for past/trauma and reexperiencing of trauma, or non-epileptic seizures	May be present; for past/trauma; reexperiencing or sometimes for actions by parts stuck in trauma time or non-epileptic seizures	Present; for acts of parts functioning in daily life (amnesia for the present) and for the past/actions of parts stuck in trauma time
Failure to recognize people or surroundings	Absent	Can be present when reexperiencing trauma	May be present	Regularly present
Fugue	Absent	Absent	May be present/actions by parts stuck in trauma time	Regularly present; actions of parts functioning in daily life and of parts stuck in trauma time

Schneiderian symptoms/ intrusions				
Pseudo-hallucinations	May be present	May be present	Regularly present	Often present
Voices; quality of voices	May be present; polarized as good/evil (1 or 2 voices)	May be present; trauma-related, e.g., abuser(s)' voice(s), sometimes children's voice	Regularly present; trauma-related, e.g., abuser(s)' voice(s), sometimes children's voice	Often present; usually several voices, sometimes described as a cacophony, male, female, children, onset hearing voices often in childhood
Thought withdrawal/ blocking	Absent	Absent	Sometimes present under the influence of dissociative parts of the personality	Frequently present under the influence of dissociative parts of the personality
Unexpected intrusive thoughts	Absent	Usually absent	Sometimes present; related to trauma-related part of personality	Frequently present; related to dissociative parts of the personality
Influences on behavior, thoughts, and emotions	Absent	Usually absent	Sometimes present; related to trauma-related part of personality	Often present; related to dissociative parts of the personality
Symptoms possibly indicating a division of the personality/dissociative parts of the personality	Absent	Mostly absent; sometimes indications for part stuck in trauma time	Present; indications of parts stuck in trauma time	Present; both parts functioning in daily life and parts stuck in trauma time
Emotional response to diagnostic assessment; dissociation; going out of contact	Absent; no difficulty with talking about dissociative symptoms	May cause anxiety; particularly when asked about PTSD symptoms	Regularly present; anxiety and ambivalence re talking about dissociative symptoms; phobia of dissociative parts of the personality	Often present; anxiety and ambivalence re talking about dissociative symptoms; phobia of dissociative parts of the personality

* Symptom profiles of patients with BPD who falsely believe they have DID or who imitate DID will be discussed in Chapter 10.

CHAPTER 9

PTSD Dissociative Subtype in DSM-5 and Complex PTSD in ICD-11

Introduction

New in DSM-5 is a separate category on trauma- and stressor-related disorders, which includes PTSD. Previously (DSM-IV-TR and earlier DSM versions from 1980 onward), PTSD was categorized in the anxiety disorders section. The DSM-5 also recognizes a correlation between PTSD and dissociative disorders. For this reason, the chapter discussing the dissociative disorders category follows the chapter on trauma- and stressor-related disorders in the DSM-5. As described in Chapter 1, the main reason for not categorizing these disorders in the same chapter was that trauma was not included as a criterion in the dissociative disorders. However, several studies with the DES and the DES-T have shown that patients with PTSD have markedly increased dissociation scores (Carlson et al., 2012; Lyssenko et al., 2018; van IJzendoorn & Schuengel, 1996; Waller et al., 1996).

CPTSD was not added as a separate classification in DSM-5, as it was in ICD-11. The criteria for PTSD have, however, been expanded to include a D criterion, "negative alterations in cognitions and mood associated with the traumatic event(s)" (APA, 2013, 2022). In addition, a subtype was added: "PTSD with dissociative symptoms," requiring individuals to meet the PTSD criteria and experience persistent or recurrent symptoms of depersonalization and/or derealization. The inclusion of this subtype of PTSD was based on research with large groups of patients with PTSD, both veterans and patients with other trauma histories (Lanius et al., 2010). Neurobiological and epidemiological research as well as symptom profiles have differentiated two PTSD subgroups: a so-called nondissociative and a dissociative group (Ginzburg et al., 2006; Lanius et al., 2010; Lanius et al., 2012; Steuwe et al., 2012; Wolf, Lunney, et al., 2012; Wolf, Miller, et al., 2012). Stein et al. (2013) conducted a large epidemiological study involving over 25,000 patients from 16 countries, in which 14% of patients with PTSD reported depersonalization and derealization symptoms. The PTSD group with depersonalization and derealization symptoms also reported more flashbacks and more amnesia (again typical dissociative symptoms) but did not report more of the other PTSD symptoms. Finally, this group showed higher rates of prior trauma, harmful childhood experiences, suicidality, and comorbid psychiatric problems before the onset of PTSD and impairment in functioning. Stein and colleagues concluded that their findings were consistent with features of complex PTSD (CPTSD) or DESNOS (disorders of extreme stress not otherwise specified), but that future research will need to clarify the relationship between CPTSD and the DSM-5 dissociative subtype of PTSD. Several studies reported a prevalence of 12% to 44% of the dissociative subtype in patients with PTSD (Armour et al., 2014; Hansen et al., 2017; Müllerová et al., 2016; Wolf, Miller, et al., 2012). Recently, Swart et al. (2020) found that 54% of patients with the dissociative subtype of PTSD had a comorbid dissociative disorder.

Although it is a step forward that the DSM-5 now formally recognizes the relationship between PTSD and dissociation, there is much more to be said about this dissociative subtype. Dorahy and van der Hart (2015) discussed limitations of the DSM-5 dissociative subtype listed as "classic PTSD." The name alone suggests that it would not be dissociative in nature, even though several important PTSD criteria, notably amnesia and flashbacks, are core symptoms of dissociation. Their second criticism is that the entire body of research was focused only on two of the negative dissociative symptoms, namely depersonalization and derealization. This is mainly because most research is based on the Clinician Administered PTSD Scale (CAPS; Blake et al., 1995) or other self-report questionnaires. The CAPS only includes a few questions about depersonalization and derealization. This is also the case in some self-report questionnaires, such as the Global Psychotrauma Screen (GPS; Olff et al., 2020). In addition, there is no consensus about whether these two symptoms are conceptually dissociative (see Chapter 1). Future research should examine the association between PTSD and the full range of positive and negative dissociative symptoms (for a detailed discussion, see Dorahy & van der Hart, 2015; Nijenhuis, 2015, 2017).

DID, OSDD-1, and PTSD Dissociative Subtype in DSM-5

The vast majority of patients with DID and OSDD-1 meet many, if not all, criteria of classic PTSD (Boon & Draijer, 1993a; Loewenstein et al., 2017; Rodewald, Wilhelm-Gößling, et al., 2011; Spiegel et al., 2011; Spiegel et al., 2013). In our study with the SCID-D in patients with DID, 80% of the total of 71 patients also met the criteria for PTSD. The remaining 20% did not meet the A criterion for PTSD because at the time of the interview there was complete amnesia for the trauma history and often also for part of their childhood. Nevertheless, this remaining 20% of participants did score on all other PTSD symptoms. They reported flashbacks, symptoms that resembled reliving traumatic experiences, and avoidance of several situations without realizing what these symptoms were related to. In addition, many symptoms of hyperarousal were mentioned, such as irritability, panic, and jumpiness interspersed with emotional numbing. Similarly, in recent research with the TADS-I, almost all patients with DID and OSDD-1 reported the entire range of PTSD symptoms.

Furthermore, almost all patients with DID and OSDD-1 (formerly DDNOS), both in the earlier SCID study and in the current one with the TADS-I reported chronic, severe depersonalization, which would mean that almost all of them also meet the criteria for the current subtype of PTSD. A differential diagnostic problem is the high comorbidity of the dissociative subtype of PTSD with the dissociative disorders (Swart et al., 2020). The diagnoses of DID or OSDD-1 can easily be missed—especially if during diagnostic testing only depersonalization and derealization are emphasized in the context of PTSD, instead of the full range of dissociative symptoms. In Chapter 7 it was noted that the dissociative subtype of PTSD is often difficult to distinguish from OSDD-1, especially in patients who are as yet unable to report on dissociative parts or who are very avoidant or say they have no parts.

Complex PTSD in ICD-11

The concept of complex PTSD (CPTSD) is not new, although it is now included in ICD-11 for the first time. Also, as evidenced by the different concepts in DSM-5 and ICD-11, there is much confusion and difference of opinion, both about what to consider complex trauma and about what CPTSD might be (Ter Heide et al., 2014, 2016). The International Society for Traumatic Stress Studies (ISTSS) formulates complex trauma as "Exposure to repeated or prolonged instances or multiple forms of interpersonal trauma, often occurring under circumstances where escape is not possible due to physical, psychological, maturational, family/environmental, or social constraints" (Cloitre et al., 2012, p. 4). This formulation is used by many clinicians.

Development of the Concept of CPTSD

Lenore Terr (1991) was the first to distinguish between what she called Type 1 and Type 2 trauma in children. This distinction is still used in clinical practice, not only in children but also in adults. Type 1 trauma concerns a one-time traumatic experience, while Type 2 trauma involves long-term, repeated traumatic experiences. Terr also described differential clusters of symptoms in children with Type 1 versus Type 2 trauma; Type 2 trauma involves more dissociation.

Herman (1992a) was the first to speak about CPTSD in adults. At the time, she called this a "syndrome of survivors of prolonged and repeated trauma." She felt that the classification of PTSD in DSM-III did not adequately reflect the much more complex picture of patients with a history of early childhood trauma, such as sexual abuse and physical and domestic violence, as well as traumas such as being held hostage, chronic war experiences, being a prisoner of war, or concentration camp experiences. This included not only the nature and severity of the traumatic experiences, but also the degree of "totalitarian control" over the victim. With Bessel van der Kolk, she grouped symptoms matching this concept of CPTSD into six categories, with the goal of creating a new diagnosis in the DSM-IV: "Disorders of Extreme Stress Not Otherwise Specified (DESNOS)" (Herman, 1992a; Herman & van der Kolk, 1987; Pelcovitz et al., 1997). The proposed diagnosis is shown in Table 9.1.

TABLE 9.1
Criteria for Disorders of Extreme Stress Not Otherwise Specified (DESNOS)
1. Alterations in regulation of affect and impulses
2. Alterations in attention or consciousness
3. Alterations in self-perception
4. Alterations in relationships with others
5. Somatization
6. Alterations in systems of meaning

Two similar diagnostic interviews were developed for the assessment of CPTSD for the field trials for the DSM-IV: the Structured Interview for Disorders of Extreme Distress (SIDES; Pelcovitz et al., 1997) and the Structured Clinical Interview for DSM-IV disorders of extreme stress not otherwise specified (SCID-DESNOS: van der Kolk et al., 1992). Worldwide, the SIDES is commonly used and considered the gold standard. There is also a Dutch-language self-report version in addition to the interview (van Dijke & van der Hart, 2002; van Dijke et al., 2018). However, the SIDES should always be preceded by an interview, such as the CAPS, which identifies PTSD.

Despite all the efforts made by Herman and many colleagues since the 1990s, neither DESNOS nor CPTSD have ever been included as independent diagnoses in the DSM, because the field trial for the DSM-IV supposedly did not provide sufficient evidence for a separate classification of DESNOS. This conclusion was not shared by van der Kolk and colleagues (2005). Internationally there is broad agreement that CPTSD calls for separate guidelines for diagnosis and treatment, as provided by the ISTSS (Bisson et al., 2019; Courtois & Ford, 2009, Ford et al., 2005; Ford & Courtois, 2020; Herman, 1992b; van der Kolk et al., 2005; ISTSS: Cloitre et al., 2012).

CPTSD Criteria in ICD-11

In ICD-11, CPTSD is categorized as a separate diagnosis from PTSD. In accordance with World Health Organization (WHO) guidelines, the diagnosis of CPTSD is simpler than the previously proposed DESNOS diagnosis. According to WHO guidelines, the simplicity of a diagnostic classification increases clinical utility and makes ICD diagnoses easier to apply in clinical practice worldwide (Cloitre, 2020). The choice of inclusion criteria is mainly based on Cloitre's (2020) concept, and when compared to the originally proposed classification by Herman and van der Kolk, it is greatly simplified (Maercker et al., 2013). CPTSD involves three clusters of PTSD symptoms and three clusters of CPTSD symptoms (see Table 9.2). Individuals are either diagnosed with PTSD or CPTSD, but not both. However, a prerequisite for CPTSD is that a person meets the criteria for PTSD. The criteria were based partly on symptoms that occurred most frequently in patients with complex traumatization in previous research (van der Kolk et al., 2005) and partly on clinical judgments of experts (Cloitre et al., 2011).

Despite some overlap with other disorders, such as BPD, CPTSD would be readily distinguishable from BPD using the ICD-11 criteria even in BPD patients with PTSD symptoms (Brewin et al., 2017; Cloitre et al., 2014, Hyland, Karatzias, et al., 2019). The following clusters of symptoms fit BPD but not CPTSD: (1) desperate attempts to avoid abandonment, (2) an unstable sense of self, (3) unstable relations and intense interpersonal relationships, and (4) impulsivity. Based on these clusters the two disorders can be distinguished (Hyland, Karatzias, et al., 2019).

When comparing the current ICD-11 criteria (Table 9.2) with the earlier DESNOS criteria (Table 9.1), the first thing to notice is that the important criterion of "changes in attention or awareness" was omitted. This omission all but eliminated the role of dissociation as a major symptom in CPTSD, which is a major limitation of the new classification. Also, the abbreviated version of the International Trauma Questionnaire (ITQ; Cloitre et al., 2018), the ITQ-12, does not include a single item on dissociation (Frewen, 2021). There is one recent study that examined the severity of dissociative experiences in a group of patients with PTSD or CPTSD based on ICD-11 criteria measured by self-report using the ITQ (Hyland, Shevlin, et al., 2019). Dissociative experiences were measured with a short version of the Dissociative Symptoms Scale (DSS), which does not focus solely on

TABLE 9.2
ICD-11 Criteria for Complex Posttraumatic Stress Disorder (CPTSD)

Exposure to an event or series of events of an extremely threatening or horrific nature, most commonly prolonged or repetitive events from which escape is difficult or impossible. Such events include, but are not limited to, torture, concentration camps, slavery, genocide campaigns and other forms of organized violence, prolonged domestic violence, and repeated childhood sexual or physical abuse.

Following the traumatic event, the development of all three core elements of posttraumatic stress disorder, lasting for at least several weeks:

- Re-experiencing the traumatic event after the traumatic event has occurred, in which the event(s) is not just remembered but is experienced as occurring again in the here and now. This typically occurs in the form of vivid intrusive memories or images; flashbacks, which can vary from mild (there is a transient sense of the event occurring again in the present) to severe (there is a complete loss of awareness of present surroundings), or repetitive dreams or nightmares that are thematically related to the traumatic event(s). Re-experiencing is typically accompanied by strong or overwhelming emotions, such as fear or horror, and strong physical sensations. Re-experiencing in the present can also involve feelings of being overwhelmed or immersed in the same intense emotions that were experienced during the traumatic event, without a prominent cognitive aspect, and may occur in response to reminders of the event. Reflecting on or ruminating about the event(s) and remembering the feelings that one experienced at that time are not sufficient to meet the re-experiencing requirement.

- Deliberate avoidance of reminders likely to produce re-experiencing of the traumatic event(s). This may take the form either of active internal avoidance of thoughts and memories related to the event(s), or external avoidance of people, conversations, activities, or situations reminiscent of the event(s). In extreme cases the person may change their environment (e.g., move house or change jobs) to avoid reminders.

- Persistent perceptions of heightened current threat, for example as indicated by hypervigilance or an enhanced startle reaction to stimuli such as unexpected noises. Hypervigilant persons constantly guard themselves against danger and feel themselves or others close to them to be under immediate threat either in specific situations or more generally. They may adopt new behaviors designed to ensure safety (not sitting with one's back to the door, repeated checking in vehicles' rear-view mirror). In complex posttraumatic stress disorder, unlike in posttraumatic stress disorder, the startle reaction may in some cases be diminished rather than enhanced.

Severe and pervasive problems in affect regulation. Examples include heightened emotional reactivity to minor stressors, violent outbursts, reckless or self-destructive behavior, dissociative symptoms when under stress, and emotional numbing, particularly the inability to experience pleasure or positive emotions.

Persistent beliefs about oneself as diminished, defeated, or worthless, accompanied by deep and pervasive feelings of shame, guilt, or failure related to the stressor. For example, the individual may feel guilty about not having escaped from or succumbing to the adverse circumstance, or not having been able to prevent the suffering of others.

Persistent difficulties in sustaining relationships and in feeling close to others. The person may consistently avoid, deride, or have little interest in relationships and social engagement more generally. Alternatively, there may be occasional intense relationships, but the person has difficulty sustaining them.

The disturbance results in significant impairment in personal, family, social, educational, occupational, or other important areas of functioning. If functioning is maintained, it is only through significant additional effort.

Source: WHO. International Classification of Diseases 11th Revision (ICD-11). icd.who.int, Feb 2022.

depersonalization and derealization (Carlson et al., 2016). The mean DSS score among patients with CPTSD was significantly higher than that of patients with PTSD alone, demonstrating that dissociation is an important factor in CPTSD.

A limitation of this study is that only two very short self-report questionnaires were used. Furthermore, the sample group consisted mainly of female respondents (93%). Of this group, 69% (n = 67) met criteria for CPTSD, 9.3% (n = 9) met criteria for PTSD, and 21.6% (n = 21) met criteria for neither of the diagnoses. All of them reported traumatic experiences, particularly physical (95.1%) and sexual violence (83.5%). More research will have to show whether the same severity of dissociative experiences occurs in other populations. Note that this sample is quite similar to groups of patients with a dissociative disorder, the majority of whom are also usually women and report similar trauma.

When comparing complex PTSD in ICD-11 with the dissociative subtype in DSM-5, it is notable that, despite legitimate criticism of the DSM-5 classification, DSM-5 does pay more attention to dissociation as a symptom than does the ICD-11 classification. Frewen (2021) noted that the DSM diagnosis is actually more similar to the original DESNOS concept than the current ICD-11 diagnosis.

DID, Partial DID, and CPTSD in ICD-11

No research has yet been done on the distinction and any overlap between CPTSD as currently formulated in ICD-11 and DID or partial DID. The only clear dissociative symptom included in the PTSD criteria in ICD-11 is the re-experiencing of the traumatic event or events in the present. This implies that both within the theory of structural dissociation and the TRASC model, there must be at least one other personality part (EP) or altered state of consciousness in addition to the part functioning in daily life (see Figure 1.1). The description of this altered state of consciousness, or rather this other part of herself as it occurs in PTSD, is beautifully expressed in the autobiography of Charlotte Delbo (1971, English translation, 1990), a French resistance fighter who was imprisoned in Auschwitz:

> [. . .] I feel that the one who was in the camp is not me, is not the person who is here, facing you. No, it is all too incredible. And everything that happened to that other, the Auschwitz one, now has no bearing upon me, does not concern me, so separate from one another are this deep-lying memory and ordinary memory. . . . Luckily in my agony I cry out. My cry wakes me, and I emerge from the nightmare, drained. It takes days for everything to get back to normal, for everything to

get shoved back inside memory, and for the skin of memory to mend again. I become myself again, the person you know, who can talk to you about Auschwitz without exhibiting or registering any anxiety or emotion. (p. 3)

In her nightmares, Charlotte Delbo is back in the then and there, reliving her experiences at Auschwitz as in the now. In the present, the self that *was in the camp* is a different self than that of today.

As described earlier, the vast majority of patients with DID or OSDD-1 meet the DSM criteria for PTSD. To assess whether CPTSD is also present according to the current ICD-11 criteria, a patient must report symptoms in the following three areas in addition to PTSD: problems in affect regulation, a negative perception of self, and problems in relationships with others.

Precisely because the ICD-11 criteria for CPTSD hardly address dissociative symptoms and do not screen for them at all when using the ITQ, there is a risk of overlooking the more complex dissociative disorders. When CPTSD and DID are present, the patient should report the cluster of dissociative symptoms in addition to the CPTSD symptoms: amnesia for traumatic experiences as well as for everyday life functioning; Schneiderian symptoms, which usually include hearing voices and intrusions of dissociative parts; and evidence of the existence of dissociative parts. When these symptom clusters are properly assessed, using the diagnostic interview will help clarify whether the CPTSD symptoms are part of a dissociative disorder.

Examples of Patients With and Without CPTSD According to ICD-11, Based on TADS-I Assessment

Part 2 of the TADS-I contains sections with questions about PTSD symptoms and the proposed criteria for the DESNOS concept. When the entire TADS-I is administered, there is sufficient information to determine the severity of PTSD and/or CPTSD symptoms in addition to the presence of a dissociative disorder. The trauma history is not included in the TADS-I and must be assessed separately in order to make a diagnosis of PTSD or CPTSD.

Chapter 6 describes three examples of a TADS-I assessment of patients with DID, partial DID, or OSDD-1. These three patients also reported symptoms consistent with the dissociative subtype of PTSD in DSM-5, while two of them also met the criteria of the ICD-11 CPTSD diagnosis. One patient did not meet the ICD-11 criteria for CPTSD, as she reported having neither a negative self-image (ICD-11, Criterion 2) nor problems in relationships with others (ICD-11, Criterion 3). The examples in Chapter 6 emphasize the importance of always properly investigating the entire cluster of dissociative symptoms in patients referred for CPTSD or the dissociative subtype of PTSD. If this is left unchecked, a more complex dissociative disorder can easily be missed. The following case reports illustrate this for CPTSD.

Case Report: A Patient With CPTSD (ICD-11)

The patient was a 30-year-old woman who had been referred for a second opinion to find out whether she might have a dissociative disorder. She was single and worked in aged care. Both her parents were psychiatric patients, and she had been removed from home by child protection services at a young age, together with her little brother. Later, she lived alternately with her father and her mother, who had divorced by then. In elementary school, she was overweight and was severely bullied. She had felt like an outsider. While at high school she had put herself on a very strict diet, and at 16 she had found a boyfriend and had felt she was noticed for the first time in her life. He had initially devoted a great deal of attention to her, giving her compliments and presents, but he turned out to be what in the Netherlands is called a "loverboy," and in the United States is known as a "pimp-boyfriend," a term used to describe young men who pretend to be boyfriends, but who act like pimps, forcing their girlfriends to have sex with other men. For over a year, he had forced her to have sex with others. At age 18, the patient had attempted suicide and had been admitted to psychiatric care; a follow-up program that provided a safe living environment had helped her detach herself from this boyfriend. The patient later lived with a new boyfriend for a period of time, but this relationship did not work out either. The patient reported that she had been too suspicious, thinking he was unfaithful because the sex between them was not going well. That was why her boyfriend had left.

General

First Impressions. The patient was a friendly woman who clearly tried to answer questions to the best of her ability. She was open in the interaction although sometimes a little verbose in her answers.

Substance Use and Medication. The patient used drugs during the period she had spent with the pimp-boyfriend, specifically speed and other party drugs; she had never used them again after that. She rarely drank alcohol, only occasionally in social settings. She was on a low dose of antipsychotic medication and sleep medication.

Possibly Trauma-Related Symptoms

Eating Problems. The patient said that she still had eating problems.

> I often feel lonely and then I start eating too much. They're not real binges; I just keep eating in the evening. At other times, I think that I am way too fat and ugly, and I barely eat for a few weeks so I lose a lot of weight. It's kind of a yo-yo effect and goes up and down a lot.

The patient reported no symptoms that might indicate a division of the personality associated with the eating problems, nor did she recognize depersonalization during binge eating.

Sleep Problems. The patient slept reasonably well with the help of medication, but when she was not on medication she had frequent nightmares, especially about the period with the pimp-boyfriend. She also reported other bad dreams involving abandonment or loneliness. Sometimes the nightmares seemed so real that she was reliving the horrible situations. The patient explained that it took time for her to regain her orientation in the now when waking up from a nightmare like that. She had tried to stop medication several times, but then she would be too anxious and would barely sleep. Apart from the above, she did not recognize any symptoms that might indicate a division of the personality.

Mood and Emotion Regulation. The patient reported being depressed regularly, especially when thinking about the future; she felt that she would not be able to achieve her dream of having a happy family with children of her own. *It's not for me, that was clear ever since I was very small and removed from my home by child protection services. I do understand that my parents were ill, but they should never have had children.* She could vividly recall her suicide attempt and described it as an act of desperation for not knowing how to ever get away from her pimp boyfriend. She had never attempted suicide after that, although she still often felt depressed.

She was easily offended and had a hard time calming down when upset. She also had difficulty with intense emotions, especially anger. She sometimes found herself being very unreasonable, even in her work, because she could not tolerate injustice.

> I can get very angry with colleagues about the way they talk about these elderly people, but they know I can be like that, so I usually get away with it or I admit that I overreacted. I suspect all of this started after the time with the loverboy [pimp-boyfriend].

The patient denied having rapid mood swings; generally she was quite even-tempered, but she had noticed that she sometimes worked on autopilot.

Anxiety and Panic. The patient reported anxiety since the experiences with the pimp-boyfriend. For a long time, she had been terrified that he might find her, and she was still vigilant. Sometimes she thought she recognized him, and then it turned out to be someone else. She also found that she still suffered from certain triggers that reminded her of him. There were many things she tried to avoid; for example, she never watched TV programs related to the subject. Every so often she might reexperience certain events, as if they were happening in the present. *It's strange, but I do not only relive the nasty things, but also how I fell for him and how sweet he was at first, but that's the very thing that makes me most afraid and wary.* She had already gone through trauma-focused treatment (Narrative Exposure Therapy [NET]; Schauer et al., 2011) and said her PTSD symptoms had decreased but not disappeared.

> When I'm home alone and feel so lonely—and this is a very old feeling—it sometimes overwhelms me again. Then I may even long for the nice side of him sometimes. I'm very crazy. I can lose myself at those times and then suddenly be reliving it all as if it were happening right now.

She had learned to seek diversion to avoid this. She described herself as hyperalert and very jumpy, and sometimes as having a *short fuse.*

Self-Injurious Behavior. The patient used to scratch her arms and bang her head during the time with the pimp-boyfriend but was no longer doing this. She explained that she used to do that quite deliberately because she had been so desperate. She did not report any symptoms of depersonalization or amnesia associated with these behaviors.

Self-Image and Identity. The patient had a low self-image and usually thought negatively about herself.

> From a very young age, I had the idea that it'd been better if I'd not existed and that I was ugly and fat. Also, surely not everyone would be stupid enough to fall for that idiot. That happens simply because I'm of little worth, and he understood that very well. This was only reaffirmed in the relationship I had after that. I was so suspicious, and I also couldn't fulfill what he wanted from me sexually.

She was not otherwise confused about who she was, although she sometimes had a hard time believing the positive evaluations she received at work. She was aware that others thought less negatively of her than she did of herself, but that did not change her thoughts. She did not experience an internal struggle, and she knew quite well what she wanted, but did not think she would be able to achieve it.

Relationships With Others. The patient had difficulty trusting others and was afraid to let people get too close.

> I have been alone since childhood, not daring to have friends over as I never knew how I would find my parents. I was ashamed of them and of our dirty house. Often, there even was no food in the house, so me and my little brother were left to ourselves. Sometimes I used to go to a neighbor who was kind. I think it was her who called Child Protective Services. My parents had so many problems of their own; they just didn't see us.

The patient now had a small network of acquaintances with whom she had superficial contact.

Sexuality. Since her partner had left her, the patient had had no sexual relations, and did not want to. She reported feeling uncomfortable and constantly ashamed of her body. She said she used to not feel much, as if shutting off. This had even been the case when she was with the pimp-boyfriend: *I just let it happen.*

EVALUATION OF POSSIBLY TRAUMA-RELATED SYMPTOMS

The section on possibly trauma-related symptoms reveals that this patient was clearly still suffering from PTSD, although she said it had decreased. However, she still occasionally was reexperiencing traumatizing events, described "negative alterations in cognitions and mood" (D criterion of the DSM-5 diagnosis of PTSD) and detachment. All of this had been exacerbated by the pimp-boyfriend experience, but part of these problems had originated earlier from the neglect as a child. She had negative beliefs about herself and thought that she had been a willing victim of the pimp-boyfriend for *being so stupid.* She avoided social contact and had difficulty connecting with others. Finally, she also mentioned symptoms of hyperarousal. Thus, she met the PTSD criteria of both DSM-5 and ICD-11.

The patient also met the CPTSD criteria of ICD-11, since (1) she mentioned affect regulation problems; (2) she had a very negative self-image; and (3) she had significant problems in relationships, including feeling suspicious and having difficulty connecting with others. In addition, she generally seemed to describe detachment. This interview did not reveal any indications of BPD; rather, the patient appeared avoidant.

The Next Part of the Interview

No evidence of a division of the personality emerged in the section of the TADS-I on possibly trauma-related symptoms, and this was confirmed in subsequent sections of the interview. The patient did not describe any memory problems or amnesia, had never heard voices, and did not identify any other Schneiderian symptoms. Neither did she endorse having dissociative parts. She did describe having recurrent depersonalization symptoms, particularly emotional detachment. Both in social situations and at work, she acted on automatic pilot a lot. She did not describe derealization but did describe absorption. When she was alone, she would sometimes lose herself in daydreaming, but since this sometimes evolved into episodes of reexperiencing she tried to avoid this at all costs.

Conclusion

The patient met the ICD-11 criteria for CPTSD and the DSM-5 criteria for dissociative subtype PTSD. Many of the CPTSD symptoms, such as negative self-image and problems in relationships with others, had evolved much earlier as a result of the unavailability of her parents and the resultant emotional neglect. PTSD had evolved later in life as a result of the trauma caused by the pimp-boyfriend and had amplified preexisting negative cognitions and beliefs. Treatment to date had focused on the trauma caused by the pimp-boyfriend, and the PTSD symptoms had diminished but not completely disappeared. The patient indicated that she was unwilling to focus treatment on the previous adverse experiences of neglect from her parents or on the feelings of shame and loneliness. She was relieved that she did not have a dissociative disorder.

Case Report: A Patient With PTSD Dissociative Subtype (DSM-5), but Not CPTSD (ICD-11)

The following is a brief example of a patient who met the criteria for the dissociative subtype of PTSD based on the TADS-I interview but who had neither a dissociative disorder nor CPTSD according to the ICD-11 criteria.

General

The patient was a 35-year-old Syrian refugee. He had reached the Netherlands after more than a year of drifting from country to country. Both his war experiences (he lost friends and barely escaped death due to violence by Assad's army) and his refugee story had resulted in severe PTSD. In Syria he had completed conservatory training and had been working in an orchestra. He was also a music teacher. Many of his relatives still lived in Syria. He had been in the Netherlands for several years and had fled together with a younger brother for whom he felt a great deal of responsibility. He spoke Dutch remarkably well.

Possibly Trauma-Related Symptoms

During the TADS-I section on possibly trauma-related symptoms, severe PTSD symptoms were particularly prominent. He reported little to no other symptoms and there was no evidence of division of the personality, such as amnesia or hearing voices. He described himself before the war as a cheerful person with many friends and a close family. His father had been a musician as well, but he had passed away. The patient had been unable to attend the funeral, which made him feel very sad. The patient used to have a clear plan for his future as a musician.

The patient described frequent flashbacks and episodes of reexperiencing his war trauma and said that sounds in particular triggered him severely. He figured that this was because, being a musician, he would be more likely to be triggered by sound than by sight. He tried to avoid anything related to war, but that was impossible because he was still in a shelter for asylum seekers, so he was in frequent contact with others with similar experiences.

No further evidence was found for the CPTSD symptom cluster of ICD-11. He described no obvious difficulties in affect regulation; he mainly felt numb. He certainly had no negative sense of self, although he sometimes did feel guilty for leaving his mother and sisters behind. He never had problems with relationships with others. He did, however, feel tense and down at times about the future, particularly because the refugee status determination procedure took so long, and the outcome was unknown. However, these are very real problems that do not fit a CPTSD criterion. In fact, the patient was trying to do as much as possible to integrate into Dutch society and build a new future and was committed to learning the language. Because of his musical talent, he succeeded in this quite well. He had a good relationship with a Dutch family who assisted him and his younger brother in many ways.

Alterations in Consciousness

Apart from reexperiencing, he described frequent depersonalization.

> I am no longer myself, the cheerful boy I was in Syria. I don't know who I am now. At best I feel nothing, no grief, nothing; then I feel completely numb. That's how I feel most of the time. It's unpleasant, but much less awful than the moments when it seems like I'm back in Syria, when I hear everything, the shooting, the bombs, the cries of fear.

Psychoform Dissociative Symptoms

The patient did not endorse any symptoms that indicate a division of the personality. He said his memories of the war were rather too intense: *I wish I was more able to forget.* He did not describe any Schneiderian symptoms and there was no evidence of dissociative parts.

Conclusion

The patient's symptoms fit the dissociative subtype of PTSD. They did not meet the criteria for a DSM-5 dissociative disorder diagnosis, nor did they meet the ICD-11 criteria for CPTSD.

CPTSD Versus Partial DID (ICD-11); or Dissociative Subtype of PTSD Versus OSDD-1 (DSM-5)

In the two examples above, both the dissociative subtype of PTSD and CPTSD are readily distinguishable from a dissociative disorder, such as DID, OSDD-1, and partial DID. None of the patients reported symptoms that might indicate a division of the personality or intrusions of dissociative parts. According to the theory of structural dissociation of the personality, PTSD dissociative subtype also involves a dissociative organization of the personality, with a part that functions in everyday life and a part that is stuck in trauma. This is called primary structural dissociation (see Figure 1.1). These two examples do not involve chronic trauma that began in childhood but rather traumatization at a somewhat later age, although in the case of the first patient many will speak of early childhood traumatization based on the severe neglect and insecure attachment. On its own, severe emotional neglect does not usually lead to PTSD or a dissociative disorder but to other mental health problems (see Chapter 11). The second patient was clearly securely attached, and his problems arose from war violence.

When physical or sexual abuse or serious threats to life occur at an early age in addition to emotional neglect, the long-term consequences are usually different. Such a trauma history usually results in CPTSD, the dissociative subtype of PTSD at the very least, but more often results in a dissociative disorder. In these cases, it is much more difficult to distinguish between CPTSD or PTSD dissociative subtype and OSDD-1 or partial DID from a diagnostic perspective, especially if there are partial memory problems (e.g., amnesia) regarding the traumatic experiences. This has been addressed through the examples provided in Chapters 6 and 7. The following is an example of a patient whose symptoms meet the criteria for PTSD dissociative subtype and CPTSD according to ICD-11, but who could also be argued to have partial DID.

Case Report: A Patient With PTSD Dissociative Subtype, CPTSD and/or Partial DID?

The patient was a 35-year-old woman who had previously been diagnosed with complex PTSD and BPD. She agreed with these diagnoses, but her clinician had concerns as to whether a dissociative disorder might also be present. In fact, the dissociative symptoms had never been properly assessed.

General

The patient had attended intensive day treatment for her borderline symptomatology and had received brief inpatient treatment with EMDR and exposure two years prior to the interview. She reported that the first week of this treatment had gone well. However, during the second week she had been overwhelmed with traumatic memories that could not all be dealt with during this short-term therapy. She still was not functioning well, and no outpatient follow-up had been provided by the facility providing the treatment.

The patient lived with a boyfriend. She had given up her studies as a dental assistant after the intensive trauma treatment, as she still suffered greatly from flashbacks and being overwhelmed by emotions.

Alcohol and Drugs. The patient reported having used drugs in the past, but not since she had entered treatment for the borderline symptomatology. Moreover, she had always consumed a lot of alcohol and still did so once every few weeks on average. On such occasions she was not able to control herself and would get drunk. The patient said she often used alcohol as a means of regulating her emotions. When she had been drinking, things did not affect her so intensely.

The patient used antipsychotics for sleep.

Possibly Trauma-Related Symptoms

Eating Problems. The patient reported no serious eating problems. She would sometimes binge eat during stressful periods, and on such occasions she would eat too much. She reported that food had a calming or soothing effect. The patient had no clear contact with her body and she could not feel when she was hungry or when she was full. There were no dissociative symptoms associated with eating that might indicate a division of the personality (such as amnesia and hearing voices).

Sleep Problems. The patient said that she did sleep with medication, although she would not really relax, and she would still be restless in her sleep. She often woke up very tired. Without medication, she would sleep very poorly and would experience numerous PTSD symptoms: agitation, flashbacks, and fear of closing her eyes to sleep for fear of having nightmares and flashbacks.

At the time of the interview, she also suffered from frequent flashbacks and reexperiencing during the day. She usually knew the meaning of the images and recognized most of them, but not all, and that would frighten her. Sometimes she did not know whether images were about something she had experienced. She said: *Sometimes there is something inside that says it really happened*. She could not say what that *something* was and thought about it as little as possible. When she would wake up from a bad dream, she would need a moment to reorient herself to the present. There had never been a time when waking up from a nightmare that she did not know where she was or who she was. Nor had she ever found any evidence of doing things at night for which she could not account.

Mood and Emotion Regulation. The patient described having very rapid mood swings that made her very tired. They would go from feeling gloomy to even gloomier and then suddenly very angry. The anger was often directed at her partner, which in turn made her feel guilty. Under the influence of the mood swings, especially when she was hyper, the patient would sometimes be very destructive, for example by overspending, having unsafe sex, or drinking. Outside her house, anger would be easily triggered; she described having a *short fuse* at times. There was sadness too, but she tried to hide these feelings: *It makes you vulnerable so people can only hurt you more.* She would get upset easily and it would be hard for her to calm down, although she improved a bit in the course of therapy. The patient reported that she could get depressed, especially since she would be home alone for entire days. She suffered from dark, negative thoughts about herself, like being good for nothing and ruining everything. She said she had never attempted suicide. She did have compulsive suicidal thoughts, but she never gave in to them. The patient acknowledged intense feelings of emptiness but not of boredom. She explained that she always had plenty to do, but that sometimes it was hard for her to commit to things and on those occasions she would be passive.

Anxiety and Panic. The patient said she was not fearful, but she did avoid certain things that made her anxious. She especially avoided things such as shopping, crowds, and high-level stimuli. She also had some specific fears, such as a fear of being alone in the dark. She avoided certain places where she had been abused. In addition, the patient described symptoms such as constant vigilance and jumpiness. When outdoors, she would continually scan her surroundings and she could become suspicious when people were walking close behind her or remained in her vicinity for a long time. In summary, she described the full range of severe PTSD symptoms.

Self-Injurious Behavior. The patient had cut herself in the past, but never to the point of requiring stitches. She had stopped doing so since starting treatment for the BPD symptoms. She had been aware of the cutting, but she had not been able to stop it at the time. She would feel somewhat alienated from herself when cutting and often did not feel the pain or not until later. It happened as if under inner coercion. At the time of the interview, she still experienced the impulse to harm herself now and then, but she no longer acted on it. Her boyfriend had an important role in her desire to have control over these impulses. The patient did not hear voices ordering her to engage in negative behaviors. She did describe that she sometimes felt a very strong inner compulsion to engage in negative behaviors, as if her behavior was influenced by something inside herself. But when she did not give in, she would feel better. It did not make her anxious to go against the impulses.

Self-Image and Identity. The patient described having a negative self-image. She was also very insecure about who she was and what her sexual identity and preferences were. In addition, she often had doubts about her own choices and the way she was or should be living her life, as well as whether she should go to therapy or not. Often there was a kind of battle going on inside her involving multiple opinions. She described a kind of thought process, not voices.

Relationships With Others. The patient described having very unstable relationships. There were a few exceptions. She had one close friend and her current boyfriend, with whom she had now been living for several years. The patient described having great difficulty trusting others; she was afraid to open up for fear of being hurt. She avoided relationships and had difficulty dealing with conflict. Her anger was problematic, but she could also get insecure and blame herself for everything. She often thought people were hurting her on purpose and described herself as someone who was easily offended. There was also a fear of abandonment. She felt that she was experiencing many problems in her relationships with others.

Sexuality. The patient generally did not like being touched, and especially not unexpectedly. During sexual contact, she would let her partner do *his thing*. She would be there, but also not there. She called this *spacing out*. Thus, the patient was not really involved during sexual contact although she did not have amnesia for it. Before this relationship, she used to have a great deal of casual sexual encounters, mostly with men and sometimes with women. She suffered from compulsive thoughts about sex more often than she would like. She was permanently confused about her sexual identity. She regarded sexuality as an ongoing problem.

SUMMARY OF THE TRAUMA-RELATED SYMPTOMS

The patient met all criteria for PTSD and CPTSD; in addition, she described many borderline symptoms. She had managed to gain significantly more control over impulsive and self-injurious behaviors. Although she did not describe any obvious dissociative symptoms that indicate a division of the personality, she did describe some dissociative symptoms that suggest this. She dissociated during sexual contact. She also had little or no contact with her body; she was not aware of being thirsty or hungry. She further mentioned that there was *something inside her* telling her that a flashback is based on a true traumatic experience that she could not remember. She could not elaborate on that *something* and seemed to avoid thinking about it. Finally, she did not describe a polarized struggle within herself, which might fit BPD, but rather a struggle between multiple opinions. Altogether, these examples could be subtle cues to division of the personality.

Alterations in Consciousness

Depersonalization and Derealization. The patient described many symptoms of depersonalization. She would often feel distant from herself and sometimes felt unable to really connect with herself. She would sometimes do things without understanding why, such as getting tattoos or piercings. She said that these things were not like her. She was aware of doing those things and could talk about them in detail, but they were impulses that she could not control during such moments. She thought that she might tend to go on automatic pilot for a while whenever things got to be too much. This was best described as a kind of short circuit in her head, as if she switched herself off and started functioning like a robot. She would also eventually be cut off from her feelings and not be able to access grief, for example, even though she knew it was there. The patient did not report derealization.

Absorption and Trance. The patient described that she could become completely absorbed in an activity and then lose her sense of time. This could happen when she was intensely preoccupied with something. She might also sit on the couch for hours without doing anything. In those instances, *the light would go out* and she would have no recollection of this afterward; however, there was no evidence that she was engaged in other activities in another dissociative part of the personality. She may have been reexperiencing. She would still find herself on the couch after a while: *I didn't even take a second cup of coffee.*

Somatoform Dissociative Symptoms

The patient did not experience problems such as fainting or loss of strength or paralysis in arms or legs. However, she did have difficulty swallowing at times. Also, as previously mentioned, she would sometimes be unable to make good contact with her body. Moreover, she said that she sometimes suffered from hypersensitivity to sound, light, and smell—fitting severe PTSD symptoms.

Psychoform Dissociative Symptoms

Amnesia. On the one hand, the patient impressed with her memory, which was pretty good. She did say, however, that she did not remember stretches of her past and that sometimes a flood of memories would recur or flashbacks of unpleasant things she had forgotten. Especially during periods with many flashbacks, she would find it difficult to know exactly what she had done on a day. Her thoughts were less present then; her sense of time would sometimes be like a sieve. But in fact, there were no indications that she had been doing things as another dissociative part of the personality. Once she had found herself out in the village where she lived, not quite knowing what she was doing there or how she had ended up there. She gave no further recent examples of amnesia for tasks and functions in daily life, and she said that stress and tension certainly affected the functioning of her memory. She also did not give the impression of deliberately withholding information, and she did not dissociate during the interview. There was amnesia for some of the traumatic experiences though.

Schneiderian Symptoms/Intrusions. The patient said that she did not hear voices. However, she described how she heard herself reading her own thoughts to herself in her head. She had been hearing this for as long as she could remember. The tone of her voice reading her thoughts could change somewhat according to the way her thoughts might change. The tone could be angrier or sadder. Her thoughts could be very argumentative among themselves. During the interview, the theme of her thoughts was mainly whether or not she gave the right answers and was being honest.

Dissociative Parts of the Personality. The patient did not feel that she was so divided that there were dissociative parts. Her partner had told her that she behaved differently, sometimes tough and at other times childish. She was not aware of this herself, but she thought it was part of her borderline symptomatology.

Diagnostic Considerations

The patient reported all the symptoms consistent with PTSD dissociative subtype and the ICD-11 diagnosis of CPTSD. In addition, she described many dissociative symptoms, particularly memory problems about the past. She also mentioned amnesia in the present time for episodes of reexperiencing traumatizing events. She reported chronic depersonalization. Although she said that she did not hear voices, she seemed to have been hearing her own voice all her life as if reading to herself. The tone of her own voice could be different. It is quite possible that these were dissociative voices after all, especially since there were several opposing opinions. The symptoms may be consistent with a dissociative disorder, such as partial DID, and even a masked presentation of DID cannot be completely ruled out.

The patient mentioned several times when she had been unable to resist an inner urge, for example to get a tattoo, which she felt was not in line with her character. This was more likely to be ego dystonic than the influence of a borderline mode. She also referred to inner urges in relation to self-harm and eating problems. These could be intrusions of dissociative parts but, based on the current information, it was still difficult to distinguish these from potential borderline modes. The patient also met the criteria for BPD.

It is not unlikely that there were at least one but possibly several trauma-related dissociative parts, given that she had frequent amnesia for reexperiencing traumatizing events, and mentioned *spacing out* during sexual contact. She would not be present at those moments. Again, OSDD-1 is difficult to diagnose because the patient reported frequent amnesia, which does not fit the current classification of OSDD-1. The ICD-11 diagnosis of partial DID might perhaps be the most appropriate. Previously, according to the DSM classification, this patient would likely have received a diagnosis of DDNOS. This example clearly demonstrates the overlap of PTSD dissociative subtype, DDNOS in DSM-IV-TR, and CPTSD in ICD-11.

Within the theory of structural dissociation of the personality, no distinction is made between the two classifications (CPTSS and OSDD-1), and it is referred to as secondary structural dissociation of the personality (see Figure 1.1). This involves one part that functions in daily life and several parts that are stuck in trauma time.

In clinical practice, I always include a detailed description of the dissociative symptoms and diagnostic considerations as I have done above.

Summary

In this chapter, I have tried to show that it is not always possible to make a clear distinction between CPTSD (i.e., PTSD based on a history of early childhood traumatization) and a dissociative disorder such as OSDD-1 or partial DID. Likewise, it is not always clear whether there is division of the personality when the patient cannot yet provide clear examples. The different classifications in the DSM-5 and ICD-11 further complicate this. Lastly, in cases of a division of the personality there is a continuum of elaboration of dissociative parts, including gradually, a more extensive life history, and a more specific sense of self, others, and the world.

Some parts, both parts functioning in daily life and those stuck in trauma time, have a very limited function. Particularly when there is secondary structural dissociation of the personality, not all parts stuck in trauma time are equally developed, with some only limited to one action, emotion, or physical sensation. All parts do preserve cognitions, emotions, and bodily sensations that need to be integrated and owned by the individual as a whole. Parts suck in trauma time, in particular, are often perceived as *not me* from the perspective of the part(s) functioning in daily life. The description by Charlotte Delbo in this chapter is a good example. However, in a diagnostic assessment, especially involving patients presenting with OSDD-1 or partial DID, it is usually genuinely unclear to which degree the dissociative parts have developed. This will only become more apparent during treatment.

Most important, regardless of the classification system, patients with PTSD should always be interviewed thoroughly about dissociative symptoms. An accurate diagnosis is necessary for making an appropriate treatment plan. The more complex the dissociative problems are, the more a clinician must take them into account. I will briefly discuss this in Chapter 11.

CHAPTER 10

Incorrect (False-Positive) DID Diagnoses and Factitious or Imitated DID

Introduction

As described in Chapter 1, most patients diagnosed with DID have previously been treated for other mental disorders. At the time of our research, Nel Draijer and I found that 71 DID patients had been treated in the mental health system for an average of 8 years and had received three different diagnoses before the diagnosis of DID was made (Boon & Draijer, 1993a). These findings have been confirmed worldwide (Dorahy et al., 2014; ISSTD, 2011; Loewenstein et al., 2017). Given the high comorbidity, many false-negative diagnoses are made: these are patients in whom DID is not recognized because there are no or insufficient questions asked about dissociative symptoms, or because there is no structured assessment done. In addition, as described in Chapters 1 and 7, patients with genuine DID usually present with comorbid symptoms rather than with typical dissociative symptoms. Lastly, the assessment of DID is further complicated by the fact that there is still skepticism, based on ignorance or prejudice, about the validity of the diagnosis. Some clinicians do not believe this diagnosis exists and therefore do not assess for it. When they do encounter DID it often concerns patients with a dramatic or implausible presentation and therefore often involves a false-positive DID. In such cases, the false-positive presentation is likely to confirm biases about DID and is not always distinguished from genuine DID by inexperienced clinicians.

A correct diagnosis obviously has implications for treatment, which is markedly different for genuine DID patients as opposed to false-positive DID patients. False-positive DID diagnoses lead to patients remaining sick for longer, with supposedly DID behavior being rewarded and sustained by clinicians (Draijer & Boon, 1999). In particular, patients with histrionic dynamics seek attention through symptomatic behavior. Balint (1968) referred to this as the "basic fault," that is, the tendency to regression as a pursuit in itself. This invokes the risk of a negative therapeutic response and progressively worsening dysregulation in terms of disability, suicidality, and hospitalization, all of which should be avoided (Draijer, 2008). In psychotherapy, treatment of false-positive DID requires a radically different approach: one that focuses on the feelings of being unseen rather than the ongoing sick role. It is increasingly common to receive referrals for patients with a suspected DID diagnosis both in specialized centers for the treatment of dissociative disorders or by experts in their own practices. On subsequent diagnostic examination, these patients are found not to have DID, and often they have neither another dissociative disorder nor CPTSS.

Sometimes such misdiagnoses may be based on previous diagnostic testing involving a structured interview, such as the SCID-D; at other times they may be based on self-report questionnaires such as the DES or DIS-Q. Often symptoms such as depersonalization, absorption, and identity confusion have been found, and an incorrect DID diagnosis subsequently is based on these. In some cases, the DID diagnosis is entirely the therapist's doing; in other cases, patients themselves, sometimes in conjunction with important others, suggest or are convinced that they have DID. Unfortunately, it is also common for patients to have been treated for DID for several years without having the disorder. Over the past two decades, I have observed this phenomenon in the Netherlands and other European countries.

In summary, there are several possible factors involved in incorrect DID diagnoses (Boon & Draijer, 1995a; Brick & Chu, 1991; Chu, 1991; Draijer & Boon, 1999; Kluft, 1987b):

1. Clinicians making incorrect DID diagnoses in patients with other mental disorders and patients who follow along or become confused about their symptoms;
2. Clinicians making an incorrect DID diagnosis in patients who are found to have another dissociative disorder and patients who follow along or become confused about their symptoms;
3. Patients who consciously or not mimic a dissociative disorder or are confused about their identity and think they have DID, and clinicians who follow along or become confused about the patient's diagnosis.

Thus, in clinical practice incorrect DID diagnoses often appear to involve combinations of mutual influencing between patients and therapists.

Earlier Research

When Nel Draijer and I began our validation study of the SCID-D in the late 1980s, only rarely did we see patients with false-positive DID diagnoses made by clinicians or patients who imitated DID. In the United States a number of colleagues had already published about simulation, or the iatrogenic creation of DID (Brick & Chu, 1991; Chu, 1991; Coons, 1978, 1988, 1989, 1991; Kluft, 1987b; Kluft 1989). However, in general there was little knowledge among clinicians about dissociative disorders or dissociative symptoms. Also, at that time the continuum concept of dissociation was accepted around the world (see Chapter 1). Clinicians did not distinguish between dissociative symptoms that indicate a division of the personality and other alterations in consciousness, such as mild forms of depersonalization, derealization, and absorption. Even today, knowledge about dissociative disorders, in particular DID, is limited. In the Netherlands this also is due to the fact that patients with severe dissociative problems are shunned in many departments in the mental health services. Thus, there is little treatment experience apart from a rather limited number of specialized departments and individual private practices. Also, as discussed in Chapter 1, there is limited attention for DID in training programs for psychiatrists and psychologists because it involves a complex and difficult assessment. It is not easy to diagnose genuine DID correctly when the clinician has little experience with the condition and does not know how a dissociative organization of the personality may present. Identification of imitated DID or correction of false-positive DID may be even more difficult as many patients who think they have DID offer the classic symptoms more or less on a silver platter, in accordance with the way these are presented in the media, the internet, or textbooks. The task of ruling out DID is most difficult when not only the patients themselves but also close friends or relatives are convinced that DID is present and sometimes join them in presenting so-called evidence.

In imitations of DID, the patient has sometimes studied DID more than the average clinician who must make the diagnosis. The diagnosis can provide primary or secondary gain in the form of attention and the support it offers. Therefore, patients do not appreciate the fact that a second opinion does not confirm the diagnosis of DID. In some cases, this diagnosis has become their identity, and they experience the second opinion as something being snatched from them.

It should be noted that in all of our research since the late 1980s, it has been found that only a very small percentage of patients consciously and intentionally mimic DID. The vast majority of patients, and often their therapists, are genuinely confused about dissociative symptoms and the diagnosis of DID. This is why I wrote earlier that the term "factitious DID" is not entirely appropriate because of the meaning attached to it in DSM-5. Hence we prefer to speak of imitation (Boon & Draijer, 1995a; Draijer & Boon, 1999; Pietkiewicz et al., 2021). A factitious disorder involves the conscious mimicry of symptoms or a disorder for internal psychological reasons, for example, the psychological need to assume a sick role. In this context termed malingering or simulation, it involves deliberate imitation with a clear external benefit (e.g., eligibility for disability and health insurance benefits or avoiding punishment). Many patients do not give the impression that this involves consciously factitious presentations or malingering, but rather an attempt to understand themselves and make sense of their serious identity problems, inner chaos, or feelings of immense emptiness. It is true that the gain is in receiving additional attention, because the diagnosis of DID elicits more fascination from many therapists than does a personality disorder. That said, in some therapists it would rather evoke more irritation while increasing the likelihood of rejection. Sadly, when a second opinion eventually rescinds the diagnosis, these patients once again feel unseen, misunderstood, and rejected—a repetition of their core issues.

Indeed, many of the DID-imitating patients we diagnosed at the time with the SCID-D, as well as new patients I examined more recently using the TADS-I, are unsure of who they are; they have identity problems and are struggling with huge insecurity issues. Sometimes gender identity issues come into play. As noted above, as children, they were often not sufficiently seen by their caregivers. At some point, in some way, they encountered the subject of dissociation or dissociative disorders, or they met a fellow patient with those problems. They started reading about it and sometimes attended conferences or self-help group meetings, and they came to believe, often along with their clinician, that they had DID. For some, DID is more interesting because the diagnosis seems more treatable than personality disorder or schizophrenia. In addition, having DID can serve as an excuse for behavioral problems or antisocial behavior.

The emergence of the internet has also contributed to an increase in imitated DID. A lot of information about DID can be found online, for example through YouTube, with numerous videos of patients with DID and social media posts by bloggers and vloggers. Furthermore, many of the videos on the internet are quite dramatic and correspond more closely to the media's theatrical portrayal of DID than to the way genuine DID presents itself (see Chapter 1).

Coons and Milstein (1994) were the first to systematically compare patients with genuine DID to patients with factitious DID. In a group of 122 patients who were consecutively registered in a clinic for the treatment of dissociative disorders, Coons and Milstein found that 10% (n = 11) were imitating DID. Compared to patients who had genuine DID (n = 50), they showed many more symptoms consistent with a factitious disorder, such as a dramatic presentation, exaggeration of symptoms, pathological lying, *la belle indifference*,[12] selective amnesia, and lying. Patients with imitated DID often refused collateral interviews,[13] whereas genuine DID patients did not refuse these interviews. Coons and Milstein pointed out that some patients gave a rather naive and simple presentation of DID and their *alter personalities*, while it was found that other patients were much more difficult to distinguish from patients with genuine DID, even by experienced clinicians. What was striking, however, was that 44% of the group of patients with genuine DID also had a histrionic presentation; this is a much higher percentage than the 4 to 6% that Kluft (1987) once described and the 11.5% that we found in our systematic study with the SCID-D (Boon & Draijer, 1993a, 1993b, 1995). Most likely, this was a select group of DID patients, since all patients were admitted to a specific clinic for dissociative disorders.

Nel Draijer and I were the first to conduct structured assessments with the aid of the SCID-D to investigate and describe a group of patients who imitated DID or were confused about it (Boon & Draijer, 1995, 2003; Draijer & Boon, 1999; see also Table 10.1). Most of these patients had been referred by a therapist for a second opinion. The study involved 36 patients (33 women and 3 men), aged 30 years on average, almost without exception with a long-standing psychiatric history; a quarter of them had been psychiatrically hospitalized more than seven times. Common symptoms included substance abuse, eating problems, mood problems, impulse control problems, suicidality, and self-injurious behavior. We subdivided the patients into two groups based on clinical phenomenology: a first group of patients with mainly borderline personality disorder and a few with another Axis I diagnosis and comorbid personality problems (n = 20) and a second group of patients with a histrionic personality (n = 16). Especially in this second group, several SCID-D symptom clusters, particularly amnesia and identity alteration, were impossible to score: the patients exaggerated standard symptoms; they cited examples (e.g., *Of course, then I lost time*) that seemed to have been taken straight out of a textbook;[14] and they were unwilling or

---

12 *La belle indifférence*, the absence of signs of distress in the patient when symptoms occur, was originally described in the 19th-century French psychiatric literature and was later described in the psychoanalytic literature as a symptom what was then termed hysteria. This presentation has long been considered an important support for the diagnosis of so-called conversion disorder but has also been found to occur in neurological disorders (Vermeulen & van der Linden, 2012).

13 Collateral interviews are structured conversations with people who know the patient well and experience and observe them closely. The purpose of such interviews is to find confirmation that certain symptoms or behaviors are not only mentioned by the patient but have also been observed by others who know the patient well.

14 Stories and symptoms as represented in the media or movies or books. These include dramatically different presentations of dissociative parts with completely different prefer-

unable to provide authentic, idiosyncratic examples in their own words. It was also striking that they often became angry when a particular answer was explored in more detail; it seemed as if it made them feel under attack. *Surely you are the expert, I don't need to explain that to you, I've already done that quite clearly*, or: *Surely you know what "time lost" is, at least I would hope!*, were some of the responses in those cases. The theme of *not being understood* by us was constantly at play in these assessments and—unlike for the patients with genuine DID—led to a specific transference and countertransference process: the clinician in the role of some sort of police detective and the patient feeling victimized by the examination method: *I feel as if I am facing a tribunal*, one patient remarked when asked to elaborate on her examples. In some cases, dissociative parts were played out dramatically. One patient ostentatiously pulled out stuffed toys, saying: *Now I will be X* [childhood name] *for a while*. For most patients in this group, DID seemed to have become their identity. The first group, mainly patients with BPD, was able to respond to the SCID-D questions in a reliable manner and appeared to be genuinely confused about dissociative symptoms. They did manage to provide authentic examples of their symptoms. Also, a number of patients in this group did have PTSD symptoms and, in addition, mainly reported depersonalization symptoms.

A small number of these patients claimed to have amnesia only for undesirable behaviors (e.g., stalking or aggression toward a partner or children) but not for behaviors that were neutral or valued positively by others. In general, the patients in this group were not defensive, or were much less so, and were willing to consider an alternative hypothesis for their symptoms. The characteristic cluster of DID symptoms, such as severe amnesia including for tasks and functions of daily life and Schneiderian symptoms, was not reported. In fact, these patients were generally found to have remarkably good memory when asked about their psychiatric history or previous treatment or about other symptoms such as eating problems or suicidality. Moreover, they were able to provide a clear chronological life history (see also Thomas, 2001).

However, depersonalization, derealization, and identity confusion did not differentiate from genuine DID in this group. This would make sense since in many cases these symptoms are inherent to BPD pathology. The description of their symptoms did, however, differ in quality and severity compared to those of genuine DID patients. In fact, they were entirely comparable to the symptom descriptions of BPD patients discussed in the pre-

ences regarding clothing, food (*one drinks coffee with milk and sugar, another black without sugar and another only with milk; one always wants to wear pink, but I hate pink*). Most people who really have DID try to cover up these kinds of differences, if present, at all costs and will not spontaneously mention them in this way during diagnostic testing.

vious chapter. The patients were mostly describing feelings of detachment. No symptoms indicating a division of the personality were reported. When assessing symptoms of identity confusion, this group reported a highly polarized *good/bad* self-image.

This was not the case in the second group: the histrionic patients who claimed the existence of all kinds of parts. In both groups, but more strikingly so in the second group, the patients spoke with great ease and openly about the dissociative symptoms and the various personalities they claimed, completely lacking the characteristic reluctance, shame, or fear of their existence. Except for this unusual and dramatic presentation, however, this second histrionic group was harder to differentiate from genuine DID patients in that they presented many examples of their supposedly severe dissociative symptoms and often reported a full cluster of symptoms seemingly indicating a division of the personality. Thus, for inexperienced clinicians, this group poses the greatest challenges.

Thomas (2001) described 18 patients with imitated DID whom she examined using the SCID-D and listed characteristics of this group. Many of these characteristics are consistent with our findings regarding the histrionic group, but less so with the presentations of the BPD patients; there are differences as well. Thomas did her research in the United States, and it seems that, as with earlier descriptions by Coons and Milstein, patients with genuine DID in her research also presented more dramatic, histrionic symptoms than patients we see in the Netherlands and in other European countries. For example, Thomas described how most of the patients with imitated DID in her study consistently used the first person singular ("I") form throughout the study, while patients with genuine DID spoke in the plural form ("we"). Interestingly, in the Netherlands and other European countries we find rather the opposite: patients with imitated DID always speak of "we," while most patients with genuine DID actually try to conceal the "we" for reasons of avoidance and shame; they are more likely to speak in the first person singular during diagnostic assessment. Only patients with genuine DID who have been in treatment for a longer period of time and who have overcome the phobia of the parts sometimes use "we." There are also a small number of patients with DID with a comorbid histrionic personality who sometimes speak in the plural form during diagnostic assessment. However, these patients also report embarrassment, shame, and fear and show confusion and ambivalence as opposed to the group with imitated DID.

Table 10.1 lists features that can help clinicians distinguish between genuine DID and imitated DID.[15]

---

15 This table is an adaptation of the table originally published in Draijer, N., & Boon, S. (1999). The imitation of dissociative identity disorder: Patients at risk, therapists at risk.

Findings Using the TADS-I

In the past 15 years, working with the IDDTS and, since 2014, with the TADS-I, I have seen an increasing number of patients with false-positive DID diagnoses. As described in Chapter 4, I have received referrals to my private practice and previously to the trauma center where I worked of patients who were suspected to have DID or another dissociative disorder. This is a selective group where the likelihood of referrals based on an incorrect suspicion and thus finding false-positive DID cases is much greater than in a general psychiatric population. There, false-negative DID diagnoses are more likely to be found. Similar to our earlier SCID-D study, the majority of referred patients appeared to be confused about their symptoms or had come to believe that they had DID—just as their referring clinicians believed in some cases. A smaller group had fully identified with the DID diagnosis. This group displayed many DID symptoms and became resentful when the diagnosis was rescinded. All patients had read about the diagnosis in books or on the internet. Some had been to meetings of self-help organizations; others had seen videoclips on YouTube. In comparison to 20 years ago, when we conducted our earlier research with the SCID-D, there is now much more information about DID publicly available (Pietkiewicz et al., 2021).

The TADS-I offers a number of advantages in determining false-positive DID diagnoses. The first and longer section of the TADS-I contains questions about possibly trauma-related symptoms, such as eating problems, anxiety, and mood problems. Although this section of the TADS-I also includes some questions about dissociative symptoms that may indicate DID, OSDD-1, or partial DID, the majority of the questions do not address those disorders. Also included are questions about PTSD and CPTSD.

In my experience over the past 15 years, the first part of the interview often already presented a clear picture of a patient in cases where a false-positive diagnosis of DID was suspected. Except for some very histrionic patients (see the case report on imitated DID in this chapter), most patients presented a clear and consistent ego syntonic I-experience narrative about their symptoms, one that did not fit a DID diagnosis. Patients had a clear memory of the onset of symptoms and the emotions associated with them. One patient, for example, had this to say about her eating problems:

> I remember distinctly when I was new in high school and going out with friends became important. I was way too fat. At home we always ate high-fat food, and my mother has always been overweight too, and

---

Journal of Psychiatry & Law, 11, 301–322. In the current table the recent TADS-I findings are also included.

TABLE 10.1
Genuine and False-Positive or Imitated DID*

Symptoms, Presentation, Function	DID	DID With Histrionic Presentation	False-Positive/Imitated DID With Borderline Presentation	False-Positive/Imitated DID With Histrionic Presentation
Possibly trauma-related symptoms	• Present • Always PTSD symptoms, often with depersonalization, and always indication of a division of the personality • Patients rarely draw attention to *other parts* of their own accord	• Present • Always PTSD symptoms, often with depersonalization, and always indications of a division of the personality • Patients sometimes speak of *other parts*	• May be present, sometimes combined with depersonalization/detachment • No indication of a division of the personality • Patients do not talk about *other parts* except in the event of aggression or self-mutilation, or other shameful behavior	• May be present, sometimes combined with depersonalization/detachment • No indication of a division of the personality • Patients often discuss *other parts* unsolicited and in a histrionic way (*Suzy has eating problems*)
Identity problems	• Present • Usually confusion and internal struggle between multiple parts, voices • In many cases tendency to minimization, especially regarding presence of parts • Predominantly negative sense of self underlying	• Present • Usually confusion and internal struggle between multiple parts, voices to which attention is sometimes drawn in a dramatical manner • Overt presentation of parts • Predominantly negative sense of self underlying	• Present • Usually severe confusion and variable polarized (good/bad) sense of self, and internal struggle • Patients sometimes experience bad side as *another part*	• Present • Usually severe confusion and highly variable sense of self, sometimes also immense inner emptiness • Patients change like chameleons in different situations and insist on speaking of parts, and may lose themselves in roles
Depersonalization, derealization, absorption, trance, daydreaming	Usually present, often severe	Usually present, often severe	May be present, sometimes also severe	May be present, sometimes also severe
Somatoform dissociative symptoms	Usually present	Usually present	Rarely reported	Sometimes substantial somatization but not of a dissociative nature

Amnesia, fugues; indirect evidence of amnesia in the present	Present, also for tasks and functions in daily life	Present, also for tasks and functions in daily life	No amnesia or sometimes exclusively for negatively perceived or shameful behavior (e.g., aggression, self-mutilation)	Patients claim to have substantial amnesia for many things, no reluctance, shame or avoidance, lots of textbook examples
Amnesia for the past	Often present for everyday activities in the past and trauma	Often present for everyday activities in the past and trauma	Not present, indeed often remarkably good memory	Patients often claim to have amnesia for the past, whereas they usually have very good memory
Schneiderian symptoms/ intrusions	• Present • Intrusions of dissociative parts, hearing voices and other symptoms	• Present • Intrusions of dissociative parts, hearing voices and other symptoms	• Rarely or not reported, sometimes hearing a (familiar) voice	• Patients often report hearing voices, but do not report other Schneiderian symptoms
Indications of a division of the personality	Evidence of parts with functions in daily life and parts stuck in trauma time	Evidence of parts with functions in daily life and parts stuck in trauma time	No evidence of dissociative parts, sometimes other part with undesired behaviors	Patients claim to have *all kinds of parts*
Presentation	• Often difficulty, fear, embarrassment answering questions about dissociative symptoms or talking about dissociative parts • Tendency to minimize and conceal or trivialize • Difficulties with accepting and acknowledging (realization) DID	• Varying presentation, sometimes shame but usually more open about dissociative symptoms and parts • Tendency to overt presentation of symptoms and parts • Symptoms have sometimes also become part of the identity • Sometimes sudden switch to another part	• No difficulty answering questions about dissociative symptoms • No reluctance, or rather comfortable speaking about symptoms, but quite able to answer clinician's questions and collaboratively considering alternative explanations for symptoms	• No difficulty answering questions about dissociative symptoms • No reluctance, but rather eager and comfortable speaking about symptoms, but quite unable to answer clinician's questions and collaboratively considering alternative explanations for symptoms • Great anger, retaliation and feeling unseen by asking more questions or examples • The patient reports or shows evidence of so-called proof of the presence of DID (e.g., drawings, different handwriting, written dialogues with *parts or switching*)

continues

Symptoms, Presentation, Function	DID	DID With Histrionic Presentation	False-Positive/Imitated DID With Borderline Presentation	False-Positive/Imitated DID With Histrionic Presentation
Nonverbal clues	Often brief moments of dissociation			
Function				
Escaping responsibility	Absent	May be present in some patients	Often present for undesired behavior	Often present for undesired behavior
Attention; being seen	Absent	May be present in some patients	Present	Present
Organizing inner world and sense of self	Absent	May be present in some patients	Present	Present
Counter-transference; feeling of irritation or disbelief	Absent	May be present in some patients	Variable	Present

* In this table, the more neutral description "false-positive/imitated DID" has been chosen because cases do not always concern consciously simulated DID. As mentioned in the introduction to this chapter, there is often mutual influencing between clinicians who may think their patients have DID and the patients themselves. Also, relatives may influence the patients resulting in DID imitations.

I was actually disgusted by that. In elementary school, none of that mattered so much, but in first year of high school I started to diet. I remember exactly what that was like, and it felt so good to get thinner and thinner. At one point, my parents became concerned. Funnily, I actually liked that because I used to feel like they had no time for me and barely noticed me. I was able to quit and I did, and I never gained that much weight again. Later, during a period when I was feeling very lonely, I did binge eat at times. That didn't last very long; I think it really had to do with that period in my life. My sister had had a serious accident at the time and that put our family in turmoil. When you binge like that you don't really realize what you are doing; you eat entire bags of candy without noticing. But I remember making sure to buy candy, especially when I was feeling bad. I was jealous of my sister who got all the attention, and I felt guilty about being jealous. Luckily, I was able to stop binge eating as well. It makes you feel so full and nauseated, I really didn't want that anymore!

When asked if she had ever noticed that she had gotten up in the night to eat when she had no recollection of doing so, she replied:

No, that has never happened, in fact I have always been a good sleeper. I sometimes have bad dreams, particularly the past few years, but never before that. The eating was something I did during the daytime, when I was feeling lonely, in my room.

What stands out in this story? First of all, there is no problem with memory: the patient was able to explain in great detail and chronologically when and why she started dieting and why she later had a period of binge eating. She was also able to discuss her emotions and motives. Finally, she made several references to how she felt physically (e.g., nice to be thin; nauseated and full after a binge). Her description shows that she knew how she felt, both emotionally and physically. Even when patients with DID are capable of describing something like dieting or bingeing, it is almost invariably another dissociative part that supposedly does it or is involved in it. The part of the person present at the interview often does not know why the dieting or bingeing started and usually indicates that they have no control over it. Depersonalization and sometimes amnesia may accompany the eating behaviors. The part of the patient present during the assessment often does not show emotion and seems very flat. Moreover, generally, patients with DID have little or no sensation in their bodies and thus tell us that they do not feel if they are hungry or are feeling full. They may hear voices giving orders to eat or prohibiting eating.

Finally, when asked about amnesia for eating during the night, the patient replied that this had never happened and spontaneously reported that she was a sound sleeper. This answer showed that she was anticipating the next part of the TADS-I, about sleep problems, and it had already become obvious that this patient did not suffer from those either. This is another finding that would be highly unusual in patients with DID, who typically have considerable sleep problems as well as symptoms of PTSD. In Chapter 5, all possibly trauma-related symptoms are extensively discussed, with examples given by patients with and without a dissociative disorder. When assessing whether a patient may have a false-positive DID diagnosis, it is advisable to read this section in Chapter 5 (Assessing Possibly Trauma-Related Symptoms: TADS-I Part 2) regularly, especially for clinicians new to assessment of dissociative disorders. In addition, the overview in Chapter 8 on TADS-I profiles in BPD is of interest. Many patients who become confused about dissociative symptoms have borderline personality problems that would include symptoms such as depersonalization on a regular basis.

Another advantage of the TADS-I in the assessment of potentially false-positive DID diagnoses is that it allows clinicians to distinguish between alterations in consciousness that do not indicate a division of the personality and dissociative symptoms that do. The group of patients and their therapists who are confused about dissociative symptoms often give examples of depersonalization, derealization, and especially absorption, but do not describe clear symptoms indicating a division of the personality—with the exception of very histrionic patients who are invested in the DID diagnosis. Some patients in the study with the TADS-I did meet the criteria for a depersonalization disorder and two patients suffered from maladaptive daydreaming, during which they would lose themselves for hours in a daydream; in fact, this was a more or less conscious choice in both, and in one patient constituted almost an addiction (Somer, 2002).

Finally, the TADS-I includes an appendix with questions in case there is a suspicion of a false-positive DID diagnosis. This section contains questions about the origins of the diagnosis, how it was previously determined, and on what symptoms DID was suspected. Also included in the appendix are questions about what it means for the patients and those around them to have the DID diagnosis and whether patients had read about the diagnosis or met others with the disorder. Some of these issues may have come up earlier in the interview, especially when asking patients about their psychiatric history.

A recent study using the TADS-I provides a detailed description of six Polish patients with a diagnosis of imitated DID (Pietkiewicz et al., 2021). Although dissociative disorders and DID are not recognized in Poland as much as they are, for example, in the Netherlands, five characteristics of these patients stood out that were very similar to those we saw in histrionic patients, using the SCID-D and now the TADS-I. These characteristics are: (1) all patients had strongly identified with the diagnosis of DID; (2) they had all read about DID or watched YouTube videos and this knowledge influenced the clinical presentation of symptoms; (3) having DID, and particularly the existence of dissociative parts, explained for them their identity confusion and conflicting ego states; (4) their supposed dissociative parts were an important topic of conversation with other people; and (5) the researcher's exclusion of the diagnosis of DID led to frustration and anger.

It is worth noting that four of the six patients told us that the diagnosis had been suggested by a clinician and that they had started reading about it subsequently. Two had come up with the idea themselves after reading about DID online.

The Phenomenology of False-Positive DID Based on the TADS-I: Case Reports

This section will discuss three different patients with a false-positive DID diagnosis. Two referred themselves for a second opinion while the third was referred by her therapist. The first two patients did not have a histrionic presentation but had both come to believe that they might have DID. The third patient presented herself clearly in a very dramatic and histrionic way and had self-diagnosed DID.

Case Report: False-Positive DID in a Patient With Bipolar I Disorder

The patient was a 40-year-old woman with a long psychiatric history. Around the age of 20, she had been admitted to a psychiatric hospital with a psychotic episode for the first time. The psychotic symptoms had been related to bipolar I disorder. She had had many involuntary psychiatric hospitalizations, each time because she had stopped taking her medication. Often, being in love was a trigger for manic decompensation. She was the oldest in a family of three children. She had a younger sister and a brother who was mentally disabled. This was a great burden on the family, because her mother did not want to have her son placed out of the home when this was in fact necessary. The patient was a good student and after high school had gone on to an agricultural college, which she had not completed due to her mental health problems. She was her father's favorite and he had hoped and expected her to carry on the farming company now that there was no son to follow in his footsteps. He had put a great deal of pressure on her. There had been no room for her to develop in her own way and do what she wanted; however, she also admired her father. Her mother had recurrent episodes of depression and her parents' marriage was not good. She did not have a good rapport with her mother. She felt a great responsibility for her younger brother, but she also felt that because of him she had not been able to leave home, even though she had very much wanted to do so around the age of 20.

A sexual assault had taken place when she was having a manic episode aged around 30. The patient now lived independently with some pets; she had a small network and saw her family very little. Her father was long deceased. Her brother had been admitted to a residential facility for the intellectually disabled after her father's death. During her last psychotic episode and hospitalization, the patient herself had begun to think that she might have been abused by her father. She had told a therapist about this. Aside from her psychotic episodes she had never had the sense that her father might have abused her, but now she had become unsure.

The patient explained that during a psychotic episode she would typically become *"really really crazy"* and receive commands through the TV or think she was a disciple of a prophet and had to save humanity. Also, she had been convinced several times that she was Mathilde Willink[16]; she had bought many extravagant clothes and incurred debt. She said she felt wonderful in her Mathilde identity. Earlier, a therapist had come to believe that she might have DID and had treated her for this disorder for several years. This therapist had taught her that she needed to care for her parts like a mother.

She explained that she had a fertile imagination and was easily influenced by suggestions from others. She had asked for a second opinion because she was distraught by the fact that a proper diagnostic examination had never taken place and because she herself at times had strong doubts about the diagnosis of DID. She repeatedly stated that her relationships with her family, particularly with her younger sister and mother, had deteriorated greatly due to her suspicions of abuse by her father.

Prior to the diagnostic examination, she had sent many email messages about her history and all her thoughts. She seemed to be hypomanic and could barely stop her streams of thought. Also, some emails prior to the diagnostic examination had been supposedly written by dissociative parts: a tough part and a vulnerable/sensitive child. The way the patient wrote about these parts did not fit genuine DID. It was a naive and childlike presentation of so-called dissociative parts.

General

First Impressions. The patient made a lucid impression. Unlike her lengthy emails, she was able to adequately answer the questions. She was articulate, reflective, and had a sense of humor. Throughout the examination,

---

16 Mathilde Willink (1938–1977) was the third wife of the Dutch painter Carel Willink. She became known as his model but also as a fashionista in extravagant creations by fashion designer Fong Leng.

which lasted over three hours, I did not see her dissociate once. Nor did she give the impression of deliberately denying or trivializing symptoms or, conversely, accentuating them and making them worse. It did become clear that tremendous confusion had developed as to whether or not she had DID and whether or not she had dissociative parts.

Possibly Trauma-Related Symptoms

The patient provided a clear and consistent ego syntonic, first-person narrative. She did not report dissociative symptoms related to the possibly trauma-related symptoms. She endorsed the typical sleep problems associated with hypomanic or manic episodes and other sleep problems when she was depressed. She reported no PTSD symptoms and no other anxiety-related symptoms. She acknowledged episodes of severe depression but had never attempted suicide. The main problems in her life had been caused by manic dysregulation. The patient had a highly variable self-image, somewhat polarized between positive and negative. She explained that she found interpersonal relationships difficult, especially when people got closer. She was afraid to lose friends or to be abandoned. She recognized a pattern of attraction and repulsion. The way she talked about her friendships was consistent with insecure attachment. The patient indicated that she had no significant problems with sexual relationships, but she did not currently have a boyfriend. In the past, though, she had been confused about her sexual identity.

Alterations in Consciousness

The patient reported some depersonalization symptoms, especially during and immediately after a hypomanic episode: *I'm not myself at all then, it feels slightly like I'm floating, everything happens like in a dream, fast but also nice, until I get really crazy, then I start thinking and doing very strange things.* She did not report chronic or severe depersonalization. The patient explained that sometimes she could be lost in thought. Especially since she was often home alone, she would fret a lot and the day could go by without her really getting anything done. She primarily described absorption symptoms occurring at home. The patient did not report derealization in daily life, but rather during psychotic episodes.

Somatoform Dissociative Symptoms

The patient did not endorse any of the symptoms in this section of the TADS-I.

Psychoform Dissociative Symptoms

Amnesia. The patient did not describe dissociative amnesia. She had never lost time, and she had never done things she did not remember afterward.

She had never had fugues. When she was manically dysregulated, her perception of time did become distorted. Also, time would pass when she would be ruminating or very much lost in thought. Then suddenly it would be much later.

Schneiderian Symptoms/Intrusions. The patient reported never having heard any voices, even during psychotic episodes. The commands during such episodes would sometimes come through the TV. Her so-called Mathilde Willink identity had first emerged during a manic episode after reading about her, around age 25. She reported no other Schneiderian symptoms.

Dissociative Parts of the Personality. The patient reported that the dissociative parts had emerged during the treatment. Prior to this treatment, she had never noticed or experienced the presence of such parts. She herself had given names to these parts during treatment; they were all girls. Since she was no longer in treatment for DID, most of the parts had spontaneously disappeared. She basically had no idea how that had happened. Her Mathilde Willink persona had mainly been there during psychotic episodes when she was younger. She had cooperated with a court order to place her under financial conservatorship around the age of 30, because at that time she had got into huge debt for the purchase of what she called *Willink clothes*. She explained that she had begun to act like a small child and speak in a child's voice. She did so with her therapists, who viewed this behavior as confirmation of the diagnosis. Clearly, none of her therapists had been very experienced with DID. Yet, the patient herself was still ambivalent about the existence of parts and sometimes, even now, she conducted dialogues in writing with both a tough and a vulnerable side of herself, to whom she had given names. She was very much aware of this; there was no amnesia for these dialogues. The typical internal struggles between dissociative parts and the shame and anxiety about them were absent. The patient's attitude in adult mode as *mom to her two internal children* also differed from what is seen in DID. There was no phobia for child parts nor any other parts. The parts rather resembled different moods, modes, or ego states.

Both prior to and immediately after the diagnostic examination, the patient had sent emails consisting of dialogues between parts, interspersed with emails in which she indicated that these parts were all learned behaviors. Her confusion and ambivalence about the existence of different parts or different modes continued for quite some time, but eventually the patient wrote that she could put the DID diagnosis behind her and move on with her life.

Conclusion

No evidence of DID was found; the patient did not describe any symptoms or any cluster of symptoms that indicated a division of the personality, other than the idea that there might be parts. If there had been dissociative parts, she also would have reported a cluster of dissociative symptoms consistent with the presence of parts. This cluster was absent. Her TADS-I findings indicated an incorrect DID diagnosis in a woman with a history of bipolar I disorder with psychotic decompensation and a fragile personality (a borderline organization). She also had a fertile imagination and was very sensitive to suggestions. The latter possibly created further confusion among her therapists. Although she herself had doubts and had asked me to conduct a diagnostic test, she had partially in her words *started living* as someone with DID. Apparently, she was unable to immediately leave behind the last few parts and continued to write dialogues between two of them.

Case Report: False-Positive DID in a Patient With Borderline Personality Disorder

The patient was a 38-year-old woman, divorced, with an 18-year-old son who had been placed out of the home when he was 6 years old. She did have a good relationship with him by the time of the interview. The patient was the oldest in a family of four children and had lived in many places in different countries during her childhood because her father had worked as a missionary. She explained that both parents had been very active in the church and that little attention had been paid to the children at home. Moreover, as the oldest, she often had to take care of her three younger brothers. At 14, while living with her family on a mission post abroad, she had been assaulted by a gardener; one of her brothers had come running into the garden, which she said had caused the man to stop. She had not dared to mention this to her parents. At 15, back in the Netherlands, she had become depressed for the first time and was referred to a Christian youth service. When she was 18, she was admitted to a psychiatric hospital after a suicide attempt and subsequently attended intensive psychiatric day treatment. She had just finished high school at the time. During this day treatment, she was diagnosed with BPD, with recurrent episodes of depression and an anxiety disorder. After completing therapy, she unexpectedly got pregnant by her first boyfriend. She married him, but the marriage did not last long. Her parents and the church condemned her unplanned pregnancy and contact with them subsequently deteriorated.

The patient had been treated almost continuously since the age of 15 with the aforementioned symptoms, but not always with the same intensity. There had also been episodes when she had functioned better. She had worked as an administrative assistant for quite some time. A few years prior to the interview, she had become unable to continue working and ended up on a full disability benefit. She hardly saw her family by that time and had joined a different church, from which she did receive support.

She had weekly psychotherapy sessions in which she had begun to focus on her childhood memories. She said she had seen many *heavy things*, especially in developing countries, such as poverty, hunger, and violence; at home there had been no support. She had started to read about trauma and dissociation and had started to recognize signs of DID in herself.

In consultation with her therapist, who had told her that she did not know enough about dissociation, she had been referred to me for a second opinion.

General

First Impressions. The patient was a friendly woman who was a little bit overweight. She was able to outline her symptoms in a lucid manner. She came across as tough, but she could also easily become emotional during the examination, especially when she talked about her loneliness, past and present. Her affect changed appropriately in relation to the topics she spoke about. There was no flattened affectivity, nor did she dissociate during the examination. She spoke about her symptoms with ease.

Substance Use and Medication. The patient recounted that she had been smoking pot while she was in day treatment, although it had not been allowed. Others did it too and asked her to join them; she did not dare say no. She had never done it again after that time. She occasionally drank wine socially.

Possibly Trauma-Related Symptoms

Eating Problems. The patient explained that she tended to snack too much and had to try very hard not to gain too much weight. She usually had control over that, but sometimes she would feel bad and on such occasions she would not be able to control herself. *At such times I'm not myself,* she explained. When asked what she meant by that, she said that she sometimes would feel as if she was floating and eat as if she was in a daze. *I experience that quite often, and it feels like I am not as present.* When the clinician asked if she knew how she got the candy, she recounted: *Yes, well, I buy that myself of course, I know quite well I shouldn't, but on such occasions I can't resist. There are so many delicious things in a grocery store!* The patient had no amnesia related to the eating problems. She did not hear voices.

Sleep Problems. She slept seven hours per night on average and was taking antipsychotics as a sleep medication. The patient reported sometimes having nightmares representing unpleasant things she had experienced in the countries where her father had been working. In her dreams, she was often lost or left alone somewhere. She did not report episodes of reexperiencing trauma or actual flashbacks, even of the sexual assault. She did dwell on her past a lot and had been thinking about it a lot since beginning to talk about her childhood in therapy. She reported no PTSD symptoms.

Mood and Emotion Regulation. The patient described highly variable moods. She could get up cheerfully, but then after any setback she would suddenly become very gloomy and passive and tend to isolate herself at home. When she was feeling well, she was quite active and worked as a volunteer at a petting farm. She had attempted suicide once at age 15 by taking a lot of acetaminophens, but never after that. She could clearly remember buying the acetaminophen and where and when she took it. She did have suicidal thoughts regularly and was afraid of dangerous, impulsive behaviors, such as the thought of crashing herself in her car, although her religious beliefs helped her to not act on such thoughts and, moreover, she had never done anything like that.

Anxiety and Panic. The patient described mainly social anxiety symptoms: she felt insecure around others, especially around her peers. In addition, she was particularly fearful of dying suddenly from a heart attack or, as mentioned, succumbing to dangerous impulses. She also feared developing close connections with others because so many relationships had been broken off. For this reason, there were many situations she avoided.

Self-Injurious Behavior. The patient had started scratching her arms during part-time treatment at age 20. She had never scratched so deeply that it was necessary to get stitches. She explained that she would scratch in a kind of daze, just like the candy binging. She would not be quite present. She had not scratched her arms for years.

Self-Image and Identity. The patient explained that she was very confused about who she was. Her sense of self would fluctuate. Her parents used to tell her that there were a little angel and a little devil inside her, because she was either very sweet or suddenly incredibly angry at times. Since she had read about dissociation, she thought these were different parts of her. She was mainly afraid of losing control of the little devil within herself. That part, she believed, could start behaving strangely and frightfully impulsively. She would sometimes have really sadistic thoughts, and these were not part of her, either. She was now especially angry with her parents who had *dragged* her from one place to another and had *forced an extremely rigid religious belief* upon her. Every time she had just settled in somewhere, they would leave again. There was a constant struggle taking place within her. *It's more of a struggle between thoughts,* she explained, *and it's always between good and evil.*

Relationships With Others. The patient was very afraid of abandonment and tended to adapt to the wishes of others. But whenever someone did something hurtful or disappointing to her, *the little devil* would come out and say very mean things. This was a shameful thing to her, but she was unable to control it. She had lost many of her friends this way. She now had stable relationships mostly with some older people from the church. The patient said she had had relationships with both men and women. Currently, she had a girlfriend with whom she was in an on-again off-again relationship.

Sexuality. She indicated that sex was not very important in her life, but sometimes her sexual feelings would be intense; on those occasions she would want sex for release. She did not mention any dissociative symptoms associated with sexual contact. She did not avoid sexuality, and it was not hard for her to talk about it either.

EVALUATION OF POSSIBLY TRAUMA-RELATED SYMPTOMS

Again, during this part of the TADS-I no evidence was found in this patient that might indicate a division of the personality, in other words, no evidence for any underlying dissociative disorder. The patient was able to tell a very ego syntonic, first-person narrative and reported no PTSD symptoms.

Alterations in Consciousness

Mild forms of depersonalization occurred regularly, especially when she was under pressure or had to accomplish something. She would sometimes have the feeling of being cut off from her emotions or acting on autopilot. Earlier during the assessment, she had reported that sometimes she was not completely present when she used to binge eat or while scratching her arm. The patient had never seen herself from a distance from outside her body.

She did mention that she could become so absorbed in her thoughts that she would lose her sense of time. She would be sitting on the couch staring ahead of her. She had never found any evidence of having gotten up and done something in the meantime; she would simply be lost in thought.

Somatoform Dissociative Symptoms

The patient explained that she often felt dizzy and used to faint frequently. The latter had not been happening lately. She wondered if that was also dissociative; she had heard a lecture online about somatoform dissociative symptoms. She especially suffered from dizziness when she felt stressed or in a large group, but not, for example, in church, where she felt safe. The patient also had frequent tension headaches. She reported no other symptoms. No evidence of so-called conversion symptoms was found.

Psychoform Dissociative Symptoms

Amnesia. Although the patient said that she had a poor memory, what was striking was precisely the detailed and chronological manner in which she was able to recount her childhood, her many relocations, and other experiences. Amnesia had also been absent when the trauma-related symptoms were explored. Upon closer inquiry, her memory problems appeared to be linked primarily to episodes of absorption. She also described difficulty concentrating when feeling tense. Since she had stopped working, she had had less structure to her days and, in addition, she had been ruminating about her childhood and possible dissociative symptoms lately. But she said she had found no evidence that she did things she could not remember afterwards, nor did she describe any fugues. She had, however, started rereading all her old diaries in the past year. She said she read things in them that made her realize how unhappy she had felt back then. She explained that she could not remember writing those things, but that she remembered very well feeling that way. For that reason, she had begun to wonder if there was another part who had done the writing.

Schneiderian Symptoms/Intrusions. The patient said that her head felt hectic with the struggle between thoughts on her Christian angel side and *that little devil*. She also thought that sometimes she could hear a very sad little child. She did not know if she really heard that, or if it was more like a feeling. Over the past year, she had come to realize how lonely she had been as a child. She did not endorse any further Schneiderian symptoms.

Dissociative Parts of the Personality. The patient believed to have at least three parts, but no clear direct or indirect indications that they existed were found.

On her own account, she spoke of her good, Christian side, her bad devil side, and a very scared and sad little girl. She had given the parts names during treatment. She did not know if these parts had separate memories, but ever since she had become so preoccupied with her childhood and with the possibility of suffering from a dissociative disorder, she had been wondering if any things had happened that she did not remember. She did not feel that the sadistic thoughts and impulses of the devil side matched her at all and did not quite understand how she could have such a part. She did recall that as a child she could sometimes suddenly be very angry, especially with her mother. This mother was relentlessly caring for others through the church and mission, but never paid attention to her sons and daughter. Anger and rage were not tolerated at home, and she recounted that she had been trained not to behave this way at home.

EVALUATION OF THE INTERVIEW AND THE DES

The patient had a very high mean DES score (57). However, during diagnostic assessment with the TADS-I, no evidence was found of dissociative symptoms indicating a division of the personality. Her responses to TADS-I questions did not at all match the high scores on the DES. However, she did not exaggerate her symptoms during the TADS-I interview and was perfectly able to respond in a nuanced manner. In fact, the degree to which she was able to talk about her life history and symptoms in a consistent and chronological manner was striking. She did not give clear examples of amnesia. The memory problems seemed to be linked to absorption. She did mention depersonalization symptoms, which occurred especially when she was tense. She said she did not hear voices; she was more troubled by highly polarized thoughts.

The way the patient described the parts did not correspond to dissociative parts in DID, but rather resembled borderline modes. It was also noticeable that there was no tension or fear to talk about the parts; rather, she seemed preoccupied with understanding herself and her parts.

She had started reading about trauma and dissociation and had also attended a few lectures organized by an association for patients with DID. That had confused her even more, because she only partly recognized herself in the stories she heard there. Also, she hardly recognized anything from what she had read about the DID patients described in the book *Coping with Trauma-Related Dissociation* (Boon, Steele, & van der Hart, 2011). In fact, she was relieved when she was told she did not have a dissociative disorder and she was able to relate to the explanation of borderline modes. Her feelings of loneliness and detachment were easily explicable based on her life history.

Case Report: Imitated DID

The patient was a 28-year-old woman who had referred herself after reading about the TADS-I study on my website. In her letter, she wrote that she had received many misdiagnoses, including BPD, and she was 100% convinced that she had DID. The incorrect BPD diagnosis had led to treatments that did not help. She was eager to qualify for a service dog because she had read that it was very helpful for patients with PTSD and DID. For this reason, she wanted an expert to confirm the diagnosis.

General

First Impressions. The patient came across as very intelligent. It was striking that she used a lot of jargon about trauma, dissociation, and DID. She was somewhat verbose and revealed her immense dissatisfaction with all the previous therapy *that had failed to understand her at all*. She recounted all that she had gone through since her mother had taken her to see a therapist when she was 10 years old eagerly and in great detail. It was an episode in which she had refused to go to school, and according to her mother she had been unreasonably angry at times, while at other times, she had been withdrawn and unapproachable, also according to her mother. At length, she recounted withdrawing into her room on purpose to taunt her mother. Her mother was never kind and *only bombarded her with annoying and strict rules*. She called her father a narcissist. When I asked how she came to this conclusion, she said she had been reading a lot about it and that his behavior fit the profile of a narcissistic personality. The patient had broken off contact with her parents and had not lived at home for a long time. She reported having had two relationships with boys who resembled her father perfectly and that one of them had abused her. She currently lived with a boyfriend who showed great understanding for her DID and who had frequent contact with her dissociative parts. She had had therapists from the age of 16, but at present she no longer needed them. She said that with the help of an international chat group for people with DID and her current boyfriend, she had come a long way and no longer needed treatment.

She was employed by an IT company but was on sick leave at the time of the assessment. She indicated that the work was actually too hard for *someone with DID*. She was happy that she would now finally be examined by an expert in the field of DID and that the diagnosis would be confirmed. It was immediately apparent that the patient had no fear or ambivalence when it came to talking about her symptoms and was eager to report on her DID.

Substance Use and Medication. The patient had never used drugs and only drank the occasional beer. She had overused benzodiazepines for some time, but she had now stopped taking them. She had also been treated with antipsychotics for several months, but she had stopped taking them because she became overweight. She said that she had been given that medication because she could be very aggressive at times.

Possibly Trauma-Related Symptoms

Eating Problems. The patient said that she had never had eating problems and added on her own accord:

Of course some (parts) eat when I am not aware. Besides, as you know with DID, everyone likes something different. But it's not a problem, because all of us together pay very close attention to our body, we totally agree on our weight.

The subject of possible eating problems is one of the first items mentioned in the TADS-I. It was remarkable that the patient immediately brought up the existence of parts and drew attention to them. In addition, a certain naive presentation and the textbook example (*everyone likes something different*) was notable. Even without obvious eating problems, DID usually involves a variety of different thoughts about eating or not eating, including what to eat and what the right body weight should be. It is unusual that there would be no struggle about this or that the body would be *looked after by all the parts together.*

Sleep Problems. The patient did not report typical PTSD problems, although she did say that she was afraid to go to sleep. Once she was asleep, however, it would always be for 8 hours of undisturbed sleep. This is unusual for someone with DID, where sleep is usually disrupted by fears, nightmares, flashbacks, or episodes of reexperiencing trauma. She explained that she had discovered she would sleep best when her boyfriend put *the part Annie* to bed: that is, a little girl who had always been lonely. Her mother never read a book to her, and she would have to go to bed by herself. Now it was nice for her boyfriend to take her to bed and read to her. She was proud to have figured this out with him.

Here it became clear that apparently the DID and the little-girl part brought her special attention from her partner and that she liked this very much. There was also no noticeable shame, which again did not fit genuine DID. Even patients with genuine DID and a histrionic personality usually have parts that would be ambivalent or ashamed about the situation. Only extremely histrionic patients do not show a lot of shame during a diagnostic interview. As described earlier, the vast majority of patients with DID would not only try to conceal DID from their partners, but also would never talk about a dissociative part in this way during a diagnostic assessment.

Mood and Emotion Regulation. The patient explained that she was hypersensitive and experienced many emotions. All parts were allegedly the same in that respect. She had not finished her psychology studies, and she had student loan debt. She was not functioning well in her job, and no one understood her except her boyfriend. Her intense emotions were appropriate to the sadness and helplessness she described. She had many arguments with the family doctor and other physicians about somatic problems, but also with the managers at her work: *Then I switch into Ariane; she can get very angry when people don't understand how we suffer.* The patient claimed to have undertaken suicide attempts in high school by going into the woods to find poisonous mushrooms. Also, the part named Ariane used to scratch her arm with a pair of compasses during that period, she said, *but we all want to live, so we don't do that anymore.* The patient went on to explain that her mood could change instantly. *But that is rapid switching,* she added.

Again, the use of jargon was notable, as was the somewhat naive presentation that *all parts would have intense emotions.* It is also worth noting that she consistently spoke in the plural form about herself ("we"). In patients with DID, there are usually parts that feel too much and parts that feel too little. It is unusual that all dissociative parts would be hypersensitive or that all would experience the same intense emotions.

Anxiety and Panic. The patient described herself as very anxious and particularly having anxiety when she was in large spaces. She did not, however, make an anxious impression. Notably, she did not get startled at unexpected noises in the building, even though she referred to herself as jumpy and hyperalert. She explained that she was working on all her bad memories in close cooperation with her parts and therefore did not have any flashbacks or episodes of reexperiencing trauma. *We know exactly what to do when someone feels bad.* She did not describe any PTSD symptoms.

The way she self-resolved all the bad memories with her parts was not characteristic for DID, especially for someone with DID who had never received treatment for it. It was as if she did not really grasp the problems and internal struggles that occur in someone with genuine DID, despite all the reading and the chatting on online. Her distressing memories were always about her father's emotional neglect and narcissistic rage. It was also noteworthy that all parts agreed on this and that there was no typical struggle between parts loyal to parents and those angry at or fearful of them.

Self-Injurious Behavior. The patient said that *she* had not been harming herself since high school but was unable to explain how the decision to stop harming herself was made by all parts.

Self-Image and Identity. The patient believed that she had achieved a great deal herself with her DID and did not endorse feelings of worthlessness. *Of course, I do have all these different desires in me, but I know them all and take them into account; who doesn't?* When asked if there was inner conflict, she described a polarized struggle between the little girl, Annie, who was sweet and gentle, and the adolescent, Ariane, who was angry.

There's a back and forth most of the time. But in the end we all want the same things and we work very well together to achieve them, and there is virtually no struggle anymore. And I take everyone into account and so does my boyfriend.

The patient described that she never complied with others and was rather contrary. That was why she had so many conflicts, she added.

This description of her self-image and identity was also very different from that of patients with genuine DID. The latter report without exception that they suffer from a negative self-image and feelings of worthlessness. Even when they are very advanced in their treatment, there is often still conflict or uncertainty associated with the painful realization of certain aspects of themselves and their histories.

Relationships With Others. The patient described very turbulent relationships with others and losing many friends because she never adjusted. She was also mistreated in previous relationships, but she used to strike back: *We fought each other to the teeth.*

But, she said, weeds do not perish and in the end things always worked out for her. She said she was not afraid of abandonment because she would always be the one to leave first. She did not want to be offended by others. She also did not feel dependent at all and felt that she had few problems in relationships with others.

What was remarkable during this part of the examination was that she had stopped speaking about parts all of a sudden and showed a rather inflated sense of self. She also genuinely seemed to have little insight into the problems she had with others.

Sexuality. The patient explained that since being abused by an ex, she had had many problems with sex. That had never been the case before. But she now had a partner who did everything she wanted and who was considerate of her. Therefore, things were going well; they did not have intercourse very often, but they did cuddle.

EVALUATION OF POSSIBLY TRAUMA-RELATED SYMPTOMS

During this first part of the assessment, there was a striking difference between the way in which the patient described her symptoms compared to a patient with genuine DID. From the very beginning, she constantly drew attention to *the others*. This is unusual for a patient who has DID. The way she talked about her dissociative parts and their interrelationships was also naive at times (e.g., *everyone works together and has the same goal*) and very different from the dissociative organization and internal conflicts in patients with genuine DID. There was no shame, reticence, or fear in talking about the parts, and the DID also seemed to have a function in the relationship with her current partner.

In the second part of the assessment, the patient provided many text-book/media examples of dissociative symptoms, such as amnesia and hearing voices. When I asked for clarification or asked her to provide examples, she became angry several times. *It feels like you don't believe me, even though you should know how it works for someone with DID. I don't have to explain that time and again, do I?!* Her answers were therefore unscorable.

Alterations in Consciousness

The patient was unable to provide clear examples of depersonalization and derealization. She explained that she was totally absent while painting and suggested that another part of her did also paint. She showed many of her paintings as evidence and explained that some were painted by herself and others by a part of her. I could not detect a clear difference in style or theme; they were all sweet paintings with themes of flowers and nature. Although she claimed that she could become very absorbed in painting and described absorption as *I'm not present at all*, she did explain in detail which paintings she liked, the colors she loved, and the things she had learned in a painting course. There was no mention of a disso-ciative barrier (e.g., amnesia or depersonalization) between herself and the painting part or parts. If it were really a separate part, it would have been more plausible that at least sometimes this part might have gone to the course or might have been present there. Genuine DID patients may describe how they sometimes watch themselves painting from a point outside their body, unable to control what is being done or even having amnesia or only very vague flashbacks of participating in an activity like that. She did not seem fully aware of how this works for someone with genuine DID.

Somatoform Dissociative Symptoms

The patient indicated that her parts would have various *conversion symp-toms*. One part was unable to swallow at times while another suffered from muscle weakness. She could say little else about it and became irritated when I probed.

Psychoform Dissociative Symptoms

Amnesia. The patient explained that her memory was like *a sieve*—with rel-atively little sieve and large holes, suggesting that she had extensive amne-sia. She said she was constantly confronted with things she must have done but was not aware of doing; for example, her internet history would show that she had read or looked things up. She also recounted finding herself in places and not knowing how she got there and, for example, occasionally finding herself in her bedroom, wrapped up in thoughts. The memory problems allegedly occurred on a daily basis. She also said she had great difficulty with the concept of time and that she often could not remember her history chronologically. The latter was in total contradiction to the first part of the interview, when she had spoken in great detail about her past and about the present. She then mentioned that no one would really notice because she could mask almost anything because she was a highly gifted person.

The nature and severity of her memory problems could not be scored on the TADS-I. I got the impression that there were no memory problems at all, but possibly some absorption issues. However, every time I asked her to further explain her memory problems, it appeared to be nonnegotiable and she would get irritated again.

Schneiderian Symptoms/Intrusions. The patient explained that she had been hearing *little voices* her entire life. They were really more like thoughts, and the voices of Annie, the little girl, and of Ariane, the angry adolescent, predominated. She said she had read in an article that people with DID hear voices at an early age and that it was different from people with schizophrenia.

Dissociative Parts of the Personality. The patient showed a drawing she had made of her inner world, as proof of the existence of the parts. It contained 12 different parts. She said the Annie part had helped with that. Her parts had come up when she and her boyfriend had watched an American series on TV about a DID patient. Both had recognized many of this patient's problems. Then she had started reading and looking for information online, before eventually coming across the chat group. This had helped her tremendously and, according to her, it became more and more clear that she had DID. The parts, she said, had different handwritings and also different hobbies. The patient laughingly explained that it was a day job to make sure they all got to do something they liked. She kept quite a record of it so that the time was divided fairly. Finally, she explained that integration was not a goal for her and her partner, because it would just make things empty and lonely. The parts also worked together very well and never had any fights, so in fact she was not bothered by them at all. In this regard, she acknowledged that she did have a different experience from some other DID patients. *I think it's because we are so sensitive and gifted. We know very well what to do by ourselves actually*, was her explanation.

In this assessment, the DID diagnosis was brought to bear from the outset. The patient consistently spoke of "we" and kept referring to dissociative parts without any reluctance. This differs in every way from the presentation by someone who has DID. This was a case of an inconsistent, superficial, and naive presentation of symptoms. The content of the symptoms was not characteristic for genuine DID either: the typical struggle between dissociative parts was missing; they all had emotions; and they all worked together. The parts did not seem to have different thoughts and feelings about her parents or different loyalties to them. All parts agreed that her mother had not cared for her and that her father was a nasty narcissist. There were clear and serious attachment problems, but those were denied by the patient. The patient seemed quite narcissistic and presented in a histrionic way. She had a hard time accepting her own dependency; she outsourced her dependency needs and her childlike desire to be cared for to the part Annie. This seemed to fit the relationship with her partner, who was happy to comply. As adults, she and her partner seemed to share little common ground. He was addicted to gaming and to pornographic movies, the patient told me, and when he was not working, he would basically be at his computer all the time. During the second part of the interview, all the dissociative symptoms were exaggerated, including evidence to support the diagnosis. Also, the patient became increasingly annoyed, and my probing for authentic examples or details about the process of internal communication between parts in her case led to defensive or angry responses.

In summary, this patient exhibited all the characteristics of imitated DID.

Conclusion Regarding These Three Examples

The patients described above suffer primarily from other psychological problems and personality pathology. They differ in terms of their motivation and degree of awareness and the acceptance that they may not be right about their presumed DID diagnosis. The first patient received the diagnosis from a clinician and then became confused herself. The two others independently came to the conclusion that they had DID. The examples also illustrate that it takes a well-trained clinician to be able to distinguish the presentation of genuine DID from factitious or imitated DID.

Discussing the Results of the Assessment With the Patient

Another challenge is how to explain to patients that they do not have DID. Words matter, so it is best to say the diagnosis cannot be established or confirmed instead of telling them: "You don't have DID!"

With the first two patients described above, this was not a problem. Both did not exaggerate their complaints; they were confused about their symptoms but were also willing to accept an explanation other than the diagnosis of DID. They did not become defensive or angry during the diagnostic examination. Although the first patient herself had strong doubts about the diagnosis of DID, it was hard for her to part with it; she wrote several more dialogues from the perspective of parts after the diagnostic examination.

Usually, the clinician is well-advised to begin the explanation to the patient as follows:

CLINICIAN: I want to explain to you now that I cannot confirm DID and would like to take all the time necessary to clarify that. After that, you may also ask me any questions that come to mind. First, I want to tell you that it is not at all strange that you have come to believe you have a dissociative disorder. There is still much confusion about the term dissociation, and people can also have dissociative or similar symptoms without having a dissociative disorder. This is very common because dissociative symptoms also occur in other mental health issues or disorders. Many people sometimes feel alienated from themselves or feel that they are not themselves when they are under pressure. Also, many people are sometimes confused about exactly who they are—especially if their parents or caregivers have not adequately seen or recognized them during childhood. And many people do not feel they are one person, but feel unsure, divided or confused inside. This doesn't only happen in DID. So again, it's really not surprising that you, or indeed your therapist, started thinking about a dissociative disorder.

After a more general introduction with psychoeducation about dissociation, attachment, and sometimes PTSD, the clinician carefully explains what the patient has reported, using the patient's own examples about depersonalization, derealization, and absorption. Next, it is good to explain why this patient's symptoms do not fit DID. This usually works well for patients in the first group, those with borderline or other mental health issues, such as those presented in Examples 1 and 2 above. However, it is almost without exception very difficult and unsuccessful with patients with a histrionic personality. For them, DID has become their new identity to which they have strongly committed, and they feel offended when that is taken away. Moreover, in this group, the DID identity also has the clear function of making them seen and of filling the inner emptiness. Often, significant others are also involved in this so-called identity. They have come to understand the other person's behavior as explained by DID. Sometimes they draw something from it themsclves (e.g., *having a special partner*), as in the case of the third patient described above, whose partner seemed to find the DID diagnosis interesting. Sometimes it also helps them to excuse troublesome or antisocial behavior. Belief in DID and living with DID can even take the form of a *folie à deux*.

For some patients the diagnosis of DID gives hope for new treatment options, particularly when they feel desperate about treatment options for the problems they actually have. For example, one young woman with schizophrenia explicitly asked me to explain to her parents that she did not have DID. She herself had her doubts and understood and accepted my explanation. But she said:

> My mother thinks schizophrenia is so appalling, she can't accept that diagnosis and she can't accept me either. She has studied DID very closely and is convinced that my voices are related to DID and she desperately wants me to be treated for DID, because that would mean there is hope. I came to believe that too, even though I didn't recognize most of the symptoms at all.

The tragedy was that this young woman felt doubly unseen by her parents. As a child she always felt she didn't matter and she felt that way again later, as young adult, because they could not accept the diagnosis of schizophrenia.

Most patients with a histrionic presentation feel hurt by the outcome of the assessment, once again unseen and misunderstood, and therefore they become enraged. Almost without exception, there is a strong reaction from patients after the assessment, sometimes expressing anger and sometimes presenting yet more spurious evidence of DID, adding that the clinician has not understood their problems at all:

> I thought you were an expert and would have understood that the voices did not allow me to tell you the half of it. You just made a judgment, when in fact you only know half of it. How can you claim to be an expert if you make such mistakes?

This is a typical reaction after a diagnostic interview where the diagnosis is rescinded. Other patients keep emailing, sometimes even as supposed different parts, to prove that the clinician was wrong. This is highly unlikely behavior for genuine DID patients, who would be ashamed or hear voices telling them things such as: *See? You are a fake, you just make it up.* Avoidance, fear, and shame would prevent them from emailing at all.

Unfortunately, to date I have not found a way to reach the third group of patients even after several consultations. As much as I have tried to convince them that it was not strange that they had come to believe they had DID, that their symptoms were very serious, and that beneficial treatment for their symptoms was indeed possible, it was mostly to no avail.

During my time working in a closed psychiatric inpatient unit, I treated two of these patients over a longer period of time. It took more than a year to establish an adequate therapeutic relationship, and only then were they able to accept an alternative explanation for their symptoms. The important thing was that when this happened, the patients were able to tell me they felt I recognized them as a person, regardless of whether they had DID or not.

Genuine or Imitated DID in Forensic Psychiatry

Earlier in this chapter, I argued that a correct diagnosis is a prerequisite for appropriate treatment, the latter being markedly different for genuine DID versus false-positive DID. Correct diagnosis may be of even greater importance within a forensic context, although this does not exclusively involve the diagnosis of DID. In many countries around the world, regardless of the legal system, the consequences of committing a crime are different if the individual had a psychiatric condition at the time they committed the crime. This is especially true for crimes such as homicide in countries where the death penalty is still in force. If a DID diagnosis is missed during forensic examinations, this not only results in the patient not receiving adequate treatment, but also in increased risk of recidivism of delinquent behavior (Nijenhuis, 1996).

Dissociative Symptoms and Disorders in Forensic Psychiatry

Patients who truly have DID are at greater risk of being accused of malingering because of the skepticism that exists regarding the diagnosis, especially if these patients have amnesia for committing the crime. Memory loss for committing a crime is a common phenomenon in serious sex and homicide crimes (Brandt, 1988; Cima et al., 2001; Cima et al., 2003; Cima et al., 2004). In the Netherlands, almost a quarter of patients committed to a forensic psychiatric facility are reported to claim amnesia for the crime (Cima et al., 2004). In crime-related amnesia, three distinct forms of amnesia are generally identified in the literature: (1) dissociative amnesia, (2) amnesia caused by an organic cause or alcohol intoxication, and (3) simulation of amnesia, primarily to avoid responsibility for the crime. However, the study by Cima et al. (2004) does not clarify which form of crime-related amnesia was involved. In their study, crime-related amnesia was not assessed using diagnostic instruments—including instruments for identifying or excluding dissociative disorders—but based on health records research.

In the United States, publications on dissociative disorders, in particular DID, in the forensic context have appeared over the course of many years (Brand, Webermann, & Frankel, 2016; Brand, Schielke, & Brams, 2017; Brand, Schielke, et al., 2017; Brown, 2009; Coons, 1991; Dinwiddie et al., 1993; Farrel, 2011; Frankel & Dalenberg, 2006; Kluft, 1987b; Lewis & Bard, 1991; Lewis et al., 1997; Ondrovik & Hamilton, 1990; Spitzer et al., 2003). Back in 1997, Lewis and colleagues described a group of 12 adult murderers with DID and a history of severe abuse in childhood (Lewis et al., 1997). Lewis herself was an experienced clinician who had conducted more than 150 psychiatric examinations of individuals suspected of or already convicted of homicide. Fourteen of them had diagnosed DID. She and her colleagues conducted very extensive examinations and found objective and independent evidence from many different sources in 12 of the patients, confirming both DID and early childhood abuse. The data collected spanned a period of time long before the offense had occurred, when there was no incentive to simulate DID. Their conclusion at the time was that DID could be distinguished from simulated DID in the forensic context, but that assessment was intensive and time-consuming. There are now more validated assessment tools both for diagnosing dissociative disorder and for detecting simulation.

Most authors agree that forensic evaluation of DID and of other dissociative disorders should be undertaken by experienced clinicians: these should have expertise in the diagnosis and treatment of these disorders outside the forensic context as well. They should use data from a variety of sources to support or exclude the diagnosis, including the results of structured diagnostic assessment and neuropsychological testing. They also should gather the most comprehensive picture possible of the person's history, including their trauma history, psychiatric and psychological treatments, and comorbidities, and possibly medical data, as was done by Lewis and colleagues (1997).

Special expertise is also definitely needed for the interpretation of results from psychological tests and assessments aimed at the detection of simulation. Brand and colleagues (2016) provide an overview of the various assessment tools commonly used in forensic examinations (Brand, Webermann, & Frankel, 2016). They conclude that psychological testing data are particularly difficult to interpret, requiring special expertise, because patients with DID, as well as other traumatized patients, often show high scores on subscales similar to patients simulating DID. Self-report questionnaires and interviews aimed at detecting malingering of psychological symptoms can be particularly problematic, especially in severely traumatized patients (Brand et al., 2006; Brand, Tursich, et al., 2014; Brand, Weber-mann, & Frankel, 2016; Rogers et al., 2009). These tools involve a variety of detection strategies including the solicitation of strange and bizarre symptoms and exaggeration or magnification of symptoms (for an overview of different detection techniques, see Walczyk et al., 2018).

Two of the most widely used and best validated instruments for the detection of simulators with mental health problems are the Structured Interview of Reported Symptoms (SIRS; Rogers, Bagby, & Dickens, 1992; Rogers, Kropp, et al., 1992) and the SIRS-2 (Rogers et al., 2010). Although these interviews are excellent for the differentiation between simulators and patients with genuine symptoms in a general psychiatric population, this is not the case for severely traumatized patients (Brand et al., 2006; Brand, Armstrong, et al., 2009; Brand, Tursich, et al., 2014; Brand, Weber-mann, & Frankel, 2016; Brand, Schielke, & Brams, 2017; Brand, Schielke, et al., 2017; Brand, Webermann, et al., 2019; Rogers et al., 2009). Although Brand and colleagues (2006) found that the SIRS identified 35% of genuine DID patients as simulators, Rogers and colleagues (2009) found that 31% of severely traumatized patients were incorrectly labeled as simulators based on the SIRS interview. For this reason, Rogers developed a special Trauma Index that was thought to be more satisfactory. According to Brand and colleagues, the Trauma Index combined with the original version of the SIRS would be the best option for patients who may have a dissociative disorder (Brand, Webermann, & Frankel, 2016). Nevertheless, they emphasize that forensic consultants should interpret the results of psychological testing including the SIRS with caution because patients with DID report many symptoms, due to their severe symptomatology, and often have elevated scores on the various tests.

Another dilemma is that some of the tools identify some common psychological symptoms as "bizarre" or "exceptional" and use them to detect simulation. This is the criticism leveled against the Structured Inventory of Malingered Symptomatology (SIMS; Smith & Burger, 1997), of which Dutch, German, and Spanish translations exist (Merckelbach et al., 2002; Cima et al., 2003). Merckelbach and colleagues do note that the instrument does not measure simulation but rather exaggeration and that not all exaggeration comes from simulation (Merckelbach et al., 2002; van Impelen et al., 2014). The instrument is now regularly used in medical insurance cases and also in forensic investigations. The questionnaire consists of 75 statements, categorized into five subscales (affective disorders, low intelligence, psychosis, amnesia, neurological disorders) of 15 items that must be answered with either "true" or "false." The statements supposedly refer to "bizarre experiences" and unrealistic symptoms. Opinions on the validity and reliability of the SIMS vary, and different cutoff points are mentioned in order to not incorrectly identify patients as simulators (van Impelen et al., 2014).

According to critics, most of the items on the SIMS consist of common medical and psychological symptoms referred to as "bizarre experiences" (Cernovsky & Diamond, 2020). These critics came to this conclusion in relation to each of the subscales (Cernovsky, Bureau, et al., 2019; Cernovsky, Mendonça, Oyewumi, et al., 2019; Cernovsky, Mendonça, Ferrari, et al., 2019; Cernovsky, Mendonça, Bureau, & Ferrari, 2019; Cernovsky & Diamond, 2020). As a result, simulators are not easily distinguished from patients with genuine medical and psychological problems, and the latter group is at high risk of being wrongly identified as simulators. Cernovsky and Diamond (2020) describe how in research using the SIMS, 82.7% of U.S. veterans with PTSD, 78.3% of patients with a serious motorcycle accident, and 72% of hospitalized psychiatric patients were incorrectly identified as simulators (false-positive cases of simulation). Patients with DID are also certainly at risk of scoring high on the SIMS and being categorized as simulators, as four of the five subscales name symptoms that are common for DID (Vissia et al., 2016). Both in DSM-5 and ICD-11, amnesia is a criterion for DID. It is also one of the scales of the SIMS. Many of the neurological symptoms may also be somatoform dissociative symptoms (e.g., SIMS item 1: *Sometimes I lose all the feeling in my hand so it's like wearing a glove;* item 64: *Sometimes my leg is "paralyzed" below the knee, and I can't move it*). Fairly general affective symptoms are also common (item 32: *I have difficulty sleeping;* item 60: *I cannot express my feelings;* item 47: *I am depressed all the time*); and finally, Schneiderian symptoms and hearing voices are prevalent in DID (SIRS subscale psychosis, with several questions about hearing voices). For this reason, this questionnaire seems inappropriate to use as a tool to distinguish patients with a severe history of trauma and/or dissociative disorder from simulators, at the present time.

For an excellent overview of and recommendations for the assessment of dissociative disorders in a forensic context, I refer to two recent articles by Brand and colleagues (Brand, Schielke, & Brams, 2017, Brand, Schielke, et al., 2017), as well as an earlier article by Frankel and Dalenberg (2006).

The Dutch Situation

Dissociative disorders are still relatively unknown in Dutch forensic psychiatry. That is, they are not often diagnosed in the context of forensic psychiatric or psychological examinations. On the phenomenon of factitious DID in the courtroom I have been unable to find any data. These are people who pretend to have DID to avoid being held accountable for the crimes they committed. In the Netherlands, this problem arises with suspects who are examined within the context of an outpatient or inpatient Pro Justitia

Report to determine the degree of culpability at the time of the perpetration of a crime and the risk of recidivism. Over 3,000 reports were drawn up in 2019, including 203 clinical reports drawn up at a national center, the Pieter Baan Center (PBC) (NIFP, 2019). At this center, accused persons are examined by court order to determine if they were in a decompensated mental state at the time they committed an offense.

Research at the PBC on diagnoses made between 2000 and 2002 shows that in 307 (90.1% male and 9.1% female) of the 355 records reviewed, a mental disorder was diagnosed (Harte, 2004). A dissociative disorder (not DID) was diagnosed only three times in that period (0.8%), as well as one factitious disorder.

More recent record reviews of virtually all individuals examined at the PBC between January 2017 and December 2019 suggest that no DSM-5 diagnoses of dissociative disorders were identified. Also, in this group (n = 619), only 1.5% of those included were diagnosed with trauma- and stressor-related disorders (Kempes & Gelissen, 2021). Thus, although these data include only a small proportion of Pro Justitia reports (i.e., only those conducted by the PBC), these data do confirm that dissociative disorders still are not frequently diagnosed. It should be noted that this says little about the actual prevalence of dissociative disorders in the forensic context in the Netherlands, but rather about the possible lack of familiarity with dissociative disorders.

During my own time working in a forensic psychiatric unit (1995–2002), I regularly drew up Pro Justitia reports, especially with defendants with a history of trauma or possible PTSD or dissociative symptoms. During that period, as well as in the 20 years since, I have never examined a defendant or convict who had feigned DID, as reported in the United States and other countries. I did see, however, a small number of forensic patients with true DID. I treated one patient in this unit with a false-positive diagnosis of DID, but this diagnosis had been made by a clinician long before this patient committed a crime. By order of the judge, the patient was admitted to my unit for a year by means of Section 37 of the Netherlands Penal Code, which at the time meant that a convicted person was mandated to treatment in a psychiatric ward for a year. The DID diagnosis played no role in the judge's decision and was not taken seriously, which was appropriate in this case. The case involved a patient with severe borderline and histrionic personality problems who had been psychiatrically hospitalized for many years. DID had become her identity and she displayed her parts in a naive, dramatic way. It took more than a year for her to give up her DID identity and feel adequately seen without this diagnosis. Only then was she able to move forward in treatment with her core problem, the chronic feeling of not being seen. The treatment would likely have failed without the legal requirement of a year-long hospitalization. Most likely, the patient would have walked away because she initially disagreed with the fact that I did not confirm the diagnosis of DID.

Case Report: Genuine Amnesia Mistaken for Simulation

The example that follows shows that amnesia is sometimes mistaken for simulation. More expertise on dissociative disorders is needed in forensic psychology and psychiatry, just as in general psychiatry.

Ms. D. had been convicted of committing homicide—with clear evidence. She had amnesia for the criminal act but did have brief flashbacks related to the crime. These flashbacks had led her to turn herself in. Prior to the verdict she was extensively observed and diagnostically assessed in a Dutch inpatient facility for the forensic assessment of serious offenders and declared fully accountable. Although she had reported having amnesia for the crime and hearing voices, a dissociative disorder was not considered. The perception was that she was exaggerating her symptoms. Interestingly, this judgment was partly based on high scores on many psychological tests (consistent with Brand and colleagues' findings about patients with DID; Brand et al., 2009), whereas she had scored low on the only self-report questionnaire for dissociation (DES). This discrepancy could be an indication for a dissociative disorder, given that she also heard voices and had memory loss. Patients who deliberately feign or imitate a dissociative disorder would rather score extremely high on the DES. Patients with dissociative disorders sometimes score low, especially if there is a lot of fear, shame, or denial of the dissociative symptoms. She was not examined diagnostically using a structured interview such as the SCID-D. After her conviction, she became increasingly anxious in prison in response to her daily recurring memory problems and the voices she heard. Her greatest fear was that she would commit another crime even after spending years in prison. She therefore wanted treatment for her symptoms in a special forensic clinic. For this reason, her lawyer requested that I reexamine her for the appeal case.

Using part of the questions from the TADS-I and the SCID-D, I examined her and diagnosed DID. She had never spoken about her symptoms before and was anxious and avoidant. When asked the questions in the section on possibly trauma-related symptoms, she already spontaneously gave examples that were indicative of a division of the personality. The examples dated from long before the crime was committed. She also showed authentic confusion and shame about these experiences. For example, when asked about sleep problems, she mentioned that she often woke up at night but would not be in her bed at all, but in the room, such as behind her computer. The last thing she would remember on such occasions was having gone to bed.

She appeared to have ordered things over the internet sometimes, and she did not remember having done so. She reported chronic depersonalization and spontaneously talked about out-of-body experiences. She reported the full cluster of severe dissociative symptoms, both somatoform (*I'm paralyzed sometimes and then I can't move the left half of my body*) and psychoform symptoms, including Schneiderian symptoms and severe amnesia—also for daily life in prison—consistent with DID. She gave examples from years earlier about amnesia in daily life, sometimes of episodes lasting a few days. From a young age she had been hearing voices that made her very anxious and that she herself originally thought were ghosts. Her family members confirmed that she had suffered from hearing voices as a child.

The patient also had a history of severe trauma that she had never talked about before. Part of this history had also been confirmed by third parties. However, she could not comment on the presence of dissociative parts; she had never thought about it before. She did dissociate several times during the examination, especially when asked about voices and dissociative parts. She would go out of contact and become unresponsive to my questions. At no point did she suggest that a part of her committed the crime. She understood that she must have done it because there was evidence. She was mainly extremely anxious about the loss of control, because she did not remember committing the crime. She also completely failed to understand what had led her to the act, even though several years had passed since. She still reported the same severe PTSD symptoms and amnesia. Her case fit the initial presentation of DID (Boon & Draijer, 1993a), as described in Chapters 1 and 7.

In the appeal case that followed, she was again examined by four independent clinicians; remarkably, all four unanimously confirmed DID. The discussion at the appeal trial focused on whether DID exists or not, after witnesses had been heard by the prosecution questioning the existence of DID. Ultimately, in this case the court concluded that there was sufficient scientific evidence for the existence of DID and also recognized the conclusions of the four experts that this patient suffered from DID. Indeed, this woman was not deemed fully criminally responsible for the crime and was sentenced to mandatory psychiatric treatment.

Incorrect Diagnoses of Imitated DID

This chapter addresses false-positive DID diagnoses in which patients, be it consciously or subconsciously, imitate DID or believe they have DID, primarily based on confusion about their identity. It may also happen, however, that a dissociative disorder is incorrectly excluded on the assumption that simulation is involved. Based on a patient's presentation and responses to the SCID-D or the IDDTS (the predecessor of the TADS-I), I have excluded DID a number of times. Years later I was told by experienced colleagues that a dissociative disorder had been correctly diagnosed after all in the patients involved. These were not patients with initial presentations of DID, but patients who—sometimes in a histrionic way—would speak of parts. They initially reported few or no PTSD symptoms, and the typical cluster of dissociative symptoms was absent during the diagnostic examination. But they did talk about *inner children*, for instance. A clear trauma history was also lacking in some of these cases. It was obvious however, that there were attachment issues and personality problems. In several cases, this had led me to believe that I was more likely dealing with serious personality problems, or with the dynamics of the unseen child.

In one case, it became clear years later that the patient had had complete amnesia for a severe history of trauma at the time of the first diagnostic assessment. At that time the patient said that she had experienced the presence of inner child parts during a previous body-focused therapy. Other than this she did not report any symptoms that might indicate the existence of DID or OSDD-1. I mention this to alert colleagues to the fact that dissociative patients can sometimes have a very atypical presentation of symptoms, such as the experience of inner child parts without otherwise recognizing or reporting dissociative symptoms. No dissociative disorder can be diagnosed in such cases. In itself, transference focused therapy (TFP), schema focused therapy, or mentalization based therapy (MBT; Batemen & Fonagy, 2004; Fonagy & Target, 1997; Fonagy et al., 2015) are good treatment options for such patients. Once in therapy, they often gradually become more aware of other dissociative symptoms and a trauma history. Subsequently, treatment should focus on the dissociative disorder.

Summary

DID often goes unrecognized and underdiagnosed for years (Boon & Draijer, 1993a, 1993b; Dorahy et al., 2014; Loewenstein et al., 2017). Nevertheless, an increasing number of patients with false-positive DID are seen. This originally occurred mainly in countries where there was already more knowledge about the diagnosis and treatment of DID. In places where there is little awareness of DID among clinicians, the emergence of the internet has allowed patients to start reading for themselves, looking for information, and thinking that they have DID (Pietkiewicz et al., 2021). Factitious or imitated DID then becomes more common, resulting in an increase of wrongly diagnosed DID. Also, some imitations are becoming increasingly professional and thus more difficult for inexperienced clinicians to distinguish from genuine DID with a histrionic presentation

(Coons & Milstein, 1994). Three studies show that imitation of dissociative disorders, particularly DID, is more common than imitation of other mental disorders (Brand, Webermann, & Frankel, 2016). In these studies, 2% to 14% of patients present with imitated DID (Coons & Milstein, 1994; Friedl & Draijer, 2000; Thomas, 2001), versus 5% to 6% of patients in a general psychiatric population (Eisendrath, 1995; Pope et al., 1982). What does this mean? On the one hand clinicians worldwide lack knowledge and need to learn how to diagnose dissociative disorders. On the other hand, however, when learning to assess dissociative disorders they may encounter patients who imitate DID. This presents a significant challenge, especially for clinicians who have little experience with what genuine DID looks like. Ideally, requiring specialized courses on assessment and treatment of dissociative disorders should be part of the general training for psychiatrists, psychologists, and psychotherapists.

CHAPTER 11

Assessment of Traumatic Childhood Experiences: Patient History and Treatment Implications

Introduction

This chapter discusses two subjects of importance for further assessment, case formulation, and treatment plan for patients. The first involves childhood traumatization. The second subject relates to the limitations of dissociative disorders classifications and the need for further assessment beyond diagnosis to determine prognosis and create tailored treatment plans. After all, patients are more than their diagnoses or clusters of symptoms. Arriving at a descriptive diagnosis is a first and necessary step, but formulating a treatment plan requires more information (Steele, Boon, & van der Hart, 2017).

Childhood Traumatization

There are different views on childhood traumatization and what it involves. The DSM-5 concept of trauma offers little guidance; it was narrowly defined as "exposure to actual or threatened death, serious injury or sexual violence," so as to avoid placing too much under this heading. The ICD-11 uses a broader trauma concept, particularly in complex PTSD where organized violence, long-term domestic violence, and repeated childhood sexual or physical abuse, among others, are identified (ICD-11, version February 2022: WHO).

DSM-5 offers an overly narrow definition when it comes to traumatic childhood experiences, as they often involve so much more. It is helpful in this regard to make a distinction between "acts of omission" and "acts of commission." Another important distinction is between one-time traumatizing events versus repetitive and chronic traumatization.

Omission Versus Commission

Acts of omission involve failure to do what should have been done. This includes serious child neglect. Neglect may be conscious negligence by one or both parents or caregivers. Usually, a lack of attention, love, comfort, care, or encouragement toward children may also be a result of the parents' own problems or insecure attachment styles (Cassidy & Shaver, 1999). Apart from attention and care, the most basic needs may also be missing, such as a roof over one's head or the financial means for schooling or development. Acts of omission are often considered a form of emotional neglect, playing an independent role in symptoms experienced in the longer term, as was shown in a large national study into the sexual abuse of girls in the Netherlands (Draijer, 1988, 1990).

In particular, a systematic lack of attention, care, and comfort may lead to what I call the trauma of the unseen child, occurring at a young age. Being unseen as a child can result in a continuous feeling of being unseen as an adult and may invoke intense feelings of worthlessness. As described in the previous chapter, both in our study with the SCID-D and the recent study with the TADS-I, a proportion of patients with cluster B personality disorders reported such histories (Draijer & Boon, 1993a). Similarly, most patients with false-positive diagnoses of DID seem to suffer primarily from not being seen (Draijer & Boon, 1999). This type of emotional neglect, although very stressful, does not meet the DSM-5 criterion A of PTSD and does not usually lead to PTSD symptoms or dissociative symptoms indicating a division of the personality, but rather to serious attachment and personality problems.

Acts of commission involve acts such as sexual abuse, physical maltreatment, extreme and bizarre punishments—for example, forcing children to eat their own vomit when they have thrown up—deliberately leaving children out in the cold for hours, or locking them up. Emotional abuse includes extreme harassment, scolding, humiliation, or making the child a witness to violence between parents or caregivers.

Acts of commission typically take place within families in which emotional neglect and/or gross negligence also occur (Draijer, 1988, 1990; Dutra et al., 2009; Schimmenti, 2018). For example, the aforementioned Dutch study of sexual abuse of girls found that emotional neglect is one of the risk factors for sexual abuse: it often precedes it and goes hand in hand with it (Draijer, 1988, 1990). The same is true for insecure attachment developing from birth from a lack of attunement: a lack of primary caregivers being sensitive to the child's needs (Fonagy & Target, 1997, 2002). The vast majority of patients with complex dissociative disorders or CPTSD report both forms of traumatization. Therefore, when taking a history of traumatic experiences, it is important to always ask about both types of experiences.

One-Time Versus Ongoing or Repetitive Traumatizing Events

Apart from differentiating acts of omission from acts of commission, it is important to consider the type of traumatization. Terr (1991) distinguished between Type 1 trauma, a one-time traumatizing event, and Type 2 trauma, involving repeated or chronic traumatization. In both types, she focused mainly on acts of commission. Type 2 trauma is invariably present in patients with complex dissociative disorders or CPTSD (Draijer & Boon, 1993a). Moreover, the abuse often continues into adulthood (Middleton, 2013, 2015). Our research with the SCID-D in the 1990s and, since then, among patients in clinical practice also confronted us with what we call Type 3 trauma: extreme sadistic organized abuse in groups (Boon, 2014; Draijer, 2003; Draijer & Boon, 1993a, 1999; van der Hart et al., 1997. See also Badouk-Epstein et al., 2018; Schröder et al., 2018). An inventory of reported trauma histories of DID patients at a Dutch trauma center revealed that a quarter of these patients reported Type 3 trauma histories (Boon, 2014).

Assessment of a Trauma History

In the DSM-5 description of PTSD (and CPTSD in ICD-11), the A criterion, exposure to a traumatizing event, is a requirement for making the diagnosis. Although dissociative disorders can be understood as trauma-related disorders (see Chapter 1), neither the DSM-5 nor the ICD-11 requires exposure to a traumatizing event as a criterion for a dissociative disorder. Thus, in order to diagnose a dissociative disorder, establishing the presence of a history of traumatic experiences is not necessary. Therefore, in developing the TADS-I, it was a deliberate choice not to ask about a trauma history, both to avoid unnecessarily burdening the patient and also to prevent the possibility that these questions might influence the rest of the interview. If clinicians want to explore their patients' trauma histories (or are required to do so in case of PTSD or CPTSD), it is best not to do this during the TADS-I session, but afterward.

For patients who do not have a complex dissociative disorder, for example in PTSD as a result of a one-time traumatizing event, it is usually possible to explore their trauma histories in a systematic way (Draijer, 2003). For this purpose, a clinician can use a clinical interview or self-report questionnaire like the ones set out below. However, the more severe the dissociative symptoms, the more difficult and complicated it will be to explore a trauma history. In general, taking an oral clinical history of what has happened in the past is preferable to the use of questionnaires. The clinician can then observe what the questions about the trauma history trigger and may intervene if necessary and accommodate the patient if the questions prove to be too burdensome.

Patients with DID or OSDD-1 generally experience great difficulty in reporting on their traumatic experiences. There may be partial or even complete amnesia for the trauma history and there is often a strong tendency to avoid the topic relating to past trauma. This is understandable, as dissociative parts of the personality may be activated or triggered by questions about the trauma history, resulting in the patient possibly relapsing or losing contact with the clinician. Internal conflicts between dissociative parts may intensify, which in turn may lead to an increase in dissociative responses, including self-injurious behavior. This may also occur after the interview. Patients may hear voices forbidding them to talk about the trauma history, because when they were children, they were threatened with consequences and warned never to tell anything to anyone.

There may also be intense internal conflicts about the truth or falsehood of the trauma history or aspects of it. Especially when the abuse took place in the family with parents or caregivers being perpetrators or accomplices, or when the patients themselves were forced to commit horrid acts, there are usually strongly conflicting thoughts and different internal realities belonging to different dissociative parts that each have a different version of what took place. *My dad was a very nice man who took me to the zoo,* next to: *My dad was aggressive, he used to drink and abuse me.* Or: *Sometimes when I went to my mother crying, she'd walk away or tell me not to get so worked up,* next to: *My mother used to bake cookies with me and she let me lick the mixing bowl; it was so good!* The different realities—of the good and the bad parent, both of which can be true—were incompatible for the child and have been kept by different dissociative parts of the personality.

Nevertheless, it is important that clinicians learn a little more about traumatic childhood experiences even for patients with a dissociative disorder. This is especially useful when making a treatment plan. This includes not only traumatic experiences such as sexual and physical abuse or other experiences of violence, but also certainly the severity of emotional neglect and the unavailability of the parents or caregivers. Unpredictability or unavailability of parents and other caregivers form the background for the development of severe attachment problems. Even a simple question such as, "What would you do after hurting yourself?" can provide information about this.

Many patients with a history of severe early childhood traumatization within the family have disorganized attachment (Cassidy & Shaver, 1999; Main & Hesse, 1990; Liotti, 1999). The section Prognosis and Indication Assessment will briefly discuss the significance of attachment problems for the indication and treatment of early childhood traumatization and dissociative disorders.

As with dissociative symptoms, there are several ways to explore trauma histories, using either self-report questionnaires or a structured interview, with the latter always being the preferred method.

Self-Report Questionnaires

Since the late 1980s, numerous self-report questionnaires have been developed to explore traumatic childhood experiences, both for the Dutch language region (Lange et al., 1995; Nijenhuis et al., 1996; Nijenhuis et al., 2002; Vanderlinden et al., 1993) and the United States and other parts of the world (Briere & Spinazolla, 2009). Most questionnaires involve fairly adequate psychometric qualities (for overviews see: Hulme, 2004; Roy & Perry, 2004; Pietrini et al., 2010). Self-report questionnaires typically contain questions on several domains, such as emotional neglect and abuse, divorce, parental loss or unavailability, physical abuse, sexual abuse, and other traumatic experiences. Several of these questionnaires have been translated and validated in numerous countries. The Traumatic Experiences Checklist (TEC; Nijenhuis et al., 1996) has been used in the current TADS-I pilot study. The questionnaire was tested with psychiatric patients and has sound psychometric qualities. It can be downloaded freely and is available in various languages at dissociativedisorder.org/sdq-tec. Another widely used self-report questionnaire for PTSD is the *Life Events Checklist* for DSM-5 (LEC-5) of which there are two different versions (Weathers et al., 2013). It has a simplified version that includes questions about 17 different types of traumatization that only require a yes or no answer. There is a distinction as to whether the individual has personally experienced the event, has witnessed it, or has knowledge of it. In the second, more extensive version, the traumatizing event or events are further explored. Although this questionnaire is widely used, it is not particularly suitable for exploring early childhood traumatization since that is not the focus of the questions.

Self-report questionnaires are widely used in clinical research. In these contexts, the questionnaires have the advantage of saving time and cost. In clinical practice, especially with patients diagnosed with or suspected of having a dissociative disorder, the preferred method is to take the trauma history yourself. As required, clinicians may use questions from self-report questionnaires such as the TEC for this purpose. A number of sound and structured interviews for taking the history of stressful childhood experiences are available as well (Bernstein et al., 1998; Bifulco et al., 1994; Bremner et al., 2000; Bremner et al., 2007; Draijer & Langeland, 1999). One of these, the Structured Trauma Interview (STI), was developed by Nel Draijer and has been used in several clinical studies (Draijer, 2003; Draijer & Boon, 1993a; Draijer & Langeland, 1999; Wildschut et al., 2014; Wildschut et al., 2018; Wildschut et al., 2019). The STI interview will be discussed later in this chapter.

General Concerns in Exploring Traumatic Experiences

Draijer (2003) described several important general concerns for clinicians to consider when exploring trauma histories. Providing structure, asking "yes/no" (closed) questions, limiting the tendency to go into too much detail, and avoiding exploration of emotions provide patients the safety to share something about their past.

Primary requirements for assessing traumatic experiences are to ask closed questions whenever possible and to clearly structure the interview. It is absolutely not about details and digressions or, as Draijer (2003, 2008) states: "You don't have to know all the details!"

It is sometimes necessary to set limits for patients who want to elaborate, which may lead to problems afterward in the form of reexperiencing trauma or having other dissociative reactions. Clinicians would also be advised to keep the interview factual and not ask for emotional responses. During the diagnostic phase, one should not explore feelings about the traumatic experiences or, more generally, about childhood, as doing so may trigger severe dissociative responses.

Patients should be clearly informed in advance that they are free to refuse if they do not want to talk about certain experiences, not even on a factual level. However, sometimes they either cannot or dare not say so or realize too late, and they lose contact with the clinician and do not seem to hear what is being asked. At such moments, the clinician will need to interrupt the diagnostic interview to help the patient regain his or her orientation in the now. It often helps to name time and place: "Today is Tuesday (date), you have come to see me (name) for an interview for the purpose of your treatment. You are in (place or address). Please look around (etc.)." Sometimes it may take a few minutes for the patient to recover, occasionally longer. Typically, the longer a patient is out of contact, the greater the internal struggle in response to the questions. Patients may also hear voices prohibiting them to say anything more. When this happens, it is advisable for the clinician to take the initiative and ask whether it would be better to skip certain questions, pause for a moment, or, in extreme cases, end the interview: "I notice that you are likely to lose contact with me, perhaps these questions are too much at this time? As I told you at the beginning of this interview, you can truly say so if you want to skip a question. Also, we can take a break or stop the interview at this time. We can always resume at a later time."

Furthermore, it is important that clinicians take it upon themselves to name the potentially shameful things, such as the sexual acts involved in the abuse, to avoid overburdening the patient with feelings of shame. However, it is not recommended to use terms such as "incest" or "rape." First, these terms are not clear; they are understood differently by different patients. Second, they may trigger unnecessary activation or denial (*My grandfather did really horrible things to me, but is it incest? I think it's a dreadful word and I don't want to think about it!*)

An important obstacle to taking a good trauma history is formed by the clinician's own emotional reaction to it. Clinicians commonly have strong emotions and physical experiences in response to hearing trauma histories (Dalenberg, 2000; Steele et al., 2017). They may be too much involved or fascinated with the traumatic backgrounds of their patients or, on the contrary, very avoidant: not wanting or not being able to listen to certain things (Draijer & Boon, 1995; Draijer, 2003; van der Hart et al., 2006; Steele et al., 2017). The latter may lead to a collusion of avoidance in treatment, with both the clinician and the dissociative patient unwilling or unable to realize the severity of the trauma history. Thus, the prerequisite for exploring traumatic experiences is the ability to recognize one's own emotional responses (called countertransference reactions) to hearing about experiences of violence and to keep them from entering the interview. Clinicians may ask themselves the following questions:

- Are there any topics I would rather not touch upon?
- Have I noticed that I tend to want to ask for details?
- Do I find myself feeling very powerless with the information I get?
- Have I had tears in my eyes while the patient was saying she did not care?
- Have I noticed physical reactions in myself, such as tension, headache, or nausea?

Answers to these questions may be taken to peer intervision or consultation with colleagues to discuss one's own countertransference feelings.

In addition, clinicians should be aware that memory is fallible or can be distorted. It is essential for clinicians to be neutral and avoid suggesting traumatic memories or ask leading questions when reconstructing patients' pasts. Patients may have no memory of the traumatic experiences, in whole or in part, for a long time and may only recover them at a later stage: so-called recovered memories. Although there has been much discussion worldwide for years about whether traumatic memories can be forgotten, there are also several prospective studies that have shown that this is indeed the case (Williams, 1994, 1995; Widom & Morris, 1997). The Dutch Health Council, an advisory committee for the government, concluded that there are both "recovered memories" and "fictitious memories." Consequently, clinicians must act carefully (Gezondheidsraad, 2004; Everaerd & Gersons-Wolfensberger, 2004).

Finally, clinicians should realize that patients with DID and OSDD-1 have two types of dissociative parts: parts with tasks and functions in daily life and parts that are stuck in trauma time and hold the traumatic memories. During diagnostic examination and the assessment of traumatic experiences, there is usually a part present that functions in daily life. Such a part often has partial and sometimes even complete amnesia for the trauma history, while other parts know the traumatizing events very well. In the mid-1990s, when the discussion about recovered memories also raged in the Netherlands, a DID patient remarked: *Of course we have never forgotten all those terrible things, that concept of recovered memories is not correct. It's just better that she doesn't know, or she wouldn't be able to function at all right now!* This comment was made by a dissociative part that was very well aware of the trauma history and by *"she should not know"* she meant the part that functioned in daily life. This part had indeed had amnesia for much of the trauma history at the time.

Research on the effects of extreme stress on memory also shows that the functioning of brain regions involved in memory can be affected (Bremner et al., 1995, 1996). In our study with the SCID-D, Nel Draijer and I found that approximately 20% of DID patients had complete amnesia for their trauma histories. Follow-up research with these patients revealed that, at the time of the SCID-D examination, they were still being abused, mostly by the original perpetrators: something they, the personality parts functioning in daily life, were unaware of at that time (Boon & Draijer, 1993a, 1993b, 1995a). The ongoing abuse was revealed later, in the course of treatment, often by dissociative parts stuck in trauma time.

We must also conclude that the increase of information about trauma and dissociative disorders via the internet and social media may result in false-positive trauma-related diagnoses and sometimes pseudomemories—also called fictitious memories—of traumatizing events. Reporting pseudomemories may also be encouraged by clinicians who are too suggestive. It is well known that memories may be instilled and that clinicians themselves may interpret that something must have happened when patients are vague or unsure.

It is always a matter of finding an optimal balance for patients to reveal something about their experiences. In doing so, clinicians must be careful and cautious—but not too cautious, as this may sometimes create more anxiety in patients and may also confirm the idea that the clinician does not actually want to hear it, cannot hear it, or does not want to know about it.

The Structured Trauma Interview (STI)

The Structured Trauma Interview (STI; 1989) was developed by Nel Draijer on the basis of the questionnaire that was used in the national incest study she conducted on behalf of the Dutch Ministry of Social Affairs (Draijer, 1988, 1990). The interview was adapted for use in clinical populations and has been used in several studies with psychiatric patients (Draijer, 1995, 2003; Draijer & Langeland, 1999; Langeland et al., 2001; Rinne et al., 2000). It is available in Dutch and English with an extensive manual, and it can be requested from the authors.

The purpose of the interview is to get an overall impression of the severity of traumatic experiences and the age at which they started. Several other questions are important in this regard (Draijer, 2003):

- Was it a one-time event or did it involve repeated or chronic experiences for years?
- Were people involved that the patient depended on, such as parents or caregivers?
- Did it involve multiple perpetrators?
- Did the traumatic experiences occur before age six or did it happen later?

It is important to get an impression of how the traumatic experiences affected the patient's personality development. Whether or not a child had a one-time traumatic experience and was able to talk about it with a parent or caregiver, or at least also had positive experiences with trusted people in the core family, makes a lot of difference. Patients with severe dissociative disorders typically report repeated sexual and/or physical abuse and usually emotional abuse or neglect. For the vast majority, their home was unsafe. Even if the parents were not the direct perpetrators, there was a lack of emotional support and safety, or the parents themselves experienced serious problems that made them unavailable to their child. In addition to sexual, physical, and emotional abuse, almost all patients report intense loneliness and lack of care, support, and attention from their parents or caregivers.

The questions in the STI cover several areas. The first questions focus on the patient's family of origin, the relationships and bonds with parents and siblings, and the impact of any parental divorce. What was the patient like as a child, and were the parents available as caregivers? Next, there are questions about physical and sexual abuse and other shocking experiences. The final questions deal with later traumatic experiences after the age of 16. When answers are affirmative, the severity of the experiences is roughly assessed. Sometimes patients provide sufficient information about this themselves and there is no need to ask more questions.

The following example is a fragment of an STI interview:

CLINICIAN: Did you always live with both your parents until you were 12 years old?

PATIENT: No, my parents divorced when I was nine. That was a very nasty situation, a messy divorce. My father was really aggressive, and the police came over frequently.

CLINICIAN: Do you remember going to elementary school, for example?

PATIENT: Not from before I was nine but after that. I kept going to the same school after the divorce. We still lived in the same house. When I see photographs from before that time, nothing comes back at all.

CLINICIAN: Can you explain that?

PATIENT: What I mean is: I can see myself in the picture, but it doesn't tell me anything. I can't remember it at all. That's a bit of a weird response to a messy divorce isn't it? I often think: I'm being ridiculous!

CLINICIAN: If you try hard, do any memories come back?

PATIENT: No, they don't really. My mom told me a story about a holiday the other day. We used to go to the mountains. That's when my dad was still around. I seem to have liked it very much. We stayed with a farmer's family. Apparently, I was allowed to go horseback riding. There were many pictures of me on a pony. I still ride horses, but I can't remember at all how I learned to do so. So that must have been before I was nine.

CLINICIAN: Can you tell me something about your mother? What kind of image do you have of her?

PATIENT: Things are better between us now.

CLINICIAN: Could you tell me a bit more about her?

PATIENT: In my memory, her behavior was very erratic. She would often be very angry with me, and I always had the feeling that she was favoring my younger sister. But of course, I only remember things from after the divorce. I think she wasn't feeling all too well herself. There was always a fear that my dad would show up. I always had to keep an eye on the kind of mood she was in when I would come home from school.

CLINICIAN: Was she ill a lot?

PATIENT: I don't know, I don't think she was ill, but she was often on the couch or in bed then.

CLINICIAN: What did you do together, did you ever play a game or have fun?

PATIENT: I don't really know, I think I avoided her as much as possible; I was afraid of her temper tantrums. I don't have all that many images of my mother from that time. I think she had to work a lot too.

CLINICIAN: Who would take care of you and your little sister?

PATIENT: My grandparents were often there. They lived nearby and they were kind.

CLINICIAN: You just mentioned that your relationship is better now.

PATIENT: Yes, at least I don't fight with her as much as I used to. Things have improved for her since she remarried. I had left home by then.

I actually have a much better relationship with my boyfriend's mom. She makes me feel much more understood and she has taken care of me so many times. I don't feel that at all with my own mother; there's always some kind of distance, but I do go and visit once in a while. I think I always used to be "the annoying child that caused problems." That's what she used to say to me. Even when my sister provoked me, I got the blame!

This childhood history shows that the patient or at least the part that was presenting during the interview has amnesia for at least part of her childhood. It also reveals a disturbed relationship with her mother, especially after the divorce. Although the patient has no recollection from before the age of nine, it seems that there may have been problems in the relationship with her mother before that.

The patient stopped seeing her father altogether and her relationship with him was even more severely disrupted. She reported a history of physical abuse and extreme violence during the time of her parents' messy divorce around the time she was nine years old. It remained unclear whether there were any other factors involved in the amnesia. However, it is not desirable for clinicians to ask further questions about this or to present hypotheses to patients. It is best to record the answers given and proceed with the interview.

Completing the interview section dealing with the stressful subject— either by tackling each subject separately, or the trauma history as a whole—is done by asking the patient whether they have ever talked about it with anyone and whether there is now someone with whom they can discuss the subject. It is important to move on to the present and to how the person is holding up in the present. This will help the patient gain some mental distance from the troubling memories and regulate their affect.

CLINICIAN: What was it like for you to talk about these experiences?
PATIENT: Well, you know, it doesn't really bother me. I have said this before. I don't feel that much. Sometimes my boyfriend wonders: "How can you talk about all these terrible things like that without feeling anything?"
CLINICIAN: Whom have you been able to talk to about it?
PATIENT: With my boyfriend and his family, but also with girlfriends. Especially after I had those seizures, I began to wonder what was happening.

A notable thing during this trauma history was that the patient appeared very depersonalized. She kept repeating that she did not feel that much, but also that she must be a simulator. So, apart from the amnesia, there was also considerable depersonalization during the STI. She had presented with non-epileptic seizures for which she also had amnesia.

A Good Treatment Plan Requires More Than a Classification of a Dissociative Disorder

This book aims to contribute to the correct classification of dissociative disorders. However, there is more to a patient than a DSM or ICD diagnosis. Classifications are no more than a list of symptoms or symptom clusters, which has its limitations: It takes more than a classification to make a good treatment plan. Still, making a correct DSM or ICD diagnosis is an important first step in treatment, precisely because many patients with a complex dissociative disorder such as DID or OSDD-1 often are treated based on a wrong diagnosis for years on end.

Appropriate Diagnosis Allows for Appropriate Treatment

As mentioned in Chapter 1, in patients with DID or OSDD-1 the treatment of the comorbid diagnosis—such as eating disorders or personality pathology—is often unsuccessful or only provides a temporary improvement of the symptoms. In such cases, clinicians are unaware that the problems are primarily related to the underlying dissociative disorder. The following case provides a good example.

Case Report: Primary Diagnosis and Comorbidity

The patient, Ms. Z., presented at a social psychiatric ward when she was 20 years old. As an adolescent she had received years of treatment in both outpatient and inpatient settings for a severe eating disorder, without much result. She repeatedly lapsed into severe anorexic behavior with life-threatening weight loss. Periodically she also suffered from losing her voice, being barely able to speak—clearly a somatoform dissociative symptom. However, a dissociative disorder was never considered at that time. She and her family received family therapy, which worsened her condition and led to increasing suicidality. After a traffic accident with her bicycle, which later turned out to be a failed suicide attempt, she developed a somatoform dissociative symptom disorder (a conversion disorder in DSM-5 terms): a partial contracture of her hand. Splints and other medical interventions offered no remedy. Because of her various somatoform dissociative symptoms and because she also heard voices, a more complex dissociative disorder was suspected. Further diagnostic assessment showed that she had considerable amnesia, including for events in the present. Eventually, it became clear that there were multiple dissociative parts with tasks and functions in daily life and many traumatized child parts.

The patient was avoidant. Anxiety and shame played a major role. Although during previous family sessions the family therapists had wondered whether there might be a family secret, this had never been explored with her on an individual level when she was treated as an adolescent. There was no known trauma history. During later outpatient treatment for the dissociative disorder, it eventually became clear that there had been prolonged and very severe sexual abuse. Multiple dissociative parts appeared to have reasons to stop eating, including one part that had once been pregnant as an adolescent and had decided not to eat again so as to prevent another pregnancy. Each time the patient reached a normal weight and her menstrual cycle recovered, this part was activated and stopped eating. The patient herself, that is, the part that was present at the treatment, was not aware of this at all and felt that she was unable to influence her eating behavior in any way. She tried to cooperate in gaining weight by eating well, but she explained:

> I'm not aware that I vomit, I have no memory of it. But sometimes, when I'm present again, I have a really bad taste in my mouth and then I know that I must have been vomiting. But I'm not doing this myself; I feel so powerless.

Ultimately, an improvement in the eating problems only occurred when the parts that were involved began to participate in the treatment and there was understanding and realization about the traumatizing event associated with not wanting to eat. The contracture of her hand could be treated once it was clear which dissociative parts were involved (Boon & van der Hart, in progress).

Evaluation and Discussion

In Chapters 1 and 5, I stated that most comorbid problems (e.g., suicide attempts, eating problems, self-injurious behavior, etc.) are held by dissociative parts of the personality that are stuck in trauma time. When these parts are not included in the treatment, as in the case described above, treatment of the comorbid symptom may at best provide a temporary improvement, but often none at all. This may happen as the part of the patient presenting for treatment is often unaware of the existence of these parts, may have amnesia for them, or does not dare to talk about them at all.

This case is just one of many that shows the importance of an appropriate diagnosis as a first step; however, much more is needed to create a treatment plan. For a detailed discussion of this, I refer to the book *Treating Trauma-Related Dissociation* (Steele et al., 2017), which includes chapters on the prognosis, case formulation, and treatment plan for patients with a complex dissociative disorder. It also contains a revised version of an evaluation checklist that I developed in the mid-1990s (Boon, 1997). Originally, this list was intended to evaluate the course of treatment and determine whether a patient had stabilized sufficiently to move on to the next stage with trauma history treatment as the focus.

Prognosis and Indication Assessment

I started treating patients with dissociative disorders around 1985 while working in a psychiatric outpatient department. Even though all patients with a dissociative disorder had serious problems, it quickly became clear that there were significant individual differences between them, which influenced their prognosis and treatment plan. Some patients were employed and had completed academic studies. Others had started receiving psychiatric treatment while still in high school and were unable to live independently. Some were married and had children and a reasonable network of friends; others were completely isolated. Some had many resources they could draw on, such as creativity, or musicality, or a great love of nature that allowed them to calm themselves. They were better able to regulate their vehement emotions as compared to others, who had great difficulty doing so and lapsed into severe self-mutilation when feeling either too much or too little (Steele et al., 2017).

Although most patients had average to above-average intelligence, there were huge differences in the extent to which they were able to reflect on themselves and others. There were also huge differences in the severity of their attachment problems and the extent to which patients were able to engage in and tolerate therapeutic relationships, another major factor determining prognosis.

Several clinicians have described how patients with DID and OSDD-1 constitute a very heterogenous group with very different treatment prognoses (Boon, 1997; Dorahy et al., 2014; Horevitz & Loewenstein, 1994; Kluft, 1993, 1994; Steele et al., 2017; van der Hart & Boon, 1997). Horevitz and Loewenstein (1994) divided such patients into three subgroups with wide differences in treatment complexity and prognosis: (1) the first group concerned high-functioning DID patients. They were often treated in private practices, had few crises, and had rarely, if ever, come to the attention of mental health services; (2) the second group consisted of patients who were found to have many comorbid disorders in addition to the dissociative disorder, such as borderline personality disorder (BPD); while (3) the third group consisted of patients who demonstrated the most pushback in their treatment and who were often still entangled in abusive relationships and engaged in a lot of self-injurious behavior.

Furthermore, the role of severe attachment problems as an important prognostic factor in the treatment of patients with complex dissociative disorders has become increasingly apparent over the past 20 years.

As one of the first in the world, Draijer (1988) highlighted the importance of emotional neglect in a large nationwide study in the Netherlands, looking into the consequences of sexual abuse of girls by relatives. The groundbreaking book, *Trauma and Recovery*, by Judith Herman, was not published until 1992 (Herman, 1992b). And at the same time, Main (Main, 2000; Main & Solomon, 1990) gave renewed attention to the early work of John Bowlby and Mary Ainsworth (Ainsworth et al., 1978; Bowlby, 1969) and added the concept of disorganized attachment. It was not until the 1990s that the impact of disorganized attachment was increasingly recognized as perhaps the most important factor in the treatment of many patients with complex dissociative disorder and a history of early childhood traumatization. Barach (1991) was the first to describe DID (then called MPD) as an attachment disorder. Liotti (1992) described the role of disorganized attachment in the etiology of DID. Indeed, many patients with complex dissociative disorder have a disorganized attachment profile.

The Diagnostic Square: A Tool for Case Conceptualization

Draijer described a two-dimensional model helpful in indication assessment for patients with a history of early childhood interpersonal traumatization (Draijer, 2003, 2008; Draijer & Langeland, 2009). The model (Figure 11.1) identifies the following main dimensions (traumatizing acts of commission and acts of omission):

- Severity of the traumatization (acts of commission, cumulative)
- Severity of the affective neglect or quality of the early attachment in the bond with parent(s) (acts of omission, which are obviously also highly traumatizing)

Determining the severity of traumatization (i.e., the vertical axis in Figure 11.1) involves a number of factors:

- At what point in the person's development did traumatization take place (what age)?
- How often did it take place (and for how many years)?
- How overwhelming was it (coercion, violence, enforced secrecy)?
- How dependent was the child on the perpetrator(s)?

The so-called trauma dimensions on the y-axis are formed by a continuum of trauma-related disorders, increasing in severity with the hypothesis that

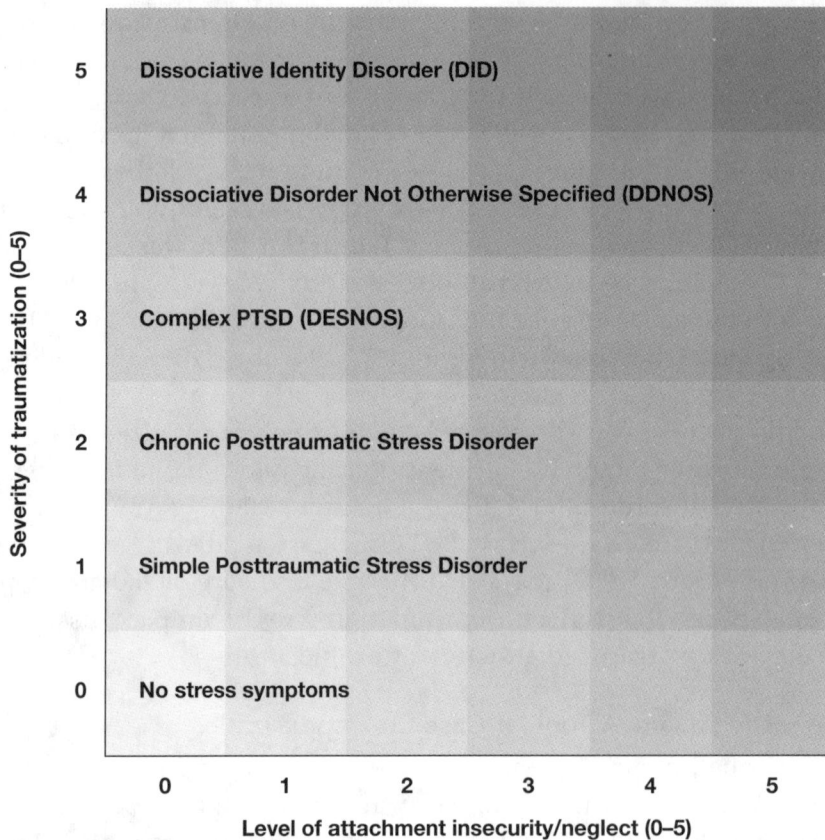

FIGURE 11.1 **The Diagnostic Square**

Source: Draijer, N., & Langeland, W. (2009). Trauma, hechting en verwaarlozing. Een tweedimensionaal model voor diagnostiek en indicatiestelling bij vroegkinderlijke traumatisering. *Cogiscope, 4,* pp. 31–38. See also: Wildschut et al., 2014.

the severity of PTSD symptoms and dissociative symptoms is related to the severity of the cumulative trauma history. The hypothesis that there is a relation between the severity of dissociative symptoms and trauma-related disorders and the severity of the trauma history was previously confirmed in our study with the SCID-D (Draijer & Boon, 1993a, 1995). Patients with DID reported the most severe trauma histories with an onset before the age of five, over many years, and often with multiple perpetrators. In most cases, there was a dependency relationship with the perpetrators. Other research studies, including research with hospitalized and outpatient psychiatric patients, have also confirmed the coherence between severity of trauma histories and severity of PTSD and dissociative symptoms (Draijer, 1994; Draijer & Langeland, 1999; Wildschut et al., 2018).

The dimension of neglect (acts of omission) is operationalized by the severity of perceived insecurity in early attachment relationships, as well as the degree of emotional neglect. Of course, acts of omission are also traumatizing. When treating patients with a dissociative disorder, it often turns out that they have experienced the emotional loss and unavailability, intentionally or subconsciously, of their parents as much worse than the actual sexual or physical abuse:

> My mother must have known about it, I think, but she did nothing to prevent it. She was just depressed, and I always had to take care of her, I was afraid she would end her life. She had already tried that once. Then I would be all alone and at his mercy. Sometimes I was longing so much for her to comfort me, that she would see that I was not well. I fantasized that we would go away together. But I guess I just didn't matter to her.

This dimension of neglect is related to the parents' attachment patterns and histories. Parents who have problems of their own or histories of traumatization, like the mother in this example, are less able or have less ability to establish secure attachment with their own children (Cassidy & Shaver, 1999). The hypothesis is that the severity of this dimension primarily affects the therapeutic relationship and thus a patient's treatment options (Draijer, 2003, 2008; Draijer & Langeland, 2009). Draijer (2003, 2008, p. 26) hypothesizes that "the greater affective neglect and attachment problems are, the more problematic the therapeutic relationship—the 'vehicle' of treatment. Also, the ability to be able to feel and realize what is going on, and to give words to it, varies with the degree of emotional neglect" (translated from the Dutch).

Validity of the Diagnostic Square

Recently, the validity of the trauma dimension of the diagnostic square was examined in a study involving 150 patients who consecutively registered at a mental health institution in the Netherlands (Wildschut et al., 2018). The patients were admitted for two different treatment programs: one group was admitted for a treatment program for trauma-related disorders (n = 49) while the other group was admitted for a treatment program for personality disorders (n = 101). All patients were thoroughly examined using structured interviews for PTSD, CPTSD (CAPS and SIDES), and dissociative disorders (SCID-D). Their trauma histories were assessed with the STI. Patients in both groups were found to have been traumatized as children. A clear relationship was found between the severity of reported traumatic experiences (acts of commission) in childhood and the severity of trauma-related disorder, as depicted in Figure 11.1. The findings support the assumption behind the trauma axis of the model, which is that the more severe the cumulative traumatization, the more complex the trauma-related disorder.

The neglect dimension was also investigated (Wildschut et al., 2020), specifically the relationship between personality disorders and reported emotional neglect. At the disorder level, a small correlation was found between the severity of reported emotional neglect and problematic personal functioning. However, evidence was found for a dimensional correlation between a lack of parental warmth and problematic functioning. This provides a first tentative support for the proposed dimensional model.

Clinical Use

For clinicians, the model presented here provides a point of departure to include the factor of insecure attachment in case conceptualization and treatment plan formulation. For the sake of clarity, it should be emphasized again that experiences on both axes are stressful for a person and can therefore be considered traumatizing. In complex dissociative disorders, such as DID or OSDD-1, it is not always easy to relate the severity of insecure attachment to, for example, functioning in daily life. On the outside, some patients perform well at work, have partners and networks of acquaintances, but still appear to have extreme difficulty in developing some degree of trust and cooperation with a therapist. Often, this does not become apparent until the patient starts treatment because it is precisely the relationship with a therapist that is an important trigger for memories of interpersonal traumatic experiences to be reactivated. Especially in patients with disorganized attachment, there is a constant internal struggle between the intense desire for attachment and the urge to protect against these desires—or deny them completely. Attachment is experienced as too threatening and has been dangerous in the past (Steele et al., 2017).

Other Factors Involved in Prognosis and Treatment Planning

Needless to say, in addition to the severity of the attachment problems and the resulting personality problems, there are numerous other factors that help determine the prognosis and treatment plan. A very important factor is the patient's own request for help. What are the patient's wishes and how realistic are they? Especially in patients with DID or OSDD-1, research has shown that patients had sometimes been treated for years without clear results because their dissociative disorder was not recognized and treated. In such cases it is important to ask why previous treatments did not lead to improvement of the disorder. For a detailed discussion of this, I refer to Steele et al. (2017).

The other factors are:

- Highest level of functioning in daily life
- Degree of comorbidity, including personality disorders
- Intensity and flexibility of psychological defense strategies
- Willingness to share personal thoughts and feelings
- Presence and intensity of trauma-related phobias
- Severity of trauma history, especially onset in early childhood and chronicity
- Ability to mentalize
- Degree of motivation and insight and willingness to take responsibility for treatment on one's own
- Degree of self-compassion
- Ability to experience positive feelings, joy, and a sense of humor
- Ability and willingness to learn to regulate and tolerate inner experiences
- Ability to accept that there are dissociative parts and the willingness to work with them
- Presence and intensity of conflicts between dissociative parts
- Persistent current abuse of the patient or of others by the patient

Concluding Remarks

Arriving at a correct descriptive diagnosis is extremely important. However, as discussed in the previous section, Prognosis and Indication Assessment, patients with complex dissociative disorder constitute a very heterogeneous group. Consequently, after diagnosis, more is needed to arrive at a proper treatment plan. It is not only the nature and severity of the traumatization, as reflected in the diagnostic square (Figure 11.1), but there are numerous other factors that must be taken into account, as detailed in this text.

After more than 30 years of experience with diagnosis and treatment of patients with a complex dissociative disorder, how do I view these differences today? More generally, dissociative patients can still be divided into groups with a different prognosis and appropriate treatment trajectory, as was done by Horevitz and Loewenstein at the time (1994). For me personally, the factors described in the previous section are a guideline, whereby I would like to emphasize that the prognosis is always determined by a combination of these factors. In addition, I have learned that there are patients who initially appeared to have a poor prognosis, which was adjusted over the course of treatment and vice versa.

The factors listed in the previous section also apply to the group of patients with ongoing abuse, at the time considered as the most serious group by Horevitz and Loewenstein (1994). It is my experience that patients who are still being abused during treatment require a long treatment trajectory. Despite such a complicating factor, it is in principle possible to successfully guide these patients in their process of breaking away from the perpetrators. But just as for patients with a history of trauma in their past, the prognosis for this group is highly dependent on the severity of the attachment problems and thus their ability to enter and maintain a therapeutic relationship (Boon, 2014).

After making the diagnosis, it is therefore of great importance that clinicians take the time to perform further assessment in order to gain more insight into the above factors. How do I look at this today? At the trauma center where I worked for many years, we also had to divide patients into different groups on the basis of various factors that determined prognosis and appropriate treatment trajectories. These factors were: (1) the severity of comorbid problems, (2) the severity of attachment problems and their possible influence on the ability to enter into a therapeutic relationship, and (3) ongoing abuse, a fact that most of the time only becomes clear during the course of a treatment because the part of the person that initially signs up for treatment usually still has amnesia for the ongoing abuse. Obviously, the more complex the patient's problems, the longer the treatment may need to continue. Of these factors, the severity of patients' attachment problems and their ability to enter into a therapeutic relationship is perhaps the most important.

If we want to offer adequate treatment—and I cannot emphasize this enough—we need to see and understand the person behind the diagnostic label.

EPILOGUE

As for many, the COVID-19 lockdowns in the years 2020–2022 put a lot of my activities on hold, but they did provide me with the opportunity to write this book. I sincerely wonder if this book would have ever come about without the pandemic. Writing the book was a long-cherished wish, but actually writing it was an entirely different proposition altogether.

While writing the various chapters, and particularly the case reports, I realized time and again how complex and intricate the diagnosis of dissociative disorders is. When I started out in the 1980s with the SCID-D assessments, it was not always clear to me what exactly patients meant when they responded to questions in the diagnostic interview. Gradually, I became more proficient in asking for clarification and also in distinguishing, for example, between memory problems caused by absorption versus those caused by the activity of dissociative parts. I also got better at recognizing the different forms of depersonalization, only some of which indicate a division of the personality.

When giving training sessions, I always tell the audience that I used to record every interview (audio or video) and that in fact, it was only while listening to these again afterward that I was able to score properly. In the beginning, it was impossible to pay proper attention to the patient and simultaneously score the interview, let alone get to a conclusion at the end of it. Also, when listening afterward, I often realized which other questions I should have asked to get a better idea of the nature and severity of a symptom. In my epilogue I want to emphasize this again for the readers, especially those who are just starting to conduct diagnostic assessments. Whatever diagnostic interview for dissociative disorders you use, it takes time and energy to make it your own. Recording the interviews and listening to these recordings afterward helped me a great deal. As I mentioned in my preface, a training course with subsequent supervision is a prerequisite. In addition, colleagues are important for intervision. After all, it takes a collective effort to better master a new diagnostic interview.

In conclusion, in the last chapter I state again that good diagnostic assessment is a prerequisite for appropriate treatment. Too many patients with complex dissociative disorders are in the health care system for far too long without the right diagnosis and without the corresponding treatment being offered. Even once the correct diagnosis has been made, there is no quick fix for these complex problems. Like many other experienced colleagues in this field I believe that good treatment for complex dissociative disorders begins with a period of stabilization and that an immediate focus on trauma treatment can be very harmful. Of course, every patient is unique and the duration of the stabilization phase will not be the same for everyone. But even during this phase, all interventions are aimed at promoting the integrative capacity of the patient. Only with thorough scientific research can the question be answered as to which patients require a shorter or longer stabilization phase. Such research must always begin with careful diagnostic assessment, in order to be sure that the patients who are included really suffer from a complex dissociative disorder. Moreover, questions about the influence of the severity of comorbidity and attachment problems must be answered.

I hope more future research will be conducted worldwide on the diagnostic assessment and treatment of patients with complex dissociative disorders.

1. Substance Abuse
2. Eating Problems
3. Sleep Problems
4. Mood and Emotion Regulation
5. Anxiety and Panic
6. Self-Injurious Behavior
7. Self-Image and Identity
8. Relationships With Others
9. Sexuality
10. Alterations in Consciousness
11. Somatoform Dissociative Symptoms
12. Psychoform Dissociative Symptoms
13. Schneiderian Symptoms
14. Symptoms That (Possibly) Indicate a Division of the Personality
15. Dissociative Parts of the Personality
16. PTSD (DSM-5)
17. Complex PTSD (ICD-11)

These TADS-I Symptom Profiles are available as free downloads from the following website: tads-i.com/download.

Symptom Profile 1

Scoring of the frequency: 1: Seldom / 2: Recurrently / 3: Monthly / 4: Weekly / 5: Daily / 0: Unclear

Assessment of subjective distress: Minor/Moderate/Severe (for explanation, please see Chapter 5)

Substance Abuse, version 1.12

Does the patient report substance abuse in the present and/or past?

☐ Yes, the patient reports substance abuse in the present and/or past, namely:

Symptoms	Frequency
☐ Excessive alcohol use present	_____
☐ Excessive alcohol use past	_____
☐ Excessive drug use present	_____
☐ Excessive drug use past	_____
☐ Excessive use of medication present	_____
☐ Excessive use of medication past	_____

☐ No, the patient has not abused alcohol, drugs, or medication, or denies such use

Clinical impression:

- Can any dissociative symptoms be explained by substance abuse?
  - ☐ Yes
  - ☐ No, that is unlikely
  - ☐ Unclear, a somatic examination should be considered

- Is the presence of everyday amnesia potentially due to excessive use of substances in the past or present?
  - ☐ Yes
  - ☐ No, that is unlikely
  - ☐ Unclear, a somatic examination should be considered

- Assessment of subjective distress:

  _____

Symptom Profile 2

Scoring of the frequency: 1: Seldom / 2: Recurrently / 3: Monthly / 4: Weekly / 5: Daily / 0: Unclear

Assessment of subjective distress: Minor/Moderate/Severe (for explanation, please see Chapter 5)

Eating Problems, version 1.12

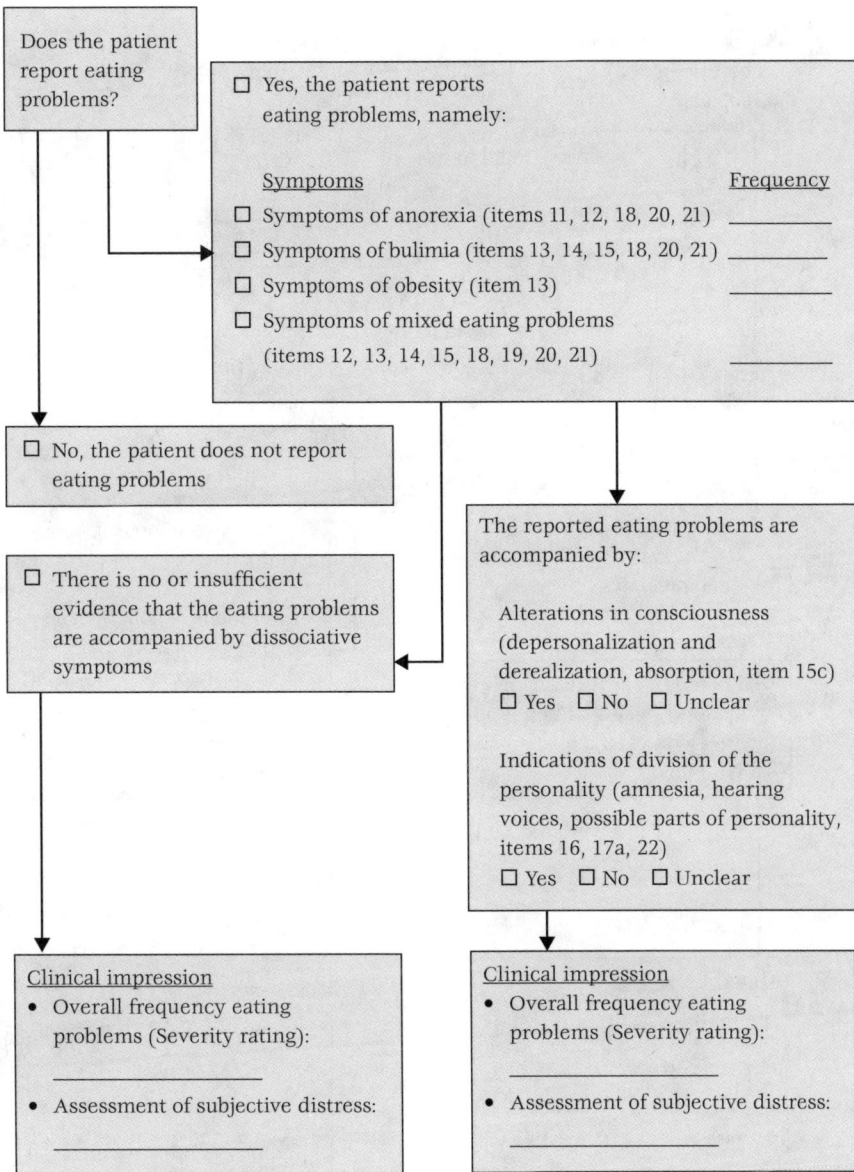

Does the patient report eating problems?

□ Yes, the patient reports eating problems, namely:

Symptoms	Frequency
□ Symptoms of anorexia (items 11, 12, 18, 20, 21)	_____
□ Symptoms of bulimia (items 13, 14, 15, 18, 20, 21)	_____
□ Symptoms of obesity (item 13)	_____
□ Symptoms of mixed eating problems (items 12, 13, 14, 15, 18, 19, 20, 21)	_____

□ No, the patient does not report eating problems

□ There is no or insufficient evidence that the eating problems are accompanied by dissociative symptoms

The reported eating problems are accompanied by:

Alterations in consciousness (depersonalization and derealization, absorption, item 15c)
□ Yes   □ No   □ Unclear

Indications of division of the personality (amnesia, hearing voices, possible parts of personality, items 16, 17a, 22)
□ Yes   □ No   □ Unclear

Clinical impression
- Overall frequency eating problems (Severity rating):

_____

- Assessment of subjective distress:

_____

Clinical impression
- Overall frequency eating problems (Severity rating):

_____

- Assessment of subjective distress:

_____

Symptom Profile 3

Scoring of the frequency: 1: Seldom / 2: Recurrently / 3: Monthly / 4: Weekly / 5: Daily / 0: Unclear

Assessment of subjective distress: Minor/Moderate/Severe (for explanation, please see Chapter 5)

Sleep Problems, version 1.12

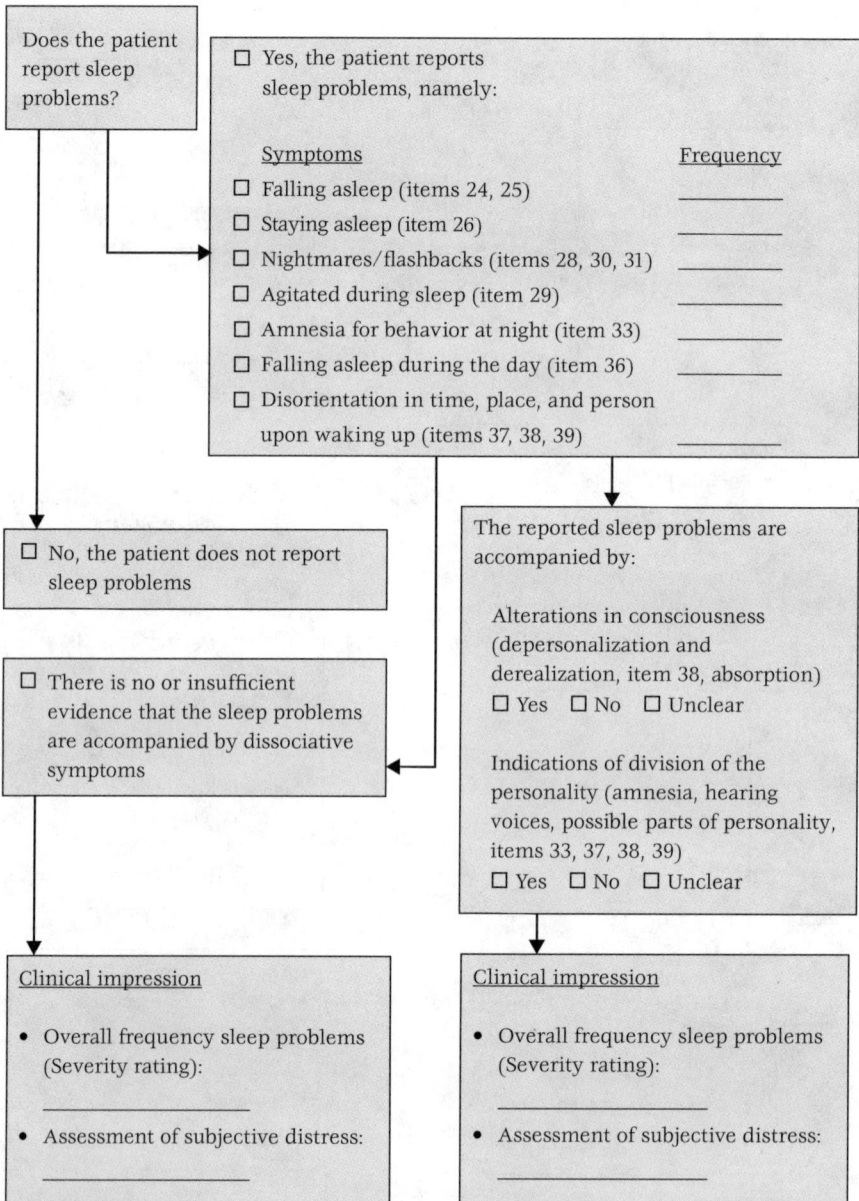

Does the patient report sleep problems?

☐ Yes, the patient reports sleep problems, namely:

Symptoms	Frequency
☐ Falling asleep (items 24, 25)	_____
☐ Staying asleep (item 26)	_____
☐ Nightmares/flashbacks (items 28, 30, 31)	_____
☐ Agitated during sleep (item 29)	_____
☐ Amnesia for behavior at night (item 33)	_____
☐ Falling asleep during the day (item 36)	_____
☐ Disorientation in time, place, and person upon waking up (items 37, 38, 39)	_____

☐ No, the patient does not report sleep problems

☐ There is no or insufficient evidence that the sleep problems are accompanied by dissociative symptoms

The reported sleep problems are accompanied by:

Alterations in consciousness (depersonalization and derealization, item 38, absorption)
☐ Yes ☐ No ☐ Unclear

Indications of division of the personality (amnesia, hearing voices, possible parts of personality, items 33, 37, 38, 39)
☐ Yes ☐ No ☐ Unclear

Clinical impression

- Overall frequency sleep problems (Severity rating):

  _____

- Assessment of subjective distress:

  _____

Clinical impression

- Overall frequency sleep problems (Severity rating):

  _____

- Assessment of subjective distress:

  _____

Symptom Profile 4

Scoring of the frequency: 1: Seldom / 2: Recurrently / 3: Monthly / 4: Weekly / 5: Daily / 0: Unclear

Assessment of subjective distress: Minor/Moderate/Severe (for explanation, please see Chapter 5)

Mood and Emotion Regulation, version 1.12

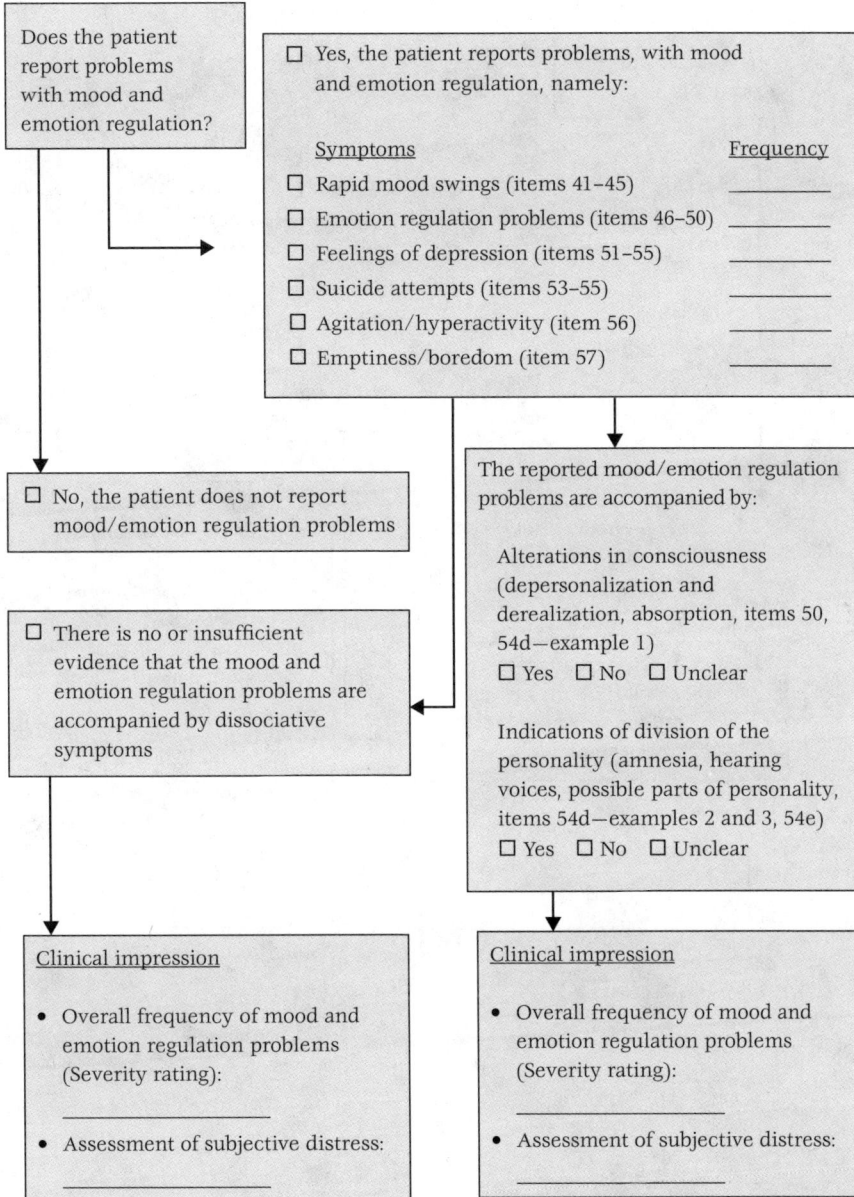

Does the patient report problems with mood and emotion regulation?

☐ Yes, the patient reports problems, with mood and emotion regulation, namely:

Symptoms	Frequency
☐ Rapid mood swings (items 41–45)	_____
☐ Emotion regulation problems (items 46–50)	_____
☐ Feelings of depression (items 51–55)	_____
☐ Suicide attempts (items 53–55)	_____
☐ Agitation/hyperactivity (item 56)	_____
☐ Emptiness/boredom (item 57)	_____

☐ No, the patient does not report mood/emotion regulation problems

The reported mood/emotion regulation problems are accompanied by:

Alterations in consciousness (depersonalization and derealization, absorption, items 50, 54d—example 1)
☐ Yes   ☐ No   ☐ Unclear

Indications of division of the personality (amnesia, hearing voices, possible parts of personality, items 54d—examples 2 and 3, 54e)
☐ Yes   ☐ No   ☐ Unclear

☐ There is no or insufficient evidence that the mood and emotion regulation problems are accompanied by dissociative symptoms

Clinical impression

• Overall frequency of mood and emotion regulation problems (Severity rating):

_____

• Assessment of subjective distress:

_____

Clinical impression

• Overall frequency of mood and emotion regulation problems (Severity rating):

_____

• Assessment of subjective distress:

_____

Symptom Profile 5

Scoring of the frequency: 1: Seldom / 2: Recurrently / 3: Monthly / 4: Weekly / 5: Daily / 0: Unclear

Assessment of subjective distress: Minor/Moderate/Severe (for explanation, please see Chapter 5)

Anxiety and Panic, version 1.12

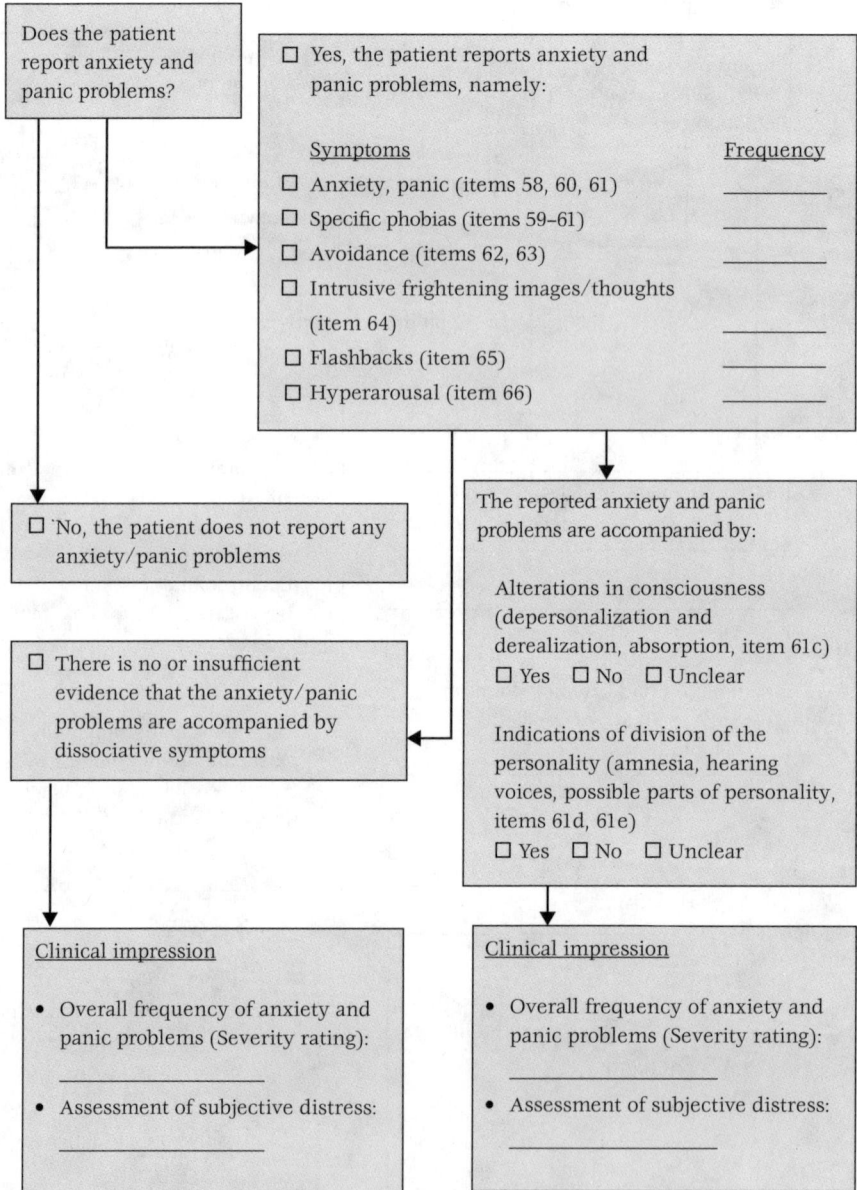

Does the patient report anxiety and panic problems?

☐ Yes, the patient reports anxiety and panic problems, namely:

Symptoms	Frequency
☐ Anxiety, panic (items 58, 60, 61)	_____
☐ Specific phobias (items 59–61)	_____
☐ Avoidance (items 62, 63)	_____
☐ Intrusive frightening images/thoughts (item 64)	_____
☐ Flashbacks (item 65)	_____
☐ Hyperarousal (item 66)	_____

☐ No, the patient does not report any anxiety/panic problems

☐ There is no or insufficient evidence that the anxiety/panic problems are accompanied by dissociative symptoms

The reported anxiety and panic problems are accompanied by:

Alterations in consciousness (depersonalization and derealization, absorption, item 61c)
☐ Yes ☐ No ☐ Unclear

Indications of division of the personality (amnesia, hearing voices, possible parts of personality, items 61d, 61e)
☐ Yes ☐ No ☐ Unclear

Clinical impression

- Overall frequency of anxiety and panic problems (Severity rating):

  _____

- Assessment of subjective distress:

  _____

Clinical impression

- Overall frequency of anxiety and panic problems (Severity rating):

  _____

- Assessment of subjective distress:

  _____

Symptom Profile 6

Scoring of the frequency: 1: Seldom / 2: Recurrently / 3: Monthly / 4: Weekly / 5: Daily / 0: Unclear

Assessment of subjective distress: Minor/Moderate/Severe (for explanation, please see Chapter 5)

Self-Injurious Behavior, version 1.12

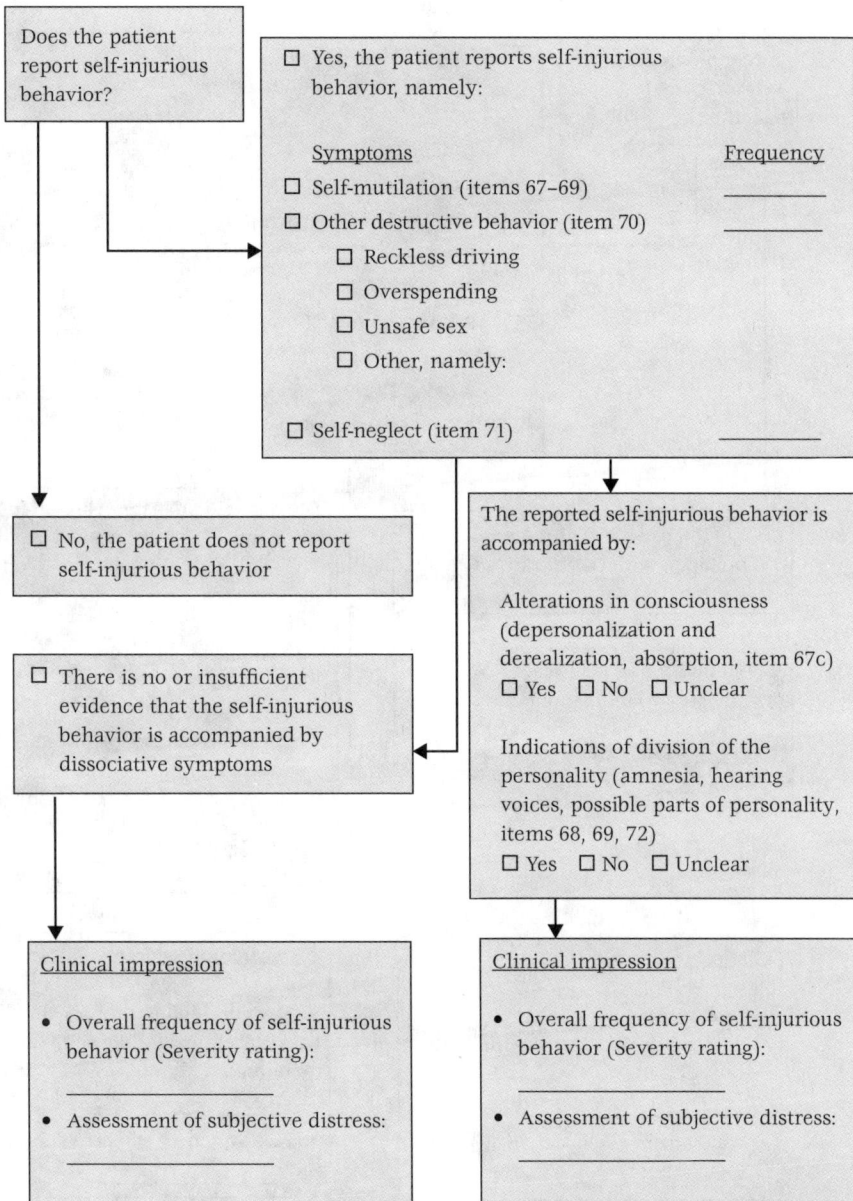

Does the patient report self-injurious behavior?

☐ Yes, the patient reports self-injurious behavior, namely:

Symptoms   Frequency
☐ Self-mutilation (items 67–69)   _____
☐ Other destructive behavior (item 70)   _____
    ☐ Reckless driving
    ☐ Overspending
    ☐ Unsafe sex
    ☐ Other, namely:

☐ Self-neglect (item 71)   _____

☐ No, the patient does not report self-injurious behavior

The reported self-injurious behavior is accompanied by:

Alterations in consciousness (depersonalization and derealization, absorption, item 67c)
☐ Yes ☐ No ☐ Unclear

Indications of division of the personality (amnesia, hearing voices, possible parts of personality, items 68, 69, 72)
☐ Yes ☐ No ☐ Unclear

☐ There is no or insufficient evidence that the self-injurious behavior is accompanied by dissociative symptoms

Clinical impression

• Overall frequency of self-injurious behavior (Severity rating):

  _____

• Assessment of subjective distress:

  _____

Clinical impression

• Overall frequency of self-injurious behavior (Severity rating):

  _____

• Assessment of subjective distress:

  _____

Symptom Profile 7

Scoring of the frequency: 1: Seldom / 2: Recurrently / 3: Monthly / 4: Weekly / 5: Daily / 0: Unclear

Assessment of subjective distress: Minor/Moderate/Severe (for explanation, please see Chapter 5)

Self-image and Identity, version 1.12

Does the patient report problems with self-image and identity?

☐ Yes, the patient reports problems with self-image and identity, namely:

Symptoms	Frequency
☐ Negative self-image (items 73, 74)	_____
☐ Insecurity (item 75)	_____
☐ Uncertain/struggle about who one is (items 76, 79)	_____
☐ Adapting to others (items 77, 78)	_____
☐ Outsider (item 80)	_____
☐ Shame/guilt (items 81, 83)	_____
☐ Helpless (items 84/85)	_____

☐ No, the patient does not report problems with self-image and identity

☐ There is no or insufficient evidence that the problems with self-image and identity is accompanied by dissociative symptoms

The reported problems with self-image and identity are accompanied by:

Alterations in consciousness (depersonalization and derealization, absorption)
☐ Yes ☐ No ☐ Unclear

Indications of division of the personality (amnesia, hearing voices, possible parts of personality, items 79c, 79d, 79e)
☐ Yes ☐ No ☐ Unclear

Clinical impression

• Overall frequency of problems with self-image/identity (Severity rating):

_____

• Assessment of subjective distress:

_____

Clinical impression

• Overall frequency of problems with self-image/identity (Severity rating):

_____

• Assessment of subjective distress:

_____

Symptom Profile 8

Scoring of the frequency: 1: Seldom / 2: Recurrently / 3: Monthly / 4: Weekly / 5: Daily / 0: Unclear

Assessment of subjective distress: Minor/Moderate/Severe (for explanation, please see Chapter 5)

Relationships With Others, version 1.12

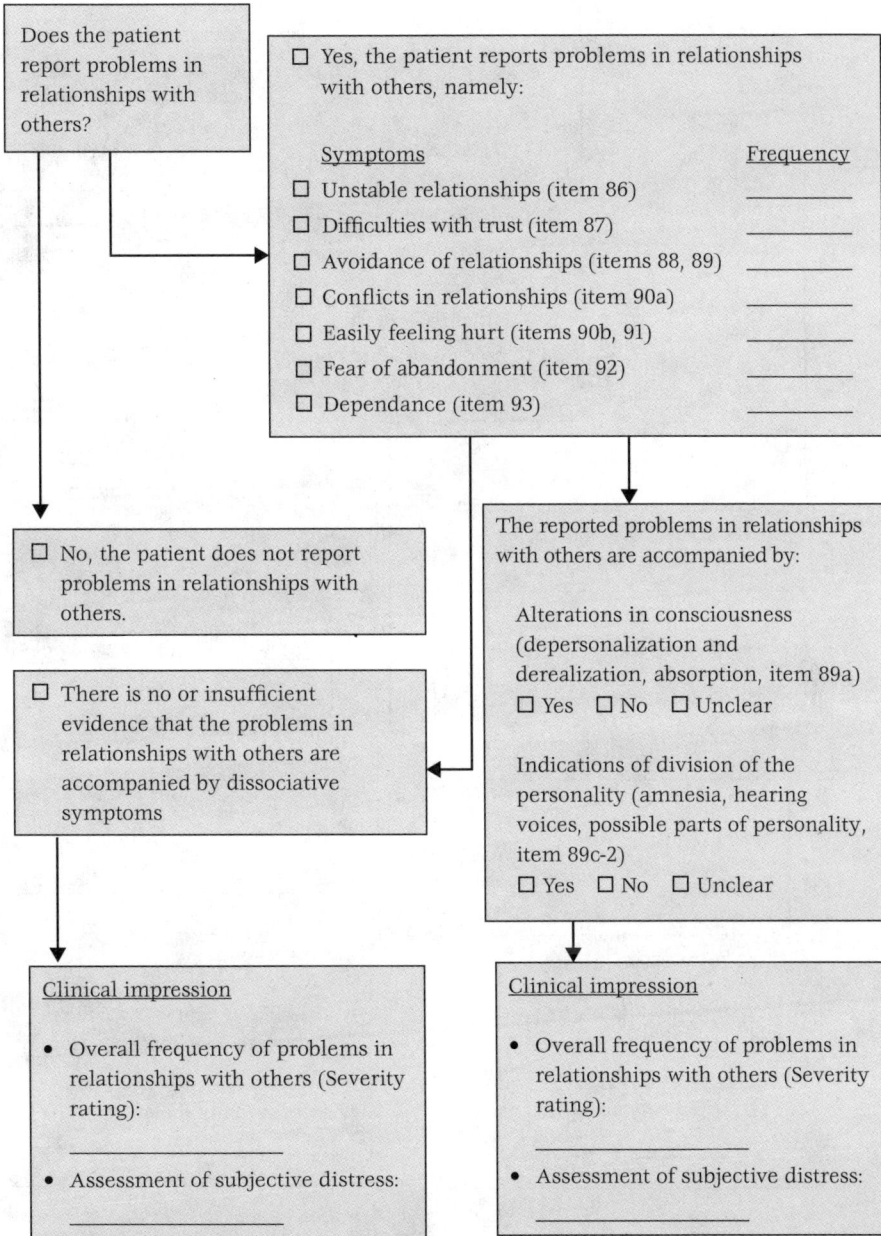

Does the patient report problems in relationships with others?

☐ Yes, the patient reports problems in relationships with others, namely:

Symptoms	Frequency
☐ Unstable relationships (item 86)	_____
☐ Difficulties with trust (item 87)	_____
☐ Avoidance of relationships (items 88, 89)	_____
☐ Conflicts in relationships (item 90a)	_____
☐ Easily feeling hurt (items 90b, 91)	_____
☐ Fear of abandonment (item 92)	_____
☐ Dependance (item 93)	_____

☐ No, the patient does not report problems in relationships with others.

☐ There is no or insufficient evidence that the problems in relationships with others are accompanied by dissociative symptoms

The reported problems in relationships with others are accompanied by:

Alterations in consciousness (depersonalization and derealization, absorption, item 89a)
☐ Yes   ☐ No   ☐ Unclear

Indications of division of the personality (amnesia, hearing voices, possible parts of personality, item 89c-2)
☐ Yes   ☐ No   ☐ Unclear

Clinical impression

- Overall frequency of problems in relationships with others (Severity rating):

  _____

- Assessment of subjective distress:

  _____

Clinical impression

- Overall frequency of problems in relationships with others (Severity rating):

  _____

- Assessment of subjective distress:

  _____

Symptom Profile 9

Scoring of the frequency: 1: Seldom / 2: Recurrently / 3: Monthly / 4: Weekly / 5: Daily / 0: Unclear

Assessment of subjective distress: Minor/Moderate/Severe (for explanation, please see Chapter 5)

Sexuality, version 1.12

Does the patient report problems with sexuality?

☐ Yes, the patient reports problems with sexuality:

Symptoms	Frequency
☐ Difficulty with physical contact (item 95)	_____
☐ Difficulty with sexual contact (items 96, 97)	_____
☐ Avoidance (items 98, 99)	_____
☐ Preoccupations (items 100, 101)	_____
☐ Having involuntary sex (item 102)	_____
☐ Confusion about sexual identity (items 103, 104)	_____

☐ No, the patient does not report problems with sexuality

The reported problems with sexuality are accompanied by:

Alterations in consciousness (depersonalization and derealization, absorption, item 97a)
☐ Yes ☐ No ☐ Unclear

Indications of division of the personality (amnesia, hearing voices, possible parts of personality, item 97)
☐ Yes ☐ No ☐ Unclear

☐ There is no or insufficient evidence that the problems with sexuality are accompanied by dissociative symptoms

Clinical impression

• Overall frequency of problems with sexuality (Severity rating):

_____

• Assessment of subjective distress:

_____

Clinical impression

• Overall frequency of problems with sexuality (Severity rating):

_____

• Assessment of subjective distress:

_____

Symptom Profile 10

Scoring of the frequency: 1: Seldom / 2: Recurrently / 3: Monthly / 4: Weekly / 5: Daily / 0: Unclear

Assessment of subjective distress: Minor/Moderate/Severe (for explanation, please see Chapter 5)

Alterations in Consciousness, version 1.12

Does the patient report alterations in consciousness?

☐ Yes, the patient reports alterations in consciousness, namely:

Symptoms	Frequency
☐ Depersonalization (item 106)	_____
☐ Derealization (items 114–121)	_____
☐ Absorption (items 122–124)	_____
☐ Trance (item 125)	_____
☐ Daydreaming/being fully immersed in fantasy (items 127, 128)	_____

☐ No, the patient does not report alterations in consciousness

Clinical impression

- Overall frequency of problems with sexuality (Severity rating):

  _____

- Assessment of subjective distress:

  _____

☐ Alterations in consciousness are not connected to another psychiatric disorder (e.g., psychoses) and/or substance abuse

☐ Reality testing is intact

Symptom Profile 11

Scoring of the frequency: 1: Seldom / 2: Recurrently / 3: Monthly / 4: Weekly / 5: Daily / 0: Unclear

Assessment of subjective distress: Minor/Moderate/Severe (for explanation, please see Chapter 5)

Somatoform Dissociative Symptoms, version 1.12

Does the patient report symptoms of somatoform dissociation?

☐ Yes, the patient reports symptoms of somatoform dissociation, namely:

Symptoms	Frequency
☐ Positive symptoms	_____
☐ Pain (items 130, 131, 133, 134)	
☐ Sensory intrusions (item 140)	
☐ Pseudo-epilepsy (item 136)	
☐ Tics (item 142)	
☐ Intrusions of motor activity (Schneiderian symptom, items 179, 190)	
Negative symptoms	_____
☐ Fainting/absences (item 135)	
☐ Loss of motor skills (items 139a, 139b, 139c, 139g)	
☐ Loss of sensory sensations (items 137, 138, 139d, 139e)	

☐ No, the patient does not report symptoms of somatoform dissociation

Clinical impression

- Overall frequency of symptoms of somatoform dissociation (Severity rating):

  _____

- Assessment of subjective distress:

  _____

☐ Symptoms of somatic dissocation are not connected to another psychiatric disorder (e.g., psychoses) and/or substance abuse

☐ Reality testing is intact

Symptom Profile 12

Scoring of the frequency: 1: Seldom / 2: Recurrently / 3: Monthly / 4: Weekly / 5: Daily / 0: Unclear

Assessment of subjective distress: Minor/Moderate/Severe (for explanation, please see Chapter 5)

Psychoform Dissociative Symptoms, version 1.12

Does the patient report symptoms of psychoform dissociation?

□ Yes, the patient reports symptoms of psychoform dissociation, namely:

Symptoms	Frequency
□ Positive symptoms	_____
□ Voices (items 163–178)	
□ Intrusive unpleasant memories (item 158)	
□ Influencing of emotions (item 188)	
□ Influencing of thoughts (items 182–184)	
□ Negative symptoms	_____
□ Amnesia (items 148, 149, 152, 153)	
□ Fugue (item 151)	
□ Thoughts removed (items 186, 187)	
□ Loss of emotions/emotions removed (item 189)	

□ No, the patient does not report symptoms of psychoform dissociation

Clinical impression

- Overall frequency of symptoms of psychoform dissociation (Severity rating):

  _____

- Assessment of subjective distress:

  _____

□ Symptoms of psychoform dissocation are not connected to another psychiatric disorder (e.g., psychoses) and/or substance abuse

□ Reality testing is intact

Symptom Profile 13

Scoring of the frequency: 1: Seldom / 2: Recurrently / 3: Monthly / 4: Weekly / 5: Daily / 0: Unclear

Assessment of subjective distress: Minor/Moderate/Severe (for explanation, please see Chapter 5)

Schneiderian Symptoms, version 1.12

Does the patient report Schneiderian symptoms?

☐ Yes, the patient reports Schneiderian symptoms, namely:

Symptoms	Frequency
☐ Voices commenting (item 171)	_____
☐ Voices arguing (items 169, 170)	_____
☐ Commanding voices (item 171)	_____
☐ Thought withdrawal (item 186)	_____
☐ Thought insertion (items 182, 183)	_____
☐ "Made" (controlled) feelings (item 179)	_____
☐ "Made" (controlled) impulses (item 179)	_____
☐ "Made" (controlled) actions or being posessed (items 179, 180)	_____
☐ Thought broadcasting (item 187)	_____
☐ Audible thoughts (item 163)	_____
☐ Delusional perception (item 181)	_____
☐ Somatic passivity (item 180)	_____

☐ No, the patient does not report Schneiderian symptoms

Clinical impression

- Overall frequency of Schniederian symptoms (Severity rating):

  _____

- Assessment of subjective distress:

  _____

☐ Schniederian symptoms are not connected to another psychiatric disorder (e.g., psychoses) and/or substance abuse

☐ Reality testing is intact

Symptom Profile 14

Scoring of the frequency: 1: Seldom / 2: Recurrently / 3: Monthly / 4: Weekly / 5: Daily / 0: Unclear

Assessment of subjective distress: Minor/Moderate/Severe (for explanation, please see Chapter 5)

Symptoms That (Possibly) Indicate a Division of the Personality, version 1.12

Does the patient report symptoms that indicate a division of the personality?

☐ Yes, the patient reports symptoms that indicate a division of the personality, namely:

Symptoms	Frequency
☐ Amnesia (items 16, 33, 54d, 68, 148, 149, 151, 152, 153)	_____
☐ Depersonalization (items 191, 192, 193)	_____
☐ Derealization (items 194, 195)	_____
☐ Changes in behavior/preferences/needs (items 196, 197, 198)	_____
☐ Loss of skills (item 199)	_____
☐ Presence of unfamiliar skills (item 200)	_____

☐ No, the patient does not report symptoms that indicate a division of the personality

Clinical impression

• Overall frequency of symptoms that indicate a division of the personality (Severity rating):

_____

• Assessment of subjective distress:

_____

Symptom Profile 15

Scoring of the frequency: 1: Seldom / 2: Recurrently / 3: Monthly / 4: Weekly / 5: Daily / 0: Unclear

Assessment of subjective distress: Minor/Moderate/Severe (for explanation, please see Chapter 5)

Dissociative Parts of the Personality, version 1.12

Does the patient experience the presence of dissociative parts?

☐ Yes, the patient experiences or acknowledges the presence of dissociative parts, namely:

Symptoms	Frequency
☐ Experiences parts (items 201–206)	_____
☐ Parts are experienced as ego dystonic (items 203, 206)	_____
☐ Parts influence behavior/actions (item 204)	_____
☐ Parts responsible for tasks in daily life (item 205)	_____
☐ Parts are experienced as ego syntonic (item 206)	_____

☐ No, the patient does not report symptoms that indicate the presence of dissociative parts, or the presence of dissociative parts is denied

Clinical impression

• The nature of the dissociative parts as described by the patient exhibits a structure which corresponds to:
  ☐ Primary structural dissociation of the personality
  ☐ Secondary structural dissociation of the personality
  ☐ Tertiary structural dissociation of the personality
  ☐ Imitated DID (items 207–214)

• Assessment of subjective distress:
  _____

Symptom Profile 16

Scoring of the frequency: 1: Seldom / 2: Recurrently / 3: Monthly / 4: Weekly / 5: Daily / 0: Unclear

Assessment of subjective distress: Minor/Moderate/Severe (for explanation, please see Chapter 5)

PTSD (DSM-5), version 1.12

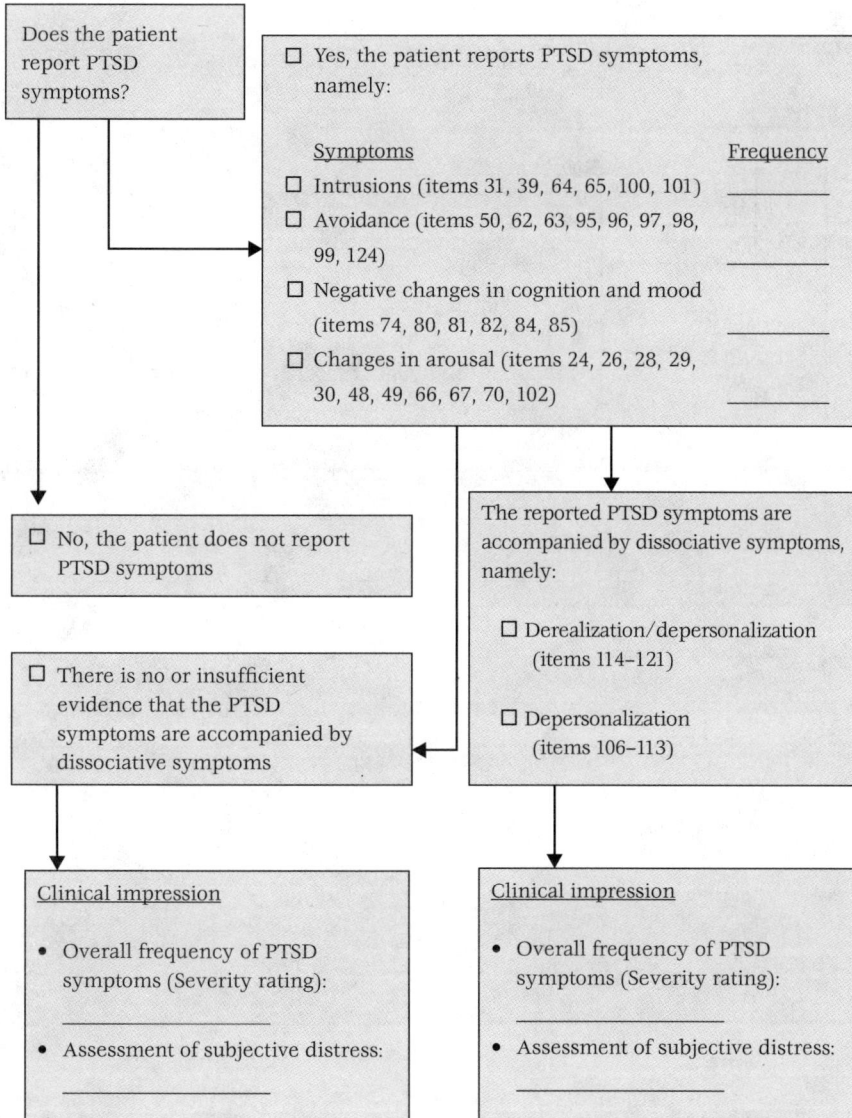

Does the patient report PTSD symptoms?

☐ Yes, the patient reports PTSD symptoms, namely:

Symptoms	Frequency
☐ Intrusions (items 31, 39, 64, 65, 100, 101)	_____
☐ Avoidance (items 50, 62, 63, 95, 96, 97, 98, 99, 124)	_____
☐ Negative changes in cognition and mood (items 74, 80, 81, 82, 84, 85)	_____
☐ Changes in arousal (items 24, 26, 28, 29, 30, 48, 49, 66, 67, 70, 102)	_____

☐ No, the patient does not report PTSD symptoms

The reported PTSD symptoms are accompanied by dissociative symptoms, namely:

☐ Derealization/depersonalization (items 114–121)

☐ Depersonalization (items 106–113)

☐ There is no or insufficient evidence that the PTSD symptoms are accompanied by dissociative symptoms

Clinical impression

• Overall frequency of PTSD symptoms (Severity rating):

_____

• Assessment of subjective distress:

_____

Clinical impression

• Overall frequency of PTSD symptoms (Severity rating):

_____

• Assessment of subjective distress:

_____

Symptom Profile 17

Scoring of the frequency: 1: Seldom / 2: Recurrently / 3: Monthly / 4: Weekly / 5: Daily / 0: Unclear

Assessment of subjective distress: Minor/Moderate/Severe (for explanation, please see Chapter 5)

Complex PTSD (ICD-11), version 1.12

Does the patient report Complex PTSD symptoms?

☐ Yes, the patient reports Complex PTSD symptoms, namely:

Symptoms	Frequency
☐ PTSD symptoms (see: PTSD symptom profile)	_____
+	
☐ Emotion regulation problems (items 46, 47, 48, 49, 53, 54, 67, 70)	_____
☐ Negative self-image (items 74–81, 82, 84, 85)	_____
☐ Problems in relationships with others (items 86–94)	_____

☐ No, the patient does not report Complex PTSD symptoms

Clinical impression

• Overall frequency of Complex PTSD symptoms (Severity rating):

_____

• Assessment of subjective distress:

_____

Introduction

The dissociative identity disorder (DID) is a polysymptomatic condition. Research into the clinical phenomenology has demonstrated that patients with DID show a coherent cluster of serious dissociative symptoms as well as many trauma-related symptoms. DSM-5 does not mention all of these symptoms as criteria. It is desirable to have an overview of a larger number of symptoms than those mentioned in DSM-5 (see Appendix 1 for an overview of Symptom Profiles for trauma-related symptoms). Moreover, the section with questions about trauma-related symptoms may already provide an understanding of whether these symptoms are associated with indications for a division of the personality.

Dissociative Identity Disorder

A. **Disruption of the Identity:** there should be clear indications of a division of the personality.

In order to assess this, please use Symptom Profiles 14 (Symptoms that [Possibly] Indicate a Division of the Personality) and 15 (Dissociative Parts of the Personality).

B. **Amnesia:** recurrent gaps in the recall for everyday events, important personal information, and/or traumatic events

For the assessment of amnesia, please use Symptom Profile 12 (Psychoform Dissociative Symptoms). It is possible that amnesia is already reported under trauma-related symptoms.

C. **Significant distress** or impairment in social or occupational functioning

For the assessment of Criterion C, use the questions on distress in Symptom Profiles 12 and 14, and possibly 1–10.

D. **Rule out the possibility that the disorder is a normal part of a broadly accepted cultural or religious practice**

This mainly concerns the possession form of DID.

E. **Rule out any physiological effects of a substance**
For the assessment of Criterion E please use Symptom Profile 1 (Substance Abuse).

Dissociative Amnesia

A. **Inability to recall important autobiographical information**
For the assessment of Criterion A, please use Symptom Profile 12 (Psychoform Dissociative Symptoms; Amnesia).
B. **Significant distress** or impairment in social, occupational, or other important areas of functioning
For the assessment of Criterion B, please use the questions on distress in Symptom Profile 12.
C. **Rule out any physiological effects of a substance**
For the assessment of Criterion E, please use Symptom Profile 1 (Substance Abuse).
D. **Rule out: DID, Acute Stress Disorder, Somatic Symptom Disorder, and Neurocognitive Disorder**

Coding note: The DSM-5 code for dissociative amnesia without dissociative fugue is **300.12**. The DSM-5 code for dissociative amnesia with dissociative fugue is 300.13.

Depersonalization/Derealization Disorder

A. **Persistent or recurrent depersonalization, derealization, or both**
For the assessment of Criterion A, please use Symptom Profile 10 (Alterations in Consciousness).
B. **Intact reality testing**
C. **Clinically significant distress or impairment in social, occupational, or other important areas of functioning**
For the assessment of Criterion C, please use the questions on distress in Symptom Profile 10.
D. **Rule out any physiological effects of a substance (e.g., a drug of abuse, medication) or another medical condition (e.g., seizures)**
For assessing Criterion D, please use Symptom Profile 1 (Substance Abuse).
E. **Rule out** that depersonalization and derealization symptoms can be explained by **another mental disorder**, such as schizophrenia, panic disorder, major depressive disorder, acute stress disorder, posttraumatic stress disorder, or another dissociative disorder
For the assessment of Criterion E, please use Symptom Profile 10.

The DSM-5 code for depersonalization/derealization disorder is **300.6**.

Other Specified Dissociative Disorder

Examples of this diagnosis, particularly OSDD-1, may also include many trauma-related symptoms in addition to the dissociative symptoms (see Part 2 of the TADS-I). The first example (OSDD-1, formerly DDNOS) appears most frequently in research studies.

OSDD-1 Chronic and Recurrent Syndromes of Mixed Dissociative Symptoms

Example 1 is a dissociative identity disturbance associated with less-than-marked discontinuities in sense of self and agency, or alterations of identity, or episodes of possession. There are no reports of dissociative amnesia.

> *For the assessment of OSDD-1, please use Symptom Profiles 10 (Alterations in Consciousness), 12 (Psychoform Dissociative Symptoms, without the amnesia items), 14 (Symptoms That [Possibly] Indicate a Division of the Personality), and sometimes 15 (Dissociative Parts of the Personality). Make sure to rule out DID.*

OSDD-2 Identity Disturbance Due to Prolonged and Intense Coercive Persuasion

This is the only dissociative disorder classification requiring a clear history of related or preceding trauma. This trauma history should be identified in a separate interview (see Chapter 11).

> *For the cluster of dissociative symptoms, please use Symptom Profiles 10 (Alterations in Consciousness), 12 (Psychoform Dissociative Symptoms), and 14 (Symptoms That [Possibly] Indicate a Division of the Personality).*

OSDD-3 Acute Dissociative Reactions to Stressful Events

This category refers to acute, transient conditions that typically last less than 1 month, and sometimes only a few hours or days. The DSM-5 describes several symptoms that may occur in these acute situations, such as somatoform dissociative symptoms, constriction of consciousness, depersonalization, derealization, perceptual disturbances (e.g., time slowing, macropsia), micro-amnesias, transient stupor, and/or alterations in sensorimotor functioning (e.g., analgesia, paralysis).

> *For the assessment of OSDD-3, please use Symptom Profiles 10 (Alterations in Consciousness), 11 (Somatoform Dissociative Symptoms), and 12 (Psychoform Dissociative Symptoms).*

OSDD-4 Dissociative Trance

For the assessment of this example, please use Symptom Profile 10 (Alterations in Consciousness; Trance). Additionally, if applicable, you may use information from the DSM-5 Cultural Formulation Interview.

Rule out the possibility that the trance experiences are part of DID or OSDD-1.

The code for DSM-5 other specified dissociative disorder is **300.15**.

Unspecified Dissociative Disorder

According to the DSM-5, this category applies to presentations in which symptoms characteristic of a dissociative disorder that cause clinically significant distress or impairment in social, occupational, or other important areas of functioning predominate but do not meet the full criteria for any of the disorders in the dissociative disorders diagnostic class.

For the assessment of unspecified dissociative disorder, please use Symptom Profile 10 (Alterations in Consciousness), and Symptom Profile 12 (Psychoform Dissociative Symptoms).

The code DSM-5 for unspecified dissociative disorder is **300.15**.

Dissociative Disorders

6B60 Dissociative Neurological Symptom Disorder

(See TADS-I Symptom Profile 11 for all the following subcategories)

It is very important to make sure that the dissociative neurological symptom is the only symptom and not part of a cluster of somatoform and psychoform symptoms.

Dissociative neurological symptom disorder is characterized by the presentation of motor, sensory, or cognitive symptoms that imply an involuntary discontinuity in the normal integration of motor, sensory, or cognitive functions and are not consistent with a recognized disease of the nervous system, other mental or behavioral disorder, or other health condition. The symptoms do not occur exclusively during another dissociative disorder and are not due to the effects of a substance or medication on the central nervous system, including withdrawal effects, or a sleep–wake disorder.

6B60.0 Dissociative Neurological Symptom Disorder, With Visual Disturbance

Dissociative neurological symptom disorder, with visual disturbance is characterized by visual symptoms such as blindness, tunnel vision, diplopia, visual distortions or hallucinations that are not consistent with a recognized disease of the nervous system, other mental or behavioral disorder, or other health condition and do not occur exclusively during another dissociative disorder.

6B60.1 Dissociative Neurological Symptom Disorder, With Auditory Disturbance

Dissociative neurological symptom disorder, with auditory disturbance is characterized by auditory symptoms such as loss of hearing or auditory hallucinations that are not consistent with a recognized disease of the nervous system, other mental or behavioral disorder, or other health condition and do not occur exclusively during another dissociative disorder.

6B60.2 Dissociative Neurological Symptom Disorder, With Vertigo or Dizziness

Dissociative neurological symptom disorder, with vertigo or dizziness is characterized by a sensation of spinning while stationary (vertigo) or dizziness that is not consistent with a recognized disease of the nervous system, mental or behavioral disorder, or other health condition and does not occur exclusively during another dissociative disorder.

6B60.3 Dissociative Neurological Symptom Disorder, With Other Sensory Disturbance

Dissociative neurological symptom disorder, with other sensory disturbance is characterized by sensory symptoms not identified in other specific categories in this grouping such as numbness, tightness, tingling, burning, pain, or other symptoms related to touch, smell, taste, balance, proprioception, kinesthesia, or thermoception. The symptoms are not consistent with a recognized disease of the nervous system, other mental or behavioral disorder, or other health condition and do not occur exclusively during another dissociative disorder.

6B60.4 Dissociative Neurological Symptom Disorder, With Non-Epileptic Seizures

Dissociative neurological symptom disorder, with non-epileptic seizures is characterized by a symptomatic presentation of seizures or convulsions that are not consistent with a recognized disease of the nervous system, other mental or behavioral disorder, or other health condition and do not occur exclusively during another dissociative disorder.

6B60.5 Dissociative Neurological Symptom Disorder, With Speech Disturbance

Dissociative neurological symptom disorder, with speech disturbance is characterized by symptoms such as difficulty with speaking (dysphonia), loss of the ability to speak (aphonia) or difficult or unclear articulation of speech (dysarthria) that are not consistent with a recognized disease of the nervous system, a neurodevelopmental or neurocognitive disorder, other mental or behavioral disorder, or other health condition and do not occur exclusively during another dissociative disorder.

6B60.6 Dissociative Neurological Symptom Disorder, With Paresis or Weakness

Dissociative neurological symptom disorder, with paresis or weakness is characterized by a difficulty or inability to intentionally move parts of the body or to coordinate movements that is not consistent with a recognized disease of the nervous system, other mental and behavioral disorder, or other health condition and does not occur exclusively during another dissociative disorder.

6B60.7 Dissociative Neurological Symptom Disorder, With Gait Disturbance

Dissociative neurological symptom disorder, with gait disturbance is characterized by symptoms involving the individual's ability or manner of walking, including ataxia and the inability to stand unaided, that are not consistent with a recognized disease of the nervous system, other mental and behavioral disorder, or other health condition and do not occur exclusively during another dissociative disorder.

6B60.8 Dissociative Neurological Symptom Disorder, With Movement Disturbance

Dissociative neurological symptom disorder, with movement disturbance is characterized by symptoms such as chorea, myoclonus, tremor, dystonia, facial spasm, parkinsonism, or dyskinesia that are not consistent with a recognized disease of the nervous system, other mental and behavioral disorder, or other health condition and do not occur exclusively during another dissociative disorder.

6B60.9 Dissociative Neurological Symptom Disorder, With Cognitive Symptoms

Dissociative neurological symptom disorder, with cognitive symptoms is characterized by impaired cognitive performance in memory, language, or other cognitive domains that is internally inconsistent and not consistent with a recognized disease of the nervous system, a neurodevelopmental or neurocognitive disorder, other mental and behavioral disorder, or another health condition and does not occur exclusively during another dissociative disorder.

6B60.Y Dissociative Neurological Symptom Disorder, With Other Specified Symptoms

This category is an "other specified" residual category.

6B60.Z Dissociative Neurological Symptom Disorder, With Unspecified Symptoms

This category is an "unspecified" residual category.

6B61 Dissociative amnesia

Essential Features

- Inability to recall important autobiographical memories, typically of recent traumatic or stressful events, that is inconsistent with ordinary forgetting.

    For the assessment of this criterion, please use Symptom Profile 12 (Psychoform Dissociative Symptoms).

- The memory loss does not occur exclusively during episodes of trance disorder, possession trance disorder, dissociative identity disorder, or partial dissociative identity disorder and is not better accounted for by another mental disorder (e.g., posttraumatic stress disorder, complex posttraumatic stress disorder, a neurocognitive disorder such as dementia).

- The symptoms are not due to the effects of a substance or medication on the central nervous system (e.g., alcohol), including withdrawal effects, and are not due to a disease of the nervous system (e.g., temporal lobe epilepsy), another medical condition (e.g., a brain tumor), or to head trauma.

    For the assessment of this criterion, please use Symptom Profile 1 (Substance Abuse).

- The memory loss results in significant impairment in personal, family, social, educational, occupational, or other important areas of functioning.

    For the assessment of this criterion, please use the questions on distress in Symptom Profile 12.

Presence or Absence of Dissociative Fugue

6B61.0 Dissociative Amnesia with Dissociative Fugue

- Dissociative amnesia with dissociative fugue is characterized by all of the features of dissociative amnesia, accompanied by dissociative fugue, i.e., a loss of a sense of personal identity and sudden travel away from home, work, or significant others for an extended period of time (days or weeks).

    For the assessment of this criterion, please use Symptom Profile 12 (Psychoform Dissociative Symptoms). Rule out that fugue states are part of DID or partial DID.

6B62 Trance Disorder

(See Part 3, Alterations in Consciousness, in particular Items 124 and 125 in TADS-I Symptom Profile 10)

*Rule out that trancelike states are a symptom of DID or partial DID, mean-
ing that the patient should not answer in the affirmative on Symptom Profiles
12, 14, and 15.*

*If a trance disorder is suspected, some additional questions should be asked
that are not included in TADS-I (e.g., restriction of movements, speech repetition).*

Essential Features
- Occurrence of a trance state in which there is a marked alteration in
  the individual's state of consciousness or a loss of the individual's nor-
  mal sense of personal identity, characterized by both of the following:
  ○ Narrowing of awareness of immediate surroundings
    or unusually narrow and selective focusing on specific
    environmental stimuli; and
  ○ Restriction of movements, postures, and speech to repetition
    of a small repertoire that is experienced as being outside of
    one's control.
- The trance state is not characterized by the experience of being
  replaced by an alternate identity.
- Trance episodes are recurrent or, if the diagnosis is based on a single
  episode, the episode has lasted for at least several days.
- The trance state is involuntary and unwanted and is not accepted as a
  part of a collective cultural or religious practice.
- The symptoms are not due to the effects of a substance or medication
  on the central nervous system (including withdrawal effects), exhaustion, or to hypnagogic or hypnopompic states, and are not due to a
  disease of the nervous system (e.g., complex partial seizures), head
  trauma, or a sleep–wake disorder.
  *For the assessment of this criterion, please use Symptom Profile 1
  (Substance Abuse).*
- The symptoms result in significant distress or significant impairment in personal, family, social, educational, occupational, or other
  important areas of functioning. If functioning is maintained, it is only
  through significant additional effort.
  *For the assessment of this criterion, please use the questions on distress
  in Symptom Profile 10 and keep in mind the influence of possible
  cultural factors.*

6B63 Possession Trance Disorder
Rule out that Possession Trance is a symptom of DID or partial DID.

*In DID and partial DID, patients usually experience the influence of internal
identities. Some patients may also experience the influence of external possess-*

ing identities (in addition to internal identities), especially when they grew up in religious communities or when there is a culture-specific explanation (e.g., devil or angels, ghosts).

Essential Features

- Occurrence of a trance state in which there is a marked alteration in the individual's state of consciousness and the individual's normal sense of personal identity is replaced by an external "possessing" identity. The trance state is characterized by behaviors or movements that are experienced as being controlled by the possessing agent.

  For the assessment of this criterion, please use Items 179 and 180 in TADS-I Symptom Profile 13.

- Trance episodes are attributed to the influence of an external "possessing" spirit, power, deity, or other spiritual entity.

- Trance episodes are recurrent or, if the diagnosis is based on a single episode, the episode has lasted for at least several days.

- The possession trance state is involuntary and unwanted and is not accepted as a part of a collective cultural or religious practice.

- The symptoms are not due to the effects of a substance or medication on the central nervous system (including withdrawal effects), exhaustion, or to hypnagogic or hypnopompic states, and are not due to a disease of the nervous system (e.g., complex partial seizures) or a sleep–wake disorder.

  For the assessment of this criterion, please use Symptom Profile 1 (Substance Abuse).

- The symptoms result in significant distress or impairment in personal, family, social, educational, occupational, or other important areas of functioning. If functioning is maintained, it is only through significant additional effort.

  For the assessment of this criterion, please use the questions on distress in Symptom Profiles 12 and 13 and keep in mind the influence of possible cultural factors.

6B64 Dissociative Identity Disorder

Essential Features

- Disruption of identity characterized by the presence of two or more distinct personality states (dissociative identities), involving marked discontinuities in the sense of self and agency. Each personality state includes its own pattern of experiencing, perceiving, conceiving, and relating to self, the body, and the environment.

  For the assessment this criterion, please use Symptom Profiles 14 and 15.

- At least two distinct personality states recurrently take executive control of the individual's consciousness and functioning in interacting with others or with the environment, such as in the performance of specific aspects of daily life (e.g., parenting, work), or in response to specific situations (e.g., those that are perceived as threatening).

   For the assessment of this criterion, please use Symptom Profiles 14 and 15.
- Changes in personality state are accompanied by related alterations in sensation, perception, affect, cognition, memory, motor control, and behavior. There are typically episodes of amnesia inconsistent with ordinary forgetting, which may be severe.

   For the assessment of this criterion, please use Symptom Profile 12.
- The symptoms are not better accounted for by another mental disorder (e.g., schizophrenia or other primary psychotic disorder).
- The symptoms are not due to the effects of a substance or medication on the central nervous system, including withdrawal effects (e.g., blackouts or chaotic behavior during substance intoxication), and are not due to a disease of the nervous system (e.g., complex partial seizures) or to a sleep–wake disorder (e.g., symptoms occur during hypnagogic or hypnopompic states).

   For the assessment of this criterion, please use Symptom Profile 1 (Substance Abuse).
- The symptoms result in significant impairment in personal, family, social, educational, occupational, or other important areas of functioning. If functioning is maintained, it is only through significant additional effort.

   For the assessment of this criterion, please use the questions on distress in Symptom Profiles 12, 13, 14, and possibly 1–10.

6B65 Partial Dissociative Identity Disorder

Essential Features
- Disruption of identity characterized by the experience of two or more distinct personality states (dissociative identities), involving discontinuities in the sense of self and agency. Each personality state includes its own pattern of experiencing, perceiving, conceiving, and relating to self, the body, and the environment.

   For the assessment of this criterion, please use Symptom Profiles 13, 14, and 15.
- One personality state is dominant and functions in daily life (e.g., parenting, work), but is intruded upon by one or more nondominant personality states (dissociative intrusions). These intrusions may be cognitive (intruding thoughts), affective (intruding affects such

as fear, anger, or shame), perceptual (e.g., intruding voices, fleeting visual perceptions, sensations such as being touched), motor (e.g., involuntary movements of an arm), or behavioral (e.g., an action that lacks a sense of agency or ownership). These experiences are experienced as interfering with the functioning of the dominant personality state and are typically aversive.

> *For the assessment of this criterion, please use Symptom Profiles 12, 13, 14, and 15.*

- The non-dominant personality states do not recurrently take executive control of the individual's consciousness and functioning to the extent that they perform in specific aspects of daily life (e.g., parenting, work). However, there may be occasional, limited, and transient episodes in which a distinct personality state assumes executive control to engage in circumscribed behaviors (e.g., in response to extreme emotional states or during episodes of self-harm or the reenactment of traumatic memories).

> *For the assessment of this criterion, please use Symptom Profiles 13, 14, and 15.*

- The symptoms are not better accounted for by another mental disorder (e.g., schizophrenia or other primary psychotic disorder).
- The symptoms are not due to the effects of a substance or medication on the central nervous system, including withdrawal effects (e.g., blackouts or chaotic behavior during substance intoxication), and are not due to a disease of the nervous system (e.g., complex partial seizures) or to a sleep–wake disorder (e.g., symptoms occur during hypnagogic or hypnopompic states).

> *For the assessment of this criterion, please use Symptom Profile 1 (Substance Abuse).*

- The symptoms result in significant impairment in personal, family, social, educational, occupational, or other important areas of functioning. If functioning is maintained, it is only through significant additional effort.

> *For the assessment of this criterion, please use the questions on distress in Symptom Profiles 12, 13, 14, and possibly 1–10.*

6B66 Depersonalization/Derealization Disorder

Essential Features

- Persistent or recurrent experiences of either or both depersonalization or derealization:
  - Depersonalization is characterized by experiencing the self as strange or unreal, or feeling detached from, or as though one were

an outside observer of, one's thoughts, feelings, sensations, body, or actions. Depersonalization may take the form of emotional and/or physical numbing, a sense of watching oneself from a distance or "being in a play," or perceptual alterations (e.g., a distorted sense of time).

○ Derealization is characterized by experiencing other persons, objects, or the world as strange or unreal (e.g., dreamlike, distant, foggy, lifeless, colorless, or visually distorted) or feeling detached from one's surroundings.

For the assessment of this criterion, please use Symptom Profile 10 (Alterations in Consciousness).

- During experiences of depersonalization or derealization, reality testing remains intact. The experiences are not associated with delusions or beliefs that the individual is being controlled by external persons or forces.

- The symptoms are not better accounted for by another mental disorder (e.g., posttraumatic stress disorder, an anxiety or fear-related disorder, another dissociative disorder, personality disorder).

For the assessment of this criterion, please use Symptom Profile 10.

- The symptoms are not due to the effects of a substance or medication on the central nervous system, including withdrawal effects, and are not due to a disease of the nervous system (e.g., temporal lobe epilepsy), head trauma, or another medical condition.

For the assessment of this criterion, please use Symptom Profile 1 (Substance Abuse).

- The symptoms result in significant distress or significant impairment in personal, family, social, educational, occupational, or other important areas of functioning. If functioning is maintained, it is only through significant additional effort.

For the assessment of this criterion, please use the questions on distress in Symptom Profile 10.

6B6Y Other Specified Dissociative Disorders

This category is an "other specified" residual category.

6B6Z Dissociative Disorders, Unspecified

This category is an "unspecified" residual category.

6B41 Complex Posttraumatic Stress Disorder

(See TADS-I Symptom Profile 17. Note: Trauma History must be assessed separately.)

Essential (Required) Features

- Exposure to an event or series of events of an extremely threatening or horrific nature, most commonly prolonged or repetitive events from which escape is difficult or impossible. Such events include, but are not limited to, torture, concentration camps, slavery, genocide campaigns and other forms of organized violence, prolonged domestic violence, and repeated childhood sexual or physical abuse.
- Following the traumatic event, the development of all three core elements of posttraumatic stress disorder, lasting for at least several weeks:
  - Re-experiencing the traumatic event after the traumatic event has occurred, in which the event(s) is not just remembered but is experienced as occurring again in the here and now. This typically occurs in the form of vivid intrusive memories or images; flashbacks, which can vary from mild (there is a transient sense of the event occurring again in the present) to severe (there is a complete loss of awareness of present surroundings), or repetitive dreams or nightmares that are thematically related to the traumatic event(s). Re-experiencing is typically accompanied by strong or overwhelming emotions, such as fear or horror, and strong physical sensations. Re-experiencing in the present can also involve feelings of being overwhelmed or immersed in the same intense emotions that were experienced during the traumatic event, without a prominent cognitive aspect, and may occur in response to reminders of the event. Reflecting on or ruminating about the event(s) and remembering the feelings that one experienced at that time are not sufficient to meet the re-experiencing requirement.
  - Deliberate avoidance of reminders likely to produce re-experiencing of the traumatic event(s). This may take the form either of active internal avoidance of thoughts and memories related to the event(s), or external avoidance of people, conversations, activities, or situations reminiscent of the event(s). In extreme cases the person may change their environment (e.g., move house or change jobs) to avoid reminders.
  - Persistent perceptions of heightened current threat, for example as indicated by hypervigilance or an enhanced startle reaction to stimuli such as unexpected noises. Hypervigilant persons constantly guard themselves against danger and feel themselves or others close to them to be under immediate threat either in specific situations or more generally. They may adopt new behaviors designed to ensure safety (not sitting with one's back to the door,

repeated checking in vehicle's rear-view mirror). In complex post-traumatic stress disorder, unlike in posttraumatic stress disorder, the startle reaction may in some cases be diminished rather than enhanced.

- Severe and pervasive problems in affect regulation. Examples include heightened emotional reactivity to minor stressors, violent outbursts, reckless or self-destructive behavior, dissociative symptoms when under stress, and emotional numbing, particularly the inability to experience pleasure or positive emotions.
- Persistent beliefs about oneself as diminished, defeated or worthless, accompanied by deep and pervasive feelings of shame, guilt, or failure related to the stressor. For example, the individual may feel guilty about not having escaped from or succumbing to the adverse circumstance, or not having been able to prevent the suffering of others.
- Persistent difficulties in sustaining relationships and in feeling close to others. The person may consistently avoid, deride, or have little interest in relationships and social engagement more generally. Alternatively, there may be occasional intense relationships, but the person has difficulty sustaining them.
- The disturbance results in significant impairment in personal, family, social, educational, occupational, or other important areas of functioning. If functioning is maintained, it is only through significant additional effort.

(Eli Somer, Jayne Bigelsen, Jonathan Lehrfeld, & Daniela Jopp, 2014)

In answering the following questions, please refer to your daydreaming activities in the last month, if not otherwise specified. Choose the option that best fits your experience. For example: Some people get so caught up in their daydreaming that they forget where they are. How often do you forget where you are when you daydream? In this example, 20% is chosen.

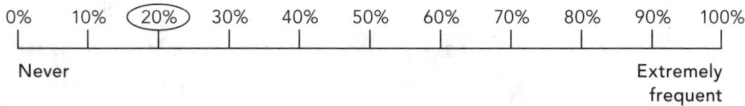

```
0%    10%   (20%)  30%   40%   50%   60%   70%   80%   90%   100%
|_____|_____|_____|_____|_____|_____|_____|_____|_____|_____|
Never                                            Extremely
                                                 frequent
```

1. Some people notice that certain music can trigger their daydreaming. To what extent does music activate your daydreaming?

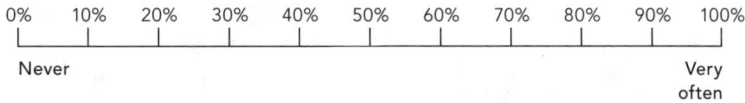

```
0%    10%   20%   30%   40%   50%   60%   70%   80%   90%   100%
|_____|_____|_____|_____|_____|_____|_____|_____|_____|_____|
Never                                                 Very
                                                      often
```

2. Some people feel a need to continue a daydream that was interrupted by a real world event at a later point. When a real world event has interrupted one of your daydreams, how strong was your need or urge to return to that daydream as soon as possible?

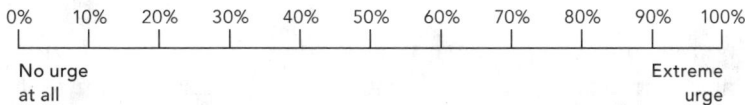

```
0%    10%   20%   30%   40%   50%   60%   70%   80%   90%   100%
|_____|_____|_____|_____|_____|_____|_____|_____|_____|_____|
No urge                                           Extreme
at all                                            urge
```

3. How often are your current daydreams accompanied by vocal noises or facial expressions (e.g., laughing, talking, or mouthing the words)?

```
0%    10%   20%   30%   40%   50%   60%   70%   80%   90%   100%
L_____|_____|_____|_____|_____|_____|_____|_____|_____|_____|
Never                                               Extremely
                                                    frequent
```

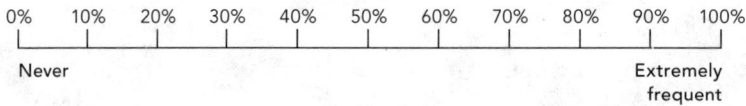

4. If you go through a period of time when you are not able to daydream as much as usual due to real world obligations, how distressed are you by your inability to find time to daydream?

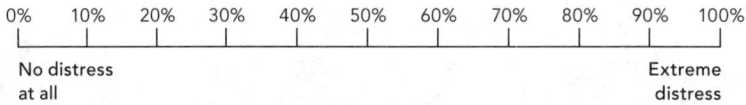

```
0%    10%   20%   30%   40%   50%   60%   70%   80%   90%   100%
L_____|_____|_____|_____|_____|_____|_____|_____|_____|_____|
No distress                                         Extreme
at all                                              distress
```

5. Some people have the experience of their daydreaming interfering with their daily chores or tasks. How much does your daydreaming interfere with your ability to get basic chores accomplished?

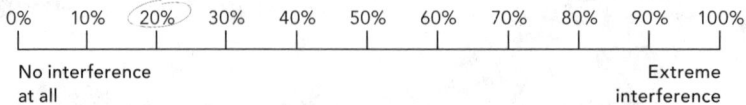

```
0%    10%  (20%)  30%   40%   50%   60%   70%   80%   90%   100%
L_____|_____|_____|_____|_____|_____|_____|_____|_____|_____|
No interference                                     Extreme
at all                                              interference
```

6. Some people feel distressed or concerned about the amount of time they spend daydreaming. How distressed do you currently feel about the amount of time you spend daydreaming?

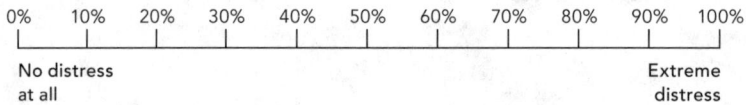

```
0%    10%   20%   30%   40%   50%   60%   70%   80%   90%   100%
L_____|_____|_____|_____|_____|_____|_____|_____|_____|_____|
No distress                                         Extreme
at all                                              distress
```

7. When you know you have had something important or challenging to pay attention to or finish, how difficult was it for you to stay on task and complete the goal without daydreaming?

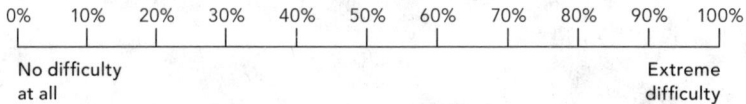

```
0%    10%   20%   30%   40%   50%   60%   70%   80%   90%   100%
L_____|_____|_____|_____|_____|_____|_____|_____|_____|_____|
No difficulty                                       Extreme
at all                                              difficulty
```

8. Some people have the experience of their daydreaming hindering the things that are most important to them. How much do you feel that your daydreaming activities interfere with achieving your overall life goals?

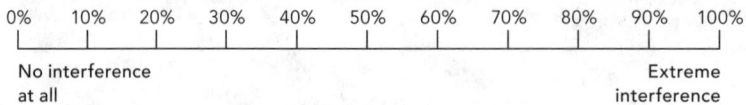

```
0%    10%   20%   30%   40%   50%   60%   70%   80%   90%   100%
L_____|_____|_____|_____|_____|_____|_____|_____|_____|_____|
No interference                                     Extreme
at all                                              interference
```

9. Some people experience difficulties in controlling or limiting their daydreaming. How difficult has it been for you to keep your daydreaming under control?

```
0%    10%   20%   30%   40%   50%   60%   70%   80%   90%   100%
|_____|_____|_____|_____|_____|_____|_____|_____|_____|_____|
No difficulty                                      Extreme
at all                                             difficulty
```

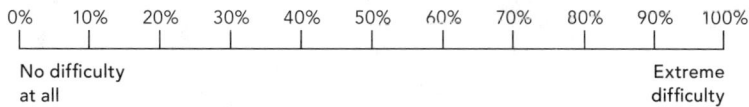

10. Some people feel annoyed when a real world event interrupts one of their daydreams. When the real world interrupts one of your daydreams, on average how annoyed do you feel?

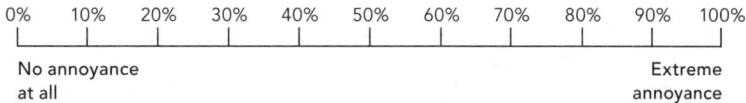

```
0%    10%   20%   30%   40%   50%   60%   70%   80%   90%   100%
|_____|_____|_____|_____|_____|_____|_____|_____|_____|_____|
No annoyance                                       Extreme
at all                                             annoyance
```

11. Some people have the experience of their daydreaming interfering with their academic/occupational success or personal achievements. How much does your daydreaming interfere with your academic/occupational success?

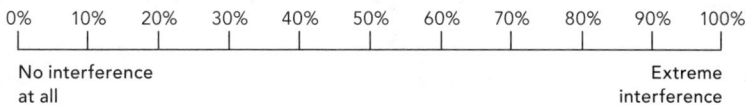

```
0%    10%   20%   30%   40%   50%   60%   70%   80%   90%   100%
|_____|_____|_____|_____|_____|_____|_____|_____|_____|_____|
No interference                                    Extreme
at all                                             interference
```

12. Some people would rather daydream than do most other things. To what extent would you rather daydream than engage with other people or participate in social activities or hobbies?

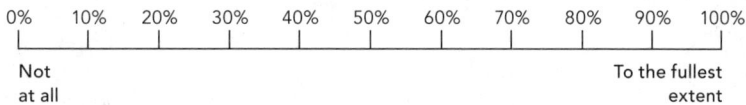

```
0%    10%   20%   30%   40%   50%   60%   70%   80%   90%   100%
|_____|_____|_____|_____|_____|_____|_____|_____|_____|_____|
Not                                                To the fullest
at all                                             extent
```

13. When you first wake up in the morning, how strong has your urge been to immediately start daydreaming?

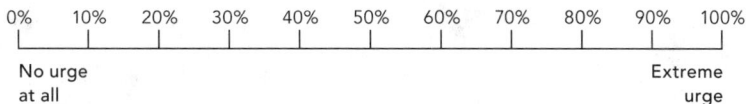

```
0%    10%   20%   30%   40%   50%   60%   70%   80%   90%   100%
|_____|_____|_____|_____|_____|_____|_____|_____|_____|_____|
No urge                                            Extreme
at all                                             urge
```

14. How often are your current daydreams accompanied by physical activity such as pacing, swinging, or shaking your hands?

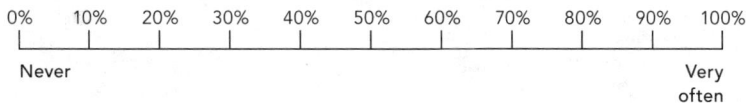

```
0%    10%   20%   30%   40%   50%   60%   70%   80%   90%   100%
|_____|_____|_____|_____|_____|_____|_____|_____|_____|_____|
Never                                              Very
                                                   often
```

15. Some people love to daydream. While you are daydreaming, to what extent do you find it comforting and/or enjoyable?

```
0%   10%  20%  30%  40%  50%  60%  70%  80%  90%  100%
└──┴───┴───┴───┴───┴───┴───┴───┴───┴───┴──┘
Not comfortable/                                    Very
enjoyable at all                             comfortable/
                                                enjoyable
```

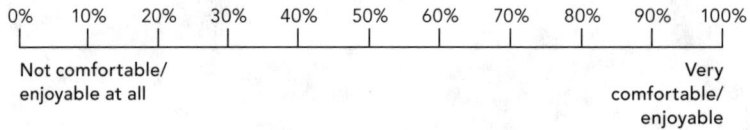

16. Some people find it hard to maintain their daydreaming when they are not listening to music. To what extent is your daydreaming dependent on continued listening to music?

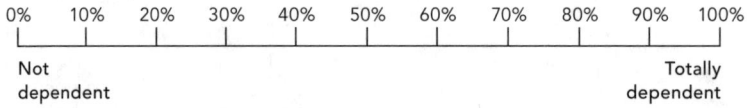

```
0%   10%  20%  30%  40%  50%  60%  70%  80%  90%  100%
└──┴───┴───┴───┴───┴───┴───┴───┴───┴───┴──┘
Not                                              Totally
dependent                                      dependent
```

17. Research with the questionnaire has shown that a cut-off score of 40 (or higher) is reason to use the Structured Clinical Diagnostic Interview for Maladaptive Daydreaming (SCIMD: Somer et al., 2017). Both instruments can be downloaded via daydreamresearch.wixsite.com/md-research.

TRAUMA AND DISSOCIATION SYMPTOMS INTERVIEW (TADS-I)

Version 1.12

Suzette Boon, PhD

Helga Matthess, MD

The most recent version of the TADS-I is available as a free download via tads-i.com/download.

CONTENTS TADS-I

Instruction for the Interviewer

This is the revised 2022 version of the semi-structured interview Trauma and Dissociation Symptoms Interview (TADS-I). The interview consists of five parts. Administering the complete interview offers you a reliable method of establishing whether your patient has a dissociative disorder. In addition, it provides information on the presence of symptoms associated with a posttraumatic stress disorder (PTSD) and with a complex posttraumatic stress disorder (CPTSD), as well as a broad range of other trauma-related complaints.

To properly administer and score the interview, it is important that you follow the instructions in Chapter 5 of *Assessing Trauma-Related Dissociation: With the Trauma and Dissociation Symptoms Interview (TADS-I)*, (Boon, 2023).

You may decide not to further explore certain parts about trauma-related complaints (sections from Part 2 of the interview), depending on the subjects on which you are focusing or the time available to you for establishing a diagnosis. Chapter 5 lists the parts that must *at least* be administered in order to reliably establish or exclude a dissociative disorder.

Each section includes a number of questions with numbers presented inside a shaded field. These are the compulsory questions within that part. Questions without a shaded field are follow-up questions for cases in which a previous question has been answered in the affirmative.

Each question is used to assess whether a certain symptom is present. This is a clinical assessment, as defined in Chapter 5 of *Assessing Trauma-Related Dissociation: With the Trauma and Dissociation Symptoms Interview (TADS-I)*, (Boon, 2023).

The quality of a symptom is determined, among other things, by how frequently the symptom is present. To this end, we use the following guideline:

Seldom	Up to 3 times in the past year
Occasionally	Between 4 and 11 times in the past year
Monthly	At least once a month in the past year
Weekly	At least once a week in the past year
Daily	At least once a day in the past year
Unclear	

The results of a pilot study with version 1.9 of the TADS-I are being processed and hopefully will be published in 2023. Versions 1.10–1.12 contain only minor changes, partly based on this study.

PART 1: GENERAL

BIOGRAPHICAL INFORMATION

Name:
Sex:
Age:
Marital status:
- ☐ Single
- ☐ Married/living together
- ☐ Divorced
- ☐ Widow/widower

Children:
Current living situation:
- ☐ Alone
- ☐ With partner and/or children
- ☐ In an institution or assisted living facility

Education (highest level completed):
- ☐ Primary school
- ☐ Secondary school
- ☐ Undergraduate
- ☐ Postgraduate

Current work situation:
- ☐ Full-time
- ☐ Part-time
- ☐ Unemployed
- ☐ On a benefit
- ☐ Retired

PSYCHIATRIC TREATMENT OR PSYCHOTHERAPY / PAST HISTORY

A   Are you currently receiving mental health treatment
from a psychiatrist or psychologist?   YES / NO / UNCLEAR

     a   What kind of treatment are you receiving?
- ☐ Out-patient
- ☐ Day treatment
- ☐ In-patient
- ☐ Other: _____

     b   How frequent are your (individual) sessions?
     c   What complaints/problems are you being treated for?

B   Have you ever had treatment before?   YES / NO / UNCLEAR

     If yes:
     a   What kind of treatment was this and how long did it continue?
     b   What was/were the reason(s) for the termination of these courses of treatment?

C   Have you ever been admitted to a psychiatric hospital
or psychiatric ward?   YES / NO / UNCLEAR

If yes:
a   For what reason(s)?
b   How long were you hospitalized?
c   How many times have you been admitted?
d   How old were you when you were first admitted?
e   How old were you when you were last admitted?

D   Do you know what diagnose(s) you were given in the past?   YES / NO / UNCLEAR

If yes:
a   What diagnoses were they?

SUBSTANCE USE AND MEDICATION

1   Do you ever consume alcohol?   YES / NO / UNCLEAR

If yes:
a   What type of alcohol do you consume?
   ☐ Wine/beer
   ☐ Liquor
   ☐ All
b   How many units do you consume per occasion?
c   How often do you consume alcohol?
   ☐ Seldom
   ☐ Recurrently
   ☐ Monthly
   ☐ Weekly
   ☐ Daily
   ☐ ?

If no:
d   Have you ever consumed alcohol in the past?   YES / NO / UNCLEAR

Instruction for the interviewer: If the patient indicates never to have consumed alcohol, you may proceed to Question 4, "Do you ever use street drugs?"

If yes:
d-1   What type of alcohol did you consume?
   ☐ Wine/beer
   ☐ Liquor
   ☐ All
d-2   How many units did you consume on each occasion?
d-3   How often did you consume alcohol?
   ☐ Seldom
   ☐ Regularly
   ☐ Monthly
   ☐ Weekly
   ☐ Daily
   ☐ ?

2 Have you ever suffered a black-out or other memory problems
as a result of alcohol?   YES / NO / UNCLEAR

If yes:
a Can you describe what that was like?

3 Have you ever been treated for alcohol problems?   YES / NO / UNCLEAR

If yes:
a Where and when?

4 Do you ever use street drugs?   YES / NO / UNCLEAR

If yes:
a What street drugs do you use?
    ☐ Soft drugs
    ☐ Hard drugs
    ☐ Both
b How much do you use on each occasion?
c How often do you use street drugs?
    ☐ Seldom
    ☐ Regularly
    ☐ Monthly
    ☐ Weekly
    ☐ Daily
    ☐ ?

If no:
d Have you ever used street drugs in the past?   YES / NO / UNCLEAR

> **Instruction for the interviewer:** If the patient indicates that he or she has never used street drugs, you may proceed to Question 6, "Are you currently using prescribed or over-the-counter medication?"

d-1 What street drugs did you use?
    ☐ Soft drugs
    ☐ Hard drugs
    ☐ Both
d-2 How much did you use per occasion?
d-3 How often did you take street drugs?
    ☐ Seldom
    ☐ Regularly
    ☐ Monthly
    ☐ Weekly
    ☐ Daily
    ☐ ?

5 Have you ever been treated for drug problems?   YES / NO / UNCLEAR

6 Are you currently using prescribed or over-the-counter
medication?   YES / NO / UNCLEAR

If yes:
a What medication do you currently use, and why?

7 Are you currently addicted to certain medication,
or are you using certain medication excessively? YES / NO / UNCLEAR

If yes:
a What medication do you use excessively or addictively?
b How much do you use per occasion?
c How often do you use this medication?
☐ Seldom
☐ Regularly
☐ Monthly
☐ Weekly
☐ Daily
☐ ?

If no:
d Have you been addicted to certain medication in the past, or
have you used certain medication excessively? YES / NO / UNCLEAR

If yes:
d-1 What medication did you use excessively or addictively?
d-2 How much did you use per occasion?
d-3 How often did you use this medication?
☐ Seldom
☐ Regularly
☐ Monthly
☐ Weekly
☐ Daily
☐ ?

Instruction for the interviewer: If there are no indications of substance abuse, you may proceed to Part 2, "(Possibly) Trauma-Related Symptoms."

8 Have you any idea in what kind of situations you use alcohol,
drugs, or medication? YES / NO / UNCLEAR

If yes:
a Can you describe those situations and how you believe
substances help you cope in those situations?

9 At what age did the problems with alcohol, drugs, or medication begin? (Different drugs
may be taken at different ages.)

If these problems have only existed in the past:
a At what age did the problems with alcohol, drugs, or medication stop?

Overall severity score SUBSTANCE/MEDICATION ABUSE

0 = Absent

1 = Minor

2 = Moderate

3 = Severe

88 = Unclear

Subjective distress score SUBSTANCE/MEDICATION ABUSE

0 = Absent

1 = Minor

2 = Moderate

3 = Severe

88 = Unclear

Is the SUBSTANCE/MEDICATION ABUSE accompanied by alterations in consciousness?

0 = No

1 = Yes

88 = Unclear

Is the SUBSTANCE/MEDICATION ABUSE accompanied by dissociative symptoms indicating a division of the personality?

0 = No

1 = Yes

88 = Unclear

PART 2: (POSSIBLY) TRAUMA-RELATED SYMPTOMS

EATING PROBLEMS

10   Have you ever had eating problems?   YES / NO / UNCLEAR

If yes:
a Can you describe these problems?

11   Have you ever lost so much weight that your doctor or others told you that you were seriously underweight?   YES / NO / UNCLEAR

If yes:
a Are you currently (seriously) underweight?   YES / NO / UNCLEAR
b What was your lowest weight? _____
c What is your height? _____

For women:
d Have you ever stopped having your periods/menstruating due to being underweight?   YES / NO / UNCLEAR

12   Have you ever been hospitalized in connection with being underweight?   YES / NO / UNCLEAR

13   Have you ever had problems with overeating?   YES / NO / UNCLEAR

If yes:
a What was your highest weight? _____

14   Does your weight fluctuate a lot over the course of a month or year?   YES / NO / UNCLEAR

If yes:
a Can you describe how much your weight fluctuates (how many lbs/kg)?

15   Have you ever suffered from binge eating?   YES / NO / UNCLEAR

If yes:
a How often do you have binges?
- ☐ Seldom
- ☐ Recurrently
- ☐ Monthly
- ☐ Weekly
- ☐ Daily
- ☐ ?

b Can you give an example of such a binge?
c Does the binging take place while you are in a daze?   YES / NO / UNCLEAR

If yes:
    c-1 Can you describe this?

16   Does it ever happen that you have no memory at all of eating (or binge eating) even though there are indications that you actually have eaten?   YES / NO / UNCLEAR

If yes:
a   Can you give an example?

17   Do you ever completely forget to eat during the day?   YES / NO / UNCLEAR

If yes:
a   Are you aware of feeling hungry or feeling "full"?   YES / NO / UNCLEAR

18   Do you ever make yourself vomit to get rid of food?   YES / NO / UNCLEAR

If yes:
a   How often do you make yourself vomit?
        ☐   Seldom
        ☐   Recurrently
        ☐   Monthly
        ☐   Weekly
        ☐   Daily
        ☐   ?

19   Do you ever suffer from spontaneous vomiting or nausea
without any physical cause?   YES / NO / UNCLEAR

If yes:
a   Can you give an example?

20   Do you ever use (or have you ever used) laxatives to help
you get rid of food you have eaten and to manage your weight?   YES / NO / UNCLEAR

If yes:
a   How often does this occur?
        ☐   Seldom
        ☐   Recurrently
        ☐   Monthly
        ☐   Weekly
        ☐   Daily
        ☐   ?

21   Have you ever engaged in excessive exercising
(several hours per day)?   YES / NO / UNCLEAR

If yes:
a   Can you give an example?

22   Have you ever heard voices or had compulsive thoughts
telling or commanding you not to eat or to eat too much?   YES / NO / UNCLEAR
a   Not eating   YES / NO / UNCLEAR
b   Eating too much   YES / NO / UNCLEAR

▨   Overall severity score EATING PROBLEMS
▨   0 = Absent
▨   1 = Minor
▨   2 = Moderate
▨   3 = Severe
▨   88 = Unclear

Subjective distress score EATING PROBLEMS

0 = Absent

1 = Minor

2 = Moderate

3 = Severe

88 = Unclear

Are the EATING PROBLEMS accompanied by alterations in consciousness?

0 = No

1 = Yes

88 = Unclear

Are the EATING PROBLEMS accompanied by dissociative symptoms indicating a division of the personality?

0 = No

1 = Yes

88 = Unclear

SLEEP PROBLEMS

23 Do you ever suffer from sleep problems?   YES / NO / UNCLEAR

If yes:

a   How often do you suffer from sleep problems?

☐ Seldom

☐ Recurrently

☐ Monthly

☐ Weekly

☐ Daily

☐ ?

Interviewer: "I will now ask you some specific questions about sleep problems."

24 Do you have trouble falling asleep?   YES / NO / UNCLEAR

If yes:

a   Can you describe this?

b   Does this involve:

☐ Worrying?

☐ Anxiety?

☐ Being afraid to close your eyes?

☐ Other: _____

25 Do you ever put off going to sleep because you are afraid to do so?   YES / NO / UNCLEAR

If yes:

a   Can you give an example?

26 Do you often wake up during the night?   YES / NO / UNCLEAR

If yes:
a How often do you wake up in the night?
b Does this happen at particular times during the night?   YES / NO / UNCLEAR
   b-1 If yes: time(s): _____
c Can you describe what wakes you up?

27   How many hours of sleep do you average per night?

> **Instruction for the interviewer:** When answering Question 28, the patient is not supposed to describe his/her nightmares in detail. What is important, is simply whether he/she remembers the nightmares.

28   Do you ever suffer from nightmares?   YES / NO / UNCLEAR

If yes:
a How often does this occur?
   ☐ Seldom
   ☐ Recurrently
   ☐ Monthly
   ☐ Weekly
   ☐ Daily
   ☐ ?
b Are you aware of the content of these nightmares?
   ☐ No
   ☐ Sometimes
   ☐ Often
   ☐ Unclear
c Do you think that the nightmares are related to past (unpleasant) events?
   ☐ No
   ☐ Sometimes
   ☐ Often
   ☐ Unclear
d Does it ever seem to you at night as if you are reliving the unpleasant
   events?   YES / NO / UNCLEAR

29   Have you ever noticed or heard from others that you are agitated
     while sleeping (e.g., screaming, fighting, talking in your sleep)?   YES / NO / UNCLEAR

If yes:
a How often does this occur?
   ☐ Seldom
   ☐ Recurrently
   ☐ Monthly
   ☐ Weekly
   ☐ Daily
   ☐ ?
b Can you describe what happens?
   ☐ Screaming
   ☐ Crying

□ Talking
□ Fighting
□ Other: _____

30 Do you ever have trouble waking up from an unpleasant dream, as if the unpleasant dream seems to continue even after you have woken up?   YES / NO / UNCLEAR

If yes:
a How often does this occur?
□ Seldom
□ Recurrently
□ Monthly
□ Weekly
□ Daily
□ ?
b Can you describe this experience?

31 Do you ever have nightmare-like visions during the day?   YES / NO / UNCLEAR

If yes:
a How often does this occur?
□ Seldom
□ Recurrently
□ Monthly
□ Weekly
□ Daily
□ ?
b Can you describe this experience?
c Do you have any idea what causes these visions?   YES / NO / UNCLEAR

32 Have you ever suffered from sleepwalking?   YES / NO / UNCLEAR

If yes:
a Can you describe this experience?

33 Have there ever been signs that you have gotten out of bed and done things during the night that you could not remember doing the following morning (without being under the influence of alcohol, drugs, or medication)?   YES / NO / UNCLEAR

If yes:
a How often does this occur?
□ Seldom
□ Recurrently
□ Monthly
□ Weekly
□ Daily
□ ?
b Can you give an example?

34 Do you use sleep medication?   YES / NO / UNCLEAR

If yes:
a   What medication do you use?
b   What effect do you think it has?
c   Can you describe this effect?

35   Do you use any other sleeping aids (for example: taking a warm
bath before you go to bed, or listening to certain music)?   YES / NO / UNCLEAR

If yes:
a   Can you describe these sleeping aids?

36   Have you ever had the experience of involuntarily falling asleep
during the day when you should have been awake?   YES / NO / UNCLEAR

If yes:
a   Can you describe this experience?

37   Have you ever awoken feeling like you were another person?   YES / NO / UNCLEAR

If yes:
a   How often does this occur?
         ☐   Seldom
         ☐   Recurrently
         ☐   Monthly
         ☐   Weekly
         ☐   Daily
         ☐   ?
b   Can you describe this experience?

38   Have you ever woken up and not recognized where you were,
even though you were in your own home?   YES / NO / UNCLEAR

If yes:
a   How often does this occur?
         ☐   Seldom
         ☐   Recurrently
         ☐   Monthly
         ☐   Weekly
         ☐   Daily
         ☐   ?
b   Can you describe this experience?

39   Have you ever woken up feeling like you were in
a time in your past?   YES / NO / UNCLEAR

If yes:
a   How often does this occur?
         ☐   Seldom
         ☐   Recurrently
         ☐   Monthly
         ☐   Weekly
         ☐   Daily
         ☐   ?
b   Can you describe this experience?

Overall severity score SLEEP PROBLEMS
0 = Absent
1 = Minor
2 = Moderate
3 = Severe
88 = Unclear

Subjective distress score SLEEP PROBLEMS
0 = Absent
1 = Minor
2 = Moderate
3 = Severe
88 = Unclear

Are the SLEEP PROBLEMS accompanied by alterations in consciousness?
0 = No
1 = Yes
88 = Unclear

Are the SLEEP PROBLEMS accompanied by dissociative symptoms indicating a division of the personality?
0 = No
1 = Yes
88 = Unclear

MOOD AND EMOTION REGULATION

40 What has your mood been like in general over the past several years?

Please describe:

41 Have you ever experienced rapid mood swings?   YES / NO / UNCLEAR

If yes:
a   How often does this occur?
   ☐ Seldom
   ☐ Recurrently
   ☐ Monthly
   ☐ Weekly
   ☐ Daily
   ☐ ?

b   Are you always aware of your mood swings?   YES / NO / UNCLEAR

If no:
   b-1 Can you describe what happens?

Instruction for the interviewer: If the patient does not report mood swings, you may proceed to Question 45.

---

42 Can you describe how the mood swings typically begin?
   ☐ Abruptly
   ☐ More gradually

      ☐ Begins with a mild feeling and progresses to a similar feeling that is more intense (e.g., content to euphoric)

      ☐ Swings between extremely intense feelings that are very different from each other (e.g., happy to enraged)

      ☐ Other: _____

  a Can you give an example?

43 Do your mood swings affect:

  a Yourself?   YES / NO / UNCLEAR

  b Others around you?   YES / NO / UNCLEAR

  c Your daily life/work?   YES / NO / UNCLEAR

  If yes:

  d Can you describe how your mood swings affect yourself, others, and your functioning?

44 Have you ever experienced strong fluctuations in your capacities or your abilities as a result of your mood swings?   YES / NO / UNCLEAR

  If yes:

  a How often does this occur?

      ☐ Seldom

      ☐ Recurrently

      ☐ Monthly

      ☐ Weekly

      ☐ Daily

      ☐ ?

  b Can you give an example?

45 Have you ever noticed that you could easily do things that you felt should be impossible, or that you are normally unable to do?   YES / NO / UNCLEAR

  If yes:

  a How often does this occur?

      ☐ Seldom

      ☐ Recurrently

      ☐ Monthly

      ☐ Weekly

      ☐ Daily

      ☐ ?

  b Can you give an example?

46 Do you get upset easily by what others would consider to be minor issues?   YES / NO / UNCLEAR

  If yes:

  a Can you give an example?

47 Do you find it difficult to calm yourself down when you are upset?   YES / NO / UNCLEAR

  If yes:

  a Can you give an example?

48 Do you ever have the feeling that you are not in control
of your behavior or emotions?   YES / NO / UNCLEAR

If yes:
a How often does this occur?
- ☐ Seldom
- ☐ Recurrently
- ☐ Monthly
- ☐ Weekly
- ☐ Daily
- ☐ ?

b Can you give an example?

49 Are there any particular emotions (e.g., anger) that you
feel you cannot control?   YES / NO / UNCLEAR

If yes:
a Can you describe these emotions?
b How often does this occur?
- ☐ Seldom
- ☐ Recurrently
- ☐ Monthly
- ☐ Weekly
- ☐ Daily
- ☐ ?

c Do you always understand the reason for these emotions, or what they are related
to?   YES / NO / UNCLEAR

  c-1 Can you tell me more about that?

50 Do you ever have the experience of feeling numb, as if you
cannot get in touch with your feelings or emotions?   YES / NO / UNCLEAR

If yes:
a Can you give an example?
b How often does this occur?
- ☐ Seldom
- ☐ Recurrently
- ☐ Monthly
- ☐ Weekly
- ☐ Daily
- ☐ ?

51 Do you ever feel depressed?   YES / NO / UNCLEAR

If yes:
a Can you give an example?
b How often does this occur?
- ☐ Seldom
- ☐ Recurrently
- ☐ Monthly
- ☐ Weekly

☐ Daily
☐ ?

52 Do you ever feel hopeless about your future? YES / NO / UNCLEAR

If yes:
a Can you describe that feeling?
b Does this feeling of hopelessness relate to your living situation? YES / NO / UNCLEAR

If yes:
b-1 Can you describe this?
c Does this feeling of hopelessness relate to difficulties
in (meaningful) relationships with other people? YES / NO / UNCLEAR

If yes:
c-1 Can you describe this?

53 Have you ever felt so desperate that you thought
about taking your own life? YES / NO / UNCLEAR

> **Instruction for the interviewer:** If the patient does not report suicidal thoughts, you may proceed to Question 56.

54 Have you ever actually tried to take your own life? YES / NO / UNCLEAR

If yes:
a What exactly did you do?
b How did the suicide attempt come to an end, or how were
you prevented from taking your own life?
c Have you attempted suicide more than once? YES / NO / UNCLEAR

If yes:
c-1 How often have you attempted suicide?
d Did the attempt(s) happen in a daze (outside your control)? YES / NO / UNCLEAR

If yes: Can you describe this experience?
☐ I felt like I was in a dream state (depersonalization/derealization)
☐ I felt like I was outside of my body, watching
☐ I heard voices
☐ Other: _____
e Has it ever happened that you had no memory at all
of trying to end your life, but you know you must have made
a suicide attempt? Can you give an example? YES / NO / UNCLEAR
f Had you been using alcohol, drugs, or medication
at the time of the attempt? YES / NO / UNCLEAR

55 a Have you ever been treated in a (psychiatric) hospital to
prevent you from undertaking a suicide attempt? YES / NO / UNCLEAR
b Have you ever been treated in a hospital as a result of a suicide
attempt? YES / NO / UNCLEAR

56 Do you ever feel hyperactive, extremely energetic,
keyed up and/or exuberant without a specific reason? YES / NO / UNCLEAR

If yes:

a   How often does this occur?
- ☐ Seldom
- ☐ Recurrently
- ☐ Monthly
- ☐ Weekly
- ☐ Daily
- ☐ ?

b   Can you give an example?

c   Have you ever done things in a hyperactive mood which you later regretted or which got you into trouble?   YES / NO / UNCLEAR

If yes:

c-1 Can you give an example?

d   When you are in a hyperactive mood, do your thoughts ever run away with you, as if you are unable to stop them?   YES / NO / UNCLEAR

If yes:

d-1 Can you give an example?

e   Do you know whether there is a connection between this hyperactive/overexcited behavior and feelings of stress and anxiety?   YES / NO / UNCLEAR

If yes:

e-1 Can you give an example?

57   Have you ever experienced severe feelings of:

a   Emptiness   YES / NO / UNCLEAR

If yes:

a-1 Can you give an example?

a-2 How often does this occur?
- ☐ Seldom
- ☐ Recurrently
- ☐ Monthly
- ☐ Weekly
- ☐ Daily
- ☐ ?

a-3 How long do these feelings tend to last?
- ☐ Hours
- ☐ Days
- ☐ Almost continually
- ☐ Unclear

b   Boredom   YES / NO / UNCLEAR

If yes:

b-1 Can you give an example?

b-2 How often does this occur?
- ☐ Seldom
- ☐ Recurrently
- ☐ Monthly
- ☐ Weekly

☐ Daily

☐ ?

b-3 How long do these feelings tend to last?

☐ Hours

☐ Days

☐ Almost continually

☐ Unclear

Overall severity score MOOD AND EMOTION REGULATION PROBLEMS

0 = Absent

1 = Minor

2 = Moderate

3 = Severe

88 = Unclear

Subjective distress score MOOD AND EMOTION REGULATION PROBLEMS

0 = Absent

1 = Minor

2 = Moderate

3 = Severe

88 = Unclear

Are the MOOD AND EMOTION REGULATION PROBLEMS
accompanied by alterations in consciousness?

0 = No

1 = Yes

88 = Unclear

Are the MOOD AND EMOTION REGULATION PROBLEMS accompanied
by dissociative symptoms indicating a division of the personality?

0 = No

1 = Yes

88 = Unclear

ANXIETY AND PANIC

58 Are you generally an anxious person?   YES / NO / UNCLEAR

If yes:

a   Can you give an example?

59 Have you ever suffered from specific fears or phobias?   YES / NO / UNCLEAR

If yes:

a   Can you describe these fears?

60 Have you ever suffered from (sudden) panic attacks?   YES / NO / UNCLEAR

If yes:

a   Can you describe such a panic attack?

b   Do you usually know the reason for a panic attack?   YES / NO / UNCLEAR

If yes:

    b-1 Can you give an example?

  c Are these panic attacks accompanied by physical
complaints such as palpitations, perspiring, hyperventilating,
and/or other complaints?   YES / NO / UNCLEAR

If yes:

    c-1 Can you give an example?

Instruction for the interviewer: When you ask Question 61, please refer to the experiences as reported by the patient in response to Questions 58–60.

---

61   When you think back on your experiences of fear, anxiety, phobia (mention the experience the patient has described):

  a When did you experience this for the first time?

  b How often do you have such experiences?
- ☐ Seldom
- ☐ Recurrently
- ☐ Monthly
- ☐ Weekly
- ☐ Daily
- ☐ ?

  c Do you ever feel alienated from yourself when you are scared?   YES / NO / UNCLEAR

If yes:

    c-1 Can you describe this?

  d Do you ever hear voices when you are scared?   YES / NO / UNCLEAR

If yes:

    d-1 Can you describe this?

  e Have you ever been so scared that you didn't know
what you were doing or had done?   YES / NO / UNCLEAR

If yes:

    e-1 Can you describe this?

62   Do you ever avoid certain situations or places out of fear?   YES / NO / UNCLEAR

If yes:

  a Which situations do you avoid?

  b Can you give an example?

  c How often does this occur?
- ☐ Seldom
- ☐ Recurrently
- ☐ Monthly
- ☐ Weekly
- ☐ Daily
- ☐ ?

63   Are there any other things that you avoid out of fear?   YES / NO / UNCLEAR

If yes:

  a Can you give an example?

64 Have you ever had frightening images or thoughts repeatedly force themselves upon your mind?   YES / NO / UNCLEAR

If yes:
a How often does this occur?
- ☐ Seldom
- ☐ Recurrently
- ☐ Monthly
- ☐ Weekly
- ☐ Daily
- ☐ ?

b Do you know where these images or thoughts are coming from, or what they mean?   YES / NO / UNCLEAR

If yes:
b-1 Can you tell me more about that?

65 Do you ever have flashbacks of negative earlier experiences?   YES / NO / UNCLEAR

If yes:
a How often does this occur?
- ☐ Seldom
- ☐ Recurrently
- ☐ Monthly
- ☐ Weekly
- ☐ Daily
- ☐ ?

b Can you give an example?

66 Do you ever suffer from:

a Jumpiness?   YES / NO / UNCLEAR

If yes:
a-1 How often does this occur?
- ☐ Seldom
- ☐ Recurrently
- ☐ Monthly
- ☐ Weekly
- ☐ Daily
- ☐ ?

a-2 Can you give an example?

b Hypervigilance?   YES / NO / UNCLEAR

If yes:
b-1 How often does this occur?
- ☐ Seldom
- ☐ Recurrently
- ☐ Monthly
- ☐ Weekly
- ☐ Daily
- ☐ ?

b-2 Can you give an example?

c   Irritable behavior or anger outbursts?   YES / NO / UNCLEAR

If yes:

    c-1 How often does this occur?
- ☐   Seldom
- ☐   Recurrently
- ☐   Monthly
- ☐   Weekly
- ☐   Daily
- ☐   ?

    c-2 Can you give an example?

d   Compulsive thoughts or actions?   YES / NO / UNCLEAR

If yes:

    d-1 How often does this occur?
- ☐   Seldom
- ☐   Recurrently
- ☐   Monthly
- ☐   Weekly
- ☐   Daily
- ☐   ?

    d-2 Can you give an example?

Overall severity score ANXIETY AND PANIC

0 = Absent

1 = Minor

2 = Moderate

3 = Severe

88 = Unclear

Subjective distress score ANXIETY AND PANIC

0 = Absent

1 = Minor

2 = Moderate

3 = Severe

88 = Unclear

Are the ANXIETY AND PANIC accompanied by alterations in consciousness?

0 = No

1 = Yes

88 = Unclear

Are the ANXIETY AND PANIC accompanied by dissociative symptoms indicating a division of the personality?

0 = No

1 = Yes

88 = Unclear

SELF-DESTRUCTIVE BEHAVIOR

67   Have you ever intentionally hurt or injured yourself (e.g., burning or cutting
yourself, or banging your head on the floor or against a wall)?   YES / NO / UNCLEAR

If yes:
a How often does this occur?
- ☐ Seldom
- ☐ Recurrently
- ☐ Monthly
- ☐ Weekly
- ☐ Daily
- ☐ ?

b Can you give an example?
c Are you aware of what you are doing when you are injuring yourself?   YES / NO / UNCLEAR
   c-1 Can you give an example?
d Do you feel that you are in control of your self-injurious behavior?   YES / NO / UNCLEAR
   d-1 Can you give an example?

> **Instruction for the interviewer:** If the patient does not report self-injurious behavior (auto-mutilation), you may proceed to Question 70.

68 Does it ever happen that you have no memory at all of injuring yourself but that you later discover that it must have happened?   YES / NO / UNCLEAR

If yes:
a Can you give an example?

69 Do you ever have the experience of watching yourself harm your body, as though you are watching someone else doing it?   YES / NO / UNCLEAR

If yes:
a Can you give an example?
b Do you experience this as if you are literally outside of your body?   YES / NO / UNCLEAR

70 Do you ever do other dangerous or self-injurious things?   YES / NO / UNCLEAR

If yes, does it involve:
a Reckless driving?   YES / NO / UNCLEAR
   a-1 How often does this occur?
- ☐ Seldom
- ☐ Recurrently
- ☐ Monthly
- ☐ Weekly
- ☐ Daily
- ☐ ?

b Overspending?   YES / NO / UNCLEAR
   b-1 How often does this occur?
- ☐ Seldom
- ☐ Recurrently
- ☐ Monthly
- ☐ Weekly
- ☐ Daily

    ☐ ?

  c Unsafe sex?   YES / NO / UNCLEAR

    c-1 How often does this occur?

        ☐ Seldom

        ☐ Recurrently

        ☐ Monthly

        ☐ Weekly

        ☐ Daily

        ☐ ?

  d Other: _____

If yes:

d-1

    How often does this occur?

        ☐ Seldom

        ☐ Recurrently

        ☐ Monthly

        ☐ Weekly

        ☐ Daily

        ☐ ?

71 Are there any other situations in which you do not take care
of yourself (e.g., failing to do things that are necessary
for your health or well-being)?   YES / NO / UNCLEAR

    If yes:

  a Can you give an example?

72 Does it ever happen that you are forced or told by
something inside yourself to behave in a self-injurious manner?   YES / NO / UNCLEAR

    If yes: Does this involve:

  a A commanding voice (or voices)?   YES / NO / UNCLEAR

    If yes:

    a-1 How often does this occur?

        ☐ Seldom

        ☐ Recurrently

        ☐ Monthly

        ☐ Weekly

        ☐ Daily

        ☐ ?

    a-2 Can you give an example?

  b Compulsive thoughts?   YES / NO / UNCLEAR

    If yes:

    b-1 How often does this occur?

        ☐ Seldom

        ☐ Recurrently

        ☐ Monthly

        ☐ Weekly

        ☐ Daily

        ☐ ?

    b-2 Can you give an example?

c   Another way?   YES / NO / UNCLEAR

If yes:
   c-1   How often does this occur?
            ☐   Seldom
            ☐   Recurrently
            ☐   Monthly
            ☐   Weekly
            ☐   Daily
            ☐   ?
   c-2   Can you give an example?

          Overall severity score SELF-DESTRUCTIVE BEHAVIOR
          0 = Absent
          1 = Minor
          2 = Moderate
          3 = Severe
          88 = Unclear

          Subjective distress score SELF-DESTRUCTIVE BEHAVIOR
          0 = Absent
          1 = Minor
          2 = Moderate
          3 = Severe
          88 = Unclear

          Is the SELF-DESTRUCTIVE BEHAVIOR accompanied by alterations in consciousness?
          0 = No
          1 = Yes
          88 = Unclear

          Is the SELF-DESTRUCTIVE BEHAVIOR accompanied by dissociative
          symptoms indicating a division of the personality?
          0 = No
          1 = Yes
          88 = Unclear

SELF-IMAGE AND IDENTITY

73   a Do you usually have a positive opinion of yourself?   YES / NO / UNCLEAR

        If yes:
           a-1 Can you describe this?

        If no:
           a-2 Can you describe what thoughts and feelings you usually have about yourself?
        b Do you think there is a difference between your beliefs about yourself and how other
           people think of you?   YES / NO / UNCLEAR

        If yes:
           b-1 Can you describe this difference?

74   If you think negatively about yourself:

    a   How often does this occur?
- ☐ Seldom
- ☐ Recurrently
- ☐ Monthly
- ☐ Weekly
- ☐ Daily
- ☐ ?

75   Are you ever uncertain about your wishes and preferences?   YES / NO / UNCLEAR

    If yes:
    a   Can you give an example?

76   Are you ever insecure or uncertain about who you really are?   YES / NO / UNCLEAR

    If yes:
    a   Can you give an example?
    b   How often are you uncertain about who you really are?
- ☐ Seldom
- ☐ Recurrently
- ☐ Monthly
- ☐ Weekly
- ☐ Daily
- ☐ ?

77   Are you ever insecure or uncertain about how you would
like to be or should be?   YES / NO / UNCLEAR

    If yes:
    a   Can you give an example?

78   Do you have a strong tendency to do what others would like you
to do, instead of standing up for yourself?   YES / NO / UNCLEAR

    If yes:
    a   Can you give an example?

79   Have you ever had the feeling that there is a struggle going on
inside yourself, or that you have strong feelings of ambivalence or inner conflict?

    YES / NO / UNCLEAR

    If yes:
    a   Can you give an example?
    b   Do you experience ambivalence or a struggle between:
- ☐ Two opinions or thoughts?
- ☐ Several opinions or thoughts?

    c   Can you hear the inner struggle in the form of voices?   YES / NO / UNCLEAR

d Have you ever had the feeling that you are observing yourself, like a spectator, while
     such a struggle is happening?   YES / NO / UNCLEAR

  If yes:
    d-1 Can you describe this?
  e Do the conflicting opinions feel like they are your own opinions? YES / NO / UNCLEAR
  f How often does this experience occur?
       ☐ Seldom
       ☐ Recurrently
       ☐ Monthly
       ☐ Weekly
       ☐ Daily
       ☐ ?

80 Have you ever had the feeling that you are a total outsider,
        don't belong, or are completely different from everyone else?   YES / NO / UNCLEAR

  If yes:
  a How often does this occur?
       ☐ Seldom
       ☐ Recurrently
       ☐ Monthly
       ☐ Weekly
       ☐ Daily
       ☐ ?
  b Can you give an example?

81 Do you sometimes feel very ashamed of yourself
        (i.e., in a way that is severe, repetitive, long-lasting, and pervasive)? YES / NO / UNCLEAR

  If yes:
  a Can you give an example?

82 Have you ever had any of the following negative feelings about yourself:
  a That you do not want people to get to know you better?   YES / NO / UNCLEAR

  If yes:
    a-1 Can you give an example?
  b That you prefer to hide from, or avoid, other people?   YES / NO / UNCLEAR

  If yes:
    b-1 Can you give an example?
  c That you prefer to hide from, or avoid, yourself?   YES / NO / UNCLEAR

  If yes:
    c-1 Can you give an example?

83 Do you ever feel seriously guilty?   YES / NO / UNCLEAR

  If yes:
  a Can you give an example?

84 Do you have the feeling that you can generally influence
        or control what is happening in your daily life?   YES / NO / UNCLEAR

If yes:
a   Can you give an example?

85   Do you ever feel very helpless in daily life?   YES / NO / UNCLEAR

If yes:
a   Can you give an example?

Overall severity score SELF-IMAGE AND IDENTITY PROBLEMS
0 = Absent
1 = Minor
2 = Moderate
3 = Severe
88 = Unclear

Subjective distress score SELF-IMAGE AND IDENTITY PROBLEMS
0 = Absent
1 = Minor
2 = Moderate
3 = Severe
88 = Unclear

Are the SELF-IMAGE AND IDENTITY PROBLEMS
accompanied by alterations in consciousness?
0 = No
1 = Yes
88 = Unclear

Are the SELF-IMAGE AND IDENTITY PROBLEMS accompanied by
dissociative symptoms indicating a division of the personality?
0 = No
1 = Yes
88 = Unclear

RELATIONSHIPS WITH OTHERS

86   Do you have stable and long-lasting relationships with other
people?   YES / NO / UNCLEAR

If yes:
a   Can you give an example?

If no:
b   Have you ever had stable long-lasting relationships in your
lifetime?   YES / NO / UNCLEAR

If yes:
b-1 Can you give an example?

87   Have you ever had serious difficulties in trusting other people?   YES / NO / UNCLEAR

If yes:
a   Can you give an example?

88   Do you avoid (close) relationships with other people?   YES / NO / UNCLEAR

If yes:

a Can you give an example?

89 When in contact with other people, do you ever experience:

a feeling alienated from others? YES / NO / UNCLEAR

If yes:
   a-1 Can you give an example?
b feeling insecure about yourself with others? YES / NO / UNCLEAR

If yes:
   b-1 Can you give an example?
c an inner conflict taking place related to your interactions with others? YES / NO / UNCLEAR

If yes:
   c-1 Can you give an example or describe what this inner conflict looks like?
   c-2 Does this involve more than one conflicting thought/voice within yourself?

90 a Have you ever had difficulties in dealing with conflicts in relationships with others? YES / NO / UNCLEAR

If yes:
   a-1 Can you give an example?
   a-2 Do you think that these difficulties are caused/influenced by different conflicting thoughts/opinions within yourself?
b Do you think you tend to feel more hurt in relationship conflicts than other people seem to feel? YES / NO / UNCLEAR

If yes:
   b-1 Can you give an example?

91 Do you ever have the feeling that people hurt you purposefully? YES / NO / UNCLEAR

If yes:
a Can you give an example?

92 Are you sometimes afraid that other people will abandon you? YES / NO / UNCLEAR

If yes:
a Can you give an example?
b What do you do to prevent this? Can you give an example?

93 Do you feel very dependent on other people? YES / NO / UNCLEAR

If yes:
a Can you give an example?

94 a How much distress and discomfort do you experience in relationships with others?

   ☐ Little or minimal distress and discomfort in interpersonal relationships
   ☐ Frequently recurring distress and discomfort in interpersonal relationships
   ☐ Ongoing distress and discomfort in interpersonal relationships

b Which of the previously mentioned problems in relationships with other people bother you the most?

- ☐ Unstable relationships
- ☐ Difficulties with trust
- ☐ Avoiding relationships
- ☐ Feeling alienated / feeling insecure / inner conflict
- ☐ Dealing with conflicts
- ☐ Easily feeling hurt
- ☐ Fear of abandonment
- ☐ Dependence

Overall severity score PROBLEMS IN RELATIONSHIPS WITH OTHERS

0 = Absent

1 = Minor

2 = Moderate

3 = Severe

88 = Unclear

Subjective distress score PROBLEMS IN RELATIONSHIPS WITH OTHERS

0 = Absent

1 = Minor

2 = Moderate

3 = Severe

88 = Unclear

Are the PROBLEMS IN RELATIONSHIPS WITH OTHERS accompanied by alterations in consciousness?

0 = No

1 = Yes

88 = Unclear

Are the PROBLEMS IN RELATIONSHIPS WITH OTHERS accompanied by dissociative symptoms indicating a division of the personality?

0 = No

1 = Yes

88 = Unclear

SEXUALITY

95 Does it bother you when you are physically touched by someone you know well?   YES / NO / UNCLEAR

If yes:
a Can you give an example?

96 Does it bother you when you are touched in a sexual way by a partner?   YES / NO / UNCLEAR

If yes:
a Can you give an example?

97 During sexual contact, does it ever occur that you:
a Become numb/feel nothing?   YES / NO / UNCLEAR
b Leave your body?   YES / NO / UNCLEAR

c	Experience (partial) amnesia?	YES / NO / UNCLEAR
d	Hear voices?	YES / NO / UNCLEAR
e	No longer recognize your partner/surroundings?	YES / NO / UNCLEAR
f	See unpleasant images?	YES / NO / UNCLEAR

98 Do you try to avoid thinking about sex?　　　　　　　　YES / NO / UNCLEAR

If yes:
a Can you give an example?

99 Do you try to avoid sexual contact and/or sexual relationships?　　YES / NO / UNCLEAR

If yes:
a Can you give an example?

100 Do you think more about sex (or topics related to sex)
than you would want?　　　　　　　　　　　　　　　　YES / NO / UNCLEAR

If yes:
a Can you give an example?

101 Have you ever been bothered by thoughts about sex
and/or sexual relationships?　　　　　　　　　　　　　YES / NO / UNCLEAR

If yes:
a How often does this occur?
　　☐ Seldom
　　☐ Recurrently
　　☐ Monthly
　　☐ Weekly
　　☐ Daily
　　☐ ?
b Can you give an example?

102 Have you ever engaged in sexual contact and/or a sexual
relationship without really wanting it?　　　　　　　　YES / NO / UNCLEAR

If yes:
a How often does this occur?
　　☐ Seldom
　　☐ Recurrently
　　☐ Monthly
　　☐ Weekly
　　☐ Daily
　　☐ ?
b Is this behavior influenced by a voice/voices or compulsive
　thoughts?　　　　　　　　　　　　　　　　　　　　YES / NO / UNCLEAR
　b-1 Can you give an example?

103 Have you ever felt confused about your gender or sexual identity?　YES / NO / UNCLEAR

If yes:
a How often does this occur?
　　☐ Seldom

□ Recurrently
□ Monthly
□ Weekly
□ Daily
□ ?

b Can you give an example?

104 Have you ever felt confused about your sexual preference?　　　YES / NO / UNCLEAR

If yes:
a How often does this occur?
□ Seldom
□ Recurrently
□ Monthly
□ Weekly
□ Daily
□ ?

b Can you give an example?

105 How much distress and discomfort do you experience with regard to sexuality?
□ Little or minimal distress and discomfort with regard to sexuality
□ Frequently recurring distress and discomfort with regard to sexuality
□ Continuous distress and discomfort with regard to sexuality

Overall severity score PROBLEMS WITH SEXUALITY
0 = Absent
1 = Minor
2 = Moderate
3 = Severe
88 = Unclear

Subjective distress score PROBLEMS WITH SEXUALITY
0 = Absent
1 = Minor
2 = Moderate
3 = Severe
88 = Unclear

Are the PROBLEMS WITH SEXUALITY accompanied by alterations in consciousness?
0 = No
1 = Yes
88 = Unclear

Are the PROBLEMS WITH SEXUALITY accompanied by dissociative symptoms indicating a division of the personality?
0 = No
1 = Yes
88 = Unclear

PART 3: ALTERATIONS IN CONSCIOUSNESS

DEPERSONALIZATION

> **Instruction for the interviewer:** In the previous part of the interview, several questions have already been posed about depersonalization. If the patient has already given examples of this, you may refer to these examples, or even skip some of the questions about depersonalization.

106 Have you ever felt very unreal, detached, or disconnected from yourself?   YES / NO / UNCLEAR

   If yes:
   a   Can you give an example?

107 Have you ever felt as if you were acting like a sort of robot or automaton?   YES / NO / UNCLEAR

   If yes:
   a   Can you give an example?

108 Have you ever felt disconnected from, or not in touch with, your emotions?   YES / NO / UNCLEAR

   If yes:
   a   Can you give an example?

109 Have you ever felt that you are not really there, as if you are not entirely present?   YES / NO / UNCLEAR

   If yes:
   a   Can you give an example?

> **Instruction for the interviewer:** If there are no indications of depersonalization, you may proceed to the next section of the interview: "Derealization."

110 How often do these experiences (mentioned in Questions 106–109) occur?
   - ☐ Seldom
   - ☐ Recurrently
   - ☐ Monthly
   - ☐ Weekly
   - ☐ Daily
   - ☐ ?

111 Do these experiences only occur when you are using alcohol, drugs, or prescription medication?   YES / NO / UNCLEAR

112 Do these experiences only occur when you are:
   a   Under pressure/stressed?   YES / NO / UNCLEAR
   b   Tired?   YES / NO / UNCLEAR

c   Dejected?   YES / NO / UNCLEAR

d   Confused?   YES / NO / UNCLEAR

e   Ill?   YES / NO / UNCLEAR

f   Anxious?   YES / NO / UNCLEAR

g   Other: _____

113   Do these experiences also occur when you are not suffering from any of the above-mentioned complaints (Question 112)?   YES / NO / UNCLEAR

____   **Overall severity score DEPERSONALIZATION**
____   0 = Absent
____   1 = Minor
____   2 = Moderate
____   3 = Severe
____   88 = Unclear
____   **Subjective distress score DEPERSONALIZATION**
____   0 = Absent
____   1 = Minor
____   2 = Moderate
____   3 = Severe
____   88 = Unclear

DEREALIZATION

114   Have you ever had the experience that people or the world around you seem unreal?   YES / NO / UNCLEAR

If yes:
a   Can you give an example?

115   Have you ever had the experience as if you are looking at the world through a haze?   YES / NO / UNCLEAR

If yes:
a   Can you give an example?

116   Have you ever felt disconnected from your friends or family, as if they were strangers?   YES / NO / UNCLEAR

If yes:
a   Can you give an example?

117   Have you ever had the experience that your own house or a familiar place seemed unreal or strange to you?   YES / NO / UNCLEAR

If yes:
a   Can you give an example?

Instruction for the interviewer: If there are no indications of derealization, you may proceed to the next section of the interview: "Absorption, Trance, and Daydreaming."

---

118 How often do these experiences (mentioned in Questions 114–117) occur?

- ☐ Seldom
- ☐ Recurrently
- ☐ Monthly
- ☐ Weekly
- ☐ Daily
- ☐ ?

119 Do these experiences only occur when you are using alcohol, drugs, or prescription medication? YES / NO / UNCLEAR

120 Do these experiences only occur when you are:

a Under pressure/stressed? YES / NO / UNCLEAR
b Tired? YES / NO / UNCLEAR
c Dejected? YES / NO / UNCLEAR
d Confused? YES / NO / UNCLEAR
e Ill? YES / NO / UNCLEAR
f Anxious? YES / NO / UNCLEAR
g Experience occurs without clear cause YES / NO / UNCLEAR
h Other: _____

121 a Do these experiences also occur when you are not suffering from any of the above-mentioned complaints (Question 120)? YES / NO / UNCLEAR

b Do these experiences occur:

b-1 While you feel alienated from yourself?
- ☐ Never
- ☐ Sometimes
- ☐ Always
- ☐ Unclear

b-2 Without feeling alienated from yourself?
- ☐ Never
- ☐ Sometimes
- ☐ Always
- ☐ Unclear

Overall severity score DEREALIZATION
0 = Absent
1 = Minor
2 = Moderate
3 = Severe
88 = Unclear

Subjective distress score DEREALIZATION
0 = Absent
1 = Minor
2 = Moderate
3 = Severe
88 = Unclear

ABSORPTION, TRANCE, AND DAYDREAMING

122 Have you ever experienced being so absorbed in a book,
a movie, or your work, etc., that you do not notice what
is going on around you?   YES / NO / UNCLEAR

If yes:
a   Can you give an example?
b   How often does this occur?
  ☐ Seldom
  ☐ Recurrently
  ☐ Monthly
  ☐ Weekly
  ☐ Daily
  ☐ ?

123 Have you ever experienced being totally absorbed in
your thoughts, without being aware that a lot of time has passed?   YES / NO / UNCLEAR

If yes:
a   Can you give an example?
b   How often does this occur?
  ☐ Seldom
  ☐ Recurrently
  ☐ Monthly
  ☐ Weekly
  ☐ Daily
  ☐ ?

124 Have you ever had experienced sitting for hours while staring
into space without thinking?   YES / NO / UNCLEAR

If yes:
a   Can you give an example?
b   How often does this occur?
  ☐ Seldom
  ☐ Recurrently
  ☐ Monthly
  ☐ Weekly
  ☐ Daily
  ☐ ?

125 Have you ever experienced being in a trance-like state?   YES / NO / UNCLEAR

If yes:
a   Can you give an example?
b   How often does this occur?
  ☐ Seldom
  ☐ Recurrently
  ☐ Monthly
  ☐ Weekly
  ☐ Daily
  ☐ ?

126 Do you have a vivid imagination?   YES / NO / UNCLEAR

    If yes:
    a Can you give an example?

> **Instruction for the interviewer:** Below you will find some questions about daydreaming. If you are under the impression that the patient often becomes lost in daydreams, you can add questions from the Maladaptive Daydreaming Scale as included in Appendix 5 of the book *Assessing Trauma-Related Dissociation: With the Trauma and Dissociation Symptoms Interview (TADS-I)*, (Boon, 2023).

127 Do you easily become lost in daydreams?   YES / NO / UNCLEAR

    If yes:
    a Can you give an example?
    b How often do you daydream?
          ☐ Seldom
          ☐ Recurrently
          ☐ Monthly
          ☐ Weekly
          ☐ Daily
          ☐ ?
    c When you are lost in your daydreams, do you stay aware
       of your present surroundings?   YES / NO / UNCLEAR
       c-1 Can you give an example?

128 a Have you ever had the experience that you are so immersed
    in a daydream (or fantasy) that it feels as if it is really happening?   YES / NO / UNCLEAR

    If yes:
       a-1 Can you give an example?
    b Can you easily shake off your daydreams?   YES / NO / UNCLEAR
    c Does it bother you when you cannot daydream, or when
       your daydreaming is interrupted?   YES / NO / UNCLEAR
    d Does your daydreaming interfere with your daily activities?   YES / NO / UNCLEAR

    Overall severity score ABSORPTION, TRANCE, AND DAYDREAMING
    0 = Absent
    1 = Minor
    2 = Moderate
    3 = Severe
    88 = Unclear

    Subjective distress score ABSORPTION, TRANCE, AND DAYDREAMING
    0 = Absent
    1 = Minor
    2 = Moderate
    3 = Severe
    88 = Unclear

PART 4: SOMATOFORM DISSOCIATIVE SYMPTOMS

129   Do you currently have any physical complaints, symptoms,
or problems?   YES / NO / UNCLEAR

If yes:
a   What are they?
b   Have you seen a doctor about these complaints?   YES / NO / UNCLEAR

130   Do you ever have, or have you ever had, complaints or pain
for which no medical cause could been found?   YES / NO / UNCLEAR

If yes:
a   What kinds of complaints?
b   How often do/did these complaints occur?
    ☐   Seldom
    ☐   Recurrently
    ☐   Monthly
    ☐   Weekly
    ☐   Daily
    ☐   ?

> Interviewer: "I will now ask you some specific questions about physical complaints."

131   Do you suffer from headaches or migraines?   YES / NO / UNCLEAR

If yes:
a   How often does this occur?
    ☐   Seldom
    ☐   Recurrently
    ☐   Monthly
    ☐   Weekly
    ☐   Daily
    ☐   ?

132   Have you ever sustained a head injury?   YES / NO / UNCLEAR

If yes:
a   What happened?
b   Did you lose consciousness?

If yes:
How long were you unconscious for?

133   Have you ever had abdominal pain (belly ache) without a
clear medical cause?   YES / NO / UNCLEAR

If yes:
a   Can you explain?

134   Have you ever suffered from one of the following:
a   Difficulty urinating?   YES / NO / UNCLEAR
b   Pain while urinating?   YES / NO / UNCLEAR

c   Sudden inability to hold your urine?   YES / NO / UNCLEAR
d   Bed-wetting?   YES / NO / UNCLEAR

135 Have you ever suffered from fainting spells or absences
for which no medical cause could be found?   YES / NO / UNCLEAR

If yes:
a   Can you describe what happened?
b   Did you lose consciousness?   YES / NO / UNCLEAR

If yes:
   b-1 How long were you unconscious for?
c   How often do you have these spells?
     ☐ Seldom
     ☐ Recurrently
     ☐ Monthly
     ☐ Weekly
     ☐ Daily
     ☐ ?

136 Have you ever had (pseudo) epileptic seizures?   YES / NO / UNCLEAR

If yes:
a   How often does this occur?
     ☐ Seldom
     ☐ Recurrently
     ☐ Monthly
     ☐ Weekly
     ☐ Daily
     ☐ ?
b   Have you ever had a neurological examination as a result of this? YES / NO / UNCLEAR

If yes:
   b-1 Were any physical causes found for these seizures?   YES / NO / UNCLEAR
c   Have you been treated for these seizures?   YES / NO / UNCLEAR

137 Have you ever had the feeling that part of your body
or your whole body was alien to you?   YES / NO / UNCLEAR

If yes:
a   Can you give an example?

138 Have you ever experienced not feeling your body (or a part of it), or that it seemed numb,
or that you could not really feel pain?   YES / NO / UNCLEAR

If yes:
a   How often does this occur?
     ☐ Seldom
     ☐ Recurrently
     ☐ Monthly
     ☐ Weekly
     ☐ Daily
     ☐ ?
b   Can you give an example? (If it only concerns a part of your body, which part?)
c   Have you ever waited too long to see a doctor as a result of this? YES / NO / UNCLEAR

139 Have you ever suffered from other (neurological) complaints for which no medical cause could be found, such as:

   a Losing your voice (partly or completely)?   YES / NO / UNCLEAR

   If yes:
      a-1 Can you describe this experience?
   b Loss of strength, or paralysis of your arms or legs?   YES / NO / UNCLEAR

   If yes:
      b-1 Can you describe this experience?
   c A total inability to move, speak, and/or respond to your environment?   YES / NO / UNCLEAR

   If yes:
      c-1 Can you describe this experience?
   d Sudden (temporary) problems with your vision or hearing?   YES / NO / UNCLEAR

   If yes:
      d-1 Can you describe this experience?
   e Being unable to smell or taste without a medical cause?   YES / NO / UNCLEAR

   If yes:
      e-1 Can you describe this experience?
   f Difficulty swallowing?   YES / NO / UNCLEAR

   If yes:
      f-1 Can you describe this experience?

140 Have you ever had the experience of being over-sensitive to stimuli, such as:

   a Sound (e.g., everything sounds very loud)?   YES / NO / UNCLEAR
   b Smell (e.g., a certain smell seems to be very intense)?   YES / NO / UNCLEAR
   c Taste (e.g., a very bad taste)?   YES / NO / UNCLEAR
   d Light (e.g., light seems to be extremely bright)?   YES / NO / UNCLEAR
   e Other: _____

141 How often do these experiences (mentioned in Questions 139–140) occur?
        ☐ Seldom
        ☐ Recurrently
        ☐ Monthly
        ☐ Weekly
        ☐ Daily
        ☐ ?

142 Do you ever suffer from involuntary movements or tics?   YES / NO / UNCLEAR

   If yes:
   a How often does this occur?
        ☐ Seldom
        ☐ Recurrently
        ☐ Monthly
        ☐ Weekly
        ☐ Daily
        ☐ ?
   b Can you give an example?

143 Are there any other physical symptoms that I have
not asked about? YES / NO / UNCLEAR

If yes:
a Can you tell me more about that?
b How often does this occur?
  - ☐ Seldom
  - ☐ Recurrently
  - ☐ Monthly
  - ☐ Weekly
  - ☐ Daily
  - ☐ ?

144 Did you have any accidents as a child? YES / NO / UNCLEAR

If yes:
a Can you describe these accidents?
a How often did such accidents occur?
  - ☐ Seldom
  - ☐ Recurrently
  - ☐ Monthly
  - ☐ Weekly
  - ☐ Daily
  - ☐ ?

145 Were you ever hospitalized as a child? YES / NO / UNCLEAR

If yes:
a Why were you hospitalized?
b How often did this occur?
  - ☐ Seldom
  - ☐ Recurrently
  - ☐ Monthly
  - ☐ Weekly
  - ☐ Daily
  - ☐ ?

Overall severity score SOMATOFORM DISSOCIATIVE SYMPTOMS
0 = Absent
1 = Minor
2 = Moderate
3 = Severe
88 = Unclear

Subjective distress score PHYSICAL COMPLAINTS, SOMATOFORM DISSOCIATION
0 = Absent
1 = Minor
2 = Moderate
3 = Severe
88 = Unclear

Part 5: PSYCHOFORM DISSOCIATIVE SYMPTOMS

AMNESIA

146 Do you generally have a good memory? YES / NO / UNCLEAR

If no:
a Can you describe any difficulties with your memory?

147 Do you ever have concentration problems? YES / NO / UNCLEAR

If yes:
a Can you give an example?

148 Are there ever periods when you have trouble remembering what you have done during the day or when you are "missing" chunks of time? YES / NO / UNCLEAR

If yes:
a Can you describe such periods?
b How often does this occur?
- ☐ Seldom
- ☐ Recurrently
- ☐ Monthly
- ☐ Weekly
- ☐ Daily
- ☐ ?

149 Are there ever periods when you have trouble remembering important events from your past? YES / NO / UNCLEAR

If yes:
a Can you give an example?
b How often do you have these memory problems?
- ☐ Seldom
- ☐ Recurrently
- ☐ Monthly
- ☐ Weekly
- ☐ Daily
- ☐ ?

c Do you have these memory problems now? YES / NO / UNCLEAR

If yes:
c-1 Can you tell me more about that?

150 Do you ever have the experience that time goes by very fast or very slowly? YES / NO / UNCLEAR

If yes:
a Can you give an example?

151 Have you ever found yourself in a place while unable to recall how you had gotten there (without being under the influence of substances)? YES / NO / UNCLEAR

If yes:
a Can you describe what happened?
b How often do you have such experiences?
  ☐ Seldom
  ☐ Recurrently
  ☐ Monthly
  ☐ Weekly
  ☐ Daily
  ☐ ?

152 Have you ever been told that you had been seen or been somewhere, without being able to remember being there yourself? YES / NO / UNCLEAR

If yes:
a Can you describe what happened?

153 Have you ever had indications or found evidence that you must have done things that you do not recall doing? YES / NO / UNCLEAR

If yes:
a Can you give an example?

154 Have you ever forgotten important personal information, such as your address, your name, or your age? YES / NO / UNCLEAR

If yes:
a Can you give an example?

155 How often do these experiences (mentioned in Questions 152–154) occur?
  ☐ Seldom
  ☐ Recurrently
  ☐ Monthly
  ☐ Weekly
  ☐ Daily
  ☐ ?

156 When you are having problems with your memory, can you usually eventually remember what you have done if you try hard? YES / NO / UNCLEAR

If yes:
Can you describe how you do this?

157 Have you ever experienced being completely unable to recall important events that you know must have happened? YES / NO / UNCLEAR

If yes:
a Can you give an example?

158 Have you ever experienced unwanted memories unexpectedly forcing themselves upon your mind even though you are trying to avoid them? YES / NO / UNCLEAR

If yes:
a Can you give an example?

159 Have you ever suddenly recalled a memory that you
had completely forgotten about?   YES / NO / UNCLEAR

If yes:
a   Can you give an example?

> **Instruction for the interviewer:** If there are no indications of memory problems, you may proceed to the next section of the interview: "Schneiderian Symptoms/Intrusions."

160 When did you first realize that you have problems with your memory or difficulties
recalling periods of time?
- ☐ In the past year
- ☐ Two to five years ago
- ☐ Longer than five years ago
- ☐ In childhood

a   Can you describe this situation?

161 Do your memory problems only occur during or after using alcohol,
drugs, or medication?   YES / NO / UNCLEAR

If yes:
a   Can you give an example?

162 Do your memory problems mainly occur when you are:

a   Under pressure/stressed?   YES / NO / UNCLEAR
b   Tired?   YES / NO / UNCLEAR
c   Dejected?   YES / NO / UNCLEAR
d   Confused?   YES / NO / UNCLEAR
e   Ill?   YES / NO / UNCLEAR
f   Anxious?   YES / NO / UNCLEAR
g   Other: _____

Can you give examples?

   Overall severity score AMNESIA
   0 = Absent
   1 = Minor
   2 = Moderate
   3 = Severe
   88 = Unclear

   Subjective distress score AMNESIA
   0 = Absent
   1 = Minor
   2 = Moderate
   3 = Severe
   88 = Unclear

SCHNEIDERIAN SYMPTOMS/INTRUSIONS

> **Instruction for the interviewer:** If it has already become obvious based on the previous parts of the interview that the patient is hearing voices, you may continue to interview the patient in keeping with that knowledge. However, make sure you ask all questions from Question 163 onward.

163 a Do you ever hear voices inside or outside your head?   YES / NO / UNCLEAR

   If yes:
   - ☐ A voice or voices inside your head?
   - ☐ A voice or voices outside your head?
   - ☐ A voice or voices both inside and outside your head?
   - ☐ Voices that sound like audible thoughts (hearing your own thoughts in your head)?

   b Can you describe the voice(s)?

> **Instruction for the interviewer:** If there are no indications that the patient is hearing voices, you may proceed to Question 179.

164 How often does this occur?
   - ☐ Seldom
   - ☐ Recurrently
   - ☐ Monthly
   - ☐ Weekly
   - ☐ Daily
   - ☐ ?

165 When did you first hear this voice / these voices?
   - ☐ Before the age of 10
   - ☐ After the age of 10
   - ☐ As an adolescent
   - ☐ As an adult
   - ☐ Following a particular stressor or incident
   - ☐ Other: _____

166 Do you hear one voice or several voices?
   - ☐ One voice
   - ☐ Several voices

167 Are there both male and female voices?   YES / NO / UNCLEAR

168 Are there also children's voices?   YES / NO / UNCLEAR

169 Do these voices talk about you among themselves without your participation?   YES / NO / UNCLEAR

   If yes:
   a Can you give an example?

170 Is there an inner discussion going on while we are
    having this interview? YES / NO / UNCLEAR

    If yes:
    a Can you describe that?

171 Do you ever hear a voice in your head that gives you orders or
    commands, or tells you what you ought to do (or ought not to do),
    or that comments on your behavior? YES / NO / UNCLEAR

    If yes:
    a Can you give an example?

172 Do you ever hear critical or punitive voices? YES / NO / UNCLEAR

    If yes:
    a Can you give an example?

173 Do you also hear voices that are kind or supportive? YES / NO / UNCLEAR

    If yes:
    a Can you give an example?

174 Do the voices have names? YES / NO / UNCLEAR

    If yes:
    a Can you give an example?

175 Have you ever heard voices outside of your head? YES / NO / UNCLEAR

    If yes:
    a Can you give an example?

176 Can other people also hear your voices? YES / NO / UNCLEAR

    If yes:
    a Can you give an example?

177 Do you think that the voices can also talk with other
    people outside yourself, for instance with a friend or with me
    (the interviewer)? YES / NO / UNCLEAR

    If yes:
    a Can you tell me more about that?

178 Do the voices have an opinion about me (the interviewer)? YES / NO / UNCLEAR

Instruction for the interviewer: Continuation following Question 163: Questions 179 and
180 may be interpreted in different ways. For example, they could refer to the feeling
of being "controlled" by dissociative parts of the personality (even if the patient has
no awareness or knowledge of dissociative parts). Possession by the devil or demons is
often also reported by patients with a dissociative disorder who grew up in/are part of a
(conservative) religious community in Western countries. Aggressive or self-injurious parts
may be understood to be demons in that case. Alternatively, non-Western patients may
also report feelings of being "possessed." In that case, it is advisable to also conduct the
Cultural Formulation Interview as included in DSM-5 (DSM-5; APA, 2013, pp. 749–759 or
DSM-5-TR; APA, 2022, pp. 860–870).

Of course, a symptom of psychosis may be involved as well (see Chapter 7 of *Assessing Trauma-Related Dissociation: With the Trauma and Dissociation Symptoms Interview (TADS-I)*, (Boon, 2023).

179 Have you ever felt that your behavior or feelings were
     influenced by something (other than an inner voice) that did
     not feel like it came from you?   YES / NO / UNCLEAR

    If yes:
    a How often does this occur?
          ☐ Seldom
          ☐ Recurrently
          ☐ Monthly
          ☐ Weekly
          ☐ Daily
          ☐ ?
    b Can you give an example?
    c Does it seem like this involves something:
       c-1 Outside yourself?   YES / NO / UNCLEAR
       c-2 Inside yourself?   YES / NO / UNCLEAR
       c-3 Other: _____
    d Can you describe this for me?

180 Have you ever had the feeling of being controlled by
     an external force or being possessed?   YES / NO / UNCLEAR

    If yes:
    a Can you give an example?

181 Have you ever received orders via the television, the computer,
     the radio, or in some other way?   YES / NO / UNCLEAR

    If yes:
    a Can you give an example?

182 Do you ever have the feeling that strange or unfamiliar
     thoughts are being put into your mind?   YES / NO / UNCLEAR

    If yes:
    a Can you give an example?

183 Do you ever have the feeling that thoughts suddenly pop up
     in your mind that do not seem to be your own?   YES / NO / UNCLEAR

    If yes:
    a Can you give an example?

184 Do you ever have (sudden) thoughts that are irrelevant
     to the current situation?   YES / NO / UNCLEAR

    If yes:
    a Can you give an example?

185 How often do these experiences (mentioned in Questions 181–184) occur?

- ☐ Seldom
- ☐ Recurrently
- ☐ Monthly
- ☐ Weekly
- ☐ Daily
- ☐ ?

186 Do you ever have the feeling that your thoughts are suddenly
removed from your head, or that your head is suddenly "empty"? YES / NO / UNCLEAR

If yes:
a How often does this occur?

- ☐ Seldom
- ☐ Recurrently
- ☐ Monthly
- ☐ Weekly
- ☐ Daily
- ☐ ?

b Can you give an example?

187 Do you ever have the feeling that your thoughts are being
broadcast so that other people can hear them? YES / NO / UNCLEAR

If yes:
a How often does this occur?

- ☐ Seldom
- ☐ Recurrently
- ☐ Monthly
- ☐ Weekly
- ☐ Daily
- ☐ ?

b Can you give an example?

188 Have you ever had sudden feelings such as sadness, anger,
or fear that seemed to come out of nowhere? YES / NO / UNCLEAR

If yes:
a How often does this occur?

- ☐ Seldom
- ☐ Recurrently
- ☐ Monthly
- ☐ Weekly
- ☐ Daily
- ☐ ?

b Can you give an example?

189 Have you ever had the experience that your feelings went away without
any obvious reason (e.g., from feeling very emotional to a state of
feeling completely numb)? YES / NO / UNCLEAR

If yes:

a How often does this occur?

- ☐ Seldom
- ☐ Recurrently
- ☐ Monthly
- ☐ Weekly
- ☐ Daily
- ☐ ?

b Can you give an example?

190 Have you ever had the experience that something inside you is
making you act in a way that is very unlike you?   YES / NO / UNCLEAR

If yes:

a Can you give an example?

Overall severity score SCHNEIDERIAN SYMPTOMS / INTRUSIONS

0 = Absent

1 = Minor

2 = Moderate

3 = Severe

88 = Unclear

Subjective distress score SCHNEIDERIAN SYMPTOMS / INTRUSIONS

0 = Absent

1 = Minor

2 = Moderate

3 = Severe

88 = Unclear

SYMPTOMS THAT (POSSIBLY) INDICATE A DIVISION OF THE PERSONALITY

191 Have you ever had the feeling that you were looking at yourself
from a distance, outside your own body?   YES / NO / UNCLEAR

If yes:

a Can you give an example?

b How often does this occur?

- ☐ Seldom
- ☐ Recurrently
- ☐ Monthly
- ☐ Weekly
- ☐ Daily
- ☐ ?

c If you are having the experience of being outside of your body,
where are you? Can you describe this?   YES / NO / UNCLEAR

d In what situations does this happen to you?

e If you are feeling as if you are outside of your body, do you see
yourself or does it feel like you are looking at another person?   YES / NO / UNCLEAR

192 Have you ever had the feeling that your body or part of your
body had changed? For example, that your body seemed to be
larger/smaller or stronger/weaker? YES / NO / UNCLEAR

If yes:
a   Can you give an example?

193 Have you ever experienced looking in a mirror and not (really)
recognizing yourself? YES / NO / UNCLEAR

If yes:
a   Can you give an example?
b   How often does this occur?
  ☐ Seldom
  ☐ Recurrently
  ☐ Monthly
  ☐ Weekly
  ☐ Daily
  ☐ ?

194 Do you ever have the experience that you do not recognize
your own house or street? YES / NO / UNCLEAR

If yes:
a   How often does this occur?
  ☐ Seldom
  ☐ Recurrently
  ☐ Monthly
  ☐ Weekly
  ☐ Daily
  ☐ ?
b   Can you give an example?

195 Have you ever been told that you did not recognize a
good friend or relative? YES / NO / UNCLEAR

If yes:
a   How often does this occur?
  ☐ Seldom
  ☐ Recurrently
  ☐ Monthly
  ☐ Weekly
  ☐ Daily
  ☐ ?
b   What did people tell you?

196 Have you ever been told that you behaved very differently
from the way you normally behave? YES / NO / UNCLEAR

If yes:
a   Can you describe what people told you?
b   Did you know what the person was referring to? YES / NO / UNCLEAR
c   How often does this occur?

☐ Seldom
☐ Recurrently
☐ Monthly
☐ Weekly
☐ Daily
☐ ?

197 Have you ever had the experience that your behavior,
tastes, or preferences suddenly change?   YES / NO / UNCLEAR

If yes:
a Can you give an example?
b Can you explain these changes?   YES / NO / UNCLEAR
c How often does this occur?
    ☐ Seldom
    ☐ Recurrently
    ☐ Monthly
    ☐ Weekly
    ☐ Daily
    ☐ ?

198 Do you ever experience inner struggles or conflicts about
what you want to do, what you feel, what you wish, what you like,
or what you expect?   YES / NO / UNCLEAR

If yes:
a How often does this occur?
    ☐ Seldom
    ☐ Recurrently
    ☐ Monthly
    ☐ Weekly
    ☐ Daily
    ☐ ?
b Can you give an example?
c Does this concern an inner struggle between:
    ☐ Two contradictory desires or opinions?
    ☐ More than two contradictory desires or opinions?
    ☐ Unclear/Other: _____

199 Do you ever experience suddenly losing certain abilities,
knowledge, or skills that you normally do possess?   YES / NO / UNCLEAR

If yes:
a How often does this occur?
    ☐ Seldom
    ☐ Recurrently
    ☐ Monthly
    ☐ Weekly
    ☐ Daily
    ☐ ?
b Can you give an example?

200 Do you ever experience suddenly having certain abilities, knowledge or skills that you do not normally possess (e.g., being able to speak a foreign language or play a musical instrument)?   YES / NO / UNCLEAR

If yes:

a   How often does this occur?
- ☐ Seldom
- ☐ Recurrently
- ☐ Monthly
- ☐ Weekly
- ☐ Daily
- ☐ ?

b   Can you give an example?

Overall severity score SYMPTOMS THAT (POSSIBLY) INDICATE A DIVISION OF THE PERSONALITY

0 = Absent
1 = Minor
2 = Moderate
3 = Severe
88 = Unclear

Subjective distress score SYMPTOMS THAT (POSSIBLY) INDICATE A DIVISION OF THE PERSONALITY

0 = Absent
1 = Minor
2 = Moderate
3 = Severe
88 = Unclear

DISSOCIATIVE PARTS OF THE PERSONALITY

Instruction for the interviewer: Questions associated with dissociative parts of the personality must only be asked if there have been clear indications over the course of the interview of the possible existence of dissociative parts of the patient's personality. For a further explanation, please refer to Chapter 5 of the book *Assessing Trauma-Related Dissociation: With the Trauma and Dissociation Symptoms Interview (TADS-I)*, (Boon, 2023).

201 Have you ever had the feeling that different parts of you exist inside you?   YES / NO / UNCLEAR

If yes:

a   Can you give an example?
b   What makes you suspect or know there are other parts of yourself?

Instruction for the interviewer: It is not uncommon for patients to feel unable or to be afraid to talk about dissociative parts of the personality, even if there is clear evidence for their existence. In such a case, you may decide to conclude the interview at this point, or to re-discuss the symptoms that indicate the existence of a dissociative part with the patient.

202 Can you tell me a bit more about those different parts or sides of your personality?

203 In what respect do these parts differ from you?
    a Can you explain?
    b Are there any parts that have a different gender to you?   YES / NO / UNCLEAR
    c Are there any parts that have a different age to you?   YES / NO / UNCLEAR
    d Do you think these parts have memories that are
       different from yours?   YES / NO / UNCLEAR

    If yes:
       d-1 What gave you that idea?

204 Do you know whether one or more parts of your personality
ever influence your behavior/thoughts/emotions without you
having any control over that?   YES / NO / UNCLEAR

    If yes:
    a Can you give an example?
    b How do you notice this?
    c Are you always able to remember this experience later?   YES / NO / UNCLEAR

205 Do you know if there are parts that take control of your behavior
and functioning in daily life (such as during shopping, taking care
of children, working)?   YES / NO / UNCLEAR

    If yes:
    a Can you describe this?

206 Do you consider such parts to belong to yourself?   YES / NO / UNCLEAR

    If yes:
    a Can you describe this?
    b How do you notice that these parts are present?
    If no:
    c Can you describe this?

APPENDIX: SUSPECTED IMITATION OF DID (OR FALSE-POSITIVE DIAGNOSIS OF DISSOCIATIVE DISORDER BY A THIRD PARTY)

> **Instruction for the interviewer:** Please ask the questions below ONLY if you suspect a false-positive diagnosis of a dissociative disorder or imitation of DID symptoms on the part of the patient. For a further explanation, please refer to Chapter 5 and Chapter 10 of the book *Assessing Trauma-Related Dissociation: With the Trauma and Dissociation Symptoms Interview (TADS-I)*, (Boon, 2023).

207 Have you ever been diagnosed as having DID by a previous
therapist / medical practitioner?   YES / NO / UNCLEAR

   If yes:
   a In what way was the diagnosis established?
   b Was a formal interview used?   YES / NO / UNCLEAR
   c Did you fill in questionnaires?   YES / NO / UNCLEAR
   d Have any therapists ever expressed doubt about this diagnosis? YES / NO / UNCLEAR
   If yes:
       d-1 Can you describe what that was like?

208 Do you think you have DID?   YES / NO / UNCLEAR

   If yes:
   a Why do you think so?

209 Have you ever read anything about the diagnosis of DID?   YES / NO / UNCLEAR

   If yes:
   a What have you read?

210 Have you ever met other people with this diagnosis?   YES / NO / UNCLEAR

   If yes:
   a How did you meet these people?

211 Do you ever go on the internet to look up information on DID?   YES / NO / UNCLEAR

   If yes:
   a Have you ever participated in a chat group with DID patients? YES / NO / UNCLEAR

212 Have you ever participated in a self-help group for DID patients? YES / NO / UNCLEAR

213 Do you have friends or relatives who think you have DID?   YES / NO / UNCLEAR

   If yes:
   a Why do they think so?
   b Do they also speak with or otherwise deal with
      other parts of your personality?   YES / NO / UNCLEAR

214 What would it mean to you if I told you that I do not think you have DID (or that I have
grave doubts as to whether you actually have DID)?

   a What would it mean to the people around you?

REFERENCES

Ainsworth, M., Blehar, M., Waters, E., & Wall, S. (1978). *Patterns of attachment*. Lawrence Erlbaum.

Akwa, G. G. Z. (2017) . Zorgstandaard conversiestoornis [Dutch Care Protocol – Conversion Disorder]. (Retrieved from www.ggzstandaarden.nl/zorgstandaarden/conversiestoornis /introductie)

Akwa, G. G. Z. (2020). Zorgstandaard dissociatieve stoornissen [Dutch Care Protocol – Conversion Disorder]. (Retrieved from www.ggzstandaarden.nl/zorgstandaarden/dissociatieve -stoornissen/introductie)

Ali, S., Jabeen, S., Pate, R. J., Shahid, M., Chinala, S., Nathani, M., & Shah, R. (2015). Conversion disorder—mind versus body: A review. *Innovations in Clinical Neuroscience, 12*(5–6), 27–33.

APA. (1980). *Diagnostic and Statistical Manual of Mental Disorders* (3rd ed., DSM-III). American Psychiatric Association.

APA. (1987). *Diagnostic and Statistical Manual of Mental Disorders*, third revised edition (DSM-III-R). American Psychiatric Association.

APA. (1994). *Diagnostic and Statistical Manual of Mental Disorders, fourth edition* (DSM-IV). American Psychiatric Association.

APA. (2013). *Diagnostic and Statistical Manual of Mental Disorders, fifth edition* (DSM-5). American Psychiatric Association.

APA. (2022). *Diagnostic and Statistical Manual of Mental Disorders, fifth edition, text revision* (DSM-5-TR). American Psychiatric Association.

Armour, C., Elklit, A., Lauterbach, D., & Elhai, J. D. (2014). The DSM-5 dissociative-PTSD subtype: Can levels of depression, anxiety, hostility, and sleeping difficulties differentiate between dissociative-PTSD and PTSD in rape and sexual assault victims? *Journal of Anxiety Disorders, 28*(4), 418–426. https://doi.org/10.1016/j.janxdis.2013.12.008

Armstrong, J. G., Putnam, F. W., Carlson, E. B., Libero, D. Z., & Smith, S. R. (1997). Development and validation of a measure of adolescent dissociation: The Adolescent Dissociative Experiences Scale. *Journal of Nervous and Mental Disease, 185*(8), 491–497.

Badouk-Epstein, O., Schwartz, J., & Schwartz, R. W. (eds.) (2018). *Ritual abuse and mind control: The manipulation of attachment needs*. Routledge/Taylor & Francis Group.

Bækkelund, H., Frewen, P., Lanius, R., Ottesen Berg, A., & Arnevik, E. A. (2018). Trauma-related altered states of consciousness in post-traumatic stress disorder patients with or without comorbid dissociative disorders, *European Journal of Psychotraumatology, 9*(1), 1544025. https://doi.org/10.1080/20008198.2018.1544025

Baker, D., Hunter, E., Lawrence, E., Medford, N., Patel, M., Senior, C., Sierra, M., Lambert, M. V., Phillips, M. L., & David, A. S. (2003). Depersonalisation disorder: clinical features of 204 cases. *British Journal of Psychiatry, 182*, 428–433.

Balint, M. (1968). *The basic fault: Therapeutic aspects of regression*. Tavistock.

Ball, J. S., & Links, P. S. (2009). Borderline personality disorder and childhood trauma: Evidence for a causal relationship. *Current Psychiatry Reports, 11*(1), 63–68.

Barach, P. M. M. (1991). Multiple personality disorder as an attachment disorder. *Dissociation: Progress in the Dissociative Disorders, 4*(3), 117–123.

Bernstein, D. P., Fink, L., Handelsman, L., & Foote, J. (1998). Initial reliability and validity of a new retrospective measure of child abuse and neglect. *American Journal of Psychiatry, 151,* 1132–1136.

Bernstein, E. M., & Putnam, F. W. (1986). Development, reliability, and validity of a dissociation scale. *Journal of Nervous and Mental Disease, 174*(12), 727–735.

Bifulco, A., Brown, G. W., & Harris, T. O. (1994). Childhood Experience of Care and Abuse (CECA): A retrospective interview measure. *Journal of Child Psychology and Psychiatry, 35*(8), 1419–1435.

Bisson, J. I., Berliner, L., Cloitre, M., Forbes, D., Jensen, T. K., Lewis, C., Monson, C. M., Olff, M., Pilling, S., Riggs, D. S., Roberts, N. P., & Shapiro, F. (2019). The International Society for Traumatic Stress Studies New Guidelines for the Prevention and Treatment of PTSD: Methodology and development process. *Journal of Traumatic Stress, 32*(4), 475–483.

Blake, D. D., Weathers, F. W., Nagy, L. M., Kaloupek, D. G., Gusman, F. D., Charney, D. S., & Keane, T. M. (1995). The development of a clinician-administered PTSD scale. *Journal of Traumatic Stress, 8*(1), 75–90. https://doi.org/10.1002/jts.2490080106

Boon, S. (1997). The treatment of traumatic memories in DID: Indications and contraindications. *Dissociation: Progress in the Dissociative Disorders, 10*(2), 65–80.

Boon, S. (2014). The treatment of clients reporting (ritual) abuse by organized perpetrator networks. *ESTD Newsletter, 3*(6), 4–13.

Boon, S., & Draijer, N. (1991). Diagnosing dissociative disorders in the Netherlands: A pilot study with the Structured Clinical Interview for DSM-III-R Dissociative Disorders. *American Journal of Psychiatry, 148*(4), 458–462.

Boon, S., & Draijer, N. (1993a). *Multiple personality disorder in the Netherlands.* Swets & Zeitlinger.

Boon, S., & Draijer, N. (1993b). Multiple personality disorder in the Netherlands: A clinical investigation of 71 patients. *American Journal of Psychiatry, 150*(3), 489–494.

Boon, S., & Draijer, N. (1993c). The differentiation of patients with MPD or DDNOS from patients with a cluster B personality disorder. *Dissociation: Progress in the Dissociative Disorders, 6*(2/3), 126–135.

Boon, S., & Draijer, N. (1995a). *Screening en diagnostiek van dissociatieve stoornissen [Screening and assessment of dissociative disorders].* Swets & Zeitlinger.

Boon, S., & Draijer, N. (1995b). Comorbiditeit bij de dissociatieve identiteitsstoornis [Comorbidity in dissociative identity disorder]. In C. A. L. Hoogduin, P. Schnabel, W. Vandereycken, K. van der Velden, & F. C. Verhulst (eds.), *Jaarboek voor psychiatrie en psychotherapie 1994–1995 [Year Book for Psychiatry and Psychotherapy 1994–1995].* Bohn Stafleu van Loghum.

Boon, S., & Draijer, N. (2003). Simulated DID: Diagnostic and treatment implications. *Proceedings of the Sixteenth Annual Fall Conference of the International Society for the Study of Trauma and Dissociation.* ISSTD.

Boon, S., & Draijer, N. (2007). Diagnostiek van dissociatieve stoornissen met de SCID-D: Mogelijkheden en beperkingen [Assessment of dissociative disorders with the SCID-D: Opportunities and limitations]. *Psychopraxis, 2007*(9), 27–32.

Boon, S., & Matthess, H. (2006). *Interview voor dissociatieve stoornissen en traumagerelateerde symptomen [Interview for dissociative disorders and trauma-related symptoms].* (Available through first author. Updated until 2012.)

Boon, S., & Matthess, H. (2016, 14 April). *The Trauma and Dissociation Symptoms Interview* [Workshop]. Fifth Biennial Conference of the European Society for the Study of Trauma and Dissociation. Amsterdam.

Boon, S., Steele, K., & van der Hart, O. (2011). *Coping with trauma-related dissociation: Skills training for patients andtTherapists.* W. W. Norton.

Boon, S., & van der Hart, O. (2022). Psychological trauma and somatoform dissociation [Not yet published].

Bowlby, J. (1969). *Attachment and loss: Vol. 1: Attachment.* Basic Books.

Bowman, E. S. (1993a). Etiology and clinical course of pseudoseizures: Relationship to trauma, depression, and dissociation. *Psychosomatics, 34*(4), 333–342.

Bowman, E. S. (1993b). Clinical and spiritual effects of exorcism in fifteen patients with multiple personality disorder. *Dissociation: Progress in the Dissociative Disorders, 6*(4), 222–238.

Bowman, E. S. (2006). Why conversion seizures should be classified as a dissociative disorder. *Psychiatric Clinics of North America, 29*, 185–211.

Braehler, C., Valiquette, L., Holowka, D., Malla, A. K., Joober, R., Ciampi, A., Pawliuk, N., & King, S. (2013). Childhood trauma and dissociation in first-episode psychosis, chronic schizophrenia and community controls. *Psychiatry Research, 210*(1), 36–42.

Brand, B. L., Armstrong, J. G., Loewenstein, R. J., & McNary, S. W. (2009). Personality differences on the Rorschach of dissociative identity disorder, borderline personality disorder, and psychotic inpatients. *Psychological Trauma: Theory, Research, Practice, and Policy, 1*(3), 188.

Brand, B. L., & Chasson, G. S. (2015). Distinguishing simulated from genuine dissociative identity disorder on the MMPI-2. *Psychological Trauma: Theory, Research, Practice, and Policy, 7*, 93–101.

Brand, B. L., Classen, C., Lanius, R., Loewenstein, R., McNary, S., Pain, C., & Putnam, F. W. (2009). A naturalistic study of dissociative identity disorder and dissociative disorder not otherwise specified patients treated by community clinicians. *Psychological Trauma: Theory, Research, Practice, and Policy, 1*, 153–171.

Brand, B. L., Dalenberg, C. J., Frewen, P. A., Loewenstein, R. J., Schielke, H. J., Brams, J. S., & Spiegel, D. (2018). Trauma-related dissociation is no fantasy: Addressing the errors of omission and commission in Merckelbach and Patihis (2018). *Psychological Injury and Law, 11*(4), 377–393.

Brand, B. L., & Frewen, P. (2017). Dissociation as a trauma-related phenomenon. In S. N. Gold (ed.), *APA handbook of trauma psychology: Vol. 1. Foundations in knowledge* (pp. 215–241). American Psychiatric Press.

Brand, B. L., & Loewenstein, R. J. (2010). Dissociative disorders: An overview of assessment, phenomenology and treatment. *Psychiatric Times, 27*(10) 62–69.

Brand, B. L., & Loewenstein, R. J. (2014). Does phasic trauma treatment make patients with dissociative identity disorder treatment more dissociative? *Journal of Trauma & Dissociation, 15*(1), 52–65.

Brand, B. L., Loewenstein, R. J., & Spiegel, D. (2014). Dispelling myths about dissociative identity disorder treatment: An empirically based approach. *Psychiatry: Interpersonal and Biological Processes, 77*(2), 169–189.

Brand, B. L., McNary, S. W., Loewenstein, R. J., Kolos, A. C., & Barr, S. R. (2006). Assessment of genuine and simulated dissociative identity disorder on the structured interview of reported symptoms. *Journal of Trauma & Dissociation, 7*(1), 63–85.

Brand, B. L., McNary, S. W., Myrick, A. C., Classen, C. C., Lanius, R., Loewenstein, R. J., & Putnam, F. W. (2013). A longitudinal naturalistic study of patients with dissociative disorders treated by community clinicians. *Psychological Trauma: Theory Research, Practice, and Policy, 5*(4), 301–308.

Brand, B. L., Şar, V., Stavropoulos, P., Krüger, C., Korzekwa, M., Martínez-Taboas, A., & Middleton, W. (2016). Separating fact from fiction: An empirical examination of six myths about dissociative identity disorder. *Harvard Review of Psychiatry, 24*(4), 257–270.

Brand, B. L., Schielke, H. J., & Brams, J. S. (2017). Assisting the courts in understanding and connecting with experiences of disconnection: Addressing trauma-related dissociation as a forensic psychologist, part I. *Psychological Injury and Law, 10*, 283–297.

Brand, B. L., Schielke, H. J., Brams, J. S., & DiComo, R. A. (2017). Assessing trauma-related dissociation in forensic contexts: Addressing trauma-related dissociation as a forensic psychologist, part II. *Psychological Injury and Law, 10*, 298–312.

Brand, B. L., Spindler, H., & Cannon, R. (2019). A Psychological assessment perspective on clinical and conceptual distinctions between dissociative disorders and psychotic disorders. In A. Moskowitz, M. J. Dorahy, & I. Schäfer (eds.), *Psychosis, trauma and dissociation: Evolving perspectives on severe psychopathology* (pp. 351–365). John Wiley & Sons.

Brand, B. L., Tursich, M., Tzall, D., & Loewenstein, R. J. (2014). Utility of the SIRS-2 in distinguishing genuine from simulated dissociative identity disorder. *Psychological Trauma: Theory, Research, Practice, and Policy, 6,* 308–317.

Brand, B. L., Vissia, E. M., Chalavi, S., Nijenhuis, E. R. S., Webermann, A. R., Draijer, N., & Reinders, A. A. T. S. (2016). DID is trauma based: Further evidence supporting the trauma model of DID. *Acta Psychiatrica Scandinavica, 134*(6), 560–563. https://doi.org/10.1111/acps.12653

Brand, B. L., Webermann, & A. R., Frankel, A. S. (2016). Assessment of complex dissociative disorder patients and simulated dissociation in forensic contexts. *International Journal of Law and Psychiatry, 49* (Part B), 197–204. https://doi.org/10.1016/j.ijlp.2016.10.006

Brand, B. L., Webermann, A. R., Snyder, B. L., & Kaliush, P. R. (2019). Detecting clinical and simulated dissociative identity disorder with the Test of Memory Malingering. *Psychological Trauma: Theory, Research, Practice, and Policy, 11*(5), 513–520. https://doi.org/10.1037/tra0000405

Brandt, J. (1988). Malingered amnesia. In R. Rogers (ed.), *Clinical assessment of malingering and deception.* Guilford Press.

Bremner, J. D., Bolus, R., & Mayer, E. A. (2007). Psychometric properties of the Early Trauma Inventory-Self Report. *Journal of Nervous and Mental Disease, 195*(3), 211–218.

Bremner, J. D., Krystal, J. H., Southwick, S. M., & Charney, D. S. (1995). Functional neuroanatomical correlates of the effects of stress on memory. *Journal of Traumatic Stress, 8*(4), 527–553.

Bremner, J. D., Krystal, J. H., Charney, D. S., & Southwick, S. M. (1996). Neural mechanisms in dissociative amnesia for childhood abuse: Relevance to the current controversy surrounding the "false memory syndrome." *American Journal of Psychiatry, 153,* 71–82.

Bremner, J. D., Vermetten, E., & Mazure, C. M. (2000). Development and preliminary psychometric properties of an instrument for the measurement of childhood trauma: The Early Trauma Inventory. *Depression & Anxiety, 12,* 1–12.

Brewin, C. R., Cloitre, M., Hyland, P., Shevlin, M., Maercker, A., Bryant, R. A., Humayun, A., Jones, L. M., Kagee, A., Rousseau, C., Somasundaram, D., Suzuki, Y., Wessely, S., van Ommeren, M., & Reed, G. M. (2017). A review of current evidence regarding the ICD-11 proposals for diagnosing PTSD and complex PTSD. *Clinical Psychology Review, 58*(Dec), 1–5.

Brick, S. S., & Chu, J. A. (1991). The simulation of multiple personalities: A case report. *Psychotherapy: Theory, Research, Practice, Training, 28*(2), 267.

Briere, J., & Spinazolla, J. (2009). Assessment of the sequelae of complex trauma: Evidence-based measures. In C. A. Courtois & J. D. Ford (eds.), *Treating complex traumatic stress disorders. An evidence-based guide* (pp. 104–123). Guilford Press.

Brown, D. P., Scheflin, A. W., & Hammond, D. C. (1998). *Memory, trauma treatment and the law.* W. W. Norton.

Brown, L. S. (2009). True drama or true trauma? Forensic trauma assessment and the challenge of detecting malingering. In P. F. Dell & J. A. O'Neil (eds.), *Dissociation and the dissociative disorders: DSM-5 and beyond* (pp. 585–594). Routledge/Taylor & Francis Group.

Brown, R. J. (2006). Different types of "dissociation" have different psychological mechanisms. *Journal of Trauma & Dissociation, 7,* 7–28.

Brown, R. J., Cardeña, E., Nijenhuis, E., Şar, V., & van der Hart, O. (2007). Should conversion disorder be reclassified as a dissociative disorder in DSM V? *Psychosomatics, 48,* 369–338.

Butler, C., Dorahy, M., & Middleton, W. (2019). The Detachment and Compartmentalization

Inventory (DCI): An assessment tool for two potentially distinct forms of dissociation, *Journal of Trauma & Dissociation, 20*(5), 526–547.

Butler, L. D. (2004). Editorial: The dissociation of everyday life. *Journal of Trauma & Dissociation, 5*(1), 1–11.

Butler, L. D. (2006). Normative Dissociation. *Psychiatric Clinics of North America, 29*, 45–62.

Cardeña, E. (1994). The domain of dissociation. In S. J. Lynn & J. W. Rhue (eds.), *Dissociation: Clinical and theoretical perspectives* (pp. 15–31). Guilford Press.

Cardeña, E., van Duijl, M., Weiner, L., & Terhune, D. B. (2009). Possession/trance phenomena. In P. F. Dell & J. A. O'Neil (eds.), *Dissociation and the dissociative disorders: DSM-5 and beyond* (pp. 171–181). Routledge/Taylor & Francis Group.

Cardeña, E., Schaffler, Y., & van Duijl, M. (2022). The other in the self: Possession, trance, and related phenomena. In M. J. Dorahy, S. N. Gold, & J. A. O'Neil (eds.) (2022). *Dissociation and the dissociative disorders: Past, present, future* (2nd ed.). Routledge/Taylor & Francis Group.

Carlson, E. B., & Armstrong, J. (1994). The diagnosis and assessment of dissociative disorders. In S. J. Lynn & J. W. Rhue (eds.), *Dissociation: Clinical and theoretical perspectives* (pp. 159–174). Guilford Press.

Carlson, E. B., Dalenberg, C., & McDade-Montez, E. (2012). Dissociation in posttraumatic stress disorder, part I: Definitions and review of research. *Psychological Trauma: Theory, Research, Practice and Policy, 4*(5): 479–489. https://doi.org/10.1037/a0027748

Carlson, E. B., Dalenberg, C., & McDade-Montez, E. (2012). "Dissociation in posttraumatic stress disorder Part 1: Definitions and review of research": Correction to Carlson, Dalenberg, and McDade-Montez (2012). *Psychological Trauma: Theory, Research, Practice, and Policy, 4*(5), 489. https://doi.org/10.1037/a0030230

Carlson, E. B., & Putnam, F. W. (1993). An update on the Dissociative Experiences Scale. *Dissociation: Progress in the Dissociative Disorders, 6*(1), 16–27.

Carlson, E. B., Putnam, F. W., Ross, C. A., Torem, M. S., Coons, P. M., Dill, D. L., Loewenstein, R. J., & Braun, B. G. (1993). Validity of the Dissociative Experience Scale in screening for multiple personality disorder: A multicenter study. *American Journal of Psychiatry, 150*(7), 1030–1036.

Carlson, E. B., Waelde, L. C., Palmieri, P. A., Macia, K. S., Smith, S. A., & McDade-Montez, E. (2018). Development and validation of the dissociative symptoms scale. *Assessment, 25*(1), 1–15. https://doi.org/10.1177/1073191116645904

Cassidy, J., & Shaver, P. R. (eds.) (1999). *Handbook of attachment: Theory, research, and clinical applications* (1st ed.). Guilford Press. (3rd ed., 2016: Guilford Press.)

Cavalletti, M., Boldrini, M. P., Catania, A., Fusco, V., Serra, N., & Tagliavini, G. (2021). Utilizzare la TADS-Interview di S. Boon e H. Matthess per la diagnosi dei Disturbi Dissociativi e Complex PTSD [Use of the TADS-Interview by S. Boon en H. Matthess for the assessment of dissociative disorders and complex PTSD]. *Rivista Sperimentale di Freniatria, 2021*(3), 79–91. https://doi.org/10.3280/RSF2021-003006

Cernovsky, Z. Z., Bureau, Y., Mendonça, J., Velamoor, V., Mann, S., Sidhu, G., Diamond, D. M., Campbell, R., Persad, E., Oyewumi, L. K., & Woodbury-Fariña, M. A. (2019). Validity of the SIMS scales of neurologic impairment and amnestic disorder. *International Journal of Psychiatry Sciences, 1*(1), 13–19.

Cernovsky, Z. Z., & Diamond, D. (2020). High risk of false classification of injured people as malingerers by the Structured Inventory of Malingered Symptomatology (SIMS): A Review. *Archives of Psychiatry and Behavioral Sciences, 3*(2), 30–38.

Cernovsky, Z. Z., Mendonça, J. D., Bureau, Y. R., & Ferrari, J. R. (2019). Criterion validity of low intelligence scale of the SIMS. *International Journal of Psychology Sciences, 1*(1), 3–5.

Cernovsky, Z. Z., Mendonça, J. D., Ferrari, J. R., Sidhu, G., Velamoor, V., Mann, S. C., Oyewumi, L. K., Persad, E., Campbell, R., & Woodbury-Fariña, M. A. (2019). Content validity of the Affective Disorder Subscale of the SIMS. *Archives of Psychiatry and Behavioral Sciences, 2*(2), 33–39.

Cernovsky, Z. Z., Mendonça, J. D., Oyewumi, L. K., Ferrari, J. J., Sidhu, G. S., & Campbell, R. (2019). Content validity of the Psychosis Subscale of the Structured Inventory of Malingered Symptomatology (SIMS). *International Journal of Psychology and Cognitive Science, 5*(3), 121–127.

Chu, J. A. (1991). On the misdiagnosis of multiple personality disorder. *Dissociation: Progress in the Dissociative Disorders, 4*(4), 200–204.

Cima, M., Merckelbach, H., Hollnack, S., & Knauer, E. (2003). Characteristics of psychiatric prison inmates who claim amnesia. *Personality and Individual Differences, 35*(2), 373–380.

Cima, M., Nijman, H., Merckelbach, H., Kremer, K., & Hollnack, S. (2004). Claims of crime-related amnesia in forensic patients. *International Journal of Law and Psychiatry, 27*(3), 215–221.

Cloitre, M. (2020). ICD-11 complex post-traumatic stress disorder: Simplifying diagnosis in trauma populations. *British Journal of Psychiatry, 216*(3), 129–131.

Cloitre, M., Courtois, C. A., Charuvastra, A., Carapezza, R., Stolbach, B. C., & Green, B. L. (2011). Treatment of complex PTSD: Results of the ISTSS expert clinician survey on best practices. *Journal of Traumatic Stress, 24*(6), 615–627. https://doi.org/10.1002/jts.20697

Cloitre, M., Courtois, C. A., Ford, J. D., Green, B. L., Alexander, P., Briere, J., Herman, J. L., Lanius, R., Stolbach, B. C., Spinazzola, J., van der Kolk, B. A., & van der Hart, O. (2012). *The ISTSS Expert Consensus Treatment Guidelines for Complex PTSD in Adults.* Retrieved on July 14, 2022 at https://istss.org/ISTSS_Main/media/Documents/ComplexPTSD.pdf

Cloitre, M., Garvert, D. W., Brewin, C. R., Bryant, R. A., & Maercker, A. (2013). Evidence for proposed ICD-11 PTSD and complex PTSD: A latent profile analysis. *European Journal of Psychotraumatology, 4*(1), 20706. https://doi.org/10.3402/ejpt.v4i0.20706

Cloitre, M., Garvert, D. W., Weiss, B., Carlson, E. B., & Bryant, R. A. (2014). Distinguishing PTSD, complex PTSD, and borderline personality disorder: A latent class analysis. *European Journal of Psychotraumatology, 5*(1), 25097. https://doi.org/10.3402/ejpt.v5.25097

Cloitre, M., Shevlin, M., Brewin, C. R., Bisson, J. I., Roberts, N. P., Maercker, A., Karatzias, T., & Hyland, P. (2018). The International Trauma Questionnaire: Development of a self-report measure of ICD-11 PTSD and complex PTSD. *Acta Psychiatrica Scandinavica, 138*(6), 536–546.

Coons, P. M. (1978). Examples of pseudomultiplicity. *Memos on Multiplicity, 2*(3), 4–5.

Coons, P. M. (1984). The differential diagnosis of multiple personality: A comprehensive review. *Psychiatric Clinics of North America, 7,* 51–65.

Coons, P. M. (1988). Misuse of forensic hypnosis: A hypnotically elicited false confession with the apparent creation of a multiple personality. *International Journal of Clinical and Experimental Hypnosis, 36,* 1–11.

Coons, P. M. (1989). Iatrogenic factors in the misdiagnosis of multiple personality disorder. *Dissociation: Progress in the Dissociative Disorders, 2*(2), 70–76.

Coons, P. M. (1991). Iatrogenesis and malingering of multiple personality disorder in the forensic evaluation of homicide defendants. *Psychiatric Clinics of North America, 14*(3), 757–768.

Coons, P. M., & Bowman, E. A. S. (2001). Ten-year follow-up study of patients with dissociative identity disorder. *Journal of Trauma & Dissociation, 2*(1), 73–89.

Coons, P. M., Bowman, E. A. S., & Milstein, V. (1988). Multiple personality disorder: A clinical investigation of 50 cases. *The Journal of Nervous and Mental Disease, 176,* 519-527.

Coons, P. M., & Milstein, V. (1992). Psychogenic amnesia: A clinical investigation of 25 cases. *Dissociation: Progress in the Dissociative Disorders, 5*(2), 73–79.

Coons, P. M., & Milstein, V. (1994). Factitious or malingered multiple personality disorder: Eleven cases. *Dissociation: Progress in the Dissociative Disorders, 7*(2), 81–85.

Courtois, C. A., & Ford, J. D. (eds.) (2009). *Treating complex traumatic stress disorder: An evidence-based guide*. Guilford Press.

Dalenberg, C. J. (2000). *Countertransference and the treatment of trauma*. American Psychological Association.

Dalenberg, C. J., Brand, B., Gleaves, D., Dorahy, M., Loewenstein, R., Cardeña, E., Frewen, P., Carlson, E., & Spiegel, D. (2012). Evaluation of the evidence for the trauma and fantasy models of dissociation. *Psychological Bulletin, 138*(3), 550–588. https://doi.org/10.1037/a0027447

Dalenberg, C. J., Brand, B. L., Loewenstein, R. J., Gleaves, D. H., Dorahy, M. J., Cardeña, E., Frewen, P. A., Carlson, E., & Spiegel, D. (2014). Reality versus fantasy: Reply to Lynn et al. (2014). *Psychological Bulletin, 140*(3), 911–920.

Dalenberg, C. J., Brand, B. L., Loewenstein, R. J., Frewen, P. A., & Spiegel, D. (2020). Inviting scientific discourse on traumatic dissociation: Progress made and obstacles to further resolution. *Psychological Injury and Law, 13*(2), 135–154 (2020). https://doi.org/10.1007/s12207-020-09376-9

Dalenberg, C., Katz, R. R., Thompson, K. J., & Paulson, K. (2022). The case study for "normal" dissociation processes. In M. J. Dorahy, S. N. Gold, & J. A. O'Neil (eds.) (2022). *Dissociation and the dissociative disorders: Past, present, future* (2nd ed.). Routledge/Taylor & Francis Group.

Dalenberg, C. J., Paulson, K. (2009). The case for the study of "normal" dissociation processes. In P. F. Dell & J. A. O'Neil (eds.), *Dissociation and the dissociative disorders: DSM-5 and beyond* (pp. 145–154). Routledge/Taylor & Francis Group.

De Waal, M. W., Arnold, I. A., Eekhof, J. A., & van Hemert, A. M. (2004). Somatoform disorders in general practice: Prevalence, functional impairment and comorbidity with anxiety and depressive disorders. *British Journal of Psychiatry, 184*, 470–476. https://doi.org/10.1192/bjp.184.6.470

Delbo, C. (1990). *Days and memory*. The Marlboro Press/Northwestern University Press. (Translation of *Mesure de nos jours*, 1971.)

Dell, P. F. (1998). Axis II pathology in outpatients with dissociative identity disorder. *Journal of Nervous and Mental Disease, 186*(6), 352–356.

Dell, P. F. (2002). Dissociative phenomenology of dissociative identity disorder. *Journal of Nervous and Mental Disease, 190*(1), 10–15.

Dell, P. F. (2006a). A new model of dissociative identity disorder. *Psychiatric Clinics of North America, 29*(1), 1–26.

Dell, P. F. (2006b). The Multidimensional Inventory of Dissociation (MID): A comprehensive measure of pathological dissociation. *Journal of Trauma & Dissociation, 7*(2), 77–106.

Dell, P. F. (2009a). The long struggle to diagnose multiple personality disorder (MPD): MPD. In P. F. Dell & J. A. O'Neil (eds.), *Dissociation and the dissociative disorders: DSM-5 and beyond* (pp. 383–402). Routledge/Taylor & Francis Group.

Dell, P. F. (2009b). The long struggle to diagnose multiple personality disorder (MPD): Partial MPD. In P. F. Dell & J. A. O'Neil (eds.), *Dissociation and the dissociative disorders: DSM-5 and beyond* (pp. 403–428). Routledge/Taylor & Francis Group.

Dell, P. F., & O'Neil, J. A. (eds.) (2009). *Dissociation and the dissociative disorders: DSM-5 and beyond*. Routledge/Taylor & Francis Group.

Dinwiddie, S. H., North, C. S., & Yutzy, S. H. (1993). Multiple personality disorder: Scientific and medicolegal issues. *Journal of the American Academy of Psychiatry and the Law Online, 21*(1), 69–79.

Dorahy, M. J., Brand, B. L., Şar, V., Krüger, C., Stavropoulos, P., Martínez-Taboas, A., Lewis-Fernández, R., & Middleton, W. (2014). Dissociative identity disorder: An empirical overview. *Australian & New Zealand Journal of Psychiatry, 48*(5), 402–417.

Dorahy, M. J., Gold, S. N., & O'Neil, J. A. (eds.) (2022). *Dissociation and the dissociative disorders: Past, present, future* (2nd ed.). Routledge/Taylor & Francis Group.

Dorahy, M. J., Shannon, C., Seagar, L., Corr, M., Stewart, K., Hanna, D., Mulholland, C., & Middleton, W. (2009). Auditory hallucinations in dissociative identity disorder and schizophrenia with and without a childhood trauma history: Similarities and differences. *Journal of Nervous and Mental Disease, 197*(12), 892–898.

Dorahy, M., & van der Hart, O. (2015). DSM-5's "PTSD with dissociative symptoms": Challenges and future directions. *Journal of Trauma & Dissociation, 16*(1), 7–28. https://doi .org/10.1080/15299732.2014.908806

Draijer, N. (1988). *Seksueel misbruik van meisjes door verwanten [Sexual abuse of girls by relatives]*. Ministerie van Sociale Zaken en Werkgelegenheid [Dutch ministry of social affairs and employment].

Draijer, N. (1990). *Seksuele traumatisering in de jeugd. Gevolgen op lange termijn van seksueel misbruik van meisjes door verwanten [Childhood sexual traumatization. Long term consequences of sexual abuse of girls by relatives]* [Thesis]. Singel Uitgevers.

Draijer, N. (1994). Dissociatie en trauma bij psychiatrische patiënten. Een onderzoek [Dissociation and trauma in psychiatric patients. A study. *Journal of Mental Disease*]. *Maandblad Geestelijke Volksgezondheid, 49*(8), 811–828.

Draijer, N. (2003). Diagnostiek en indicatiestelling bij (een vermoeden van) seksueel misbruik in de voorgeschiedenis: State of the art [Assessment and indication in (suspected) history of sexual abuse: State of the art]. In N. Nicolai (ed.), *Handboek psychotherapie na seksueel misbruik* (pp. 21–45). De Tijdstroom.

Draijer, N. (2008). Een razend verlangen naar betekenis. Over hysterie bij een borderline organisatie van de persoonlijkheid [A raging desire for meaning. On hysteria in a borderline organization of the personality]. In J. Dirkx & W. Heuves (eds.), *Hysterie: Psychoanalytische beschouwingen* (pp. 83–99). Boom Uitgevers.

Draijer, N., & Boon, S. (1993a). Trauma, dissociation and dissociative disorders. In S. Boon & N. Draijer, *Multiple personality disorder in the Netherlands* (pp. 177–194). Swets & Zeitlinger.

Draijer, N., & Boon, S. (1993b). The validation of the Dissociative Experiences Scale against the criterion of the SCID-D, using receiver operating characteristics (ROC) analysis. *Dissociation: Progress in the Dissociative Disorders, 6*(1), 28–37.

Draijer, N., & Boon, S. (1995). De anamnese van traumatische jeugdervaringen [The assessment of childhood traumatic experiences]. In S. Boon & N. Draijer, *Screening en diagnostiek van dissociatieve stoornissen* (pp. 119–128). Swets & Zeitlinger.

Draijer, N., & Boon, S. (1996). Knelpunten in de differentiële diagnostiek van de dissociatieve identiteitsstoornis [Difficulties in the differential diagnosis of dissociative identity disorder]. *Tijdschrift voor Psychiatrie, 1996*(2), 108–122.

Draijer, N., & Boon, S. (1999). The imitation of dissociative identity disorder: Patients at risk, therapists at risk. *Journal of Psychiatry & Law, 27,* 423–458. https://doi.org/10 .1177/009318539902700304

Draijer, N., & Langeland, W. (1999). Childhood trauma and perceived parental dysfunction in the etiology of dissociative symptoms in psychiatric inpatients. *American Journal of Psychiatry, 156*(3), 379–385.

Draijer, N., & Langeland, W. (2009). Trauma, hechting en verwaarlozing: Een tweedimensionaal model voor diagnostiek en indicatiestelling bij vroegkinderlijke traumatisering [Trauma, attachment and negligence: A two-dimensional model for the assessment and indication in early childhood traumatization]. *Cogiscope, 4,* 31–38.

Draijer, N., Langeland, W., & Boon, S. (2012). Klinische diagnostiek van complexe traumagerelateerde stoornissen [Clinical assessment of complex trauma-related disorders]. In E. Vermetten, R, Kleber, & O. van der Hart (eds.), *Handboek Postttraumatische stressstoornissen* (pp. 491–510). De Tijdstroom.

Draijer, N., & van Zon, P. (2013). Transference-focused psychotherapy with former child soldiers: Meeting the murderous self. *Journal of Trauma & Dissociation, 14,* 170–183.

Dubester, K. A., & Braun, B. G. (1995). Psychometric properties of the Dissociative Experiences Scale. *Journal of Nervous and Mental Disease, 183,* 231–235.

Dunn, G. E., Ryan, J. J., & Paolo, A. M. (1995). A principal components analysis of the Dissociative Experiences Scale in a substance abuse population. *Journal of Clinical Psychology, 50*(6), 936–940.

During, E. H., Elahi, F. M., Taieb, O., Moro, M. R., & Baubet, T. (2011). A critical review of dissociative trance and possession disorders: Etiological, diagnostic, therapeutic, and nosological issues. *Canadian Journal of Psychiatry, 56*(4), 235–242. https://doi.org/10.1177/070674371105600407

Dutra, L., Bureau, J., Holmes, B., Lyubchik, A., & Lyons-Ruth, K. (2009). Quality of early care and childhood trauma: A prospective study of developmental pathways to dissociation. *Journal of Nervous and Mental Disease, 197*(6), 383–390. https://doi.org/10.1097/NMD.0b013rd3181a653b7

Eisendrath, S. J. (1995). Psychiatric aspects of chronic pain. *Neurology, 45*(12), 26–34.

Ellason, J. W., Ross, C. A. (1995). Positive and negative symptoms in dissociative identity disorder and schizophrenia: A comparative analysis. *Journal of Nervous and Mental Disease, 183*(4), 236–241.

Ellason, J. W., Ross, C. A., & Fuchs, D. L. (1996). Lifetime axis I and II comorbidity and childhood trauma history in dissociative identity disorder. *Psychiatry, 59*(3), 255–266.

Ensink, B. J., & van Otterloo, D. (1989). A validation study of the DES in the Netherlands. *Dissociation: Progress in the Dissociative Disorders, 2*(4), 221–223.

Espirito Santo, H., & Pio-Abreu, J. (2009). Portuguese validation of the Dissociative Experiences Scale (DES). *Journal of Trauma & Dissociation, 10*(1), 69–82. https://doi.org/10.1080/15299730802485177, Available through SSRN: https://ssrn.com/abstract=2999136

Everaerd, W., & Gersons-Wolfensberger, D. C. M. (2004). Commentaar op advies van gezondheidsraad op hervonden herinneringen [Comments on Health Council advice on recovered memories]. *Nederlands Tijdschrift voor Geneeskunde, 148*(33), 1620–1622.

Evren, C., Şar, V., Karadag, F., Gurol, D. T., & Karagoz, M. (2007). Dissociative disorders among alcohol-dependent inpatients. *Psychiatry Research, 152*(2–3), 233–241.

Farina, B., Liotti, M., & Imperatori, C. (2019). The role of attachment trauma and disintegrative pathogenic processes in the traumatic-dissociation dimension. *Frontiers in Psychology, Section Psychology for Clinical Settings, 2019*(10), 00933. https://doi.org/10.3389/fpsyg.2019.00933

Fonagy, P., Luyten, P., & Bateman, A. (2015). Translation: Mentalizing as treatment target in borderline personality disorder. *Personality Disorders: Theory, Research, and Treatment, 6*(4) 380–392. https://doi.org/10.1037/per0000113

Fonagy, P., & Target, M. (1997). Attachment and reflective function: Their role in self-organization. *Development and Psychopathology, 9,* 679–700.

Fonagy, P., & Target, M. (2002). Early intervention and the development of self-regulation. *Psychoanalytic Inquiry, 22*(3), 307–335.

Foote, B., & Park, J. (2008). Dissociative identity disorder and schizophrenia: Differential diagnosis and theoretical issues. *Current Psychiatry Reports, 10*(3), 217–222.

Foote, B., Smolin, Y., Kaplan, M., Legatt, M. E., & Lipschitz, D. (2006). Prevalence of dissociative disorders in psychiatric outpatients. *American Journal of Psychiatry, 163*(4), 623–629. https://doi.org/10.1176/appi.ajp.163.4.623

Foote, B., Smolin, Y., Neft, D., & Lipschitz, D. (2008). Dissociative disorders and suicidality in psychiatric outpatients. *Journal of Nervous and Mental Disease, 196,* 29–36.

Ford, J. D., & Courtois, C. A. (eds.) (2020). *Treating complex traumatic stress disorders in adults.* Guilford Press.

Ford, J. D., & Courtois, C. A. (2021). Complex PTSD and borderline personality disorder. *Borderline Personality Disorder and Emotion Dysregulation, 8*(1), 1–21.

Ford, J. D., Courtois, C. A., Steele, K., van der Hart, O., & Nijenhuis, E. R. S. (2005). Treatment of complex posttraumatic self-dysregulation. *Journal of Traumatic Stress, 18,* 437–447.

Frankel, A. S. (2009). Dissociation and dissociative disorders: Clinical and forensic assessment with adults. In P. F. Dell & J. A. O'Neil (eds.), *Dissociation and the dissociative disorders: DSM-5 and beyond* (pp. 571–583). Routledge/Taylor & Francis Group.

Frankel, A. S., & Dalenberg, C. (2006). The forensic evaluation of dissociation and persons with dissociative identity disorder: Searching for convergence. *Psychiatric Clinics of North America, 29,* 169–184.

Fraser, G. A. (1993). Exorcism rituals: Effects on multiple personality disorder patients. *Dissociation: Progress in the Dissociative Disorders, 6*(4), 239–244.

Frewen, P. A. (2021, April). *The relevance of dissociation in PTSD: Subtype, comorbidity, or component?* [Webinar]. ESTD.

Frewen, P. A., Brown, M. F. D., & Lanius, R. A. (2017). Trauma-related altered states of consciousness (TRASC) in an online community sample: Further support for the 4-D model of trauma-related dissociation. *Psychology of Consciousness: Theory, Research, and Practice, 4*(1), 92–114.

Frewen, P. A., Hegadoren, K., Coupland, N. J., Rowe, B. H., Neufeld, R. W., & Lanius, R. (2015). Trauma-Related Altered States of Consciousness (TRASC) and functional impairment I: Prospective study in acutely traumatized persons. *Journal of Trauma & Dissociation, 16*(5), 500–519.

Frewen, P. A., & Lanius, R. A. (2014). Trauma-related altered states of consciousness: Exploring the 4-D model. *Journal of Trauma & Dissociation, 15*(4), 436–456.

Frewen, P. A., & Lanius, R. A. (2015). *Healing the traumatized self: Consciousness, neuroscience, treatment* (1st ed.). W. W. Norton.

Freyd, J. J. (1994). Betrayal trauma: Traumatic amnesia as an adaptive response to childhood abuse. *Ethics & Behavior, 4*(4), 307–329.

Friedl, M., & Draijer, N. (2000). Dissociative disorders in Dutch psychiatric inpatients. *American Journal of Psychiatry, 157,* 1012–1013.

Friedl, M. C., Draijer, N., & De Jong, P. (2000). Prevalence of dissociative disorders in psychiatric in-patients: The impact of study characteristics. *Acta Psychiatrica Scandindinavica, 102,* 423–428.

Frischholz, E. J., Braun, B. G., Sachs, R. G., Hopkins, L., Shaeffer, D. M., Lewis, J., Leavitt, F., Pasquotto, J. N., & Schwartz, D. R. (1990). The Dissociative Experiences Scale: Further replication and validation. *Dissociation: Progress in the Dissociative Disorders, 3*(3), 151–153.

Frischholz, E. J., Braun, B. G., Sachs, R. G., Schwartz, D. R., Lewis, J., Schaeffer, D., Westergaard, C., & Pasquotto, J. (1991). Construct validity of the Dissociative Experiences Scale (DES): 1. The relationship between the DES and other self-report instruments. *Dissociation: Progress in the Dissociative Disorders, 4,* 185–188.

Fromm, E. (1965). Hypnoanalysis: Theory and two case excerpts. *Psychotherapy: Theory, Research and Practice, 2,* 127–133.

Gast, U., Oswald, P., Zündorf, F., & Hofmann, A. (2000). *Das strukturierte klinische Interview für DSM-IV-Dissoziative Störungen. Interview und Manual* [The structured clinical interview for dissociative disorders in DSM-IV: Interview and manual]. Hogrefe.

Gast, U., Rodewald, F., Dehner-Rau, C., Kowalewsky, E., Engl, V., Reddemann, L., & Emrich, H. M. (2003). *Validity and reliability of the German version of the Multidimensional Inventory of Dissociation (MID-D): Preliminary results* [Paper and presentation]. 2003 Conference of the International Society for the Study of Trauma and Dissociation.

Gast, U., Rodewald, F., Nickel, V., & Emrich, H. M. (2001). Prevalence of dissociative disorders among psychiatric patients in a German university clinic. *Journal of Nervous and Mental Disease, 189,* 249–257.

Gezondheidsraad (2004). *Omstreden herinneringen [Contested memories]* [Advice to the Minister of Health, Welfare and Sport]. Publication nr 2004/02. Gezondheidsraad, onafhankelijk wetenschappelijk adviesorgaan voor regering en parlement [Health Council, independent scientific advisory body to the Dutch government and parliament]. https://tinyurl.com/mr3hsjwv

Giesbrecht, T., Lynn, S. J., Lilienfeld, S. O., & Merckelbach, H. (2008). Cognitive processes in dissociation: An analysis of core theoretical assumptions. *Psychological Bulletin, 134*(5), 617–647. https://doi.org/10.1037/0033-2909.134.5.617

Ginzburg, K., Koopman, C., Butler, L. D., Palesh, O., Kraemer, H. C., Classen, C. C., & Spiegel, D. (2006). Evidence for a dissociative subtype of post-traumatic stress disorder among help-seeking childhood sexual abuse survivors. *Journal of Trauma & Dissociation, 7*(2), 7–27.

Goodwin, J., Hill, S., & Attias, R. (1990). Historical and folk techniques of exorcism: Applications to the treatment of dissociative disorders. *Dissociation: Progress in the Dissociative Disorders, 3*, 94–101.

Gysi, J. (2020). *Diagnostik von Traumafolgestörungen: Multiaxiales Trauma-Dissoziations-Modell nach ICD-11* [Assessment of disorders caused by trauma: Multiaxial Trauma-Dissociation-Model in accordance with the ICD-11]. Hogrefe.

Hansen, M., Ross, J., & Armour, C. (2017). Evidence of the dissociative PTSD subtype: A systematic literature review of latent class and profile analytic studies of PTSD. *Journal of Affective Disorders, 213*, 59–69. https://doi.org/10.1016/j.jad.2017.02.004

Harte, F. M. (2004). Het wetenschappelijk onderzoek [Scientific research]. In F. Koenraadt, A. M. W. Mooij, & G. M. Mulbregt (eds.), *De persoon van de verdachte: De rapportage pro Justitia vanuit het Pieter Baan Centrum [The person of the suspect: The report pro justitia from the Pieter Baan Centre]*. Wolters Kluwer.

Hecker, T., Braitmayer, L., & van Duijl, M. (2015). Global mental health and trauma exposure: The current evidence for the relationship between traumatic experiences and spirit possession, *European Journal of Psychotraumatology, 6*, 1. https://doi.org/10.3402/ejpt.v6.29126

Herman, J. L. (1990). Discussion. In R. P. Kluft (ed.), *Incest-related syndromes of adult psychopathology* (pp. 289–293). American Psychiatric Press.

Herman, J. L. (1992a). Complex PTSD: A syndrome in survivors of prolonged and repeated trauma. *Journal of Traumatic Stress, 5*(3), 377–391.

Herman, J. L. (1992b). *Trauma and recovery: The aftermath of violence: From domestic abuse to political terror.* Basic Books.

Herman, J. L., Perry, C., & van der Kolk, B. A. (1989). Childhood trauma in borderline personality disorder. *American Journal of Psychiatry, 146*, 490–495.

Herman, J. L., & van der Kolk, B. A. (1987). Traumatic antecedents of borderline personality disorder. In B. van der Kolk (ed.), *Psychological trauma* (pp. 111–126). American Psychiatric Press.

Holmes, E. A., Brown, R. J., Mansell, W., Fearon, R. P., Hunter, E. C., Frasquilho, F., & Oakley, D. A. (2005). Are there two qualitatively distinct forms of dissociation? A review and some clinical implications. *Clinical Psychology Review, 25*(1), 1–23.

Holtgraves, T., & Stockdale, G. (1997). The assessment of dissociative experiences in a non-clinical population: Reliability, validity, and factor structure of the Dissociative Experiences Scale. *Personality and Individual Differences, 22*(5), 699–706.

Horevitz, R. P., & Braun, B. G. (1984). Are multiple personalities borderline? An analysis of 33 cases. *Psychiatric Clinics of North America, 7*(1), 69–87.

Horevitz, R., & Loewenstein, R. J. (1994). The rational treatment of multiple personality disorder. In S. J. Lynn & J. W. Rhue (eds.), *Dissociation: Clinical and theoretical perspectives* (pp. 289–316). Guilford Press.

Howell, E. F., & Blizard, R. A. (2009). Chronic relational trauma disorder: A new diagnostic scheme for borderline personality and the spectrum of dissociative disorders. In P. Dell & J. O' Neil (eds.), *Dissociation and the dissociative disorders: DSM-5 and beyond*. Routledge/Taylor & Francis Group.

Hulme, P. A. (2004). Retrospective measurement of childhood sexual abuse: A review of instruments. *Child Maltreatment, 9,* 201–217.

Hunter, E. C., Charlton, J., & David, A. S. (2017). Depersonalisation and derealisation: Assessment and management. *British Medical Journal, 356*(j745). https://doi.org/10.1136/bmj.j745

Hunter, E. C., Sierra, M., & David, A. S. (2004). The epidemiology of depersonalisation and derealisation. A systematic review. *Social Psychiatry and Psychiatric Epidemiology, 39,* 9–18.

Huntjens, R. J. C., Rijkeboer, M. M., & Arnzt, A. (2019a). Schema therapy for dissociative identity disorder (DID): Rationale and study protocol. *European Journal of Psychotraumatology, 10*(1), 1571377. www.ncbi.nlm.nih.gov/pmc/articles/PMC6383624/

Huntjens, R. J. C., Rijkeboer, M. M., & Arntz, A. (2019b). Schema therapy for dissociative identity disorder (DID): Further explanation about the rationale and study protocol. *European Journal of Psychotraumatology, 10*(1), 1684629. https://doi.org/10.1080/20008198.2019. 1684629

Huntjens, R. J. C., Rijkeboer, M. M., & Arntz, A. (2020). Schematherapy in DID: Treatment length and related studies on dissociative amnesia. *European Journal of Psychotraumatology, 11*(1), 1711638. https://doi.org/ 10.1080/20008198.2020.1711638

Hyland, P., Karatzias, T., Shevlin, M., & Cloitre, M. (2019). Examining the discriminant validity of complex posttraumatic stress disorder and borderline personality disorder symptoms: Results from a United Kingdom population sample. *Journal of Traumatic Stress, 32*(6), 855–863.

Hyland, P., Shevlin, M., Fyvie, C., Cloitre, M., & Karatzias, T. (2019). The relationship between ICD-11 PTSD, complex PTSD and dissociative experiences. *Journal of Trauma & Dissociation.* https://doi.org/10.1080/15299732.2019.1675113

International Society for the Study of Trauma and Dissociation [ISSTD] (2011). Guidelines for treating dissociative identity disorder in adults, third revision. *Journal of Trauma & Dissociation, 12,* 115–187.

Janet, P. (1889). *L'automatisme psychologique: Essai de psychologie exp é rimentale sur les formes inf é rieures de l'activit é humaine.* Paris: Félix Alcan. Reprint: Paris: Société Pierre Janet, 1973. English edition: *Catalepsy, memory and suggestion in psychological automatism and subconscious acts, anesthesias and psychological disaggregation in psychological automatism.* New York/London: Routledge, 2021.

Janet, P. (1894/5). Un cas de possession et l'exorcisme moderne [A case of possession and modern exorcism]. *Bulletin de l'Université de Lyon,* Dec. 1894–Jan. 1895, 41–57. Also in P. Janet (1898). *Névroses et idées fixes* [Neuroses and idée fixes] (Vol. 1, pp. 375–406). Félix Alcan.

Janet, P. (1898). Le traitement psychologique de l'hystérie. [The psychological treatment of hysteria]. In A. Robin (ed.), *Traité de thérapeutique appliqué* [Treatise on applied therapeutica] (pp. 140–216). Rueff. Also in P. Janet (1911), *L'état mental des hystériques* [The mental state of hysterici] (pp. 619–688). Félix Alcan.

Janet, P. (1907). *The major symptoms of hysteria.* Macmillan. (Reissue of the edition of 1920, 1965. Hafner.)

Janet, P. (1935). Réalisation et interprétation [Realisation and interpretation]. *Annales Médico-Psychologiques, 15*(2), 329–366.

Karadag, F., Şar, V., Tamar-Gurol, D., Evren, C., Karagoz, M., & Erkiran, M. (2005). Dissociative disorders among inpatients with drug or alcohol dependency. *Journal of Clinical Psychiatry, 66*(10), 1247–1253.

Kate, M. A., Jamieson, G., Dorahy, M. J., & Middleton, W. (2021). Measuring dissociative symptoms and experiences in an Australian college sample using a short version of the Multidimensional Inventory of Dissociation. *Journal of Trauma & Dissociation, 22*(3), 265–287.

Kempes, M., & Gelissen, N. (2021). Het wetenschappelijk onderzoek [Scientific research]. In T. den Boer, J. E. Beekman, & F. Koenraadt (eds.), *De persoon van de verdachte: De rapportage pro Justitia vanuit het Pieter Baan Centrum [The person of the suspect: The report pro justitia from the Pieter Baan Centre]* (pp. 235–257). Boom Uitgevers.

Kihlstrom, J. F. (1992). Dissociative and conversion disorders. In D. J. Stein & J. E. Young (eds.), *Cognitive science and clinical disorders* (pp. 247–270). Academic Press.

Kihlstrom, J. F., Tataryn, D. J., & Hoyt, I. P. (1993). Dissociative disorders. In P. J. Sutker & H. E. Adams (eds.), *Comprehensive handbook of psychopathology* (2nd ed., pp. 203–234). Plenum.

Kluft, R. P. (1984). An Introduction to multiple personality disorder. *Psychiatric Annals, 14,* 19–24.

Kluft, R. P. (1985). Natural history of multiple personality disorder. In R. P. Kluft (ed.), *Childhood antecedents of multiple personality.* American Psychiatric Press.

Kluft, R. P. (1987a). First-rank symptoms as a diagnostic clue to multiple personality disorder, *American Journal of Psychiatry, 144*(3), 293–298.

Kluft, R. P. (1987b). The simulation and dissimulation of multiple personality disorder. *American Journal of Clinical Hypnosis, 30*(2), 104–118.

Kluft, R. P. (1987c). An update on multiple personality disorder. *Hospital and Community Psychiatry, 38,* 363–373.

Kluft, R. P. (1988). The phenomenology and treatment of extremely complex multiple personality disorder. *Dissociation: Progress in the Dissociative Disorders, 1*(4), 47–58.

Kluft, R. P. (1989). Iatrogenic creation of new alter personalities. *Dissociation: Progress in the Dissociative Disorders, 2,* 83–91.

Kluft, R. P. (1991). Multiple personality disorder. In A. Tasman & S. M. Goldfinger (eds.), *The American Psychiatric Press Annual Review* (Vol. 10, pp. 161–188). American Psychiatric Press.

Kluft, R. P. (1993). Multiple personality disorder. In D. Spiegel (ed.), *Dissociative disorders: A clinical review* (pp. 17–44). Sidran Press.

Kluft, R. P. (1994). Treatment trajectories in multiple personality disorder. *Dissociation: Progress in the Dissociative Disorders, 7*(1), 63–76.

Kluft, R. P. (2006). Dealing with alters: A pragmatic clinical perspective. *Psychiatric Clinics of North America, 29*(1), 281–304. https://doi.org/10.1016/j.psc.2005.10.010

Kluft, R. P., Steinberg, M., & Spitzer, R. L. (1988). DSM-III-R revisions in the dissociative disorders: An exploration of their derivation and rationale. *Dissociation: Progress in the Dissociative Disorders, 1*(1), 39–46.

Korzekwa, M., & Dell, P. (2022). Is dissociation an integral aspect of borderline personality disorder, or is it a comorbid disorder? In M. J. Dorahy, S. N. Gold, & J. A. O'Neil (eds.) (2022). *Dissociation and the dissociative disorders: Past, present, future* (2nd ed.). Routledge/Taylor & Francis Group.

Korzekwa, M., Dell, P., Links, P., Thabane, L., & Fougere, P. (2009). Dissociation in borderline personality disorder: A detailed look. *Journal of Trauma & Dissociation, 10*(3), 346–67. https://doi.org/ 10.1080/15299730902956838

Korzekwa, M. I., Dell, P. F., & Pain, C. (2009). Dissociation and borderline personality disorder: An update for clinicians. *Current Psychiatry Reports, 11*(1), 82–88.

Kundakçi, T., Şar, V., Kiziltan, E., Yargiç, I. L., & Tutkun, H. (2014). Reliability and validity of the Turkish version of the structured clinical interview for DSM-IV dissociative disorders (SCID-D): A preliminary study. *Journal of Trauma & Dissociation, 15*(1), 24–34. https://doi.org/10.1080/15299732.2013.821434

Laddis, A., & Dell, P. F. (2012). Dissociation and psychosis in dissociative identity disorder and schizophrenia. *Journal of Trauma & Dissociation, 13,* 397–413.

Laddis, A., Dell, P. F., & Korzekwa, M. (2017). Comparing the symptoms and mechanism of "dissociation" in dissociative identity disorder and borderline personality disorder. *Journal of Trauma & Dissociation, 18*(2), 139–173.

Laferrière-Simard, M. C., Lecomte, T., & Ahoundova, L. (2014). Empirical testing of criteria for dissociative schizophrenia. *Journal of Trauma & Dissociation, 15*(1), 91–107.

Lange, A., Kooiman, K., & Huberts, L. (1995). Childhood unwanted sexual events and degree of psychopathology of psychiatric patients: Research with a new anamnestic questionnaire (the CHUSE). *Acta Psychiatrica Scandinavica, 92*(6), 441–446.

Langeland, W., van den Brink, W., Draijer, N., & Hartgers, C. (2001). Sensitivity of the Addiction Severity Index physical and sexual assault items: Preliminary findings on gender differences. *European Addiction Research, 7*(4), 193–197.

Langeland, W., Draijer, N., & van den Brink, W. (2002). Trauma and dissociation in treatment-seeking alcoholics: Towards a resolution of inconsistent findings. *Comprehensive Psychiatry, 43*, 195–203.

Langeland, W., Draijer, N., & van den Brink, W. (2004). Psychiatric comorbidity in treatment-seeking alcoholics: The role of childhood trauma and perceived parental dysfunction. *Alcoholism: Clinical and Experimental Research, 28*(3), 441–447.

Lanius, R. A. (2015). Trauma-related dissociation and altered states of consciousness: A call for clinical, treatment, and neuroscience research. *European Journal of Psychotraumatology, 6*, 27905. https://doi.org/10.3402/ejpt.v6.27905

Lanius, R. A., Brand, B., Vermetten, E., Frewen, P. A., & Spiegel, D. (2012). The dissociative subtype of posttraumatic stress disorder: Rationale, clinical and neurobiological evidence, and implications. *Depression & Anxiety, 29*, 701–708.

Lanius, R. A., Vermetten, E., Loewenstein, R. J., Brand, B., Schmahl, C., Bremner, J. D., & Spiegel, D., (2010). Emotion modulation in PTSD: Clinical and neurobiological evidence for a dissociative subtype. *American Journal of Psychiatry, 167*(6), 640–647.

Leavitt, F. (1999). Dissociative experiences scale taxon and measurement of dissociative pathology: Does the taxon add to an understanding of dissociation and its associated pathologies? *Journal of Clinical Psychology in Medical Settings, 6*(4), 427–440. https://doi.org/10.1023/A:1026275916184

Lewis, D. O., & Bard, J. S. (1991). Multiple personality and forensic issues. *Psychiatric Clinics of North America. 14*(3), 741–756.

Lewis, D. O., Yeager, C. A., Swica, Y., Pincus, J. H., & Lewis, M. (1997). Objective documentation of child abuse and dissociation in 12 murderers with dissociative identity disorder. *American Journal of Psychiatry, 154*(12), 1703–1710.

Lilienfeld, S. O., Kirsch, I., Sarbin, T. R., Lynn, S. J., Chaves, J. F., Ganaway, G. K., & Powell, R. A. (1999). Dissociative identity disorder and the sociocognitive model: Recalling lessons of the past. *Psychological Bulletin, 125*, 507–523. https://doi.org/10.1037/0033-2909.125.5.507

Liotti, G. (1992). Disorganized/disoriented attachment in the etiology of dissociative disorders. *Dissociation: Progress in the Dissociative Disorders, 5*, 196–204.

Liotti, G. (1999). Disorganization of attachment as a model for understanding dissociative psychopathology. In J. Solomon & C. George (eds.), *Attachment disorganization* (pp. 291–317). Guilford Press.

Liotti, G. (2009). Attachment and dissociation. In P. F. Dell & J. A. O'Neil (eds.), *Dissociation and the dissociative disorders: DSM-5 and beyond* (pp. 53–65). Routledge/Taylor & Francis Group.

Lipsanen, T., Saarijärvi, S., & Lauerma, H. (2003). The Finnish version of the Dissociative Experiences Scale-II (DES-II) and psychiatric distress. *Nordic Journal of Psychiatry, 57*(1), 17–22.

Loewenstein, R. J. (1991a). An Office Mental Status Examination for complex chronic dissociative symptoms and multiple personality disorder. *Psychiatric Clinics of North America, 14*(3), 567–604.

Loewenstein, R. J. (1991b). Psychogenic Amnesia and Psychogenic Fugue: A Comprehensive Review. In A. Tasman & S. M. Goldfinger (eds.), *Annual Review of Psychiatry, 10*(9), 189–222.

Loewenstein, R. J. (2018). Dissociation debates: Everything you know is wrong. *Dialogues in Clinical Neuroscience, 20*, 229–242.

Loewenstein, R. J., Frewen, P. A., & Lewis-Fernández, R. (2017). Dissociative disorders. In

B. J. Sadock, V. A. Sadock, & P. Ruiz (eds.), *Kaplan & Sadock's Comprehensive Textbook of Psychiatry* (10th ed., Vol. 1, pp. 1866–1952). Wolters Kluwer/Lippincott Williams & Wilkins.

Loewenstein, R. J., & Goodwin, J. (1999). Assessment and management of somatoform symptoms in traumatized patients: Conceptual overview and pragmatic guide. In J. Goodwin & R. Attias (eds.), *Splintered reflections: Images of the body in trauma* (pp. 67–88). Basic Books.

Longden, E., Branitsky, A., Moskowitz, A., Berry, K., Bucci, S., & Varese, F. (2020). The relationship between dissociation and symptoms of psychosis: A meta-analysis. *Schizophrenia Bulletin, 46*(5), 1104–1113. https://doi.org/10.1093/schbul/sbaa037.

Lynn, S., Lilienfeld, S., Merckelbach, H., Giesbrecht, T., & van Heugten, D. (2012). Dissociation and dissociative disorders: Challenging conventional wisdom. *Current Directions in Psychological Science, 21*(1), 48–53. https://doi.org/10.1177/0963721411429457

Lyssenko, L., Schmahl, C., Bockhacker, L., Vonderlin, R., Bohus, M., & Kleindienst, N. (2018). Dissociation in psychiatric disorders: A meta-analysis of studies using the dissociative experiences scale. *American Journal of Psychiatry, 175*(1), 37–46.

Maercker, A., Brewin, C. R., Bryant, R. A., Cloitre, M., Reed, G. M., van Ommeren, M., Humayun, A., Jones, L. M., Kagee, A., Llosa, A. E., Rousseau, C., Somasundaram, D. J., Souza, R., Suzuki, Y., Weissbecker, I., Wessely, S. C., First, M. B., & Saxena, S. (2013). Proposals for mental disorders specifically associated with stress in the International Classification of Diseases-11. *Lancet, 38*, 1683–1685. https://doi.org/10.1016/s0140-6736(12)62191-6

Main, M. (2000). The organized categories of infant, child and adult attachment: Flexible vs. inflexible attention under attachment-related stress. *Journal of the American Psychoanalytic Association, 48*, 1055–1095.

Main, M., & Hesse, E. (1990). Parents' unresolved traumatic experiences are related to infant disorganized attachment status: Is frightened and/or frightening parental behavior the linking mechanism? In M. T. Greenberg, D. Cicchetti, & E. M. Cummings (eds.), *Attachment in the preschool years: Theory, research, and intervention* (pp. 161–182). University of Chicago Press.

Main, M., & Solomon, J. (1990). Procedures for identifying infants as disorganized/disoriented during the Ainsworth Strange Situation. In M. T. Greenberg, D. Cicchetti, & E. M. Cummings (eds.), *Attachment in the preschool years: Theory, research, and intervention* (pp. 121–160). University of Chicago Press.

Martinez, A. P., Dorahy, M. J., Nesbit, A., Palmer, R., & Middleton, W. (2020). Delusional beliefs and their characteristics: A comparative study between dissociative identity disorder and schizophrenia spectrum disorders. *Journal of Psychiatric Research, 131*, 263–268.

Merckelbach, H., Devilly, G. J., & Rassin, E. (2002). Alters in dissociative identity disorder: Metaphors or genuine entities? *Clinical Psychology Review, 22*(4), 481–497.

Middleton, W. (2013). Ongoing incestuous abuse during adulthood. *Journal of Trauma & Dissociation, 14*, 251–272.

Middleton, W. (2015). Tipping points and the accommodation of the abuser: Ongoing incestuous abuse during adulthood. *International Journal for Crime, Justice and Social Democracy, 4*(2), 4–17.

Middleton, W., & Butler, J. (1998). Dissociative identity disorder: An Australian series. *Australian & New Zealand Journal of Psychiatry, 32*, 794–804.

Moskowitz, A., Dorahy, M. J., & Schäfer, I. (eds.) (2019). *Psychosis, trauma and dissociation: Evolving perspectives on severe psychopathology.* John Wiley & Sons.

Moskowitz, A., Heinimaa, M., & van der Hart, O. (2018). Defining psychosis, trauma, and dissociation: Historical and contemporary conceptions. In A. Moskowitz, M. Dorahy, & I. Schäfer, *Psychosis, trauma and dissociation: Evolving perspectives on severe psychopathology* (pp. 7–29). John Wiley & Sons.

Moskowitz, A., & van der Hart, O. (2020). Historical and contemporary conceptions of trauma-related dissociation: A neo-Janetian critique of models of divided personality. *European Journal of Trauma & Dissociation, 4*(2). https://doi.org/10.1016/j.ejtd.2019.02.004

Mosquera, D., Gonzalez, A., & van der Hart, O. (2012). Borderline personality disorder, childhood trauma and structural dissociation of the personality. *Revista Persona, 11*, 44–73.

Mosquera, D., & Steele, K. (2017). Complex trauma, dissociation and borderline personality disorder: Working with integration failures. *European Journal of Trauma & Dissociation, 1*, 63–71. https://doi.org/10.1016/j.ejtd.2017.01.010

Müllerová, J., Hansen, M., Contractor, A. A., Elhai, J. D., & Armour, C. (2016). Dissociative features in posttraumatic stress disorder: A latent profile analysis. *Psychological Trauma: Theory, Research, Practice, and Policy, 8*(5), 601.

Mychailyszyn, M. P., Brand, B. L., Webermann, A. R., Şar, V., & Draijer, N. (2021). Differentiating dissociative from non-dissociative disorders: A meta-analysis of the Structured Clinical Interview for DSM Dissociative Disorders (SCID-D), *Journal of Trauma & Dissociation, 22*(1), 19–34. https://doi.org/10.1080/15299732.2020.1760169

Myers, C. S. (1940). *Shell shock in France 1914–18*. Cambridge University Press.

Myrick, A. C., Webermann, A. R., Loewenstein, R. J., Lanius, R., Putnam, F. W., & Brand, B. L. (2017). Six-year follow-up of the treatment of patients with dissociative disorders study. *European Journal of Psychotraumatology, 8*(1), 1344080. https://doi.org/10.1080/20008198.2017.1344080

Najavits, L. M., & Walsh, M. (2012). Dissociation, PTSD, and substance abuse: An empirical study. *Journal of Trauma & Dissociation, 13*(1), 115–126.

NIFP (Nederlands Instituut voor Forensische Psychiatrie en Psychologie [Dutch Institute for Forensic Psychiatry and Psychology]) (2019). NIFP-richtlijn ambulant forensisch psychologisch onderzoek en rapportage in het strafrecht, volwassenen en jeugdigen [NIFP guideline outpatient forensic psychological assessment and documentation in criminal justice, adults and juveniles]. NIFP.

Nijenhuis, E. R. S. (1996). Dissociative identity disorder in a forensic psychiatric patient: A case report. *Dissociation: Progress in the Dissociative Disorders, 9*, 282–288.

Nijenhuis, E. R. S. (2000). Somatoform dissociation: Major symptoms of dissociative disorders. *Journal of Trauma & Dissociation, 1*(4), 7–32.

Nijenhuis, E. R. S. (2004). *Somatoform dissociation: Phenomena, measurement, and theoretical issues*. W. W. Norton. (Original publication 1999.)

Nijenhuis, E. R. S. (2009). Somatoform dissociation and somatoform dissociative disorders. In P. F. Dell & J. O'Neil (eds.), *Dissociation and dissociative disorders: DSM-IV and beyond* (pp. 259–277). Routledge/Taylor & Francis Group.

Nijenhuis, E. R. S. (2010). The scoring and interpretation of the SDQ-20 and SDQ-5. *Activitas Nervosa Superior, 52*(1), 24–28.

Nijenhuis, E. R. S. (2015). *The trinity of trauma: Ignorance, fragility, and control: Vol. 1. The evolving concept of trauma*. Vandenhoeck & Ruprecht.

Nijenhuis, E. R. S. (2017). Ten reasons for conceiving and classifying posttraumatic stress disorder as a dissociative disorder. *European Journal of Trauma & Dissociation, 1*(1), 47–61.

Nijenhuis, E. R. S., Spinhoven, P., van Dyck, R., van der Hart, O., De Graaf, A., & Knoppert, E. A. M. (1997). Dissociative pathology discriminates between bipolar mood disorder and dissociative disorder. *British Journal of Psychiatry, 170*(6), 581–581.

Nijenhuis, E. R. S., Spinhoven, P., van Dyck, R., van Der Hart, O., & Vanderlinden, J. (1996). The development and psychometric characteristics of the Somatoform Dissociation Questionnaire (SDQ-20). *Journal of Nervous and Mental Disease, 184*(11), 688–694.

Nijenhuis, E. R. S., Spinhoven, P., van Dyck, R., van der Hart, O., & Vanderlinden, J. (1997). The development of the somatoform dissociation questionnaire (SDQ-5) as a screening instrument for dissociative disorders. *Acta Psychiatrica Scandinavica, 96*(5), 311–318.

Nijenhuis, E. R. S., & van der Hart, O. (2011). Defining dissociation in trauma. *Journal of Trauma & Dissociation, 12*, 469–473.

Nijenhuis, E. R. S., van der Hart, O., & Kruger, K. (2002). The psychometric characteristics of the Traumatic Experience Checklist (TEC): First findings among psychiatric outpatients. *Clinical Psychology & Psychotherapy, 9*(3), 200–210.

Nijenhuis, E. R. S., van der Hart, O., Schlumpf, Y. R., Vissia, E. M., & Reinders, A. (2019). Considerations regarding treatment efficiency, dissociative parts and dissociative amnesia for Huntjens et al.'s Schema therapy for dissociative identity disorder. *European Journal of Psychotraumatology, 10*(1), 1687081. https://doi.org/10.1080/20008198.2019.1687081

Nilsson, D., Lejonclou, A., & Holmqvist, R. (2019). Psychoform and somatoform dissociation among individuals with eating disorders. *Nordic Journal of Psychiatry*. https://doi.org/10.1080/08039488.2019.1664631

Olff, M., Bakker, A., Frewen, P., Aakvaag, H., Ajdukovic, D., Brewer, D., Elmore Borbon, D. L., Cloitre, M., Hyland, P., Kassam-Adams, N., Knefel, M., Lanza, J. A., Lueger-Schuster, B., Nickerson, A., Oe, M., Pfaltz, M. C., Salgado, C., Seedat, S., Wagner, A., & Schnyder, U. Global Collaboration on Traumatic Stress (GC-TS) (2020). Screening for consequences of trauma – an update on the global collaboration on traumatic stress. *European Journal of Psychotraumatology, 11*(1), 1752504. https://doi.org/10.1080/20008198.2020.1752504

Ondrovik, J., & Hamilton, D. (1990). Multiple personality: Competency and the insanity defense. In *Proceedings of the 1990 Conference on Multiple Personality and Dissociative States*. Akron.

Pelcovitz, D., van der Kolk, B., Roth, S., Mandel, F., Kaplan, S., & Resick, P. (1997). Development of a criteria set and a structured interview for disorders of extreme stress (SIDES). *Journal of Traumatic Stress, 10*, 3–16.

Piedfort-Marin, O., Tarquinio, C., Steinberg, M., Azarmsa, S., Cuttelod, T., Piot, M. E., Wisler, D., Zimmermann, E., & Nater, J. (2021). Reliability and validity study of the French-language version of the SCID-D semi-structured clinical interview for diagnosing DSM-5 and ICD-11 dissociative disorders. *Annales Médico-psychologiques, revue Psychiatrique. 180*(6), S1-S9. https://doi.org/10.1016/j.amp.2020.12.012

Pietkiewicz, I. J., Bańbura-Nowak, A., Barłóg, M., Duszkiewicz, R., Tomalski, R., & Nęcki, S. (2019). *Out-of-body experiences in a clinical group: An interpretative phenomenological analysis* [Paper and presentation]. 7th Biennial ESTD conference.

Pietkiewicz, I., Banbura, A., Tomalski, R., & Boon, S. (2021, 6 May). Revisiting false-positive and imitated dissociative identity disorder. *Frontiers in Psychology*. https://doi.org/10.3389/fpsyg.2021.637929

Pietrini, F., Lelli, L., Verardi, A., Silvestri, C., & Faravelli, C. (2010). Retrospective assessment of childhood trauma: Review of the instruments. *Rivista die Psichiatrica, 45*(1), 7–16.

Pilton, M., Varese, F., Berry, K., & Bucci, S. (2015). The relationship between dissociation and voices: A systematic literature review and meta-analysis. *Clinical Psychology Review, 40*, 138–155.

Pope, H. G., Jonas, J. M., & Jones, B. (1982). Factitious psychosis: Phenomenology, family history, and long-term outcome of nine patients. *American Journal of Psychiatry, 139*(11), 1480–1483.

Putnam, F. W. (1985). Dissociation as a response to trauma. In R. P. Kluft (ed.), *Childhood antecedents of multiple personality*. American Psychiatric Press.

Putnam, F. W. (1989). *Diagnosis and treatment of multiple personality disorder*. Guilford Press.

Putnam, F. W. (1997). *Dissociation in Children and Adolescents: A Developmental Perspective*. Guilford Press.

Putnam, F. W. (2006). Dissociative disorders. In D. Cicchetti & D. J. Cohen (eds.), *Developmental Psychopathology* (Vol. 2, pp. 657–695). Wiley Online. https://doi.org/10.1002/9780470939406.ch18

Putnam, F. W. (2016). *The way we are: How states of mind influence our identities, personality and potential for change*. International Psychoanalytic Books.

Putnam, F. W., Guroff, J. J., Silberman, E. K., Barban, L., & Post, R. M. (1986). The clinical phenomenology of multiple personality disorder: 100 recent cases. *Journal of Clinical Psychiatry, 47,* 285–293.

Read, J., van Os, J., Morrison, A. P., & Ross, C. A. (2005). Childhood trauma, psychosis and schizophrenia: A literature review with theoretical and clinical implications. *Acta Psychiatrica Scandinavica, 112*(5), 330–350.

Reinders, A., Marquand, A., Schlumpf, Y., Chalavi, S., Vissia, E., Nijenhuis, E., Dazzan, P., Jäncke, L., & Veltman, D. (2019). Aiding the diagnosis of dissociative identity disorder: Pattern recognition study of brain biomarkers. *British Journal of Psychiatry, 215*(3), 536–544. https://doi.org/10.1192/bjp.2018.255

Reinders, A. A. T. S., Nijenhuis, E. R. S., Quak, J., Korf, J., Haaksma, J., Paans, A. M. J., Willemsen, A. T. M., & Den Boer, J. A. (2006). Psychobiological characteristics of dissociative identity disorder: A symptom provocation study. *Biological Psychiatry, 60*(7), 730–740. https://doi.org/10.1016/j.biopsych.2005.12.019

Reinders, A., & Veltman, D. J. (2020). Dissociative identity disorder: Out of the shadow at last? *British Journal of Psychiatry, 219*(2) 413–414. https://doi.org/10.1192/bjp.2020.168

Reinders, A. A. T. S., Willemsen, A. T. M., Vos, H. P. J., Den Boer, J. A., & Nijenhuis, E. R. S. (2012). Fact or factitious? A psychobiological study of authentic and simulated dissociative identity states. *PLoS One, 7*(6), e39279.

Renard, S. B., Huntjens, R. J., Lysaker, P. H., Moskowitz, A., Aleman, A., & Pijnenborg, G. H. (2016). Unique and overlapping symptoms in schizophrenia spectrum and dissociative disorders in relation to models of psychopathology: A systematic review. *Schizophrenia Bulletin, 43*(1), 108–121.

Rinne, T., Westenberg, H. G., Den Boer, J. A., & van den Brink, W. (2000). Serotonergic blunting to meta-chlorophenylpiperazine (m-CPP) highly correlates with sustained childhood abuse in impulsive and autoaggressive female borderline patients. *Biological psychiatry, 47*(6), 548–556.

Rodewald, F. (2005). Diagnostik dissoziativer Störungen [Assessment of Dissociative Disorders] [Dissertation]. Hannover Medical School.

Rodewald, F., Dell, P. F., Wilhelm-Gößling, C., & Gast, U. (2011). Are major dissociative disorders characterized by a qualitatively different kind of dissociation? *Journal of Trauma & Dissociation, 12,* 9–24.

Rodewald, F., Wilhelm-Gößling, C., Emrich, H. M., Reddemann, L., & Gast, U. (2011). Axis-I comorbidity in female patients with dissociative identity disorder and dissociative identity disorder not otherwise specified. *Journal of Nervous and Mental Disease, 199,* 122–131.

Roelofs, K., Keijsers, G. P., Hoogduin, K. A., Näring, G. W., & Moene, F. C. (2002). Childhood abuse in patients with conversion disorder. *American Journal of Psychiatry, 159*(11), 1908–1913. https://doi.org/10.1176/appi.ajp.159.11.1908

Rogers, R., Bagby, R. M., & Dickens, S. E. (1992). *Structured interview of reported symptoms: Professional manual.* Psychological Assessment Resources.

Rogers, R., Kropp, R. P., Bagby, M. R., & Dickens, S. E. (1992). Faking specific disorders: A study of the Structured Interview of Reported Symptoms (SIRS). *Journal of Clinical Psychology, 48*(5), 643–648.

Rogers, R., Payne, J. W., Correa, A. A., Gillard, N. D., & Ross, C. A. (2009). A study of the SIRS with severely traumatized patients. *Journal of Personality Assessment, 91*(5), 429–438.

Rogers, R., Sewell, K. W., & Gillard, N. D. (2010). *Structured Interview of Reported Symptoms (SIRS): Professional manual* (2nd ed.). Psychological Assessment Resources.

Ross, C. A. (1995). Diagnosis of dissociative identity disorder. In L. M. Cohen, J. N. Berzoff, M. R. Elin, L. M. Cohen, J. N. Berzoff, & M. R. Elin (eds.), *Dissociative identity disorder: Theoretical and treatment controversies* (pp. 261–284). Jason Aronson.

Ross, C. A. (1996). History, phenomenology, and epidemiology of dissociation. In

L. K. Michelson & W. J. Ray (eds.), *Handbook of dissociation. Theoretical, empirical, and clinical perspectives* (pp. 3–24). Springer.

Ross, C. A. (1997). *Dissociative identity disorder: Diagnosis, clinical features, and treatment of multiple personality.* John Wiley & Sons.

Ross, C. A. (2019). Dissociative schizophrenia: A proposed subtype of schizophrenia. In A. Moskowitz, M. Dorahy, & I. Schäfer, *Psychosis, trauma and dissociation: Evolving perspectives on severe psychopathology* (pp. 321–335). John Wiley & Sons.

Ross, C. A. (2011). Possession experiences in dissociative identity disorder: A preliminary study. *Journal of Trauma & Dissociation, 12*, 393–400. https://doi.org/10.1080/15299732.2011.573762

Ross, C. A., Anderson, G., Fleisher, W. P., & Norton, R. (1991). The frequency of multiple personality disorder among psychiatric inpatients. *American Journal of Psychiatry, 148*(12), 1717–1720.

Ross, C. A., Duffy, C. M. M., & Ellason, J. W. (2002). Prevalence, reliability and validity of dissociative disorders in an inpatient setting. *Journal of Trauma & Dissociation, 3*, 7–17.

Ross, C. A., Ferrell, L., & Schroeder, E. (2014). Co-occurrence of dissociative identity disorder and borderline personality disorder. *Journal of Trauma & Dissociation, 15*(1), 79–90.

Ross, C. A., Heber, S., Anderson, G., Norton, G. R., Anderson, B., Del Campo, M., & Pillay, N. (1989). Differentiating multiple personality disorder and complex partial seizures. *General Hospital Psychiatry, 11*, 54–85.

Ross, C. A., Heber, S., Norton, G. R., Anderson, B., Anderson, G., & Barchet, P. (1989). The dissociative disorders interview schedule: A structured interview. *Dissociation: Progress in the Dissociative Disorders, 2*, 169–189.

Ross, C. A., Heber, S., Norton, G. R., & Anderson, G. (1989). Differences between multiple personality disorder and other diagnostic groups on structured interview. *Journal of Nervous and Mental Disease, 177*(8), 487–491.

Ross, C. A., & Keyes, B. (2004). Dissociation and schizophrenia. *Journal of Trauma & Dissociation, 5*, 69–83.

Ross, C. A., Kronson, J., Koensgen, S., Barkman, K., Clark, P., & Rockman, G. (1992). Dissociative comorbidity in 100 chemically dependent patients. *Hospital and Community Psychiatry, 43*, 840–842.

Ross, C. A., Miller, S. D., Reagor, P., Bjornson, L., Fraser, A. F., & Anderson, G. (1990a). Structured interview data on 102 cases of multiple personality disorder from four centers. *American Journal of Psychiatry, 147*, 596–601.

Ross, C. A., Miller, D. S., Reagor, P., Bjornson, L., Fraser, G. A., & Anderson, G. (1990b). Schneiderian symptoms in multiple personality disorder and schizophrenia. *Comprehensive Psychiatry, 31*, 111–118.

Ross, C. A., Norton, G. R., & Wozney, K. (1989). Multiple personality disorder: An analysis of 236 cases. *Canadian Journal of Psychiatry, 34*, 413–418.

Roy, C. A., & Perry, J. C. (2004). Instruments for the assessment of childhood trauma in adults. *Journal of Nervous and Mental Disease, 192*, 343–351.

Şar, V. (2011). Epidemiology of dissociative disorders: An overview. *Epidemiology Research International, 2011*, 1–8. 404538. https://doi.org/10.1155/2011%2F404538

Şar, V., Akyuz, G., & Dogan, O. (2007). Prevalence of dissociative disorders among women in the general population. *Psychiatry Research, 149*, 169–176.

Şar, V., Alioğlu, F., & Akyüz, G. (2014). Experiences of possession and paranormal phenomena among women in the general population: Are they related to traumatic stress and dissociation? *Journal of Trauma & Dissociation, 15*(3), 303–318. https://doi.org/10.1080/15299732.2013.849321

Şar, V., Akyuz, G., Kugu, N., Ozturk, E., & Ertem-Vehid, H. (2006). Axis I dissociative disorder comorbidity in borderline personality disorder and reports of childhood trauma. *Journal of Clinical Psychiatry, 67*(10), 1583–1590. https://doi.org/10.4088/jcp.v67n1014

Şar, V., Dorahy, M. J., & Krüger, C. (2017). Revisiting the etiological aspects of dissociative identity disorder: A biopsychosocial perspective. *Psychology Research and Behavior Management, 2017*(10), 137–146. https://doi.org/10.2147/PRBM.S113743

Şar, V., Kundakçi, T., Kiziltan, E., Yargic, I. L., Tutkun, H., Bakim, B., Boskurt, O., Özpulat, T., Keser, V., & Özdemir, Ö. (2003). The Axis-I dissociative disorder comorbidity of borderline personality disorder among psychiatric outpatients. *Journal of Trauma & Dissociation, 4*(1), 119–136.

Şar, V., & Oztürk, E. (2019). Psychotic symptoms in dissociative disorders. In A. Moskowitz, M. J. Dorahy, & I. Schäfer (eds.), *Psychosis, trauma and dissociation: Evolving perspectives on severe psychopathology* (2nd ed., pp. 195–206). John Wiley & Sons.

Şar, V., Taycan, O., Bolat, N., Özmen, M., Duran, A., Öztürk, & E., Ertem-Vehid, H. (2010). Childhood trauma and dissociation in schizophrenia. *Psychopathology, 43*(1), 33–40.

Scalabrini, A., Cavicchioli, M., Fossati, A., & Maffei, C. (2017). The extent of dissociation in borderline personality disorder: A meta-analytic review. *Journal of Trauma & Dissociation, 18*(4), 522–543. https://doi.org/10.1080/15299732.2016.1240738.

Schäfer, I., Aderhold, V., Freyberger, H. J., Spitzer, C., & Schroeder, K. (2019). Dissociative Symptoms in Schizophrenia Spectrum Disorders. In A. Moskowitz, M. Dorahy, & I. Schäfer, *Psychosis, trauma and dissociation: Evolving perspectives on severe psychopathology* (2nd ed., pp. 179–195). John Wiley & Sons.

Schäfer, I., Harfst, T., Aderhold, V., Briken, P., Lehmann, M., Moritz, S., Read, J., & Naber, D. (2006). Childhood trauma and dissociation in female patients with schizophrenia spectrum disorders: An exploratory study. *Journal of Nervous and Mental Disease, 194*(2), 135–138.

Schäfer, I., Langeland, W., Hissbach, J., Luedecke, C., Ohlmeier, M. D., Chodzinski, C., Kemper, U., Keiper, P., Wedekind, D., Havemann-Reinecke, U., Teunissen, S., Weirich, S., & Driessen, M. (2010). Childhood trauma and dissociation in patients with alcohol dependence, drug dependence, or both-A multi-center study. *Drug and Alcohol Dependence, 109*(1–3), 84–89. https://doi.org/10.1016/j.drugalcdep.2009.12.012

Schäfer, I., Reininghaus, U., Langeland, W., Voss, A., Zieger, N., Haasen, C., & Karow, A. (2007). Dissociative symptoms in alcohol-dependent patients: Associations with childhood trauma and substance abuse characteristics. *Comprehensive Psychiatry, 48*(6), 539–545. https://doi.org/10.1016/j.comppsych.2007.05.013

Schauer, M., Schauer, M., Neuner, F., & Elbert, T. (2011). *Narrative exposure therapy: A short-term treatment for traumatic stress disorders*. Hogrefe Publishing.

Schimmenti, A. (2018). The trauma factor: Examining the relationships among different types of trauma, dissociation, and psychopathology, *Journal of Trauma & Dissociation, 19*(5), 552–571. https://doi.org/10.1080/15299732.2017.1402400

Schlumpf, Y. R., Nijenhuis, E. R. S., Chalavi, S., Weder, E. V., Zimmermann, E., Luechinger, R., La Marca, R., Reinders, A. A., & Jäncke, L. (2013). Dissociative part dependent biopsychosocial reactions to backward masked angry and neutral faces: An fMRI study of dissociative identity disorder. *Neuroimage Clinical, 3*, 54–64.

Schneider, K. (1959). *Clinical Psychopathology* (5th ed.). Grune & Stratton.

Schröder, J., Nick, S., Richter-Appelt, H., & Briken, P. (2018). Psychiatric impact of organized and ritual child sexual abuse: Cross-sectional findings from individuals who report being victimized. *International Journal of Environmental Research and Public Health, 15*(11), 2417. https://doi.org/10.3390/ijerph15112417

Scott, J. G., Ross, C. A., Dorahy, M. J., Read, J., & Schäfer, I. (2018). Childhood trauma in psychotic and dissociative disorders. In A. Moskowitz, M. Dorahy, & I. Schäfer (eds.), *Psychosis, trauma and dissociation: Evolving perspectives on severe psychopathology* (pp. 143–159). John Wiley & Sons.

Sierra, M., & Berrios, G. E. (2000). The Cambridge Depersonalisation Scale: A new instrument for the measurement of depersonalisation. *Psychiatry Research, 93*(2), 153–164.

Simeon, D. (2009). Depersonalization disorder. In P. F. Dell & J. A. O'Neil (eds.), *Dissocia-*

tion and the dissociative disorders: DSM-5 and beyond (pp. 435–444). Routledge/Taylor & Francis Group.

Simeon, D., Knutelska, M., Nelson, D., & Guralnik, O. (2003). Feeling unreal: A depersonalization disorder update of 117 cases. *Journal of Clinical Psychiatry, 64*, 990–997.

Smith, G. P., & Burger, G. K. (1997). Detection of malingering: Validation of the Structured Inventory of Malingered Symptomatology (SIMS). *Journal of the American Academy of Psychiatry and the Law Online, 25*, 183–189.

Somer, E. (2002). Maladaptive daydreaming: A qualitative inquiry. *Journal of Contemporary Psychotherapy, 32*, 197–212.

Somer, E., & Dell, P. F. (2005). Development of the Hebrew-Multidimensional Inventory of Dissociation (H-MID): A valid and reliable measure of pathological dissociation. *Journal of Trauma & Dissociation, 6*(1), 31–53. https://doi.org/10.1300/J229v06n01_03

Somer, E., Lehrfeld, J., Bigelsen, J., & Jopp, D. S. (2016). Development and validation of the Maladaptive Daydreaming Scale (MDS). *Consciousness and Cognition, 39*, 77–91. https://doi.org/10.1016/j.concog.2015.12.001

Somer, E., Soffer-Dudek, N., Ross, C. A., & Halpern, N. (2017). Maladaptive daydreaming: Proposed diagnostic criteria and their assessment with a structured clinical interview. *Psychology of Consciousness: Theory, Research, and Practice, 4*(2), 176–189. https://doi.org/10.1037/cns0000114

Somer, E., Somer, L., & Jopp, D. S. (2016a). Childhood antecedents and maintaining factors in maladaptive daydreaming. *Journal of Nervous and Mental Disease, 204*, 471–478. https://doi.org/10.1097/NMD.0000000000000507

Somer, E., Somer, L., & Jopp, D. S. (2016b). Parallel lives: A phenomenological study of the lived experience of maladaptive daydreaming. *Journal of Trauma & Dissociation, 17*, 561–576. https://doi.org/10.1080/15299732.2016.1160463

Spanos, N. P. (1994). Multiple identity enactments and multiple personality disorder: A sociocognitive perspective. *Psychological Bulletin, 116*, 143–165.

Spiegel, D., & Cardeña, E. (1991). Disintegrated experience: The dissociative disorders revisited. *Journal of Abnormal Psychology, 100*(30), 366–378.

Spiegel, D., Lewis-Fernández, R., Lanius, R., Vermetten, E., Simeon, D., & Friedman, M. (2013). Dissociative Disorders in DSM-5. *Annual Review of Clinical Psychology, 9*(1), 299–326.

Spiegel, D., Loewenstein, R. J., Lewis-Fernández, R., Şar, V., Simeon, D., Vermetten, E., Cardeña, E., & Dell, P. F. (2011). Dissociative disorders in DSM-5. *Depression & Anxiety, 28*(9), 824–852. https://doi.org/10.1002/da.20874

Spitzer, C., Liss, H., Dudeck, M., Orlob, S., Gillner, M., Hamm, A., & Freyberger, H. J. (2003). Dissociative experiences and disorders in forensic inpatients. *International Journal of Law and Psychiatry, 26*(3), 281–288.

Spitzer, C., Spelsberg, B., Grabe, H., Mundt, B., & Freyberger, H. J. (1999). Dissociative experiences and psychopathology in conversion disorders. *Journal of Psychosomatic Research, 46*(3), 291–294.

Steele, K., Boon, S., & van der Hart, O. (2017). *Treating trauma-related dissociation: A practical, integrative approach.* W. W. Norton.

Steele, K., Dorahy, M., & van der Hart, O. (2022). Dissociation versus alterations in consciousness: Related but different concepts. In M. J. Dorahy, S. N. Gold, & J. A. O'Neil (eds.). (2022). *Dissociation and the dissociative disorders: Past, present, future* (2nd ed.). Routledge/Taylor & Francis Group.

Steele, K., Dorahy, M., van der Hart, O., & Nijenhuis, E. R. S. (2009). Dissociation versus alterations in consciousness: Related but different concepts. In P. F. Dell & J. A. O'Neil (eds.), *Dissociation and the dissociative disorders: DSM-5 and beyond* (pp. 155–170). Routledge/Taylor & Francis Group.

Stein, D., Koenen, K., Friedman, M., Hill, E., & Kessler, R. C. (2013). Dissociation in post-traumatic stress disorder: Evidence from the World Mental Health Surveys. *Biological Psychiatry, 73*, 302–312.

Steinberg, M. (1991). The spectrum of depersonalization: Assessment and treatment. In A. Tasman (ed.), *Annual review of psychiatry: Psychiatric update, 10* (pp. 223–247). American Psychiatric Press.

Steinberg, M. (1994a). *Structured Clinical Interview for DSM-IV Dissociative Disorders (SCID-D)*. American Psychiatric Press.

Steinberg, M. (1994b). *Therapist's guide to the Structured Clinical Interview for DSM-IV Dissociative Disorders (SCID-D)*. American Psychiatric Press.

Steinberg, M. (1995). *Handbook for assessment of dissociation: A clinical guide*. American Psychiatric Press.

Steinberg, M. (2004). Systematic assessment of posttraumatic dissociation: The Structured Clinical Interview for DSM-IV Dissociative Disorders. In J. P. Wilson & T. M. Keane (eds.), *Assessing psychological trauma and PTSD* (2nd ed., pp. 122–143). Guilford Press.

Steinberg, M. (2019). Advances in clinical assessment: The differential diagnosis of dissociative identity disorder and schizophrenia. In A. Moskowitz, M. J. Dorahy, & I. Schäfer (eds.), *Psychosis, trauma and dissociation: Evolving perspectives on severe psychopathology* (2nd ed., pp. 335–349). John Wiley & Sons.

Steinberg, M., Cicchetti, D., Buchanan, J., & Hall, P. (1993). Clinical assessment of dissociative symptoms and disorders: The Structured Clinical Interview for DSM-IV Dissociative Disorders (SCID-D). *Dissociation: Progress in the Dissociative Disorders, 6*(1), 3–15.

Steinberg, M., Cicchetti, D., Buchanan, J., Rakfeldt, J., & Rounsaville, B. (1994). Distinguishing between multiple personality disorder (dissociative identity disorder) and schizophrenia using the Structured Clinical Interview for DSM-IV Dissociative Disorders. *Journal of Nervous and Mental Disease, 182*(9), 495–502.

Steinberg, M., Rounsaville, B., & Cicchetti, D. (1990). The structured clinical interview for DSM-III-R dissociative disorders: Preliminary report on a new diagnostic instrument. *American Journal of Psychiatry, 147*, 76–82.

Steinberg, M., Rounsaville, B., & Cicchetti, D. (1991). Detection of dissociative disorders in psychiatric patients by a screening instrument and a structured diagnostic interview. *American Journal of Psychiatry, 148*(8), 1050–1054.

Steinberg, M., & Spiegel, H. D. (2008). Advances in assessment: The differential diagnosis of dissociative identity disorder and schizophrenia. In A. Moskowitz, I. Schäfer, & M. J. Dorahy (eds.), *Psychosis, trauma and dissociation: Emerging perspectives on severe psychopathology* (pp. 177–189). Wiley Blackwell.

Steuwe, C., Lanius, R. A., & Frewen, P. A. (2012). Evidence for a dissociative subtype of PTSD by latent profile and confirmatory factor analyses in a civilian sample. *Depression & Anxiety, 29*, 689–700.

Swart, S., Wildschut, M., Draijer, N., Langeland, W., & Smit, J. H. (2020). Dissociative subtype of posttraumatic stress disorder or PTSD with comorbid dissociative disorders: Comparative evaluation of clinical profiles. *Psychological Trauma, 12*(1), 38–45. https://doi.org/10.1037/tra0000474

Tamar-Gurol, D., Şar, V., Karadag, F., Evren, C., & Karagoz, M. (2008). Childhood emotional abuse, dissociation, and suicidality among patients with drug dependency in Turkey. *Psychiatry and Clinical Neurosciences, 62*(5), 540–547.

Ter Heide, F. J. J., Mooren, T. M., & Kleber, R. J. (2014). Complex trauma en Complexe PTSS, Wat is het en wie heeft het [Complex trauma and Complex PTSD: What is it and who has it]. *Tijdschrift voor psychotherapie, 40*(5), 347–359.

Ter Heide, F. J. J., Mooren, T. M., & Kleber, R. J. (2016). Complex PTSD and phased treatment in refugees: A debate piece. *European Journal of Psychotraumatology, 7*, 286–287.

Terr, L. C. (1991). Childhood traumas: An outline and overview. *American Journal of Psychiatry, 148*, 10–20.

Thomas, A. (2001). Factitious and malingered dissociative identity disorder: Clinical features observed in 18 cases. *Journal of Trauma & Dissociation, 2*(4), 59–77.

Tobin, S. M. (2019). *Exorcism, deliverance, and psychotherapy from a catholic-christian perspective: A critical literature review* [Dissertation]. Azusa Pacific University.

Tschöke, S., Uhlmann, C., & Steinert, T. (2011). Schizophrenia or trauma-related psychosis? Schneiderian first rank symptoms as a challenge for differential diagnosis. *Neuropsychiatry, 1*(4), 349.

van der Hart, O. (2000). *Psychic trauma: The disintegrating effects of overwhelming experience on mind and body* [Lecture]. 66th Beattie Smith Lecture, University of Melbourne, Department of Medicine.

van der Hart, O. (2021). Trauma-related dissociation: An analysis of two conflicting models. *European Journal of Trauma & Dissociation, 5*(4), 100210. https://doi.org/10.1016/j.ejtd.2021.100210

van der Hart, O., Boon, S., & Heijtmajer Jansen, H. (1997). Ritual abuse in Europe: A clinician's perspective. In G. A. Fraser (ed.), *The dilemma of ritual abuse: Cautions and guides for therapists* (pp. 137–166). American Psychiatric Press.

van der Hart, O., Boon, S., & Op den Velde, W. (1991). Trauma en dissociatie [Trauma and dissociation]. In O. van der Hart (ed.), *Trauma, dissociatie en hypnose.* Swets & Zeitlinger.

van der Hart, O., & Dorahy, M. J. (2009). History of the concept of dissociation. In P. F. Dell & J. A. O'Neil (eds.), *Dissociation and the dissociative disorders: DSM-5 and beyond* (pp. 3–26). Routledge/Taylor & Francis Group.

van der Hart, O., Nijenhuis, E. R. S., & Steele, K. (2006). *The haunted self: Structural dissociation of the personality and treatment of chronic traumatization.* W. W. Norton.

van der Hart, O., Nijenhuis, E., Steele, K., & Brown, D. (2004). Trauma-related dissociation: Conceptual clarity lost and found. *Australian & New Zealand Journal of Psychiatry, 38,* 906–914. https://doi.org/10.1111/j.1440-1614.2004.01480.x

van der Hart, O., & Spiegel, D. (1993). Hypnotic assessment and treatment of trauma-induced psychoses: The early psychotherapy of H. Breukink and modern views. *International Journal of Clinical and Experimental Hypnosis, 41*(3), 191–209.

van der Hart, O., Van Dijke, A., Van Son, M., & Steele, K. (2000). Somatoform dissociation in traumatized World War I combat soldiers: A neglected clinical heritage. *Journal of Trauma & Dissociation, 1*(4), 33–66.

van der Hart, O., Witztum, E., & Friedman, B. (1993). From hysterical psychosis to reactive dissociative psychosis. *Journal of Traumatic Stress, 6*(1), 43–64.

van der Hart, O., & Witztum, E. (2019). Dissociative psychosis: Clinical and theoretical aspects. In A. Moskowitz, M. Dorahy, & I. Schäfer, *Psychosis, trauma and dissociation: Evolving perspectives on severe psychopathology* (pp. 307–321). John Wiley & Sons.

van der Hoeven, R., Broersma, M., Pijnenborg, G. H. M., Koops, E. A., Van Laar, T., Stone, J., & Van Beilen, M. (2015). Functional (psychogenic) movement disorders associated with normal scores in psychological questionnaires: A case control study. *Journal of Psychosomatic Research, 79,* 190–194. https://doi.org/10.1016/j.jpsychores.2015.06.002

van der Kolk, B. (2014). *The body keeps the score.* Penguin Publishing Group.

van der Kolk, B. A., Hostetler, A., Herron, N., & Fisler, R. E. (1994). Trauma and the development of borderline personality disorder. *Psychiatric Clinics of North America, 17*(4), 715–730.

van der Kolk, B., Pelcovitz, D., Herman, J. L., Roth, S., Kaplan, S., & Spitzer, R. L. (1992). *The Disorders of Extreme Stress Inventory* [Unpublished instrument].

van der Kolk, B. A., Roth, S., Pelcovitz, D., Sunday, S., & Spinazzola, J. (2005). Disorders of extreme stress: The empirical foundation of a complex adaptation to trauma. *Journal of Traumatic Stress, 18,* 389–399.

van Dijke, A., Hopman, J., & Ford, J. D. (2018). Affect dysregulation, psychoform dissociation, and adult relational fears mediate the relationship between childhood trauma and complex posttraumatic stress disorder independent of the symptoms of borderline personality disorder. *European Journal of Psychotraumatology, 9*(1), 1400878. https://doi.org/10.1080/20008198.2017.1400878

van Dijke, A., & van der Hart, O. (2002). *The Dutch self-report version of the Structured Interview for Disorders of Extreme Stress (SIDES-r-nl)* [Unpublished manual]. Universiteit Utrecht.

van Duijl, M. (2014). *Spirits, devils and trauma. Dissociation in south-west Uganda.* Boekenplan.

van Duijl, M., Kleijn, W., & De Jong, J. (2013). Are symptoms of spirit possessed patients covered by the DSM-IV or DSM-5 criteria for possession trance disorder? A mixed-method explorative study in Uganda. *Social Psychiatry and Psychiatric Epidemiology, 48,* 1417–1430. https://doi.org/10.1007/s00127-012-0635-1

van Duijl, M., Kleijn, W., & De Jong, J. (2014). Unravelling the spirits' message: A study of help-seeking steps and explanatory models among patients suffering from spirit possession in Uganda. *International Journal of Mental Health Systems, 8,* 24.

van Duijl, M., Nijenhuis, E., Komproe, I., Gernaat, H., & De Jong, J. (2010). Dissociative Symptoms and reported trauma among patients with spirit possession and matched healthy controls in Uganda. *Culture, Medicine and Psychiatry, 34,* 380–400. https://doi.org/10.1007/s11013-010-9171-1

van Dyck, R. (1992). Zin en onzin over multipele persoonlijkheid [Sense and nonsense about multiple personalities]. *Trans, 8*(1), 26–32.

van IJzendoorn, M. H., & Schuengel, C. (1996). The measurement of dissociation in normal and clinical populations: Meta-analytic validation of the Dissociative Experiences Scale (DES). *Clinical Psychology Review, 16*(5), 365–382.

van Impelen, A., Merckelbach, H., Jelicic, M., & Merten, T. (2014). The Structured Inventory of Malingered Symptomatology (SIMS): A systematic review and meta-analysis. *Clinical Neuropsychologist, 28*(8), 1336–1365.

Vanderlinden, J., van Dyck, R., Vandereycken, W., Vertommen, H., & Jan Verkes, R. (1993). The Dissociation Questionnaire (DIS-Q): Development and characteristics of a new self-report questionnaire. *Clinical Psychology & Psychotherapy, 1*(1), 21–27.

Vanderlinden, J., Vandereycken, W., van Dyck, R., & Vertommen, H. (1993). Dissociative experiences and trauma in eating disorders. *International Journal of Eating Disorders, 13*(2), 187–193.

Vissia, E. M., Giesen, M. E., Chalavi, S., Nijenhuis, E. R. S., Draijer, N., Brand, B. L., & Reinders, A. A. T. S. (2016). Is it trauma or fantasy-based? Comparing dissociative identity disorder, post-traumatic stress disorder, simulators, and controls. *Acta Psychiatrica Scandinavica, 134*(2), 111–128.

Walczyk, J. J., Sewell, N., & DiBenedetto, M. B. (2018). A review of approaches to detecting malingering in forensic contexts and promising cognitive load-inducing lie detection techniques. *Frontiers in Psychiatry, 9.* 00700. https://doi.org/10.3389/fpsyt.2018.00700

Waller, N., Putnam, F. W., & Carlson, E. B. (1996). Types of dissociation and dissociative types. A Taxometric analysis of dissociative experiences. *Psychological Methods, 1,* 300–321.

Watkins, J. G., & Watkins, H. H. (1997). *Ego states: Theory and therapy.* W. W. Norton.

Watkins, H. H., & Watkins, J. G. (1993). Ego-state therapy in the treatment of dissociative disorders. In R. P. Kluft & C. G. Fine (eds.), *Clinical perspectives on multiple personality disorder* (pp. 277–299). American Psychiatric Press.

Weathers, F. W., Blake, D. D., Schnurr, P. P., Kaloupek, D. G., Marx, B. P., & Keane, T. M. (2013). *The Clinician-Administered PTSD Scale for DSM-5 (CAPS-5)* [Assessment measure]. www.ptsd.va.gov/professional/assessment/adult-int/caps.asp#obtain

Welburn, K. R., Fraser, G. A., Jordan, S. A., Cameron, C., Webb, L. M., & Raine, D. (2003). Discriminating dissociative identity disorder from schizophrenia and feigned dissociation on psychological tests and structured interview. *Journal of Trauma & Dissociation, 4,* 109–130.

Widom, C. S., & Morris, S. (1997). Accuracy of adult recollections of childhood victimization, part 2: Childhood sexual abuse. *Psychological Assessment, 9*(1), 34.

Wildschut, M., Langeland, W., Smit, J. H., & Draijer, N. (2014). Survivors of early childhood trauma: Evaluating a two-dimensional diagnostic model of the impact of trauma and neglect. *European Journal of Psychotraumatology, 5,* 21824. https://doi.org/10.3402/ejpt.v5.21824

Wildschut, M., Swart, S., Langeland, W., Hoogendoorn, A., Smit, J. H., & Draijer, N. (2019). Profiling psychopathology of patients reporting early childhood trauma and emotional neglect: Support for a two-dimensional model? *Psychological Trauma: Theory, Research, Practice, and Policy, 11*(5), 525.

Wildschut, M., Swart, S., Langeland, W., Smit, J. H., & Draijer, N. (2018). A trauma-spectrum approach: Quantifying a dimensional model of trauma-related and dissociative disorders. *JSM Anxiety and Depression, 3*(1), 1024.

Wildschut, M., Swart, S., Langeland, W., Smit, J. H., & Draijer, N. (2020). An emotional neglect-personality disorder approach: Quantifying a dimensional transdiagnostic model of trauma-related and personality disorders. *Journal of Personality Disorders, 34*(2), 250–261. https://doi.org/10.1521/pedi_2019_33_381

Williams, L. M. (1994). Recall of childhood trauma. A prospective study. *Journal of Consulting and Clinical Psychology, 62,* 1167–1176.

Williams, L. M. (1995). Recovered memories of abuse in women with documented child sexual victimization. *Journal of Traumatic Stress, 8,* 649–673.

Winnicott, D. W. (1960). Ego distortion in terms of true and false self. In *The maturational processes and the facilitating environment: Studies in the theory of emotional development* (pp. 140–152). Karnac Books (2005).

Wolf, E. J., Lunney, C. A., Miller, M. W., Resick, P. A., Friedman, M. J., & Schnurr, P. P. (2012). The dissociative subtype of PTSD: A replication and extension. *Depression & Anxiety, 29,* 679–688.

Wolf, E. J., Miller, M., Reardon, A., Ryabchenko, A., Castillo, D., & Freund, R. (2012). A latent class analysis of dissociation and PTSD: Evidence for a dissociative subtype. *Archives of General Psychiatry, 69,* 698–705. https://doi.org/10.1001/archgenpsychiatry.2011.1574

World Health Organization Classification of Mental and Behavioral Disorders (WHO) (1992). *The ICD-10 Classification of Mental and Behavioral Disorders.* World Health Organization, Division of Mental Health.

World Health Organization Classification of Mental and Behavioral Disorders (WHO) (2019). *The ICD-11Classification of Mental and Behavioral Disorder.* World Health Organization, Division of Mental Health.

Young, J. E., Klosko, J. S., & Weishaar, M. E. (2003). *Schema therapy.* Guilford Press.

Zanarini, M. C., & Jager-Hyman, S. (2009). Dissociation in borderline personality disorder. In P. F. Dell & J. A. O'Neil (eds.), *Dissociation and the dissociative disorders: DSM-5 and beyond* (pp. 383–402). Routledge/Taylor & Francis Group.

Zanarini, M. C., Ruser, T., Frankenburg, F. R., & Hennen, J. (2000a). The dissociative experiences of borderline patients. *Comprehensive Psychiatry, 41,* 223–227. https://doi.org/10.1016/S0010-440X(00)90051-8

Zanarini, M. C., Ruser, T. F., Frankenburg, F. R., Hennen, J., & Gunderson, J. G. (2000b). Risk factors associated with the dissociative experiences of borderline patients. *Journal of Nervous and Mental Disease, 188*(1), 26–30.

Zingrone, N. L., & Alvarado, C. S. (2001). The Dissociative Experiences Scale-II: Descriptive statistics, factor analysis, and frequency of experiences. *Imagination, Cognition and Personality, 21,* 145–157.

INDEX

Note: Italicized page locators refer to figures; tables are noted with a *t*.

Schneiderian symptoms/intrusions (*continued*)

    tactile hallucinations, 62*t*, 64–65

    TADS-I and assessment of, 109*t*, 131 (box 5.6), 135, 391–95

    TADS-I profile, for BPD patients without PTSD or CPTSD, 212–13

    thought broadcasting, 68

    thought insertion, 62*t*, 67

    thought withdrawal, 62*t*, 67

    various presentations of DID, OSDD-1, and partial DID associated with, 178*t*

    visual hallucinations, 62*t*, 64

Schuengel, C., 88, 98, 204

SCID-D. *see* Structured Clinical Interview for Dissociative Disorders (SCID-D)

SCID-DESNOS. *see* Structured Clinical Interview for DSM-IV disorders of extreme stress not otherwise specified (SCID-DESNOS)

SCID-D-R. *see* Structured Clinical Interview for DSM-IV Dissociative Disorders, Revised (SCID-D-R)

SCIMD. *see* Structured Clinical Diagnostic Interview for Maladaptive Daydreaming (SCIMD)

SCL-90, 41

screening

    advisability criteria for, 86–87

    followed by diagnostic interview, 103

    see also screening tools

Screening and Assessment of Dissociative Disorders (Boon & Draijer), xiv

screening tools

    Cambridge Depersonalization Scale, 99

    DES-Taxon, 98

    Detachment and Compartmentalization Inventory, 101

    Dissociation Questionnaire, 98–99

    Dissociative Experiences Scale, 87–98, 102

    Dissociative Symptoms Scale, 100–101

    Multidimensional Inventory of Dissociation, 99–100, 101

    Somatoform Dissociation Questionnaire, 99, 102

    summary of, 101–2

    use of, 87

SDQ-20. *see* Somatoform Dissociation Questionnaire-20 (SDQ-20)

secondary structural dissociation, 5, *6*, 37, 53–54, 176, 177, 244

second opinions, 249, 250

seizures. *see* non-epileptic seizures

selective amnesia, in DSM-5, 29*t*

self-image and identity

    anxiety symptoms and, case report of patient with, 196

    conversion disorder with attacks or seizures (DSM-5) and, case report of patient with, 168

    CPTSD (ICD-11) and, case report of patient with, 234–35

    depersonalization/derealization disorder and: case report of patient with, 164

    DID and, case report of patient with, 140–41

    differentiating dissociative disorders from BPD and, points to consider, 210 (box 8.1)

    dissociative neurological symptom disorder with non-epileptic seizures (ICD-11) and, case report of patient with, 168

    factitious (or imitated) DID and, case report of patient with, 271–72

    false-positive DID in patient with borderline personality disorder and, 265–66

    genuine and false-positive or imitated DID and, 254*t*

    high-functioning patient with DID, initially presenting with partial DID: case report, 149

    OSDD-1 or partial DID and, case report of patient with, 158

    personality disorders and, 221

    PTSD dissociative subtype, CPTSD and/or partial DID, case report of patient with, 241

    TADS-I and questions about, 107, 109*t*, 110, 111, 123–26, 371–74

    TADS-I profile, for BPD patients without PTSD or CPTSD and, 211

    various groups of BPD patients with/without CPTSD and/or dissociative disorder and, 221*t*

self-injurious behavior, 11, 22, 30, 206, 290, 299

    conversion disorder with attacks or seizures (DSM-5) and, case report of patient with, 168

    CPTSD (ICD-11) and, case report of patient with, 234

    depersonalization/derealization disorder and, case report of patient with, 164

    DID and, case report of patient with, 140

Suzette Boon, PhD, is a clinical psychologist and psychotherapist specialized in the treatment of chronic traumatization and dissociative disorders. She translated and validated the Dutch version of the Structured Clinical Interview for DSM-IV Dissociative Disorders (SCID-D) and received a PhD for her thesis "Multiple Personality Disorder in the Netherlands" in 1993. She has worked within the mental health field on outpatient and inpatient psychiatric units. In the last seven years before her retirement, she worked at a top reference trauma center. She is currently working in private practice. She is a trainer and supervisor and teaches in many different countries. She is cofounder of the European Society for Trauma and Dissociation (ESTD) and was the first president of this Society.

The International Society for the Study of Trauma and Dissociation (ISSTD) granted her the David Caul Memorial Award in 1993, the Morton Prince Award in 1994, and the President's Award of distinction and the status of fellow in 1995 for her contributions to diagnosis, treatment, research, and education in the field of dissociative disorders. In 2009 she received the Life Time Achievement Award from ISSTD.

She has published several books, book chapters, and many articles on the diagnosis as well as treatment of dissociative disorders. She has developed a skills training manual for patients with a complex dissociative disorder. The English version of this manual, *Coping With Trauma-Related Dissociation*, was written with coauthors Kathy Steele, MN, CS, and Onno van der Hart, PhD, and published in March 2011. With these authors, she also wrote the book *Treating Trauma-Related Dissociation: A Practical, Integrative Approach* (Steele, Boon, & van der Hart, 2017). Both titles won the Pierre Janet Writing Award of ISSTD in 2011 and 2017, respectively.

The Trauma and Dissociation Symptoms Interview (TADS-I) that she has developed is a semi-structured interview for the assessment of complex dissociative disorders and trauma-related symptoms. A validation study has been started. She wrote this book, *Assessing Trauma-Related Dissociation: With the Trauma and Dissociation Symptoms Interview (TADS-I)*, on the use and background of this interview.

suzetteboon.com